William and Mary

William and Mary

HENRI AND BARBARA
VAN DER ZEE

ALFRED A. KNOPF
New York
1973

Contents

Illustrations

A Court Ball at The Hague in 1686, by D. Maret
(*Rijksmuseum, Amsterdam*)

The departure of William's fleet from Hellevoetsluys in November 1688
(*Rijksmuseum, Amsterdam*)

The Battle of the Boyne, July 1690
(*Rijksmuseum, Amsterdam*)

William at the Boyne, by J. Wijck
(*Collection Groeninx van Zoelen, Het Huys ten Donck, Ridderkirk*)

Hampton Court
(*Mansell Collection*)

Kensington Palace
(*Mansell Collection*)

Henry Sidney, Earl of Romney
(*By permission of Viscount de L'Isle,*
V.C., K.G., from his collection at Penshurst Place, Kent)

William Bentinck, Earl of Portland, by Hyacinthe Rigaud
(*National Portrait Gallery, London*)

William's mistress, Elizabeth Villiers, from a portrait by an unknown artist
(*Earl of Jersey*)

Arnold Joost van Keppel, first Earl of Albemarle, by Sir Godfrey Kneller
(*National Portrait Gallery, London*)

Louis XIV, by de la Haye
(*Radio Times–Hulton*)

John Churchill, Duke of Marlborough, after Sir Godfrey Kneller
(*National Portrait Gallery, London*)

Czar Peter the Great, by Sir Godfrey Kneller
(*Her Majesty Queen Elizabeth II*)

Charles Talbot, twelfth Earl and only Duke of Shrewsbury
(*National Portrait Gallery, London*)

William shortly after the Coronation in 1689, by J. Gole
(*Rijksmuseum, Amsterdam*)

Daniel Finch, second Earl of Nottingham
(*National Portrait Gallery, London*)

Charlotte Elizabeth (Liselotte), Duchess of Orléans, by Largillière
(*Mansell-Bulloz*)

Sir Thomas Osborne, first Earl of Danby, by Sir Peter Lely
(*National Portrait Gallery, London*)

Acknowledgements

The authors gratefully acknowledge the support and encouragement we have received in the writing of this book.

In particular, we should like to thank Mr. Russell Braddon for his initial enthusiasm; Mr. Douglas Matthews, Deputy Librarian of the London Library, for his constant guidance; and Mr. Michael Borrie, Assistant Keeper of MSS in the British Museum, for initiating us into the Museum's treasure-stores.

Our studies of the Royal homes have been greatly aided by Dr. John Hayes, Director of the London Museum; and Mr. J. M. A. Muntenaar, Hoofd, Alg. Zaken, Rijksmuseum Paleis Het Loo.

For the illustration of this book, we have been very much helped by Miss de Hoop Scheffer of the Rijksprenten-kabinet in Amsterdam, and by Dr. Roy Strong and Mr. Richard Ormond of the National Portrait Gallery.

It would of course have been impossible to write this book without the patient help of the staffs of the London Library and the British Museum, the Koninklijke Bibliotheek, and the Library of the Rijks universiteit in Leiden, etc.

Invaluable assistance was given to us by the Dutch Ambassador in London, Baron W. Gevers; Dr. Sylvia England; Mr. Norman Goode; Countess Alexander Shuvalov; Mrs. Patricia Perez; and Miss Ineke Jager.

Finally, the authors are immensely grateful to their Editors, of *De Telegraaf* in particular, whose indulgence made the writing of this book possible.

A Note on Dates

Throughout the seventeenth century England, following the Julian calendar, was ten days behind the Continent, where the calendar reforms introduced by Gregory XIII were observed. This ten-day time-lag increased to eleven days in 1700: in addition, the Julian year was officially dated from 25 March, instead of 1 January. Thus 12 February 1675 New Style on the Continent, was 2 February 1674 Old Style in England. Contemporaries travelling or corresponding between England and the Continent appear to have sorted out the complexities of this situation without much trouble, switching easily from one calendar to another. Occasionally, to avoid confusion, they dated their letters both ways — 2/12 February. Historians and biographers, on the other hand, have not always found it so easy to avoid confusing themselves and their readers. We have followed their standard practice by dating events happening in England according to the Old Style, and events on the Continent according to the New Style, except when they are viewed in an English perspective.

NORTH

SEA

Groningen
Leeuwarden
FRIESLAND
GRONINGEN

Hoorn
Alkmaar
Kampen
Haarlem
Amsterdam
OVERIJSSEL
Scheveningen
Leiden
Nearden
Zutphen
Rijswijk
UTRECHT
GELDERLAND
The Hague
Utrecht
Dieren
Den Briel
Arnhem
Dordrecht
Nijmegen
Grave
Cleve
ZEELAND
Breda
Middelburg
THE GENERALITY
SPANISH
Flushing
GELDER-
LAND
Ostend
Sluys
Antwerp
Roermond
Nieuwpoort
Bruges
Dunkirk
FLANDERS
Ghent
Mechlin
Cologne
Calais
Dixmude
Oudenaarde
Brussels
Louvain
Maastricht
Ypres
Courtrai
BRABANT
Aix-la-Chapelle
St.Omer
Ath
Enghien
Waterloo
Limburg
Tournai
Steenkerk
Liege
Bouvines
Soignies
Seneffe
Fleurus
Spa
Condé
Mons
Namur
Valenciennes
Binche
Charleroi
Arras
Cambrai
BISHOPRIC OF LIEGE

LUXEMBOURG
Treves
Luxembourg

0   50   100 miles

THE NETHERLANDS IN THE SECOND HALF OF THE
SEVENTEENTH CENTURY

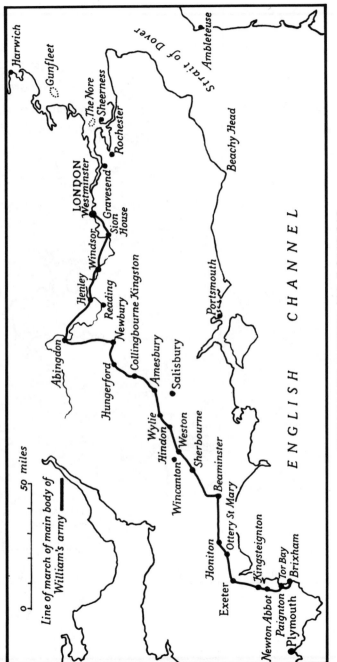

WILLIAM'S ROUTE TO LONDON

THE IRISH CAMPAIGN

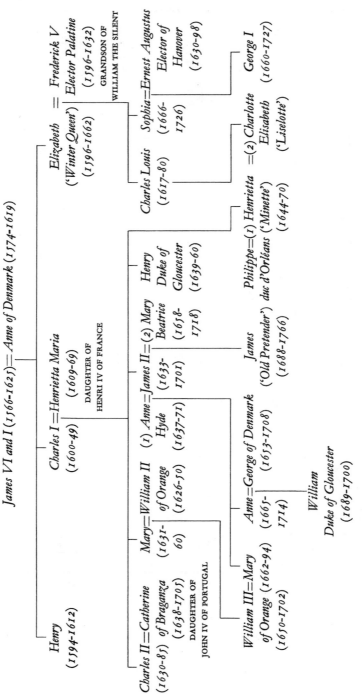

HOUSE of STUART

James VI and I (1566-1625) = Anne of Denmark (1574-1619)

Henry
(1594-1612)

Charles I = Henrietta Maria
(1600-49)   (1609-69)
             DAUGHTER OF
             HENRI IV OF FRANCE

Elizabeth = Frederick V
('Winter Queen') Elector Palatine
(1596-1662)   (1596-1632)
                  GRANDSON OF
                  WILLIAM THE SILENT

Charles II = Catherine
(1630-85)   of Braganza
             (1638-1705)
             DAUGHTER OF
             JOHN IV OF PORTUGAL

Mary = William II
(1631- of Orange
60)   (1626-50)

(1) Anne = James II = (2) Mary
Hyde   (1633-   Beatrice
(1637-71) 1701)   (1658-
                       1718)

Henry
Duke of
Gloucester
(1639-60)

Charles Louis
(1617-80)

Sophia = Ernest Augustus
(1666-   Elector of
1726)   Hanover
          (1630-98)

George I
(1660-1727)

William III = Mary
of Orange   (1662-94)
(1650-1702)

Anne = George of Denmark
(1665-   (1653-1708)
1714)

James
('Old Pretender')
(1688-1766)

Philippe = (1) Henrietta
duc d'Orléans ('Minette')
               (1644-70)

= (2) Charlotte
Elisabeth
('Liselotte')

William
Duke of Gloucester
(1689-1700)

HOUSE of ORANGE

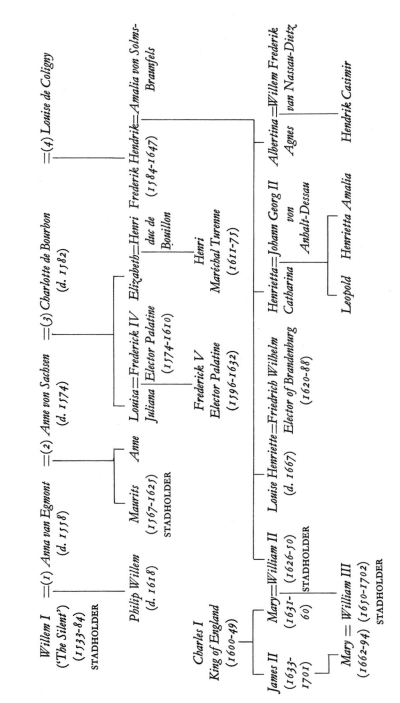

William and Mary

CHAPTER I

Death and Birth

Eight days after William II, Prince of Orange, died of small-pox and two days after large areas of his country, the Dutch United Provinces, were laid waste by its eternal enemy and friend the sea, William III of Orange was born in The Hague.* It was 14 November 1650, the nineteenth birthday of his mother Mary Stuart. She had hardly had time to recover from the shock of her husband's sudden illness and death, and the room where she gave birth was hung in black. The State bed specially constructed to honour this occasion so vital to the Orange dynasty was not even used: its splendour had seemed inappropriate.*

Mary's labour had begun at half past two in the afternoon, and her mother-in-law, Princess Amalia of Orange, had hurried to her bedside when they sent her the news. Grief for once had united these two women between whom there had never been any affection. "At half past eight her Royal Highness gave birth to a healthy young prince, God be blessed and give him a long life," wrote her Steward Johan van Kerckhoven, Heer van Heenvliet.* Mary's confidante and aunt, the exiled Queen Elizabeth of Bohemia – the Winter Queen – remarked that the confinement had gone through "verie happilie".

Legend almost immediately grew up about the young prince's birth: a maidservant reported that when a gust of wind snuffed out the three candles in the room she saw three circles of light glowing round the baby's head.* The Dutch people were ready to believe it: for most of them the important news was that there was once more a Prince of Orange. Every scrap of information about him was eagerly circulated, and when on the third day of his life three doctors had to be consulted about his feeding, it was at once feared that he had been poisoned by enemies of the House of Orange.* Those inside the Household knew better. The baby had refused the breast of his wet-nurse for twelve hours and was growing weak. She was replaced by another wet-nurse, Mrs. Lesley, and a few hours later Heenvliet was able to report with much relief

*An asterisk indicates that a reference for the passage will be found in the Notes on pages 487–513.

that "the Prince had sucked heartily and brought up plenty of wind".*

It was his mother who gave more concern. The death of her husband, followed so swiftly by the birth of their only child, had prostrated the young woman. *"Elle avait failli succomber à son deuil et à ses couches,"* wrote Brasset, the French Resident at The Hague.* Her favourite brother, Charles II of England, still a king in exile, sent anxiously from Scotland to Heenvliet's English wife for news. "How my sister does for her health, whether my nephew be lusty or strong, whom he is like and a hundred such questions, I desire an answer of under your hand, because a less evidence will not satisfy the curiosity I have for those I am so much concerned."

The death of William II had been a blow for Charles too. He had liked his brother-in-law, who had offered his hospitality in his own entertaining circle of merry diplomats, officers and actresses in The Hague, and who had broken to him the news of the execution of his father Charles I in 1648, when he was his guest at the palace of Honselaersdijck.

They had met for the first time in 1642, when William came to London to marry Charles I's eldest daughter Mary. This alliance with the influential and Protestant Dutch House of Orange was the sort of gesture Charles urgently needed to make. The strong influence of his Roman Catholic wife, Henrietta Maria, had poisoned his relations with Parliament and people. The wedding between the fifteen-year-old boy and the nine-year-old girl made, however, very little stir, and even less attention was paid to her departure to Holland in February 1642 – England was on the brink of civil war.

The young bride arrived at The Hague with her mother Henrietta Maria and a formidable pack of English attendants. She looked forward to seeing her handsome husband again, but her mother had already filled her with prejudices against the Calvinist Dutch. It was even rumoured that the Queen wanted to abduct her daughter to France before the marriage was consummated. William's mother Amalia had been too quick for her and – still according to rumour – hurried the young pair into bed.

A few months later Henrietta Maria left The Hague. She took from the despised Dutch a large sum of money to help her husband's cause; she left behind a daughter she had effectively brainwashed into a lifelong dislike of the Dutch, and an intense hostility towards her ambitious mother-in-law Amalia. Already, in the first year of the marriage, "there were reports of a violent scene in which she showed her mother-in-law contempt, hatred and dissatisfaction."* Amalia was a proud woman, like her daughter-in-law; and however great may have been the satisfaction of marrying her son into the English Royal family, she was constantly irritated by the deferential homage she and her husband were compelled to pay to this unfriendly but Royal child.*

For a woman like Amalia, it was galling to be constantly reminded by her daughter-in-law that she had been a mere lady-in-waiting to the Winter Queen, Elizabeth, when in 1625, twenty-three years old, she had caught the eye of the thirty-nine-year-old Frederik Hendrik, who had just succeeded his brother Maurits as Stadholder of Holland.

The relationship of the two women worsened when in 1647 Frederik Hendrik died and William II was nominated Stadholder of the United Provinces.† Mary violently resented the strength of Amalia's influence over her husband, who in political matters was still treated by her as a child. During the negotiations that led to the Peace of Westphalia in 1648 William wanted to keep the French alliance and fight on against Spain. His mother, who had received a splendid pair of ear-rings from the French statesman, Cardinal Richelieu, was at first of the same view, but the even more impressive gift of two estates from the Spaniards made her change sides, and it was her opinion that triumphed.* A separate peace treaty was signed, which after eighty years of war with Spain gave the seven United Provinces their formal independence at last. The French had to fight on alone.

William was humiliated and Mary shared his feelings. She loved her spoiled and unpredictable husband, in spite of his constant attentions to pretty French actresses and his passion for gambling. And now, thanks to Amalia's intrigues, she was confronted with a man frustrated in his political and military ambitions, and very bored by inaction.

His opportunity came in the spring of 1650, when after two years' discussion about the reduction of troops in the United Provinces, one of the seven States, Holland, took unilateral action. In defiance of the Republic's "constitution" they disbanded their military forces without waiting for general agreement. The result was a conflict which culminated in the arrest of six leaders of the opposition party, usually known as the Loevesteiners, followed by an attempt by the Stadholder to subdue Amsterdam by force. But the city had been alerted well in advance, and

---

† *Stadholder:* literally "lieu-tenant", the holder of a town, or governor. The term is taken from the time when an emperor or king appointed a representative to rule over distant provinces. In the United Provinces the title was in fact not hereditary, and a stadholder had theoretically only limited powers: no right to declare war, to levy taxes, to raise troops and no power over life and death. He was allowed to appoint municipal magistrates and shared with the States of the provinces the right of military appointments. He also had the right to arbitrate between the States.

the coup was a fiasco. William picked up the pieces as well as he could. After three days of talks, Amsterdam gave in on the question of troops and the situation seemed almost normal again. But the renewed resentment of Amsterdam and the Loevestein party against the Stadholder was to have expensive consequences for the House of Orange.

For the moment there was nothing the Prince could do. Amsterdam had been compelled to give way, but his attempt to impose his personal authority had been a failure. He retired to his country estate at Dieren in Gelderland to indulge a family passion, hunting. It was October 1650, a wild and wet month. Day after day he spent hours in the saddle chasing boar and deer in the dense Veluwe forests, while Mary, who was expecting her first child within the next weeks, remained at The Hague.

On 29 October he rejoined her there, feverish and unwell after a seven-hour hunt. Three days later he became seriously ill. The doctors diagnosed smallpox. For fear of infection his desperate wife was not allowed to see him, although his mother Amalia – having had the disease – visited him. Five days of agonized uncertainty crawled by, and on 6 November Heenvliet, meeting the doctor on the stairs, had the message whispered in his ear: "The Prince is dead, or as good as dead."* Before he saw the Princess he took a stiff drink, but he still lacked courage to tell her the truth. The Prince, he said, had been given a cordial: the doctors were waiting to see if he responded. Then he left Mary weeping in the arms of her former governess, his wife Lady Stanhope.

At nine in the evening William died, but it was hours before anyone felt brave enough to break the news to Mary. Heenvliet walked up and down till two in the morning, when it was decided that Doctor Brunwon should tell her. On his return he reported that the Princess Royal was "in bed, sad and inconsolable".* Elizabeth of Bohemia, who had hurried to console her favourite niece, wrote a few days later to her son Charles Louis, the Elector Palatine: "My poore neece is the most afflicted creature that ever I saw and is changed as she is nothing but skin and bone. . . ."*

While the young expectant widow and the Dutch people mourned their Prince, his opponents rejoiced. His prisoners from Loevestein were freed and a little poem found in the offertory plate in a church gave savage expression to their feelings:

> *The prince is dead.*
> *My gift is vast,*
> *More glad this year*
> *Than eighty past.**

The enemies of the House of Orange felt that their moment had come. At last they could shake off Orange pretensions to power and run their own affairs. A resolution passed by Holland, the most influential of the seven United Provinces, to defer decision about the next Stadholder "until the Royal Princess should be delivered" was hurriedly changed into vaguer terms, "to leave everything as it is at the moment, until a future decision of the Provinces."*

The common people, as always violently pro-Orange, hardly realized what was happening. When William III was born on 14 November, "the bells were rung, and the populace showed great joy, making it clear that they expected nothing else but that the Prince would be sovereign."*

His grandmother, the Dowager-Princess, had no such illusions. She grasped at once what the "patrons of real liberty" – as her son's opponents had styled themselves – had in mind. She seized the initiative before her daughter-in-law had fully regained strength, and in a bid to fortify her own position wrote to the Provinces to remember the new-born prince, "when the appointment of Stadholder will be deliberated."* This bold move met with no encouragement, and it quickly became apparent to Amalia that her grandson's future position was in danger. Moreover far from being able to count on the support of the family, she had to deal with the intrigues of her own son-in-law, Count Willem Frederik van Nassau-Dietz, Stadholder of Friesland and now of Groningen and Drente as well and with those of Johan Maurits van Nassau-Siegen, the intelligent and colourful former governor of Brazil, now Stadholder of the Rhenish provinces of Brandenburg. Both of them were eager to obtain the Captain- and Admiral-Generalship of the seven provinces, ranks that normally went together with the Stadholdership of Holland and Zeeland; and Sir Constantyn Huygens, the famous Dutch poet and secretary of Princess Amalia, wrote sadly of this division of family loyalties:

> It is deplorable and indeed heartbreaking for good and honest people to see, after God in His infinite mercy had wished to console the most illustrious House of Orange-Nassau, in the extremity of its afflictions, by the fortunate birth of a male heir, that . . . this precious child, its unique visible support, should prove unhappily to bring about its division.*

The same words applied to the country. That became clear when a great Convention of the States' representatives was held in The Hague. On 18 January 1651 three hundred delegates listened to a passionate plea that they should "allow their thoughts to dwell on a form of

government after the example of the oldest Republic, that of the
Hebrews, which for 450 years never appointed a permanent governor,
but chose a new leader for every campaign."* These words, uttered by
versemonger Jacob Cats who, as Raadspensionary of Holland, was the
most important man in the most important province, made an enormous
impression.

Four provinces were sufficiently convinced by them to remain
Stadholder-less. It was victory for Holland; it was revenge for the
Amsterdammers. From now on they would rule the loosely bound
provinces. And they had no intention of ever again yielding their
supremacy. When in March of that year England, quiet and strong under
Cromwell, proposed to the Dutch a new alliance which was almost a
merger between the two countries, the offer was indignantly rejected.
Even though after the death of William II the United Provinces had
recognized Cromwell, this was going too far. Cromwell's two ambassadors were coolly received by the Regents, while the populace of The
Hague were plainly hostile, shouting "Regicides" after their coaches.*
They left hurriedly.

The popular demonstration had not been entirely spontaneous: it
was incited by, among others, Mary's second brother, James Duke of
York. This impetuous young man, after a tremendous row with his
exiled mother in Paris, had been staying with his sister at The Hague to
comfort her in these sad times.

In that same month of March he was the chief mourner at the funeral
of Mary's husband, who had lain in state since November at the Binnenhof. A day later than planned because of bad weather, the cortège set out
from The Hague to Delft, where William II was buried in the tomb of
his forefathers in the church of St. Ursula. Heenvliet wrote with relief in
his diary that evening that for once a family occasion had passed off in
"quiet and without disputes".*

The christening of little William two months earlier, in contrast, had
been the occasion for a violent family quarrel. Already relations between
Mary and her mother-in-law, never particularly cordial, had been
embittered by a dispute over the guardianship of the baby and the
administration of William's estates. The two women could not even
agree over the names to be given to the child. Amalia understandably
thought that he should be given the family names of Willem Hendrik,
while Mary wanted to call him Charles. On 15 January, while everybody
waited in the Grote Kerk in The Hague, the argument was still raging.
Amalia's victory was a foregone conclusion: the day before, the Winter
Queen had written that the names of her "little nephue" would be

William Henry.* But the row held up the ceremony for two hours and Mary was so angry that she refused to attend.

If Mary stayed away, the rest of the family presented a solid front for the occasion. Besides the Winter Queen and her children, there was Count Willem Frederik van Nassau-Dietz, Count Johan Maurits van Nassau-Siegen and William's aunt Louisa, Electress of Brandenburg. There were representatives of the Dutch and English nobility, and envoys from foreign courts. The church, draped in black mourning, was packed, and the sermon, preached on the text "Suffer little children to come unto me," was inaudible. The Reverend Tobias Tegnejus gave up in the middle, and his admonition to the Regents, who stood godfather, to admit the prince eventually to the honours of his forefathers was lost. While the Winter Queen held William, the baptism was performed by the Reverend Herman van der Linden, and the Dowager Princess looked proudly on. The Regents, meanwhile, noted with fury that the christening robes were lined with pretentious royal ermine,* and Mary gave further proof of her lack of tact when they called on her after the ceremony. She received them coldly, standing in front of her bed, and refused even to touch the golden casket they offered her, which contained a Letter of Credit for 5000 guilders.*

Immediately after the christening the storm about William's guardianship blew up again. Mary wanted sole custody on the basis of an unsigned and undated will of her husband. "It was", she argued, the only honour that her husband "had left her to maintain respect for her person".* On 30 May, the High Court did in fact award custody of the child to the Princess Royal, and appointed her brother-in-law, Friedrich Wilhelm, Elector of Brandenburg, as guardian for the administration of the Prince's estates and the supervision of his education.

Her mother-in-law of course immediately objected, and her party was strengthened when the Elector of Brandenburg and his wife arrived in The Hague on 24 June. This intelligent and blunt son-in-law was no great admirer of Mary, who had refused, as a Royal Princess, to yield to his wife the precedence that was her due. He and his wife therefore made a point of going to see the little William while they knew Mary to be at church. The Princess was furious, but worse was to come. Two days later, Friedrich Wilhelm published a bitter criticism of the "misunderstandings created by people of ill-will in this illustrious House at a time when, following the death of its head, it most needed to be united and at peace. . . ."*

Mary counter-attacked vigorously. She published an answer in which she said that a personal meeting between the people involved seemed to her a more appropriate way to resolve their present differences. A week later she complained to delegates of the High Council that her brother-in-law had treated her in a way "a King would not wish to treat a demoiselle."* She asked them at the same time to speed up the hearing of the appeal of the Dowager-Princess, and the decision came on 29 July: the High Court appointed Amalia joint guardian with Mary and the Elector; and they added a fourth, the Duke of Landsberg, a distant relation.

It was Mary's turn to ask the Court to reconsider. But the President of the Court made another suggestion which Mary, Amalia and the Elector, tired of the long struggle and short of funds, accepted on 13 August 1651. The Princess Royal was given one-half share in the guardianship of William, and the Dowager-Princess and the Elector the other half together.

Amalia left the next day with her daughter and son-in-law for a short holiday at Aix-la-Chapelle, relieved and triumphant.* She had won an important voice in the upbringing of the little Prince and in the administration of the estates. If she had been excluded from the guardianship altogether, she would have been, with her small income of 39,000 guilders, a person of little importance.

Mary herself was disappointed by the verdict and another blow soon followed. Given the almost royal style she felt obliged to keep up, the 100,000 guilders allowed her annually by her marriage contract together with the income of 50,000 guilders from the will of her husband, were barely adequate, and she appealed to the States-General for a pension of 40,000 guilders. Holland's refusal was a decisive snub – "the province was not now so eager for the favour of the said princess that they would buy it so expensively."*

Their veto meant drastic economies for Mary and her household, a difficult task for Constantyn Huygens, who in October was appointed Counsellor and Treasurer to the Prince of Orange. Amazingly, his appointment was signed by both Mary and Amalia, in spite of his well-known loyalty to the Dowager-Princess, whom he glowingly described as "the most useful and indispensable tutor that could possibly be chosen for the Prince".*

Perhaps the heat was now taken out of the battle. Relations between the two women were never again as bitter as they had once been, and in December Amalia, drinking chocolate with Mary and the Winter Queen, made a demonstration of goodwill. She talked about "my great affection" for her daughter-in-law, saying that she would leave her completely free in the education of her child.*

Thus ended the year in which the family affairs of the little Prince of Orange seemed to be settled. At the same time it had, however, become clear that the Regents of the Republic had no intention of submitting to a Prince of Orange ever again. As a force in Dutch and European affairs, the House of Orange seemed extinct.

In France, on the contrary, after the exhausting years of La Fronde, the House of Bourbon now returned to full glory. On 7 September 1651, the thirteen-year-old Louis XIV had proclaimed his coming of age. In Parlement he announced that in accordance with the law of the state, he wished to take the government on himself.

CHAPTER II

The Triumph of Amsterdam

THE EXCLUSION OF THE BABY PRINCE OF ORANGE from the traditional role of his family was a break with seventy years of Dutch history. It was under the leadership of an Orange prince, William the Silent, that the Netherlands first rose to shake off the Spanish yoke in the sixteenth century; it was under the leadership of his two sons, Prince Maurits and Prince Frederik Hendrik, that the seven northern provinces – Holland, Zeeland, Friesland, Groningen, Utrecht, Gelderland and Overijssel – achieved their independence. During that time the family had enjoyed an unique position in Dutch affairs. As one Orange prince after another succeeded to the title of Stadholder to six of the seven provinces, and military commander of the whole United Republic, both the country and the family came to regard these honours as their hereditary right. To the Dutch nobility, the common people and the outside world, the Oranges seemed more and more like a Royal family.

The Orange-Nassau family was indeed an impressive dynasty, of German origin. William the Silent had been born Prince of Nassau-Dillenburg. At the age of eleven he had inherited the Royal title of Prince of Orange, together with the little principality in the south of France that went with the name. Orange-Nassaus had married into the reigning families of Europe. As a result of one such match, the tiny Prince William III had as great-grandparents on his mother's side James I of England, Anne of Denmark, Henri IV of France and Marie de Medici.

The wealthy merchant classes of the United Provinces, republicans at heart, were not impressed by all this royal glory. They accepted the Stadholder in times of danger; but when peace returned they preferred to run their own affairs, and in a sense they had created their own administrative aristocracy, the "Regenten", whose hold of office had become virtually hereditary too. The Regents had almost absolute power in local affairs, and represented their towns in the seven provincial "Staten", the Councils that had once governed the provinces for the King of Spain. During the war for independence they had established their autonomy, and the seven Provinces were in effect a very loosely knit federation held together only by a contract made in Utrecht in 1579, which stipulated that they should not make war separately nor desert each other when war broke out.

To the outside world the United Provinces spoke with one voice, that of the States-General at The Hague, an assembly of delegates from the seven provincial States. But the States-General had little real power, because every delegate was bound by the instructions of his province, and resolutions had to be voted unanimously to be valid. And in times of crisis the system had a disastrous weakness: as every delegate had to refer important decisions to his own States, precious time was often lost. It was a form of government which often earned for the country the mocking name of the "Disunited Provinces".

Fortunately for the Dutch they seldom lacked a strong man to impose his personality on affairs. Either it was a prince of Orange, or it was the highest official of wealthy and domineering Amsterdam, the Raads-pensionary: the two had often worked together, but their interests as often clashed. Holland, and specially Amsterdam, was preoccupied with trade and the expansion of her commercial influence – her unenviably high contribution of 60 per cent to the common funds was sufficient proof of her success – while the Orange family was more interested in political and military influence in the affairs of Europe. As Sir Winston Churchill once wrote:

> There were, indeed, two Hollands – the pacific, and at times Francophile, Holland of Amsterdam, and the Holland which adhered to the memory and lineage of William the Silent. . . . No Government, French or English, could tell which of these Hollands would be supreme in any given situation.*

In the first years of the 1650s it was unquestionably the pacific and mercantile Holland of Amsterdam that prevailed. Amsterdam was now at the peak of its wealth and influence, eloquently expressed by the great baroque Town Hall completed in 1655 and sometimes described as the Eighth Wonder of the World. Like all the houses in the city it was built on piles sunk deep into the soggy ground – 13,569 supported it.

Amsterdam as a whole lived up to its reputation. It was a beautiful city, its many canals curving round in a series of graceful loops between the river Amstel and the broad waters of the IJ that flowed out into the Zuider Zee. The canals were lined with tall, gabled, brick houses, and the streets, unusually broad for that age, were paved with French cobbles over which the sledges, used for goods, and the coaches rattled.

Visitors were always immediately struck by the cleanliness of the town, though many burghers tended to use the canals as a convenient litter-bin, "which causes ill scents and fumes and which is a nasty thing". Fines for such behaviour were high, and the "hardie fellow" that dared to break the glass of the streetlamps which Amsterdam was still the only European city to possess, was either whipped or had his hand cut off in punishment.

Another thing foreigners always noted was the absence of beggars. The poor were taken care of by the City Council, as were orphans and the aged. The city's social services were advanced by seventeenth-century standards, and as a traveller wrote: "The charity of this renowned city is very great, even beyond example, and above comparison. They are continually giving to the poor."*

The Amsterdammers could afford to be charitable. Their city was the financial capital of Europe and its wealthiest trading centre. Its harbour was always a forest of masts, and its citizens such enthusiastic merchants that an Amsterdammer who was accused of trading with the enemy in wartime, defended himself and his city: "Burghers of Amsterdam are free to trade everywhere . . . If it were necessary to pass through hell in pursuit of gain, I would risk burning my sails."*

Their slogan "Trade but no crusade" was not admired by everyone. The exiled French philosopher Descartes remarked, in spite of Amsterdam's hospitality and charity: "In this great town where apart from myself there dwells no one who is not engaged in trade, everyone is out so much for his own advantage that I could live my whole life here without meeting a mortal being."

It was an exaggeration, but the Dutch preoccupation with trade was forgivable. Commerce had been their guarantee of independence: it had financed their struggle for freedom from Spain. In the seventy years of their existence, the United Provinces had built up from almost nothing a maritime and commercial empire which surpassed that of the Portuguese, rivalled that of Spain, and created anxious jealousies across the North Sea in England. A century ago there had been no Dutch merchant navy. In 1650 it was by far the biggest in Europe and Dutch merchant shippers were "the common carriers of the world", trading as far afield as China, Japan and the Americas.

Nearer home, they had a virtual monopoly of the important Baltic grain trade: the number of Dutch ships passing the Sound outnumbered the English by thirteen to one. Another source of wealth was the North

Sea itself with its cod and haddock, and Dutch herrings were a gastrono-
mic luxury in France.

As early as 1602 they had glimpsed the enormous commercial
potential of the Far East and set up their own chartered East India
Company, the V.O.C., which was given a monopoly of Dutch trade and
navigation in that part of the world.

The creation of a West India Company followed nineteen years later
with the monopoly of the American and African trade. In 1652 Jan van
Riebeeck assured the Dutch East route by planting the flag on the Cape
of Good Hope – a station for refreshment and revictualling on the
routes to the Far East. It was the birth of South Africa.

Mary Stuart was not impressed by the commercial success of the
Republic. For her the Dutch were no better than *nouveaux-riches* and
living in Holland was still for her "the greatest punishment in this
world". Since the death of her husband there was little in her life to make
her think otherwise. The Hague was now a "court without a king" and
the place had lost much of its gaiety and brilliance. In any case, Mary no
longer had the means to be extravagant. She lived quietly with her little
son, now a healthy toddler, in the Binnenhof, the family palace. The
States had allowed her to go on living in the large and splendid apartments in this palace traditionally occupied by the Stadholder. On one
side these rooms overlooked the still waters of the Vijver, on the other
side a courtyard and the Hall of Knights, the last surviving fragment of a
medieval castle now hung with trophies of the Spanish War. The other
buildings in this complex had been constantly modernized, and contained not only the palace but the richly furnished rooms where the
States of Holland and the States-General had their offices.

From time to time Mary took her son to the family house of
Honselaersdijck, more a luxurious mansion than a formal palace, or to
the castle Teylingen at Breda, which gave William one of his many titles
and later caused Louis XIV to call him, condescendingly, "*le petit Sieur
de Breda*".

Spurning Dutch company as she did and at odds with her mother-in-
law, Amalia, Mary would have been a very lonely woman without the
company of her favourite aunt, Queen Elizabeth of Bohemia. This
daughter of James I had lived in The Hague in poverty and exile for
years, ever since her husband had been driven out of Bohemia after a
brief rule of one winter. The "Winter Queen" as she was called, was a
lively, frivolous woman who cared more for Mary than for her own six
children. In her company Mary relaxed, showing a wit and an ease of
manner which she never displayed for the Dutch. And it was with this

pleasant aunt that after the death of William II Mary now and then ventured outside the Binnenhof. "My neece and I have been in the kermess together and to see the Dutch plays all incognito", wrote Elizabeth in May 1652.*

Occasionally Mary entertained English friends at the Binnenhof, but she had learned from bitter experience that she had to be cautious in her choice of company. When the Earl of Buckingham, the agreeable libertine who was her brother Charles's favourite companion, came to The Hague in 1651, rumours of a flirtation between him and Mary were soon circulating. After a stern warning that the people "even in the barges" were gossiping about them, Mary reluctantly sent him away.*

Other members of the exiled English court always found the doors of her palaces open, and, when in 1652 war between the Republic and Cromwellian England broke out, these refugees from the Protector gathered at The Hague around her, hoping that a Dutch victory would mean their return to England.

This war had been inevitable ever since the English Parliament passed a series of Navigation Acts in October 1651.

To such a trading country as the Dutch these Acts amounted to a declaration of war. By them England prohibited imports carried in ships other than British, or those of the country of origin. In the state of tension thus created between the two countries, only a spark was needed; and flashpoint came on 29 May 1652 when the Dutch admiral, Tromp, in the act of lowering his flag to a fleet of fifteen British ships in the Channel, was fired on by their Admiral Blake. The Dutchman hesitated, then retaliated, and after a day-long sea-battle, retired with the loss of two ships. The States-General angrily censured Tromp. War had been the last thing they wanted: their navy was ill-prepared and unequipped, the ships undermanned, and what they dreaded almost more was that now, as in any time of crisis, the people would instinctively look to the House of Orange for leadership even if its prince was only eighteen months old.

Their worst fears were realized. Two years and twelve sea-battles later, the grass was sprouting in the once neat streets of Amsterdam, the country swarmed with beggars, the Dutch carrying trade was at a standstill. And in Zeeland and Gelderland in the years 1653 and 1654 there were riotous popular demands to have William made Stadholder, under the slogan:

> *Even if our Prince is small*
> *He'll be Stadholder after all.**

In May 1663, William was given his own Household of twenty-nine persons, and to celebrate this Charles II – who himself had volunteered to serve in the Dutch navy* – made his little nephew Knight of the Garter, focussing public attention on him. When William and his mother went to Breda the following month there were huge demonstrations. Back at The Hague, William had to be held up at the windows of the Binnen-hof to the cheering crowds outside. Even the local militia joined in the shouting, and the worried States-General had to send troops to restore order. "In later years it will seem unbelievable that a warlike nation in its embarrassment sought refuge with a small boy not yet out of his swaddling-clothes"; so wrote an indignant States of Holland man in a pamphlet.*

But the hour of the Orange Prince had not yet come. At the height of the crisis another personality made itself felt. It was Johan de Witt. In March 1653 he was provisionally named Raadspensionary of Holland, and in August he was sworn in for this "gilded slavery", with the warning from friends: "If you accept this office you must expect to be put in your coffin not whole but in pieces."* Born into a Regent family in Dordrecht in 1625, he already had the habit of authority. His father and grandfather had both been Burgemeesters of Dordrecht, his uncle had been Pensionary, and he himself, after studying at Leiden University and long travels through France and England, became Pensionary of Dordrecht at the age of twenty-five. He was a tall, rather solemn young man, simply but carefully dressed, who liked to study mathematics and translated Corneille's *Horace* from French into Dutch for his amusement. As well as his own countrymen, he impressed the foreign diplomats who had dealings with him – "*Un esprit prompt et hardi*"; "it's impossible to find a more experienced or finer man".*

He had the anti-Orange sentiments natural to his class, and in his case they were strengthened by family experience: his father Jacob de Witt had been one of the six Loevesteiners thrown into prison by William II during the Amsterdam crisis of 1650. But he was a Republican by conviction as well as by birth. For him the sovereignty of the States was not to be challenged, and the supremacy of Holland was natural and realistic. The exclusion of the Orange family, he believed, was essential to the preservation of the Republic, and when in January 1654 Cromwell suggested that an Act of Exclusion of the Orange family in perpetuity should form part of a peace treaty, it was to be expected that De Witt – now half a year in office – should readily agree.

The Act itself was passed on 1 May by the States of Holland, who had been sworn to secrecy, but news of it soon leaked out and the other provinces were indignant. Justifying his independent action, De Witt said: "Holland was compelled to it by force of necessity because Cromwell refused to agree to a peace treaty without this secret promise from Holland."* Public opinion was not placated. "On carts and in barges this work was attacked in the most furious terms . . ." and many of the Dutch believed that this Act of Exclusion was a deliberate "Apple of Discord" thrown to them by Cromwell in the hope of making a rift in the Union, after which they would call for his protection.*

The two Princesses, Amalia and Mary, were astonished and angered. They sent a memorandum to the States-General asking them to annul Holland's action and reminding them of the "long and faithful services of the Orange family, and the tender and innocent years of Prince William".* But it was too late. The States of Holland replied to the Princesses that they had acted not out of enmity against the House of Orange but of *evidente necessiteit.**

Amalia herself, who had shown sympathy with the popular demon-strations, received a severe reprimand from De Witt. "My Lords of Holland will take care . . . that the rabble shall not again behave insolently in the streets . . . my Lords know well by whom and for whose sake all this was done and planned." Amalia, much mortified, shut herself up with a "little fever". Mary took it all more calmly. She declared: "With things as they are, I can only be patient and accept the situation as long as I live in this country."*

She had another reason for resentment. One of the unwritten con-ditions of the peace treaty signed at Westminster on 5 April 1654 was that in the future her brother Charles, now living in Spa in the Spanish Netherlands, was not allowed to enter Holland. Instead Mary had to travel to see him and this summer she joined him for a long holiday. His court in Spa was almost penniless, but they amused themselves enor-mously nevertheless. "There is not a day or night but there are balls and dansinge", it was reported to Cromwell.

Amid all this gaiety, Mary did not forget her little son. In July she sent detailed instructions to his governess Mrs. Howard, telling her that William was to be available to callers every day between eleven and three, and that he was to be taken to his grandmother's pretty little palace in the woods outside The Hague, Het Huis ten Bosch, when the weather was fine enough.*

Perhaps it was on one of these outings to his grandmother that William had an accident one day in August, when on the bridge leading to the Princess of Orange's house his coach overturned. "But God be thanked, there was no hurt, onelie the coache broken," wrote the Queen of Bohemia on 31 August 1654. She had taken him into her own carriage and brought him home.*

The party at Spa, in the meantime, had broken up when Kate Killigrew, one of Mary's ladies-in-waiting, died of smallpox. Mary travelled into Germany with Charles, stayed in Aix-la-Chapelle, then returned at last in October to Holland, where she began to look about for a new lady-in-waiting. Among the English exiles at The Hague was the seventeen-year-old Anne, daughter of her brother's Chancellor Sir Edward Hyde. She was a lively girl of character, and Mary took her in her service. Elizabeth of Bohemia commented: "I heare Mrs. Hide is to come to my neece in Mrs. Killigrew's place, which I am verie glad of, she is verie fitt for itt and is a great favorit of mine."* Less pleased was Anne's father, "who did in Truth perfectly detest" the appointment.

Anne herself obviously enjoyed her new life, and when Henry, Duke of Gloucester, came to stay with his elder sister Mary at her castle of Teylinge, she joined happily in the festivities. When she appeared at a fancy-dress ball dressed as a shepherdess, the Winter Queen described her as "verie handsome in it, none but her mistress looked better than she did".*

A year later Anne travelled with Mary to Paris, a visit the Princess had planned for years and for which she offered the excuse that she wanted to discuss the affairs of Orange with Louis XIV. Frederick von Dohna, the Governor of the little principality left to her by her husband, had always refused to acknowledge her claim on it, and she hoped that Louis XIV would give her his support. Her real object, however, was to see her mother again after thirteen years, to amuse herself in Europe's most civilized court, and even – so rumour had it – win Louis XIV as a husband. On that score at least, her visit was a failure.* She stayed almost a year and only returned when she heard that William had fallen ill. In Bruges the news reached her that it was no worse than measles, a reason for her to extend her holiday for a few weeks.

During her long absence, William celebrated his sixth birthday and was allowed his first pocket-money – fifty guilders a month.* His Household was increased and his uncle, the Stadholder of Friesland, gave him two horses which, together with a horse given by another uncle, the Elector of Brandenburg, were stabled at Honselaersdijck. A travelling preacher who saw the little boy at this age described him in his diary: "We have seen the young Prince . . . a handsome young gentleman, very lively." He had been wearing a black moire silk skirt, following Dutch custom, and a small black hat with a white feather. But to the preacher's astonishment, he was still being carried around in the arms of a nurse.* What struck most people was his "Reservedness and Moderation"* in public. After the christening of her nephew Hendrik Casimir on 10 January 1655, Elizabeth of Bohemia had already noted: "My little nephue was at the super and satt verie still all the time: those States that were there, were verie taken with him."*

Now, on his sixth birthday, as usual, the people flocked to pay their respects to their small Prince. Most striking among them was the little daughter of the fervent Orangist Jan Zoet. She was dressed from head to foot in orange, white and blue.

From that day life took on a new aspect for William. While his mother was still absent in Paris, the Dowager-Princess had appointed the Reverend Cornelius Trigland – a *"ministre Flamand"* – as Chaplain, with the responsibility of "educating and instructing him in the fear of God, and the true Christian reformed religion". Trigland, who instructed him for one and a half hours every day, was as impressed by his pupil as everyone. He found in him a *"divinum ingenium*, an excellent character, and purity of behaviour". Sometimes he would find the boy on his knees at prayer in his bedroom.

For his secular instruction the French artist Abraham Ranguineau, who painted his pupil several times, had been chosen. These two men, together with the governess Mrs. Walburg Howard van Kerckhoven, Heenvliet's second daughter by his first marriage and a "matron adorned with prudence, piety and most chaste manners",* had to follow as much as possible the careful instructions drawn up by Constantyn Huygens in 1654. In this *Discours sur la nourriture de Son Altesse Monseigneur le Prince d'Orange*, four hundred and twelve paragraphs set out in the minutest detail how the Prince was to be prepared for the great offices of his ancestors which "by turn of the wheel of time" would be restored to him. Sound health was an essential, so Huygens prescribed plenty of fresh air, a simple diet and exercise at ball-games or riding – but until he was a little older, it was to be a wooden horse only. The suggestion that the Prince should as far as possible be kept out of the hands of doctors, who "often ruin their patients by medicines", was one that William never forgot.

His spiritual health was equally insisted on. He was to be kept free from all *"bigotterie et devotion exterieure"* but he was to attend church services regularly, read the scriptures and the psalms, and compose a private prayer. He was to be instructed in the *"vertues et vices"*, and taught to resist temptation, particularly *"lesquels s'exercent au jeu, au vin et avec les dames"*. Above all, he was to be trained in rigid self-control, essential for his difficult position in Dutch affairs. As Huygens prophetically put it, "*Qui est maistre de soy mesme, il est maistre de touts autres.*" With the same eye to his future, he was to be trained to command the respect of the States and not to abuse his position to create political conflict. He was not to deceive, but not forbidden to dissemble. And finally, he must learn to regard politics and military affairs as part of his everyday life.*

One of the first fruits of this education was the letter in French he wrote around that time to Charles II. His uncle had often sent him affectionate little notes. Now, probably with the help of Trigland, it was William's turn. He started with the endearing excuse that if he had not written before, it was not "by lack of good will but from my incapacity, not having been able to handle the pen". He promised his uncle to follow his advice "to rouse myself to study, following from afar your example and that of other great men, who particularly distinguished themselves by having happily married letters and sciences together with arms, and who achieved salutary law-giving with great feats . . ."* Charles was amused by this epistle that breathed the high-minded sentiments of William's instructor. He was touched as well, because he was very fond of this little nephew. So much so, that Mary could not hide her jealousy.

"You are so partially kind to him," she wrote her brother once reproachfully, "that I fear at last my desiring your kindness to him will turn to jealousy he may take some from me." Carried away by her strong feelings for her brother, she exaggerated her detachment from her son by stating: "I must assure you, that I shall obey all your commands except that of loving him (though he is my only child) above all things in the world, as long as you are in it. . . ."*

Mary's love for her brother was as constant as her anxiety about his future. In 1659 after the death of Cromwell she financed abortive attempts to recover his crown by selling some of her jewels and pawning for 30,000 guilders a beautifully cut diamond called the "Little Sancy" of 39 carats, set in a bed of silver and worth 80,000 guilders.* In defiance of the States ban, Charles made occasional secret visits to her, but news of them usually leaked out, and George Downing, a bitter enemy of the Dutch who had been sent to The Hague in January 1658 as Cromwell's ambassador, made it his business to hurry the young man out of the country. With relish he reported to London in June 1658 that his protest to De Witt had caused Charles II to leave Dutch territory "a little sooner than he intended".*

The young Prince, who had heard Downing's intrigues discussed at home, made his own gesture of protest. In May 1658 he was being driven through the streets of The Hague when Downing approached in his coach. The ambassador "would not give way, till the gathering of people frightened him".

Mary's brother continued in the meantime to visit her in Breda.* Charles was not the only trespasser. Another constant visitor was her younger brother James, who had as keen an interest in visiting Mary as the Princess Royal had once had in welcoming Charles: during Mary's visit to Paris, James's eye had fallen on her lady-in-waiting Anne Hyde, and Mary herself had developed a "kindness" for Harry Jermyn, one of Charles's dissolute courtiers and an ugly but irresistible womanizer.

Mary's involvement had been short-lived – Charles put an end to it after a blazing row with his sister – but James continued his wooing, and during a lively house-party at Honselaersdijck in the summer of 1659 he was able to admire Anne dancing at a masked ball and playing in a French comedy. His aunt Queen Elizabeth of Bohemia wrote of this performance that "Nane Hyde . . . is the chief of our players; she doth act verie well."*

At eight years old, William was much too young to take part in these frolics. He was studying hard in preparation for his departure to Leiden University. Founded by his great-grandfather William the Silent, it was the oldest university of the United Provinces and one of the most distinguished in Europe. The Prince was not to be enrolled as an ordinary student, but to receive private tuition in his own rooms in the one-time convent of St. Barbara, now called the Prinsenhof. As his governor, Mary appointed Frederik van Nassau, Heer van Zuylestein. This was a tactical victory over Amalia, who had good reasons for resenting the nomination.* Zuylestein was the illegitimate son of her husband Frederik Hendrik, and married to an Englishwoman Mary Killigrew, one of Mary's ladies-in-waiting, by whom he was said to be dominated. In spite of these grave defects, even Amalia could not deny that he was an "*homme de cœur, de sens et d'esprit*",* and accepting her defeat she travelled together with William and Mary to Leiden, the "garden of Holland", where the Prince, to the irritation of the Regents, was given a solemn reception by the University and wild acclamations by the people.

Of course it was "Constanter" Huygens who had drawn up further detailed instructions for this next stage of his education. Zuylestein, with the help of Trigland and a new tutor, the Frenchman Chapuzeau, was to pay much attention to the formation of the Prince's character. The boy was inclined to be irritable or impatient, due "to his natural disposition or the liberty of his first infancy" and Zuylestein was to check this. (The French Ambassador de Thou had already noted "*quelque sémence de fierté*" in the young Prince.) This streak of petulance was probably accounted for by Mary's regular and long absences, and by his health which was "not of the most robust". He suffered from asthmatic attacks and had now grown up into a thin, pale boy with a hollow chest and a cough. Huygens told Zuylestein to take great care of his physical well-being, send him to bed not later than ten, and see that he had the right food and took enough exercise. This exercise included fencing, ball-games and riding, and Bernard Duka instructed him in dancing. Once again, as he had done five years earlier, Sir Constantyn emphasized how important it was for William to learn how to handle people and situations, so that those "ill-disposed to him lose their rancour", while those who love him should love him more and more. Courtesy and good manners were to be the rule, and offenders promptly punished so that "he may see how persons of honour hold such incidents in loathing".

As in the first instructions, the chief emphasis was on religion. He must go to church twice daily, once to the French and once to the Dutch.

The languages he studied were Latin, French and, perhaps not surprisingly, Dutch: in his mother's household Dutch was the language of the servants, only French or English being spoken. Other subjects were music, drawing, writing, modern and ancient history, and geography. During a lesson in this last his teacher, describing the British Isles as "a little world in themselves", drew from William the remark: "I wish I had a little world like that." His tutor, amused, asked "And what would you do with it if you had, Highness?" "Give it to me and I will show you," replied William.*

He was also to be instructed in current affairs by reading the Gazettes, and his military education was not forgotten. Anthony Smets, the Prince's librarian, saw him coming on his own to borrow books like Hexham's *Principles of the Military Art*, Gheyn's beautifully illustrated *Wapenhandelinge van Roers, Musquetten ende Spiesen* – which William pre-ferred in a French translation, bound in blue satin – and military classics like Caesar's *Commentaries*. The history of his own family fascinated him. Mary had once shown him a book called *Effigien van Prinsen en Princessen van Orange*. Now eight years old he came back to borrow this handsome red-velvet bound album.*

Study, however, was from time to time interrupted by pleasant distractions. On 17 November there was a trip to The Hague to say goodbye to his mother who was going to Breda and to meet a lively little girl two years younger than himself, whom everybody called Liselotte. She was Charlotte Elisabeth, daughter of Charles-Louis, Elector Palatine, who had come to pay a visit to her grandmother, the Winter Queen, together with her aunt Sophia, the Duchess of Osnabrück, later Electress of Hanover, with whom she had lived since her parents separated. William and the girl took to each other at once. They played together at the Binnenhof, and sixty years later Liselotte, the fat and ageing widow of the Duc d'Orléans, still remembered asking the young William during that visit who was the lady "with such a fiery nose"? The boy answered giggling: "That is the Princess Royal, my mother." Liselotte, who had promised her aunt to be on her best behaviour, was horrified, but Anne Hyde came to the rescue and sent the children off by themselves to play "all sorts of games".

They were rolling over a Turkish carpet when Liselotte was summoned to go home with her grandmother Queen Elizabeth. "I took one leap and rushed into the drawing-room but the Queen was already in the antechamber. However, I was not scared." She tugged at Mary's dress to attract her attention, performed a pretty curtsey and walked out, mimicking the stately exit of the Winter Queen to the great amusement of the whole Court.*

Her grandmother, who adored Liselotte, noticed with delight the "great acquaintance betwixt the little Prince and her".* They had been so pleased with each other that the grown-ups began to wonder if they might not make an excellent match when they were a little older. But Liselotte confided to William's former governess Mrs. Howard: "I think it will go with me as with that little poodle dog that is promised so much and sent to his kennel after all." And, indeed, nothing came of these expectations.*

Another more important alliance was, however, successfully concluded that same month: France and Spain signed the Peace of the Pyrenees. For Louis XIV this was the occasion for a stately tour through his whole country. Among the halting places on this journey was the strongly fortified city and principality of Orange, dominating the hills of Provence not far from Avignon. For the French King, Orange was a thorn in his side, a foreign and Protestant enclave in the heart of French territory, and a refuge for French malcontents.

With the sovereign of the tiny state still a minor and powerless, Louis thought the moment had come to eradicate this nuisance. Before his own arrival troops had been sent to blockade the town, and on 20 March 1660 its corrupt governor, Frederick von Dohna, brother-in-law of Amalia, who for ten years had opposed Mary's claims, surrendered it to the French in return for a handsome present.

A week later Louis made his grand entrance. He walked the streets, concealing his indignation at the sight of the huge bastion that towered over the town, and when he had climbed to the top of it, tugged out a tiny fragment of stone and dropped it over the parapet. The fortifications, his gesture signified, were to be destroyed. By July his orders had been carried out. And William was notified that the French protectorate would last until he came of age. In the meantime, the revenues would be paid to Louis.

The Dowager-Princess protested in vain, "the French King telling her that he was not bounde to doe anything for her consideration, having not forgott how she disobliged him at the treatie of Munster".* Mary herself complained bitterly to the French ambassador, whom she summoned to Honselaersdijck.*

But that for the moment was all that could be done. Louis XIV knew perfectly well that the Orange family would not have the support of the States in this question, and the faint and formal protest of the High Mightinesses, as the Dutch deputies were styled, was brushed off contemptuously by the French statesman Cardinal Mazarin with the words: "that the King did more for the interests of the Prince of Orange than those who spoke for him".*

This rape of his principality was an affront that William never forgave Louis XIV.

CHAPTER III

William Alone

I N APRIL 1660 Charles II was at last invited to return to his kingdom. Cromwell was dead. His son Richard was not strong enough to impose the republican ideal on a country essentially royalist. And the English Parliament now voted overwhelmingly for the restoration of their monarchy.

Overnight the young King became the most popular guest of the Dutch. The Regents, who for six years had forbidden him even to enter the United Provinces, flocked to the Orange castle at Breda to do him honour. They were joined by hundreds of Englishmen, and the little town was so overcrowded that one of the States Deputies complained about the rising prices and the shortages. He wrote to the States that if the King did not leave Breda soon, half England would come to the town. And he urged them to be lavish in sending in supplies of food, especially marmalade, "to preserve the reputation of the state".*

Nobody could accuse the Regents of being stingy. Amsterdam lent Charles 20,000 guilders until funds arrived for him from England, and they invited him to The Hague for a magnificent reception. A delighted and triumphant Mary was always at his side, together with the Dukes of York and Gloucester. Her son William met them in Delft and sat on his uncle James's knee in the coach for their glorious entry into The Hague. Charles was lodged in the small palace of Johan Maurits van Nassau-Siegen, where fine troops of horses guarded him, and he was fêted and feasted wherever he went. He remarked drily, later on, that he had never been treated better anywhere. And as his aunt Elizabeth of Bohemia wrote to her son: He "was receaved with the great joye and affection that can be. If he were their own King the States could doe no more to him."*

The climax of the celebrations was a dinner given in his honour by the States-General. Mary sat radiant at his right side, while William had a seat next to his uncle Henry of Gloucester. It seemed a great reconciliation between the States and the Orange family, and between Holland

and England. As Johan de Witt put it: ". . . his majesty could judge with what affection and zeal they would in future cherish and maintain the union and close friendship between your Kingdom and this Republic." And Charles, in an equally gracious reply, made it clear that past injuries were now forgiven and forgotten, taking "into consideration that the Dutch had been forced to treat with people who, having revolted against his father, were equally persistent against him." But he assured De Witt: "Now you will have to do with men of honour."*

Inevitably, William's future was touched on in discussions between Charles and De Witt. The Raadspensionary understood very well that the position of the Orange family had been strengthened by Charles's restoration. He had anticipated the young King's intervention in the affairs of his nephew, and had his answer ready. "With a free people, events must be allowed to take their own course."* To his relief and Mary's disappointment, Charles let the matter drop for the moment, only recommending the interests of his sister and her son – *"deux personnes qui me sont extrêmement chères"* – to the care of the States.

His tact was lavishly rewarded by the Dutch. They presented him with the collection of pictures bought at the sale of Charles I's treasures by a Dutchman, restoring to the English crown many of the most precious paintings now in its possession. Other gifts were a beautiful yacht and the great State bed which had been destined for the confinement of the Princess Royal but never used because of mourning for William II. They had bought it back from Mary for 100,000 guilders.

By the time Charles left, the States-General had spent one and a half million guilders to do him honour, while he had cost the States of Holland another 600,000 guilders. Not everyone thought the money well spent. Deputy Stellingwerff from Enkhuizen remarked: "It would have been better to employ the money . . . in the purchase of cannon, cannonballs and the munitions of war."* But the more general feeling was that "if the devil himself were sovereign of Great Britain, it would be necessary to live on friendly terms with him."

On 2 June Charles left Holland. Mary, William and the Queen of Bohemia went with him to Scheveningen, where he boarded the naval yacht the *Naseby*, now rechristened the *Royal Charles*. Huge crowds – more than 100,000 people, some said – watched his departure from the dunes. As the Dutch *Mercurius* remarked: "The whole population seemed to have met by appointment . . . a King who had been seen some months before walking in the streets of The Hague without attracting the least attention from passers-by."* Aboard the ship, Charles dined for the last time with his sister and her son. He urged her to visit him as soon as possible in London, and to bring William with her. Then the *Royal Charles* set sail for England.

Her brother's restoration had given fresh heart to Mary and fresh hope to the Orange family. She felt confident enough now to introduce William officially to Amsterdam, where they arrived on 15 June. The anti-Orange and anti-English city gave them an unexpectedly warm reception. Triumphal cars paraded tableaux showing scenes from Nassau and "Stuwaert" history. One of them, however, was not much appreciated by Mary. It represented the beheading of Charles I so vividly that the Princess Royal was deeply shocked and almost fainted when she saw the poised axe.*

It was the first encounter between William and Amsterdam, and on this occasion the traditional conflict between the Orange family and the republic's most powerful city were forgotten. Perhaps not surprisingly the frail nine-year-old boy hardly seemed an immediate threat to Amsterdam's supremacy.

From Amsterdam, Mary and William went on to Haarlem and another enthusiastic welcome. A special treat for the Prince was a visit to the rich merchant Gabriel Marcelis at Overveen. After feasting him on "rare fruits and everything that was new, delicate and attractive", his host let loose a hare in his conservatory. It was William's first hunt. The *Mercurius* reported that the hare "was immediately pursued with great energy and caught by the prince."* Back in The Hague, they found a band of small boys waiting to greet William outside the Binnenhof, with wooden swords and orange plumes in their hats. William solemnly reviewed his troops, invited them in, and presented each of them with a gingerbread cake.

Mary's campaign was a success. In August Zeeland proposed to make the Prince Stadholder of Holland and Zeeland, and Captain and Admiral-General of the United Provinces, with effect from his eighteenth birthday. Friesland supported the proposal. Johan de Witt, under pressure from public feeling, gave in enough to offer, at the request of the Dowager-Princess, that the States should now make themselves responsible for the Prince's education.

Mary wanted them to go further and commit themselves to William's future Stadholdership. De Witt, irritated by her tactless insistence, complained bitterly to the French ambassador de Thou that she would do better to devote herself to the upbringing of her son, so that he would be able to serve the State when he was old enough. He thought it the height of folly to promise a child of nine or ten such important responsibilities, to which one day he might not be equal.*

The Raadspensionary was in fact still completely opposed to the idea of an Orange resurgence. He was convinced that their exclusion was in the best interests of the State, and he boasted to Beverwaert, the Dutch envoy in England, "I am not surprised that I have the reputation . . . of being opposed to the interests of the Prince of Orange, for I have at all times placed them after those of the State."

The Princess Royal, eager to leave for a visit to England, ceased protesting and accepted a compromise. Holland would adopt William as a Child of State, make themselves responsible for his maintenance and education, and train him for those offices which they refused to promise him. At the same time the Act of Exclusion was repealed, and Mary declared that she considered this a first step to a "further and complete" restoration of Orange power. It was 29 September, and on the following day she left for England.

William accompanied his mother when she left The Hague at half past nine in the morning, and they arrived at Hellevoetsluys at six in the evening. While she waited for the tide, Mary wrote a last letter to the States-General begging them to take care of "the being who is dearest to us in the world".*

Next day news reached her of the death from smallpox of her younger brother the Duke of Gloucester. Overwhelmed, she withdrew to her cabin where she spent the last hours completely alone. At three in the afternoon, her ship the *Tredagh* sailed, leaving the small boy she had called her *Piquinino* waving goodbye from Den Briel.

· The departure of the Stuart Princess was not much regretted by the Dutch. She had always disliked them and they had returned the feeling. The thin dark-haired girl with her sullen and discontented face had even alienated the Orange party by her arrogance. In his Instructions from the French government, Ambassador de Thou was told that Mary "does not readily condescend to demonstrations of goodwill and kindness" which would have been in the interests of her son's position, and this not because she lacked intelligence or love for her child, but because – thanks to her English upbringing and her character – she thought such behaviour beneath her.* She took the loyalty of the Orangists for granted, and it seems never to have crossed her mind that her fanatical Stuart loyalties and her constant junketings abroad could damage her son's interests. "It breaks my heart," Hyde wrote, "to see how negligent she is of old friends."*

Her haughty snubbing way was notorious. Two young Dutch Orangists who once called on the Princess in Bruges noted: "She received us in her customary manner, that is to say, coldly and without saying a word."* Almost as damaging to the Orange cause were her constant quarrels with the Dowager-Princess. "Everything that is advised by the mother-in-law was opposed by the daughter-in-law, although she was often told that only unity could serve the interests of the Prince."* From the Orange point of view, accordingly, Mary's absence in England, where she intended to stay, could only ease the situation.

Without his mother William celebrated his tenth birthday on 14 November. The magistrates from The Hague invited "the instrument of great hope for this State" – as they liked to call the Prince – to a banquet in the Oude Doelen. Later in the day, he was the guest of the local militia in the Nieuwe Doelen where the mayor of The Hague hung round his neck the heavy gold chain of the Golden Fleece, once presented to the militia by Charles V of Spain.

According to the London diarist Samuel Pepys, who had met him during Charles's stay at The Hague in June, the Prince was now "a very pretty boy", who lived modestly with his small household.* Another contemporary writer who had seen him in Leiden was struck by the simplicity of his clothes and daily life, and impressed by the boy's *"vivacité d'esprit et un certain air de grandeur"*.* Monsieur de Monconys described him as "very good-looking, his face long but well shaped, his eyes soft, his nose aquiline, and his intelligence keen".* Those who had met him reported that he talked well, but rarely. He was an excellent listener, never interrupted, and when he answered it was always to the point. Already he was the centre of a court. Foreign diplomats and distinguished visitors to The Hague made a point of calling on him, and this small boy kept open table "for the resort of such of the States or officers of the army, or other noble persons, who frequently repaired thither", wrote Clarendon.*

The common people of Holland adored him, and the French envoy de Thou wrote to Paris: "At ten years, the prince must nevertheless be considered as the heir to the name and the affection of the people of this country. . . . If this affection and love, which at the moment fills the people, lasts and grows stronger, it can be said that as long as he has the drive, the ambition and the will to become sovereign of the State, he could well succeed."*

THE JOURNEY OF HIS MOTHER Princess Mary had had an ill-omened start. Her ship the *Tredagh* ran aground on the sandbanks outside Margate and there were fears for her safety. The King, who was waiting for his sister at Gravesend, heard she was stranded and came to meet her in his own barge.* She was home after an absence of eighteen years, but much had changed. The death of her brother the Duke of Gloucester had plunged the English court into mourning, and at the same time a family scandal raged around her other brother, the Duke of York.

But nothing could repress for very long the gaiety of Whitehall. It was obvious that Charles "that known enemy to virginity and chastity" was King. As the Comte de Gramont wrote in his memoirs, it was "an entire scene of gallantry and amusement, all the politeness and magnificence, which the inclination of a Prince, naturally addicted to tenderness and pleasure, could suggest. The beauties were desirous of charming and the men endeavoured to please."* The dazzling Barbara Palmer whom Charles brought back from exile as his mistress – her complaisant husband was soon created Earl of Castlemaine – was the reigning belle of the Court.

The Whitehall style was extravagant. Everybody was dressed in the very latest fashion – five years later London counted, for example, 10,000 ribbon-makers – and the women glittered with jewellery, sometimes more than £40,000 worth at a time. Gambling was an obsession, and the loss of £100 at the tables was considered a trifle. The Londoners found it all great fun, and it was even more fun to be able to watch it at close quarters – Charles kept open house and was usually accessible to those who wanted to ask a favour, pay their respects or simply have a look at their King.

Mary ought to have enjoyed it all very much. But her pleasure was spoiled by the scandal that James had created at Court by announcing that he was secretly married to Mary's lady-in-waiting Anne Hyde, the girl he had met in Paris in 1656 and often visited at The Hague. Mary was horrified by the idea of her brother marrying "one of her servants" and humiliated by the prospect of having to give precedence to this daughter of a middle-class lawyer. James's mother, Henrietta Maria, arrived in person from Paris to prevent, with her authority, "so great a stain and dishonour to the Crown" as this marriage.* She threatened that "whenever that woman shall be brought into Whitehall by one door, she would instantly quit it by another."* And her threats and intrigues very nearly succeeded. With the help of gentlemen of the Court, she spread rumours that James – who had confessed that he had secretly contracted to marry Anne at Breda on 24 November 1659 and lived with her as his wife – had not been the only lover of the now-pregnant girl. One of Henrietta Maria's supporters was Tom Killigrew, who detested Anne's father, the prosy straitlaced Clarendon. He boldly declared that "he had had the honour of being upon the most intimate terms with her. He affirmed that he had found the critical minute in a certain closet built over the water, for a purpose very different from that of giving ease to the pain of love."

It was too much for Charles. He called his brother and forced him to put an end to the scandal. The wedding was performed in private on 3 September 1660 by the Duke's Chaplain Dr. Drowther, at Worcester House, the home of Anne's father. Afterwards, in front of witnesses and before Clarendon's disapproving eyes, Charles gestured to Anne and asked two of his friends to pay their respects to "his sister, the Dutchess of York".

But the marriage was not made public despite Anne's pregnancy, and Henrietta Maria made a final effort. She persuaded her courtier Sir Charles Berkeley to "reveal" that Anne and he had been secretly betrothed. The Duke of York, who already regretted his misalliance, was only too willing to believe him. He swore never to see Anne again and "was resolved to deny that he was married". Only after the child was born on 22 October did Berkeley confess his slander, whereupon James wrote to Anne that "he would speedily visit her", telling her to take care of his son.* Henrietta Maria admitted defeat, especially after Mazarin had written threatening that unless she remained on good terms with her sons and their ministers, she would not be allowed to come back to France.*

The family unity was restored and on 1 January 1661 Pepys could report in his Diary that the Duke of York brought his Lady "to wait upon the Queene [mother], the first time that ever she did since that great business; and the Queene is said to receive [her] with much respect and love".*

Mary did not live to witness the reconciliation. Just before Christmas she had fallen ill of smallpox, the disease that had killed her husband ten years earlier. "As soone as she fell sick, she saide she shoulde dye, but was not at all afrayed of it and rather seemed willing to dye" wrote her aunt the Winter Queen later. Death came on Christmas Eve – "she made a verie godlie end." A few days later, she was buried next to her brother Henry in the Stuart vault in Westminster Abbey.* On the day of her death she made a will in which she left her son 150,000 guilders, and all the jewels given her by her husband. She asked Charles and Henrietta Maria "to take upon them the care of the Prince of Orange, my son, as the best parents and friends I can commend him unto . . . praying God to bless and make him a happy instrument to his country's good."*

The will was to create great difficulties for William, and not many of the clauses were fulfilled. The family jewels, for instance, "those which I found in his father's cupboard", disappeared, one expensive pearl necklace going to the new Duchess of York; a whole boxful was taken back to France by the Queen Mother; and Mary's most precious jewel, the Little Sancy which she had pawned a year ago to finance her brother, had to be redeemed years later by William.

Charles appeared to have forgotten his sister's many loans to him and the unpaid dowry, and had the effrontery to claim from the Princess-Dowager in Holland the sum of 200,000 guilders to pay off her servants and her creditors.

News of Mary's death was slow to reach The Hague: Holland had been ravaged by one of the worst storms in its history, disrupting communications with England.* When they were restored Charles II received a letter from his nephew in The Hague, "my first in the Latin tongue". Even the cynical King must have been deeply touched by the words praising him as "a Prince who is a paragon of our age, a Prince who is my uncle and guardian and who now holds my precious mother in his treasure-house."*

Not until 3 January did William learn that he was now an orphan. Queen Elizabeth of Bohemia rushed "in her first burst of sorrow" to Leiden, and folded "the desolate boy in her arms". William was inconsolable and his health collapsed under the strain. For days following, he suffered from asthmatic attacks, violent headaches and fainting spells so severe that his life seemed in danger. And the Dutch, remembering now only that Mary had been the mother of their young Prince, grieved with him. "All heere from the highest to the lowest are verie sorrie for here" wrote Elizabeth.*

Their grief, unlike William's, was short-lived, and in England it was the same. Two months later a courtier wrote from London: "The Princess Royal is more forgotten here than ever before."*

When William finally recovered from his illness he was still so weak that he needed a harness to support his back, and returning to his studies at Leiden he found that he was once more the subject of a battle over his guardianship. Mary's will had offended the States-General in every aspect. De Witt exclaimed: "The Princess Royal makes a will and not only does not make her son universal heir, but hardly leaves him a stiver; she recommends him to the care of the King her brother and the Queen her mother, but does not even mention the States . . . to whom she had once entrusted her child as his chief guardian."*

He asked Charles II to relinquish the guardianship to the State of

Holland, and the King at first agreed. Representations hurriedly made by Amalia made him change his mind, and De Witt wrote exasperated: "If the matter cannot be settled in that way, or in some similar manner, then it seems best to me for their noble High Mightinesses to wash their hands of it."* Charles was unmoved, and gave the Princess-Dowager his share of the guardianship with complete control over the Orange estates and the Prince's education. He reasoned that princes were needed "when princes are educated".

Johan de Witt angrily refused from that moment all the States' responsibility for William's education, and even stopped his grants. He explained years later in a conversation with a Frenchman, that if the States had formally insisted on undertaking his guardianship at this time, it would have been impossible to refuse him the hereditary Orange offices, "and the people, who already love him too much, at this time when it's too early to judge how he will be, might force the magistrates to give him a power too great and too prejudicial to the liberty of the country, which, sustained by his alliances in England and elsewhere, could one day be its ruin."*

William was old enough to understand what was going on. He now appeared to have recovered completely from the first shock of his mother's death, and in April 1661 was taken for a holiday at Cleves. Before he left, he said goodbye to the Winter Queen, who was going back to England where she died in February 1662. After their last meeting in The Hague, she wrote to her son on 11 April:

> Yesterday my little nephue was heere to take his leave of me, he is sent for to Cleve and goes this morning . . . My nephue is verie inquisitive of her [Liselotte] he liked her verie well but she could not abide him. He mends strangely and grows verie strong, you cannot imagine the witt he has, it is not a witt of a child who is suffiçant, but of a man. . . . He is a verie extra-ordinarie childe and verie good natured.*

At Cleves, William stayed with his uncle Friedrich Wilhelm, the Elector of Brandenburg, who was charmed with him and called him "*das liebste Kind*" that he knew, and very intelligent for his age. Here for the first time in his life William went on a real hunt and killed a boar with the help of his uncle,* an enormous thrill for the ten-year-old boy. His health improved very much during this holiday, and two doctors who examined him at Cleves suggested that he could exchange his heavy back-support for a lighter brace. But his constitution remained shaky, and his poor health was always a source of anxiety to his supporters. As one of them said, "Many of the Regents of today would be reassured by his death, because they fear that otherwise there will be changes in the future."*

William's health also worried his uncle Charles II, who made inquiries from time to time. The Dowager-Princess, sending him news, had a personal motive at first for keeping in touch with him. At forty-two Charles was the most eligible bachelor of Europe and Amalia still hoped that the King would marry her youngest daughter Marie. But the King had never forgotten the way she snubbed him when, still in exile, he had asked for the hand of her elder daughter Henrietta. And her hopes were finally dashed in May 1662 when he married Catherine of Braganza, of whom Dryden later wrote that "her greatest fault was her being educated a Catholic; her greatest misfortune bearing the King no children; and her greatest foible an excessive love of dancing."*

Three weeks earlier Charles's sister-in-law, the Duchess of York, who in 1660 had lost the little son born immediately after her marriage, was "brought to bed of a girle", reported Pepys, "at which I find nobody pleased."*

The girl was born at St. James's Palace. The date was 30 April 1662, and her godparents were Prince Rupert and the Duchesses of Buckingham and Ormonde. She was named Mary after her great-great-grandmother, the Queen of Scots.

CHAPTER IV

War and Peace

O N 9 MARCH 1661, between two and three in the morning, the great Cardinal Mazarin died. He had been virtual ruler of France for more than a decade. Now Louis XIV, nineteen years old, decided that it was time for him to govern France on his own. "You will assist me with your advice when I ask for it", he told his astonished ministers. He was a born ruler and government for him was always supremely enjoyable: "I do not know what other pleasures we would not give up for this one."

In the same year he married Maria Theresa, daughter of Philip V of Spain, and already his acquisitive eye, wandering over the map of Western Europe, had paused at the Spanish Netherlands, the barrier between France and the United Provinces. But he was in no hurry yet, and in April 1662 France concluded a treaty offensive and defensive with the United Provinces to last for twenty-five years.

The following year he sent the able and likeable Godefroi, Comte d'Estrades to The Hague. The ambassador opened secret discussions with De Witt about a possible partition between the two countries of the Southern Netherlands. He found De Witt evasive. The Raadspensionary had many sympathies for France but no desire to see Louis XIV a neighbour. His principle was: "*Amicus Gallus non Vicinus*".* The question was dropped by France for the time being. At the same time, negotiations about the principality of Orange dragged on in Paris. After the death of the Princess Royal, Louis had offered to return it to William without waiting for him to come of age. One of his conditions was, however, that the Governor should be a Roman Catholic. Amalia refused, and in 1661 sent her confidant Sir Constantyn Huygens to Paris with instructions to remind the King "that the Princes of Orange have always been the servants of the Kings of France, but never their subjects and still less their slaves."* An often exasperated Huygens was compelled to remain three years in Paris before a settlement was finally reached in 1664.

Amalia accepted a Roman Catholic Governor, and on 25 March 1665 the French troops at last marched out of the town.

William was deeply angered by the contempt the French King displayed in the Orange affair. He made the only protest he could when, driving along the Voorhout in The Hague on 6 May 1664, he encountered the French ambassador's coach. The narrowness of the street meant that one of them would have to give way, but d'Estrades, as the representative of The Most Christian King, refused to budge. So did William. It was a repetition of the Downing incident. A crowd gathered round the two coaches "with great murmurings and menaces which might have gone to very unfortunate extremes if I had not intervened promptly, having been warned by Sieur de Zuylestein," wrote Amalia to Huygens. She gave the young Prince orders to leave his coach and go with her on foot. He obeyed, his coach turned round, and the French ambassador was at last able to proceed. But the incident was the talk of The Hague – particularly crowded at this time because of the annual *kermess*, the great fair – and d'Estrades protested vigorously.*

It was not the only occasion on which William made life difficult for Amalia. At fourteen years, he was showing an increasing strength of character, a headstrong independence, and Amalia – who loved him as her *"prouber enfant"* – was beginning to be almost afraid of him. She "dares scarce herself to speake anything to him that shee thinks wil displease him," wrote Downing to Clarendon.* She herself complained in a letter to Huygens that the Prince refused to sit still while Adriaan Hanneman for the sum of 1508 guilders was making two portraits of him for Queen Dowager Henrietta Maria and the Duchess of York. And a year later she had to give an order to the painter Johan Mijtens "to make no paintings for the Prince without the approval of her Highness", as he had taken the habit of buying without asking her.*

The Dowager-Princess, now in her sixties, obviously found her responsibilities heavy, and she faced them almost alone. The States still refused to have anything to do with William's education. His uncle the Elector of Brandenburg, one of his guardians, lived too far away to be of much help. His other guardian, Charles II, had shrugged off his commitment. And the only other relative to whom she could turn for advice, his uncle Willem Frederik, the Stadholder of Friesland and Groningen, died in October 1664, accidentally shot through the head by his own bullet. He left a young widow Albertina Agnes and an only son, the seven-year-old Hendrik Casimir.

But the lack of guardians to whom he could turn was by this time a matter of indifference to the young William, who more and more had his

own small set of friends. One of them in particular received his entire
confidence. He was Hans Willem Bentinck, who had joined the Prince's
Household as a page in 1664. William had taken an immediate liking to
the young boy, who was a year older than himself and had an open face
and easy manners. He came of an old Dutch family – the Bentincks could
trace their ancestors back 300 years – and was the third of nine children.
His father was Bernhard Bentinck, Lord of Diepenheim and Drost
(Bailiff) of Deventer, his mother Anna van Bloemendael. Life in his large
noisy Gelderland family had given the young redheaded page a confidence and warmth which the withdrawn Prince found very appealing. He
went almost everywhere with William, and was soon promoted. When
the rhyming chronicler Coenraet Droste saw the two together in 1665 at
the wedding breakfast of Elizabeth Ruysch, daughter of the Registrar of
the States-General, the sixteen-year-old page had already become a
Cornet and a key figure in the Household set, so important for William.
And in 1667 he represented the Prince at the funeral of his uncle Willem
Frederik.

To his household William was a thoughful master. The moral instructions of Sir Constantyn had left their mark, and William, with perhaps
an excessive zeal, urged good behaviour on them. Even after they left
his Court, his concern followed them. In the summer of 1665 he twice
wrote earnestly to one of his former pages, Johan Theodor, Baron van
Friesheim, who had joined the army: "I hope that you haven't become a
drunken debauchee; as far as women are concerned, I fear you were
debauched long since . . ." and again: "Abstain as far as possible from
drink and especially from women. . . ." He threatened him: "If you don't
follow this advice as much as you can, you will never have my friendship."*

For all his earnestness William knew how to relax as well. The French
diplomat Jean Herault de Gourville remembered later in his Memoirs
how in 1665 he often used to join William at card-parties with the ladies
of The Hague. When the parties broke up with the withdrawal of the
ladies at eight o'clock, William had the habit of inviting himself to the
houses of his male friends, where they played on for another hour or two.
Protocol was sometimes waived, as when Gourville, who had boasted
how good his chef was, gave a dinner-party in a friend's house in the
country to show off his talents. He invited some of the ambassadors with
the Prince and they all agreed beforehand that "on the arrival each guest
should relinquish his official character and his rank, an arrangement
which was faithfully carried out."*

Much of the Prince's time was devoted to riding and hunting, already a passion with him. For the theoretical side, the Marquis of Newcastle had given him in 1658 a book *Concerning the Exercise of Horse-Riding*, but Sir Constantyn, when he returned in 1664 from his three-year absence in Paris and Orange, was appalled by his style. As he wrote to a friend, "I found my once-small Master grown so big and strong that I couldn't stop myself protesting that he had been allowed to develop such bad habits while hunting, which he loved insanely, without even being taught the art of riding."* And to correct these bad ways the Sieur d'Orival, a "very expert Cavalerizzo", was hired from Paris.

In all other ways, Huygens was delighted with his pupil. "My master is no longer a child, thanks be to God. I see with astonishment, how in so few years he has grown and matured in body and mind. As he is a very handsome Prince, he certainly promises great things, worthy of his birth."*

It looked as if those "great things" might be asked of him very soon. The second Anglo-Dutch war started in 1665, and once again the Dutch people, led by the pro-Orange clergy, looked to William. "I will go and return to my first husband; for then was it better with me than now," was the text out of Hosea on which the Reverend Lantman preached at The Hague. The States of Holland reprimanded the pastor sharply, but it was difficult to stem the tide.* Even in the States-General requests were made that William should be appointed Captain-General, with the French Marshal Turenne given the actual command. Both Louis XIV and De Witt were against this idea.

Another proposal came nearer to realization. While De Witt was absent quelling one of the many mutinies that had broken out in the fleet, the States-General by a vote of five to three accepted a proposal to send William to England as head of a peace delegation. Charles II had been careful not to mention the question of his nephew's position in his Declaration of War,* but it was widely believed in the United Provinces that his secret reason for war against the Dutch was anger and resentment at his nephew's exclusion. Sending William to him as their official representative seemed the obvious way to appease him. De Witt returned in time to have the proposal dropped.

Whatever personal motives Charles may have had for disliking the Dutch, this war had long been inevitable for economic reasons. The interests of the two trading and fishing countries, separated only by the North Sea, were constantly clashing. The English envied and resented those "Dutch butterboxes" with their fast-growing colonial empire in the Far East and the New World. The Dutch had laid hands on vast areas of the once-rich empire of the Portuguese, leaving them in possession of

Ceylon, and only Goa in India. They had been obliged to hand back Brazil to the Portuguese in 1661, but they had collected eight million guilders in exchange. Their colony on the Cape of Good Hope was flourishing. They had lost Formosa to the Chinese pirate Coxinga in 1662, but compensated themselves by the conquest of Palembang and Macassar. And in the heart of the English colonies in America, they had helped themselves to a piece of land and called it Nieuw Nederland. From Virginia north to the St. Lawrence the English, however, recognized no claims other than their own, and the small Dutch territory with its ten thousand inhabitants and its capital Nieuw Amsterdam, run by the dictatorial Peter Stuyvesant, was a thorn in their side. Downing in The Hague always ignored its existence, and when on 12 March 1664 Charles had given Nieuw Nederland to his brother James, and the Dutch had protested, the Ambassador had behaved as though he did not know what they were talking about.*

Over the years and round the oceans of the world, the navies of the two countries fought an intermittent running battle, seizing each other's merchant ships. Nearer home, petty grievances accumulated. The English were furious that the republican Dutch still gave shelter to Cromwellian refugees, resentful that the States refused to send them an envoy with the status of ambassador, and insulted by the vicious Dutch press campaign against the Duke of York, the conqueror of Nieuw Nederland. As far as the English were concerned, in short, to be a Dutchman at this time was to be a monster. In an English broadside, he is described as a "Lusty, Fat Two-legged Cheeseworm: a creature that is so addicted to eating butter, drinking fat drink, and sliding, that all the world knows him for a slippery fellow."

The Dutch, for their part, accused the English of atrocities, "of frying Dutchmen by the fire and cutting off the noses and eares of others".* And this time they had prepared themselves for war. When in April 1665 the English Parliament asked Charles for redress for "the dishonours, indignities and grievances" they suffered from the Dutch, the United Provinces had a strong fleet ready.

The first battle of the Second Anglo-Dutch War took place in 1665 off Lowestoft, when Admiral Van Wassenaer van Obdam encountered the English fleet commanded by the Duke of York, England's Lord High Admiral, with Prince Rupert and Montague. The Dutch were defeated; two thousand of their men were taken prisoner, they lost nineteen ships, and Admiral Obdam and his Vice-Admiral were both killed.

The Dutch were spared a worse blow when De Ruyter, returning with the Dutch treasure fleet from the West Indies, successfully evaded the

English fleet in the Channel by sailing north and taking refuge in the Norwegian harbour of Bergen. The Danes, who, for a half-share of the booty, had promised the English not to intervene when they attacked, opened fire nevertheless on the English fleet: the orders had not arrived in time. Charles had no choice but to declare war on the Danes as well: the Dutch had gained an ally.

The final disheartening blow for the English fell on 26 January 1666 when France declared war on them in observance of her treaty with the Dutch of 1662. But even the entry of France and Denmark into the war on the Dutch side could not save Raadspensionary De Witt from growing unpopularity, and a gesture to Orangist feeling was obviously needed. In April De Witt announced that William was to be made a "Child of State" at last. At the same time he seized the opportunity to remove the English influence from William's education by dismissing his Household. Amalia co-operated by begging Holland officially, at De Witt's request, to take on the education of her grandson. William never forgave her action, through which at one stroke he lost his entire entourage. Only Bentinck was left of the small circle that for William had been a substitute family.

The loss of his governor Zuylestein hurt him most. He even swallowed his pride and paid a visit to d'Estrades, the French ambassador, to beg him to intervene with De Witt. "He came to me three days ago," wrote d'Estrades to Paris, "and implored me with tears in his eyes to talk to M. De Witt into letting him keep De Zuylestein. He offered that for his sake he would be willing to put himself into the hands of M. De Witt and consider him as his father. . . ." Zuylestein would send his English wife away and not see her again till peace with England was restored, promised William, who protested: "They do me wrong if they think I have any dealings with the King of England. I am a child of State, so how could I have any attachments save with the States and their friends and allies?"*

He wrote asking his new Governor, Van Ghent – the former ambassador to France and a pleasant but rather coarse man – not to take on his new charge. He promised him somewhat arrogantly that "neither you nor your family shall suffer in your estate if you do this." Van Ghent accepted nonetheless, and William – as usual in time of great emotional strain – fell seriously ill. D'Estrades reported: "*Le Prince d'Orange en est malade de regret, jusqu'à ne quitter ni sa chambre, ni son lit.*"*

When he reappeared in public, he was completely master of himself again. He had, however, no intention of making life easy for his new Household, and at once demanded a complete reorganization of his finances and the administration of his estates, knowing very well how this would discredit Amalia. She had been responsible for them, but he found that she had sold parts of his land below the usual rates and many of his debts were unpaid – "Tho' his own Expences, in Proportion to his Rank, were inconsiderable, his very Butcher and Baker had not been paid for Years together."*

To De Witt he showed a different face. The statesman visited him every Monday to instruct him in affairs of government, and on one of these occasions Gourville, who was present, noted how the Prince paid *"des amitiés à M. De Witt"*. Gourville showed his astonishment and William afterwards explained that he had no choice. Gourville remarked admiringly that *"il en savait beaucoup pour son âge."** D'Estrades sized him up shrewdly in a letter to Lionne, the French Minister for Foreign Affairs: "He is a great Dissembler, and omits nothing to gain his Ends." But he added "the Prince had Capacity and will have Merit."*

After a while, his relationship with De Witt appeared to be based on a genuine affection and respect, so much so that Amalia anxiously reproached him with it. But William answered coolly that it was her own doing. He enjoyed De Witt's lessons which, he later said, gave him "very just notions of everything relating to the State". The young Prince and the elder statesman sometimes played tennis, and one deputy remarked jokingly, seeing the two together: "They had better take care that the State did not become the Child of William."*

All this time his prestige in his own country was growing, and the fact did not go unnoticed in the courts of Europe. In at least three of them, the mothers of marriageable princesses began to put forward their daughters' claims. The interest of Princess Leopoldine of Innsbruck was only rumoured. Two other princesses made a definite move. The Princess Emilia van Tarente travelled to The Hague with her daughter Charlotte. They met the young Prince several times, but Charlotte was not very much taken with the boy, who teased her by trying to snatch off her bonnet.* At the same time the Duchess Sophia of Osnabrück remembered the childhood attachment between her niece Liselotte and the Dutch Prince of whom "everyone speaks well". She wrote to Liselotte's father, Charles-Louis of the Palatinate: "I believe that my niece would be as happy with him as with a German Prince, if she can't get at least the King of Sweden or a future Elector of Brandenburg."* Her father had nothing against the idea, and Sophia began to make discreet enquiries about the dowry and Liselotte's pin-money.

William was not interested. The war with England was still raging, and the summer campaign of 1666 was about to start. The Dutch fleet, eighty-five ships strong, was ready to set sail, and on the eve of their departure in May William made an official visit to raise the morale of the navy. The sailors gave him a rousing welcome. A few days later they encountered the British navy in full strength at North Foreland, and one of the bloodiest sea-battles of the century followed. It lasted four days of shifting fortunes, but when De Ruyter, on 14 June, hoisted the red flag for a general attack, the English finally gave way and retreated. Dense fog suddenly came up and made pursuit of them impossible, De Ruyter declaring: "God did not wish to destroy them completely, only to punish their insolence."* Casualties were enormous on both sides. The Dutch lost three admirals and 800 men. They had 1200 wounded, and four vessels were destroyed. The English lost seventeen ships – six were carried as prizes to Holland – while 5000 seamen were killed and 3000 taken prisoner. The English gave public thanksgiving for what they claimed as a victory, but every other nation awarded the victory to the Dutch.

The English hastily re-fitted their fleet, and in August they had their revenge. They beat the Dutch in another sea-battle at Dunkirk on 4 August, and followed this up a fortnight later by a sudden swoop on the island of Terschelling where they set fire to 140 richly loaded merchant ships.

During these last disasters, William had been absent at Cleves, and when he returned to The Hague at the end of September, he discovered that some of his supporters had been recklessly plotting with the English in his favour. The chief conspirator was a Frenchman Buat, Seigneur de Fleury de Coulan, a boisterous and loyal companion of William's, who for some weeks had been acting as go-between for De Witt and the English Foreign Minister Arlington, who were exploring the possibilities of peace. At the same time he had been conducting his own secret correspondence with Arlington, offering to secure the best possible terms for the English in exchange for their support of the Prince's claims. The correspondence was discovered when Buat, with incredible carelessness, handed De Witt a letter for him from Arlington, together with one marked for the plotter himself. He was arrested, and accused of holding a secret and treasonable correspondence with foreign ministers. William, who knew nothing of the plot, was forced to sign a document which disowned the plotters, and Buat was executed. The other plotters were Admiral Cornelius Tromp, who was dismissed, and two politicians from Rotterdam, who fled to England.*

There they found a country for which the war was becoming an almost unbearable burden. Since April 1665 the Dutch had had a terrible ally in London itself: the Great Plague. By June of the first year the death-rate was 600 a month and the Court had fled Whitehall to seek refuge in Oxford. By August 1666 more than 26,000 people had died of it, and the disease sapped at national morale and resources alike.

The Great Fire of London in September 1666 was the *coup de grâce*. It started on a Sunday night at Pie Corner in the City of London, with a high wind fanning the blaze, and engulfed the City in "a most horrid malicious bloody flame, not like the fire flame of an ordinary fire," reported Pepys who was a horrified witness.* His fellow-diarist John Evelyn described how the stones of St. Paul's flew around like grenades while the melted lead flowed down the street. "The very pavements glowing with fiery rednesse, so as no horse nor man was able to tread on them."* In a desperate effort to check the fire, whole rows of houses were blown up in its path, and by 6 September it was finally spent. Years later Londoners were still accusing the Roman Catholics of having lit the fire, and the Duke of York in particular: in 1680 he tried to stop these rumours, and had a certain Mr. Pilkington convicted and ordered to pay damages of £100,000.

In reality James had behaved with the greatest courage, and together with his brother Charles had personally directed the battle against the fire. They had just returned to London after the Court's long absence on account of the Great Plague. While "London might well be said to be all in tears", and grass sprouted in the streets of Whitehall, the Court had been amusing itself as usual in Oxford. The cynical Anthony à Wood noted their way of life there with scorn: "Though they were neat and gay in their apparell, yet they were very nasty and beastly, leaving at their departure their excrements in every corner, in chimneys, studies, colehouses, cellers. Rude, rough, whoremongers; vaine, empty, carelesse..."*

They had even had their usual scandal. It involved the Duke and Duchess of York, now the parents of two little girls, Mary and her sister Anne, born on 6 February 1664. Mary especially had grown up into an enchanting little girl, whom James liked to show off in public, playing with her as Pepys once saw – "with great pleasure . . . like an ordinary private father".*

But there was in fact little "ordinary" happy family life for the York ménage, as the scandal of that winter of 1665–6 had made clear. While the Duke was at Oxford his wife Anne, left behind in York, was said to have encouraged the advances of James's Groom of the Bedchamber, Henry Sidney. "Beau Sidney", as everyone called him, was the handsomest man at Court, an easygoing and agreeable charmer. He was "greatly in love" with Anne, according to Sir John Reresby who believed Anne to be innocent. James did not. He returned hurriedly to York, suspecting her "to be nought with Mr. Sidney" and banished him from the Court, thus giving the greatest publicity to the whole affair. For many days after he did not even speak to her. His jealous indignation was thought a little unreasonable by the Court: he himself was a conspicuously unfaithful husband.

ON 17 SEPTEMBER 1665, Philip IV of Spain had died. He was succeeded by his feeble and invalid son Charles II, and his widow became Regent. Nobody expected the young King to live very long, and Louis XIV married to Charles's sister Maria Theresa, began to see interesting possibilities in the situation. His wife had renounced her claims on the Spanish throne at her marriage, but her dowry had never been paid. Louis XIV waited eighteen months, but in 1667, while the Republic and England were fighting each other and after he had given notice to the Spanish Queen-Regent that he was claiming his wife's dowry, he sent Marshal Turenne with 47,000 men into the Spanish Netherlands in May. Within three months all the principal fortresses, among them Charleroi, Tournai, Lille and Courtrai, were in his hands.

All Europe wondered in alarm what was to stop Louis XIV claiming the whole Spanish inheritance eventually. De Witt was especially concerned. There was a Dutch saying that a good neighbour is better than a distant friend, and the Raadspensionary firmly believed it. France now looked like neither. Louis had had the effrontery to ask the Dutch to help him with troops, in fulfilment of their treaty obligations. De Witt, caught in his own trap, refused in alarm. His whole policy, based on the French alliance, had now collapsed and he decided to accept Charles's offer for peace negotiations.

The delegates of the two countries met at Breda, but the English were reluctant to make useful concessions. To force their hand, the Dutch made a show of strength and sent their entire fleet to sail proudly along the English coast, while the English fleet stayed at home for lack of money. The ships of the States were so numerous that a friend of Pepys exclaimed: "By God, I think the Devil shits Dutchmen." Worse was to come. On 19 June 1667 seventeen Dutch ships sailed up the Medway, raided Sheerness, and hoisted the flag of the United Provinces over the naval dockyards.

Three days later, they sailed on and taking advantage of a spring tide and a north-easterly wind, sent a fireship running down to break the boom at Chatham. Admiral Van Ghent, assisted by De Witt's brother Cornelius, captured England's pride, the battleship the *Royal Charles*, which was towed away to Holland, and burnt four other ships. After sailing as far as the castle at Upnor, the squadron returned triumphantly to rendezvous with the rest of the great Dutch fleet, cruising under De Ruyter's command at the mouth of the Thames.

There was panic in London. Charles felt humiliated, but a month later the Peace of Breda was a fact. It was impossible to make out from it who had won the war. Nieuw Amsterdam was forever lost to the Dutch and renamed New York, but Surinam, the private colony of Zeeland and for long a bone of contention between the two countries, was confirmed in the possession of the United Provinces. The Navigation Acts were somewhat softened on the point of Rhine traffic. Otherwise they were unchanged. Shortly afterwards, England concluded peace treaties with France and Denmark as well.

In England, one casualty of the war was the father of the Duchess of York, Chancellor Clarendon. His criticism of its conduct and his attacks on Court extravagance had been so outspoken that King and Parliament for once made common cause. Clarendon was impeached, and he went into exile in Paris. In the Netherlands, the principal victim of the war seemed likely to be William of Orange. Johan de Witt, having asserted his leadership by the Peace of Breda, now felt strong enough to abolish the office of Stadholder for Holland. In the Perpetual Edict, passed in secret on 5 August 1667 by the States of Holland, the other Provinces were also asked never to appoint a Captain- or Admiral-General as Stadholder. The distribution of magisterial offices, traditionally a function of the Stadholder, was given to the towns. In January 1668 the Edict was ratified. But not everybody was convinced of its perpetuity. Vivian, Pensionary of Dordrecht, scraped a penknife over the document, explaining: "I'm testing what steel can do to parchment."* And a contemporary historian wrote: "Never has displeasure against Holland and De Witt been more evident."*

William did not react. Unperturbed, he went on with the preparations for his "Ballet de la Paix", a combined play and dance to celebrate the Peace of Breda, for which he paid out of his own pocket. Statesmen, diplomats, nobles, in short *toute La Haye* was invited for one of the two interminable performances on 7 February 1668 in the stables near the Binnenhof. One of the guests was Cosimo, heir to the Grand Duke of Tuscany, a withdrawn hypochondriac who, however, seemed to have amused himself well enough on this occasion. In his *Travels* his secretary relates:

The spectacle started with the appearance of several characters, smartly dressed, according to the subject that they represented . . . they performed a ball of twenty-four people, including the Prince of Orange himself, richly attired, after the ancient Roman fashion, very rich dressed, and with a flourish of hat and feathers on the head, all with the utmost comeliness and very well regulated.*

Droste described the opening scene: "To begin with, the Goddess of War was represented there who had divided Great Britain and ourselves by discord, and after the peace being restored again bound to one another, Prosperity and Peace were found among the people. The Prince of Orange himself represented Mercury, and imparted the tidings to the spectators."* William appeared also as a Swiss, a shepherd, and finally, dressed as a Dutch peasant woman.

The play was not quite the innocent entertainment it seemed. There were moments when it sounded more like an Orange Manifesto, full of hidden allusions to the Prince and his position. William himself declaimed:

> *Another time will come*
> *In which a rightful call*
> *Will turn my arms elsewhere,*
> *Fulfil my wishes all.*

Another actor was made to say:

> *He is prudent and no fool,*
> *His ambitions he can rule.**

It was hardly surprising that the "Ballet de la Paix" was not a great success with the Regents. Even William's own supporters were not enthusiastic, and the rigid Dutch pastors in particular, normally so pro-Orange, were offended by this display of frivolity.

But at least one spectator raved about it afterwards. Cosimo had been the subject of special attention from William, who in the intervals came down in his Roman dress to greet the twenty-six-year-old Tuscan Prince, and afterwards, "having danced a good deal . . . had the fine courtesy to come down from the stage to sit with H. H. using towards him the most obliging and polite manners. Nor did he depart until invited to dance by a lady."

Cosimo particularly admired the great elegance and verve of the "eighteen-year-old Prince gifted with beauty, deportment and self-assurance".*

CHAPTER V

Visit to England

WILLIAM'S APPARENT MOOD OF RESIGNATION after the Perpetual Edict was mainly for show. In secret he was preparing his next move. Sir Constantyn Huygens, who visited Middelburg in February 1668 to settle some affairs for Amalia, used the occasion to arrange with the Pensionary of Zeeland, Pieter de Huybert, an unpleasant surprise for De Witt and the Loevesteiners. In September Huygens returned to Zeeland, this time with William in his company.

The Prince's governor Van Ghent knew nothing of it. While he was hunting in Breda, he received a letter from William telling him that he was coming to join him. Instead, William travelled with Johan-Maurits of Nassau to Bergen-op-Zoom and crossed from there by boat to Rammekens. Sir Constantyn was sent to Middelburg to notify the States of the Prince's arrival, and a coach drawn by six horses was immediately sent to fetch him. The news spread fast. While the States assembled in the ancient gothic abbey, former residence of the Counts of Zeeland, the crowds massed in the streets outside. "The streets are nearly impassable; roofs, windows, even trees and masts are black with spectators; the Abbey is so full of people on foot and in carriages that it was hardly possible to reach the Prince's apartments," wrote a proud Huygens to Amalia.*

The secret planning beforehand and the crowds gathered on that 23 September had a purpose now made clear: William III had decided to assume his hereditary title of First Noble of Zeeland. "We will follow the same measures as our august ancestors who contributed towards laying the foundations of this glorious Republic", were the opening words of his first public speech, which he knew would ring round the Republic. "By conferring on me today the dignity of First Noble you will not confine the proof of your affection for my person within the limits of your Province, for you consider this a way to arouse in all the other provinces the sentiments which have animated yourselves." It was a defiant challenge of De Witt's authority.*

Afterwards he stayed for two hours at the windows of his apartment while the crowds cheered and the militia fired salvoes in his honour. In the evening there were fireworks. After a visit next day to Flushing and Veere, he departed from Zeeland, leaving behind as his representative the unscrupulous bastard-grandson of Prince Maurits, Adriaan Willem van Nassau, Heer van Odijk.

Returned to The Hague, he asked his grandmother to bring his minority to an end. Amalia agreed, and asked William's uncles, the English King and the Elector of Brandenburg, for their consent, pointing out that his status of minor was inconsistent with his new dignity. In any case, she added, the burden of guardianship was now too much for her after many *"interruptions de ma santé"*.* Neither of her two co-guardians had any objection, and on 25 October she announced her decision to the States-General and the States of Holland. Louis XIV was also notified that the Prince of Orange was now of age. In her memorandum to the States-General, she explained that one of her reasons for ending William's minority was so that he could gain valuable experience administering his own estates with the help of his "Domein-Raad". This Council met every Tuesday to deal with the affairs of more than thirty territories scattered over Western Europe which made up William's inheritance. From now on, the Prince presided over their meetings.

The Orange property was immense. Apart from the principality of Orange itself, William owned six manors in Franche-Comté, and the hereditary burgraveship of Besançon in France. In Germany there was Nassau, together with Katsenellenbogen and Dietz, an impressive principality. There was Vianden in eastern Luxembourg, Meurs in Westphalia, Lingen in the Bishopric of Munster – where William later founded a university.

Most of his properties were in the United Provinces: Buren (the place from which the Orange family often derives its incognito to this day), Veere, Flushing, Doesburg, Lingdam, Naaldwijk, Breda, Grave, Willemstadt, Giertruedenberg and Diest. In the Spanish Netherlands, Herstal and St. Vith were among William's possessions. The revenue from all these domains, in some years more than a million guilders, flowed into one treasure-chest supervised by the Domain-Council. One third of it was re-invested in the estates, one third was put by as reserve, and the rest was used for education and religion.

The States of Holland, already outraged by the Zeeland incident, did their utmost to hinder William's assumption of these administrative responsibilities. Fearing the convincing demonstration of his abilities that such a role would allow, they announced that he was not officially of age and that businessmen and traders must have no dealings with him.

But they could do nothing to stop him taking over the running of his own Household, and on his eighteenth birthday he issued new and detailed instructions, which he had composed himself with great care, for its management. Extravagance and waste were to be eliminated as far as possible, and pilfering checked. Special care was to be taken of the younger members of the staff and household. The hours of meals were fixed, and the provisions for the tables – plentiful but not luxurious – were detailed. John Blair, a Scotsman, was put in charge of accounts, which were to be checked weekly with William, or in his absence with the Hofmeester. The eight-page memorandum suggested a prudent pater-familias, concerned that his family should be well looked after. And it was evidence of that "good plain sense, with show of application if he had business that deserved it" which an Englishman noted in him at that time.*

The author of these words was Sir William Temple, the new English ambassador to The Hague. He had arrived in August 1668 to conclude the negotiations which would result in the Triple Alliance between England, the United Provinces and Sweden. He was then forty years old, a protégé of the Earl of Arlington, Charles's Secretary of State. This warm and civilized prototype of the English country gentleman had known and liked Holland for years. He admired the Dutch and had a great respect for De Witt. It was therefore with a certain reserve that he first approached the Prince of Orange, whose goodwill he had instructions to cultivate. Charles, who after the peace of Breda sent William four horses as a gift, had gone so far as to order him to give the young Prince precedence, and William accepted this with pleasure after some demur. The older man and the eighteen-year-old took to each other at once, and Temple sent a glowing account of him to London.

> I find him in earnest a most extreme hopeful prince, and, to speak more plainly, something much better than I expected, and a young man of more parts than ordinary, and of the better sort; that is, not lying in that kind of wit which is neither of use to oneself nor to anyone else . . . and that with extreme good, agreeable humour and disposition, and thus far on his way without any vice; besides being sleepy always by ten o'clock at night, and loving hunting as much as he hates swearing, and preferring cock-ale before any sort of wine. [In other words] A Prince of many virtues.*

Temple grasped at once the enormous hold of the young man over the Dutch people, which "was not to be dissolved or dispersed by any medicines or operations, either of rigour or of artifice".* He also understood that De Witt's position was not as strong as the Dutchman believed. In 1655 De Witt had married Wandela Becker, and thus united himself with one of the wealthiest and most influential families of Amsterdam. If De Witt had a fault, it was his nepotism, and there were growing complaints that more and more political posts were being concentrated in one family. De Witt, unperturbed by criticism, was more concerned by the menace of France: since the Peace of Aix-la-Chapelle on 2 May 1668, Louis XIV was master of a formidable line of fortresses in Flanders, stretching from the North Sea to Charleroi.

De Witt still hoped to keep France at bay by the Triple Alliance, unaware that Louis XIV – that King "who expects not only to be gazed at but adored by the whole world"* – was already working on his Grand Design. It was nothing less than the destruction of Dutch power. He was more than irritated by the arrogant behaviour of these *petits commerçants*, as he contemptuously called them. And while De Witt and Temple were thrashing out the last details of the Triple Alliance, the French King was putting out the first feelers in London about a pact between himself and the English King, of which the object was the ruin of the Dutch Republic. He found Charles ready to listen, but, as the King pointed out, Parliament would certainly vote him ample funds for an attack on France, but not a penny to be used against Holland. Louis took the hint and in the end Charles was offered an annual subsidy of about £166,000. An important point in the discussions was the future of their relation, the Prince of Orange, as a letter from Vienna of 2 January 1669 mentions: "I have been astonished to learn from well-informed sources . . . that the French have offered the King of England that if he stands by and lets them move against the . . . United Provinces, he will make the Prince of Orange sovereign there."* The letter-writer must have had excellent sources, but even he had no knowledge of another clause in the treaty now being discussed. By this clause, to be kept secret between the two kings, Charles undertook "being convinced of the truth of the Catholic faith . . . to declare himself a Catholic . . . as soon as the welfare of the realm will permit." At the same time he promised to make the utmost efforts to convert England to Catholicism.

This secret deal between Charles and Louis undid in one stroke all Temple's careful work on the Triple Alliance. But of this the diplomat was completely unaware, and on 25 January 1669, when Charles informed his brother James of his romanizing plans, a burgher of The Hague wrote that the Ambassador, together with the Prince of Parma and the whole population of the Residentie, was enjoying the Dutch winter pleasures. The ice in the canals and lakes this year was so hard that "people drive over it in twenty and thirty coaches one behind the other".* When in the spring of the following year, however, Temple learned that Charles had had long meetings in Dover with his sister Henrietta, married to Louis's brother, the Duc d'Orléans, he began to have an inkling of the truth.

The witty and captivating Henrietta, called Minette by Charles, had been the emissary of her brother-in-law Louis XIV. For the last two years she had acted as informal go-between for the two kings, and Louis left her the honour now of having the Treaty signed. The French court moved to Flanders on 28 April 1670, ostensibly for a grand tour of the annexed fortresses. At Lille, Henrietta left for Dunkirk and made the crossing to Dover. On 12 June she returned in triumph with her brother's signature to the paper, leaving behind – as an extra compliment from Louis XIV to Charles II – the pretty, doll-faced Louise de Kéroualle.

Henrietta was well received at Versailles, but fell ill a few days later after drinking a glass of chicory water, and died on 19 June. As usual at that time, it was immediately rumoured that she had been poisoned – in this case by the Duchess of York, who had been envious of the great attentions Charles paid to his sister at Dover. "The Prince of Orange would be well advised for that reason not to go to England," commented a Dutchman. "He too might easily be served with something indigestible."*

The Prince had, in fact, been invited to come to England in April, and Arlington had hoped that he might even be present at the Dover meeting. Nobody at the English court seemed yet to have grasped that William could never be persuaded to acquiesce in the destruction of the Regents' republic, even if he were to be rewarded with its sovereignty. He was first and foremost a Dutchman. In any case, he had been too busy to accept the invitation. His supporters had been hard at work, and on 31 May he made his solemn entrance into the Council of State, an advisory body without much influence. For the young man it was nevertheless an important step which meant that Holland recognized his majority and his status. A friend of De Witt saw the danger to their party and sighed: "I greatly regret that we have laid the first stones of an edifice which menaces both our liberty and our persons."* Louis sent his warm congratulations and, sharing the illusions of the English Court, added his hopes that this advancement was "soon to lead to another and higher one".*

The Prince of Orange attended the Council meetings almost daily. They had taken away the great State chair of the Orange princes to indicate that he was no more than an ordinary Councillor, but they could not, to their annoyance, prevent the members flocking respectfully round him.* William, who had almost immediately sacked his governor Van Ghent, claimed that his seat in the Council gave him the right to membership of the States-General, but De Witt foiled his bid. Seeing that for the moment there was no more to be hoped for, the Prince decided now to accept his uncle's invitation to come to England.

He tackled the question with his usual caution, "being of opinion that the said journey may bring some prejudices in these countries to the interest of His Highness if the same should be without good effect," explained his special emissary to Arlington.* The man William had picked for this mission was his personal physician Dr. Rumph, and the Prince impressed on him so strongly the need for secrecy that the doctor, disguised in a black wig, met Arlington only late at night, in the darkness of the Minister's garden.*

He had been sent to ask for Charles's reassurances on two points. The first concerned the enormous, long-standing debts of the Stuarts to the Oranges, money "of which his Highness had so greate neede, that without the said payment his princely house kould not possibly subsist." Rumph explained that if his Highness returned from England without payment of at least part of the debt it would be a damaging blow to his prestige. The second point had to do with the protracted Anglo-Dutch negotiations then taking place in London about trade in the Far East. The talks were going badly, and William feared that if they broke down while he was in England, "the ill-afectionated should putt all the fault upon his Highnesse".*

On the first question Arlington was reassuring. After consulting the King he told the physician, at their second stealthy meeting, that it was "his Majesty's intention to give his Highness complete satisfaction". About the trading talks, Charles was unable to be so obliging, since too many commercial interests were involved. After a third meeting the physician returned to Holland with an invitation for the beginning of October. Arlington had added a personal message: the Prince would do well to come to England and show himself to the people. Charles II was childless, the Duke of York's children were few and delicate, and his "ageing and corpulent Duchess" was unlikely to have more. It would not take "a miracle" to give William the Crown of England one day.*

THE INVITATION HAD BEEN SINCERE, and in October Charles II sent over Thomas Butler, Earl of Ossory, to escort William back to London. His departure was dogged by difficulties and delays. The Dutch navy failed to salute the English Royal yachts at Hellevoetsluys, and the States had to offer their excuses; the Deputy of Dordrecht protested violently at William's reference to Charles, in his parting message, as "our" uncle, a form to be used only by royalty.* And when on 1 November the party, which included Bentinck, Zuylestein and Huygens among others, reached Den Briel, storms made it impossible to set sail and they had to return to The Hague. After four days of impatient hanging about they set out for Calais, but learning that the storms had calmed a little, turned back and finally sailed from Den Briel in the *Henrietta*.

The rough and unpleasant crossing lasted thirty-six hours, and not till 8 November, at nine o'clock in the evening, did they land at "Marigat". William's first night on English soil was spent in a coaching inn at Rochester. Next day he posted on to Gravesend, where the waiting Royal barge took him on to Whitehall.

The King's welcome for the nephew he had last seen in 1660 as a ten-year-old boy was particularly warm. When William tried to kneel and kiss his hand, "as is the English habit", his uncle stopped him and "kissed him with tears in his eyes".* The Londoners lit bonfires – their usual sign of excitement – and there were fireworks in the evening.

The Dutch Prince was accommodated in the Cockpit, one of the finest sets of apartments in Whitehall. Charles had planned to give him the lodgings of the baby Duke of Cambridge, James's only son, and his sisters Mary and Anne. But their mother was so indignant at the idea of a son of a brother of the King being turned out for the son of a sister of the King that Charles gave in. William made no appearance of minding, and paid a polite visit to the ailing Duchess, the former lady-in-waiting of his mother.

A round of entertainments was laid on for him. He went hare-coursing twice with the King, and twice fox-hunting with his uncle James. Invitations for dinners poured in, he visited Parliament, and he went several times incognito to the revels at the Temple.

It was all typically in the informal style of Whitehall, that Palace "ill-Built and nothing but a heap of Houses erected at diverse times, and of different Models which they made Contiguous in the best Manner they could for the Residence of the Court".* This straggling complex of buildings, at the heart of which stood Inigo Jones's magnificent Banqueting Hall, contained more than two thousand rooms, divided into a series of apartments and offices for the King, his court and his government. They were lavishly furnished, but as the Dutchman Droste immediately noticed, they were filthy, and "all the carpets are faded and stained".* Nobody bothered to clean them. When Charles sauntered about there was always a pack of little spaniels following him. They were allowed complete freedom, and the bitches pupped and gave suck in any corner of the palace, "which render'd it very offensive, and indeede made the whole Court nasty and stinking".* Droste was horrified when he saw that the King, crowned and robed, had to carry his dogs himself out of the Council Chamber when their barking drowned his speech. And he was disgusted to see all the dogs leaping up around Charles's dinner-table and being fed the heads of hares and partridges or the leg of a chicken which they chewed noisily on the chairs.*

The reigning beauty of this splendid but squalid Court was Louise de Kéroualle, later Duchess of Portsmouth. This former lady-in-waiting of Henrietta of Orleans, still a new face at Court, was "a very fine woman and as most thought sent over" by Louis XIV "on purpose to ensnare the King who was easily taken with that sort of trap".* Like most of Charles's mistresses, she was appointed Lady of the Bedchamber to the long-suffering Queen Catherine of Braganza, and had completely supplanted Barbara Castlemaine, now Duchess of Cleveland, whom Charles, after enduring ten years of her tantrums, had packed off to France with a fat pension and the message, "make the least noise you can, and I care not who you love".*

It was not a Court in which William could feel at ease. The ladies found him grave and formal, and complained that "he did not make up to them enough".* He struck Charles's dissipated set as impossibly self-controlled and sober, and one evening, at a supper given by the Duke of Buckingham, Charles could not resist giving his nephew much more to drink than he was used to. "The prince did not naturally love it, but being once entered, was more frolic and merry than the rest of the company." To their surprise he broke the windows of the Maids of Honour's rooms, "and had got into some of their apartments had they not been timely rescued".*

But on the whole, William made an excellent impression. Evelyn, who was struck by his resemblance to his mother and his uncle the Duke of Gloucester, thought that he had "a manly, courageous, wise coun-tenance".* As the guest of the City of London one evening, William compelled respect by his sober and dignified bearing, and in the dazzlingly dressed-up company, he stood out for the simplicity of his clothes and the lack of a wig. The ladies commented: "What a nice young gentleman he looked, not like those popinjays."* And when William, on 6 December, made a visit to Cambridge, Alderman Newton wrote in his diary of this "well-countenanced man with a smooth and smeager plump face and a handsome head of hair of his own".*

William went on to Cambridge after staying with the Court at Newmarket Races – where all his expenses, amounting to £1846 10*s*. 5½*d*, had been paid by Charles.* In the old university town, he was awarded an honorary degree, "*in Magistrum Artis, pro honore Academiae*". A lesser degree was given to "*Gulielmus Bentecc*".

It was Oxford's turn on 29 December. The Prince travelled down by way of Windsor, where he paid a brief visit to Prince Rupert. When his mud-caked coach reached the town, it was nearly dark, and students and professors welcomed him with torches. Next day the Prince, wearing a scarlet academic gown, received the degree of Doctor in Civil Laws.

On the last day of the year he returned to London which he found buzzing with the latest sensation. Six men on horseback had made an armed attack on Ossory's father, the distinguished old Duke of Ormonde, and he had had a very narrow escape. Another unpleasant scandal called for William's personal attention. Two of the men in his retinue, Captain de la Sale and the Heer van Valckenburg, had a blazing row. The Prince intervened but could not prevent a duel in which de la Sale was killed. Van Valckenburg was summoned before six English and six Dutch judges, pleaded self-defence and was acquitted.*

It was now February 1671, and William began to think of going back to Holland. The main object of his visit, the repayment to him of the Stuart debts, looked like being achieved after Sir Constantyn Huygens and the Treasury had done some hard bargaining. Contrary to Charles's promise, nothing had been prepared, Parliament had not voted any funds for payment, and the English even haggled over the sums in question. William claimed 2,400,000 guilders, but Charles worked it out at only 1,800,000 – 400,000 for Mary's dowry, 500,000 for William's father's loan to him, and as interest, 900,000 guilders. Huygens finally accepted this figure, and the King promised to pay 400,000 guilders within the next six weeks, and the rest in instalments of 200,000 half-yearly. It was soon to become clear once more what Charles's promises were worth: in March 1672 only 200,000 guilders had been repaid – after the deduction of £325 commission for the civil servants involved.*

Charles may have been a bad debtor, but he was certainly a generous and attentive host. William's entertainment cost him about £100 a day, and as a Christmas present he gave his nephew twenty magnificent English riding-horses and a collection of exotic birds. He loved to show his guest around, and after William's installation as Knight of the Garter on 8 February, he took him to "Heipark" to review his Foot and Horse Guards in their splendid uniforms.

On 28 February the Prince was back in The Hague at last, after a crossing even more stormy and unpleasant than the journey out. With almost everybody aboard seasick, they had to take shelter in the little port of Veere, where they went ashore and warmed themselves after the freezing journey before going on to Den Briel. From here barges towed them to Delft, where a coach waited to take William home to the Binnenhof. Next day he had recovered sufficiently to attend a service at the Kloosterkerk, where the crowds gave him a wholehearted welcome.*

The Prince was delighted to be home again. He had not been much impressed by England, and he had not enjoyed the court life of Whitehall. Perhaps the only person from whom he had parted with real regret was Thomas Butler, Earl of Ossory. This thirty-six-year-old nobleman had been one of the party that accompanied William during his stay in England. They had certainly met before in Holland – Ossory had been married since 1659 to Emilia van Beverwaert, a second cousin of William – but on this last visit a deep sympathy and friendship had grown up between them.

Ossory was the eldest son of the Duke of Ormonde, born in the ancestral castle of Kilkenny. The Ormonde family had almost beggared themselves in the Royalist cause, and Ossory himself had spent a great deal of his youth in exile in Paris and in Holland, where he remained until the Restoration. He was a man for whom nobody seems to have had anything but praise – a universal favourite, perfect courtier and perfect gentleman. He was the darling of Whitehall, where he was lovingly known as "the gallant Ossory", and from the Restoration onwards no court occasion seemed complete without him: he had been a witness of the Duke of York's marriage with Anne Hyde, and had held the mantle at Charles's Coronation. In Paris "he had distinguished himself by his skill in manly exercises", and when he took part in the Four-Day Battle at sea against the Dutch in 1665, his conspicuous courage made him the idol of the seamen, who called him "the preserver of the navy". At the most dissolute court in Europe, Ossory's personal life was untouched by scandal, though no one ever dreamed of calling him a prig, and if he had one weakness, it was a pardonable one – he loved gambling.

William with his intense reserve never made friends easily, and at first sight it might have seemed that the solemn young Prince had little in common with the accomplished and popular courtier sixteen years his senior. But Ossory himself was a much more serious person than most people imagined; the two men had many interests and tastes in common. And in Ossory's company William's reserve disappeared entirely, to reveal a warmth and spontaneous affection which few people glimpsed in the withdrawn Prince of Orange, but which breathed from every line of the constant correspondence between the two men which began after William's return. In Ossory William had left more than a friend at Whitehall: he had left an ally in a court whose good faith, he knew only too well, was not to be relied on.

For the moment at least, all was friendship and harmony, and the Dutch ambassador in London sent an eloquent account of their ex-pupil's success to the States-General. He had been "extraordinarily esteemed and had gratified all by his wisdom, generosity and politeness".*

But if Charles had been, as he told the French ambassador Colbert de Croissy, "much satisfied" with the Prince of Orange, in one respect he was severely disappointed. During talks with the Prince they had touched on religion and he had hinted in confidence at his own conversion. He described the Protestants as "a factious body" and urged his nephew to "take more pains to enquire into these things better and not be led by his Dutch blockheads".*

The Prince's response had been so discouraging that Charles had not dared raise the subject of the Treaty of Dover. As Colbert reported to Louis, the English King found William "so passionate a Dutchman and protestant, that even although your Majesty had not disapproved of his trusting him with any part of the secret, these two reasons would have hindered him".*

That his nephew had been born a Dutchman Charles knew. That he could have grown up into a Dutch patriot had not until now entered the King's calculations. He never completely trusted him again.

CHAPTER VI

Clouds over Europe

THREE DAYS BEFORE HE LEFT ENGLAND, William of Orange had stood godfather to another little York Princess, born on 9 February and christened Catherine.* She was the tenth child that Anne Hyde bore the Duke of York, and only four of them still lived. Three little Dukes of Cambridge, one Duke of Kendal, and one unnamed son had died in their infancy or immediately after birth. A girl, Henrietta, had survived only eleven months.* Of the four that remained, the new-born girl and the four-year-old Duke of Cambridge were delicate, and seemed unlikely to live for long. "*Mala stamina vitae*" commented Court physician Dr. Willis – a remark that cost him his job.* But nine-year-old Mary and her six-year-old sister Anne were growing up into reasonably healthy young girls, although the younger girl had been sent to France the year before to consult a specialist about her eyes.* Mary had the same weakness, but to a lesser degree.

It is not certain that she met her cousin William during his visit to London, but already rumours suggested that he had come "to pretend to the Lady Mary".* His mother had been married at the same age, but neither her father nor William had any idea of such a match at this time.

The Duke and Duchess of York lived in St. James's Palace, a brick-built Tudor home which still looked out over meadows at one side and which Cromwell had used as stables. Charles had given it to his brother after the Restoration. But Mary spent most of her childhood in the Old Palace at Richmond, remote from the quarrels between her parents and the decadence of the Court. Until she was five years old, she was some-times taken to stay at York House, in Twickenham, the country home of her grandparents. These visits, however, came to an end in 1667, when her grandmother died and her grandfather, Chancellor Lord Clarendon, was banished to France.*

At Richmond, Mary and her sister Anne were in the charge of Colonel Edward and Lady Frances Villiers, and they grew up together with the seven lively Villiers children. Lady Frances, who had been appointed Lady Governess to the York children in 1661, almost certainly owed her appointment to her husband's niece, Barbara, Charles's notorious mistress Lady Castlemaine. Lady Frances was a gentle, warm-hearted woman who spoiled her charges a little; discipline was not too strict in this home, which most of the time lacked a father. Colonel Edward Villiers had been made Governor of Teignmouth Castle in Devonshire and was not often at Richmond.

Mary's small Household consisted of a nanny, Mrs. Mary Langford whom she called her Mam, Mrs. Anne Walsingham, two dressers, a rocker, Mrs. Jane Leigh, a sempstress, a laundress, Mrs. Elizabeth Brookes, and a Page of the Back Stairs.* She was given the education of a wealthy heiress of the time. Peter de Laine gave her lessons in French at which she was very good, and for her drawing lessons Anne had chosen the miniature-painter Gibson, a dwarf who was married to a dwarf but had nine full-sized children. Initially, he did not find her a very promising pupil. Her Household also included a Singing Master at £100 a year, and its most highly-paid member was the Dancing Master who earned £200 a year – a Frenchman who had already taught her grandparents, Charles I and Henrietta Maria, and her father to dance. This elderly man was still a brilliant teacher: Mary was an excellent dancer for the rest of her life. Pepys noted when she was only seven: "I did see the young duchesse, a little child in hanging sleeves, dance most finely, so as almost to ravish me, her ears were so good.'*

As was usual in this age, the two girls spent very little time with their parents, and their mother in any case was often ill. Anne Hyde was an unhappy woman who had realized almost immediately that her marriage – subject of such a major court scandal in 1660 – was a failure. She was humiliated by James's continual infidelities with a series of mistresses so little attractive that one of them once remarked: "I wonder for what qualities he chooses his mistresses. We are none of us handsome and if we have wit, he has not enough himself to find it out."* Even after ten years of marriage she could not accept his inconstancy, and her jealousy, obvious to everyone, made her a general object of pity and derision. When the Duke of York's closet was broken into one day in March 1669 and papers were found to be missing, it was immediately rumoured that "the Duchess hath done itt, to looke out for love letters".*

Like many frustrated and unhappy women, she was an enormous eater by way of compensation, "one of the highest feeders in England," wrote Gramont, who went on: "It was really an edifying sight to see her at table. The Duke, on the contrary, giving way to new caprices, exhausted himself by his inconstancy and was gradually wasting away whilst the poor Duchess, gratifying her good appetite, grew so fat and plump that it was a blessing to see her."* Her "extraordinary stomach" and excessive weight may have been partly responsible for her poor health, but there is some suggestion of another cause, syphilis. Many contemporaries thought James suffered from it, pointing to the sickliness of most of Anne's children, the repeated miscarriages of his second wife, and the inability of his two daughters to bear healthy children. Bishop Burnet, the famous but anti-Jacobite historian, mentions it, and several foreign diplomats in London allude to it in their despatches.* And while no medical proof exists, his wife Anne often suffered towards the end of her life from sores that broke out "in severall places of her face and body" and obliged her to retire from public.*

Hardly anybody ever thought her a handsome woman, but she was impressive in other ways. "She had a majestic air, not much beauty, a great deal of wit," wrote Gramont. And Burnet called her "a very extraordinary woman", with "great knowledge and a lively sense of things".* In spite of her ordinary birth, she had filled her new role of Royal duchess immediately with an air of grandeur which "made her be considered as if born to support the rank which placed her so near the throne".* Some people thought she overdid it – the proudest woman in the world, Pepys called her – and her haughty imperious manner made her many enemies. Her meddling in the business of James – about whose life she was writing a book – was widely resented. She turned up in his offices at the Admiralty, sat in "like Queene Elizabeth" on the Council meetings, and made arbitrary decisions about wages and prices. Mr. Povy, the former Treasurer of Tangier, was one of her victims: he complained to Pepys that he was "like to lose his £400 a year pension of the Duke of York", while she herself was laying aside £5000 a year to invest in jewels.*

Her investments were certainly not the only strain on the York finances. James's many mistresses and their offspring cost him plenty of money, and eventually he had a complete illegitimate family to provide for. In 1665, at the time when he furiously dismissed Henry Sidney as his wife's suspected lover, he had begun his own long-lasting liaison with Arabella Churchill, one of the Duchess's maids of honour. She bore him many children, of whom four survived: one of them was James Fitz-James, later Duke of Berwick, born in 1670.

In that same year the health of the Duchess of York was declining rapidly, although she was still well enough in May to go with the rest of the Court to Dover to meet Madame, Charles's sister Minette. It was a long absence from the children, and a member of her Household, Teague Power, wrote to her: "I hope your Sweet Highness will soon return to the little children," adding, "the parks look very thin, the King and Duke not being there, and the Queen's chapel strange when she is praying at Dover."* By Christmas, pregnant again, Anne was a sick woman who spent most of her time in bed, where William of Orange came to visit her. The birth of Catherine, her tenth child, was too much for her. Seven weeks later, on 30 March 1671 she left her sickbed for dinner at Burlington House in Piccadilly. She ate voraciously as usual but on coming home to St. James's, she collapsed and the doctors were sent for. They diagnosed cancer of the breasts, and could only pronounce that she was dying. Blandford, the Bishop of Worcester, came at once to her sickbed and asked her: "I hope you continue still in the truth?" Desperately she answered him: "What is the truth?" repeating the last word.* The bystanders noted that Blandford did not give her the last blessing of the Church of England – he was in fact one of the few people who knew of her secret conversion to Roman Catholicism, having discussed with her at great length her doubts and difficulties.

Anne had first shown interest in the Roman Church in 1665, possibly hoping, as Burnet suspected, to conciliate her husband – already Roman Catholic – after the Sidney affair. Her brother Laurence Hyde took another view. He wrote later that after her father's banishment in 1667, she had succumbed in her loneliness to the Roman Catholic influence at Court: her sister-in-law Catherine of Braganza was an ardent Catholic, the King was a recent, if secret convert, and her husband was rapidly turning into a proselytizing bigot. To the last moment, however, she never made her conversion public, perhaps knowing that by doing so "I must necessarily lose all the friends and the credit that I have."* Her silence might also have been occasioned by her uncertainty: Catholicism had given her no peace of mind and her death struggles were agonizing. She died on 31 March with her husband at her bedside, crying "Duke, Duke, death is terrible." An eye-witness said later: "She was full of unspeakable torture and died (poor creature) in doubt of her religion, without the sacrament . . . like a poor wretch."*

The Court went into mourning, but the black hid only indifference, and not much respect was shown even to her dead body. "None remembered her after one weeke, none sorry for her; she was tossed and flung about and everyone did what they would with the stately carcase."*

For the Princesses Mary and Anne the death of their mother meant that more than ever they became "children of state", as James once bitterly said. Already for a long time a gulf had yawned between him and his two daughters, who at the order of Charles were being carefully educated in the religion of the Church of England. The King, knowing too well that popery at Court might lead to trouble in the country, had appointed the Bishop of London, the ex-soldier Dr. Henry Compton, as their governor. He was assisted by Dr. Edward Lake, Archdeacon of Exeter, and the two clergymen did their work well: the girls grew up pious and sincere Protestants, with neither sympathy nor understanding for their father's religious belief. The death of their mother made the breach almost complete.

WHEN THE NEWS of Anne Hyde's death reached her nephew William of Orange he himself was lying seriously ill in the Castle of Loevestein.* As he had only recently returned from London, his opponents in Holland – "who would have liked him dead" – hinted darkly about his sickness that he "must have brought it back from England", in the hope "that if he died, they would be free of suspicion".* He was suffering from a badly infected and swollen throat, but on 9 April it was announced that he was out of danger. And soon he returned to The Hague to send Ossory, as a belated present for so much kindness during his stay in England, a "bason and ewer of massy gold". A few days later he resumed his attendance at the Council of State.

It was now becoming painfully clear to him that if his visit to England had been worthwhile for his personal reasons, it had achieved nothing for his country. The cordiality of Charles II to his nephew did not extend to the States, and relations between England and the United Provinces had worsened over the last eighteen months. Temple, still busily constructing his lifework, the Triple Alliance, was constantly being pestered by Charles's petty grievances against the Dutch, such as the fact that the *Royal Charles*, captured in Chatham, was on public show at Den Briel and, the King had heard, used as an alehouse. The harassed States-General decided to be conciliating; the arms were taken off the *Royal Charles* and her name changed.

More genuine differences arose during discussions between Van Beuningen and the English about trade in the Far East. The English demand to trade freely in that part of the world where the Dutch had a near-monopoly, was considered preposterous at The Hague, and they themselves protested about the English occupation of Surinam in defiance of the Peace of Breda.

Some inkling of England's true intentions had dawned on the puzzled De Witt when, in the summer of 1670, rumours of the secret

Anglo-French Treaty at Dover reached The Hague. The Raadspensionary questioned Temple about them; still ignorant of the London switch in policy the ambassador exclaimed in horror: "If ever such a thing should happen I will never have any part in it."* His recall to London on 1 September 1670 strengthened the fears of De Witt, who a few months earlier had already spoken despairingly of England as "a nation fickle in everything but its love of change".*

Temple's patron Arlington told him that his recall was only temporary. But when, on his return, the Minister kept him waiting for an hour and a half, and the King confined his conversation to polite enquiries after the Prince of Orange, Temple realized that Arlington, a man whom he almost hero-worshipped, had used him to double-cross the Dutch. His mission had been worse than a farce.

Temple's embassy was not officially ended, however, until May 1671, and his wife's journey home in August on board the royal yacht *Merlin* was made the occasion of a new incident. Since the *Merlin* was not a man-of-war, the Dutch fleet failed to salute her. Her captain had had instructions to be as provocative as possible, and fired off his guns, but the Dutch admiral, Van Ghent, after a polite enquiry if this was a signal of distress, refused the challenge. The captain asked Lady Temple's advice and like a good diplomat's wife, she told him to carry out his instructions regardless of her children's safety. But he sailed on, and when he returned to London was thrown into the Tower for having compromised England's honour. Yet another English protest was made to the Dutch.

This apparent touchiness was in fact part of a deliberate campaign to swing English public opinion round against the Dutch, and to provoke the States into acts of hostility. "Our business is to break with them and yet lay the breach at their door", declared Arlington,* who deliberately exacerbated Anglo-Dutch relations by appointing as ambassador Sir George Downing, a man they knew and hated. His simple brief: "to embitter matters to the point of rupture". Downing arrived with a long string of grievances and demands, varying from trade disputes to the flag incident of August, and plunged into his task with such enthusiasm that Charles had to write restraining him. The fuse was to be a slow-burning one. "I would have you use your skill so to amuse them, that they may not finally despair of me, and thereby give me time to make my selfe more ready and leave them more remisse in there preparations," said the King.

But in spite of English provocations, De Witt was still blind to the dangers of his country's situation. When the Dutch ambassador in

Paris, Pieter de Groot, sent him alarming reports about Louis's preparation for war, the Raadspensionary, who believed that the French conquest of the United Provinces would be contrary to English interests,
was convinced that England would come to their help at the crucial
moment, and most Dutchmen shared this comforting view. Even
William, in the summer of 1671, wrote to his friend Ossory: "All the talk
here is of the war and the great preparations that the King of France is
making to attack us. I hope that the King will not abandon us, and that he
stands by the treaties that he made with the States. It's in his own interest
not to see us destroyed."* By the end of the year, his illusions were
fading. "I beg you to tell me if you are going to be our friends or not.
Everyone here doubts it more and more",* he told the Englishman.

At about the same time he reported to Ossory: "There are great
struggles going on here to make me Captain-General."* In the growing
uncertainty about England's intentions, Gelderland had proposed this
promotion for the Prince to the States-General in November 1671, in
the hope of appeasing Charles II. Such a move would also please the
Elector of Brandenburg, who was wavering between the French and
Dutch sides. De Witt objected violently to giving William such important powers: "The remedy is worse than the disease", he wrote to De
Groot in Paris, explaining his fear that it would lead to *"absolute dependitie"*
on England.*

A compromise was found: William would be made Captain- and
Admiral-General for a single campaign, but he refused. And Temple's
successor, the detested Downing, wrote to London on 19 January 1672:
"The business of the Prince of Orange stands as it did, even his best
friends in Holland it selfe doe advise him not to accept the Office of
Generall as it is now tendered by them of Holland."* William himself
knew perfectly well that the appointment would give him no real
authority, and that if he failed he would be discredited for good.

The futile discussions and delays were intolerable to the young
Prince, and he was unable to sit by and watch his country imperilled by
De Witt's inertia. In great secrecy he sent Gabriel Sylvius, the former
secretary of his mother, to see his uncle with a proposal which justified
De Witt's worst suspicions. "If his Majesty would kindly tell me what he
desires, I shall do my utmost to procure it for him . . . in spite of Pensionary De Witt and his cabale." William coolly anticipated what might
happen if this peace mission to Charles was crowned by success. It
would mean the downfall of De Witt: "I and my friends will be at the
head of affairs." If this happened, Sylvius was to assure Charles, England
would then have a faithful ally in the United Provinces under William.

This astonishing offer, however, was qualified. It was made on the assumption that the King "was not already too much engaged with France"; and Charles's demands would not be considered if they went against "the foundations of the Republic".*

During Sylvius's mission to London, the States-General renewed Holland's offer to make William Captain- and Admiral-General for a single campaign, but this time they added the provision that the appointment would be confirmed on his twenty-third birthday. It was good enough for William for the time being, and he accepted on 25 February.

When the news was announced The Hague went wild. Hundreds of people swarmed into the streets, cheering and singing "with such pleasure that it is hard to describe".* In the great courtyard of the Binnenhof boys built a huge bonfire, shouting "*Viva Orangie*", and others crowded into the palace to see their hero eat his dinner. In the chaos a little orphan boy from Leiden lost his hat and burst into tears. The Prince heard of this and sent him a ducaton, which speculators immediately offered to buy off him for two others. He proudly refused. Even the sweets thrown to the crowd became prized souvenirs.*

A week later, the new Captain- and Admiral-General invited the States of Holland to dinner. "The banquet of H. H. was lavish, and amongst other things were 40 partridges, 24 pheasants, and six cocks in every platter." For the dazzled company, there was an out-of-season treat: on this freezing winter evening they were offered a huge tub full of fresh asparagus, which had cost the Prince eighty guilders. Their host went out of his way to be pleasant to these men, for so long his opponents, who now "were very gay and cheerful" while many of them kissed the Prince's hand as they reeled away at one in the morning after a dinner that lasted eight hours.*

News arriving during the banquet that Downing, who had fled from Holland, had been thrown into the Tower on his return to England, spoiled no one's pleasure – "as that gave them reasons for good hope".*

These hopes were ill-founded. When the envoy of the States to London, Meerman, arrived in February to offer the English a complete settlement of all their grievances, there was no response. And Charles rejected with the same indifference the mediation that William had offered between him and the States. In a letter congratulating him on his promotion to Captain-General, he stalled: "I have made no haste to answer what you commanded Silvius to say to me, because I am far from believing you could effect what you should undertake; it is enough you have done your own business as well. I must drive mine in the usual and open way. . . ."*

The States – and William of Orange – at last understood that they had to prepare not only for war with France but with England too. "You can easily believe how heartbreaking I find this business", wrote William to Ossory.*

CHAPTER VII

The Disaster Year

"THERE'S A GOOD JOKE about the Dutch going round", wrote Madame de Sévigné from Paris in June 1672. "Holland is a countess of about a hundred years old; she is very ill, and she has four doctors at her bedside: they are the Kings of England, France, Spain and Sweden. The King of England says, Show me your tongue. . . . Ah! what a foul mouth! The King of France feels her pulse and says, She needs a good bleeding!"*

The Paris witticism summed up perfectly the attitude of the two kings towards the tiny republic they had set out to destroy. On 6 April 1672 Charles II declared war on the United Provinces, followed a day later by Louis XIV. While the English King pestered the Dutch with his complaints and protests, his French cousin had been preparing himself thoroughly and openly for his Grand Design – the humiliation of the "cheesemongers" who had dared to question his claims in the Spanish Netherlands.

As early as the beginning of 1671, urgent reports of French military preparations, sent to De Witt by the Dutch Ambassador in Paris, Pieter de Groot, had fallen on deaf ears. The Raadspensionary was the more willing to be deluded since a war with France would inevitably mean the restoration of the Orange Stadholder.

Even at the beginning of 1672, the Dutch still seemed unconscious of any danger. "We have no notion of war any more", a Dutchman warned De Witt.* And a commission sent that April by the States-General to report on the state of the eastern IJssel line of fortresses came back with alarming news: the Republic's key defence line in the east had been so much neglected that many of the ramparts had become promenades lined with houses, the guns had been removed or rusted away, and the garrisons were almost unmanned.* Worse still, there was little money available for military needs, and as a result pay was in arrears throughout the army, discipline was non-existent, and strong guards had to be posted in some garrisons to stop the troops deserting. The Republic's supplies of weapons and ammunitions were dangerously low; through the treachery of an Amsterdam banker, François-Michel le Tellier, Marquis de Louvois, the French Minister of War, had been able to buy up almost all the powder, lead and matches in the country. Of the Republic's defences only the fleet – a total of 130 ships lying in the ports under the command of Admiral De Ruyter – was ready for action.

On the international front also the Dutch position was dangerously weak. As late as April the only ally the Republic had found was a reluctant Spain; and not until May did the Elector of Brandenburg sign a defence treaty with the States, and then only after the payments of huge subsidies. Ranged against the Dutch were not only the French and the English, but also the Archbishop-Elector of Cologne and Bernard van Galen, Prince-Bishop of Münster, known in the Netherlands as "the scourge of God".

As always at times of danger the Dutch people, realizing how defenceless De Witt and his "cabal" had left them, now turned to the Prince of Orange, their new Captain-General, as their only hope. He himself had toured the fortifications and was deeply shocked by what he saw. Back in The Hague, he assembled a Grand Council on 6 April and urged that emergency measures should be taken at once, including the conscription of every man between the age of eighteen and sixty. A fortnight later he travelled to his hunting lodge at Dieren near Doesburg, one of the key fortresses along the IJssel line, to take up his command – and found that only half of the promised 18,000 troops had materialized. But he still refused to lose heart. "If they hear that the enemy has crossed the IJssel," he declared, "they can believe that I am dead."*

While at Dieren, he received a letter from Charles II, dated 22 May, in which the English King shamelessly pointed out that his nephew ought to be grateful to him: "If this war had not fallen out, I am confident you had not so soon . . . been in the post you are at present." He added that their correspondence must cease for some time "upon this misunderstanding between the States and me".*

A few days later the Sun King left Paris at the head of the most powerful French army ever assembled: more than 120,000 superbly-trained men, under the command of veterans like Turenne, Condé and Luxembourg, prepared – as Voltaire put it – to crush "a young Prince in poor health, who had seen neither siege nor combat, and about 25,000 wretched troops".* Led by Louis in person, these glittering armies swept north through the Spanish Netherlands, past Charleroi towards the fortresses in Cleves, which fell one after another. Even William found it difficult not to despair – "nobody can expect that with just a handful of men we can prevent the passage of the IJssel by such a powerful force".*

Only the Dutch fleet under De Ruyter heartened the dispirited people a little. On 7 May, watched by dense crowds on the beaches of Suffolk, it had beaten the combined French and English fleets under the Duke of York at Sole Bay. Evelyn, who saw the English fleet a few days later, found it so "miserably shattered" that it made him reflect about the folly of war, "loosing so many good men, for no provocation but that the Hollanders exceeded us in industrie, and in all things but envy".*

The good news of Sole Bay, however, was soon forgotten in the Republic. On 10 June, Louis XIV with his armies reached the Rhine at Elten. The post on the Dutch side, the Tolhuis, had been left almost undefended when its commander, the French officer Comte de Montbas, had abandoned it without William's permission. The furious Prince had hurriedly sent off a mere 2000 troops to try to hold it, and it was against this handful of men that the French army, under the eyes of Louis XIV, fought the *Bataille de Tolhuis*, so much glorified in French military history.

It began when the French cavalry plunged into the Rhine to ford it at a spot pointed out by a Dutch traitor. The current was so strong that the horses were swept off their legs, while the Dutch fired on them from the banks, and many of their riders, including several young noblemen, were shot dead or drowned. Another squadron of cavalry attempted the crossing, tightly bunched together, and successfully reached the other side. Condé followed his men in a small boat, together with his nephew the Duc de Longueville, and the French now poured over in strength. At first it looked as if the heavily outnumbered Dutch would surrender quickly when Condé demanded it, but at that moment his slightly drunken nephew shot one of their officers, shouting "no quarter for this rabble. . . ." He was instantly felled by a Dutch bullet. The Maréchal, standing close by, was wounded by another bullet in the hand, and the simple crossing turned into a bloodbath as the French fell in fury on the Dutch and slaughtered 1500 of them, themselves losing 300 men.

News that the French had crossed the Rhine reached William at Dieren, and on 14 June he decided it was hopeless to try and hold the eastern front, telling a deputy of the States of Holland, "We can't stay here and let Holland fall."* After Utrecht had slammed its gates on him and refused to defend itself, he fell back with his 10,000 men behind Holland's own defences, the Water Line – the ring of sluices that as a last resort could be opened to flood the countryside in the path of an invader. Amsterdam at least was safe for the time being, but within one month the Dutch had lost two of their seven provinces to the French, while the Bishops of Munster and Cologne, assisted by Luxembourg, had captured Overijssel. It looked as though the two northern Provinces of Friesland and Groningen, together with Holland and Zeeland, must soon follow.

The Dutch panicked. "The government lost its head, the people its heart, the country its hope," is the famous summary of the condition of the Dutch in this *Rampjaar* – the Disaster Year – of 1672. One burgher described how in Amsterdam ordinary life came to a standstill. "Everyone seemed stunned and subdued; everyone found his house too small and suffocating, so he rushed out into the streets where he found no comfort, only tears and misery." Shops, banks, schools and courts shut down, and only the churches stayed open, "too small for the fearful souls who sighed more than they prayed".* Dutch bonds fell from 100 to 30, V.O.C. shares dropped from 572 to 250, and by July Government bonds were unsaleable.

A government as unpopular as De Witt's could not hope to keep the situation under control, and rioting now broke out everywhere. Worse still, many of the peasants opposed the opening of the locks and the cutting of the dykes that flooded fields and farms, essential to create a water barrier between Holland and the French. The militia was called in, but the sabotage went on, and at the same time the water-level that year was so low that the French mocked: "The Hollanders have only given us a demi-bain, because there is not enough water to flood the countryside."*

For them this watery country was a constant source of astonishment. As a French military expert wrote in his *Géographie Militaire*: "If you look at the map of Holland, it is difficult to understand how such a country can exist. It is impossible to tell whether land or water dominates. . . . Holland is a triumph of man over the sea, an artificial man-made country."*

But fortunately for the Dutch, Turenne, who had taken over command when Condé was wounded at Tolhuis, did not immediately grasp the importance of water in the Dutch defence system, and failed to secure Muyden, the little town near Amsterdam where the main sluices were housed. The Marquis de Rochefort, sent to take it with 4000 troops, was driven off by the resistance of 500 men under the resolute command of Johan Maurits van Nassau. Not until much later did the French realize that they had missed their greatest chance of taking Amsterdam and the rest of Holland. In that month of June, they still believed they had the province at their mercy. When an embassy, sent by the States-General, reached French headquarters at "Huis te Keppel" at Doesburg on the twenty-second to enquire what the French terms were, Louis XIV refused to see them. He dismissed them contemptuously, telling them through Louvois not to return without offers of their own, and full powers to negotiate.

The embassy, led by Pieter de Groot, hurried back to The Hague. But in the few days of their absence, the scene there had completely changed. On 21 June De Witt had been attacked and stabbed in the street near his office. He was not dangerously wounded, but he was obliged to stay at home for the next few weeks, and temporarily at least Holland's most eloquent advocate of appeasement was silenced.† Even more important, there had been a dramatic change in the position of the Prince of Orange. On the day that De Witt was assaulted, William, at the request of the magistrates of Dordrecht, who could no longer control the rioting crowds in their city, had arrived on a visit and toured the city fortifications. But if the anti-Orange councillors hoped that his mere presence would calm the people, they were disappointed. While the Prince was dining with them at the Peacock Inn, the crowds broke into the hall and shouted to the Prince to know what was going on. He answered that he was perfectly satisfied, and was prepared to leave when they pushed him back into the inn and threatened the City magistrates that they would not be allowed to go before they had declared the Prince of Orange Stadholder. Two pastors were dragged out of the crowd to absolve William and the magistrates from their oath to observe the Perpetual Edict, and a resolution offering William the Stadholdership of Holland was signed. The only signature missing was that of De Witt's brother Cornelius, who was in bed at home after he had been attacked like his brother Johan. The rabble surged round to his house, and at the pleading of his terrified wife Cornelius signed, adding the letters V. C. – constrained by force. The crowds compelled him to scratch them out again, and now at last they allowed the Prince to depart. As he took his leave of the magistrates, his only words were: "Gentlemen, I am sorry for you."*

The news from Dordrecht travelled fast, and by nightfall Rotterdam, Gouda, Haarlem and Delft had followed the city's example. On 2 July it was the turn of Amsterdam. "This afternoon the City Council assembled and accepted the Resolution to offer the Prince of Orange the Stadholdership of Holland . . ." wrote an enthusiastic member of Amsterdam's civic militia in his diary of the *Rampjaar*.* In the City Hall the Secretary held the Perpetual Edict in the flame of a candle, and as the stench of

---

† Three of De Witt's attackers escaped to the Prince's army. A fourth – Jacob van der Graeff – was caught and executed on 29 June.*

burning parchment spread through the room, one of the Regents remarked, "This Edict stinks." His colleague added: "It should never have been made."*

Opposition of a few last towns to the Prince's elevation was soon swept away, and on 4 July, at four o'clock in the morning, the States of Holland voted that the twenty-one-year-old Prince should be proclaimed Stadholder and Captain- and Admiral-General of Holland. Zeeland followed suit immediately, and four days later William was proclaimed Captain- and Admiral-General of the whole Republic for life.

William showed almost no emotion when they brought him the news. He was now absolute master of as much of his country as was not in French hands – "King only without the name" – and it was not a time for rejoicing. The whole country was in an uproar: De Groot, after a second journey to Doesburg, had now returned to The Hague with the terms on which Louis was prepared to offer peace, and their harshness had provoked even the defeated and demoralized Dutch into a wave of national indignation. The French King, they learned, was demanding Maastricht, the Generality lands of Brabant and Limburg, and part of Gelderland; preferential trading treatment for France; an enormous indemnity of sixteen million guilders; and liberty of worship for Dutch Catholics who were to be admitted freely to public office. As a reminder of their defeat, the Dutch were to send a yearly embassy to the Sun King to present him with a medallion commemorating their gratitude for his kindness in returning their country to the States.

They were terms which would have left the Republic humiliated, defenceless and impoverished, and De Groot found both the Prince and the States-General unwilling even to consider them. The wretched ambassador was accused of trying to sell his country, and eventually had to flee to England.

The French had been confident that the Dutch would accept – "Unless I'm mistaken, they will sign everything", wrote Louvois to his father – but they waited in vain for De Groot's return.*

The English peace terms, arriving twelve days after the French, met with the same response at The Hague. Charles II had contributed nothing to the French victories on land, and his fleet had been defeated by the Dutch at sea. Nevertheless he now asked for an indemnity of a million guilders, important trading concessions in the East Indies, the Zeeland island of Walcheren, and £10,000 to be paid by the Dutch annually for the right to fish herring in English coastal waters. And once more Charles demonstrated how little he knew his nephew, when he demanded that the Prince should be made sovereign.

News of the English terms was followed by a special embassy from Charles consisting of Arlington and Buckingham. The two Englishmen were enthusiastically welcomed by the Dutch people who now, as always, believed that English hostility to Holland would melt away when the King's nephew was made Stadholder.* But they were to be disappointed – as were the English envoys.

At their first meeting with the Prince, at his headquarters at Nieuwerbrug, they at once broached the question of his sovereignty, as Charles had instructed them. The English King had long dreamed of setting up his nephew as the grateful puppet ruler of the United Provinces, dependent on England. He had insisted on making it one of the provisions of the Treaty of Dover, and now more than ever he thought the time was ripe for such a move. But William heard the proposition coolly: "he liked better the position of Stadholder which the States had given him . . . he believed himself obliged in honour and confidence not to prefer his interests before his obligations."*

He went further. During a long evening's discussions with the English envoys, the Prince set out to convince them that England's alliance with France was not in their country's best interests. Arlington, unpersuaded, went to bed, but William and Buckingham sat on talking and drinking into the small hours, and the Prince finally talked Charles's merry envoy into drafting a treaty between England and the United Provinces. Arlington, next morning, took one look and tore it up immediately. Then he tried once more, together with a jaded Buckingham, to convince William of the personal advantages to him in making peace with England now. They were warmly seconded by William's friends, Bentinck and Zuylestein, who made no secret of their feelings – "they would readily see a dozen of the States hanged if the country had peace and the Prince were sovereign of it", they assured the two Englishmen. But they were curtly silenced by William: "the country had trusted him and he would never deceive or betray them for any base ends of his own."*

The two envoys now packed up and prepared to leave for discussions with Louis XIV, but when the time came for farewells, Buckingham could not restrain himself from asking the Prince in amazement: "Surely you see that everything is lost?" William's only reply was: "My Lord, my country is indeed in danger, but there is one way never to see it lost, and that is to die in the last ditch."* He realized that there was nothing to be hoped for from the English.

His grandmother Amalia had come to the same conclusion. When Buckingham paid her a courtesy visit at The Hague, he talked to her of the affection the English felt for the Dutch. "We do not use Holland like a mistress, we love her like a wife", said Buckingham. Amalia, who was not uninformed about the Duke's reputation, answered drily: "*Vraiment je crois que vous nous aimez comme vous aimez la vôtre.*"*

The two English ambassadors then travelled to French headquarters at Heeswijk, where the French persuaded them without much difficulty not to make separate peace terms with the Dutch. The two sets of peace terms were accordingly put together in one daunting package, and sent off to the Prince. When he studied them, he had to be restrained from throwing them angrily into the fire. Next day he went to The Hague to report on them to the States-General.

Even now the young man, who had been in his high position for a mere two weeks, refused to consider the possibility of defeat, and his speech to the disheartened deputies was that of a great statesman. The proposals put forward by the enemy should be rejected – "he had rather be cut in pieces than accept them."* He was convinced that even if Holland itself were lost, the Hollanders might survive – a thought which the nineteenth-century historian Macaulay elaborated into a visionary scheme of a mass-migration to the Far East:

> Liberty and pure religion, driven by tyrants and bigots from Europe, might take refuge in the furthest isles of Asia. The shipping in the ports of the Republic would suffice to carry 200,000 emigrants to the Indian archipelago. There the Dutch Commonwealth might commence a new and more glorious existence.*

There is no evidence that William actually presented this romantic scheme to the States, but it perfectly conveyed the new mood of courage and defiance he had inspired in the United Provinces, and the Dutch were now determined to fight on.

The Stadholder made a last effort to detach his uncle from the French alliance. In a personal letter to Charles II he offered to try to secure for him all he had asked, and even agreed to accept the sovereignty for himself, but only on condition that peace was first restored, and that the Dutch themselves should accept him as sovereign.* But the English King was not satisfied: he had wanted a solid base in the Republic, and since William failed to make any mention of it, he rejected his nephew's secret proposal, admonishing him in suave fatherly terms: "Bethink yourself well what will become of you when the war shall be ended, if I have not a good footing in that country to stand by you against the designs and machinations of those that shall find themselves thrown out of the government."*

William did not reply – there was other work to do. In mid-August, he visited Amsterdam and toured the flooded country around the city. Returning that evening after his trip, the guards who came to inspect the boat found the exhausted Stadholder dozing, but when the city fathers apologized for disturbing him, the Prince replied laughing: "I wish that all my soldiers were as vigilant and attentive." Next day he left the town, and so many of its citizens crowded round to shake his hand that he had to break away – "I cannot give my hand to you all," he told them, "but I give you my heart."* Everywhere he went, indeed, he gave fresh hope and courage to his countrymen, who saw that they now had a determined leader.

OPPOSITION TO ORANGE RULE, however, was still alive, and when Charles warned his nephew that the Loevesteiners, now discredited and out of power, would stop at nothing to bring about his downfall, the English King was not far wrong. Their hatred of William was so notorious that it gave a disreputable barber, by the name of Willem Tichelaar, enough confidence to call on De Witt's brother Cornelius with "a plan important for the State" – the assassination of the Stadholder. He accused the Prince of being in secret alliance with the English insinuating that "His Highness would perhaps marry the daughter of the Duke of York."*

It was not the first time that a match between William and Mary had been talked about. The States ambassador Dijkvelt had returned from London at the beginning of that year with the impression that the English Court saw it as the best way to bring the Prince round to its side. And the anti-Orangists began citing the suggested match as proof that England had made a war on their country for no other reason that to establish the Prince.*

Cornelius de Witt knew what kind of man he was dealing with in Tichelaar – three years earlier he had punished him for rape and perjury and he now indignantly declined his offer. The barber retaliated by accusing Cornelius himself of plotting to kill the Prince of Orange. Cornelius was at once arrested and taken for trial to The Hague, where he was accused – in addition – of cowardice, incapacity, treason and misuse of the country's money. Similar charges were already circulating in pamphlet form against his brother Johan, the Raadspensionary, who was still recovering from the attempt on his life. In the current pro-Orange mood of the country, no accusation against the De Witts was too monstrous to be believed.

Johan de Witt, deeply wounded by the charges that he had misused the secret service funds and neglected the army, knew that only one man could save him. He wrote to William, enclosing a particularly vicious pasquinade and asking him to refute such slanders. The Prince let four days go by before he answered in freezing terms. "I can assure you that I have always despised reports which have started in this manner, since not only my family, but I myself, have several times been attacked with a freedom and avidity beyond all bounds."

On the question of the secret service funds, the Prince declined to comment: "I have no knowledge of it." Coming to the much more serious accusation that De Witt had failed to equip the army properly, William's faint praise was damning. "I cannot and do not doubt that you took such care of the army and the navy . . . as the condition of affairs and of the times would allow." He refused to be drawn into an argument about the responsibility for all the deficiencies – "I am so taken up with business in these unhappy and troublesome times that I have involved myself as little as possible in looking into the past. You will therefore find a much better justification in your own past acts and wisdom than in anything you can obtain from me." He signed this letter, which was in effect De Witt's death warrant, "your affectionate friend William Henry, Prince of Orange".*

De Witt's career was finished. On 1 August he went to see the Stadholder and tendered his resignation to him. The Prince pointed out coolly that it was a matter for the States, but that he would raise no objections. And three days later the Raadspensionary, after nineteen years in power, formally resigned his office. The usual effusive formula of thanks from the States was, on William's advice, omitted.

If De Witt had had any hopes of a quiet and dignified retirement, they were soon dashed. His brother Cornelius was in the Gevangenpoort prison next to the Binnenhof, waiting for his trial. At his first hearing he had denied all charges, and his judges had ordered him to be racked in the hope of extracting an admission of guilt. To no purpose: when on 19 August he appeared in court, the evidence against him was so meagre that he could only be sentenced to banishment and ordered to pay all costs. The Dutch were indignant and astonished. "If he is not guilty, let him go free," was the general comment, "but if they sentence him to banishment, he must be guilty, and if he is guilty, punish him with a well-deserved death."*

Tichelaar, Cornelius's accuser, released the day after the verdict, had no difficulty whipping up to fury the crowds gathered round the Gevangenpoort. Cornelius, preparing himself to leave the prison and his

country, heard the uproar and probably in panic and fear, sent a message
to his brother that he wanted to see him. Johan left the barber's chair
where the messenger had found him, and hurried to the Gevangenpoort
and his brother's bedside. The two De Witts were now the prisoners of
the maddened crowds. The civic militia found it impossible to restrain
the rabble, and the cavalry, under the command of Captain Tilly, was
sent to the assistance of the militia. They succeeded in restoring calm, but
not for long. Under orders from two States deputies, who feared an
invasion by riotous farmers and seamen from outside The Hague,
Tilly and his cavalry were sent away to guard the town gates. "I will
obey," the Captain said, "but the De Witts are dead men."* There was
nothing now to stop the crowds. They stormed into the prison where
they found Johan sitting in his brother's cell reading the Bible to him.
Cornelius, a sick and tortured man, was lying on the bed where only a
month earlier De Witt's assailant De Graeff had scratched the words
"*Nescit mens hominum fati sortisque futurae*" (the mind of men is ignorant
of the fate that awaits them).* The mob hesitated a moment, then fell on
the two men, who were dragged out into the street. Within minutes it
was all over. The brothers were killed by musket shots and their bodies
viciously mutilated. What remained of them was strung up from a lamp-
post, to be secretly removed that night by friends. Their hearts, hacked
out of their chests, were put on show, and pieces of their clothes sold as
souvenirs.*

The Prince of Orange was at Alphen after an inspection of Woerden,
one of the five key-posts in the Water Line, when news of the murder
reached him. "I have never seen him more overwhelmed", wrote
Bentinck fifteen years later.* And when his friends rejoiced openly in
De Witt's death, he was silent. But next morning, after travelling to The
Hague, the Prince told the States-General nevertheless that "he knew
not whether to proceed" against the culprits: they were too numerous
and some of them too important.

In the end, William did not raise a finger against any of those involved in the murder; on the contrary, two of them, Tichelaar and the
Hague silversmith, Hendrik Verhoeff, were eventually paid off by him
with handsome annual pensions of 400 and 600 guilders respectively. A
third culprit, Van Banchem, was promoted to Baljuw, head of the local
police, of The Hague. He was a scoundrel whose behaviour became such
a public scandal that eventually in 1674 the local pastors excluded him
from communion. When William heard this he took no action, explaining that "he had loved him because he had always protected his house."
But six years later not even the Prince could save him from the gallows.

Many of William's critics, both at the time and since, have accused him of complicity in a plot against the De Witts. They point to the rewards he gave three of the murderers; to the sudden and needless visit to Woerden – some even stating that he returned incognito to The Hague to be a witness of the murder – to the fact that Tilly's orders to withdraw were signed by a friend of his who hated De Witt intensely. However suggestive these facts, no evidence that the Prince was directly involved has been found. It is, however, undeniable that, as a modern Dutch historian says: "William was a good hater, and he did not have it in him to be magnanimous towards De Witt."*

The French diplomat Gourville wrote in his memoirs that the Prince, while he had given no orders to have the De Witts killed, admitted to him much later: "*Je ne laissai point de m'en sentir un peu soulagé.*"* He may not have approved the manner of De Witt's death, but it rid him of a man who had been, and might well be again, the determined leader of all Dutch opposition to him, and whose policies he considered responsible for his country's misfortunes. He made not the slightest effort to protect De Witt against the fury of the Dutch and by rewarding the murderers, he gave his tacit approval to the crime. Morally speaking, he cannot be acquitted of complicity.

After this explosion of mob violence, the atmosphere at The Hague remained tense for weeks, and there were real fears that there might be other victims on both sides. In September, when it was rumoured that the Prince, making an evening visit to his grandmother Amalia, at Huis ten Bosch, had been assassinated, everybody believed it and there was uproar in The Hague. The Prince was alive and untouched, but the man accused of the plot, François Focanus, a cousin of De Witt, was arrested, thrown into the Gevangenpoort and released only when no evidence could be found.

AT THE NEWS OF DE WITT'S DEATH, Charles's hopes of a settlement with the Dutch revived. He wrote in haste to his "deare Nephew" on 30 August: "The last letters having brought us the news of the people having murdered De Witt and his brothers as the authors and occasion of the war makes it plaine to me, they are infinitely desirous of a peace." He proposed an immediate meeting at Dunkirk between Dutch and English ambassadors with full powers, and offered to persuade Louis to send an ambassador as well.* To this informal approach William, after some delay, gave a very formal answer. He sent a personal envoy to Charles, Frederik van Rheede, declining his proposal. "It is impossible to oblige the people to a peace jointly with France, and . . . he did not even wish it for several reasons."* Charles was surprised that his nephew's answer was, as he said,

> without the least signification that my offers were acceptable to you, upon which I have taken the liberty to speake my minde very freely to Mons. de Reede, and I hope you will take it for a great marke of my kindnesse to you, that I have done so. I assure you, if I loved you lesse, I would have taken another course. After all, you are the best judge what is good for you and that poor people . . .*

William's intransigence infuriated not only Charles but the English Secretary of State as well. Arlington hinted that if the Prince persisted in a policy with regard to England which the Dutch obviously no longer supported, he might meet the same fate as De Witt. William, unimpressed, answered angrily: "Don't imagine that your threats to have me torn in pieces by the people frighten me very much; I am not in the least faint-hearted by nature. . . ."*

All this time, the Prince was working "night and day" trying to build up his army, and with encouraging results. He now had a force of 30,000 drilled, well-equipped and disciplined troops, and he had a set of loyal commanders under him. Most of them were young Dutch noble-men, who were his friends and with whom he had grown up, like Godart van Ginckel, later Earl of Athlone, and Walgrave van Nassau-Usingen. There was Zuylestein, his former governor, and his son Willem Frederik, a pleasant but indolent young man and a great gourmet. There were the two grandsons of Prince Maurits: Hendrik van Nassau, Heer van Ouwerkerk, an insignificant but enthusiastic young man, and his brother Maurits Lodewijk van Nassau, the handsome Heer van La Leck.* And William, as always, leaned heavily on Hans Willem Bentinck, once his page and now his inseparable friend and aide.

The loyalty and courage of all these young men was beyond question, but their experience of actual warfare, like that of William himself, was almost non-existent. Pitted against commanders like Luxembourg, Turenne and the great Condé, they looked like boys. There was only one veteran commander on William's side, and he was old enough to be the Prince's grandfather: Johan Maurits van Nassau-Siegen, the "Brazilian", the desperate and heroic defender of the sluice-gates at Miden.

In an effort to give his command a little more backbone, the Stad-holder now invited Georg Friedrich Count von Waldeck to be his second-in-command. Waldeck, who had commanded the Brandenburg armies for years, was a seasoned soldier, a thorough organizer and a tough disciplinarian. He was also a tetchy, difficult man who could be outspoken in his complaints and his criticism of his new young Commander-in-Chief. But for all these faults, he became a solid and faithful second for the Prince until the end of his military career. It was an excellent choice.

Politically too, William was now well seconded; he had been shrewd and lucky enough to find a brilliant successor to Johan de Witt in Caspar Fagel. The new Raadspensionary was a man of forty-three, an able lawyer who had become Pensionary of Haarlem in 1663. As a protégé of De Witt, and a sturdy Republican, he had been appointed Griffier or Clerk of the States-General, and in this function had been one of the proposers of the Perpetual Edict. The war had shattered his respect for De Witt, and the fighting spirit of the Prince of Orange, in such contrast to the fainthearted Regents, won Fagel over to the Stadholder's side. After De Witt's resignation, Fagel was elected his successor on 23 August.

William appreciated this adroit statesman, whose first piece of advice on taking office gave him absolute power in Holland: changes in the magistrates throughout the Province – proposed by Fagel and authorized for just this one occasion by the States – turned Holland into an Orange stronghold, not always in the local interest.*

THE AUTUMN OF 1672 was one of the wettest anyone in Holland could remember. The crops were spoiled and conditions in the camps of the unseasoned Dutch soldiers became so desperate that both men and horses died of hunger and disease. Morale was lower still on the French side. Louis XIV had returned at the end of the campaign to his own country where 20,000 soldiers slaved to realize the ultimate expression of his grandeur, the palace of Versailles. The troops he left behind under the command of François-Henri de Montmorency, Duc de Luxembourg, had been idle for weeks, and their only distraction, pillaging the surrounding countryside, was stopped by Louvois who was afraid that if it went on, Louis's new Dutch subjects would be unable to pay their taxes.

The Frenchmen detested the flat watery country, and the September rains completed their misery. "The rain falls without stopping", wrote Luxembourg to Paris. "It's not that the weather was fine up to now; but at least we had one hour of rain and one without it. At the moment it falls as if they were pouring it out of buckets, and I assure you that a man needs to be made of iron to bear it."

These rains turned Holland, behind its Water Line, into an impene-
trable bastion for the French. Luxembourg complained: "All the roads
are impassable, and nobody would dream of moving about unless he'd
turned into a duck."* But the Dutch forced the Maréchal to "move
about". After a failed attempt to take Naarden, William turned to attack
Woerden instead. Luxembourg, moving rapidly to prevent the recapture
of this little town, was halted by Zuylestein. Next day, 12 October, Dutch
treachery made it possible for the French commander to attack Zuylestein
from the rear, and the Dutch commander with his small force, refusing to
surrender, was routed and he himself literally hacked to pieces. William's
daring initiative had proved a failure and the Dutch troops were driven
back. William had not only lost his first battle, but also the man who had
been like a father to him.

Five days after this defeat, the Prince held a council of war at which
he proposed that the Dutch should attempt a breakout to the south. He
kept the details of his plans secret, and when one of his adjutants asked
if he was allowed to know, the Prince asked smilingly if he could keep a
secret. The man assured him that he could. "So can I," replied William.*
He left Rotterdam on 2 November with 10,000 horse and 3000 foot and
marching through Roosendaal reached Maastricht, where he swung
south for a surprise attack on Charleroi, an important French depot. It
very nearly succeeded – the garrison was weak, its commander absent –
but a sudden frost made it impossible to dig the trenches necessary for an
attack, and in the end the only tangible result of the expedition was the
sacking of the small town of Binche nearby.

If the campaign failed in its military objective, however, it warned
the French that the Dutch armies were led by an enterprising commander
– his initiative had for a moment caused genuine worry to the French,
and in Paris even Louis XIV had felt *"une furieuse inquiétude après une
action si hardieuse"*.*

But the Stadholder's anxiety very soon exceeded that of the French.
On his way back to his headquarters in Alphen, he received news that the
frost which had defeated him at Charleroi had given Luxembourg the
opportunity he had been waiting for to invade Holland. Luxembourg's
preparations had started as soon as William left for the south, an excellent
moment the Maréchal judged to attempt "some small undertaking which
will discredit the Prince of Orange, and show the country that he would
have done better to remain here defending it than embark on distant
adventures."*

He had distributed skates to his soldiers and trained them to move
about and fight on ice, but the weather refused to co-operate until

Christmas. Then suddenly it froze hard, and the Water Line turned into a highway over which Luxembourg's armies marched and skated into Holland on 27 December. The only order the Maréchal gave his long-idle and frustrated troops was said to be: "Go, my children, plunder, murder, destroy and if it be possible to commit yet greater cruelties, be not negligent therein. Let me see that I am not deceived in my choice of the flower of the King's troops."*

His men did not hesitate to obey him, and reports of French atrocities spread fast, creating panic everywhere. In Amsterdam every citizen spent that night in vigil, heavily armed, with so many torches blazing that it was almost as light as day. In The Hague they frantically chopped down trees to build barricades, and only in Leiden the populace forced their mayor to wait outside the gates for Luxembourg, key in hand.

A sudden thaw saved Holland. Luxembourg had to give up his plans to march on The Hague and decided to return to Utrecht, making a detour to fall on the defenceless towns of Bodegraven and Zwammerdam. A few hours later both towns were smoking ruins. More than two thousand people were dead, most of them burned alive in their own homes after the women had first been raped. "We lit the village and grilled all the Hollanders in it", boasted Louvois later. And Luxembourg admitted with glee that he had taken a particular pleasure in watching the Prince of Orange's house at Bodegraven go up in flames.

The ice was melting rapidly away and the retreat turned into a flight. The French soldiers scrambled through water that came up to their waists and sometimes to their shoulders. Many of them drowned, and in Amsterdam it was said that Luxembourg had fallen into the water and broken his leg. The rumour was exaggerated; Luxembourg only caught a severe cold.

The dispirited French reached Nieuwerbrug, and to their great surprise found this vital key point undefended – another of William's commanders, Colonel Pain-et-Vin, had deserted his post, and the French regained Utrecht unopposed.

By the time William returned to his headquarters at Alphen, the last Frenchman had left the province of Holland. The terror-stricken Dutch greeted their Stadholder with overwhelming relief. "The joy was so great that the cheering could be heard hours away." The Prince himself immediately visited Bodegraven and Zwammerdam, grimly touring the ruins and comforting those who had survived the massacre. In Bodegraven only three houses were still standing, and in one of them he found a tiny baby alive and crying. He ordered his men to take it away and have it carefully looked after.*

His fury at Luxembourg's expedition now fell on Pain-et-Vin, who was court-martialled and sentenced to life imprisonment. After William's stront protest the court reviewed their sentence, and ordered the death penalty. Pain-et-Vin was at once executed.

With the French invasion and their immediate withdrawal Holland's *Rampjaar* of 1672 came to an end. For the Hollanders Luxembourg's expedition had been a harrowing experience and for Louis XIV a useless and costly enterprise. It had hardened William's determination to drive the French back within their own frontiers, and even if his attempt on Charleroi had been unsuccessful, his prestige in Holland was greater than ever. French atrocities had convinced the most faint-hearted in Holland that Louis must be resisted; terror had united the Dutch behind their Stadholder.

CHAPTER VIII

The European War

At the beginning of 1673 the war was still no more than a military confrontation between Holland and France. But if the situation of the Dutch was not as desperate as it had been, the Prince of Orange realized that the four free provinces needed help from outside to survive. During the seasonal lull in fighting that winter always brought, he devoted all his energies to recruiting allies. At The Hague he was continuously closeted with the ambassadors of Spain and the Empire, but the Spanish were obsessed with the fear that once they had committed themselves to war with France the Dutch would pull out and leave them to it. And the Emperor, although he resented Louis's claims on Habsburg territories, had Turkish armies at his doorstep and a depleted treasury.

While these fruitless negotiations dragged on, another blow fell. The Elector of Brandenburg had always been a faint-hearted ally, but when Friedrich Wilhelm married again after the death of his first wife, William's aunt Louisa, Holland lost him completely. His second wife, Dorothea, the Dowager-Duchess of Brunswick-Luneburg, had strong French sympathies, and by June 1673 the Elector had made his peace with the French.

It was a dark hour for the Republic. Her old allies had abandoned her, and her new ones still hesitated to commit themselves. A print on sale in The Hague at this time expressed the country's disheartened and bitter mood. It showed a Dutchman being pulled one way by a Frenchman and the other way by an Englishman, while the Emperor and the Elector of Brandenburg rifled his pockets, and a Spaniard in the background made fun of him. "People great and small say 'that's the exact state of our affairs, and that's how they treat us' ", gloated a Frenchman to Louvois.*

The proud French felt themselves masters in Europe, and when the armies of Louis XIV moved north-east in May 1673, parading through the still neutral Spanish Netherlands, the King and his Court went with them. It was more like a triumphal progress than the opening of a campaign. Louis was about to be entertained by a favourite spectacle – "Big sieges please me more than the others," he was fond of saying. His choice had fallen on Maastricht, a key Dutch fortress on the Meuse with a garrison of 5000 men. It held out for nearly a fortnight before surrendering on 30 June. The King, who had been accompanied by his wife Maria Theresa and his mistress Madame de Montespan returned much satisfied. The capture of Maastricht had re-emphasized French military superiority, and for the Dutch it was another defeat.

Once more, as in the previous year, the only good news for the Republic was at sea. In Michiel de Ruyter and Cornelius Tromp the Dutch had possibly the two greatest admirals of the age, but the grumpy Tromp had not fought for years – as a fervent pro-Orange man, he had been excluded from service by De Witt. When William came to power, Tromp was reluctant to serve under De Ruyter's orders, and William demonstrated a diplomatic talent of the first order by reconciling the two men. Under their joint command, the most impressive fleet in Dutch history sailed out in May 1673 after an inspiring message from the Prince of Orange had been read out to the sailors. "The eyes and hearts of all the inhabitants of these countries, of all the Christian world indeed, follow this Fleet."*

There were brief skirmishes at sea in June, but in August the combined Anglo-French fleet suddenly appeared off the Dutch coast at Scheveningen with 4000 troops on board, ready to land. On 12 August William hurried to his fleet to encourage them in person, and nine days later De Ruyter with 111 ships engaged the 140 ships of the invader. While the Battle of Kijkduin raged between the English and the Dutch – the French were little more than onlookers – the churches all over Holland were packed. All through the long summer day the sea battle continued, and only after sunset did the English and French withdraw. The threat of an invasion disappeared with them over the horizon. De Ruyter commented with satisfaction: "The enemy still has some respect for the Seven Provinces."*

At last the tide seemed to be turning, and the Dutch case certainly looked more hopeful when on 30 August, at The Hague, William signed three separate treaties with Spain, with the Empire, and with the Duke of Lorraine. His persistence and patience at the conference table had paid off. "*La guerre de Hollande est finie; la guerre Européenne commence*", was the general verdict.*

By his treaty with the States, the Emperor bound himself to supply an army of 30,000 men, while the Republic would raise 20,000 and pay the

Emperor high subsidies. The Spanish promised by their treaty to declare war on France if a last peace effort failed. The prospect of such allies put fresh heart into the Dutch, and on 6 September William moved his army towards Naarden, the important fortress-town near Amsterdam, still in French hands. Luxembourg, with greatly depleted forces in Utrecht, had to look on while the Dutch recaptured the town five days later. It was William's first military success.

A month later he was on the move again, determined to prove to the French that Dutch confidence was now fully restored. He had chosen Bonn as his objective, where his small army of 12,000 men would combine with the forces of the Emperor to besiege the city. For the first time the Prince took with him his young secretary, Constantyn Huygens, the son of the great Constanter, who had persuaded William to give him the job a year earlier. The young man had none of the great qualities of his father or his brilliant scientist brother Christian. As his later journals show, Constantyn was a rather humourless and discontented man, more often preoccupied with his bowels than concerned by the great events around him. But at this time he was still young and keen on his new job, and his journal of this campaign is sometimes almost poetic in its brief glimpses of the Dutch armies poised before Bonn. "All the cavalry was under arms . . . H. H. was sitting by a fire at the edge of a little pine wood. A drummer wounded before Rheinbach died there under the pines. It was a beautiful night", he wrote one night during the siege.*

Bonn held out for eight days before capitulating on 12 November. News of the victory caused a sensation throughout Europe. The States-General immediately sent a message to the Prince, in which they thanked him "for all his trouble and his labour . . . the whole world will be convinced with us that it is more glorious to restore affairs from a desperate state than to preserve those which are in a good state." They urged the Prince, who had been fighting in the first ranks, to be careful of his own person: if not for his sake, at least because "the accidents that might befall your Highness would mean the total ruin of the state."*

The capture of Bonn was more than a victory for the Allies. It was a warning to Louis XIV that he could no longer dictate his own terms to a Europe that was beginning to unite against him. As he wrote regretfully in a memorandum, "I was master of a part of Holland; but my troops were far away from me, I had enemies for neighbours, frontiers completely open, mighty opponents at sea, and reasons for disquiet on every side. Thus I was forced to resign myself to losing my distant conquests."* And at the end of October Louvois sent orders to Luxembourg to evacuate the United Provinces. Louis's minister added "while the

Prince of Orange is muddying his boots in Flanders, you may abandon Vreeswijk and Woerden, pulling down the fortifications . . . let Woerden be looted if it is not prepared to pay a considerable sum, and set on fire and utterly destroy all the houses of Vreeswijk."*

Other towns were more fortunate: they were merely obliged to pay up huge sums as ransom. Luxembourg had already helped himself in the spring to the spoils of war. He had sent crates full of paintings, fine old tapestries and beautiful porcelain back to France by barge, guarded by Dutch soldiers whose captain was assured that the boats would "bring back fine wines for the Prince of Orange".*

On 8 December, William returned from his campaign in the south to find his country free again. He had hoped to reach his palace Noordeinde at The Hague without being noticed, but news that he was back spread through the town like wildfire, and the crowds gathered outside the palace, shouting for the "Redeemer of the Fatherland". They would not go away until they had seen him, and he was forced to appear repeatedly at the window to acknowledge the delirious cheering of his people.

ON THE OTHER SIDE OF THE NORTH SEA that same autumn, William's uncles Charles II and James, Duke of York, faced mounting criticism from Parliament and people. The war against Holland was unpopular. It had cost England a great deal of money, it had led to two humiliating defeats at sea, and it was bad for trade. The King and his brother were dangerously isolated in their pro-French sympathies. The French ambassador in London, Charles Colbert, Marquis de Croissy, reported to Louis XIV: "there are none of your subjects who wish you better success in all your undertakings than these two Princes do, but it is also true that you cannot count upon any friends in England except these two."* Even in the court itself William had his sympathizers. According to a charming but improbable story the little Princess Mary was once found beating out the rhythm of the Dutch national anthem on the table with her fingers. When she was reproved, she said defiantly: "I'm for the Dutch and against the French."*

But Charles was not to be deterred by mounting criticism in his country. By one of the clauses of the Treaty of Dover he had promised to do what he could to restore Catholicism in England, and early in 1673, as a first step, he had issued a Declaration of Indulgence suspending the penal laws against Dissenters and Roman Catholics. There were stormy scenes in Parliament, assembled in February 1673 by Charles to vote supplies for the Dutch War. Arlington began to fear that in their present mood they would refuse the King the money he needed, and urged the King to drop his Declaration. Charles told Louise de Kéroualle, his beautiful French mistress and Louis's spy, that he was seriously considering dissolving Parliament and making his own peace with the Dutch. As he had intended, the news was immediately reported to Louis XIV, who wrote urgently to Charles asking him to drop his Declaration of Indulgence. The English King, having demonstrated his desire to carry out the Treaty of Dover, graciously complied with Louis's request: it was seldom possible for him to please the French King and his own antiFrench parliament simultaneously. Colbert wrote happily to Louis on 20 March: "This Prince, who was almost resolved on Thursday in the evening to dissolve his Parliament . . . assured me that your Majesty's sentiments had always more power over him than all the reasonings of his most faithful ministers."*

For the moment Charles – and Louis – could relax. Parliament dutifully voted funds for carrying on the war, to the great disappointment of William of Orange. But for Charles there was a price to pay: Parliament passed the Test Act, which virtually excluded Roman Catholics from office under the crown. His brother James, the Lord High Admiral, was its most important victim.

It had been known for some time now that the Duke of York was a declared Catholic, a fact that up till then had not much worried the English. He still attended services in the Church of England, and his two daughters, next in line to the throne after himself, were being brought up staunch Protestants. But that summer, after his dismissal, rumours that he was thinking of marriage again and that he was looking for a Roman Catholic princess, changed everything. If such a marriage produced a son, he would not only be a Roman Catholic but Heir Apparent to the throne.

The task of tracking down a possible bride had been entrusted by James to Lord Peterborough, who found it a delicate and difficult mission. Some of the dozen or so princesses on his short list were not attractive enough, others were not pious enough. The perfect catch seemed to be the Princess of Innsbruck, Claudia Felicitas, equally famous for her face and her fortune. But the long negotiations were abruptly wound up when a more important candidate appeared on the scene – the Emperor Leopold I. Finally Peterborough's roving eye fell on the pious and beautiful Mary Beatrice d'Este of Modena, a healthy fifteen-year-old. James's envoy was enchanted by her, and sent a lyrical description back to London. "She was tall and admirably shaped, her hair black as jet, so were her eyebrows and her eyes, but the latter so full of light and sweetness, as they did dazzle and charm too . . . in the whole turn of her face, which was of the most graceful oval, there were all the features, all the beauty, that could be great and charming in any human creature."*

James, delighted, instructed him to arrange the match, but the girl who had always wanted to become a nun, was horrified at the news. She had hysterics for the next two days, and had to be kept in bed by force. The Pope wrote her comforting words: "The orthodox faith reinstated by you in a place of honour might recover the splendour and security of former days, an effect . . . which might become due to the victory of your piety"* – not for nothing was she to be nicknamed in England "the Daughter of the Pope"* – and Mary Beatrice's objections were overruled. She and her mother set out for England, pausing to greet the French King at Versailles, where that connoisseur of feminine beauty gave her a particularly warm welcome. He greeted her at the foot of the staircase – an exceptional honour – and showed off in person his grand new gardens and his almost completed palace to the young girl. When she left, he told her that he looked on her as his god-daughter, and presented her with a brooch worth £8000.

Her first meeting with the husband to whom she had been married by proxy was less of a success. The fifteen-year-old girl burst into tears at the mere sight of him, as she was often to do in the first weeks of their marriage. Years later, she confessed that in the beginning she had not loved her husband at all.* James, on the contrary, was completely carried away by her. Shortly after the marriage, the Italian envoy in London reported: "The Duke loves her tenderly and does nothing without informing her." He had immediately presented their pretty young stepmother to his two daughters Mary and Anne, saying teasingly that he had brought them a new playmate. His new wife was indeed only four years older than his elder daughter.

At first Mary had been deeply shocked by the news of her father's marriage to a Catholic princess, and bursting into tears, had refused to be comforted even by her preceptor, the Canon of Windsor, Thomas Doughty. Her careful training in the Protestant faith by Bishop Compton had borne excellent fruit: Piously she exclaimed: "Whatever happens, I hope that my sister and I will keep our fidelity to God and our religion unblemished."*

She was not the only one displeased by the marriage, concluded on 21 November. "The nation was much troubled at the match, she being a strict Papist, and the match carried on by the interest of the French King."* For once the Londoners failed to light their customary bonfires.* The House of Commons had even voted against it, but James had been too quick for them.

To counterbalance this dangerous new Catholic influence in the Royal family, there were now almost inevitably renewed suggestions that Mary should be married to her cousin William of Orange, Europe's emerging Protestant champion.* Such a match was of course out of the question while the two countries were at war, but it seemed clear that Charles would have to come to terms with the Dutch soon. Parliament was more anti-French than ever, and Louis's secret presents of money and crates of champagne to selected M.P.s had no effect. When Charles needed more money for the Dutch war, they dug their heels in and refused to vote it. The continuation of the war was impossible, and on 19 February 1674 the Peace of Westminster was signed.

The Dutch conceded the flag, and returned New York in exchange for Surinam. They also paid an indemnity of £200,000, most of which was earmarked for immediate payment of Charles's debts to William. From the English point of view the profits of the war seemed derisory compared to the terms William had offered only a year earlier to his uncle, who saw this as a personal defeat and humiliation. The present of a lion and tiger sent to him by William could not make up for the £4 million war indemnity he had turned down in 1673. And as if to underline the new strength of his nephew, the States of Holland and Zeeland had voted early in February to make William Hereditary Stadholder. Charles was obliged to put the best face on it he could. Graciously he wrote: "I would let you know . . . that although my own affairs obliged me to hasten the peace, I could not have had much comfort or security in it if it had not seen you so established."*

When a chance presented itself of a revenge, however, Charles could not resist. The French raised troops freely in England, but the Stadholder was not allowed to do so. And as an act of personal spite, he refused William permission to visit England, while his old friend Ossory was forbidden to go to Holland and join the Dutch army. It was a bitter disappointment for the Prince, who after the conclusion of peace had dashed off a happy letter to his friend begging him to come over. "In the name of God, my dear Mylord, do so because certainly one of the things I most want in the world is to see you and show you our army and that we are all not '*des quoquins d'Hollandais*'."*

After Charles's refusal, William wrote bitterly to Ossory, "They slight me . . . I must have patience. I hope the time will come when they will wish to treat me better and not with so much disdain."*

Not many rulers in Europe dared to laugh at the Prince of Orange these days. At twenty-three he had become the heart and leader of a mighty coalition against France. One by one, he had detached Louis's allies from him. After the King of England, it was the turn of the fiery Bishop of Münster, Bernard van Galen, who signed a treaty with the Dutch on 24 April. He was followed by the Electors of Cologne and of Mainz, and the Dukes of Brunswick and Luneburg; and last, even the Elector of Brandenburg came back to his old ally. It was a formidable achievement – a tribute to the personality of a young man who in just two years had snatched from Louis XIV the supremacy of Europe in the diplomatic field.

Now the time had come to attempt a victory over France on the battlefield too. At the beginning of the summer campaign of 1674, the Prince of Orange even toyed with the thought of taking the war into Louis's own country. He discussed it over dinner with his friends and told one of them, Count Starenberg, when he complained about the wine: "Before the summer is over, you shall drink excellent wine in Champagne itself." The invasion never took place, but Starenberg got his champagne all the same. Taken prisoner by the French and brought to Rheims, he toasted the Prince of Orange ironically: "I shall trust the Prince's word as long as I live."*

The fact was that the French still had two advantages over the allied coalition, which time and again saved the day for them: they had first-class military leaders, and they had a united command. William, on the other hand, had to operate with a set of second-rate commanders who could seldom be got to work together. The Imperial commander Charles Comte de Souches was particularly difficult. He was much older than the Prince, and jealous of his position, a fact that on 11 August 1674 nearly proved fatal for the Allies.* They had planned a combined attack on Binche, but Souches moved his 20,000 men off much earlier than they had agreed. William had no choice but to follow, while the Spanish cavalry were left behind in the rear. The French commander Condé, not far away with 40,000 men, saw his chance and pounced.

William wheeled his troops immediately to face the French near the small village of Seneffe. Although he was driven back with heavy losses, he made another desperate stand a little further west. The French forces were at first overwhelmingly superior but Souches's hurried return made it a more equal struggle, and the battle raged until ten that night. It was Condé who broke off the action and withdrew. William, writing of the "happy success of the battle", reported proudly to the States: "We can say with truth that we have kept the field longer than the enemy."* To his grandmother Amalia he wrote soberly: "The combat lasted from ten in the morning until the evening at the same hour; it was very rough; we have lost many people, and the enemy, who were unable to win an inch of terrain from us, lost not less; . . . their only advantage was to have taken most of our baggage train."*

Describing the battle in a letter to Ossory, the Prince said modestly, "I did very little."* Both the French and his own men would have contradicted him with fervour. Condé, who claimed to have won – Te Deums were sung in Notre Dame in Paris – was deeply impressed by William's skill and his personal courage. "The Prince of Orange," he told Louis XIV, "has acted in all respects like an old captain, except in venturing his life too much like a young one." Souches for once forgot to be resentful and praised William generously for the "skill of a veteran commander, the courage of a Caesar, and the fearlessness of a Marius",* and an English eyewitness reported: "None was more forward than the Prince of Orange, who, all along, fought in the heat of the battle, animating his men by his own example."*

In William's life the day of Seneffe was of profound significance. For the first time he had succeeded, if not in beating, at least in halting the mighty French army under the almost legendary Condé in an open battle with inferior forces. On that day he discovered something within himself that stamped him for the rest of his life: a passion for battle that was even greater than his love for hunting, and many times stronger than his interest in politics. As Burnet later would say: only on the battlefield did the Prince really come to life. "He was all fire . . ."*

His personal courage was indeed astonishing. He was constantly in the front lines, and wherever the battle was hottest his slight figure, with the Star of the Garter glittering prominently on one shoulder, could be picked out by his men – and by his enemies. He encouraged them, crying: "Come on, children." When friends urged him not to expose himself so recklessly, he was amazed: "It's my duty to do so." His soldiers may not have loved him for his severity, but they admired him for his courage and followed him where they would not have followed anyone else. Seneffe showed him a new destiny. He wrote afterwards to Temple: "I dare to say without vanity, that life will always be less dear to me, than the satisfaction of living up to the expectations men have of me."*

After his losses at the Battle of Seneffe William and other allied commanders worked hard to rebuild their armies. Reinforcements arrived from Holland but the divisions in the allied command made it difficult to attempt anything more that year. When on 20 September the Allies and the French at Oudenaarde faced each other again, Souches refused to fight and left for Ghent. William complained bitterly at Vienna about this piece of sabotage. It was infuriating for him to see "Matters in general so ill managed, and so little Probability . . . to do any great Things this Campaign."*

Nevertheless, he hated to admit defeat, and on 9 October he made a last effort to achieve something before winter came. He joined those Allied troops that had been besieging Grave since June. It was the last French outpost in the Republic, commanded by the Marquis de Chamilly. The arrival of the Prince and his forces transformed the situation, and on 26 October, after the Dutch had repeatedly stormed the town with heavy losses, the French capitulated. William returned to The Hague. The campaign had certainly not been unsuccessful: the Allies had stood up to Condé and William had retaken Grave. But so much more might have been done if there had been unity in the Allied command. As the Prince wrote to Ossory: "I have nothing to reproach myself with, I have done everything in my power, but I have been very badly seconded."*

In Madrid and Vienna the same conclusion had been reached. It was evident that the Allied armies needed one man as commander, and William's outstanding conduct in the campaign made him the obvious choice. In November the new twenty-four-year-old Stadholder of the United Provinces was nominated Generalissimo of the European coalition against France.

CHAPTER IX

The Princess of England

"THE DUTCH . . . whose principal interest was commerce, would go no farther in the war, than the Prince of Orange would carry them." At the end of 1674 this was the general view in Europe.* The Dutch anxiety for peace was a constant worry to the Allies, who were afraid of being let down by them; the Prince's determination to go on making war was equally exasperating to France and England.

Sir Leoline Jenkins, Charles's foreign minister, reported from The Hague to the Privy Council in May that in his view, William's "Inclinations were to be at the Head of an Army; the Spaniards, and the young Men about him, encourag'd these Inclinations . . ." Sir Leoline added: "He had some personal Resentments against the French King . . . and a State of War was besides a State of Security for him against the Loevestein Faction."* He forgot to mention and did not understand that William's policy was based quite as strongly as De Witt's on one principle: France could be a friend, but never a neighbour. The presence of French troops in the Flanders garrisons was unacceptable to him.

Undiscouraged by Sir Leoline, Charles sent an embassy to Holland at the end of the summer campaign. One of the two envoys was Ossory, whom William was delighted to see again. The other was Arlington, the former Secretary of State, now Lord Chamberlain: a thoughtless choice on Charles's part. Arlington was a witty, arrogant man, but the Prince had not forgotten Arlington's threat to have him torn to pieces like the De Witts. He was also infuriated by the condescending manner of the older man, who treated him, he felt, like a child. It was a bad start to the talks, and Arlington afterwards complained that he had found the Prince "dry and sullen or at the best uneasy".*

The offer of mediation that Arlington brought led to nothing. The French had already made it clear that they would accept peace only if they could keep their conquered territories, and William pointed out that the States treaty with Spain obliged the Dutch "to see things restored to the Terms of the Pyrenean Treaty" – in other words, the French must give up their Flanders fortresses.*

Charles had another card to play, however: the marriage of William to Princess Mary, heir to the English throne after her father James. It was an arrangement which, thought Charles, would make almost everybody happy. The English Parliament and people would be delighted by it, the Prince would be won over to his side and it would raise William's prestige in the Courts of Europe. It was Ossory who was given the delicate task of sounding out his friend on the subject.

The moment seemed well chosen. For the last two years, the Prince had been completely absorbed by the political and military affairs of his country, and now at last things were going better. But when Ossory hinted that a proposal from William for his cousin Mary would be well received by the English Court, the Prince's only answer was "not yet". He assured Ossory that it was "his highest ambition as soon as war was over", but at the present time he had more important things to do. "I cannot leave the battlefield nor believe that it would be agreeable for a lady to be where the battlefield is."*

Privately he felt that Mary at twelve was much too young to make him a wife. And most important of all, he was anxious – though he did not admit it – to do nothing which could suggest to his allies in Europe and his connections in the English opposition that he was wavering in his loyalties.* For William the promise of increased prestige was a doubtful one too. Information had reached him from England suggesting resistance to the idea of Mary, grand-daughter of a commoner, on the English throne. At the dinner table about this time, the Prince had discussed the question of the succession, suggesting that "if the Duke of York came to die before the King, there would be an argument whether his daughters should have precedence to the throne before him".* Neither had he forgotten that Mary was the daughter of Anne Hyde, "his mother's maid".

It was soon clear that the missions of both Arlington and Ossory were failures. The former had to report to London that the Prince had turned down the offer of mediation, the latter that he had rejected the match. Charles and James were angry and disappointed, and they were particularly mortified by Ossory's manner of handling his task. He had had careful instructions from Charles not to make an offer of the Princess's hand, merely to give it as his personal opinion that Charles and James might consider a marriage proposal if it came from William. Instead he had discussed it in frank, straightforward terms and thus laid the King and James open to a snub from their nephew.

The two envoys were understandably in no hurry to return to the wrath of their master, and The Hague was a most pleasant refuge. They were both married to daughters of Lodewijk van Nassau, Heer van Beverwaert, the bastard son of Prince Maurits. Ossory's wife was Emilia, and Arlington's Elisabeth. Together with their wives' brother Odijk, and another, younger sister, Charlotte, who had come over with them from England, they formed a pleasant family group around the Prince. A round of parties, balls, hunts and card-evenings was organized to celebrate their reunion, of which the witty Lotte was the centre. William was very much taken with this lively and intelligent girl – who had something in her humour and conversation "very agreeable to the prince".* But it was his friend Bentinck who fell violently in love with her, and long after her departure his despairing appeals reached her through William's letters to Ossory. All in vain: Lotte never married.*

Despite the confidential nature of Ossory's mission, the States-General were well aware what was going on. After the Peace of Westminster at the beginning of 1673, their ambassador Van Rheede van Amerongen had, like his predecessors, reported that "very important gentlemen of quality" in London had spoken to him about the desirability of an engagement of the Princess Mary and Prince William of Orange.* The States were not too enthusiastic about such a close tie between England and Holland, but nevertheless preferred a match with Mary to no match at all.

They had made it clear in February 1674, when they gave William the hereditary Stadholdership, that they hoped he would look for a wife. Their request to Europe's premier bachelor had had swift consequences. William's uncle in Brandenburg proposed a match with the widowed Queen of Poland, the sister of the Emperor. A marriage with this Princess of Radziwill would give William the Polish crown and his uncle a staunch ally in the east. But the Prince of Orange had not been interested.

He himself had made a gesture to please the States: he asked the Dutch ambassador in Copenhagen, the Heer van Werkendam, to take a close look at one of the Royal Danish Princesses, who might be "worthy H. H.'s care for the continuation of an esteemed family". The ambassador wrote hurriedly back that the princess in question was "well-made and well-shaped, pleasant in her conversation and full of majesty, mixed with sweetness".* But the Prince had left it at that.

There was, however, no peace for him. After the States and Charles it was now the turn of Louis XIV to make a marriage offer. He did it in a manner even more devious than Charles. D'Estrades, now governor of

Maastricht, was sounding out Dutch opinion through Johan Pesters, a delegate from Utrecht. He had been instructed by Louis to ask casually – "as if it is your own idea" – during one of his talks with Pesters, if the Prince did not feel inclined for a marriage with a French princess. He was even permitted to insinuate that *"Princesses de mérite"*, closely related to the King, were available.* Told of this offer, the Prince learned with astonishment that the particular princess Louis had in mind was Mademoiselle de Blois, his daughter by his first mistress, Louise de la Vallière. Scornfully William rejected the offer: "The Princes of Orange marry the legitimate daughters of Kings and not their bastards."* The relationship of William and the French King was already becoming tinged with strong personal hostility.

Louis certainly did not suppose that a match between his daughter and the Prince of Orange would turn his greatest rival and opponent into a faithful ally; but he was very anxious to prevent William marrying into the English Royal family. He had already taken his own shrewd precautions at Whitehall. A year earlier, on his instructions, a French attaché in London had hinted to James that a marriage between his daughter and the thirteen-year-old Dauphin was not out of the question. James had jumped at the idea, and talked about it proudly and often.* At the French embassy it was very well known that other matrimonial plans had already been made for the Dauphin, but they were careful not to disillusion James. They even spread a discreet rumour or two; as late as 1677 Secretary of State Sir Joseph Williamson was told by a German diplomat that he had heard of a definite contract of marriage between the two.*

In the gossipy *Secret History of Whitehall*, published in 1678, is a story of a plot to confront the English with the match as a *fait accompli*. "The Duke should use all the power and interest he had with the King to let his daughter, the Lady Mary, take a voyage into France to take the waters of Bourbon; or else to consent she might be privily sent away by the Duke, as against his knowledge and will, and then they would get her speedily married." Another idea was that the French King should send an embassy to Charles to ask his permission for the marriage and if he refused, "the Duke should contrive a way to get her seized and shipped off".*

The young Princess probably heard these rumours: she had an eager ear for Court gossip and plenty of opportunities for hearing it. Her family circle was a much closer one since James's second marriage to Mary Beatrice, and – unusually in that age – Mary and her sister Anne dined often at their father's table. Their stepmother, still a young girl

herself, spent plenty of time in their company when James's business or
amorous adventures took him away from home. Mary's nanny Mrs.
Langford – "Mam" – was part of the family, and she was an inordinate
gossip who never stopped to consider whether Court scandals were fit
for ten-year-old ears. When Mary played with her friends, the heartless
intrigues and the vicious chatter of Whitehall were the common topics
of their conversation. Her best friend and confidante was a girl eleven
years older than herself, Frances Apsley, daughter of her father's
Treasurer, Sir Allen. Frances did not always have time for the adoring
little Princess who when they were apart bombarded her with excited
notes, full of devotion and gossip. One of her first letters preserved tells
in a childish scrawl, and in a spelling appalling even by seventeenth-
century standards, the news that her preceptor Dr. Doughty has a mistress.

> I am half mad & have bin so ever since yesterday morning that is to say
> my mam put me in such a good humore then with talking to doctor douty
> about his mrs that I have continued so ever since I hope you will not shuw
> it I mean my letter to anybody. [In a postscript she added another titbit:]
> . . . if I had any nuse to tel you I wold but hear there is none worth a chip
> but what there is I wil that is that Dr D. mrs is come to dine with him may
> be, she is his W.*

The little princess followed the complicated intrigues raging at
Whitehall with fascinated curiosity. When Charles's bastard son, the
Duke of Monmouth, was caught having an affair with a certain Mrs.
Needam, Mary wrote:

> They both beged very hartely that they wold not tel . . . The duke of
> munmoth that they wold not tel his wife & mrs Nedam that they wold tel
> nobody of it but espetialy Mrs Jenings . . . but mrs Trevors maid sad the
> divel take her if she did not tel mrs Jenings the first time she see her . . .
> then Mrs Worsley told the dushes . . . then the dushes hering of it was
> mighty angry at it & now Mrs Needam is gone away & says nobody shal
> never heer of her more . . . The Duches of Munmouth they say dos take it
> mightily to harte . . .*

Sometimes Mary was more than an onlooker in the diversions of
Whitehall. In December 1674 a masque called *Calysto* was performed at
Court, acted by ladies only. The twelve-year-old Mary took the title
role because she was "the exact and perfect character of chastity and
therefore a very proper character for Mary to represent". Evelyn watched
it in some disapproval: "Saw a comedy at night at court, acted by the
ladies only, amongst them Lady Mary and Ann, his Royal Highnesses
two daughters . . . they were all covered with jewels."* Whether it was a

very suitable entertainment for a young girl to take part in is questionable. Evelyn's great friend Margaret Blagge, a lady-in-waiting to Queen Catherine and an earnest young prig, was miserable at being involved in it herself and wrote to him: "I am extremely heavy for I would be free from that place and have nothing to do in itt at all: but it will not be, for the play goes on mightily, which I hoped would never have proceeded further . . ."*

Mary's letters to Frances show clearly how much influenced the young girl was by the decadent atmosphere of the court. Her girlish attachment, for instance, is translated into precocious terms of passion. While she called herself "Clorine", Frances was christened Aurelia or "my dear husband" and scenes of jealousy were frequent.

Her sister Anne, a plain and stolid girl, copied Mary and was always trying to get Frances's attention for herself. Sometimes she succeeded, leaving Mary dreadfully upset and writing to Aurelia: "She has tryumpht over a rival that wonce was hapy in your love til she with her aluring charmes removed unhapy Clorine from your heart." It is the exaggerated language of the novels and plays of the time, which Mary obviously devoured eagerly and imitated in her unschooled English. Unconsciously the hyper-romantic girl lived her own romance, and melodramatically announced once to her "dear husband . . . this is the last time I shall cal you so answare this letter that I may have own letter of your dear hand wrighting to look upon . . ." With sad satisfaction she compared her own state with the heroines of her romances: ". . . while pore unhapy I sate reading of a play my heart was ready to brake for I was read where Massanissa come first to Sophonisba and thought that saene so like my misery it made me ready to cry . . ."*

The misunderstandings never lasted long, and when Mary heard that Frances had a kindness for a certain "mr Sute", she rushed to assure her possessively that her love was "a thousand times more longer better . . . more than ever the constantest love had for his Mrs . . ." and she offered herself to be "your dog in a string your fish in a net your bird in a cage your humbel trout".*

It is plain that this adolescent daydreaming was the expression of an enormous capacity for love and devotion. Mary was a warmly affectionate child, even towards her slow-witted and tiresome sister Anne. In spite of occasional scenes, she had the protective attitude of the elder sister towards her and they sometimes shared their friends. One of these was Barbara Villiers, now Mrs. Berkely. Lady Frances Villiers, their governess and Barbara's mother, found this friendship between her grown-up daughter and her two royal pupils unsuitable and forbade it. The girls had to write to her in secret and one day they were nearly found out, when the governess came in just as Anne's letter was being sealed by her friend Sarah Jennings. Mary jumped up blushing and with great presence of mind asked Lady Frances what she thought of her new "manto". The governess was not fooled and asked sternly what Sarah was doing. Mary told her a white lie: Sarah had invented a new way to seal letters and was demonstrating it to them. Lady Villiers let it go with the remark that Sarah was a "very ingenius" girl.*

The year 1675 brought Mary another sister. Her stepmother gave birth to her first child, Catherine Laura, and Mary, who adored the baby at first sight, was godmother at the christening in January. James was less enthusiastic and wrote to his nephew William: "I believe you will not be sorry to hear of the Duchess being safely delivered . . . it is but a daughter."* A daughter, of course, was not a threat to Mary's claims on the Crown and James perhaps assumed that the man who had just been offered her hand would find this news reassuring. His concern was needless, as Ossory's reports from The Hague made clear at that time.

WHEN IN THE AUTUMN OF 1674 the Prince had told his friend that he was too busy to think about marriage, he had certainly not exaggerated. With Fagel as his right hand he had to deal with an incredible range of political, military and administrative problems. These heavy responsibilities had turned him into a serious and authoritative young man, respected by friend and foe. "Such a perfect model of a prince, of whom we and our children have reason to expect so much good", is only one admirer's opinion.* And his nephew Henrik Casimir, Stadholder of Friesland and Groningen, was always having his cousin's excellent example forced down his throat by his governor, who pointed out to him that "H. H. is vigilant, sober, asks advice from wise men and follows it, . . . does not gamble or curse, is dutiful and hardworking."*

To anyone who did not know William, indeed, he sounded too good to be true, but his close friends, like Bentinck and Ossory, knew him as a warm and generous person, who lost all his chilling reserve in their company. Only with them was he able to relax, sitting talking for hours over supper. With his character and in his position he did not make friends easily, but to the handful of people that mattered to him he was faithful and considerate.

There was a feminine streak in him, and he was always particularly attracted to young men with good looks, dash and flair. As long as they were gallant and loyal to him, he could overlook many failings. He was

fond of giving them presents and titles, and it was to Hans Willem
Bentinck, who, it was related, earned the Prince's favour by "showing"
him an inn-keeper's daughter, that William most loved to be lavish.* In
1672 Bentinck was made "Gentleman of the Chamber" and Equerry,
and in December 1674 the Prince offered him part of the money to buy
his villa "Sorghvliet" between Scheveningen and The Hague. Bentinck,
who loved gardening, turned it into a little paradise.* The young nobleman from Gelderland certainly earned his rewards: this now somewhat
stilted and formal but gentle person almost wore himself out for William.
The Prince, who always wanted the people he loved around him, was
rarely seen without Bentinck at his side, and some people called him
mockingly William's slave. The only time during the day that he could
consider his own was when the Prince gave audiences.

Bentinck gave the most striking proof of his devotion to William
when on 3 April 1675 the Prince fell dangerously ill. To the consternation
of the Dutch it was announced that he was suffering from smallpox, the
disease that had killed his father and his mother. For days he hung
between life and death, and he said later, "I never called in those 16 days
and nights but Bentinck answered."* Twenty years later the Venetian
ambassador in London heard how William in fact owed his life to this
friend: "When . . . the Prince of Orange, was in danger of death from
smallpox, the doctors believed that the violent progress of the disease
could only be stopped if a young man of the same age, lying in bed with
the Prince, exposed himself to the dangerous contagion of his illness."
Bentinck had immediately volunteered and the warmth of his body made
the Prince sweat so heavily that the smallpox broke out. The Prince
recovered, but Bentinck, after contact with the "dangerous fluids",
fell ill himself.*

Temple, at that time back in The Hague as English ambassador,
praised William's companion highly. "I cannot here forbear to give
Monsieur Bentinck the character due to him, of the best servant I have
ever known in prince's or private family." The Englishman had been
closely involved himself as William would only eat food from his
kitchen; in those days, when poisoning was a common crime and often
suspected after a sudden death, Temple ran a considerable risk. If the
Prince had died, "I believe we could not have left alive", he wrote in his
memoirs. The frenzied Dutch would have torn him to pieces. Fortunately
for Temple and to the great joy of most Dutchmen, William was sufficiently recovered by 21 April to hear a sermon in the Kloosterkerk and to
dine on the twenty-second at Temple's house. His doctors attributed his
recovery to the "great evenness of his temper and constancy of mind",*

and the general relief in the United Provinces was expressed by Fagel: "Good God, what would have been our plight if H. H. had been taken from us?"

The news of the Prince's illness had caused concern far beyond the Dutch borders. The Elector of Brandenburg had sent some remedies for William, his nephew and former ward; the King of England and the Duke had sent two envoys "to enquire into the state of his health",* and even the French King displayed anxiety. He asked daily for news, and after William's recovery Louvois wrote to d'Estrades that the King "had learned the good tidings with great pleasure", adding that "the conduct of the Prince during the last few years has in no way extinguished the sentiments of friendship H. M. has always had for him."* Ossory wrote in distress how he had longed to come over "*au premier alarme*" but that the King had not allowed it.*

The smallpox had interrupted preparations for the campaign of 1675, and William wrote in despair to Waldeck: "What weighed on me most, during my sickness, was that for three weeks I was not able to deal with any business at all. You can imagine how much there was waiting for me, but heaven wants me to be patient. In the last two days I have started work again, but I find it a great strain." He was very much alarmed for his friend Bentinck, still dangerously ill, and although he was trying desperately to get the army ready in time for the rendezvous on 6 May at Bergen-op-Zoom, he feared that without Bentinck to help him it might be too much for him. He asked Waldeck to come to the rescue: "The work is piled up."*

Tired and still weak, he went to the army in May, and for the rest of the summer pursued the French in the Spanish Netherlands without much enthusiasm, unable to prevent the reoccupation of Dinant and Huy and the conquest of a great part of Limburg.

While on campaign he suffered a personal loss too. His grandmother, the Dowager-Princess Amalia, died on 8 September at the age of sixty-three. The relations between her and her grandson had improved over the last years, and although he had never quite forgiven her behaviour at the time when De Witt had dismissed his governor Zuylestein, she was still the last of his close family circle. Bentinck wrote to Fagel from Flanders: "H. H. is very much grieved about it and although by reason of her great age one had long seen it coming, nevertheless this loss and the impossibility of being with her at the last affected H. H. deeply, and the more so because he thought that those who should have been present, had neglected their duty."*

The Prince was mistaken: Amalia had died alone by her own choice.

Her two daughters, the widowed Princess Albertina Agnes and the Duchess of Zimmern, had sent a message to their dying mother to ask if she would like them to come to her at The Hague. "She said no; they would only weep and torment themselves at her bedside, which would disturb her", related Sir Constantyn Huygens.*

She left her grandson her charming palace outside The Hague, "Het Huis ten Bosch", and she was buried in December at Delft, next to her husband Frederik Hendrik.

Her death saddened William's home-coming in the autumn, and he left almost immediately for his new palace at Soestdijk and a week's hunting. He was very much in need of his favourite distraction after a year that, as he felt it, had gone so badly for him. At home he still seemed as popular as ever – the Dutch "have an insane passion for the Prince of Orange", wrote Sophia of Hanover, "they kiss the ground where he passes, and the horse he rides on"* – but the man in the street was beginning to wonder why his country was still at war. He had to pay for enormous armies, but they won no victories, and a general impression was growing that the war with France was a private affair of the Prince. They accused him of being too eager for glory.

William in fact longed for peace quite as much as his people. In a letter to Ossory he explained that "all Christendom" would be very unhappy if the peace was not made that winter.* But he clung to his guiding principle: "Europe must be made free from the French."

He was particularly hurt by the mounting criticism of his generalship. He had never had the chance of fighting under an experienced general, and this defect was obvious. The French joked: "The Prince of Orange can at least boast that no general of his age had raised so many sieges and lost so many battles." And he himself said once: "I would willingly give part of my provinces to have served some campaigns under the Prince de Condé."*

It was not all they reproached him with in the United Provinces. Many of the Dutch suspected that their ambitious Prince was aiming at complete sovereignty, and they were not entirely mistaken. The States of Gelderland who, like Utrecht, had elected the Prince their Stadholder after liberation from the French, had offered him in January 1675 the historic title of Duke of Gelderland, giving him almost absolute power in this province. The Prince had at first been eager to accept, and his friends, delightedly drinking to the health of "the Duke", urged him to do so.

But reaction in Holland and Zeeland, however, was so hostile that he hesitated. Many of the Regents feared that a Duke of Gelderland would pay too much attention to his territory, and would expect the same honour from the other states. In Amsterdam there was a rush on the banks: three million guilders were withdrawn and the East India shares fell more than 30 per cent. Disconcerted, the Prince consulted the other States and from Zeeland there came a stern reply asking him outright to reject the title. "The peace and welfare of his country," they wrote him, "no less than his own credit and honour demanded it, following the example of Gideon, who refused a similar offer made to him by God's people out of gratitude for his having delivered them out of the hands of the Midianites."*

Jan Rothe, one of the Prince's most violent critics, rhymed:

> *The Prince a Duke, the people slaves;*
> *The States of the country abject knaves;*
> *The English flag in Holland waves.**

William understood that in the circumstances he had no choice but to reject the offer of Gelderland. The French diplomat Gourville told him, a few years later, how astonished he had been that the Prince should think of making himself sovereign of a province, given the fiercely republican views of the Dutch. According to Gourville William explained that "it was not long ere he saw this himself but that it was not extraordinary that at his age he should have false views, especially as he had no person about him who could rectify his ideas."*

He had not, however, been able to resist a tart reply to the States of Zeeland. If they wished to compare him with Gideon the Deliverer, he wrote, they should not forget that in the words of God: "The children of Israel were not generous to the house of Gideon after all he had done for Israel."*

CHAPTER X

Fading Hopes

I N THE SPRING OF 1676 the Prince of Orange was an anxious man. It was known that the French, as strong and determined as ever, were gathering an enormous army for their summer campaign, and their first blow might be struck at any moment. The Allies, on the other hand, had had little effective consultation, and their armies would not be ready for some time, even if all the promised troops actually materialized. Last year the Allies had assembled – on paper at least – a formidable army, while France had had only the so-called neutrality of England as an ally. For all that, the few military honours of the campaign had gone to France. This year's campaign might well go worse, the Allies would lose heart, and the coalition so carefully built up would disintegrate. Studying the situation, William saw England as the joker in the pack. Properly played, she might still turn the fortunes of the game.

If William needed English support, Charles was just as much in need of his nephew. The King's pro-French policy had made him increasingly unpopular with the people, and the attitude of his brother James in religious matters had worsened the situation. The Roman Catholic Duke refused that year to attend the Easter service at Whitehall Chapel for the first time, "to the infinite grief and threatened ruin of this poor nation".* He even went further, making a semi-public declaration that he would never more come under the roof of Whitehall Chapel, but would hear Mass in his wife's chapel.* The possibility of excluding him from the succession was now being openly talked about – "so strong was the national distaste for his religion and his second marriage".*

For English Protestants the outlook was certainly alarming: Mary Beatrice might well produce a male and Roman Catholic heir, and rumours that James's eldest daughter Mary, brought up a good Protestant, was the prospective bride of the Dauphin, were discussed everywhere. No action on Charles's part would do more to restore his own popularity and quieten his kingdom than marrying his niece to the Protestant Champion of Europe, the Prince of Orange. These considerations helped William to make up his mind.

One day in April, the Prince called Temple, the English envoy, to Honselaersdijck. He told him straight away about his decision to ask for Mary's hand and strolling through the beautiful palace gardens, they discussed for two hours, in all openness, the various aspects of a marriage between William and the Princess. The Prince explained that the English opposition "who pretended to be much his friends" were opposed to the match, which they felt would discredit him in the country and identify him with the "dispositions and the designs of the court". He added that "his friends there did not believe the government could be long without disturbance, unless they changed their measures." He asked for Temple's candid opinion, as a friend.

The ambassador had an almost fatherly affection for the young man, and the Anglo-Dutch alliance, which this match would further, was the cornerstone of his political creed. Understandably he now did his best to encourage the Prince, protesting that he saw the political situation in much too dark colours. Temple did not believe that the marriage could harm William's standing in England, feeling as he said, that the crown "stood upon surer foundations than ever it had done in former times", and he urged the Stadholder to go ahead.

William, however, had other doubts. It was unusual, he knew, for a prince who was contemplating an advantageous political marriage to be worried about "personal particulars". But he confided to Temple "without any sort of affection, that he was so, and in such a degree, that no circumstances of fortune or interest would engage him, without those of the person, especially those of humour and disposition." He admitted that he might not be an easy man to live with, and certainly not for "such wives as were generally in the court of his age; that if he should meet with one to give him trouble at home it was what he should not be able to bear, who was like to have enough abroad in the course of his life; and that, after the manner he was resolved to live with a wife, which should be the best he could, he would have one that he thought likely to live well with him, which he thought chiefly depended on her disposition and education."

Temple went back to The Hague with the request, that "if I knew any thing particular of the Lady Mary in these points, he desired me to tell him freely."* A few days later William handed the ambassador letters for his uncles Charles and James, asking them for permission to visit England. Lady Temple, just about to sail to London, had the two letters entrusted to her together with a more delicate task: to send back a full personal account of Mary.

This private matter dealt with, it was more than time for the Prince to leave for the battlefield. The French had launched an unusually early campaign by a surprise siege of the strong fortress Condé on the Schelde.

It was a warning to William that after the muted showing of last year Louis XIV was back in the field with all confidence and glory. When the Prince arrived at headquarters in Roosendaal on 11 April, the picture the Allied forces presented was sadly different. Only a fifth of the promised 25,000 Spanish troops had arrived, and the Imperial army could not be expected for weeks yet. His own soldiers were assembled, but money for their pay and supplies was short. Nine days after his arrival at the army the Stadholder wrote Fagel from Brussels that he was desperate and that he only hoped that "God, who has helped us so often, will save us again."

In this grim mood he marched his armies south-east to meet the enemy. The French had occupied the town of Condé on 22 April in the approving presence of Louis and was now on its way to Bouchain, already under siege by other French forces. When William finally caught up with them, the main body of the army under the personal command of the Sun King was drawn up at Valenciennes. While Louis XIV looked down from the heights of Heurtebise, the Prince ordered his 50,000 men to prepare for battle. It was Sunday 10 May, and the weather was hot and beautiful. Both King and Prince rode along their lines, inspecting their troops. Then came a long pause, interrupted after a few hours by three hesitant cannon-shots from the French. The allied guns did not reply and silence fell again.

While the soldiers waited and wondered, discussions were raging at headquarters on either side. Both commanders wanted to attack, but they were alone in their wish. William's advisers pointed out that the French were not only numerically superior, but had an advantage in their position. In the other camp Louis's advisers, especially Louvois, felt that defeat would be a fatal blow to the prestige of the French King, and Louis, who in any case preferred sieges to battles, was obliged to give in. When night fell, troops on both sides were still being kept in battle order and they had to wait for another twenty-four hours before they were allowed to make camp. That same day William wrote to Fagel: "It's the most beautiful sight in the world, to see two such mighty armies so near each other."* Two days later he found the sight only frustrating. He had to admit that the French position was stronger, but was nevertheless angry that his commanders did not allow him to attack. Even more infuriating, on 12 June, while he was held up at Valenciennes, Bouchain fell into the hands of the French.

On the morning of the eighteenth it was all over. The allies woke up to find that in the darkness of the night the French had silently broken camp and withdrawn. In Paris it was explained that the Prince of Orange – "an adventurer who is compelled to hazard everything" was not a worthy opponent for his Most Christian Majesty.* It was the nearest the two men – Europe's greatest adversaries now and for the rest of their lives – ever came to meeting.

If French opinion was critical of Louis XIV after this retreat, the Dutch were equally dissatisfied with their Stadholder, and William, very conscious of this, now decided on a bold move. Maastricht, a frontier-fortress at the most south-eastern point of the Netherlands, was occupied by the French, who were using it as a raiding base. William determined to relieve it, and on 7 July he arrived with his army in front of the town, which had been strongly fortified by France's greatest siege expert, Sebastian le Prestre de Vauban. The Prince had hardly enough troops to begin the siege, his own engineer Ivoy was ill, and a more experienced general would have bided his time. But William was young and desperate. Three times he stormed the town, displaying his usual reckless courage and getting wounded by a bullet in his arm – it was all to no avail. When at the end of August Maastricht was still in French hands, he conceded defeat and his demoralized army straggled away in torrential rain, con-stantly harassed by the French and greeted with derision by the people in the surrounding villages. William's humiliation was complete.

By the time he returned to The Hague his popularity was at its lowest ebb. Sophia of Hanover reported: "*Le Prince d'Orange est présentement plus haï qu'aimé.*"* He himself was mortified and "*extrêmement mélancholique*". He began to despair of success and wrote to Waldeck: "It's impossible for me to imagine a greater nightmare."* His temper was not improved when Charles's answer to his proposal to come to London arrived. The King did not refuse outright to give him the hand of his niece Mary, but he would not permit William to come to England before peace with France was made. Depressed and disappointed the Prince retired to Dieren to restore his spirits by days spent furiously hunting.

In a letter to his friend Ossory, written at the end of September, some of his resentment still lingered, but though he referred to "all the mis-fortunes I have suffered this campaign" the tranquillity of Dieren had relaxed him enough to allow him to worry about less momentous matters, such as the condition of his stables. As usual he was short of good hunters, and since English horses were considered the best, he asked Ossory "to buy two good horses that have run with hounds, but aren't yet spoiled".*

For the Prince of Orange, hunting was always more than a gentleman's pastime. It was in his blood and he snatched at any occasion to enjoy it. He needed it physically – the rushing air was relief for his weak chest and lungs. He needed it mentally – the tension of the hunt took his mind off business or personal cares. He loved the hours on horseback and the easy male company – he only invited those he liked. The majestic beauty of the Veluwe forests and the informality of his little hunting lodge had a special appeal for him. At Dieren he hunted day after day for hours at a time, and even drenching rain could not stop him. He loved boring his friends with the details of a good day – when Bentinck was absent on these occasions he could rely on William for a long account:

> We went after a stag, as I wrote that we meant to. Batiste had found one in Warnsborne thicket; we almost caught up with him at Doreweert, from there he went to the Old Wood, the Pampel, the Langerhout, through the Wood of Hoog Soeren, over the Wolf's Heath and Utteler's Heath and from there to Staveren swamp and we took him trying to get into Putten Wood. It was a very strenuous hunt, having lasted five and a quarter hours without anyone dropping out and using up all our relays of horses; the horses were none the worse for it and there were no falls.*

During one of those hunts in November that year the Prince arrived unexpectedly at the house of the Heer van Amerongen. The lady of the house was absent, but a quick-witted steward welcomed William on her behalf and served the hungry crowd with pork-hotpot, a hearty peasant dish of mashed potatoes, turnips, onions and pork. William loved it and still talked about it years later.*

While he hunted at Dieren, only a few kilometres away at Nijmegen the Allies and the French were sitting round the conference table to discuss peace terms. The conference had started much against the wish of the allies of the United Provinces, and only the threat that the Dutch might conclude a separate peace had brought them to Nijmegen. But a general absence of enthusiasm was evident: for its first months the conference had devoted itself to squabbles about protocol, and it looked as though the talks might drag on interminably without achieving anything.

The Prince of Orange now made another effort to secure Charles's intervention, and called his trusted friend Temple to emphasize how effective this could be: "All men knew France was not in a condition to refuse whatever terms his Majesty resolved on, or to venture a war with England in conjunction with the rest of the allies; that the least show of it was enough to make the peace."*

Charles reacted rapidly with a long letter to his nephew. He began by proposing a defensive alliance between their two countries, which interested William. The rest of the King's letter was less welcome. There could be no question, according to Charles, of France giving up any of her conquests in Flanders – on the contrary, Spain was peacefully to hand over other towns in the south-west too.

The Prince could not believe his eyes and burst out indignantly to Temple, who had shown him the letter, that he would rather die than agree. He added that he recognized the hand of the French ambassador in London and that the terms were his.*

The severity of the English terms made it clear that nothing was to be expected of discussions with Charles and the Prince refused also to have any further dealings with the French. They had offered him a personal bribe: the Duchy of Limburg, which would give him the title of Duke. The gift included Maastricht too, a strengthening of the Dutch defences. William had turned this offer over in his mind but realized now that a peaceful solution was not yet possible and that the war must go on. "He was in it and must go through it", he told Temple, and in a final letter to his uncle he wrote politely that he had put his proposal for a defensive alliance before the States-General. "They have asked me to assure H. M., that they wish H. M. had already at this present time the kindness to overwhelm them with this honour. . . ." Ironically he quoted the pious hope of the States, that the "current war and all the accidents which must infallibly accompany it, would not make it impossible to see the fulfilment of this alliance.'*

If the Allies had discussed peace at Nijmegen, they had forgotten to talk war at The Hague, and the summer campaign of 1677 now looming seemed likely to be as disastrous as that of the previous years, thanks to the inertia of the Allies. There was a long delay before the Allied armies had assembled at Breda, and French troops under Louis's brother Monsieur, the Duc d'Orléans, had used the opportunity to besiege St. Omer, while Louis himself was on his way to Cambrai. The Prince rushed his 30,000 men southward as soon as they were ready and after a week's march he reached Mont Cassel, to the north of St. Omer, and prepared for battle. Next day he crossed the river Peene to discover that the French forces, encamped at the other side of the river, had received reinforcement during the night. The engagement that followed was not so much a battle as a rout. The French were far in the majority and only the tenacity of the Prince kept his troops in the field. He was constantly on the move to encourage his men, had two horses killed under him, and a bullet tore away a piece of his sleeve, but all his bravado could not stop his army disintegrating. Desperately he tried to hold them together with threats and promises – one fleeing soldier was slashed over his face by the Prince, who shouted in blind fury: "I'll mark you, so that I will be able to hang you later."* The Duke of Monmouth, the bastard son of Charles II, saw it all and was full of admiration for the Prince. He told a friend in The Hague later: "Nothing so brave which is not due to the conduct and valour of the Prince of Orange at the battle of Mont Cassel. He held up and maintained the cause and spirit of his army when all was near lost but the courage of this vigorous commander."*

Defeat was inevitable and, abandoning the baggage, William's army fled, leaving rich treasures for the victorious French. All William's cannon, all his munitions and fifty-four of his standards were captured, reported Luxembourg. He himself seized the rarest prize – the Prince of Orange's tent and personal baggage, in which were found his gold plate and a set of magnificent maps of all the strongholds of Europe. Louvois wrote greedily, begging the maps as his share of the booty and urging Luxembourg to hide them carefully in case anyone else spotted them.*

William's defeat allowed the French to help themselves at leisure to two towns which the Prince had offered them in his own peace proposals four months earlier: St. Omer and Cambrai fell shortly after Mont Cassel.

It was now clear to the Allies that the war with France could never be won on the battlefield; their armies were not strong enough and they complained openly about the leadership of William, who was – according to an understatement of Huygens – "*un peu embarrassé*".* He was so much embarrassed, in fact, that he thought it worth attempting another approach to Charles, and on 10 June he sent Hans Willem Bentinck – "*l'homme que j'estime le plus de mes gens*" – to London with lengthy instructions.

Since February of this year Parliament had been putting enormous pressure on Charles to declare war on France, and anti-French feeling was violent. "They are ready to sell their shirts off their back, to keep the Netherlands from being seized upon by us", reported the French ambassador in London, Honoré Courtin, to Paris after he had vainly spent nearly £3000 attempting to buy M.P.s.* But Charles had answered by proroguing Parliament, telling his Lord High Treasurer, Sir Thomas Osborne, Earl of Danby, that "now to turn his arms against France would not look well nor just to the world".* And to Courtin he boasted: "that at the bottom England enjoyed a profound tranquillity and enriched herself, while all the neighbouring states were drained or ruined by the war."*

It was hardly surprising, therefore, that William's envoy met with little or no response at the English Court, when he stressed the "*méchant état*" of the Low Countries and suggested that they could not survive without the English King's intervention. Bentinck, with his frank engaging manner, made an excellent impression on Charles, and everyone agreed that his tact did much to smooth over matters. All his diplomacy, however, could extract little more from the King than some polite phrases, and he encountered the same courteous stonewalling when he touched on a more delicate question, the price of Charles's alliance if he entered the war on the allied side. Not even the offer of Dunkirk could tempt the King, who was actually – although neither Bentinck nor William knew it – negotiating another secret agreement with Louis by which he promised not to recall Parliament for a further year, in return for another French subsidy.

Bentinck returned in the end almost empty-handed, but he had wrung one vital concession out of Charles – the Prince of Orange was to be allowed to pay a visit to England even before peace between the Allies and France was made. With pro-Dutch feeling running so high in the country, Charles could hardly refuse, and after some days of hesitation he gave reluctant assent.

Bentinck had been carefully instructed not to mention the word marriage, but Charles knew as well as William himself that a visit made it almost a foregone conclusion. Everyone at the English Court had been talking about it for months. In December 1676 Lady Chaworth had written to her brother Lord Roose with the latest Whitehall gossip: "Here is no niewse but balls and plays and the King having a sledge after the Muscovit fashion . . . The Prince of Orange they now say shall come this winter in order concluding a match with him and Lady Mary by the King's great inclination to it, though the Duke likes it not . . ."* In January and February of 1677 it was common talk everywhere. English pamphlets advertized ways for helping the Netherlands: "the first being the speedy arrangement of the marriage of the Prince of Orange and the Lady Mary".*

The most enthusiastic promoter of the match was Charles's Lord Treasurer. Danby was a country squire as well as a politician, with enormous influence and standing among the landed gentry of his native Yorkshire. He was thus in a position to understand how much Charles's pro-French policies – and his brother's avowed Roman Catholicism – had alienated the wealthy landed and middle classes from the Crown. The policy he tried to urge on Charles was based on breaking with France, re-establishing friendly relationship with the Dutch, and promoting

Protestant interests at home. And the match between William and Mary was the cornerstone of this policy. He had been told by Lady Temple, immediately after her arrival in England in April 1676, that the Prince of Orange was at last "inclined for the match" and from this moment he worked hard to persuade the King to agree to it, asking for instance "many Lords and other people of importance in the North and in other parts far from London to write him letters in which they expressed their anxiety and fear" of popery, which letters he took with a worried look to the King.*

Danby was not the only man who was delighted to hear that Charles at last allowed his nephew to come over to England. Ossory, who had been one of Bentinck's hosts in London, was no less pleased. The Prince himself wrote to announce his coming: "I'm overjoyed to know that the King has indicated that he would consent to allow me at the end of this campaign to make a journey to England, if I have not my head broken between then and now. I hope to embrace you there although I would have preferred to do so here in the army."*

Unexpectedly this wish was granted by Charles. On a day in August, while William was besieging Charleroi, Ossory appeared at his head-quarters in the company of the Duke of Monmouth and a young soldier called John Churchill. For William it made a pleasant interlude in a siege that was beginning to look hopeless. Shortly after he and the Spanish armies had arrived before the town, Luxembourg had materialized with a strong army and cut off all possibility of reinforcement. The Spanish were nevertheless anxious to attempt the town, but William's military advisers were solidly against it and to the fury of the Spaniards he pulled out his troops on 14 August. In self-justification he wrote to the States-General: "I prefer to sacrifice my personal glory rather than be the occasion of so much misfortune as would have resulted from an attack."*

Perhaps for the only time in his life, he was accused of cowardice and the Spanish spread the story that he had only raised the siege on instructions from Charles, pointing to Ossory's presence as proof. The Prince rejected these accusations scornfully and wrote to Fagel: "That I, after all I have done for the Spaniards, should be suspected of double dealing, is intolerable . . ."*

Indignantly he retired with his friends to his camp at Sombref, where he soon forgot his resentment in the pleasure of Ossory's company. They hunted together, swapped military experiences and sometimes sat up late at night arguing about religious matters, such as predestination and the Calvinist teaching on good works. They were not always so serious: Huygens had to wait up until two in the morning once while the two friends indulged in a gambling session. Like every other host William loved to show off the beauty spots of the surrounding countryside, taking Ossory to see the junction of seven great Roman roads at Bavay and the famous exotic gardens of Enghien.*

By the time Ossory and his friends took their leave William was beginning to think seriously about his coming trip to England and the possible consequences of it.

He was always keenly interested in the furnishing and running of his own houses. Now he would be bringing home a wife to be their mistress and he wanted them to look as fine as possible, choosing hangings, tapestry and sculptures. In Brussels and Antwerp he searched the art markets for painting, and he found three that he liked and bought. Two were by Rubens, *Pomona and Vertumnus* and *Venus rising from the sea*; the other was *Velvet* by Breughel.

He was in a hurry. At the end of August Bentinck had already received encouraging news from Danby: "I find the King extreame desirous to see the Prince and when itt can bee with H. H. convenience . . ."* And on 18 September the final invitation arrived. It was brought to Soignies, where William was staying, by Laurence Hyde, the brother of the first Duchess of York, Anne Hyde. The Prince wrote immediately to Fagel that Hyde had come with interesting proposals, "which I cannot confide to the paper", and that he was returning to The Hague.* There he arrived on 23 September to find another letter, this time from his uncle James, who reported that the royal yachts to collect William would be sailing at the end of the week and that the King and he looked forward to see their nephew at Newmarket.*

On 8 October, at a special session of the States of Holland, the Stadholder asked for permission to go to London for three or four weeks. Permission was given and the Prince sailed with a small company for England on the seventeenth, leaving Holland buzzing with speculation about the possible outcome of his trip.

CHAPTER XI

The Marriage

NEWMARKET IN 1677 was hardly more than a village, consisting of two hundred houses set on the gentle slopes of a hill and surrounded by the flat Cambridgeshire countryside. In the middle of the town stood Charles's palace, rebuilt in 1670, and in Evelyn's astonished words, "mean and hardly fit for a hunting house . . . without any court or avenue, like a common one".*

Twice a year the whole Court moved to Newmarket for the race meetings, and the town became dreadfully overcrowded, with the nobility scrambling for rooms. It was a very informal holiday: Charles strolled around like a private person, with his little spaniels at his heels. He hawked, went to the races and the cockfights, and often dropped in on the local theatre.

To this merry and raffish Court, still presided over by the lovely Duchess of Portsmouth, Charles welcomed his nephew William on 9 October. The Prince of Orange had come straight from Harwich in the carriage Charles had sent for him, while his company of friends and servants rode in thirty-two splendid coaches, each drawn by six horses. So eager was he to get to Newmarket – "like a hasty lover", as Temple hopefully remarked – that he caused great disappointment at Ipswich by refusing to stop for the magnificent dinner the mayor had prepared for him, and he ignored the well-meant welcome waiting for him in almost every town he drove through.*

For the first days in Newmarket, William's visit seemed almost entirely social, with little talk about politics and no talk at all about a marriage. For once in his life, William exerted himself to play the courtier. He appeared at the King's *levées* and *couchées*, and went out of his way to be agreeable to his uncle James.

All these convivialities fooled nobody, and the Court, buzzing with speculation about the real reason for his visit, found it all as fascinating as the horse-races, and laid bets on the outcome. But as Secretary of State

Sir William Coventry commented drily in a letter to Laurence Hyde: "The State and horse-politics resemble one another: those appear most confident that know least."*

A few days after his arrival, and after some general political discussion which revealed to Charles that William was much more eager for a peace with France than he had expected, the young Prince abruptly raised the question of a marriage with Mary. He made it clear at the same time, moreover, to his shocked uncles, that "he was resolved to see the young princess before he entered into affairs".*

Charles insisted on settling the political questions first. James, for his part, described his nephew bitterly to Barillon as "a self-opinionated young man, who had been badly brought up".* Barillon heartily agreed; with a certain foresight, he warned James that the Prince of Orange, married to Mary, would be the idol of England and the personal ruin of his father-in-law.*

All the same, William got his way. The Court at Newmarket packed its bags earlier than had been planned, and moved back to Whitehall. As Charles said to Temple, he supposed his nephew's whims must be humoured. William went as James's guest to stay at Whitehall, where the Duke of York's fine set of rooms on the ground floor, overlooking the river, were specially fitted up for him.* Once at Whitehall it was easy to arrange an informal meeting with his young cousin Mary, who lived at St. James's. The impression she made on him can easily be guessed: at the earliest possible moment afterwards, he went straight to his uncles and asked their permission to marry her.

William was delighted with "her person and all those signs of such a humour as had been described to him upon former enquiries".* Lady Temple had been a reliable witness. Mary was not only a well-bred and charming girl, but pretty too, something which to William's critical eye was almost as important.

If he hoped for Charles's immediate consent, however, he was disappointed. The King had long since realized that the marriage could be a useful diplomatic weapon, and he made it plain that political matters must be settled first. William found this unacceptable and made the fact clear. He felt strongly that although this match might be a political affair, it would be undignified for him to appear to bargain about it. "It shall never be charged against me that I sold my honour for a wife", he told his friend Temple.

The deadlock seemed complete, and after a few days of waiting for a decision from his uncles, William wrote irritably to Fagel instructing him to send over a ship so that he could cut short his fruitless visit.*

He called Temple, his confidant, to his room one evening, where he told him that he was planning to return to Holland. In a bitter outburst he exclaimed that he regretted ever coming to England, and had decided to give up the whole idea of the marriage. It was now up to Charles, he declared, to decide what their future relationship should be: he personally felt that if they were not to be great friends, they must be great enemies. Temple, who remembered that William was on excellent terms with the English Opposition leaders, understood exactly what he meant – especially when William asked him to report their talk to Charles. After this the Prince retired, looking "the most melancholy I ever saw him in my whole life", as Temple said.*

Next morning Temple went straight to Charles to tell him about William's angry threats. To his astonishment Charles answered unexpectedly: "Go and tell the Prince he may have his wife. I was never deceived in judging a man's honesty by his looks and if I am not mistaken in the present instance, the Prince is one of the honestest men in the world." He asked Temple to inform Mary's father the Duke of York and William himself.*

Charles's decision was not quite so spontaneous as it seemed. A shrewd judge of men, he had already understood that the marriage must evidently be conceded before politics could be usefully discussed. And while Temple had been listening to William's angry speeches the night before, the King had had a conversation on the same subject with the new French ambassador Paul Barillon d'Amoncourt, Marquis de Branges.

The Frenchman had been watching events with growing concern, and had come to see the King after supper in the splendid apartments of the Duchess of Portsmouth. To his dismay, he learned that Charles had made up his mind to agree to the match. As a defence, the King pointed out that he had had very little choice in the matter. Louis XIV might be deeply offended by this breach of his expensive trust in the English King but it was partly Charles's close friendship with him that had made the marriage unavoidable. Many of his subjects knew now that their special relationship had as its objective the conversion of England to Catholicism. "It is my brother the Duke of York's conduct that hath given rise to all these suspicions", explained Charles.

The match, he went on to suggest, might even have positive advantages from the French point of view. It would detach William from his friends among the anti-French English Opposition; it might arouse the distrust of William's allies in Europe; and it was certainly highly unpopular with the Catholic Spanish.*

Barillon, understandably, was not impressed. He afterwards told James that he was disgusted to think that "the eldest daughter of the Crown should sleep in Protestant arms".*

James's reaction was one of acute disappointment. A few days earlier he had told Barillon that he knew perfectly well what was going on, but that the marriage was bound to fall through since the King had promised never to dispose of Mary's hand without his consent. He ought to have known his brother better: Charles, told of this conversation, was unmoved. "It is true", he said cheerfully, "that I gave my brother such a promise, but God's-fish, he must consent."*

And, of course, James did consent. Faithful to his own belief in the absolute authority of a king, he set aside his personal feelings and pointed out pompously to Temple, who brought the news: "The King shall be obeyed and I would be glad all his subjects would learn of me to obey him. I do tell him my opinion upon anything, but when that is done and I know his pleasure upon anything, I obey him."*

William learnt the news from Temple with uncharacteristic enthusiasm. He took his old friend in his arms, saying that he had made him the happiest man in the world.

The last to be told was the young bride herself. On the afternoon of 21 October, Mary's father dined at Whitehall and afterwards returned to St. James's where he led his eldest daughter into her closet. There he broke the news of the marriage to her, "whereupon her Highness wept all afternoon and all the following day".*

Her tears were understandable. A royal Princess could expect to have little or no say in the choice of her husband, but knowing as much did not make it easier to submit when the moment came. The fifteen-year-old Mary was now faced – at a few days' notice – with marriage to a man she had hardly met, and who was clearly disliked by her father. Separation from family and friends, and life in an unknown country, did nothing to make the prospect seem more attractive.

She was given little time to come to terms with the idea. Two days later, Charles and James formally presented William to her. In a good-natured attempt to cheer up the occasion, Charles joked, "It is not good for a man to be alone: I will give you a helpmeet." James, with his more leaden humour, reminded the Prince that "love and war do not agree very well together".*

Then father and uncle withdrew, leaving the couple together with Mary's governess, Lady Frances Villiers. The conversation that followed, as the dismayed, red-eyed girl studied her cousin, must have been constrained.

To look at, they were an ill-matched couple. Mary was a beauty, tall and already statuesque, with the white skin and abundant dark hair of the Stuart women, and large brown eyes. A debutante this year, after her rather secluded youth, she was dressed according to the latest fashion: her tight-bodiced silk gown showed off a tiny waist.

At 5 feet 6½ inches William was almost a head shorter than his cousin, who was 5 feet 11 inches. Although he was only eleven years older, he must have seemed to her almost middle-aged, with his asthmatic cough and slightly stooping figure. He was unfashionably dressed, and while periwigs had been in fashion for at least a decade, the elegant English Court noted with astonishment that he still preferred his own thick brown hair.* He seemed to have forgotten much of his English, and spoke with a strong Dutch accent.

In personality as much as in looks, the two presented a striking contrast. William was reserved and quiet, with a chillingly formal manner: hiding his feelings had become almost second nature to him. Mary was a high-spirited and childishly romantic girl who loved to chatter. The cousin she saw could hardly have been less like the ideal man of whom she had dreamed.

Deeply shocked, she could hardly wait to summon her "dear husband", Frances Apsley, to talk it over with her. In an agitated note she appealed, "If you do not come to me sometime, dear husband, that I may have my bellyfull of discourse with you, I shall take it very ill . . . for I have a great deal to say to you concerning I do not know how to set in the letter. If you come you will mightily oblige your faithful wife Mary Clorine. . . ."*

WITH THE MARRIAGE QUESTION DECIDED, William and Charles were now determined to work out a formula for peace. They sat down to negotiations, but at first it looked as if there was little hope of agreement: Charles, with his own commitments to Louis, made an effort to drive a wedge between William and his allies by persuading him to make a separate peace with France. This peace once made, the French King, older now and lazy, would have achieved all he wanted, reasoned Charles. He would turn his attentions to the pleasures of Court and the diversion of building Versailles.*

William understood his uncle only too well. Drily he agreed that a separate peace would indeed give Louis exactly what he wanted: a split among the Allies. But he thought it unlikely that once the French King had got this, he would be content to sit back and give his mind to palaces. From his experience, William knew that a break-up of the Allied coalition would simply whet Louis's appetite for further conquest.

There was only one effective way to check him: a treaty acceptable to all the Allies, which would guarantee a strong Flanders frontier.

Danby and Temple urged the same arguments on the English King. Charles himself, well aware that he would eventually have to confront a violently anti-French Parliament – his debts were £2 million and French subsidies were completely inadequate – at last reluctantly accepted William's point of view.

Fairly rapid agreement was now reached on a number of points. France was to restore Lorraine to its Duke and hand back to the Dutch the key frontier town of Maastricht, in exchange for Philipsburg. The question of Franche-Comté, which contained some of the Orange family estates, took longer to settle, but at length William agreed that it should be left in the hands of the French, hoping that such a concession on his part might encourage Charles to be more tractable about Flanders. The King was delighted. On 31 October he declared optimistically that it was only a question of "one town more or less in Flanders", and peace would be made.*

Meanwhile, the news of the match and the King's announcement that it would be immediately consummated, was celebrated all over the country. "I could not imagine a greater expression of joy could happen to all sorts of people", said a report from Plymouth to Secretary of State Sir Joseph Williamson. In Chester – he learned – the news "was joyfully received by this city, who caused the bells to ring and made bonfires, accompanied by the firing of great guns from the castle".*

In London, the heavy-hearted Princess Mary received a string of official and pompous deputations coming to congratulate her on her good fortune. October 29 was Lord Mayor's Day, and there was the traditional civic procession through the streets of London to the Guildhall, where the windows had been taken out, and splendid Turkish carpets flung over the ledges, "so that the ladies could lean out". William and Mary, and all the Royal family, watched from under a Canopy of State at the house of Edward Waldo, who was afterwards knighted by Charles,* while the livery companies in their ceremonial dress streamed past. The procession started at nine and lasted all morning. Afterwards the new Lord Mayor, Sir Francis Chaplin, entertained his Royal guests at a banquet so lavish that one Dutch guest wrote afterwards: "If I were to describe to you the number of the dishes and how they were built up in pyramids, as also the amount of venison and pies, you would not believe it."*

Two days earlier, William had sent his companion Stangerland, an alderman of Delft, to Amsterdam to ask the States of Holland for their consent to his marriage. He wrote that in response to their often repeated wish that he should marry, he had now addressed himself to the Lady Mary, "for the service of the country". His request was not just a formal courtesy. The wealthy States had made him an annual allowance of 40,000 guilders on condition that he did not marry without their approval: they had also promised him a present of 800,000 guilders on his wedding, if he observed this condition.*

The Regents of Holland had never had much enthusiasm for an Anglo-Dutch alliance in which Holland was bound to take second place. They were even less enthusiastic now: they wanted peace at any price, and this match did not improve the prospects of it. Their consent was by no means a foregone conclusion* and when Stangerland returned to Whitehall – only a couple of hours before the wedding ceremony – to report that there were no objections, William was much relieved.

He left it to the Dutch ambassador, Van Beuningen, to inform the States-General in lyrical terms: "The extraordinary qualities of Mevrouw Princesse give to this happy alliance the utmost perfection. All those who know her unanimously agree that her Highness possesses not only the graces that please the eye, but also exceptional goodness of heart."*

That at least was reassuring news for those Regents who remembered William's mother, another Stuart princess who never bothered to disguise her contempt for them and for Holland in general. Nevertheless, as a Danish diplomat at The Hague commented, "the joy at the news of the Prince's marriage was neither complete nor widespread, and the acclamations were for the most part false."*

The Dutchman in the street had no such reservations: he was honestly delighted by the news of his Prince's marriage. Ships arriving from Holland in England all brought news that "the generality of the people there are very well satisfied. . . ."*

THE DAY OF THE WEDDING CAME. It was Sunday, 4 November, and the twenty-seventh birthday of the Prince of Orange. The ceremony, a private family affair, took place in Mary's apartments in St. James's at nine o'clock in the evening.

Smallpox was raging through the Court at the time, and kept away two people particularly dear to Mary: her sister Anne and her governess Lady Frances Villiers. The Archbishop of Canterbury, who should have officiated, was another victim: his place was taken by Henry Compton, Bishop of London.

One way and another, it was a subdued occasion. The bridegroom looked gloomy and the bride was in tears. James was stern-faced. Only Charles, who instead of her father gave her away, made any attempt at cheerfulness. Always "apter to make broad allusions upon anything that gave the least occasion than was altogether suitable", he now produced a string of coarse pleasantries.* With an eye on the heavily-pregnant Mary of Modena, whose child was born two days later, he called out to Compton: "Come, Bishop, make all the haste you can lest my sister the Duchess of York should bring us a boy and then the marriage would be disappointed." It was a witticism to make William wince.

When the Prince, uttering the words, "With all my worldly goods I thee endow", placed a handful of gold and silver coins on the open Bible, the King told his niece jokingly to "gather it up and put it in her pocket for it was all clear gain".*

After the blessing, Mary was undressed by Queen Catherine, her stepmother Mary of Modena and the Duchess of Monmouth, and put to bed, while the guests ate cakes and drank hot posset in the next room. Then William climbed into bed beside her, and the couple received the congratulations of the Court and the corps diplomatique. It was time for a final *bon mot* from Charles. As everybody left the room, the King closed the bed-curtains with the words: "Now nephew to your work. Hey! St. George for England!"*

At Versailles, a different account of William's wedding night was soon being retailed by the scandalmongers. Liselotte, once herself a serious candidate for marriage with William, and now the unfortunate wife of Monsieur, wrote gleefully to her aunt Sophia: "it was said that William went to bed in woollen drawers. When Charles suggested that he take them off, he replied that since he and his wife would have to live together for a long time, she would have to get used to his habits. And", continued Liselotte with relish, "instead of having supper with the English Royal family, he went to eat in town and kept the King and the bride waiting until midnight. When the King asked him what had kept him so long, he replied that he had been gambling. . ."*

Louis XIV received the news less lightheartedly. Three days after the marriage, William sat down to write to him: "I believed it my duty to make known to your Majesty that the King of Great Britain and Monsieur the Duke of York have had the goodness to accept the suit I made for the eldest daughter of his Royal Highness, and that accordingly I married her last Sunday. I trust that your Majesty will not be displeased by the liberty I take in informing him of this, despite all the misfortunes of the present time. . ."*

In public Louis commented viciously, "Two beggars are well matched." In private he was as shattered "as if it had been the loss of an army". And to James he wrote reproachfully: "You have given your daughter to my mortal enemy." For once he had been outmanoeuvred by William of Orange.*

THE DAY AFTER THE WEDDING, Bentinck came to call on Mary bringing with him a small chest full of jewels, William's wedding present to her. They were splendid: among them was a string of huge pearls which she can be seen wearing in almost all her portraits, diamond clasps, and a ruby ring "which she came to value above her kingdom".

The value of the jewellery was estimated at £40,000, the exact sum of Mary's dowry as stipulated in the marriage contract. If the jewels were a mere day late in arriving from Holland, however, many letters had to cross the North Sea later before William ever received a penny of the dowry. The first quarter was due six months after the wedding, and the remainder over the next eighteen months, but only part of it was ever paid, and that months overdue.

On his side, William undertook to give Mary £10,000 a year, and another £2000 as pocket-money, for her *"menus plaisirs"* as the contract, drawn up in French, put it. She was also entitled to two residences, one at The Hague and one in the country, and she was to be allowed her own Church of England services.

The question of children was carefully considered in the contract. No child of the couple was to marry without the consent of the King of England, in view of their possible succession to the English throne. If William died first, Mary was to be free to return to England, but she was only to be allowed to bring her personal possessions with her if there were no children.*

It was all very prosaic and businesslike, as might be expected of a marriage arranged for reasons of state. But at least one person at Court – if only in the line of duty – was prepared to see it in a romantic light. The ageing court poet Sir Edmund Waller had composed an elaborate epithalamium for the occasion:

> *. . . To her the Prince that did dispose*
> *Such mighty armies in the field*
> *And Holland from prevailing foes*

Could so well save, himself does yield.
Not Belga's fleet (his high command),
Which triumphs where the sun does rise,
Nor all the force he leads by land
*Could guard him from her conqu'ring eyes.**

It was a nice essay in poetic fantasy. But those who had followed the years of diplomacy, the weeks of bickering and haggling, and the tense hurried ceremony of that late autumn Sunday evening, can have had no such illusions.

CHAPTER XII

Mary in Holland

"THE PRINCE IS A VERY FOND HUSBAND, but she is a very coy bride, at least before folkes."* That was the comment in Whitehall after the marriage. It seemed that the Princess had begun to adapt herself to her new situation: at times she even looked as though she was enjoying it. "This pretty lady seemth pretty well plesed," was another comment.* While the festivities went on for a whole week – during which time every honest person at Court was said to be in a chronic state of intoxication* – the newly-married couple sat to Peter Lely, the Dutch painter who had made a name for himself at the English Court.

But the precarious understanding between William and Mary was short-lived. It was discovered that Mary's younger sister Anne, who had been too ill to be present at the wedding, was suffering from smallpox. The Prince, who had had too much experience of this dreadful disease, begged his wife to leave her home in St. James's, where Anne was lying sick, and to join him in his lodgings at Whitehall, but she obstinately refused to leave her home till the last minute. Her chaplain Dr. Lake had to take his leave of her at this time since he was in attendance on the sickroom, and when he came to see Mary he found her very upset, "her eyes full of tears, herself very disconsolate, not only for her sisters ill-nesse, but also for some discontent occasioned by the Prince's urging her to remove her lodgings to Whitehall." She struggled for self-control, but when she thanked him for all his kindness, she began to cry and "so turned her back and went into her closet".*

The Prince had other things to vex him beside the tears and sulkiness of his adolescent bride. Two days after the wedding, the Duchess of York's baby was born, and to the delight of James it was a boy, his first by her. The child – "little but sprightly and likely to live"* – was christened the next day, and Charles and the Prince of Orange were joint godfathers. The baby was given the name Charles and the title of Duke of Cambridge. His arrival not only meant that England now had what everyone dreaded – a Catholic heir to the throne; it also removed Mary and William one step from the throne.† It was not surprising that after the christening William began to feel he had had enough of Whitehall's festivities and civilities, and that the sooner he could get the partings done with and his emotional young wife to Holland, the better it would be for them both. He could not decently hurry away, however, before the birthday celebrations of Queen Catherine of Braganza on 15 November, so their departure was finally fixed for late in the evening of that day. At the ball Mary looked ravishing, richly dressed and wearing all the beautiful new jewels that William had given her. The courtiers noted, however, that the Prince had not called on her at St. James's that day, paid little attention to her and danced only once with her.

At eight o'clock the Princess changed into travelling clothes and said goodbye to all her family,* but a sudden easterly wind springing up prevented their departure and to William's irritation, next day the couple were still in London, where 'the Court began to whisper the Prince's sullennesse and clownishnesse".*

He had to suppress his impatience for another four days. Not until the morning of Monday the nineteenth, when the wind veered to the west, could the Prince and Princess of Orange embark. Mary, who had been weeping all morning, asked the Duchess of Monmouth to visit her sister Anne and to accompany her to chapel, now that Anne was the only Protestant in the Royal family. She left two letters to be given to Anne as soon as she was well enough to read them.* She also wrote a farewell letter to her friend Frances Apsley, for her still a more "deare husband" than the Prince of Orange. "I hope you will . . . not forget your pore Clorine," she wrote sadly, "that loves you better then can be exprest . . . if you shoud not belive your one treu wife which I hope you do she no way to show it but by wrighting to you so that if you wil not belive her She must dy condemned."*

Mary had not been able to control her tears when she said goodbye to Catherine of Braganza earlier that morning at Whitehall. The Queen, remembering her own misery, "comforted her with the consideration of her condition when she came into England, and had never till then seen the King", but Mary, with naive logic, replied: "Madam, you came into

---

† The baby lived only one month before dying of the prevalent smallpox. It was said that his step-sister Anne had given him the disease by kissing him, and his nurse Mrs. Chambers was also blamed for giving him entirely the wrong treatment: "He might have lived many years had not mrs Chambers . . . struck in the humour which broke forth under his arm and at his navell instead of putting a cole leaf to draw it out . . . and the duke was never known to grieve so much at the death of any of his children."*

England; I am going out of England."* Her parting with the Duchess of
York, her stepmother, was sadder still. No difference in religion had
hindered a warm affection growing up between the two young women,
and they "wept both with that excesse of sorrow" that William swore
that no matter what the weather, he would not return "to make a second
scene of grief".*

The King and the Duke of York accompanied the couple down-
stream in the splendid Royal barge as far as the little village of Erith,
where they dined.* And after Charles and James had said their farewell,
Mary and William went on board the yacht *Mary*, where Captain
Gunman waited to greet them. They sailed immediately for Holland,
but got no further than Sheerness before the wind changed again.
They decided to go ashore and the Prince sent off a messenger to
Charles telling him of the delay.* The following morning he set out with
Mary in the direction of Canterbury, but they were only half-way there,
at Bobbing, when messengers from Whitehall caught up with them
with an invitation from Charles to return to London to wait for a favourable wind there.* James, who prided himself on being an experienced
sailor, wrote, "For my Sonne" by the same messenger: "I feare the wind
is sett in NE and will continu so till the full moone, which will not be till
wensday night." He begged him, like Charles, to return to town: "it
would be a great satisfaction to me, and to all here, to have you with us
as long as you stay in this country."*

No invitation could have given William less pleasure in the circumstances, and he made up his mind to travel on to Canterbury, "where I
will stay for farther Orders; which I hope will not oblige me to bring the
Women back with me to London, which I can never do without the
utmost Trouble", as he wrote hastily to Danby from the coaching-inn.*

Charles accepted the decision: soon after his arrival at Canterbury,
William received another note from the King telling him that "now that
you are advanced so farr and resolved to embark at Margatt, I thinke you
will do well not to come hether, for it will be a troublesome journey this
ill wether and, if the winde should change, as you are comming hither,
you may chance to loose a good passage."*

James, it turned out, had been right about the wind. Twice in the
next few days the whole party embarked, and twice they had to come
ashore again. William became more and more impatient, writing to
Waldeck that he was "extremely vexed at being here for such a long
time away from business". Safely away from Whitehall, however, he
relaxed a little, and soon began to enjoy a small court of his own. On
Sunday he attended service at Canterbury Cathedral, and the local

notabilities came to pay their respects to their new Protestant Prince, to the vexation of the Court at Whitehall.

William had expected to have no further travelling expenses in England after leaving London. Instead he had to pay for the best possible travel and accommodation for a party of at least sixty, for several days, and his funds were running low. He sent Bentinck to the Mayor of Canterbury to borrow some money but he was politely refused, and it was the Dean of the Cathedral, Dr. Tillotson, who came to the rescue with a loan – a kindness which William and Mary never forgot.*

Most of this time Mary stayed quietly in her room. She was homesick, and letters from London plunged her into fresh misery: Anne was still dangerously ill, and even more distressing was the news that her beloved governess Lady Frances Villiers had succumbed to smallpox. Her death was not only a personal loss to Mary; the young Princess had counted on taking her to Holland as the head of the English household of forty people allowed her by her marriage contract. The formation of this household had presented problems enough – there had been a great scramble "especially among the old ladies and the young beggarly bitches" for a place – and by the time of her departure sickness had taken its toll of her company. Lady Frances's husband, Sir Edward Villiers, who was to have been her Master of the Horse, had also fallen ill. Her nurse Mrs. Hemlock had had to stay behind to look after a sick father, and Mistress Anne Trelawney, one of her Maids of Honour, was detained by the same reason.* The only consolation now after Lady Villiers's death was that there were at least some faces familiar from her childhood around her, like the three Villiers sisters, Anne, Elizabeth, and Katherine, and Mary's old "mam" Mrs. Langford, while Lady Sylvius, "a most pious and virtuous lady", accompanied her husband Sir Gabriel, who was made "Hofmeester" or Steward of the Orange Household.*

At last on Tuesday the twenty-seventh the wind changed with the full moon and it looked as if the party could sail next morning, but not before the Prince, too, had had bad news from London. Danby sent him the latest reports about the reaction of France to the peace terms hammered out by Charles and William. There was nothing official yet, but according to rumours they were unlikely to be favourably received. Surprisingly it had been the Duke of York who had reacted the most vigorously, remarking, "that in case they do not agree to the proposition . . . the King ought to lett the King of France know, that unless hee would forbear any further conquests in Flanders, hee could not hinder England from coming into the War."* And with this last report to brood over, the Prince and Princess of Orange left Margate on Wednesday morning at ten o'clock. They sailed in separate ships – Mary in the *Katherine*, William in the *Mary* – and the crossing was so rough that on the *Katherine* everybody was sick, except the bride.

It had been the intention to land at Rotterdam, but thick ice had made the port impassable. Instead the whole wretched party was transferred into sloops, which brought them to the little fishing village of Terheyde late on Thursday afternoon. The Prince himself carried his exhausted young wife up the beach where only a few curious villagers greeted them; but there were no carriages waiting and the bedraggled company had to walk over three miles of very bad road before coaches hastily summoned from The Hague could pick them up. Immediately they drove to Honselaersdijck, where an alerted household had fires blazing, candles burning and a hot meal ready.*

Only five days' rest was allowed Mary before public life claimed her again: The Hague had prepared a tremendous reception for her and her husband, and the Dutch people were eager to see their Stadholder's bride. It was the sort of occasion William normally detested – all formalities and speeches – but Mary was full of curiosity to see these strange Dutch, so much hated and laughed at in Whitehall, and Holland's "First Village" – as The Hague was called.

When on 14 December the couple were driven to The Hague in a golden coach drawn by six piebald horses, it was raining, but not enough to damp the festive mood of the town. On the bridge at the entrance of The Hague twelve companies of the civic militia were drawn up as guard of honour. The coach stopped and a 31-gun salute was fired, while the guards fired their muskets into the air. Twelve young girls from the Orphanage and twelve from the Workhouse, all dressed in white, surrounded the coach, scattering sweet herbs and singing songs of praise as the Prince and Princess of Orange drove slowly into town. The streets were lined with cheering crowds and decorated with garlands and arches loaded with oranges. The most impressive one stood in front of the Town Hall and showed two clasped hands and the slogan "O that the dowry of this royal marriage might be peace".*

The first impression Mary made on the Dutch was one of beauty. The rhymer Droste, who watched the splendid entry, wrote afterwards lyrically: "She was beautiful, young and good and praised by everyone." The Hagenaars noticed too the regal bearing of the young girl.*

The couple drove to the Binnenhof, another new home for Mary and as spectacularly decorated as the rest of the town. In the evening it was illuminated and from platforms in the Vijver fireworks blazed into the sky; one of the set-pieces showed two angels carrying a ring with the crowned letters W. H. and M.; another showed a golden lion with a sword in one hand and a laurel branch as the symbol of victory in the other. William and Mary watched the dazzling display from a window of the Binnenhof. It ended in a final spectacular tableau – Jupiter and Mars descending from Heaven.*

Next day the States-General offered them a formal reception. The Regents were still slightly stunned by the fact of the marriage and by the speed at which it had all happened. Whatever they may have suspected, William had kept his intentions exceptionally secret, and his request at the beginning of November for their consent to the match had been their first official notification. Even the Raadspensionary, Caspar Fagel, who was more closely in the Prince's confidence than most, had remarked to the Imperial ambassador in The Hague, Kramprich, that the news of the marriage had been a surprise to him, because only six days after William's arrival in England, the Prince had sent urgently for ships to take him back to Holland.* Shortly before William's departure Fagel had assured a diplomat that a marriage would not be discussed at all: Louis XIV, according to his information, had sent three million florins to England to promote a match between Mary and the Dauphin, and the King of Sweden was also asking for her hand.*

All the same, the States were prepared to give their Stadholder's bride a warm welcome and Mary, who had all the easy Stuart charm, did her best to respond with "gaiety of temper and fluency of conversation".* William had coached her carefully beforehand: she was to observe English Court protocol and only kiss on the cheek the wives of the nobles and the unmarried ladies who were her husband's relations. The other ladies were only offered her hand to kiss, a distinction that shattered the proud Dutch Regents. The husbands protested and some of the wives burst into tears. The Prince was short with them, asking if they were noble. When they said no but claimed that their office gave them equal rank with the nobility, he shrugged and dismissed them: "No office ennobles its possessors."*

It was the only incident which marred the two-day welcome, and when Mary returned with her husband to Honselaersdijck, everybody agreed that this Stuart princess was a great improvement on the last, William's mother.

The Prince had found it harder than his wife to respond to the smiles and the cheers. As he wrote to his friend Ossory on the day of the reception: "Here we are at The Hague with the general acclamation of everyone. I have been unable to participate in this joy, having received yesterday the news of the taking of St. Ghislain" by the French.*

In spite of this new French success in Flanders, William decided to remain at home with Mary for as long as possible, although as he wrote to Waldeck defensively, the decision was entirely his own, "not being married to the sort of woman, who would prevent me from doing my duty".*

"WHAT GREATER HAPYNES is there in the world then to have the company of them on loves to make your hapynes compleat . . .", Mary had written to Frances Apsley a year earlier. She had added sentimentally: "I could live & be content with a cotage in the contre & cow a stufe peticot & wastcot in sumer & cloth in winter a litel garden to live upon the fruit & herbs it yeilds. . . ."*

The house which would now be her home, Honselaersdijck, was certainly no country cottage. This beautiful house, which became Mary's favourite among all her Dutch homes, stood on the site of a thirteenth-century castle given to William's grandfather prince Frederik Hendrik in 1629. The castle had been pulled down and in its place a graceful manor in the Dutch Renaissance style was built of pale Leiden brick and roofed with slate. One of its designers was the architect of Amsterdam's famous Town Hall, Jacob van Campen, and Honselaersdijck was reckoned the most beautiful private house in the Republic. English visitors compared it with the Palais du Luxembourg in Paris, only objecting that the rooms were rather small for a prince's house.* But they were charmingly furnished and by squalid Whitehall standards the palace was luxurious and comfortable, with running hot water in the bathrooms and an air of spotless cleanliness everywhere.

Mary had the whole left wing and William had filled it with some of the prettiest pictures in his collection. Her little study overlooking the garden, hung with pale yellow and violet satin, embroidered with gold and silver, had a copy of Van Dyck's *Madonna and Child* on the walls. In her Audience Chamber, with its pale blue flowered damask, a painting by Honthorst of William's grandmother Amalia as Diana stood out. And Amalia reappeared as Diana in another painting in Mary's Bed Chamber. The walls of this room were covered with green damask trimmed with gilt cord. The curtains were of the same material – but their lining was said to be of poor quality. The furniture was of English lacquer, and the painted ceiling showed Virtue, Labour and Vigilance. The dressing-room was fitted out in gilded leather, and the French painter Duval had decorated it with flowers and cherubs.

The palace was only seven miles from The Hague, overlooking the

Westland dunes, and the drive out to it was a popular excursion for Hagenaars and foreign visitors. Sometimes they might see the Prince and Princess dining together in public in the great first-floor dining-room with its painted ceiling by Pieter de Grebber showing shepherds and shepherdesses disporting themselves. At other times they might be received by the Prince in his Audience Chamber which was hung with red and gold serge and had the revolutionary new sash-windows. Visitors could stroll through the Great Gallery with its many portraits of William's ancestors – Henri IV of France, James I of England, Philip III of Spain, and their wives – or admire the greatest treasures in the palace, two Rembrandts, *The Burial* and the *Resurrection of Christ*, painted in 1639, for which Frederik Hendrik had paid 1244 guilders.

The gardens of Honselaersdijck were famous. Entering them over a bridge the first thing one saw was a fountain with four intertwined dolphins spouting water and supporting a shell on which stood Cupid. In the inner garden, surrounded by a canal, statues of classic beauties like Flora, Cleopatra and Helen, bought in France, were displayed. In one corner William had reinstalled the little menagerie that his mother had been unable to keep up through lack of money. It contained, among other curiosities, a spotted Indian cat, an elk, and "several fowles most of them brought from England", but few of these survived the damp Dutch climate. Later, Droste mentioned seeing ostriches there and Huygens wrote to his brother Christian in Paris about a previously unheard-of little creature he had seen there – a chameleon, given to William by Bentinck. At the end of the gardens rose the dark backdrop of the forests.*

Honselaersdijck was only one of many residences of the Prince of Orange. The most important was still the Binnenhof, which had been left unchanged since William's birth. He found it dark and stuffy and too cramped for a court, certainly after his marriage. He tried to extend his quarters, partly by building on and partly by reclaiming some of the rooms used as offices by the States-General – in 1678 the States-Greffier was turned out of his registry-office to make room for one of the *"joffers"* – or ladies-in-waiting – of the Princess.* The Prince also owned the Oude Hof at Noordeinde in The Hague, which he used as an annexe for guests, and Het Huis ten Bosch which he had inherited in 1675 from his grandmother Amalia. When he was away, the House in the Woods was Mary's refuge, almost her dream cottage – "a small ordinary house half an hour walk out of town", its special charm being a pleasant garden with "a lively statue of Cleopatra applying the asp".*

In the south of the United Provinces was another Orange family residence, the castle of Breda, mainly used by William as a staging-post on his journeys to the Spanish Netherlands. He had a castle in Buren, a mansion in Geertruidenberg, a palace in Brussels and a palace in Soestdijk, but of all these scattered places outside The Hague, the only one he was making use of at this time was the last. He had bought Soestdijk, halfway between Amsterdam and Amersfoort, as a country house in 1674 from the son of Amsterdam's Burgemeester Cornelis de Graeff van Zuidpolsbroek, with the idea of turning it into a hunting-castle. He had purchased great tracts of countryside around it, and the States of Utrecht had made him Lord of the Manor of that part of the province.* A contemporary called it "a very pretty box . . . the lodgings are small but neat; good gardens curiously planted and made up . . . five hundred head of deer; a pretty engine or mill . . . very fine walks and rows of trees about it."* Sir Constantyn Huygens, making an inspection tour of all the Prince's properties in 1678, found it a fine house, but suggested that the Prince ought to fill up the empty white niches in the outside walls with painting on canvas – he had done the same in his own house and they had lasted thirty-eight years. He noted that the house was filled with paintings and thought that the hall at least would be much nicer *"bien tout blanc et vuide"*.*

He gave a much less favourable account of William's neglected castle at Buren, which was badly in need of repairs. The castle itself was still structurally sound, but the bridge leading to it might collapse any day, and parts of the walls were crumbling into the moat. "I can't restrain myself imploring Your Highness not to let this castle fall into ruins which your grandfather furnished and decorated with so much care and expense."*

Almost as decrepit was William's favourite hunting-lodge at Dieren, described at this time as "an old and ill-kept house surrounded by a dry and over-grown moat". Visitors entered it by a bridge leading to a great courtyard circled with low buildings and a wall pierced by windows "from which the iron bars are missing or bent". On the left of the courtyard were the stables, the kitchens and the wash-house. Straight ahead was the principal lodge, with a stone staircase curving up to the great hall hung with antlers "in the manner of the old nobility". It was obvious to any visitor that the house, not far from the river IJssel and set in hilly country on the edge of the Veluwe forests, was chosen for its hunting facilities rather than for its elegance.*

The interest their Stadholder took in the choice and furnishing of some of his houses – in which hobby he was soon eagerly joined by Mary – was very much a feature of the national character. Foreigners were always struck by the care and cleanliness of Dutch homes, while in the second half of the nation's Golden Age even the sober and Calvinist Dutch had started to build themselves statelier houses and country mansions, with "plantations, gardens, greenhouses, fountains, cascades, game reserves, everything in perfect order".* Foreigners also commented on the simple elegance of the town houses, where the furniture was "so clean and in order that it looks as if it is exhibited and not for use".*

The inhabitants of these houses were considered rather heavy-going by the rest of Europe. An Englishman warned travellers "not to expect civility from the Dutch, who pretend not to much breeding".* Even Temple, a great admirer of the United Provinces, had to admit that the people thought more about profit than honour, had more brains than soul, and more goodness than high spirits. The witty Frenchman Saint-Evremond, who spent a few years in Amsterdam, agreed completely with him. "We find here", he wrote in 1665, "fewer polite persons than men fit for business; and more good sense in the management of affairs than delicacy in conversation." Missing the frivolous elegance of Paris, he complained that "Infidelity, which passes for a gentell merit in agreeable courts, is reckoned the foulest of all vices by this honest nation, which is . . . unexperienc'd as to refin'd pleasures, and a polite way of living." He commiserated with the husbands, who "reward the fidelity of their wives, by a great subjection; and if a Man . . . should affect to be Lord and master in his own house, the wife wou'd be pitied by all her neighbours . . . and the Husband exclaim'd against as a very ill-natured fellow."*

Saint-Evremond found more to admire in Dutch tolerance in religious matters: "The difference of religion, which in other places raises so many commotions, does not in the least ruffle here the minds of people; every-one seeks heaven after his own way."* Not astonishingly the number of religions and sects in Amsterdam was legion, and it was one of the few cities in Europe where the Jews – who called it Mokum (The Place) – were not compelled to live in ghettos. The city was a haven for victims of religious persecution from all over Europe and the seventeenth-century English poet Andrew Marvell could write:

> *Hence Amsterdam, Turk, Christian, Pagan, Jew,*
> *Staple of sects and mint of schism grew;*
> *That Bank of conscience, where not one so strange*
> *Opinion but finds credit and exchange.**

The leading sect was the Calvinist Dutch Reformed Church, but as it was not the official State religion, it had little influence in political matters, and unlike the Puritans in England its leaders had never been able to impose orthodox rules of conduct on the people by law. The fact that its 2000 pastors were traditionally Orange supporters had further diminished their political status under De Witt. But on the minds of the people their influence was enormous, and their support had contributed greatly to the elevation of William in 1672.

Mary had wept at the prospect of living among the Dutch in their unknown country. As she gradually discovered Holland over the first few tranquil weeks of her marriage, she came to appreciate it and to feel at home there. In contrast to that other Mary Stuart, William's mother, who had never overcome the prejudices impressed on her in her childhood, Mary had learned to have a mind of her own, and as one of the small Protestant minority in the English Royal family she was not afraid to assert it. At Whitehall she had seldom heard the Dutch – or William himself – discussed except in terms of contempt and abuse, and now she was open-minded and generous enough to correct the prejudices she had been taught. The Dutch, she found, were warm-hearted if stiffly polite, and her husband less reserved than he had seemed in England. Back in his own country, surrounded by a circle of loyal and admiring friends, the key figure in state affairs and treated everywhere by people almost as king, he was a very considerable person, relaxed, assured and sometimes amiable. Mary had grown up yearning to fall in love, as her childish romance with Frances Apsley had revealed. William was the first man she had come to know intimately, and it was almost inevitable that this warm-hearted, impressionable girl should be in love with her husband before many weeks were out.

Already in January the first reports reaching London suggested that she was settling down happily, growing "somewhat fatt and very beautiful withal".* The only complaint of her former chaplain Dr. Lake was that, contrary to his advice, she sometimes played cards on Sunday, which he was afraid might offend the strict Dutch.*

Her English Household at Honselaersdijck were adapting themselves, like their mistress, to a new Dutch way of life, and at the end of January William could report to Danby that "mr Bentinck will needs follow his Master's example and has a mind to marry Madam Villars".* The wedding between Mary's lady-in-waiting Anne Villiers and Bentinck took place in February in The Hague, in the presence of the Prince and Princess of Orange, who settled an annuity of 8000 guilders on the bride.*

A month later it was announced that Mary was pregnant. The famous Dutch doctor Jacob Senaer was called in to attend the Princess and

happy preparations were made for a possible Orange heir, right down to
the cradle. In spite of her condition, Mary went with her husband to
Rotterdam when his presence was urgently needed at army headquarters.
Her uncle Laurence Hyde was present there at "a very tender parting on
both sides" – he had never seen the Prince so demonstrative, so easy and
so cheerful.* The long holiday with his wife had made a new man of him.
For the first time in years he had not been bothered by State affairs and
even Fagel, when at the end of January he had been obliged to ask him
for advice, had felt it necessary to excuse himself profusely for breaking
in on "the little leisure Your Highness allows yourself".*

But the French had invested Namur, and the Allied armies on the
battlefields in Flanders waited for their commander. Mary was agonized
to see him go. For the first time she began to realize that she was married
to a soldier as well as a statesman, and she was terrified by the thought of
the constant danger he would be in. She wrote in some confusion to
Frances Apsley: "I supose you know the Prince is gone to the Army but
I am sure you can geuse at the troble I am in . . . I am sure I coud never
have thought it half so much . . . I thought coming out of my own contry
parting with my friands and relations the greatest that ever coud as long
as thay lived hapen to me but I am to be mistaken that now I find till this
time I never knew sorow . . . for what can be more cruall in the world
than parting with what on loves and nott ondly comon parting but
parting so as may be never to meet again to be perpetually in fear . . . for
god knows when I may see him or wethere he is nott now at this instant
in a batell . . . I recon him now never in safety ever in danger . . . oh
miserable live that I lead. . ."* It was a letter still in the high-flown style
of Clorine, but it revealed a new Mary; it was her first open admission of
love for William, who had now in her heart supplanted Frances as "my
deare Husband".

The parting was not as final as she feared. The Prince, after a visit to
Mechlin, travelled to Antwerp on 20 March, and the Princess hurried
south to join him. The two spent a fortnight together and, regardless of
her pregnancy, Mary spent her days busily exploring another new town
in the company of Lady Inchiquin, who had taken the place of the late
Lady Villiers.

At the beginning of April, she had to say goodbye to William and
make the slow jolting coach-journey back to The Hague, where she
arrived on the third. A bare three weeks later, she was off again on the
long trip to Breda to see her husband. Gabriel Sylvius, her steward,
thought it the height of folly for a woman in her condition to be dashing
around the country and his forebodings were realized when a few days

later, to everybody's disappointment, it was reported that the Princess had had a miscarriage. The news was sent to Whitehall at once, and James wrote reprovingly: "Pray let her be carefuller of herself another time."*

There was no need to urge caution on the Princess. When she became pregnant again soon afterwards, she stayed quietly at home. And the hurried journeys to join her husband during campaigns were given up for good.

CHAPTER XIII

Peace in Europe

O N 2 8 J A N U A R Y 1 6 7 8 Charles II announced proudly in his newly-assembled Parliament "that he was entered into a strict alliance with the Prince of Orange" to fight the French. The Commons were enthusiastic and wary. They thanked him "for the care he had expressed of the Protestant religion in marrying his niece to the Prince of Orange", but his request for funds sufficient to equip a fleet of 90 ships and an army of 30,000 men was conditionally rejected.* Only if the King would bind himself and the Allies to driving France back behind its frontiers of the 1659 Treaty of the Pyrenees would they actually vote the money.

Charles pretended indignation, but secretly he was much relieved. While Lord Feversham discussed officially in Paris the tough peace terms of William and the English King, the latter had sent his own envoy, Ralph Montagu, privately to Louis XIV with a message expressing his real intentions: to remain France's ally if it were made worth his while. The French ministers Pomponne and Louvois expressed Louis's gratitude in the usual way. If Charles would use the new influence he claimed to have over the Prince of Orange "to prevail with him to recede from such High Terms, as are propos'd", he would be well rewarded. If he could persuade the Prince of Orange not to insist on Valenciennes, Condé and Tournai, "your Majesty should be paid as much as if these Places were your own; and although such a Sum of Money as this would be hard to return, it should be put into Wedges of Gold, and so put into Bales of silk, and sent over in a Yatcht. . . ."*

But the French King, unlike the Allies, was not waiting for the results of Charles's mediation, and his armies – more enormous than ever – were ready to give Europe fresh surprises. On 7 February he left his winter pleasures behind to head 160,000 men. Versailles went with him: the Queen, Madame de Montespan, a score of other pretty women, and for the first time his two "historiographers", Racine and Boileau. It

was their task to immortalize the glory of this final campaign against
Europe.

The French King appeared before Ghent on 4 March and so forced
William to break off his honeymoon. Ghent fell after five days, followed
two weeks later by Ypres, and it began to look as if Flanders would be
swallowed up in one big swoop. Only the active intervention of England
could save the Allies, but in spite of the Anglo-Dutch Treaty, signed on
10 January 1678, this help was slow in coming and when in May Louis
XIV offered a month's truce to the States, they eagerly accepted in spite
of William's protests. Sophia of Hanover wrote optimistically: "The war
between the Sun and the frogs is ended."*

It was a personal defeat for the Prince of Orange, whose prestige in
Holland had weakened rapidly. His insistence on continuing the war and
his increasingly autocratic manner had reopened a gulf between him and
the governing classes, while his marriage to an English princess, however
popular she might be, had awakened old Dutch fears of too much
dependence on England, and of William's personal ambition. "There are
strong fears that he will make himself sovereign", wrote the well informed but somewhat biased Duchess Sophia.*

The States-General majority vote for the truce was a great relief for
Charles, who seized on it immediately as an excuse for further inaction.
Danby wrote to William in the end of May: "Nobody here will beleeve
itt reasonable for us to ingage – who are out of the war – untill wee can
be assured that you, who are already in itt, shall not abandon us, when
you think fitt. . . ."* For William, abandoned by the States and England,
nothing else was left than to become a helpless spectator of developments
at the conference table at Nijmegen, and with Mary he retired to Honselaersdijck. But not for long: when everything seemed ready for the
signing of the peace treaty, d'Estrades dropped a bombshell. France
would restore none of the towns in Flanders before the Allies disarmed
and made peace with Sweden. On those conditions the States indignantly rejected the terms as unworkable. At one stroke the Prince's
credit was restored and he left Honselaersdijck to join the Dutch army
in the south. He could not conceal his satisfaction in a letter to Ossory
who just had visited him: "You will not be sorry to hear of the new
obstacle to the conclusion of peace, which could cause war to go on, at
least if you remain firm and we do too."*

Charles, who had concluded with Louis a secret treaty of non-
intervention on payment of the usual subsidies, was now no longer able
to resist the pressure of the Commons and public opinion. He sent Sir
William Temple to The Hague and on 25 July England and the Republic

signed a pact, which obliged Charles to enter the war against the French if a satisfactory peace was not agreed by 11 August.

This sudden stiffening of the opposition took the French by surprise; they realized that their demands had gone too far, and they were now confronted with an alliance strengthened by a newly purposeful England. At the eleventh hour – in this case midnight on 10 August – the French climbed down and signed a treaty of peace and commerce with the Dutch which made no reference to Sweden. Spain and the Emperor were not mentioned in it. The Dutch negotiators were so delighted that they rushed through the sleeping streets of Nijmegen knocking up the inhabitants to tell them the good news.

The Duke of York wrote to William on 14 August: "We were very much surprised this day to hear by express from Nijmegen that the peace was only signed by the Dutch and the French, without the Spaniards . . . I believe it was what you did not expect. . . ."*

As he wrote, the Prince had not even heard the news. Very strong forces under Luxembourg were blockading Mons, and on the day the Franco-Dutch treaty was signed, he had set out for its relief with 45,000 men and the support of an English detachment under his friend Ossory. He reached the town on Sunday, 14 August, and to the surprise of the unprepared Luxembourg, who himself knew that the treaty had been signed, attacked at once. A bitter battle followed that raged from two in the afternoon till ten at night. The French fought back brilliantly, and the wooded slopes above Mons were soon covered with wounded and dying. The Prince himself had a very narrow escape. When a French officer was on the point of shooting him at close range, Ouwerkerk killed the Frenchman just before he fired. William later presented his friend in gratitude with a pair of gold-mounted pistols.

The English regiments distinguished themselves, and Ossory in particular "behaved in such a manner, as almost countenanced the Wonders of Poetry and Romance . . . expos'd to all the Fire of the Enemy, as if he had been invulnerable, as well as invincible".* Two bullets pierced his armour, but he escaped unhurt.

All the courage and fire of the Allied troops could not, however, stop the French regaining most of the ground they had lost, and when the last daylight went and battle was broken off, only the abbey, Luxembourg's headquarters, was still in Allied hands. But daylight on 15 August broke on an unexpected sight: Luxembourg had withdrawn during the night, leaving the field with all the French wounded and supplies to the Prince of Orange. Victory, it seemed, was with the tired Allies.

Bentinck sent his adjutant the same morning to his wife Anne with a hastily scribbled note to inform her "of a very great and bloody battle which took place here after dinner, in order that you may assure Madame the Princess of the perfect health of his Highness".*

The battle once over, the passionate arguments about whether it ought to have taken place at all now began. While Luxembourg had known that peace terms had been signed, the Prince of Orange in a letter to Fagel dated 15 August stated: "I can declare before God that I only heard this afternoon, by your letter of the 13th, that the peace was concluded."* Many of his contemporaries, however, asserted, that he knew of the signing of the treaty, and was therefore responsible for a massacre. Hieronymus van Beverningk, the Dutch negotiator, conceded later that the message he had sent to the Prince might have been intercepted, but a close friend related many years afterwards that William himself admitted receiving some letters from Nijmegen a few hours before the battle, but he had stuffed them in his pocket, careless of what they contained.* According to the account of Gourville, the Prince told him that even if he had not received official notification of the peace, he knew it was a certainty. But he had reflected that that "might be a reason for Monsieur de Luxembourg not to be on his guard", and that if he did not succeed in beating him, "he would give him a good lesson".*

The French in any case had given the impression that if they could occupy Mons before the peace treaties were ratified, they would keep the fortress, and William's action had at least saved this gateway to Brussels.

Now that the war was over the two men who had confronted each other at the head of armies so often in the last six years were curious to meet in person. The Prince of Orange took the initiative and sent Luxembourg a brief note saying that he would like to see him. A rendezvous was arranged for 20 August on a field between the two armies, not far from the Abbey of St. Denis. The two commanders with their distinguished retinue greeted each other cordially and politely, but the French thought that William's bow was not quite as low as that of Luxembourg. They exchanged compliments and found that they had at least one thing in common: a great regret that warring was over, that their services would no longer be needed, and that from now on hunting would be their main occupation. Luxembourg afterwards commented cruelly: "The Prince of Orange shed bitter tears over the peace. He might just as well shed a few for having made war so unluckily."*

It was their last confrontation for several years. The following day both armies withdrew simultaneously by agreement. The long war between the Republic and France was over. A month later the Spaniards signed their treaty with France at Nijmegen. Louis XIV was victor: he kept Franche-Comté – a financial blow for William who lost his domain there – and twelve towns in the Spanish Netherlands. Only the Emperor fought on. For all his half-hearted support during the war, he now felt he had been left in the lurch, and his ally the Elector of Brandenburg wrote in fury to the States-General that if the danger ever should return, nobody would help the Dutch after this experience. The Emperor too was finally compelled to make peace, sacrificing two towns, Fribourg and Nancy, to the French. The Sun King's triumph was complete.

IF WILLIAM WAS UNHAPPY about the outcome of the war and frustrated by the end of the fighting, Mary was only relieved to have her husband safely home again. She had not been at all well since her first miscarriage, and during the summer months she had suffered from occasional slight feverishness, and from her childhood ailment of sore eyes. But the main cause of her ill-health was certainly not physical. She missed William very much when he was away, she fretted about him constantly when he was on campaign, and she was tortured by fear when she knew he was likely to be engaged in battle. This painful anxiety, which she had experienced for the first time this summer, undermined her health; and in London her family worried about her. Her father, the Duke of York impatiently waited for news of her by each post: "The Holland letters are not yet come. I long very much for them, being in pain to know how my daughter does, having heard by the last letters that she had not been well", was a repeated theme of his letters.*

But Mary had another reason to be glad of William's return. Late in July she had begun to believe that she might be pregnant again, and her doctor Jacob Senaer had confirmed her hopes. After the disappointment of that spring, she still hardly dared to believe it, but on 9 August, in a letter almost incoherent with happiness, she had written to confide her hopes to Frances: 'I would hardly give me self leave to think on it, nor no body to spake of it nott so much as to my self . . .'' She had not yet told her stepmother the Duchess of York, she added, and she begged Frances: "for god sake if you love me dont tell it because I would nott have it known yett for all the world since it cannott be above 6 or 7 weeks att most and when ever you do heer of it by othere people never say I said anything of it to you. . . ."*

Understandably, after the publicity about her first miscarriage, Mary would have liked to have kept her hopes a secret until they were certainties. But inevitably the news leaked out, and in September Mary's

family heard it and planned a pleasant surprise for her. James wrote to
William from London to announce a visit: "We came hither last Wednesday, and are preparing to go to Newmarket at the beginning of next
week . . . whilst we shall be out of town the Duchess and my daughter
Anne intend to make your wife a visit very incognito, and have yet said
nothing of it to anybody here but His Majesty, whose leave they asked,
and will not till the post be gone."*

Mary Beatrice was particularly anxious to see her step-daughter now
that she was pregnant again. Her experiences in England had not
differed much from those of Mary in Holland, and besides, as she wrote,
"I love her as if she were my own daughter." She admitted also to a
little curiosity to see the Dutch country, and Anne was longing to see
this sister who had not even been married when they last met.* The Royal
ladies planned to travel incognito with "little company", and sent on a
courier, Robert White – so the Duke told William – to try and rent a
house for them as near the Court as possible. Their stay would be short,
only as long as the English Court stayed at Newmarket. The Duke ended
his letter with a solicitous warning for Mary: "I was very glad to see . . .
that my daughter continued so well and hope now that she will go out
her full time. I have written to her to be careful of herself, and she would
do well not to stand too much, for that is very ill for a young breeding
woman."*

The ladies arrived a week later in the company of the Duchesses of
Monmouth, Richmond and Buckingham, and the Countess of Ossory.
Ossory was to have escorted the party, but much to William's disappointment he had to go to Ireland on family business. William went out of his
way to make the visit a success, putting up the company in style at his
own expense and entertaining them lavishly. Not a rented house but his
palace at the Noordeinde in The Hague was specially fitted up for them,
and as both he and Mary were relaxed and happy at the prospect of the
child they believed she was expecting, the Duchess of York left highly
gratified by William's hospitality and delighted to have seen her favourite
step-daughter in such good health and spirits. James wrote to thank the
Prince on her behalf, and to assure him that his wife was "so satisfied
with her journey and with you as I never saw anybody; and I must give
you a thousand thanks from her and from myself for her kind usage by
you: I should say more on this subject, but I am very ill at compliments
and you care not for them."*

Ossory, returning from Ireland, heard glowing accounts of the trip,
and reported them to William, who answered: "You will easily be
persuaded how joyful I was to learn that Madame [Mary Beatrice] is

pleased with her journey. For my part, I was also pleased with her, which is very impertinent for me to say."*

Soon after this happy family party, however, Mary's hopes of a child were shattered once more. To husband and wife it was a bitter blow, made worse by rumours that she had never been pregnant, and that her hopes had been imagination from the start. The news was a great disappointment to the Dutch people: they were eager to see an heir to their beloved Prince of Orange, and they had come to love his English princess. Many of them had had a chance to see her for the first time early that summer, when she made a series of little tours through the country. Inevitably, she had chosen for these journeys Holland's most important means of transport, the *trekschuit* or passage-boat, a horse-drawn barge big enough to hold thirty or forty people. It was a slow but comfortable way to travel – never faster than three miles an hour – and as the boat slid along through Holland's flat green countryside, Mary and her ladies amused themselves by playing cards or working at their embroidery.

At home she had fixed hours during which she received company, and the Dutch ladies thronged to call on her in The Hague, or to make the trip out to Honselaersdijk. Droste described how she was reverently waited upon, the Dutch ladies standing even when they played cards with her. From time to time the Prince made an appearance, talking very freely with those present. At Honselaersdijck Mary, who had always been a great walker, strolled through the gardens talking pleasantly to her friends and to acquaintances.* She created in the Stadholder's Court an atmosphere of warm and graceful dignity. The Marquis d'Ausson, a French Huguenot, who saw her at this time, wrote: "Her manners, beautiful though they were, never failed to inspire respect."* The Princess of Orange, still only seventeen years old, was already a woman with style. She had great charm, she could be very merry company, and she was always a great chatterer, but nobody forgot her position. Burnet later made a vivid vignette of her "an open and native Sincerity, which appeared in genuine Characters, in a free and unconstrained manner . . . an air of what is Genuine that is soon seen . . . It looks Noble, without Strains or Art . . . a charming Behaviour, a genuine Sweetness, and the Sprightliness as well as the Freedom of good Humour."*

She knew how to be tactful. When once at a reception, a diplomat made his bow to her and his wig was left entangled in the chandelier, the Princess was the only one not to laugh. On another occasion, while she was dining in public, a little boy came running right up to her table.

The Court was embarrassed by this breach of protocol but Mary laughed heartily and allowed the child to stay with her for a while.

Stories like these went the rounds of the United Provinces and made her very popular. Even the Protestant pastors almost forgave her her love of plays and Sunday card-games, since the Stadholder's Court was one of the few in Europe at this time untouched by scandal. As the Marquis d'Ausson said later, "Her conduct has always been exemplary from start to finish."* Only the irrepressible Liselotte, the sister-in-law of Louis XIV, ever suggested otherwise. Years later, she gossiped in one of her many letters about the frequent visits that the French ambassador d'Avaux at one time paid to the Princess.* But these rumours were unknown to the Dutch – they only felt her sincerity and saw her piety. She was very anxious to set a good example, and when everybody flocked one Sunday to see a ship lying wrecked on the sands at Scheveningen, Mary pointedly did not go to see it herself until the next day.

All these good qualities might not have made quite as deep an impression if she had not also been a very attractive young woman. She had bloomed since her marriage: "she had a clear pale complexion, black hair, a high and open brow, large eyes that protruded slightly, a well-proportioned nose, cheeks a little too full low down, white teeth, a deep red mouth, a beautiful throat, a slender and shapely figure, and a deportment, an air and manners full of sweetness and majesty."*

She had been married for a year now, and in that year she had learned a great deal about the difficult, unpredictable husband she had come to love so devotedly. She knew that he had already made a life of his own, long before he married, composed of politics, battles, hunting and the company of his circle of close male friends; and she understood that in this life there was little place for her. Women, indeed, had never played an important part in William's life; he was unaccustomed to their company, finding male society vastly preferable, and his own Household, since the death of his mother, had always been exclusively male. Apart from an episode involving an innkeeper's daughter mentioned by Huygens in 1677, there had never been so much as a rumour that he was sexually involved with a woman up to the time of his marriage. He was typically a man who gave himself in his friendships rather than in his love affairs, and the impression he makes at this time of his life is of a man not very much interested in sex. All his capacity for passion and most of his energy was spent on the battlefield or in the chase. He would rush to Dieren for a short and furious spell of hunting as other men would go on a debauch, only coming home when he was exhausted, and going to bed almost immediately with the words *"j'ay sommeil"*.

Back at home, deprived of these outlets, he became short-tempered and irritable. His secretary Huygens reported these moods frequently in his journals: His Highness was *"un peu mélancolique"*, or he had *"une petite langueur"*. More pleasant moods are recorded with a note of surprise: "H. H. spoke to me with some sort of civility, more so than normally", followed a day later by another note of this unusual good temper: "H. H. still treated me with kindness."*

The Prince's manners were devoid of charm. "His behaviour was solemn and serious, seldom cheerful and but with a few", said Burnet. "He spoke little and very shortly and most commonly with a disgusting dryness, which was his character at all times."* Those he knew well were used to his rather brusque and offhand manner, concealing a real affection. They were used also to occasional displays of appalling temper – those fits of impatience of which the old Sir Constantyn Huygens had warned his tutor when William was still a young boy.

His health was not calculated to sweeten his temper. "He was always asthmatical and the dregs of smallpox falling on his lungs, he had a constant dry cough."* His body, "thin and weak", had the perpetual stoop of a man with weak lungs, and some of his contemporaries go so far as to describe him as being hunchbacked. When he was twenty-four years old Pieter Schenk, a doctor from Amsterdam, met the young Prince dressed in farmer's clothes. He told him he recognized him nevertheless and when the Prince asked him how the doctor answered tactlessly: "I know you by your hump."* The reaction of the Prince is not recorded.

But if his physique was not impressive, his power of endurance could be remarkable on occasion. Nobody saw him ever tired during battles and hunts, he could go without sleep for days on end and live as rough as any of his soldiers. During campaigns his personal comfort mattered very little to him. Not for him the silk tents and elaborate pavilions of the Sun King. He slept wherever was handy, in a farmhouse or a neighbouring castle, enjoying also very often the hospitality of nuns in the Spanish Netherlands.

Long spells cooped up in town, on the other hand, had a disastrous effect on his health. His asthma became worse, his cough more penetrating and his skin resumed its normal pallor. His great dark eyes, the most striking feature in his face, would then stand out again. "Bright and sparkling", Burnet calls them, others found them commanding. And indeed his whole face with its high brow and aquiline nose, like "a Roman eagle", conveyed an impression of great authority, which made people forget his lack of inches. His manner discouraged familiarity: "He had observed the errors of too much talking, more than those of too cold a silence", as Burnet put it.*

He was no courtier, and the English Household of his wife often got on his nerves – a fact he took no trouble at all to conceal. He was irritated by their chatter and their intrigues, so characteristic of Whitehall, and so unwelcome under his own roof; they in turn found him rude and boorish.

At first sight, Mary and he had very little in common, and it needed all her love and patience to build up some sort of life for them together. But she was intelligent enough to realize that if she could play no part in his ordinary working life, she could at least offer him an oasis of tranquillity in the midst of his preoccupations, a gentle and soothing companionship in his domestic life. She soon developed the same passionate interest as William in their palaces and the gardens, and if he did not share her taste for music – "he had no other relish for any other musick than the trumpet or drum"* – they both loved and appreciated fine paintings.

William has often been reproached with the fact that he did not patronize artists – only from 1682 onwards did he appoint Robert du Val as Court-painter and Curator of his collections – but he was an avid buyer of paintings, many of which were commissioned by him, and he always took a personal interest in the hanging and arrangement of his collection. Mary herself, in spite of her childish lack of promise, seems to have developed a pleasant amateur talent. Her portraits in miniature were much admired, as was her embroidery, but much later both of these became a strain on her weak eyes and eventually had to be given up.*

Alone together, Mary and William talked English. Although it was his mother's language, the Prince had a marked accent which he never lost. Mary herself tried loyally to learn Dutch, and if she never mastered it completely, she liked to use it. Years later she proudly told William of an official letter she had written in Dutch "with much ado", and in letters to her Dutch friends, she occasionally dropped in little phrases like *"ben ick nu niet soet?"* – "am I not sweet?"*

They both spoke French fluently, while William was able to converse reasonably easily in German and had a smattering of Italian and Spanish too, picked up in the course of his military campaigns. But in other respects his education had been perfunctory, and nobody would have described him as an intellectual. One day when he found his wife deep in study of the seventeenth-century divine Hooker, and the early Christian writer Eusebius, he laughed at her, hinting that she was too much under the influence of Dr. Richard Hooper, her chaplain, who had arrived at the beginning of 1678, and to whom William had taken an almost immediate dislike on account of his Anglican prejudices and his interfering ways. Hooper was a High Churchman with a strong prejudice against Dissenters and the tolerant Calvinism of the Dutch alike. He was shocked to find that Mary had no private chapel of her own for Anglican worship, and William was irritated when she meekly agreed with Hooper and allowed her dining-room to be converted into a chapel, dining henceforth in a dark and poky parlour.*

But although the Prince made no secret of his antipathy for the man, he came regularly every Sunday evening when he was at home to hear the sermon preached by Hooper – "one of the first rank of pulpit men in the nation".* And if he mocked at the Anglican trappings in Mary's chapel, kicking once at the Communion stool and asking rudely what was the use of that thing, he gave his wife complete freedom to worship as she thought right. He himself was no bigot. His belief in God was firm if tinged with a melancholy fatalism, and his piety was simple and strong. His faith was a source of deep inner strength to him, and it gave him the conviction to carry to the end of his days the burden he had taken up in 1672; the struggle against the hegemony of oppressive Catholic France.

It was a cause which, after the peace of Nijmegen, seemed hopelessly lost.

CHAPTER XIV

The English Rival

FOR THE TOLERANT DUTCH, as for William, the power of Roman Catholicism was embodied in their mighty and menacing neighbour Louis XIV. To the average Englishman, Roman Catholicism was something far less substantial and much more terrifying. Those two simple words conjured up nightmares of Jesuits and dark plots, of the Spanish Inquisition and bloody persecutions. Only in such a country, in such a mood, could the Oates conspiracy have had such a sensational impact.

It first exploded in the autumn of 1678, when two apparently reputable university doctors, Titus Oates and Israel Tonge, laid before Charles II and his Ministers the details of a plot "of some eminent Papists for the destruction of the King and introduction of Popery".* Oates was closely examined by the Privy Council, with the King listening attentively, and as a result of his charges several arrests were made. Among them was the Duke of York's personal secretary, a Catholic named Coleman. When his rooms were searched, a box of papers was found hidden which contained a correspondence with the Papal Nuncio highly damaging to James.

Oates had struck oil: all his wildest assertions of a Catholic plot to massacre Protestants were now believed, and hysteria gripped the country. For weeks London lived in a state of constant terror. The militia were called out, cannon were wheeled into position round Whitehall, guards were posted in the cellars of the Houses of Parliament, and hundreds of Catholics were arrested and thrown into prison, including some distinguished Catholic peers.

The Roman Catholics at Court did their best to keep up an appearance of calm. When the Queen's birthday came round on 15 November it was celebrated as usual, and Evelyn noted admiringly, "I never saw the Court more brave."* Charles had had to swallow accusations that his Catholic wife had tried to poison him, and all the Catholic servants of the Court had to be dismissed.

But the principal victim, of course, was the Duke of York. Even sober and intelligent men like Evelyn held him indirectly responsible for the present reign of terror: "the truth is, the Roman Catholics were exceedingly bold and busy everywhere, since the Duke forebore to go any longer to the chapel."* When a Parliamentary committee later examined James's letters, they found that "the Duke had written thrice to the Pope", the last time "to excuse his consenting to marry his eldest daughter to the Prince of Orange. . . ."*

The House of Lords asked that he should withdraw himself from the King's Counsels, which James now did. The House of Commons wanted him to withdraw from the Court altogether, "but some argued that to be dangerous, lest he might be persuaded to put himself at the head of the popish party."* Others wanted him banished from the country. And finally, at one point in the debate, an M.P. called William Sacheverell rose to make a more drastic suggestion: that by the decision of Parliament, James should be excluded from the succession to the throne.

Sacheverell was a member of the minority Opposition in the House of Commons, once known as the Country Party and now, under the fiery leadership of the Earl of Shaftesbury, beginning to be called Whigs. It was a party which represented the strong middle-class electorate, many of them Dissenters and Puritans, and all of them anti-Roman Catholic. The Whigs were strongly opposed to excessive Court influence, and mainly anti-French. Shaftesbury, a great believer in "what the stars foretell", was a brilliant leader whose influence over the mobs made Charles call him resentfully "the greatest whoremaster in England".

Shaftesbury's opponents in Parliament were the Court Party, much bigger and – by definition – enjoying almost a monopoly of power. Around this time they too were coming to have a new nickname – the Tories – and they were Anglican, Royalist and aristocratic by tradition. The forty-eight-year-old Danby, appointed by Charles as his Chief Minister in 1675, was their leader. He was a great administrator and a political manager of genius, who had been the prime mover of the Anglo-Dutch alliance and the instigator of the marriage of Mary to the Prince of Orange. Such was his love for power, nonetheless, that he had allowed himself to be persuaded by Charles, the previous spring, to negotiate the secret subsidy treaty with Louis XIV. It was his downfall: before the year was over Shaftesbury, exploiting the anti-Catholic hysteria created by the Oates plot, had him impeached by the House of Commons for treasonable dealings with France. Charles dissolved Parliament – which had sat since the Restoration in 1661 – in an attempt to save his Chief Minister. But the elections that followed produced a strong

Whig majority in the House of Commons, and Danby's reign was over.

Their strength in the new Parliament that assembled in March 1679 made the Whigs confident enough to insist on the banishment of the Duke of York, and this time Charles gave way. That same month, James and Mary Beatrice arrived in The Hague where the Prince greeted them hospitably, turning out his personal guards to do James royal honours and paying all their expenses. If they had not been travelling incognito, he told Ossory, he would have made even more fuss of them.* But in fact, at this particular juncture, they were embarrassing guests for him, and he was relieved when they moved on to Brussels a few days later, found a house there, and settled down to sit out James's exile.

It looked as though it might be lengthy. In May of that year, Shaftesbury and the Whigs boldly introduced the first Exclusion Bill, which laid down that if the King died without issue, the Crown was to pass to the next Protestant in line to the throne. At first sight, the Bill seemed wholly to William's advantage, since it made his wife next in line to the throne. But it soon became clear that the Whigs had other ideas.

William's connections with Danby and the good relations that still existed between him and the Court had discredited him in Whig eyes, and they were beginning to turn their attention to Charles's illegitimate son, the thirty-year-old Duke of Monmouth. From their point of view, this darling of the people would make the perfect puppet king.

From the moment Monmouth had arrived in England in 1662 as a thirteen-year-old boy, he had captured the hearts of the public. Charles himself was enchanted with this offspring of his liaison in exile with Lucy Walter, the daughter of an officer – this "new Adonis", as Gramont called him. Monmouth had the dark, sensitive, rather feminine good looks which many women find irresistible, and at an early age he became "the universal terror of husbands and lovers". Charles heaped honours and titles on him – Duke of Orkney, Duke of Monmouth, Knight of the Garter – gave him princely lodgings in Whitehall, cheerfully forgave him all his youthful scrapes, and in 1663 found him the richest heiress in three kingdoms for his wife – Lady Ann Scott, whose name he took. Monmouth was certainly spoiled, but he grew up a delightful young man and undeniably a brave one; in 1672 he commanded the 600 English troops for Louis XIV against the Dutch, and in 1678 he distinguished himself fighting on the Dutch side against the French at Mons.

Unluckily for him, Monmouth's dazzling personal charms were not matched by any great intelligence. A shrewd old courtier summed him up: "Most charming both as to his person and engaging behaviour, a fine courtier, but of a poor understanding as to cabinets and politics, and given wholly up to flatterers and knaves by consequence."* In short, he was the perfect tool for the unscrupulous Whigs, and with the help of the rabble they made the most of him in their war on James, spreading rumours of documentary evidence that Charles had in fact been married legally to Lucy Walter and that Monmouth was accordingly legitimate and therefore rightful heir to the Throne.

James, watching these Whig antics from Brussels with growing consternation and fury, wrote gloomily to William that "except his Majesty begins to behave himself as a king ought to do, not only I but himself and our whole family are gone."* His brother did not disappoint him: Charles had unexpectedly strong views on the issues at stake. He had already made a formal declaration in Council that he had never been married to any woman but the Queen, to defeat the pretensions of Monmouth, and he made it known that although "he would be content that something were enacted to pare the nails . . . of a popish successor . . . he would not suffer . . . the right line of succession of the Crown inter-rupted . . ."* After the Exclusion Bill had passed its second reading in the House of Commons in May, he at once prorogued Parliament and then dissolved it in July.

For the moment, the Crown had weathered the crisis, and two new advisers for Charles now emerged: Sir George Saville, Marquis of Halifax, and Robert Spencer, Earl of Sunderland. Halifax was a brilliantly intelligent man who had earned his nickname, The Trimmer, by his independence of party allegiance; Sunderland was an unscrupulous career-politician with a strong instinct for survival. For all their differences both men were united in one aim – to preserve the hereditary monarchy, threatened as it was by Shaftesbury's Exclusion policy and the Whig promotion of Monmouth. And to counterbalance this last threat, they determined to push the Prince of Orange forward into the limelight as an impeccable Protestant with strong legitimate claims to the throne.

One of their first acts was to persuade the King to send Henry Sidney, uncle of Sunderland, as envoy to the States of Holland. Charles agreed, and before his departure Sidney was carefully briefed by Sunder-land and Halifax. He was as much their envoy to William as Charles's to the States, and they spelled out his mission in detail for him. Sidney noted on 6 June that Sunderland and he had had a long conversation about the Prince, "and particularly that we thought it would be very good for him and every body else, for him to come over in October, and take his place at the [Privy] Council and in the House of Peers . . . we thought it would be a great strengthening to our party."*

Sunderland, who knew that the Duke of York would not sit back while his nephew stole his thunder, also discussed possible tactics for the Prince: "He thinks it necessary for him [William] to see the Duke before he comes over; but it must be a good while before, or else it will give great suspicion here. When he does see him, he is to persuade him either to turn protestant himself, or else not to take it ill of him if he falls into that interest, which is the only thing that can support him and his daughter. . . ."* William's excellent relations with his Catholic father-in-law, in other words, were to be played down, and it was decided at the same time that Mary should be kept in the background for the time being, and sever her contacts with the exiled Duke and Duchess of York.*

For this delicate mission, Sidney was a good choice. He was much liked by William, who had already met him in England; and as a man known to have voted for the Exclusion Bill, he was politically "clean". In addition, he had a personal grudge against the Duke of York, who thirteen years earlier had dismissed him from Court on suspicion of a liaison between him and James's first wife, Anne Hyde.

Sidney was a handsome and dissipated charmer and now, at the age of thirty-nine Burnet described him as "a man of sweet and caressing temper . . . no malice in his heart but too great a love of pleasure". A confirmed bachelor, he had "some adventures that became very public".* A later comment from Swift was less kind: "An idle, drunken, ignorant rake, without sense, truth or honour".*

He arrived on 16 July 1679 in Holland, and two weeks later went with the English envoy at The Hague, Sir Leoline Jenkins, to Dieren, where he met the Prince. In his diary he noted: "I found him in an ill house, but in a fine country; after he had talked awhile with the ambassador, he took me into his bed-chamber, where I staid above two hours." The Prince made no secret of his curiosity about Court gossip and political developments in London. "He asked me many questions, and I informed him of every thing, much to his satisfaction."*

On his return to The Hague, Sidney wrote back to London his impressions of the Prince, who "has more credit than ever he had, and by everybody that I speak to, I find he hath: I am sure he deserves it, for he had abundance of good qualities." But there could be no question of getting down to political matters as yet: "It will be a fortnight or three weeks before he comes hither, and till then he will spend most of his time a-hunting, and thinks little of business, but ever of his friends. . . ."*

William certainly had reasons for being preoccupied with his friends that summer. Anne Villiers, the wife of Bentinck, had fallen seriously ill at the same time as Bentinck's mother. His friend had left William to be with his own family, and as always anxious letters pursued him daily. "God grant that they are now better and that you may return as soon as possible. It is impossible to express to you with what grief I left you this morning and how much I was touched at seeing you in the state in which you were, and in what anxiety. I do not know how to live without you and if ever I have felt that I love you it is today." William's love for Bentinck was possessive: "I adjure you to return immediately Mme. your wife is out of danger." An offer to come down in person to Bentinck's house Sorghvliet – " as it is impossible to me to be any longer absent from you when you are in such distress" – three weeks later was rather coolly declined by a preoccupied Bentinck, who was able at last to report that his wife was out of danger.*

There were those in the Orange Household who felt that William might have spared more of his solicitude for his own wife. At his first visit to Dieren Sidney had written reassuringly to the Duke of York that he had found her looking "so well that I cannot believe she wants any remedies. . . ."* He had obviously seen her during a spell of good health and spirits, but for Mary such times began to be sadly rare that year. The damp climate of The Hague did not seem to agree with her, and since winter she had suffered frequent attacks of a tertian fever that left her shivering, aching and very much depressed in spirits; by Easter she had had nearly a dozen attacks, and even after a spell of rest and country air at Dieren she had not succeeded in shaking off the fever completely.

But as usual, the root cause of Mary's ill-health was psychological: her relations with William had deteriorated during the last long cold winter, and Mary Beatrice, visiting her briefly in March, had been shocked by the change in the Orange Household since their happy autumn visit. "No further hope of a child", Mary Beatrice had written indignantly off to Italy, "since she had passed the nine months since her pregnancy in great loneliness which strongly displeases us."*

Since Mary, loyallest of wives, would certainly never have made such confidences herself, her stepmother had clearly been listening to the tattle of the young woman's Household with all their prejudices against William. But only the evident unhappiness of Mary could have made such gossip credible, and the letters she wrote to her friend Frances Apsley over this winter and spring are a vivid and poignant expression of her sadness and sense of desertion. Though they are addressed to her former "dear husband" of fantasy, passages in them read like a plea addressed to her real husband, written by someone in a state of uncontrollable emotion.

The rather formal tone of the newly and happily married Mary of 1677 and early 1678 was exchanged for the incoherent and unpunctuated outbursts of a woman who feels she is no longer loved. "I do not now mourn a dead lover but a false one" are strong words to address to a friend who had not written for some time. Unable to communicate with her reserved and withdrawn husband, it is from Frances that she begs for attention and understanding.

> I waited day after day still wishing for a letter [,] thought every minit an hour . . . each hour an age butt finding att the last twas all in vain I in dispare satt down to ritt this letter hoping my just rage should make me say such thing as woud provoke to ritt something [that] shoud kill me quite that with my lattest breath I might bles the Author of my death . . . if I had butt on kind look from you I should dye happy. . . .

She ended this letter pathetically with an outcry: "I know I never can desarve your love nor never can love you halve so well as I shoud . . ."

The much older Frances seems to have sensed the desperation in this letter, probably written in the beginning of 1679, and to have replied with words of love and encouragement. At any rate on 28 March Mary, possibly also cheered by the short visit of her stepmother, wrote back much more calmly: "I resolved to put all mallancolly thought out my head that my joy may be the greater that I have this way left of telling you how much I love you. . . ." And in May, staying at Dieren for a short rest after another feverish attack, she had pulled herself together sufficiently to remember her earlier outpourings with some embarrassment: "I need nott desire you nott to show my letters for that I think you were allways kind enough to hide them. . ." *

Perhaps by this time William had learned to adapt himself to the inactivity of peace. Throughout that winter he had been a frustrated man with no campaigns to plan and a wife whose pregnancies turned out to be false alarms, who was constantly unwell, and whose emotional demands he found himself unable to meet. He urged her now to try the cure at Aix-la-Chapelle, and in mid-August he accompanied her from Dieren as far as Maastricht, seeing her go with a certain relief. From Maastricht he wrote to Ossory that she had just recovered from yet another attack of the same fever, and that he hoped it was the last. "For my part, I shall try to divert myself hunting, to recover my spirits from the mortification of seeing from my window so many Frenchmen lodged here."*

Mary stayed nearly a month at Aix-la-Chapelle, and apparently the waters were a success: she joined the Prince at the family castle of Breda on 10 September, and William was delighted to see how completely recovered she appeared; "a kind meeting" observed Sidney, who was present at their reunion.*

She found the Prince preoccupied with the political affairs of England. A few weeks earlier, Charles II had been taken suddenly and dangerously ill. The Duke of York, summoned by Sunderland, had hurried back incognito to England, but had found his resilient brother already half-way to recovery. Charles was now completely out of danger, and the panic and confusion into which his illness had plunged the nation were fast subsiding. But the crisis had brought vividly home to many people – and to no one more so than to the Prince of Orange – the confusion and uncertainty in which England's affairs were likely to continue until the succession question had been satisfactorily settled.

If Charles had died, it was plain, James would have been proclaimed immediately as rightful heir to the throne, and England would have a Roman Catholic king. But would he be allowed to reign uncontested? It seemed unlikely: Monmouth, heavily backed by the Whigs, was consolidating his popularity in England; the skill with which he had put down a Scottish rebellion, and the mercy he had afterwards shown, had made him the idol of two kingdoms.

To the Tories, at least, the threat seemed real enough and their envoy Sidney hurried again to Honselaersdijck early in September to convince the Prince of the need for action: he must pay a visit to England – and the sooner the better – to assert his own perfectly legitimate claims to the throne, and make himself better known to the people. The Prince was at first reluctant to believe that such a visit could do any good. But although he could not be convinced that the Duke of Monmouth would ever have the crown, Sidney gained the impression that he "would be very willing to be put into a way of having it himself".* And when they discussed the question of Exclusion, Sidney found that the Prince now favoured the idea and was prepared to give it his public support. He was also pleased with the suggestion which Sidney put forward: that on visiting England he should accept the title of Duke of Gloucester, join the Privy Council and take his seat in the House of Lords; although, as William pointed out, there was a difficulty to be got round – as a Dutchman, he could hardly swear allegiance to the King of England.*

William had hardly made up his mind to the journey when one of the reasons for it disappeared: Charles, taking advantage of the wave of new-found popularity that his recovery had stimulated, finally steeled himself to banish his favourite son, and Monmouth in person turned up at The Hague. "This change at the Court makes it unnecessary for me to go to England", William told Sidney.* In his relief at Charles's unexpected

display of firmness he could afford to be gracious. He gave Monmouth a
hearty welcome, offered him the use of a house in town, took him hunting
and begged him to consider Holland his home for the time being. He also
studied the young man with care – and summed him up as a lightweight,
whose threat to his own prospects could be dismissed. The young man's
lack of reserve and caution in his chatter astounded the Prince. Monmouth was full of his own popularity and his plans, which he talked
about freely to Sidney. William commented airily that if Monmouth
"thought of the crown, he could not be his friend in that, but in everything else he would".*

But if the threat of Monmouth could be discounted, it was now the
Duke of York who presented a real and imminent danger. William was
seriously worried by the growing influence his father-in-law seemed to
have over Charles, and when the King allowed James to return home –
though he was to be sent to Scotland – the Prince was obviously unhappy. A conversation he had with the Duke, who came to The Hague in
October to collect his family, did not change his mood for the better.
During this long talk James was outspoken in his attacks on the present
Parliament, expressing his view that the King would be better off with
no Parliament at all.* In that case, as William knew only too well,
Charles would be obliged to turn to Louis XIV for money, and French
influence over Charles's foreign policy would be paramount again, at
the worst possible moment. The French had recently offered the Dutch
a new treaty by which they undertook never to attack the Spanish
Netherlands again in exchange for a full political and economic association between France and the United Provinces. The proposal had been
warmly welcomed by William's traditional opponents, the Loevestein
republicans, and it was beginning to look as though Louis might succeed
in establishing his ascendancy over both England and the Republic
without striking a single blow.

When James, with Mary Beatrice, took his leave on 9 October,
accompanied as far as Maassluis by Mary and William, he left a highly
anxious Prince behind him. And a fortnight later William's worst fears
seemed confirmed when Sidney reported to him that Charles had prorogued Parliament. "He was much troubled", reported Sidney to
London, "and said we were all undone; that we could not expect the
States would take any better measure till they saw us better settled. . . .
He thinks we intend to fall in with France . . . and he has great reason to
suspect it. The Ambassador sent him word that there was money lately
going into England."* Every hope William had ever had of uniting England and the United Provinces in opposition to France seemed shattered.

But he was to be spared at least the personal humiliation of the Franco-Dutch Treaty. At the last minute the Dutch took fright when Louis XIV tactlessly alluded to the decisive trading advantages France hoped to reap by it. Sidney, who together with William had been working hard to persuade the Dutch of the treaty's disadvantages, made the most of Louis's indiscretion, and the French proposal was referred to the towns in January 1680; in other words it was pigeon-holed indefinitely.

For the first time the arrogance of the Sun King had played into the hands of the Prince of Orange. It was not to be the last time.

CHAPTER XV

The Exclusion Crisis

A FTER HER CURE AT AIX-LA-CHAPELLE, in the summer of 1679, the Princess of Orange seemed completely recovered, able to take up once more the supervision of the Orange Household. And that autumn and winter she welcomed with her usual charm and grace a continuous stream of guests, including Monmouth, the Yorks, and two aunts of William, the Princess of Anhalt and the Duchess of Zimmern, both sisters of his father. There were one or two balls, and at one of them the dancing went on till seven in the morning – hardly surprisingly, Mary looked very weary next day.*

But such revels were rare. The Stadholder's Court lived very simply most of the time, and by European Royal standards it was a modest enough establishment. Mary reigned over a Household staffed by thirteen noblemen, twenty-four Household officials, twenty-six footmen, twenty-two pages, thirty-two manservants, twenty-seven Swiss guards, three chambermaids and fifteen kitchen staff. Except on state occasions, when they dined together in public, she and the Prince dined separately, the Prince with Bentinck, Ouwerkerk and occasional guests, the Princess in her own apartments with Lady Inchiquin, her eight ladies-in-waiting, her chaplain and her steward Sir Gabriel Sylvius.

Such frivolities as there were in court circles at The Hague were confined to dinner-parties at the Bentincks and Odijks, card-playing evenings in the Princess's apartments, occasional tea-parties – tea was still an expensive new fashion – and late supper-parties from time to time. Sidney, used to the non-stop round of gaiety and pleasure at Whitehall, had been dreading a tedious winter, but he was pleasantly surprised by the warm and homely gatherings. And at times of great dullness Mary's English Maids of Honour often came to the rescue with invitations to supper for the celebrated Beau.

The Prince himself, it seemed, could never have enough of Sidney's company, continually inviting him to join the party at Soestdijk or

Honselaersdijck, and sometimes himself dropping in unexpectedly on the Envoy. "On Saturday", Sidney wrote to Sunderland, "he did me the honour to come and dine with me, where we had but an indifferent entertainment as you may imagine, for he let me know of his coming but an hour before; all yesterday he was a-hunting, and today he hath sent me a buck and some gibier, which he intends to eat at my house tomorrow."*

Sidney was exactly the kind of man William was most at his ease with – unaffected, straightforward, and perfectly charming – and Burnet wrote later that he earned from the Prince "the highest measure of his trust and fancy that any Englishman ever had". By the spring of 1680, the English envoy seemed almost one of the Orange Household. And it was to him that Sir William Temple wrote anxiously on 13 March: "Pray, when you write, say one word of the Prince's and Princess's health, just what you find them both; for you know I am much concerned in them, and hear very different reports, especially of the last. . . ."*

Mary was indeed very ill again. Before a week had passed the whole Household was alarmed, and dismayed enquiries after her flowed in daily to Honselaersdijck, where nobody could think of anything else. On 18 March Sidney noted in his diary, "We talked much of the Princess' illness, and her not being likely to live . . ." and next day he reported: "They brought me word that the Princess had had a very ill night, and was worse than she had been."* William was very anxious about her, sending almost daily reports to his father-in-law, who was then in Edinburgh, and not until 4 April, nearly two weeks later, could he at last write more encouraging news. James replied in great relief, "I was very glad to find . . . that my daughter was somewhat better, and hope by your next to heare that she mends a pace. . . ."* But it was at least a week before the Princess was recovered enough to be considered out of danger.

The illness of the Princess had intensified all the latent sympathy and pity which some members of her Household had long felt for her. They resented the Prince's brusque manner and his impatience with her bouts of ill-health; they sensed her unhappiness and felt that her husband neglected their beloved Princess. One of the Prince's most outspoken critics was Dr. Thomas Ken, who had succeeded Dr. Hooper as Mary's chaplain the previous year. Ken was "extremely devout and passionate, with little learning or judgment", wrote a contemporary of him unkindly, and William seems to have taken one of his instant dislikes to this saintly man, who returned it with interest.*

Now, at this moment, Ken determined to act with heroic zeal. "Dr

Ken was with me", noted Sidney on 31 March. "I find he is horribly unsatisfied with the Prince, and thinks that he is not kind to his wife; he resolved to speak with him, though he kicks him out of doors."* Sidney himself stayed well out of the affair, too loyal and tactful even to record his own views in his diary or in letters back to London. But he was one of those sympathetic people whose manner invites confidences, and a few days later he had to listen to more angry criticisms of the Prince's unkindness to Mary, when Ken came to see him again in the company of an equally indignant Sylvius. "Both complain of the Prince, especially of his usage to his wife, they think she is sensible of it, which doth contribute to her illness." They thought that she might recover more quickly if she were away from her unkind husband: "They are mightily for her going into England, but they think he will never give his consent."*

Whether the two men finally summoned up the considerable courage necessary to repeat these reproaches to the Prince's face, Sidney does not record. William was the last man to tolerate patiently such interference in his private affairs, and Mary herself, always the soul of discretion and loyalty whatever her personal feelings, would have been horrified by it. At any rate, the Household eventually settled down again after these upheavals, and perhaps William had been genuinely shaken by his wife's dangerous illness: no more complaints of his behaviour to Mary are recorded by Sidney, and Mary's letters to Frances Apsley in the summer and autumn that followed are those of a busy, cheerful woman.

For the next few months, in any case, the Prince had little leisure to spare for his domestic problems. He was deeply concerned by his country's isolation and lack of dependable allies in the event of another attack from France – a possibility that could not be ruled out; and there was little in the English political scene to give him any comfort. Monmouth was back in London, being made much of by the Whigs, and the foolish young man was deeply involved in conspiracies and cabals against the Court. Sidney discussed the situation with Sunderland on a brief return visit to London in June, and the two men agreed that the Prince might achieve much by a visit to London now, which would project him in the public eye as an acceptable alternative to Monmouth and James: William, they thought, "setting up for the Protestant religion, will have more followers than the Duke of Monmouth, who intends to play that game".*

But they found it as hard to convince the Prince as a year earlier. Soon after Sidney's return to Holland, he dined at Honselaersdijck and tried to talk William into it. But the Prince, who had clearly thought long and hard about the question, was not to be persuaded. He said that he could not imagine, reported Sidney, "what good he can do by it; that he hath no acquaintance nor no party; that for his own particular, he knows that if he should come over, and the King and the Parliament did not agree, he should be absolutely undone in this country."* Finally, since Charles II's health seemed excellent, William felt that there was no immediate urgency for the visit, and he asked that the whole question should be shelved until after a tour of the German principalities that he planned for the autumn, when he hoped to draw some of the German rulers into a new anti-French coalition.

He did not admit it to Sidney, but there was another reason why he was anxious to postpone the English visit for the time being. Prolonged inaction and anxiety had had their usual effect on him, and his health had been poor and shaky since the spring. At the beginning of August, after another spell of illness, he went off to Dieren where he hoped that a month of hare-hunting and freedom from business would restore him to his usual resilience and energy. But after only a few days there, he heard shattering news from England: "My Lord Ossory lies desperately ill of a malignant fever. I think he is rather better than he has been, but the physitians have very little hope of his recovery. . . ."* And shortly afterwards, news came of Ossory's death, and its causes. Fever alone had not killed him. The forty-one-year-old Ossory with his intense family loyalty to the Crown and his long record of devoted service to his country, had been overwhelmed by his nomination as Governor and General of the English forces in Tangier. The title sounded impressive, but the task given to Ossory was virtually a suicide mission – Charles had already made up his mind to abandon this untenable outpost, part of his wife's dowry – and Ossory was only sent to add a little lustre to the inevitable English withdrawal, and to shoulder public responsibility for it. He was not even to be given a competent force; nobody expected them to survive the Moorish onslaughts.

Evelyn, a great friend of his, had met Ossory in the Privy Gallery at Whitehall one July morning, on the eve of his departure, and had been shocked by the young man's state of mind. The indifference with which Charles seemed prepared to consign him to his fate, "certainly tooke so deepe roote in his mind, that he who was the most void of feare in the world (and assur'd me he would go to Tangier with 10 men if his Majesty commanded him) could not beare up against this unkindness." Later the same day, Ossory went with the King to a Livery banquet in the City, "but finding himselfe ill, tooke his leave immediately of His Majesty and came back to his lodging. . . . His disorder turn'd to a malignant fever, which increasing after all that six of the most able physicians could do, he became delirious, with intervals of sense, during which Dr. Lloyd . . . administer'd the holy sacrament. . . ."*

The death of "the universal darling of mankind" was deeply mourned by the English. "His Majesty never lost a worthier subject, nor father a better or more dutiful son; a loving, generous, good-natured and perfectly obliging friend . . ." wrote Evelyn sadly.*

For William the death of this man he had so much admired and loved was a deeply-felt shock, as his letter of condolence of Ossory's widow, Emilia van Beverwaert, makes plain in its moving simplicity:

> The loss you have suffered is so great that only God can give you consolation. I hope He will give you strength enough to endure such a mortal blow. For my part it has so deeply touched me that I can assure you that no man in the world so much shares your fitting grief. I have lost one of the greatest friends that I had in the world, whose memory will always be as dear to me as his person was . . .*

As always in times of grief or strain, William plunged into a violent spell of hunting, to distract his thoughts. Sidney who went to visit him at Dieren found a restless Prince who could hardly bear to stay in the same place. Between days spent hunting or shooting, he proposed a number of brief journeys, visiting the fortifications of Zutphen where Sidney's gallant ancestor Sir Philip – the Ossory of Elizabeth's reign – had lost his life, or travelling to try the sport at Hockfoors, in another part of the country.* Mary saw little of her husband that summer, and he had not been back with her at Honselaersdijck for very long before he was off again towards the end of September for the long-planned visit to the German States. He did not take her with him, but travelled with her as far as Soestdijk: she had chosen to spend the weeks of his absence there quietly, seeing almost no company and building up her health.

William had planned this German tour in the hope of drawing the Elector of Brandenburg, the Duke of Zell, and his brother the Duke of Hanover into an alliance against France, together with Spain and England. The last two countries had signed a Guarantee Treaty in June, but the States-General had refused, and if he succeeded now in persuading the German Princes to join forces, his own position vis-à-vis the pro-French Regents of Amsterdam would be considerably strengthened. From Soestdijk William went on to visit Lingen, one of the most depressed and under-developed territories among his possessions, where a few years earlier he had opened a Latin school. And on 22 September he arrived at Epdorf in Zell where he was warmly welcomed by Duke Georg Wilhelm of Brunswick-Lüneburg, his host for the next three weeks. William was still in poor health, suffering severely from the hemorrhoids that often plagued him and catching a bad cold. Towards the end of his stay he even had a fainting-fit at supper one evening.* He found Duke Georg's court highly agreeable, however, and flung himself with relief into the distractions it offered. He hunted, danced, and gambled away fortunes at basset in the company of his host with such zeal that Waldeck, who had accompanied him, grew more and more disapproving: the Prince, he grumbled to Huygens, was devoting himself "so much to amusement and the pleasure of hunting" that he would find it impossible to settle down to serious matters again. It reminded him, said Waldeck darkly, of the King of Sweden, who had become so completely debauched, "doing nothing but running to the brothels from dawn till dusk" that he never had a moment for business.*

The Prince, however, knew perfectly well what he was about, and when he left Epdorf on 15 October, he had made a friend of Duke Georg for life. From Zell, he went on to Brandenburg, where the old Elector, his uncle and former guardian Friedrich Wilhelm, waited for him outside the town. Escorted by six squadrons of cavalry, the two men drove to Potsdam, where the Elector had built himself a handsome new palace, for a two-day stay before moving on to Berlin. Here for the first time William met his cousin Friedrich, the Electoral Prince, not a very considerable man by contrast with his impressive father, even though the Elector was now an old man crippled with gout. William thought the second son Ludwig far more intelligent and promising, and told de Rébenac, the French ambassador in Berlin, that he looked on him almost as a son, hinting that if he himself remained childless, the boy might eventually be made his heir. William knew he could count on de Rébenac to pass on this interesting information to the Electorals. It was a hint that William had taken to dropping on occasion, in the hope of luring possible allies to his side, but this time he found it ineffectual. During political discussions with his uncle, the Prince soon realized that the pro-French influence of Electress Dorothea was as strong as ever, and that the Elector himself had vivid and bitter memories of how the Dutch had let him down in 1678.

From Berlin, the Prince travelled on through Magdeburg and Helmstadt to Hanover. In almost every large town on his route, a reception committee waited to greet the celebrated Stadholder, and William grew so bored with their long-winded speeches that eventually he instructed Huygens to reply on his behalf, while he himself disappeared.* At Wolfenbüttel, the eccentric Duke August entertained him to a dinner that – according to Huygens – was bad and indifferently served, while a chapel choir deafened the guests with their "great noise": William had much to endure in the cause of gaining German friends for his country.*

On 29 October, the Prince at last reached Hanover. Here he met again the Duchess Sophia, who fifteen years earlier had come to The Hague with her little niece Liselotte and attempted to make a match between her and William. Liselotte was now the wife of Louis XIV's brother, and Sophia herself was a stout middle-aged lady, but she was as entertaining and amusing as ever. She needed her sense of humour: her husband Duke Ernst August, brother of the Duke of Zell, was a bad-tempered and rather stupid man, who had taken as his mistress the wife of his first Minister, Count Platen. And he had also established what was later to become a Hanoverian tradition in England: he was hardly on speaking terms with his son.

The reception laid on for the Prince at Hanover far outshone those of Zell and Brandenburg. In the five days William spent at the Court of the Duke, there was hardly a moment without a ball, a comedy or, of course, a hunt. In one day the party boasted of having shot 145 wild boars. But from William's point of view, the visit could be counted a success in social terms alone. As in Berlin, the political conversations he had with the Duke and Count Platen proved unproductive. And another project of William's was a failure too. He had hoped to encourage the idea of a marriage between Mary's younger sister Anne and the Duke's second son, Georg Ludwig. He had earlier told Sidney that he believed the match would be an excellent thing for the Protestant cause in England, and he had worked hard at it ever since, sending Gabriel Sylvius over to Hanover as matchmaker.* He was well aware of how important the Platen influence was at the Duke's Court, and during this visit made the Count a present of £5000 and risked offending the Duchess Sophia by attending a supper organized by Countess Platen. It was all in vain. Sylvius later explained to Huygens that the Duke was unwilling to allow his children to marry "for fear of appearing old".*

One way and another, the Prince could not look back on his German tour with much satisfaction when he left Hanover on 4 November to rejoin Mary at Soestdijk.

Her weeks there had been very quiet. "I live heer ondly upon working walking and riding wch ar my chife & ondly devertions" she had written to Frances Apsley early in October, and she had time for more letters, writing to Frances's mother to compliment her on another daughter's giving birth to a son, as well as to Frances herself again.* In this second letter, she complained of Frances's constraint: "I have had such a grave ceremoniel letter from you", she wrote reproachfully, "that if anything woud make me dout of your love it woud be that . . . pray dear husban leave of your complyment & ritt to me with the same freedom we have ever used & I hope ever shall for I do love as much as I allways did & allways shall for no distance is capable of changing a heart so treu as mine . . ." She was just going to catch rabbits, she went on: "my whole time heer has been taken up since I am come with such sort of devertions for this place afords no other . . ."* Even for Mary with her love of a quiet life, Soestdijk without William had been dull, and she was glad to have his uninterrupted company for a week before they travelled back together to The Hague.

Almost immediately he was once more overwhelmed by the complications of English politics. Monmouth had returned to England at the beginning of the year, and in September – with the encouragement of the Whigs and in defiance of Charles's orders – he had made an almost Royal progress through some of the more restless parts of England, accompanied by a hundred armed and splendidly-equipped men. A deeply disturbed James had reported to his daughter how Monmouth had been received in Oxford: "the rabble cryed 'a Monmouth, no York, no Bishop, no Clergy, no University'."* But, however much Charles loved this young man, he refused absolutely to declare him his legitimate heir, telling Shaftesbury, the leader of the Monmouth faction: "I had rather see him hanged at Tyburn than I would confess him to be my heir."* And in October he had decided to teach him a lesson. Monmouth, in the middle of his Royal progress, was suddenly arrested at Stafford.

The arrest of Monmouth was by no means the end of the Duke of York's troubles. He had written to William in September, "from severall hands I am informed that those of the Lord Shaftesburys and D. of Monmouths party do positively intend to impeche me, so sone as the Parliament sitts."* The King shared this view – the Duke having "of late so exasperated the people that they can scarce heare his name with patience"* – and Charles could only save his brother from the Tower by a new banishment. James had no choice but to obey the King, and make the long journey to Scotland once more, portentously declaring to William: "I am afraid he will sone repent the measures he now takes, for I see nothing but ruine to himself and monarky by following them."*

A week later Parliament had met, and the Whigs had immediately introduced an Exclusion Bill: both Houses had been completely absorbed by the Exclusion debate ever since, and William's return to The Hague, early in November, had been impatiently awaited by Sunderland and Sidney. The latter arrived at The Hague two days later, and was almost immediately closeted with the Prince, giving him a detailed account of affairs in England and of the growing Monmouth movement. Sidney urged the Prince for the third time to come over to London himself in order to assert his strong claims and persuade Charles to accept Exclusion in his favour. But William again declined resolutely. He had supported earlier Exclusion proposals which merely struck out Roman Catholics from the Succession. The Whig ardour now for the second Bill, worded in deliberate vagueness to leave the way open for Monmouth, made him suspicious. In any case he thought it extremely unwise to be in London while the debate still continued; it might give the impression that he lent his personal support to Whig proceedings against the Duke of York, and in favour of Charles's bastard son.*

Sunderland was frantic at the Prince's refusal. His wife wrote passionately to her uncle, Henry Sidney: "If the Prince will not come, he must never think of anything here. . . . If there be nothing to fix on, 'tis certain the Duke of Monmouth must be the King; and if the Prince thinks it not worth going over a threshold for a kingdom, I know not why he should expect any body should for him."*

William, however, quietly celebrated his thirtieth birthday on 14 November in Holland with a ball at the Bentincks', waiting patiently for the result of the Exclusion debate in London. The Bill had been passed by the violently Whig House of Commons, and carried up in triumph to the Lords. It was Halifax who, with Charles listening anxiously, saved the day. Sooner than bow to the prospect of mob rule under Shaftesbury, he was prepared to accept a Roman Catholic king, and the Bill was defeated by his eloquence. Four days after William's birthday, the news reached Holland. The prospect of more unrest in England rocked the Amsterdam Stock Exchange, and the East India shares – always a barometer of public confidence – fell sharply. But the Prince himself heard the news with a certain relief; and he had at least the satisfaction of knowing that his decision not to be in London at the time had been the right one – he would have cut "a pretty figure".*

The news that followed caused him more concern. With the Exclusion Bill rejected, England faced the possibility of a Catholic monarch, and the Lords now began to discuss ways of limiting his prerogatives by legislation – a step that, as William at once grasped, presented an even greater threat to the power of the Crown than the Exclusion Bill. He sent off a letter of vigorous protest to Sir Leoline Jenkins: "I hope that his Majesty will not incline to suffer such a thing . . . it must not be imagined that, if they had once taken away from the Crown such considerable prerogatives as are talked of, they would ever return again."*

Van Leeuwen, William's envoy in London, found little support for these protests, but he had even more alarming news for the Prince: the number of Monmouth supporters seemed to be rising with every day of uncertainty. While at the beginning of the session, not more than ten M.P.s were openly behind the Duke, now – thanks to the generous distribution of French gold by ambassador Barillon – they were stronger than ever. The movement received fresh impetus when on 28 November Monmouth openly appeared again in the streets of London, shortly after James's departure for Scotland, to be greeted with frenzied enthusiasm by the mobs. His popularity seemed to have reached a new peak, and Jenkins wrote angrily to William: "The Duke of Monmouth was feasted yesterday . . . by the seafaring men in the skirts of this city. As [he] returned home he had the usuall acclamations from one end of the City to the other."*

Charles took the news calmly, although he admitted to Van Leeuwen that he was astonished that there were still rulers prepared to have dealings with such madmen as the English, but he believed that everything would end in good harmony.* Less optimistic observers, like the level-headed Halifax, were already talking openly of civil war.*

In the Republic, there was deep concern, and the States-General decided on a bold gesture. They drew up a Plea for Unity between King and Parliament, called the Insinuation, in which they pointed out to Charles II that measures such as the Exclusion Bill had been accepted by kings before, even if not acted on. Their meaning was plain: to prevent a civil war, and for the sake of Europe and Christendom, Charles would do well to accept Exclusion. The Plea was sent off to England, and immediately translated and widely distributed by Sunderland.

When Charles read it he exploded with rage at this interference in his domestic affairs. He accused the States, his envoy in Holland Sidney, the Prince of Orange and Sunderland, of attacking his prerogative; and many of the Dutch shared his understandable vexation. One States deputy remarked that the paper was "the imprudentest thing ever writ".* William, who had actually been closely involved in its drafting, now realized that he had gone too far, and sheltered behind Fagel, writing to the Duke of York that he was certainly not for Exclusion; what he wanted was a reconciliation and a compromise.*

CHAPTER XVI

A Wasted Journey

THE END OF 1680 found the Prince of Orange still balancing the pros and cons of a visit to England, and unable to make a decision. Should he wait for a declaration from Charles that in principle he would accept some measure of Exclusion? If he went, ought Mary to go too? Would Charles imagine that a visit at this time was part of a plot carefully concocted with Sunderland – or with Monmouth? Finally the pros won: he would go. He would take a small party of advisers and some of his officers with him; he would give a few dinners to the right people. If the longed-for peerage were offered to him, he would take the Test and Supremacy oaths, and some formula for avoiding the oath of Allegiance would no doubt be worked out too. Sidney was asked to apply to London for permission for him to come to England.*

It was too late. A few days afterwards, news came of yet another of Charles's unpredictable *tours de force*; he had dissolved Parliament and thrown out Sunderland, still at this time a staunch Williamite and Exclusionist. And the King made it known to William that with new elections coming, it was better to wait.

The new elections returned yet another strongly Whig House of Commons. At Charles's orders, and to everyone's astonishment, Parliament was assembled at Oxford – that staunchly Royalist city – on 21 March 1681. Here, at a safe distance from the pro-Monmouth mobs of London, the King suggested his own solution: James was to be banished, and after the death of Charles, Mary, or William, or both jointly, should be made Regent for the Duke's lifetime. The Whigs protested against this not very practical compromise, known to be the work of Halifax: they insisted on complete Exclusion. Charles briskly dissolved Parliament again. The comedy was finished. In his pocket was the promise of three years' supply from the French King. Once more, Louis XIV's intrigues had paid off handsomely. His erring ally was once again his remittance-man.

French diplomacy was busily at work in the United Provinces too. The French ambassador at The Hague, Jean Antoine de Mesmes, Comte d'Avaux, had been instructed when he took up his post in 1679 to cultivate the goodwill of the Regents, and especially of the Loevesteiners. The Prince of Orange and all his relations were to be ignored and even slighted, if the occasion presented itself. In his first objective, d'Avaux was completely successful. Groningen and Friesland, together with Amsterdam under Burgemeester Valkenier, were soon working smoothly with him in the hope of bettering trading relations with France, and perhaps clipping the Stadholder's wings at the same time. D'Avaux found his second instructions much harder to carry out. Versailles, as usual, misjudged the Prince, who was not a man to be put out by diplomatic pin-pricks – the Binnenhof was not Versailles – and d'Avaux persevering against his own better judgment, made himself the laughing-stock of The Hague on one occasion. He appeared in the Princess's drawing-room one December evening while everyone was playing basset. Mary rose to greet him with her usual charm, asked him if he wanted to play, and seated herself again. D'Avaux ostentatiously made no reply to her greeting, which caused a sensation in the room, then looked about, saw another great armchair in a corner, and pointedly went and sat in it. After a few minutes he rose and went to the table to play.

The Hague buzzed with his extraordinary behaviour next day, and all his friends begged the embarrassed Frenchman for an explanation. He explained "that he was not to be wondered at, for he had positive orders from his master, that, whenever the Princess sate in a great arm chair, he should do so too; and that, if there were but one in the room, he should endeavour to take it from the Princess and sit in it himself."*

The Prince of Orange, if anything, was amused by the incident. A scandal in his own Household, a little later, caused him far more concern. Jane Wroth, one of Mary's Maids of Honour and a flighty girl, had had a short-lived affair with William's cousin Zuylestein. For the Dutchman, it had been no more than a passing flirtation, and he was dismayed and horrified to learn, weeks later, that she was pregnant; the more so since negotiations were nearly complete for his marriage to a beautiful and wealthy young woman called Elizabeth Pompe. Jane had hidden her condition as long as possible, but inevitably some of the Maids of Honour had become suspicious, and their talk eventually reached the Princess's ears. Mary sent for her and cross-questioned her kindly, promising to help her, but Jane Wroth in a panic denied the whole story, and Mary, inexperienced as she was, believed her. Somehow or other, Jane managed to keep her condition hidden until the baby was almost due, when she turned to Mary's meddling old governess, Mrs. Langford, for help. All she wanted was lodgings where she could have the child in secret, but Mrs. Langford, who adored a scandal and a good gossip, pointed out that if she did so, Zuylestein would certainly never marry her, and soon afterwards the story was all over Court.

Mary's chaplain Dr. Ken now intervened. He got hold of Zuylestein, persuaded him into admitting his paternity, and worked on him so successfully that he was finally, very reluctantly, married to Jane Wroth just in the nick of time to save her honour, in the lying-in chamber itself.

Mary and William were away in Amsterdam, where they had gone to see the new Italian Opera, when all this happened. At their return, they were presented with a *fait accompli*, and William's rage was terrible. Zuylestein was one of his closest friends, and a member of the proud house of Nassau. Now his prospects of a brilliant marriage were destroyed just because some nobody of a Maid of Honour had not had the sense and decency to resist his advances when he chose to make eyes at her. The Prince's fury fell chiefly on Dr. Ken, through whose meddling the situation was now beyond retrieving, and he threatened the chaplain with dismissal.* Ken bravely stood his ground, pointed out that only the Princess could dismiss him, and then tendered his resignation to her. Eventually things were smoothed over, and Ken stayed. But it gave Mary's English Household another pretext for abusing the Prince behind his back, and it increased William's dislike and mistrust of his wife's servants. For a woman of Mary's loyalties it was a painful situation, and both husband and wife were glad to escape from it for a hunting trip to Hummeling in northern Germany in the spring. The invitation, this time for the Prince and Princess together, was from the Dukes of Zell and Hanover, and the party spent a week in the hunting lodge of Georg Wilhelm.

THE VISIT THAT THE PRINCE OF ORANGE at last paid to London in August 1681 was chiefly intended as a fence-mending operation: both Godolphin and Sidney had written to warn him how dangerously low his standing was at Court. Charles was still vexed by his nephew's ambiguous attitude on the Exclusion question, and infuriated by the Dutch Insinuation. William's obstinate insistence on appointing Sidney to the command of the English regiments in Holland as successor of Ossory, in the teeth of his uncles' expressed preference for a candidate of their own choosing, had given deep offence, as had his outspoken pro-

William at the age of four,
from a commemorative medal.

William's father, William II of Orange.

William's mother, Princess Mary Henrietta Stuart,
painted as a widow by B. van der Helst.

The birth of William III.

William as a boy of seven,
by Cornelius van Ceulen.

William at the time of his marriage.
A detail from the portrait
of 1677 by Sir Peter Lely.

William in old age.

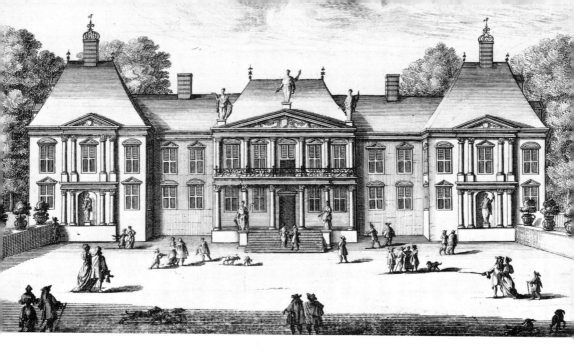

*The Palace of Honselaersdijck near The Hague where William
and Mary spent the first happy months of their marriage.*

*The dinner given in the Mauritshuis, The Hague,
by the States to Charles II in May 1660. Charles occupies
the place of honour, on his left his sister Mary,
on his right the 'Winter Queen'. Turning to look out
of the picture is the young Prince William of Orange.*

Charles II (1630–1685),
uncle to both William and Mary.

Catherine of Braganza (1638–1705),
Queen Consort of Charles II.

James II (1633–1701).

Anne Hyde (1637–1671),
first wife of James II and mother
of Mary, in about 1670.

Mary shortly after her marriage in 1677.

Mary as Diana in a Court masque, painted by Sir Peter Lely. She took part in the masque, watched by a shocked John Evelyn.

Mary as Queen.

Mary with a Negro page-boy.
In the background, the Palace at Honselaersdijck.

*William at the age of 26,
with his close friend and confidant
Hans Willem Bentinck.*

*Thomas Butler, Earl of Ossory (1634–1680),
William's faithful friend and staunch supporter
at the English court.*

Sir William Temple (1628–1699),
English Ambassador to Holland,
who took an almost paternal interest
in the young William.

Mary Beatrice of Modena (1658–1718),
second wife of James II,
in a boy's riding habit.

*James, Duke of Monmouth. His attempt
to oust William from the succession
ended in the defeat of Sedgemoor
and the Bloody Assize.*

*Frances Apsley,
the 'Aurelia' of an impassioned correspondence
with Queen Mary.*

Princess, later Queen, Anne (1665–1714),
and her son the Duke of Gloucester.

Johan de Witt, the Dutch Raadspensionary
whose long opposition to William's
appointment to the office of Stadholder
culminated in his own murder.

Sarah Jennings, Duchess of Marlborough,
whose intrigues caused the rift
between Anne and Mary.

Caspar Fagel, De Witt's successor
and William's right-hand man. He was a
fervent supporter of the Glorious Revolution.

Amalia van Solms as a widow.

Antonius Heinsius, the Raadspensionary who ruled Holland during William's long absences in England.

tests against the appointment of Bevil Skelton as new English ambassador to The Hague.

Godolphin urged restraint and submissiveness on the Prince: "That good understanding between the King and Your Highness, which is so necessary for you both, and which every day . . . I see more and more likely to decline . . . I am afraid will be quite lost at last, if your Highness will not please to make use of all your prudence and all your temper . . ."*

Sidney, whom Charles was too angry to see now on the Prince's account, sent his own warning from London: William was suspected at Court of close association with the extreme Whigs, and it was believed, he wrote "that you have a constant correspondence with those (they call) his enemies; that you drive a contrary interest . . . He [Halifax] and my Lord Hide do both complain of your letters being too high and too sharp, and say if you had writ in a more gentle style, it would have had a better effect with the King." Both men felt it was high time for the Prince to come over, wait on Charles, and "endeavour to set yourself right in his good opinion".*

William had also written to ask his old friend Sir William Temple for his views on the proposed visit. Temple, now living in happy retirement at Sheen and devoting himself to his great hobby of gardening, protested that he had been out of it all for too long for his views to be of any value. But he had known the Prince a great deal longer than Sidney, and he gave a guarded verdict. He could not, he said, see any prospects of agreement between uncle and nephew on the major issues that divided them; nor did he think there was much prospect of personal relations between them being improved by the meeting.*

Undeterred, the Prince nevertheless asked Charles for permission to come over, and the King reluctantly agreed, explaining to the French ambassador Barillon that he could hardly do otherwise, since a refusal would have been considered by everyone as confirmation of his secret understanding with France. On 25 July, William received his consent, travelled to The Hague, and asked the States in turn for their permission to go. He asked it not only for himself, but for the Princess too: her gentle charm might have done much to ease the situation. But when he sailed five days later, Mary stayed behind. It was at once said that she was pregnant again, and the rumours followed him to England. Five days after his arrival, a newsletter asserted confidently that "The Prince of Orange has acquainted his Majesty that the Princess is with child."*

After the Prince's arrival on 2 August at Margate, he went to Whitehall and straight on to Windsor to join the King and the Court. Almost immediately he had a long conversation with Charles about the Exclusion crisis, William urging that Parliament should be recalled. The King pointed out that the first act of the House of Commons would be to present a new Exclusion Bill, and asked his nephew point-blank for his views on the subject. William told him that he "abhorred" Exclusion and Limitations alike. In that case, the King asked drily, how did he propose to reconcile these contradictions? William, who had been leading up to this question, immediately replied that he "desired time to consider, and leave to speak to whom he pleased about it", which was given to him on the spot.*

Next day he went up to town where he stayed at Arlington House, magnificently entertained at the King's expense. Separately, he had long talks with the three men who might be considered as the party leaders of the time: Sunderland, Halifax who was now Charles's most trusted adviser, and the Whig Arthur Capel, Earl of Essex. These talks revealed to William the width of the breach between Charles and the Whigs, and the hopelessness of trying to bridge it. Indeed, the stubbornness of the Whigs on Exclusion made it pointless for Charles ever to summon a Parliament again. That he could afford not to do so for the time being was partly thanks to the subsidies from Louis XIV, but it was also because of a popular reaction in his favour after the violence of the Whig attacks and the terrifying spectre of civil war that they had raised. Charles had taken advantage of this reaction by having Shaftesbury arrested in July on a charge of treason: he was eventually acquitted, but his power had gone for good and he died in 1683, an exile in Holland.

In the intervals of his talks with English political leaders, the Prince of Orange was much courted in town. He was "treated very splendidly by the Duke of Albemarle", and on another evening went gambling and lost £3000 at basset, never a lucky game for him.* He was also invited to be the guest of honour of the Lord Mayor of London at a Guildhall banquet, an invitation he accepted with delight. Great preparations were made, but on the day itself, the Prince "received an Express from His Majesty to come presently to Windsor".* On former visits of the Prince, the City of London had been on excellent terms with Charles, but now they were notoriously Whig and had shown themselves fervent supporters of Monmouth. Their invitation was thus singularly interesting to William, but his acceptance of it was scarcely tactful in the circumstances. He received the King's message, however, with fury and embarrassment, pointing out that he had been the City's guest on both his previous visits, and announced defiantly; "He had promised and he would go."* Charles thereupon sent him a royal command to wait on him at Windsor, and this time the Prince dared not disobey, setting off reluctantly, while the Secretary of State, Laurence Hyde, carried his excuses to the Lord Mayor.

At dinner, his bad temper and disappointment were obvious to everyone. He even forgot his manners so far as to complain about the food at dinner, to which Edward Seymour hit back that the wine the Prince had served to them on a previous occasion had been very in-different too. William, who had brought this French wine with him from Holland, had had to pay heavy English import duties on it, and his temper was not improved by Seymour's comment. Charles was much amused. As he observed, the Prince "loved not to be convinced".*

Next day the entire incident was repeated. The Lord Mayor sent his two Sheriffs to invite the Prince again. William promised to come, and the King summoned him to Windsor once more; "whereupon his Highness sent his own Secretary to excuse it, and left the Lord Mayor under a very great Disappointment."*

One way and another, it was obvious that the visit had not been a success. William had, however, learned one thing of interest: Charles was sceptical of James's ability to keep the crown when he had it. "Whenever the Duke of York should come to reign, he would be so restless and violent that he could not hold it for four years to an end", the King told his nephew prophetically.* Reading the letters James sent him from a turbulent Scotland, William could only agree. Their blind despotic tone was alarming: "[The King] is not so absolut master as I could wish and as he aught to be, but still he is in a much better posture than he was some tyme since, and when the Parliament was sitting," wrote James in one letter.* In another, he stressed his conviction that the King was better off with no Parliament, adding: "I hope in a short tyme he will be as much master, as he was presently after his restoration."*

He strongly disapproved of his son-in-law's even talking to the Whig leaders – "the less you have to do with such kind of people is no doubt the better" – and as soon as he heard how unproductive these talks had been, he wrote with evident satisfaction: "I have been sorry to see you have been so ill informed of affairs in England, and by such misinforma-tion to have countenanced some people that will never be true friends to you nor none of our family. . . ."*

Before leaving England on 15 August, William made a last attempt to salvage something from this disastrous venture. Louis XIV was showing ominous signs of activity in the Spanish Netherlands, threaten-ing more Spanish fortresses and especially Luxembourg. Together with the Spanish ambassador in London, Don Pedro Ronquillo, he did his utmost to elicit a public promise of support from Charles against the French, at a specially called meeting of the Cabinet Council. But Charles refused to be drawn. All they could get out of him was that he would call a Parliament if and when France attacked the Spanish Netherlands.

With this vague promise, William had to be content. He paid a last call on Sunderland, who had been for eighteen months the brains, heart and head of the "Williamite" party in England, to thank him for his support and express his real regret at the Minister's fall from power – he had been dismissed by Charles for his Exclusionist views earlier that year.* Then, accompanied by Sidney as far as Harwich, he left for Holland.

In retrospect, he was obliged to admit that Temple had been his only good adviser. He regretted bitterly ever having embarked on such an unsatisfactory expedition. Two months earlier, Godolphin had still been able to write to him from England of "the love and esteem, and the natural inclination which people have for you here".* How much of this, he wondered, had survived his public humiliation by Charles in the incident of the Lord Mayor's dinner, which had, once more, given everybody the impression that he was completely under his uncle's thumb? At the Court, on the other hand, he had lost much of the good-will and credit of a year earlier by his consortings with Whig politicians with whom, nonetheless, he had found little common ground.

From now on, his relations with the English King were marked by an increasing coolness.

CHAPTER XVII

Conflict with Amsterdam

THE PRINCE OF ORANGE returned from an unsuccessful political mission in England to a domestic disappointment in Holland: after all, Mary was again not pregnant. It was one of the last occasions on which the possibility of her having a child was even rumoured. Two pregnancies of the young Princess had ended in miscarriages, and others had turned out to be phantom ones, like those of her unhappy ancestress Mary Tudor. In the Courts of Europe it was suggested that none of them had been genuine, and that sterility had been her father James's legacy to her. The indefatigable gossip Sophia of Hanover put the blame on William – he was obviously impotent – and she was not the only one to believe it.* A wild story circulated "heard from a Dutchman, a friend to the Prince and his family, that in his immature age, some considerable Persons took care, thro' the means of a Page, and an ill woman or two, that the Prince should not abound in Posterity to claim the Stadholdership."*

Mary did her best to make up to her husband for these recurring disappointments by being a gentle and undemanding wife. She saw very little of him during the daytime, but he almost always came to her apartments at nine in the evening for supper with her, when she made a point of never talking business with him. "I saw him so full of it that I thought, and he has told me so himself", she wrote later, "that when he could get from it he was glad to come to me and have his thoughts diverted by other discourse."* She realized that he preferred to be distracted "with pleasing Jests, that might revive him with innocent Mirth",* rather than answering her ignorant questions about his affairs.

In these early years, both she and her husband underestimated her political intelligence. As Burnet wrote later: "Her Humility and Modesty did really depress Her too much, in her own Eyes: and . . . she might too soon be made to think that the Reasons which were offered to Her by others, were better than her own."* It certainly never occurred to the Prince to talk over political questions with his young wife, even after his visit to England, when his relations with her father and her uncle were involved. He would not have expected her to grasp the complications of Charles's devious domestic and foreign policy.

The English King had given the Prince of Orange a vague promise of support if France should once more attack the Spanish Netherlands, but William knew only too well that all Charles's sympathies were with France, and that only Parliament could compel him to send active support to the Dutch. He had now reigned without one for six months, and intended to do so for the rest of his life; peace and quiet in Europe were therefore his first object, to be secured by whatever concessions to Louis's ambitions might be necessary.

The extent of these ambitions was becoming plainer every day. The French King had set up in 1679 a number of Chambres de Réunion, staffed by competent lawyers, with instructions to investigate all possible claims that the King of France or his relations might have on territories outside France. In the summer of 1681, the Chambre de Réunion at Metz had unearthed a French claim on the county of Chiny, part of the duchy of Luxembourg which belonged to the Spanish crown. It had been immediately occupied by the French who then blockaded the city of Luxembourg. A few weeks later, at the end of September, Louis briskly seized Strasbourg, with its commanding position on the Rhine.

William's alarmed indignation found no echo in the United Provinces; Strasbourg "was too far to be of any importance", thought the Dutch.* And Charles II seemed almost equally disinclined for action. He made the token gesture of instructing the English ambassador in Paris to protest jointly with the Dutch envoy against French acts of aggression, but when this mild reproof was brushed aside by Louis XIV, Charles was content to let matters slide for the moment. The States-General, however, had been sufficiently alarmed by the French moves in Luxembourg to send one of the Amsterdam Regents, Van Beuningen, to London to discuss a renewal of the Triple Alliance between themselves, England and Sweden. And the Prince of Orange himself now made a revolutionary proposal: all European countries, including France, should join in an Association with the aim of safeguarding all existing frontiers. This first attempt to realize the vision of a League of Nations conceived by the Stadholder of a tiny Republic created a sensation in Europe, and the French were seriously alarmed.

Louis described the Association as a personal insult, the more so since Charles II seemed genuinely attracted by this means of preserving the quiet of Europe so necessary to his own domestic calm, and began to use it as a lever at Versailles. Pressed by Van Beuningen, he gave his word that "he would recall Parliament and enter into the Treaty of Association if the [French] King did not raise the blockade of Luxembourg."* William made the most of this promise, publicizing it throughout the United Provinces, and the French ambassador at The Hague, D'Avaux, saw that William's brilliant diplomacy had succeeded not only in persuading the States to sign the Treaty of Association with Sweden, but also in immediately voting for an increase of 12,000 men in the Dutch army.

The idea of a League of Nations came to nothing in the end. D'Avaux successfully discouraged the Amsterdammers, and the plan was shelved in the States, while in England the French offered Charles an extra million to the subsidy of that year, sufficient for the King to lose his interest.*

It was now clear that the Prince's obstinacy alone stood between the French and their conquests, and it was hardly surprising that a French plot against his life was discovered at this time. According to stories that circulated in the Republic, William's box at the theatre in The Hague was to be blown up when he went to watch his group of French players. It was also said that some French dragoons, famous for their ruthlessness, had crossed the border to murder or kidnap the Prince. Some evidence of the plot was discovered and one French actor, Guillaume Marcouseau, found it wiser to flee back to his country. Another plotter, a French officer in the service of the States, La Garigue, was arrested but pardoned by the Prince. The news of the plot or plots reached London soon afterwards and Laurence Hyde, Charles's Secretary of State, wrote to the Prince: "We were all extremely surprised yesterday with the news from The Hague of a designe of seizing on your Highnesse and carrying you away; I know not what to make of it. . . ."*

THE YEAR 1682 OPENED DISASTROUSLY for the United Provinces. It rained continually all winter and "the greatest part of Zeeland was laid under water, several towns and villages with their inhabitants, were drowned." Another report told how the sea "breaking through the dykes . . . overflowed . . . villages, cattle . . . thousands of persons . . . the like has not been known in the memory of man."* The floods lasted for weeks and the Republic's losses were estimated even greater than those inflicted by the last war.

James, hearing about the personal financial losses of his son-in-law, offered his sympathy: "I never heard of so many dismal stories", he wrote on 11 February, "I am very sorry you had so great a share of the losse."*

William, preoccupied by the European situation, had no time to brood over more personal matters. For the last few months he had been battling in the States-General about the small army of 8000 men he wanted to send to the help of the Spanish in the Low Countries. D'Avaux's intrigues had been so successful that the Province of Holland, led by Amsterdam, persistently blocked him in the States-General, and the Prince now decided to attack the States of Holland directly.

During the early months of 1682 he forced them to debate the matter twenty times over, sending the deputies back to their towns to consult their councils afresh every time they failed to agree, but to no avail: Amsterdam, skilfully manipulated by d'Avaux, refused to give in. The Prince, frustrated to the point of fury, now turned his pent-up irritation on Charles II who, he felt, did not deal firmly enough with Versailles. "All our troubles come from England, which has accepted its own subjection, and will be the cause of all Europe's", he burst out to the new English ambassador, Thomas Chudleigh, who arrived in February at The Hague.* Chudleigh's appointment had been a fresh grievance in the circumstances. He was described by d'Avaux as "a man of small wit, ill-bred and unreliable",* and William, who thought nothing of him, did not bother to pick his words in discussion with him, describing the King's behaviour as "insupportable" and "inexcusable", words which, reported immediately to Charles, gave great offence. Halifax, who saw his efforts to deflect Charles's French sympathies threatened by William's plain speaking, begged him to be more guarded: "I am sure you will forgive me, if I move your Highness . . . to take some paines . . . to excuse anything that might bear an unkind interpretation."*

William's uncompromising attitude, however, achieved its object. When the Spanish, in secret concert with him, threatened to break off trading relations with England if the King refused the help promised by the Anglo-Spanish Treaty of 1680, the pressure was too much for Charles. And it was probably partly due to his representations at Versailles that in March 1682, Louis climbed down. The French blockade of Luxembourg was raised, and the Sun King piously explained that since Christendom was menaced by the Turks massing at the gates of Vienna, he would no longer insist on France's claims by force of arms, but submit them to arbitration by England.

"It is generally believed that the vigorous attitude of the Dutch had more to do with it than the Great Turk", commented William drily.* Charles was equally eager to claim the credit, and Halifax wrote to William in April: "Since the King hath had such a part in bringing this about, he deserveth all imaginable encouragements from his allies."*

On the surface, the Sun King was taking his diplomatic defeat gracefully, and if his military glory seemed dimmed for the moment, he could dazzle in other ways. In May 1682 Louis XIV – since 1680 styled "The Great" – took formal possession of Europe's most impressive palace. On the sixth of that month, Versailles officially became the seat of the monarchy and the government of France. Tens of thousands of workmen had been labouring on it for years, and it was still more of a building site than a palace. But inside it looked all splendour, even if it was so draughty and cold that in winter the huge fires filled the rooms more with smoke than heat, and the wine froze on the Royal table.*

This display of magnificence was not enough to soothe Louis's injured pride, and he decided that it was time for the public humiliation of his presumptuous little Dutch opponent. On 14 August he sent the Marquis de Montanegre, with a French army, to seize possession of the principality of Orange. The Marquis had orders to demolish the fortifications that had been rebuilt when Orange was restored to its Prince after the Peace of Nijmegen in 1678. This affront was "legalized" by the Chambre de Réunion at Metz, which stated that the title to Orange was in fact vested in the Abbot of Orléans, a descendant of the family of Châlons to whom the principality had once belonged.*

The Prince who, a year earlier, had lost two of his domains, Viande and St. Vith, when the French occupied Chiny, learned of the new occupation of Orange on 2 September during a hunting holiday at Hooge Soeren. "*Hé bien, messieurs, les Français m'accommodent bien*" he exclaimed at the dinner-table, and talked of nothing else during the meal. His friends had never seen him so angry. He repeated four or five times that "he was obliged to be patient until he was in a position to take his revenge, and that he hoped not to die before he had the means of doing so."* Solemnly he swore that he would one day make the Most Christian King feel what it was to have exasperated a Prince of Orange.*

His furious outburst was soon common knowledge in The Hague, and d'Avaux asked him to disavow his threats against Louis. William refused point-blank. From that time onwards, D'Avaux was *persona non grata* at William's court, and the Princess's drawing-room saw him no more.* Louis knew how to repay an insult. When William was summoned to appear before a French council to defend his claim to Orange, the summons was addressed to "*Messire Guillaume, Comte de Nassau, demeurant à la Haye en Hollande*".*

William appealed to his uncle in England, but the King had not forgiven him the pressure he had brought to bear on Whitehall in the Luxembourg question, and he hardly bothered to hide his glee and indifference. Lord Preston, the English ambassador in Paris, made a half-hearted protest, but readily accepted the French explanation that it was "a private business and that it doth in no way regard the affairs of Europe".* Exasperated by Charles's negative attitude, the Prince made no effort to hide his resentment, and when Lord Cornbury, son of Rochester and nephew to James, came to visit him in October, he was received with freezing hostility. During an official dinner the Prince had to give for him, William did not address a single word to this amiable young man who sat next to him, and who was so distressed by his treatment that he was almost in tears when the dinner ended.*

Until March 1683 the Prince waited to see if Charles would make a move in the question of Orange. Finally, the King made a vague promise of diplomatic support, and Antonius Heinsius, Pensionary of Delft, was sent to Paris to argue the matter.* He had been picked by the unenthusiastic States-General for his brilliant legal abilities, they claimed, but it was also because, as a leading Holland man, the young Heinsius belonged to the anti-Orange clan and was unlikely to embarrass Holland by pressing William's claims too strongly. In Paris, as it turned out, no English help was forthcoming, and in the end Heinsius made his protest alone, reminding Louis "that the Prince was absolute master in his state, and that no one could rightfully pull down the walls of the capital of his principality".*

The protest fell on deaf ears, and much later that year Preston reported to London: "Monsieur Heinsius, finding that he can obtain nothing in this court in the affair of Orange, did on Tuesday last demand his audience of congé."* If Heinsius had failed in his mission, however, it had at least one consequence of enormous importance for William. The Pensionary was so much alarmed by what he had seen and heard of French expansionist ambition that he returned a resolute Williamite, to the horror of d'Avaux.

Charles could afford to be apathetic in the Orange question: by the spring of 1683 he was almost immune to political pressures from William, since his once-powerful opponents, the Whigs, were now virtually silenced. England had swung decisively to the right, and almost every political stronghold in the nation – even the City of London – was now in Tory hands. By the beginning of 1683 Charles's ministry was solidly Tory too, led by Sunderland who had now returned to his old French allegiance. And in March the demoralized Whigs suffered the final blow: the discovery of a plot to assassinate Charles and James on their way back to London from Newmarket. Three distinguished Whig leaders, Lord Russell, the Earl of Essex and Algernon Sidney, were arrested.

They all disclaimed knowledge of the murder plans, but there was just enough evidence against them of involvement in the Rye House plot to have them executed, a fate that Essex escaped by cutting his throat.

The Prince of Orange sent a letter to his uncles politely congratulating them on their escape, but in the Republic it was well known that he was sceptical of the threat to his uncles' lives. He told confidants that "this plot was no more than a thing contrived to destroy the most honest people in England",* so that Charles could ally himself with France. His scepticism was based on a letter he had received on 2 March from Charles who, with all the confidence of his growing political strength, had tried to persuade his nephew to give in to French claims in the Spanish Netherlands, pointing out that with the Emperor entirely preoccupied with the Turks on his eastern frontiers, there was little to stop the French King helping himself to what he wanted.* William took his time to reply. When at last he did so, he summed up in the course of a passionate but somewhat confused letter the principles on which his life-long opposition to France was based. "Experience, and the lamentable sequel to the Peace of Nijmegen, have made it clear that to come to terms with an overwhelming Power, without those who have reason to fear it putting themselves in a condition to counter it by sound alliances among themselves, is no more than a deceitful appearance of peace and quiet."*

Shortly before he wrote, Charles had announced a match between Mary's sister Anne and Prince George of Denmark, younger brother of the Danish King Christian V. And in his letter, William did not hide his resentment at the proposed marriage. As a king's son George would have precedence over William; as a Protestant, he would have a rival claim to popularity in England; and as a Dane, he was France's ally. His choice was all the more offensive to William since the suitable match he himself had proposed – with Prince Georg of Hanover – had fallen through, thus destroying his hope of tying England to Hanover, a reliable Protestant ally of his own. Instead, the marriage concluded on 28 July 1683 appeared a pro-French match, made – it was said – "no nearer to heaven than Versailles".*

As it turned out, there was no need for William to fear his new brother-in-law as a potential rival. The description Evelyn gave of the young Dane was one of the kindest – "of few words . . . somewhat heavy, but reported to be valiant".* Charles put it more tersely: "I have tried him drunk and I have tried him sober, and drunk or sober there is nothing in him." And George himself wrote a little later, to a friend, "We talk here of going to tea, of going to Winchester, and everything

else except sitting still all summer, which was the height of my ambition";
and he sighed, "God send me a quiet life somewhere."*

If William had been in England himself for the wedding, he would
have sized George up at once: but Charles had refused him permission to
come, and instead he sent Bentinck over with a compliment, while he
himself snatched at the chance of a break at Dieren with Mary. His letters
followed Bentinck to England, full of news and requests. The gardens at
Dieren were looking splendid. "Everything had grown exceedingly well,
but little fruit . . . the melons spoiled by the rain which has been heavier
here than in Holland."* He planned a surprise for the Princess – a ring
set with a lock of her own dark hair, made by the Court jeweller Loofs,
and he warned Bentinck: "Do not tell the Princess that I have written
to you nor about the ring."* In another letter he asked Bentinck to buy
him a good hunter – a commission given to almost all his friends when
they went to England – and also, if possible, a nice steady mount for
Mary.'*

From the peace of Dieren, he was able to write almost casually about
the siege which, on 13 July, the Turks had laid to Vienna, throwing all
Europe into panic: "the alarm which the ill turn of events in Hungary has
given us has much abated, since the whole business is not as bad as we
believed" referring rather sneeringly to the 3000 Tartars of whom so
much fuss had been made.*

But Vienna's preoccupation with these Tartars had consequences that
he did not foresee: Louis took advantage of it in September to send troops
to Flanders and blockade Luxembourg again. As usual, the French King
had picked his moment brilliantly. Since the Rye House plot had broken
the Whigs, he knew he could count on Charles's support. Besides,
September was generally recognized as the end of the campaigning
season. Louis's activity was the more surprising since the French Court
was still in mourning after the death of his Queen Maria Theresa on 30
July.

The Spanish declared war, and called on Charles to come to the
rescue. The English King's only reaction was a suggestion that they
should raze the fortifications of Luxembourg and simply hand it over.
"'Tis what they [the Spanish] might have long expected", James wrote to
William, "and I believe it had happened sooner had not the King inter-
posed; and if where you are, people had been of this mind . . . this
invasion had not been, and all christendom had been in peace."*

His illusions were shared by Amsterdam, and when the new Governor of the Spanish Netherlands, the energetic Count de Grana, asked for
the 8000 troops that the Dutch were bound by treaty to supply, Amster-

dam refused. Fagel interfered and sent the troops off after an uncon-
stitutional majority vote in the States-General. The Stadholder proposed
immediately that a further 8000 men should be raised. Amsterdam
rejected the suggestion: it was the start of a new phase in the long and
bitter struggle for mastery in the Republic.

The Regents of Amsterdam had for years been convinced that the
so-called "Barrier" of the Spanish Netherlands between the Dutch and
France, on the importance of which the Stadholder so strongly insisted,
simply created an unrest and uneasiness out of which "the Prince of
Orange would always extract some advantage". In their view, "it would
be much more useful for the States to live in peace and to be neighbours
of His Majesty without defiance or alarm; to make commerce flourish and
to enjoy their freedom than to ruin themselves keeping up armies which
were useless to them, and which might serve the Prince of Orange as a
means for subjecting them. . . ."* These pacific fantasies were encouraged
to the utmost by d'Avaux, who was on excellent terms with Amsterdam's leaders; and William found himself in constant conflict with what
was virtually a fifth column of France in his own country.

His passionate anger at Amsterdam's latest refusal to co-operate
vented itself on one of the city's Burgemeesters, Van Beuningen. The
eccentric Regent, sent to London in 1681 to negotiate the anti-French
Triple Alliance, had fallen under the spell of Charles's complaisant
attitude towards Louis, and at William's insistence he had been recalled
in February 1683. He was now one of the most outspoken of the Prince's
critics in Amsterdam, and William told friends that he deserved to have
his head thrown in front of his feet. He was determined never to give in
to *"ces coquins d'Amsterdam* – or my name is no longer William".*

D'Avaux, in the comforting knowledge of Amsterdam support,
presented France's ultimatum to the States-General in November. Spain
must either give up Luxembourg or hand over a number of important
towns including Beaumont, Courtrai and Dixmude. The States of
Holland promptly voted in favour, telling the Prince that "commerce
being the pillar of the state", they wanted to be able to get on with it in
peace. William retorted that "he agreed that it was necessary to think of
preserving trade, but not to do it in such a way that one ruined the rest of
the country."* Amsterdam, unconvinced, obstinately voted against the
expansion of the Dutch armies, and the motion was lost.

As a last resort, the Stadholder decided to exert personal pressure on
the stubborn Amsterdammers. On 15 November, taking with him a
deputation of twenty-two men, he rode into Amsterdam where he settled
down for a six-day stay at the city's expense, and a series of consultations

with the Regents followed. The gulf was too wide to be bridged. At a
final confrontation, one of the Burgemeesters summed up their relentless
opposition to the Prince's power: "even if the City of Amsterdam had had
the intention of changing its mind it would not do so, in order to leave
one instance to posterity, when not all the efforts of the Prince of Orange,
nor even his own presence, had succeeded in changing the free resolution
of the Council of the City of Amsterdam."* The Prince walked out
seething with fury. Refusing to be present at the splendid dinner they had
prepared for him, he had his horses saddled at once and left without
another word.

Amsterdam itself was a little dazed by its own courage in opposing
the Stadholder, having vivid memories of the tactics employed by
William's father in 1650. Guards were posted on the walls, the guards on
the gates were tripled and given firearms, and 600 men were employed to
break the ice and keep the canals open. Van Beuningen took to moving
around the city with a strong bodyguard,† and alarm turned to panic
when it was rumoured that the Stadholder was about to bombard the
town and had already stationed 5000 men in nearby Naarden. But
William had not forgotten 1650 either, and remembering his father's
defeat when he attempted force on Amsterdam, decided to try other
tactics. Well aware of the close understanding between the Regents and
d'Avaux, he had the envoy's courier stopped and relieved of his papers
on 9 January 1684. Among them was a letter of d'Avaux to Louis
XIV which, when decoded, revealed the names of two co-operative
Regents and the extent to which these two "well-intentioned" were
prepared to acquiesce in French plans. At a session of the States-General,
William dramatically produced the letter and the two deputies fled back
to Amsterdam.

The results were all that he hoped. Crowds gathered in the streets
shouting that Amsterdam had sold their country to France and that the
Regents ought to be treated as the De Witts had been. But before
William could take advantage of this change in public feeling, Louis XIV
again seized the initiative. On 17 February, just as his armies moved
forward to besiege Luxembourg, he dangled a glittering offer before the
eyes of the Dutch, the English and the Brandenburgers: a Twenty Years'
Truce. William protested that the offer was merely a trap, designed to lull
the Republic into a false sense of security so that the French could repeat
their tactics of 1672 at their leisure – "then it will become clear whose

† The resentment of the Prince of Orange pursued Van Beuningen for the rest of his life
and together with the loss of his fortune eventually unhinged his mind. He died in a private
asylum.

head is more firmly placed on his shoulders, and who has done his duty or not."*

All his eloquence was in vain. On 4 June 1684 Luxembourg capitulated, and twenty-five days later the Republic signed the Treaty of Ratisbon with France. Spain, now completely isolated, followed on 20 August, handing over Luxembourg, while the Emperor, signing the same day, sacrificed Strasbourg to the French. For the Prince of Orange, it was perhaps the greatest diplomatic defeat of his career. "If God does not take upon himself the protection of this poor people and her neighbours", he warned, "in a short time all will be over."* And with the prediction that "France will take more in peacetime than she did by war", he retired to Dieren to find what distraction he could on the hunting-field, leaving Louis XIV – for the moment at least – to pursue his dream of a "Fifth Universal Monarchy".*

CHAPTER XVIII

The Fall of Monmouth

THE PRINCE OF ORANGE had hardly arrived at Dieren when the Duke of Monmouth appeared unexpectedly. The young man had been deeply implicated in the Rye House Plot the previous year, and had only escaped trial by going into hiding. At a secret interview with his father, Monmouth had denied all knowledge of the murder plot – "I wish I may die this moment if it ever entered in my head", he protested* – and he had readily signed the paper Charles laid before him, promising never again to be guilty of similar indiscretions, only to retract it on the day of Sidney's execution. Even Charles with all his indulgence for this adored and wayward son could not overlook his offences this time, and Monmouth had been banished, going first to Brussels. Now he had made his way to The Hague, following in the footsteps of a stream of English refugees, and the Prince of Orange at once made him a warmly welcome guest.

William had always liked this agreeable young charmer, and although he was unable to take his ambitious designs on the English throne very seriously, Monmouth was still a potential rival and while he was under the Prince's own roof, he could keep an eye on him. It was possible, too, that Charles might be appeased and gratified by kindness paid to his son which he himself could not now afford to show.

But when Monmouth's whereabouts became known, the first letters arriving from the English Court were of furious protest. James was particularly indignant. He had got into the habit of slipping little political sermons into his letters to his daughter Mary and now he wrote: "It scandalises all loyal and monarchical people here, to know how well the Prince lives with, and how civil he is to the Duke of Monmouth . . . and in this affair methinks you might talk with the Prince (though you meddle in no others) . . ."*

According to d'Avaux, Mary burst into tears on reading this angry letter. She exclaimed that she was not mistress of her own conduct and that since the Prince had ordered her to be civil to the Duke of Monmouth, she must obey him.* But d'Avaux's spies in the Orange household were apt to tell him stories that he wanted to hear.

Soon afterwards, it was Charles's turn to protest. He sent instructions to the English envoy Chudleigh, who called on the Prince at the beginning of July. William sent an account of their conversation to Bentinck: "Mr. Chudleigh came to tell me that he had an order from the King to inform me that his Majesty took ill my having seen the Duke of Monmouth . . . in a manner so insolent . . . that if I had not had consideration for his character, I would not have suffered it as I did."* Relations between Chudleigh and the Prince had been icy for some time, and William protested strongly to Whitehall about the envoy's impertinence. Chudleigh was recalled for discussions about the incident, but when he returned to The Hague, it was with instructions to break off relations with the Prince altogether.*

The Prince was uncertain whether to take these demonstrations of Charles's displeasure at their face value. On his last visit to England, the King had told him that letters not sealed with his personal signet were intended chiefly for public consumption only, and none of his letters of protest about Monmouth had carried this seal. William ignored them, and Monmouth remained at Dieren as his honoured guest. There was another consideration. By entertaining Monmouth in the teeth of his uncles' displeasure, William made it clear to the world that he was not to be dictated to by them, since they had done nothing for him over the last few years.

By their trafficking with France they had sold Europe down the river, and in personal terms they had let their nephew down. They had refused to stand by him in the Orange question, they had never paid Mary's dowry, they had consistently tried to bully him into supporting their point of view, and by their withdrawal of public support over the last few months, they had dangerously weakened his position in the Republic. He had no reason to be grateful to them, and no cause to respect their wishes.

Charles and James were perfectly aware of the hardening in William's attitude, and James wrote in hurt reproach at the beginning of October:

> You may be sure that I shall do my part in what concerns you, but it is necessary you do yours to satisfy the King; and pray consider, whether he had any reason to be satisfied with several things you have done for some time past. I could say more to you upon this subject, but am not encouraged to do it, since I have found that you have had so little consideration for

things I have said to you, which I thought of concern to our family, though you did not.*

The French ambassador delightedly reported to Versailles this rift in the English Royal family: "The Duke of York remains of the opinion that the Prince of Orange and the Duke of Monmouth flatter themselves with the hope of being able to bring about a rising in one of the three kingdoms."* Charles himself was too shrewd to swallow such an unlikely tale, but when the Dutch ambassador in London, Van Citters, desperately tried to convince him of the Prince's good intentions in this affair, the King told him cynically that it was too much to expect of him: "as if a man going into a brothel should ask me to believe and accept the excuse that he had done no wrong because he had only gone in to convert people."* And Charles remained "as dissatisfied as ever with the conduct of William of Orange". William, even though Monmouth had returned to Brussels two months earlier, refused to climb down. On 9 January 1685, he wrote to Van Citters: "I shall never make any difficulty over making every submission to the King which he shall ask for, or over asking his pardon for any offence which he may have taken; but to admit guilt when I am sure I have not acted badly, is a thing that cannot be asked of me or of any honourable man, and something to which I shall never be brought."*

The letter was barely written when Monmouth reappeared unannounced and uninvited at The Hague late at night. He was immediately received by the Prince, who had a long conversation with him. Monmouth told him that he had been to England on a secret visit, and had had a meeting with Charles at the beginning of December. The King, William learned, had been unable to hide his pleasure at seeing his favourite son again, and had pressed his hand warmly; even the Duke of York had given him a grudging welcome. He had left again with a promise that he would be allowed to return in February. Monmouth thought that the King was now convinced of his innocence in the Rye House plot, and as his rather juvenile diary reveals, he seriously believed that Charles, with the help of Halifax, was prepared to deceive and betray his brother James in order to save his bastard's skin. William was left with the impression that pro-Dutch influence, in the shape of Halifax and Monmouth, was regaining the ascendancy at the English Court, and that James's influence was no longer so powerful as it had been.*

In the circumstances, Monmouth was a welcome guest indeed, and Mary, preparing to go to bed, was sent a message by her husband to get

dressed again and receive Monmouth in her apartments. He was given the
beautiful neighbouring Mauritshuis as his lodging, and one of the gayest
winter seasons The Hague had ever seen now got under way. Everybody
was delighted with Monmouth, whose winning charm and good looks
made him such an attractive guest, and d'Avaux reported to Versailles
what extraordinary attentions were being paid to him: "There were
continually new balls and new parties; four or five days ago they were
sledging on the ice with the Princess of Orange at one of the Prince's
houses which is three leagues from The Hague; and when they danced,
it was the Duke of Monmouth who led out the Princess of Orange."

D'Avaux dwelt suggestively on the remarkable attentions Monmouth
paid to his young hostess and cousin:

> He went regularly every day to the dinner of this Princess, although she
> eats alone and in private, and afterwards he dined with the Prince of
> Orange. It was even remarked that the Princess, who went out walking on
> foot in public places, went nearly every day in the "mail" which is a very
> agreeable wood at the gates of The Hague, and that M. Monmouth was
> very regularly there, and nobody could understand how the Prince of
> Orange, who is the most jealous man alive, permitted all the airs of
> gallantry which were observed by everyone between the Princess of
> Orange and M. de Monmouth.*

D'Avaux was shocked by her sudden frivolity:

> They even made her behave in a manner unbecoming in a Princess and
> which I should call ridiculous in an ordinary woman, for in the great frosts
> of that year the Prince of Orange obliged her, through the great com-
> plaisance she has for him, to learn to skate on the ice, since M. de Mon-
> mouth also wished to learn. It was a most extraordinary thing to see the
> Princess of Orange with very short skirts partly tucked up, and iron skates
> on her feet, learning to slide now on one foot and now on the other.*

But in February these gaieties came to a sudden end. On the twelfth
of that month, Charles had a stroke. Only the day before, Evelyn had
seen the King sitting and joking with three of his mistresses, Portsmouth,
Cleveland and Mazarin. Four days later, he was dead, after having
secretly received the last rites of the Roman Catholic faith, at Portsmouth's
urging. He had ruled over England for a quarter of a century, and he
was heartily mourned by a nation that had learned to live, according to
the disapproving Evelyn, "in a wanton peace, minding nothing but
luxury, ambition, and to procure money for our vices".*

As soon as the first reports of Charles's death reached him, William
called Mary to his room to break the news to her. She was now Heiress

Apparent to the English crown, and her status in the United Provinces underwent an immediate change. For the first time since 1660, when William's mother had returned to England, the wife of a Stadholder was served at table on bended knee. Monmouth, who learned the news from Halifax, was shattered by this sudden end to his hopes, and scribbled in his diary sadly "O cruel fate". With James on the throne, there was no chance that he would be allowed to return to England, and for William his presence now could only be an embarrassment, as the Prince did not hesitate to make plain: Monmouth must leave, and as soon as possible. He gave the dejected young man a handsome sum of money, suggested that he go to Vienna and serve in the Emperor's army, and strongly advised him not to be drawn into plots against the new King. Monmouth swore to both William and Mary that he would not think of it, and in the beginning of February he left The Hague.

James himself had written briefly to his nephew with the news of his accession: "I have only time to tell you that it has pleased God Almighty to take out of this world the King my brother . . . and that all the usual ceremonies were performed this day in proclaiming me King in the City and other parts."*

Rioting, sedition and civil war had been widely expected when James succeeded Charles, and military precautions were taken in many parts of England as soon as the news of the King's serious illness first became known. But Sir John Reresby, the Governor of York, noted in his diary with relief and surprise on 10 February 1685: "The King was proclaimed at nine in the morning by my Lord Mayor, myself and the high sheriff . . . being done with all the signs of peace and satisfaction that could be, not only in York, but afterwards throughout the country and indeed the whole kingdom."*

On the day of his accession, James summoned the Privy Council and its members waited apprehensively to hear what bad news he might have to break to them. To their amazement, he made a moderate speech, promising to preserve the government in Church and State "as it is now by law established". The councillors could not believe their ears. One of them got up respectfully and asked if they might have his words in writing. James graciously assented, and the text of his speech was rushed to the printers.

On 23 April the new King was solemnly crowned at Westminster Abbey. There were, of course, plenty of superstitious people around to note one or two sinister omens. Henry Sidney had to step forward to prevent the Crown falling off James's head at one moment; one of the poles supporting the canopy broke; "and the same day a part of a window in one of the London churches, on which the royal arms were beautifully painted, suddenly fell down in a very unaccountable manner."*

Towards the end of May his first Parliament assembled, after a General Election that was a triumph for James. The discredited Whigs were hardly represented – "not above 40 members but such as he himself wished for", commented the King happily – and the new House of Commons was enthusiastically Royalist. His opening speech was firm but conciliating. He confirmed his widely published promise to defend and support the principles of the Church of England; he undertook to "invade no man's property" and told them that in return he expected them to settle the revenues on him for life. "At every period of this the House gave loud shouts", and dutifully granted him for life the biggest income ever enjoyed by an English king.*

James was now in his early fifties, a tall, well-built man with a long horsey face always framed in a blond wig, and a slight stutter. He lacked the easy-going charm of his brother Charles, and expected deference and great respect. Like many rather stupid men he had no sense of humour, and a fixed obstinacy, which he took for firmness, was a very marked trait in his character. "Firm to the point of pig-headedness", said one observer. The French ambassador who had heard him say: "I know the English, you must not show them any fear in the beginning", commented on this autocratic streak.* "He suffers very impatiently the least contradiction. He is very pleased at being complimented on bold displays of power."*

On the credit side James was a brilliant administrator, a hard worker and a straightforward man with a feeling for government. If England had a navy at all in the eighties it was entirely thanks to her Lord High-Admiral the Duke of York with the naval secretary Samuel Pepys. And Evelyn was deeply impressed when he saw the new King in September – such "infinite industry, sedulity, gravity . . . that I cannot but predict much happiness to the nation".*

In the first few months of his reign, indeed, it seemed as if there was a new James. He was very intent on business, and cut his hunting down to once a week. He sent a shiver of horror through Whitehall by announcing that he was going to reform the Court from "swearing, drinking and wenching";* and to set a good example, he sent his Protestant mistress Catherine Sedley packing. The strain was too much for him, however, and before the year was out, he had gone sneaking back to Mrs. Sedley, whom he now created Countess of Dorchester and set up in style in St. James's Square, to the great distress of Mary Beatrice and her priests. And in the end his whole ambitious scheme for moral reform amounted to little more than the abrupt dismissal of his brother's favourite, the Duchess of Portsmouth, who was instructed to pay her debts before she left for France.

On the political front, James's most significant move was to downgrade the moderate and pro-Dutch Halifax from Lord Privy Seal to the Lord Presidency of the Council. The anti-Dutch Sunderland remained Principal Secretary of State, and the two most important offices were filled by the brothers of his first wife, both of them ardent Royalists and loyal supporters of the Anglican church. Henry Hyde, second Earl of Clarendon, became Lord Privy Seal, while his younger brother Laurence, Earl of Rochester, was made Lord Treasurer.

Not only in England but throughout all Europe there was great curiosity to see what policy James would follow. William was anxious to establish good relations with his uncle, as much for his own position in the Republic as for the safety of Europe, and he sent Ouwerkerk to London to pay his compliments and respects to the new King. To his surprise, these advances were graciously received, although James made three stipulations: the Prince must abandon Monmouth, purge the English regiments in Holland of those officers whose loyalty to James was suspect, and – most important of all – he must moderate his hostility to France. William replied that he had already sent away Monmouth, and was perfectly willing to part with any disaffected officers. Concerning France, he offered some vaguely-phrased assurances.

For the present, it was good enough for James, who wrote back in friendly terms of his hope that "for the time to come, the same confidence will be established between us, as our near relation and the good of our family requires".* As a gesture of goodwill, the odious Chudleigh was recalled from The Hague, and replaced by Bevil Skelton. It was not much of an improvement. Skelton's silliness and indiscretion soon made him the laughing-stock of the *corps diplomatique* at The Hague – d'Avaux dismissed him as "*un homme fort léger et fort inconstant*" – and William came to detest him quite as much as his predecessor.

But James's attitude at least seemed encouraging. He was an Englishman and a patriot as Charles had never been, and in the past he had shown an occasional streak of independence in his dealings with France. Now he gave the impression that he wanted to steer a course of his own. When Louis XIV sent Barillon to him with the news that he had 5,000,000 livres ready if James needed it, the King told the ambassador with tears in his eyes: "It is the part of the King your master alone, to act in a manner so noble . . ."* But after Parliament's unexpected generosity such funds were not needed. And this financial independence strengthened him in the belief that he might one day play the role of the great arbiter of Europe. This role was a possibility as long as Protestant England was solidly behind him, and as long as he could keep his religion a private matter.

The new English King, however, was a Roman Catholic with all the fanaticism of the convert. His brother Charles, who knew him better than anyone, had once remarked prophetically: "My brother will lose his kingdom by his bigotry and his soul for a lot of ugly trollops."*

"I AM NOW SO MUCH IN LOVE with retired life, that I am never like to be fond of making a bustle in the world again", wrote the Duke of Monmouth in the spring of 1685.* Only weeks later, on 24 May, he sailed from the isle of Texel off Holland with a 32-gun frigate, three smaller vessels and a band of eighty-two followers. In the lockers were arms for 5000 men. The most foolhardy invasion in England's history was under way. During his stay in Brussels English refugees together with the Earl of Argyll, who had lived in exile since 1681 in Friesland's capital, Leeuwarden, had worked on the vanity of the gullible young man. They were prepared, they told him, to go to England and risk their lives for him. Monmouth was much moved: "How can I avoid exposing my own person, when others are so forward in exposing theirs in my cause?"*

He bought weapons and ships, for which his mistress and great love Henrietta Wentworth sold her jewels. While the small force gathered in Amsterdam harbour, Skelton asked the Regents in that town to have the ships detained, but they had already left for Texel. Amsterdam, after some delay, referred him to the States-General, and Monmouth sailed unhindered. Argyll had left a month earlier.

On 11 June the Duke landed at Lyme in Dorset, where the people flocked around him. He at once published a declaration, calling the King his "mortal and bloody enemy" and accusing him of responsibility for the Great Fire of London, the Popish plot, the assassination of the Earl of Essex and the poisoning of Charles II. He declared himself born in wedlock and the legitimate heir to the throne. "He cast his usual spell over the common people, who swelled his small army at every stage of its progress."

As soon as the news of the landing reached the Prince of Orange, he realized that James was bound to suspect him of complicity, and he at once sent Bentinck to London with a memorandum, drawn up in William's own handwriting, in which he offered every possible service he could render him. If James thought he might be useful, William was willing to come to England himself, and he would in any case send over the six English and Scottish regiments from Holland.* Bentinck crossed to England in spite of terrible storms and reached Whitehall two days later. James was delighted by the offer of the regiments but he had no desire to see his famous son-in-law leading them. William, who was genuinely anxious for the fast-spreading rebellion to be put down, was not happy with this reaction but he was at least reassured about the King's suspicions of him. There were already rumours going around the English Court that Monmouth was assisted by the French – he paid in French coins – and Bentinck, who did not hesitate to improve on these rumours in a conversation with James, could report to the Prince that the King believed him.*

The Western Rising looked far more menacing from Holland than it did in England, and William sent repeatedly for news. He was particularly worried by the small size of the army sent to oppose Monmouth under the inexperienced Feversham, and after Argyll had been defeated in Scotland he wrote to Bentinck: "I cannot imagine that Monmouth will be as easily overcome as Argyll. I much fear that they despise him too much and that thus they may be deceived."*

His fears were needless. When on 5 July the army of Monmouth, swollen to 6000 men, faced Feversham's troops on the plain of Sedgemoor, the battle that followed soon turned into a rout. Monmouth's army of untrained, half-armed peasants had attacked the Royalist troops at midnight, and for a moment this surprise assault seemed likely to be successful. But Feversham's troops under the able command of the rising young John Churchill were too much for them, and by sunrise they were running for their lives. More than 1500 bodies were left behind on the bloody plain.

It was the end of the road for Monmouth. A day later he was discovered hiding in a ditch, betrayed – according to legend – by the faithfulness of one of his dogs, who having lost his master followed his scent.* Monmouth was in a state of nervous collapse, trembling and crying, and said later that he had never enjoyed a night's rest nor eaten a meal in quiet since the day of his landing. The *London Gazette* published the latest news on 8 July 1685: "His Majesty has just now received an account that the late Duke of Monmouth was taken this morning in Dorsetshire, being hid in a ditch."* The King was deeply relieved, though he made a point of not showing his delight.* William made no secret of his joy, writing to Bentinck: "God be praised for the good success that the King's troops have had against the rebels. I am sure that this affair has now been satisfactorily dealt with and that the reign of the King will be a happy one, which God grant. . . ."*

Monmouth had picked the worst possible moment for his rebellion. James had done nothing yet to lose the goodwill of Parliament and country, or to suggest that pro-Catholic measures were imminent. And in any case the next in line for the crown was still the reliably Protestant Mary, with her Dutch husband. When Monmouth landed Parliament had voted unanimously to stand by James with their lives and fortunes, and – more to the point – they granted him an immediate £400,000 for the suppression of the rebellion, while a price of £5000 was put on Monmouth's head.

He now himself had to pay the price of his reckless venture. He was taken to London, where he knew that death was waiting him. The rebel who only weeks earlier had styled himself King, now begged James abjectly for an audience. "I am sure, when you hear me, you will be convinced of the care I have of your preservation, and how heartily I repent of what I have done." James, who had no intention of sparing him, granted him an interview at which Monmouth completely lost control of himself, and grovelled in tears at James's feet, asking him for "mercy and compassion".* The King remained unmoved, but Monmouth was not a Stuart for nothing. He pulled himself together in time to make a brave end and on 15 July "he carried himself with great sedateness of mind on the scaffold, and told them he was not afraid of death."*

In an account sent to Holland it was related how, when he arrived at the block, Monmouth first felt the axe, to see if it was sharp enough. He was about to offer the executioner Jack Ketch twenty guineas for his grisly service, but his steward stopped him and suggested that instead he should offer him five now, with the promise of the other fifteen to be paid by his steward if he did the job well. A ghastly scene followed: "I saw him given five blows with the axe, probably out of malice", wrote an eye-witness in the huge crowd that roared its horror and rage on Tower Hill. When Monmouth gave him an agonized look, Ketch flung down his axe in disgust. He had to be ordered to take it up again, and to finish his appalling job with two more blows.*

Thus ended this quondam Duke, darling of his father and the ladies, . . . a favourite of the people, of an easy nature, debauch'd by lust, seduc'd by crafty knaves who would have set him up only to make a property, and took the opportunity of the King being of another religion, to gather a party of discontented men. He fail'd, and perish'd. He was a lovely person.

It was his epitaph, written sadly by one of his sternest critics, John Evelyn.*

The revenge the King now took on the dead man's followers in the West Country was as bloody as the execution on Tower Hill. His Lord Chief Justice George Jeffreys went down in person to supervise what James referred to as "his campaign in the West", and a horrifying judicial massacre followed. More than 300 peasants were hanged, and their bodies left to rot on gibbets by the roadside or in the market-places of towns. Jeffreys was later heard to boast, "with a sort of brutish pleasure, that he hanged more men than all the judges of England since William the Conqueror".* At least 800 people were deported to the West Indies.

Even in that callous age the work of Jeffreys and his assistants – already known as the "Bloody Assizes" – horrified many. Mary's former chaplain, Dr. Thomas Ken, went to James to beg him with tears in his eyes to put a stop to the dreadful butchery. The whole air of Somerset was tainted with death, he said, but the King remained "hard as the marble chimney pieces of Whitehall".* Years later the dying Jeffreys told a chaplain: "I was not half bloody enough for him that sent me thither."*

The memory of the Bloody Assizes haunted the West Country for years to come, but for James it was merely the successful closing of an incident. It had confirmed his belief in "bold displays of power" and in the importance of firmness. He had taken advantage of the crisis to raise his regular army from 6000 to 30,000, Parliament was docile and the nation regarded him after Monmouth's defeat with awed respect and terror. "Henceforward he was determined to be the unquestionable ruler of his land and to revive the pristine glories of the divine right of Kings."*

For William also, the disappearance of Monmouth had far-reaching consequences. From now on any opposition to the policies of James would crystallize naturally around the person of the Prince of Orange. But at the moment there seemed little prospect of such opposition and James was confident enough to send back to Holland the six Scottish and English regiments. Before they left the Londoners poured out to admire these impressive soldiers in their camp at Blackheath – "excellently clad and well disciplined" – and James also, bringing his wife, came in person to see them exercise.* He always liked the sight of a fine army, even if they were Dutch trained.

CHAPTER XIX

Scandal at Court

"I WAS VERY SORRY to find my daughter had got sore eyes", wrote the Duke of York to his son-in-law William early in 1684, "but was glad to know by a letter I had from her . . . that she was better."*

Mary suffered all her life from a weakness in her eyes, which easily became inflamed, infected and painful, making it impossible for her to read, write letters or do close work, and in 1684 they gave her a great deal of trouble. William wrote to James from Dieren in mid-July, reporting that Mary's eyes were so sore that she had been let blood in an effort to give her some relief, and a month later they were still troubling her. She was preparing to take a spa-water cure in the hope of improving them.*

Apart from this chronic ailment, however, the Princess's health was now excellent, and there was no more talk of the feverish chills, the rheumatic bouts, and the agues to which she had been so prone when she first came into Holland. Her new life evidently suited her down to the ground. She liked the pleasant formality and orderliness of her life at The Hague, and she was making her own friends now among the Dutch ladies, with whom she could practise speaking her husband's language. Perhaps even better, she loved escaping to one of their country homes – to the intimacy of Dieren, or the small pretty palace of Soestdijk with the fields and woods around it, where there were no ceremonial occasions or formal visits to take up her time, and she could devote it happily to making plans for the gardens, or improvements for the house, or going on long country walks. She was happiest in the country when William could be there with her. She had learned to accept his long absences on military exercise, in conference with the Allies, touring his estates or attending to political affairs, but she never got used to them, or to the way in which he might suddenly be called back from the country at a moment's notice. Once in the summer of 1683 she had travelled to Dieren to join him, arriving on Saturday only to find that he himself had to leave the next day. "My wife was bitterly disappointed . . . and I not less so . . ." William wrote to Bentinck in London.*

By the summer of 1685, there was a new favourite among the Prince's country residences. William always enjoyed rebuilding, improving and adding to his many inherited homes. Now for the first time he was about to build a new palace, Het Loo, which if it lacked the crushing splendours of Versailles, should have its own beauty and dignity. In the autumn of 1684, he had bought the small castle Het Oude Loo – The Old Forest – from Johan Carselis van Ulft. It was within hunting distance of the lodge at Dieren, set in the same wild wooded country, and he and Mary spent much of the summer there commuting between the two houses. The new Loo palace, near the old castle, was designed by Jacob Romans to be built in Dutch brick, with great formal gardens inspired by the famous French landscape gardener, Le Nôtre, who had laid out the grounds of Versailles. The couple spent hours discussing plans for the house itself, for William's picture gallery and Mary's porcelain cabinets, for her special small garden below the windows of her apartment, and for the aviary she wanted to install there.

Mary occasionally brought some of her friends to keep her company at the old castle while William was absent hunting. Among them was a young Englishwoman, Lady Mary Forester, then living at The Hague with her husband. Lady Mary had been presented to the Princess in the formal manner dictated by protocol at The Hague, and she sometimes came to the Princess's evenings, sitting politely at the basset table. Mary had found her pleasant enough to invite her to Het Loo, and away in the country, with protocol left behind, she turned out to be lively, good-humoured company, energetic enough even to keep up with a great walker like Mary, and full of delicious Whitehall scandals. In October 1685 she and her husband were, however, returning to England, and Mary wrote sadly to her on the twenty-ninth: "I had bin very glad your concerns and your condition would have permited you to stay longer since I have learnt to know you to well to be willing to louse you quite . . . since you have been at Loo working, walking and ramping, you must not wonder if I shoud have bin vry glad to have found you still at the hague . . ." Mary had not known that the young wife was pregnant at the time, and recalling the day when they had played at hide and seek in the little wood nearby, she added reproachfully, "If I had then knowne your conditione you had never got the reputation of as good a walker as myself, at least we had nevr pased ditches as we did together . . ."*

Another of her friends, Frances Apsley, had been married since 1682 to Lord Bathurst, and while Mary still kept up the correspondence with her "dear Aurelia" the fond little "dear husban" had disappeared. It is difficult to keep up an intimate friendship over a long distance, and from the tone of the letters it is clear that the two girls had long since become young married women with other attachments. Mary was in any case a bad correspondent. Almost all her letters start with excuses that any poor letter-writer will recognize: "I have bin so taken up these three weeks that I have bin at The Hague that I have not had a moment time to my self or els I would have write soner . . ."* Another begins: "I have not time to say much at present to my dear Aurelia . . ."* And most of the letters now contained little more than shopping commissions for exotic fabrics or fashionable accessories from smart London shops that she could not find at The Hague or Amsterdam.

Mary was very fashion-conscious – naturally enough for a girl who had grown up at the court of Charles II. Like any young wife she liked to look pretty for her husband, and as First Lady of Holland she was a natural fashion-leader; any new style she wore was copied. Mary felt this as a responsibility – "I am here as a schoolmistris amongst this people", she had remarked smiling to Huygens* – and once when Frances proposed the latest fad, she had to refuse it. "It was not because I had not heard of them", Mary defended herself, "but because I would not bring up such a fashion heer which the pursses could not bear."*

In a letter of October 1685 she asked for "blake razed satin" for a gown, insisting that the border be left plain around the edge to be embroidered "that I can have done heer very well". The material was to be sent as soon as possible by post – "I am in great hast for it & therefore desire you woud louse no time."*

The gown had been in fashion since the early 1680s. It had a close-fitting bodice with elbow length sleeves, and its fully gathered skirt was worn open down the front to show off the pretty flounced chemise underneath of which the long frilled or ruffled sleeves were also visible at the elbow. These gowns were often edged with a richly embroidered border or trimmed with thick fur. Frances sent the black satin off promptly together with a bill for one pound, ten shillings and two pence, but Mary now needed some more accessories to go with it: "2 cotten peticotes a pair of sleeves such as may be worn now & a rolle or what els you may call it I know not but I mean sich a thing as is worn upon the head with a blacke gowne . . ."*

It is impossible to believe that this busy young woman, who visited Amsterdam together with her husband at the end of 1684, was seen on a sleigh ride in The Hague in January 1685 and was the cheerful hostess of her cousin Monmouth in February, was the pathetic prisoner d'Avaux had described to Louis XIV in the beginning of that year. According to him she never left her apartments from the moment she got up till eight o'clock at night, except in the summer when she went for a walk once every eight days. Nobody was allowed in her room, not even the ladies-in-waiting or her Maids of Honour, of whom two were appointed every day to guard her with instructions not to leave her. He added again that the Prince was the most jealous man in the world since he not only forbids visits from men but from women as well.* The obvious explanation for this extraordinary letter is that the French ambassador had fallen under Mary's spell but had been firmly kept at arm's length by her. Years later he would even boast to Liselotte that Mary, while in Holland, had been "*un peu coquette*" and that he met her secretly in the apartments of one of her Maids of Honour, "Mme de Tresslaire" (Mrs. Trelawney). "The Prince of Orange heard about it and threw her out on another pretext", so was d'Avaux's story.*

In October 1685 Mrs. Trelawney was indeed dismissed from the Prince's Court, but the "other pretext" had been the actual reason. For years William had disliked her as one of the intriguing and gossiping members of Mary's English Household, and now she took her revenge: she was one of the busybodies who revealed to the Princess that William had been having an affair for some time with another Lady-in-Waiting, Elizabeth Villiers.

The relationship between William and "Betty" had been going on for years. The Villiers girl had come over with Mary in 1677, and as early as 1679 rumours about her and William had reached Paris. Unlike Charles, James and Louis in their amorous affairs, the Prince of Orange had gone out of his way to keep his attentions to Elizabeth as discreet as possible, but it is highly improbable that Mary was not aware of what was going on, and everything suggests that she first knew of it in the spring of 1680. It was at that time that Mary reacted characteristically for her in moments of emotional crisis: she fell seriously ill and seemed to have lost her will to live. At the same time too, many of her entourage had been complaining about the Prince's unkindness and indifference. She had recovered slowly and eventually she came to terms with the situation. She was, after all, a child of her times, when adultery was openly paraded at the English and French Courts and made a subject of her nursery chatter. In love with William, she was shocked and deeply hurt, but by 1685 they had worked out their own *modus vivendi* and the two gave every appearance of being a close and happy couple.

It was only when her father James – embarking on his romanizing policies in England in spite of opposition from his daughter and son-in-law – began in the autumn of that year to meddle in their domestic affairs, that she was compelled unwillingly to take public notice of it. It seems probable that he aimed at the breaking-up of his daughter's marriage only in order to destroy the Prince's influence in English political affairs: the idea that she might subsequently be married again to the widowed Louis XIV – as was rumoured a few years later – seems far-fetched even by James's standards.* Equally improbable is the suggestion, in Madame de Zoutelandt's colourful memoirs, that Mary wrote complaining about the affairs to her father. James had other informants. For some time now the less trustworthy members of Mary's English Household had been encouraged by him to relay domestic gossip from the Orange household, particularly anything which might be damaging to the Prince, and they had been happy to oblige.

The leading informer was Mary's recently appointed chaplain, Dr. Covell, ably assisted by Anne Trelawney, Mary's old nanny Mrs. Langford, and her son, who was Dr. Covell's assistant. They were constantly in touch with Skelton, the English ambassador that William already disliked, and their unpleasant revelations went back to James by the diplomatic bag. Encouraged by the King's interest, they decided to put the facts of the Villiers affair before the Princess, who for years had successfully concealed her awareness of it. She was pained and humiliated to find that it had now become public knowledge and in her distress – according to Daniel de Bourdon – she played into the hands of the English intriguers by taking a foolish step. When William came late to bed – the couple slept together, unusual in Royal ménages of that time – he usually explained that he was sitting up dealing with correspondence. The next time this happened, Mary made a pretence of going to bed but put on a wrapper and stationed herself near the staircase leading to the apartments of the ladies-in-waiting. "She waited till at two o'clock the Prince appeared, who, surprised to find her still up, heaped reproaches on her to which she only replied with tears and withdrew to her bed which the Prince did not come to for several days."*

This scene was duly reported to James, and he seized the opportunity to represent vividly to his daughter the wrong and the injury that was being done to her position and her trust. The triumph of her Household was not lost on the Prince, who was furious that they had dared to interfere in his private life. "He knew very well the sweetness and good nature of his wife, and readily understood that some one had been embittering her spirits and feeding her jealousy." He kept a careful watch and discovered that Mrs. Langford and her son, the chaplain, and Anne Trelawney, were all sending reports to England through Skelton.

One day, while the Court was staying at Dieren, he went off on a hunting trip but left instructions that any messenger leaving the Court was to be stopped and searched. The ruse worked, and a day later a footman was discovered on his way to Skelton with a packet of letters. He was instructed to continue his journey and to say nothing, while the Prince examined the letters. He was horrified by what he read.

One of the letters was from Dr. Covell himself to Skelton, and it was strange language for a clergyman:

"Your Honour may be astonished at the news, but it is too true the Princess' heart is like to break; . . . we dare no more speak to her. The prince hath infallibly made her his absolute slave, and there is an end of it." The chaplain realized that when Mary came to the throne "the Prince will for ever rule the roast", and he deplored the fate of Skelton, so much disliked by the Prince and only protected from his displeasure by James's life. As he said spitefully, "I wonder what the devil makes the Prince so cold to you. None but pimps and bawds must expect any tolerable usage here. I beseech God preserve the King many and many years." Even Mary – whose natural good spirits had evidently reasserted themselves after the first shock – did not escape the chaplain's malice: "she . . . counterfeits the greatest joy, and looks upon us as dogged as maybe", and the letter ends disapprovingly, "The Princess is just now junketing with Madame Bentinck and Mrs. Jesson in Madame Zuy-lestein's chamber."*

After reading this and the other letters the Prince sent for his wife to his study. What was said between them was overheard by no one, but Daniel de Bourdon, who was close friends with one of the companions of a lady-in-waiting, makes a plausible guess at it. Once alone with Mary, the Prince asked "whether she was aware that there were people attempting to destroy their unity and to drive her to a scandalous separation by making her believe falsehoods. She replied that although, if the truth were to be told, she had had reason not to be too happy for some time now, she had nevertheless shut up her sorrow in her heart, without having told anyone of it, and that if someone had been touched and moved to intervene, it had not been her doing, that she knew very well how to suffer in silence."

"Well," said the Prince, "you protect thus those of your household who dare to sow dissension between us, and who by false reports, make you doubt of my fidelity to you." "Have I not reason to do so?" she asked. "No," said the Prince, "and I swear to you by all that is most sacred that what has caused you pain was simply a distraction, that there has been no crime; but there are servants of yours, for whom I have done everything I could, who betray me, and if you believe the oath I make before God, never to violate the trust I swore to you, you must abandon them to my just indignation."

The Princess – still according to Bourdon – was completely disarmed by his assurances, burst into tears and threw herself into his arms, protesting that she had no knowledge and no part in the correspondence of her servants, and telling him to act as he thought fit. The Prince then interviewed the culprits privately. Mrs. Langford and her son were sent for, and at first put up a stout defence, claiming that they had done no more than inform a father of his daughter's grief. But the Prince refused to listen, and ordered them abruptly to pack their cases and be ready to leave in two hours. They were forbidden to write or see their mistress again, and were shipped off to England, together with Anne Trelawney and Dr. Covell.*

Mary resented their meddling quite as much as her husband did, and she saw them go without regret. In her next letter to Lady Bathurst, at the beginning of December, she mentioned the departure of Mrs. Langford, "my Mam haveing put herself out of a conditione of ever doing anything more for me of wch I have not spoke its being a thing for wch I was good natured enough remembring what she had bin to me to be sory for at first, but her behaviour has bin such as has given me but just cause to forget that . . . when what is past cant be recaled the lesse one thinks of it the beter."*

Bentinck, William's favourite, had not escaped the malicious tongues of the scandalmongers, who suggested that he took advantage of his position and lacked due respect for the Princess. Mary was certainly not very pleased with him at this time –, but for a quite different reason. As far as can be deduced, the blunt and plain-spoken Bentinck had not only given Betty – the sister of his wife Anne – but the Prince as well a piece of his mind, another intervention Mary had not appreciated.

He wrote a long description of all these events to his friend Sidney in London.

You will be very much surprised to hear of the changes which have been happening in our Court. His Highness, having seen by chance a letter which made clear that Dr Covell had for a long time been the malicious spy of the house, who reported many things invented to be hurtful; upon which H. R. H. Madame dismissed him with no other punishment on account of his position; and as it was evident that Mrs Langford and Miss Trelawney were acting in concert with him, Madame sent them off this morning as well. Its a terrible thing that people can be wicked enough to wish harm on those who give them their living, but it is still worse to think that a Minister could be capable of that. The second Chaplain Langford was also in the plot.

Bentinck begged Sidney to tell him what the reaction had been in London to all the stories, and he confessed his fear that it was still not over.*

Whether or not Mary believed William's assurances, it was plainly impossible for her to keep Elizabeth Villiers in her Household now that the scandal had become public, and Betty was sent back to England. Madame de Zoutelandt, perhaps not very reliably, relates how when the Prince went out hunting one day, the Princess took this opportunity to send Miss Villiers to London on the pretext that she was to deliver a letter from Mary to the King. Arrived at Harwich, Betty had suspected something, and looked for a boat to take her back to Holland.* Certainly Elizabeth Villiers was sent back to England, but in view of the stories circulating in London, it was her father Sir Edward Villiers who wrote begging the Prince and Princess to let her return to The Hague, which she did.

Mary naturally refused to receive her, and she settled down with her sister Katherine, married to M. de Puissars. Bentinck was indignant and complained to Sidney, "I have no reason to be proud of my brother-in-law." His wife Anne was forbidden to visit the Puissars, and he himself told Betty of "the pain and resentment that I have in seeing that by her own choice and the wish of her father she pursues a course of conduct so opposed to her interests, to her honour and to what she promised me in speaking."*

The next step was to get rid of the English ambassador Skelton, and William himself dealt with the matter. He wrote a stiff letter to the Earl of Rochester, which he hoped would be shown to James, telling him the whole story of the correspondence between Dr. Covell and Skelton that he had discovered. "I consider that I have good reason to complain of Mr. Schelton . . . you can judge well whether after this I can continue to live on good terms with him, I hope that the King will do me the kindness to remove him from here. . . ."*

James was incensed by William's request and Barillon recorded his outburst: "The Prince of Orange shows clearly his bad will towards him when he is so much upset by the knowledge that his minister is informed of what goes on in the house of his daughter and son-in-law."* In the circumstances, however, he could hardly insist on Skelton remaining at The Hague, and the envoy was recalled. But in spite of William's request that Covell should be punished by his bishop, the ex-chaplain on his return became Vice-Chancellor of Cambridge University where four years later the Prince and he came face to face again. Covell found himself under the painful necessity of praising him, in an oration of welcome, as a saint and saviour of his country. But it was noticed by the onlookers that he could not meet the King's eyes.*

As Bentinck had feared, the drama of October 1685 was not the end of the affair. The fascination that Betty had for the Prince was not to be broken off so easily. None of their correspondence, if there was any, has survived, and little is known about their relationship, but it was generally assumed that it was physical, and if Bourdon was accurate in saying that the Prince assured Mary that it was not, it was the lie of a man who could not face hurting his wife with the truth.

Elizabeth was the eldest of the eight Villiers children, and probably seven or eight years older than Mary. An ungainly young woman, with a bad complexion and a squint that everyone noticed at once, she certainly could not be described as a beauty. Her figure, however, was quite good, and her best point was her long white neck.* Certainly it was not her looks that attracted the Prince, but even her severest critics had to admit that she was witty, intelligent and an excellent talker – exactly the sort of woman that always appealed to William.

When he had first known Mary in 1677, the Princess was a tearful, emotional and sentimental girl of sixteen. Elizabeth was then in her early twenties, independent, cool and clever. She was arrogant although not vain, and her portrait suggests a woman of humour and detachment. But like William himself, her reserved manner hid a genuine warmth and generosity.

When the Prince made his first advances, she had done her best to discourage him, even enlisting as an ally Mary's private secretary d'Allonne. But William had been persistent and had sent away another suitor of the girl, a Scottish captain Wauchope or Wauchon, after one of the Prince's friends, the nobleman Adriaan van Borssels van der Hoogh, had refused to interfere.*

After the Scotsman had disappeared – Van Ginckel met him in 1692 fighting with James's army against William and reminiscing in tears about his life in Holland – the way had been clear for the Prince. For the Court the only visible clue was that William came more often to Mary's dinner table when he knew that Betty was to be there. He enjoyed talking to her, and discussed state affairs with her as he could not with Mary. She had a woman's insight and a man's shrewdness – years later she could keep Swift talking till far into the night.

After the discovery, and Betty's return to The Hague, the possibilities of their meeting were much more limited. Madame de Zoutelandt tells that Elizabeth often went to see the Prince incognito, "her head wrapped in a scarf in the Flemish fashion", passing through Bentinck's apartment on her way to see the Prince. In view of Bentinck's attitude during the crisis, this story can be dismissed as fantasy. But other friends of William were more complaisant, and he certainly continued to see her at the Puissars', at Zuylestein's house or elsewhere.

The affair was to last for over fifteen years, but in the long run it seems to have become more cerebral than physical. After the scandal of 1685, at any rate, their relationship was tacitly accepted by the Court as something known but not to be commented on. The Orange Household settled down again.

CHAPTER XX

A Crown at Stake

The Villiers crisis was a major upheaval in the Orange Household, but it was insignificant by contrast with events now taking place in France. On 2 October 1685 Louis XIV revoked the Edict of Nantes, thus officially depriving French Protestants of their freedom to worship, and unleashed a ruthless persecution. The campaign against the one-million-strong French Huguenots had already begun on a minor scale in 1679, when some of their rights of worship were taken away from them, followed in 1680 by the terrible dragonnades. Three hundred temples were closed down and mixed marriages forbidden. Over the next few years Huguenot churches, schools and hospitals were closed, and the Revocation of the Edict of Nantes set the final seal on a process that was already well under way.

In every north European country the reaction was one of horror, and even the Pope criticized the eldest daughter of the Church, as France liked to describe itself. At Versailles the storm of anger was ignored, and the Sun King, who had so often defied all Europe, continued unmoved along the course he had plotted. In fact he was that year a very sick man, acting under the strong influence of Madame de Maintenon, the former governess of his bastard children. This bourgeois widow had first ousted his reigning mistress, Madame de Montespan, and then became his morganatic wife – probably in the middle of 1685 – after the death of Queen Maria Theresa. Formerly a Protestant, Madame de Maintenon was now an ardent Roman Catholic, who shared to the full Louis's conviction that France could only be glorious and united if it had one religion.

At no time in his life had Louis been particularly moderate or merciful, but now terrible physical suffering had turned him into a highly irritable man. Unlike the Prince of Orange, who never took much notice of his doctors, the King of France was very much a victim of his,

believing that it was his duty to his people. As a result, he had to endure
the most extravagant medical treatments of that time – blood-lettings,
ferocious purges that sent him to his commode as many as nineteen
times a day, nauseating medicines to be swallowed. In the autumn of this
year, it was a tooth that plagued him. It was extracted but was followed
by an abscess, infection of the jawbone and sinusitis. To ease his agony,
the doctors pulled out all his upper teeth, destroying part of his palate and
breaking his jaw. They cauterized the gaping incision several times over
with a red-hot coal, but from that time on he always had to drink with
care, or the fluid ran out of his nose.*

Suffering as he did, he had no pity for the desperate Huguenots.
Evelyn wrote of "The French persecution . . . raging with the utmost
barbarity, exceeded even what the very heathens us'd . . . on a sudden
demolishing all their churches, banishing, imprisoning and sending to the
gallies all the ministers; plundering the common people . . . taking away
their children; forcing people to the Masse, and then executing them as
relapsers; they burnt their libraries . . . eate up their fields and substance."*

In spite of the fact that they were forbidden to leave the country, at
least 200,000 Huguenots left everything they had in the world to flee for
refuge to England, Holland, Denmark and Brandenburg; and soon it
was clear that France's loss was Europe's gain. Many of the Huguenots
were superb craftsmen, specialists in luxury light industries like silk-
weaving, paper-making, and the working of fine leather, of which France
had once had the monopoly, and the welcome they were given in other
countries was certainly not entirely disinterested. As early as 1682 the
United Provinces had offered the refugees generous tax concessions, and
Amsterdam relaxed its closed-shop policy and gave them the right to
work in the city, building 1000 houses to offer them at low rents.

The Dutch were particularly incensed because their own compatriots,
who had settled in France, were victims of persecution and were not
allowed to leave the country.

In the circumstances, Amsterdam's pro-French feelings cooled
considerably. D'Avaux warned Louis that in consequence the position
of the Prince of Orange had been very much strengthened, but Louis,
nursing his toothache, refused to listen. As a fresh insult to the Prince,
he had decided on the total destruction of the last Protestant bulwark
in France. In spite of the levelling of the walls in 1682, and the confisca-
tion that followed, the little principality of Orange had always remained
a Protestant enclave, and the Huguenot refugees had flocked to it, in a
pathetic belief that they would be safe there. As an inevitable consequence
of the Revocation of the Edict of Nantes, on 24 October Louis sent a

body of dragoons to occupy Orange with all the cruelty for which they were notorious.

Their commander, the Comte de Tesse, was shocked to find how popular the Prince of Orange still was. "You cannot imagine the extent to which these people were and still are infatuated with the Prince of Orange, his authority and Holland", he wrote to Louvois,* who encouraged him to eradicate these feelings and Protestantism at the same time. De Tesse carried his orders out with brutal efficiency. He imprisoned the pastors, burnt every bible he found, pulled down the small temple and forcibly converted to Roman Catholicism those inhabitants that had not fled.*

News of the French cruelties reached Holland, and the Prince and Mary asked the King of England immediately to take up the Orange case with Louis. James obliged at first but soon desisted when the French King told him point blank: "The King . . . acknowledged no sovereignty of Orange to belong to the Prince . . . that it was his incontestably."* Barillon was instructed to drop a hint in London: "I must believe that the King of England will not take up this question, especially as the interest of our religion does not permit that this town shall remain longer in heresy."*

Confronted with French intransigence James had to write to Mary that "he could do no more in that matter unless he should declare war upon it; which he could not think fit for a thing of such small importance."* Mary, who had been totally disillusioned by the behaviour of her father in the Villiers affair, later complained: "The only thing I ever asked the King, my father, to do was to use his influence with the King of France to prevent the seizure of the Principality of Orange. But my father preferred to join with the King of France against my husband."*

The hopes of an independent English policy which James had encouraged in the first half year of his reign were by this time fading fast. In August of 1685 at Halifax's instigation the existing treaties between England and the United Provinces had been renewed, and the Prince of Orange and his father-in-law seemed on such excellent terms that in Holland it was happily commented: "The King has declared that he will henceforth look upon him as his successor."*

But these were surface cordialities only. James had not lost his old mistrust of his clever son-in-law and even now he showed it in petty ways, refusing him, for instance, the courtesy style of Royal Highness in England. And by midsummer England and the Prince of Orange had begun to realize that James, like the King of France, had his own Grand Design. Soon after the execution of Monmouth in July he announced that he intended to repeal the Test and Penal Acts, which excluded Roman Catholics from all public office, together with the Habeas Corpus Act. But he planned to go much further, as he proudly revealed to Barillon, who reported to Louis: "This Prince has thoroughly explained to me his intentions with regard to the Catholics, which are to grant them entire liberty of conscience and the free exercise of their religion; this is a work of time and it can be brought about only step by step."*

If James had told the ambassador that he had to proceed carefully, he forgot his own words very soon. In the early autumn of 1685 he appointed some Catholic officers in his army, and in a council meeting he announced that he wanted the Roman Catholics to resume their seats in the House of Lords. Halifax objected strongly, and at a private interview James tried to persuade him to change his mind. Halifax refused and on 21 October the King dismissed him from office with "kind expressions". When the House of Commons met again in November, the M.P.s sent the King an address reminding him of the existence of the Test Act. James was surprised and displeased, but he was even more shocked by the plain speaking of the Lords on the same subject. The Bishop of London, Dr. Compton, was one of those who spoke strongly against James in the debate and although he had spoken "with all the respect imaginable to the King" his name was struck off the list of Privy Councillors and he ceased to be Dean of the Chapel Royal.*

The unruly Parliament was dealt with in the same summary manner: on 20 November James prorogued it indefinitely, thus effectively driving all opposition underground.

It was becoming clear that James was completely obsessed with his Grand Design, and that this obsession warped his judgment and clouded his reason. Both the dismissal of Halifax and the prorogation of the Parliament were understandably received with particular concern in the United Provinces. William knew from long experience that England without a Parliament could never be an ally, and Raadspensionary Fagel wrote to Heinsius – in England as a special envoy at this time – that he should appeal to the Parliamentary leaders not to be too violent in their dispute with the King. "It seems to me that the quiet of Europe hangs on a good understanding between His Majesty and his Parliament", stated Fagel.*

But it was fruitless to urge moderation on Protestant leaders in England while hundreds and thousands of Huguenot refugees were taking their horror stories into every other country in Europe. The English, like the rest of Europe, were deeply shocked by their persecution, and James at first shared the general horror, contributing £500 out of his own pocket to a relief fund, and ordering a proclamation to be read in the churches in which he condemned the religious policy of the French King. But this reaction was short-lived. His old mistrust of the Prince of Orange soon reasserted itself, and at the beginning of January 1686 Barillon reported with satisfaction to Paris that James suspected his son-in-law of plotting against him with the English Protestant leaders. "The King of England regards the Prince of Orange as his enemy", wrote Barillon's colleague, Bonrepaus, that month; adding later: "The King of England can scarcely hide his hatred for and jealousy of the Prince of Orange."*

At the same time, James abandoned his appearance of sympathy for the Huguenots. He apologized to Louis XIV for the anti-French terms of his proclamation, and ordered the public burning of a book, written by the French Protestant minister Jean Claude, describing the suffering of the Huguenots. The King's Council protested, but James answered blandly: "My resolution is taken. It has become the fashion to treat Kings disrespectfully; and they must stand by each other. . . ."*

The attitude of the King aroused increasing alarm in England. The Roman Catholics were coming out more and more into the open, in defiance of the law and with the brazen connivance of the King. When in April a Catholic chapel was opened in Lime Street, in the heart of the City, and rioting broke out, the Lord Mayor was summoned by James and told "to take care of the peace of the citty, or otherwise he should be forced to send some assistance to them".*

Catholics were appointed to more and more public posts, and in the Hales case in June, a carefully-rigged test case, eleven out of the twelve hand-picked judges found that the King was entitled to exercise his power to dispense with the laws of the land. In the same month the Dean of Norwich, Rector of St. Martin-in-the-Fields, preached an anti-Catholic sermon and the King ordered the Bishop of London to suspend him. When Dr. Compton refused, he was suspended himself "during his Majesty's pleasure".*

The Princess of Orange, as Heiress Apparent to the throne, had shown a new interest in English affairs during the last year. She had already intervened in the Orange question, and now she ventured to protest to her father about his treatment of the Bishop who had confirmed and married her. She was snubbed for her pains, and James wrote back "reflecting severely on the bishop, not without some sharpness of her meddling in such matters".*

Up till now, the correspondence between James and the Prince and Princess of Orange had been superficially polite. In these times of growing unrest in England, the King discussed in detail the sore eyes of his daughter and the shingles of his wife, ending usually: "As for news there is very little stirring here."* But in the summer of 1686 a sharper note crept in with this exchange about Compton, and rumours began to circulate that James wanted to exclude Mary from the succession. These rumours were based on a document which the Dutch ambassador in London, Van Citters, got hold of in the same summer. It was called "A remonstrance made to the King of England by his Council" and it advocated the exclusion of Mary. Her sister Anne, apparently more pliant and docile than her older sister, was to be converted to Roman Catholicism and take her place.

James flatly denied such a plan to Van Citters, telling him that the document was a forgery; and on a later occasion he told him that his affection for his eldest daughter would prevent him entertaining such an idea. But nobody had forgotten that when James had come to the throne he had given her "no appointments to support the dignities of a King's Daughter . . . nor did he send her any presents or jewels, which was thought very indecent."*

The scheme against Mary must have struck the Prince and Princess of Orange as unrealistic, since they were certain that Anne would never become a Roman Catholic. In April, when Mary had asked her sister for her views on Catholicism, Anne had replied stoutly: "I must tell you that I abhor the principles of the Church of Rome . . . the doctrine . . . is wicked and dangerous, and directly contrary to the Scriptures and their ceremonies – most of them – plain, downright idolatry."* When later in the year James had grace said by a priest at his dinner-table, Anne made a habit of looking another way, "which the King observing, one day he came to me and asked whether I did it on purpose or by chance . . . he said it was looking upon them as Turks, and looked disrespectfully to him . . . he said also he would not torment me about it, but hoped that one day God would open my eyes. . . ."*

Anne's attitude might have made it clear to the English Court that it would be difficult ever to convert her, but as Barillon wrote on 23 September to Paris: "Hope has not been given up of eventually finding a way to make the crown pass to a Catholic Heir."

Any man of sense would have realized the impossibility of sweeping out Mary, Anne and William from the throne, but to an obstinate visionary like James, one bill to exclude all Protestant heirs, passed by a Parliament packed with Catholics, was not out of the question. In that case the succession would pass to Marie-Louise d'Orléans, the eldest daughter of James's sister Henrietta and Monsieur, now Queen of Spain.

If James had seriously entertained such a fantastic scheme, another obvious move for him would have been to have his marriage to his first wife Anne Hyde declared null, thus making both Anne and Mary illegitimate. By a sinister coincidence one Edward Getthing was taken to court in November 1686 accused of making precisely this suggestion. He pleaded guilty but was fined only the derisory sum of £500.* Similar libels on James in the previous reign had earned fines of up to ten thousand pounds.

All these rumours and scandals had again brought the matter of succession into the limelight. Both James and William probably assumed that the crown would effectively be William's when the time came and it might have been expected that the question would have been discussed in detail between William and Mary. But according to a Scottish refugee in The Hague, Dr. Gilbert Burnet, who had come to know the Prince and Princess very well, it seemed not even to have been mentioned between them.

Burnet had fled England in 1684, touring Europe and writing political tracts on what he found. His writing had come to the notice of William, who invited him to visit him at The Hague in 1686. He was a generous and good-natured busybody with an underdeveloped sense of tact. Few men would have dared, in a private conversation with the Princess of Orange, to allude to a question so delicate as the position of her husband when she came to the throne.

But Burnet by his own account did and when he later revised his memoirs he included an account of an astonishing conversation with Mary. "She, who was new to all matters of that kind, did not understand my meaning, but fancied that whatever accrued to her would likewise accrue to him in right of marriage."* Burnet explained that this was not the case; as matters stood William would be no more than the husband of the Queen. And even more boldly he asked her to consider whether a man like the Prince would enjoy such a role. Mary was horrified and Burnet proposed his solution . . . "the remedy, if she could bring her mind to it, was to be contented to be his wife, and to engage herself to him, that she would give him the real authority as soon as it came into her hands, and endeavour effectually to get it to be legally vested in him during life." Burnet added very impertinently: "This would lay the greatest obligation on [William] possible, and lay the foundation of a perfect union between them, which had been of late a little embroiled."

Mary, he reported, was stunned by what she had learned and Burnet asked her to think it over carefully before committing herself to any decision. But she had made up her mind almost immediately and told Burnet: "She would take no time to consider of anything by which she could express her regard and affection to the Prince." She asked Burnet to report the whole conversation to her husband and bring him to her on his return from hunting.

The next day Burnet, still by his own account, was present at a crucial moment in the nine-year old marriage of the couple. He brought the Prince to Mary, who "in a very frank manner told him, that she did not know that the laws of England were so contrary to the laws of God, . . . She did not think that the husband was ever to be obedient to the wife; she promised him he should always bear rule: and she asked only, that he would obey the command of, Husbands love your wives, as she should do that, Wives be obedient to your husbands in all things". Burnet commented in satisfaction that both seemed very pleased with him, but he was a little hurt by the Prince's failure to acknowledge his good service.

The Prince is said to have told another friend later, however, that in all the nine years he had been married to the Princess he never had the confidence to ask her to consider this question, which Burnet had now helped to settle in one day.

If Burnet had the courage to interfere in so personal a matter now, it may have been because the couple were already in his debt. A little earlier he had been able to unmask a plot to kidnap the Prince. A friend of his at The Hague, Mr. Fatio, a celebrated mathematician, had had a lodger, "a brutal Savoyard, who was capable of the blackest thing", and who had already been convicted for murder. This person had noticed one of the Prince's habits which made him particularly vulnerable to an abduction attempt. The Prince had a sand-yacht, built by the famous Simon Stevin, in which on windy days he loved to skim over the flat beach of Scheveningen. He never took more than one other person and a couples of pages on the chariot. The Savoyard wrote to the French minister Louvois with a plan: "He offered to go in a small vessel of twenty guns, that should lie at some distance at sea and to land in a boat with seven persons besides himself and to seize on the Prince and bring him aboard, and so to France."

Louvois at once had shown interest and called him to Paris, sending money for his journey. The plotter could not resist boasting about it, and showed the letter to Mr. Fatio before he left for Paris. Burnet rushed to the Prince with his discovery. "He was not much moved at it", but the Princess was very worried and with the help of Fagel had an official request from the States addressed to him to take a body-guard wherever he went. The Prince, who was "very regardless of himself", complied reluctantly.

Burnet soon got to know William very well, and studied him shrewdly. What struck him immediately was that although the Stadholder "put on some appearance of application", he had a hatred for paper work. "This put him on a perpetual course of hunting", wrote Burnet, who looked on that "as a flying from company and business". He was also struck by the strength of William's feelings about Louis XIV. "The depression of France was the governing passion of his whole life."

Like everyone else, Burnet had quickly fallen under the Princess's spell. Soon after his arrival he wrote to a friend in Glasgow a letter in which he described her as the "most wonderfull person that I ever knew . . . She has a modesty, a sweetness, and a humility in her that cannot be enough admired. She has a vast understanding and knows a great deal."* Burnet was one of the first to appreciate that the Princess in spite of the limited education she had received had an excellent mind. "She had great knowledge, with a true understanding", he remarked and with his encouragement she began her political education.

"She knew little of our affairs, till I was admitted to wait on her. And I began to lay before her the state of our Court, and the intrigues in it, ever since the Restoration; which she received with great satisfaction, and shewed true judgment, and a good mind, in all the reflections that she made. . . ."* From now on Mary read far more about history, when the condition of her eyes allowed it, and certainly it was at about this time that in her own small way she first began to play an active part in English politics with her letters of remonstrance to her father.

What impressed Burnet most, however, was Mary's goodness. "She has a true and generous notion of the Christian religion, and her life is an example to all the world."* Mary's chaplain Stanley, writing to Dr. Henry Compton in May of this year, had said much the same thing. "The Princess is exemplary, constant and regular in her public devotions."

Unusually for Mary's chaplains, Stanley was also very much taken with the Prince, who he noted "hath come severall times whilest we were in the country, officially on Sundays in the afternoon to prayers, and three or four times to sermon". He found William very sympathetic to the Anglican faith – "he professes an approbation and esteem for our Church". Clearly the Prince had changed his mind about the Anglican rites which he had once disapproved so strongly, knowing very well that his new interest would be reported to Protestant circles in England, and these reports could not have been more glowing. Stanley summed up:

"I cannot but think him an extraordinarily good tempered person and for ought that I can perceive, well affected to the church."*

If William was anxious to make a good impression on English Protestants, however, he was still careful to avoid giving his father-in-law James a pretext for displays of resentment. In August 1686, his uncle the Elector of Brandenburg and his wife Dorothea came to the Mookerheide, on the heath at Limburg, for a review of the Dutch armies. Originally it was planned that Mary should accompany William and be hostess. To avoid protocol difficulties – strictly speaking, Mary as the daughter of a reigning King should have taken precedence over the Brandenburgs – the Princess would simply make a casual appearance at the review. But James heard of it, and made his displeasure known. The idea was given up and Mary stayed at home.*

The review went off very well. The Prince of Orange played host gracefully, riding hat in hand alongside the Brandenburg carriage and explaining every point about his troops. It was remarked how well drilled they were, and William revealed afterwards to a flattered Monsieur De Rébenac, the French ambassador to Berlin who was also present, that the army of the French King had been his example. He reassured the Frenchman – these troops were formed to prevent war, not to make it. If it was up to him, the Prince said, the world would always be at peace. The French ambassador was slightly sceptical and replied: "People, having such high ideas of his merit, would find it hard to believe that he had such a great love of repose."*

Another guest at the Mookerheids was Prince Philip Wilhelm, the eldest son of the Elector and his second wife. William, who had taken an immediate liking to this boy in 1680, invited him to come and stay with Mary and him in The Hague. In the autumn, the sixteen-year-old Prince arrived on a visit that was to last a year. The Dutch liked him very much and affectionately christened him Flip. He was guest of honour at the great ball on William's birthday on 14 November, he was shown around Holland, and fêted everywhere. His stepbrother Ludwig – about whom the Prince of Orange had once said that he regarded him as his son – died during Flip's stay and soon there were rumours going round that Philip Wilhelm had replaced Ludwig as candidate for the Orange succession in the Republic. Whether the Prince really meant to make him his successor or not is unknown. But although William and Mary in private had not given up hope of having children, it was generally assumed that there would be none and the Prince was perfectly prepared to exploit this belief when it suited him – in this case, in the hope of converting the Elector of Brandenburg from his French sympathies to the allied cause.

In the same autumn of 1686, William received a more important guest. Lord Mordaunt, a leading Whig peer, visited Holland with the King's permission and came at once to call on the Prince of Orange. During one of their conversations, he pressed the Prince to take matters in England into his own hands, and encouraged him to believe that a bloodless revolution, which would replace James with William and Mary, would be easy to bring about. The cautious William found the project completely unrealistic at this stage. But he promised that he would follow events in England carefully; that he would arrange his affairs in the Republic so as to be free to act when necessary; and finally, he assured his guest that if the King of England should threaten "to change the established religion, or to wrong the princess in her right, or to raise forged plots to destroy his friends", he would attempt what he could.*

Mordaunt had hardly left when another visitor from England arrived, William Penn, the well-known Quaker. It was James who had sent over this honest but naive man to put across as persuasively as he could James's own plans for abolishing the Test and Penal Acts, and for getting out of the Prince and Princess of Orange a public declaration of support for these measures of Toleration. James had come far since the early days of his reign when he had told Barillon his plans to relieve the Catholics with the support of the Anglican clergy – "which he regards as the royalist party".* He now knew that he could only rely on the Catholics themselves – and not all of them very wholeheartedly – and on Dissenters such as the Quakers, who suffered from the penal laws.

In Holland Penn hinted at a magnificent bonus for the Prince's co-operation: James would join the alliance against France. William needed nobody to spell out to him the facts of English political life – Parliament would vote against the King on the Test question, and without Parliamentary support James would never be able to turn against France. In any case, even if James's offer had been worth anything, William would have lost all credit with the English opposition by agreeing. He stated his own position clearly: he was for the repeal of the Elizabethan penal laws according to which Catholics were heavily fined for not attending Anglican services, where priests and those who attended Mass could be punished for treason. These laws had been, on the whole, a dead letter for years now, but they could still be used on occasion to harass Catholics. He told Penn that he "readily consented to a toleration of popery, as well as of the dissenters, provided it were proposed and passed in parliament, and he promised his assistance, if there were need of it, to get it passed." But the Test Acts were for William another matter.

"He looked on [them] as such a real security and indeed the only one, where the king was of another religion, that he would join in no counsels with them that intended to repeal those laws. . . ."* The Test Act of 1673 – "the black charter of Protestantism" – excluded everyone from civil or military office under the crown, who refused to take the sacrament according to the rites of the Church of England.

James was disappointed by William's reaction, but he went ahead with his plans undeterred. Foreign diplomats in London were astonished by his reckless zeal. "Politics were on the gallop" noted the Imperial ambassador, who observed that "the King seems determined to push on in religious matters as far as he possibly can."* Barillon, another shrewd observer, reported James's growing autocratic attitude: "The discontent is great and general; but the fear of incurring still worse evil, restrains all those who have anything to lose. The King openly expresses his joy at finding himself in a situation to strike bold strokes."*

He wrote this in July just after James had openly defied public opinion and the law by appointing four Roman Catholics to his Privy Council, and by establishing an Ecclesiastical Commission for the government of the Church of England, feared and dreaded by the Anglicans for its dictatorial nature. In October a Roman Catholic, Richard Talbot, the Earl of Tyrconnel, became Lord Lieutenant of Ireland with greatly increased powers, and in December 1686 James dismissed Lord Rochester when he refused to turn Catholic, and replaced him as Treasurer with a commission of five, two of whom were Catholics.

The Earl of Chesterfield expressed the feelings of the country when he wrote at the end of that year: "Though we have now a Prince, whose study is his country's glory, whose courage would give him lustre without a throne, whose assiduity in business makes him his own chief minister, yet heaven, it seems, hath found a way to make all this more terrible than lovely."*

CHAPTER XXI

The Turning Tide

THE NEW YEAR OF 1687 started appropriately with a display of good intentions: an exchange of ambassadors between England and the States-General with the object of trying to compose the differences between the two countries. James sent Ignatius White, the Irish Marquis d'Albeville, while the States envoy, personally chosen by William, was Everard van Weede van Dijkvelt.

D'Albeville was a Roman Catholic adventurer, one of the many second-rate talents on which James had to fall back on in his efforts to romanize his public service – there simply were not enough trained and educated Catholics available. He was, in Burnet's words, "a most contemptible and ridiculous man, who had not the common appearances of decency or of truth".* And even Barillon and Bonrepaus, the two French envoys in London, and D'Avaux at The Hague, who had secretly bought his services, wondered if he was worth the money.

Dijkvelt, by contrast, was an able and sympathetic man – the most influential statesman in Utrecht – with a considerable diplomatic reputation. Burnet described him as "the smoothest man that ever was bred in the Commonwealth", and he had great charm and polish, together with a warmly sympathetic manner that inspired people to talk freely to him. His instructions were "to expostulate decently but firmly with the king upon the methods he was pursuing both at home and abroad; and to see if it was possible to bring him to a better understanding with the prince . . . to assure all the church party, that the prince would ever be firm to the Church of England . . . to assure them [the dissenters] of a full toleration; and likewise of a comprehension, if possible, whensoever the crown should devolve on the princess."* In addition to these guidelines, Dijkvelt had a secret and delicate mission from the Prince, "To try all sorts of people and to remove the ill impressions that had been given of the prince."* In other words, he was to sound out possible supporters for William.

D'Albeville's instructions were to discover where William now stood in the question of the Test Act. The Prince did not make it easy for him, avoiding a meeting by going to Dieren for hunting, from where Mary and he followed events with growing concern. Almost every mail brought disquieting reports from Dijkvelt, especially the news that James, determined to wait no longer for the approval of his son-in-law and Mary, had told the Dutch envoy: "neither she nor the Prince could oppose his unalterable plans without displeasing him; their duty was to deserve a continuance of good will by an entire submission to his judgment." On 14 April 1687 the King made his Declaration of Indulgence. "The prisons were opened to thousands of the best men in England, and everywhere public worship was freely resumed. . . ."*

William, who personally wished that England could enjoy the same religious tolerance as his own country, was political realist enough to understand that James was dangerously ahead of his time. His action was seen by the Church of England as a direct attack on the social structure of the country. But even now the Prince hesitated over the best way of explaining his objections to his father-in-law,* and it was only after Dijkvelt returned in June and brought his report, that William wrote on the seventeenth of that month. He began by stating that he disliked persecution, but added that he was determined never to do anything to the disadvantage of his religion, and that for that reason could not lend himself to what the King wished of him.*

James made a last effort and instructed D'Albeville to approach the Princess directly. He received exactly the same response. It was underlined later for him by the Prince: "Even if he were to lose everything, including his wife's claim to the throne, he would never consent to what the King intended."* "The King of England was more embittered against him than ever before", reported Bonrepaus from London to Paris,* and James himself made this plain to William in one of the shortest letters he ever wrote to him. "As the reasons I asked Dijkvelt to put before you have not been able to convince you, obviously no letter of mine would do so and I shall spare myself the trouble."*

William was, however, encouraged in his stand by a bundle of letters Dijkvelt brought back for him from England. The leaders of the Opposition in England had not been content with sending William verbal assurances of their devotion to the Prince, they had put it in writing. Some of the most distinguished men in England – among them Halifax, Danby, Compton, Admiral Herbert, Shrewsbury, John Churchill and even a Tory like Nottingham – made it clear that they looked on William as the man who might eventually save England. As the popular Shrewsbury put it: "The great and only consolation we have left is that you are so generous to countenance us in our misfortune. . . ."*

The most significant of these letters was written by John Churchill at the instructions of Princess Anne. Mary's younger sister had made plans to come over to The Hague for a visit, but her father had considered this too dangerous and had forbidden it. In silent protest, Anne retired from court and paraded her Protestantism as publicly as possible. In Churchill's letter she proudly proclaimed it. "She was resolved by the assistance of God to suffer all extremities, even to death itself, rather than to be brought to change her religion . . ."*

Churchill, whose wife Sarah Jennings was known to dominate her mistress Princess Anne completely, thought it advisable to add an oblique assurance. "I think it may be a great ease to Your Highness and the Princess to be satisfied that the Princess of Denmark is safe in the trusting of me, I being resolved, although I cannot live the life of a Saint, if there ever be occasion for it, to show the resolution of a martyr."*

Anne's decision to retire from Court was a shrewd one, as became more and more apparent. Roman Catholic influence was growing daily, while the number of Protestant courtiers thinned. The Royal Household trooped off daily to hear mass in the Catholic chapel, recently splendidly fitted up with marble and tapestries. Grace was heard at every meal and when the first Papal Nuncio in England since the time of Mary I, Ferdinand, Count of Adda, made his official entry in 1687 and appeared at Court, James to everyone's horror fell on his knees before him. Even Pope Innocent XI thought that James was going too far too fast. The King listened reluctantly to his criticism, but when the ambassador of Catholic Spain, Don Pedro Ronquillo, made the same point, he bit back: "Is it not the custom in Spain for the King to consult with his confessors?" "Yes Sir," replied Ronquillo drily, "and that is the very reason our affairs succeed so ill."

These indications of James's religious fervour were duly reported to The Hague, and gave increasing doubts of James's mental stability. But William was perhaps more diverted than alarmed when he heard of the King's latest plan for an attack on the Protestant Dutch, with the object of "destroying heresy everywhere". The plan was revealed to the Pope by James's ambassador at Rome, the inept Lord Castlemaine, and caused general astonishment. France and England, with the support of the Pope, James proposed, would fall upon the Dutch "without any declaration of war, treating them as a company of rebels and pirates, who had not a right, as free states and princes have, to a formal declaration of war".*

When it came to William's ears he could not seriously believe that James was planning such an attack but it was an indication of the way in which his troubled mind was moving and the Prince filed it for future reference.

"THE KING IS STILL ASSURED that he shal have a house of Commons to his licking, and doubts not of getting such a party in the House of Lords, as wil doe what he semes to desire" wrote one Fitzpatrick to the Prince of Orange on 1 September 1687.* James had dissolved Parliament two months earlier and set out, with his wife Mary Beatrice, for a Royal progress which was also an election campaign. While the Queen went to take the waters at Bath, James turned southwards, pausing at Winchester where Charles II had begun the building of a spectacular new palace designed by Christopher Wren. From there he went on to inspect his navy and channel fortresses, and he joined Mary Beatrice at Bath at the end of August.

On the day Fitzpatrick wrote to William, James travelled north by way of Gloucester and Shrewsbury, reaching Chester on 5 September, where he met Tyrconnel, his commander of Ireland. The handsome Earl known at Whitehall as "lying Dick Talbot", had been one of James's favourites for years, often playing the role of pander to the King's sexual adventures. But as Macaulay waspishly remarked: "Talbot was not only welcome at the Palace when the bottle or the dice box was going around, but was heard with attention on matters of business."* And the business discussed at Chester was highly important: how Ireland could be turned into a Roman Catholic fortress. Tyrconnel was building up a Roman Catholic army and civil service, and James was already considering the possibility of separating Ireland from England, if the English remained obstinately Protestant. It was even strongly rumoured, as the Dutch ambassador Van Citters had reported to the Prince of Orange in October 1686, that James was planning to give Ireland its own Catholic king, and had in mind the seventeen-year-old Duke of Berwick, his bastard son by Arabella Churchill.*

But he had not given up hope of a legitimate Catholic heir for England, and the end of his tour he made a pilgrimage to the miraculous well of St. Winifrede at Holywell near Chester, where he publicly prayed for a son. It had been many months since Mary Beatrice had last shown signs of pregnancy, and England devoutly hoped that James's prayers would not be answered.

Politically, his tour had been a disappointment. The King had hoped for demonstrations of national support for his policy, and they had not been forthcoming. "I hear in all the King's progress very few of the gentry wayted one his Majesty", wrote Fitzpatrick to the Prince.* But James was still not unduly worried about the coming elections. With the help of Sunderland, the ground had been so carefully prepared that he looked forward to a Parliament filled with obedient yes-men. The corporations of cities up and down the country had been packed with his supporters; Lords Lieutenant hostile to his policy had been replaced; and during all this autumn a final effort was being made. The Lords Lieutenant of every county were instructed to put three questions to every man of influence or standing in local affairs.

The first question was an outrageous defiance of Parliamentary privilege: if you are elected as M.P. will you support the repeal of the Penal Laws and the Test Act? The second question was as impertinent: will you use your influence to elect a member so pledged? Only the third question was innocuous, asking for an undertaking to live "friendly with those of all persuasions, as subjects of the same Prince, and good Christians ought to do".

The reaction of the country amounted to a national condemnation of James's policy. Most of the Lords Lieutenant refused even to put the questions and when they were asked only the third question was answered affirmatively in most cases. Van Citters summed up the results in a letter to The Hague: the leaders of the nation and the nobility were adamant in their refusal to see the Test Act abolished.

All this time the Prince of Orange had kept silent. If he had made it privately known to the King where he stood on the question of religious freedom, he had never yet made a public statement, despite continuous pressure from James's opponents. Rumours in England that the Prince now consented to the repeal of the Test Act as well as the Penal laws, however, made William look for an opportunity to reassure the English.

Fagel had been corresponding with a certain James Stewart, a Scottish dissenter who had lived in The Hague but had returned to London, reconciled with James through Penn the Quaker. Stewart had become a fervent supporter of James's policy for religious freedom, and now undertook the conversion of the Prince of Orange. In his letters to Fagel he urged him to win the Prince over and make a statement on the question.

In November William at last obliged, but not in the way Stewart had intended. He called on the help of Burnet – "who not only had a profound knowledge of English affairs, but I can think of no one more suitable to translate it"* – and composed together with him a reply ostensibly from Fagel that was in effect William's manifesto. In it he declared himself in favour of toleration of all dissenters, including Catholics, and the abolition of the Penal Law. He remained, however, opposed to the repeal of the Test Act. James was one of the first to see Fagel's letter and he read it with irritation, "being in no way satisfied with the distinction made of the Test from the Penal laws", wrote Stewart to Fagel.*

It was at this time that James seems first to have thought of his daughter Mary as a possible convert to Roman Catholicism – perhaps even a more docile subject for his efforts than her sister Anne – and he now set about the task of enlightening her with enthusiasm. He had heard, he wrote to her at the beginning of November, that she had mentioned to D'Albeville her curiosity to know what had motivated his own conversion, and he explained it to her at some length. It was mainly the devotion of Catholics of all classes which had first impressed him; and it was the Church's claim to infallibility which finally won him over. Mary wrote back in guarded terms, declining direct discussion of such a thorny subject, but James replied more insistently, at the same time asking D'Albeville to press her for a definite answer. Yielding to these pressures, Mary shut herself up in her study on 26 December, re-read James's letter carefully, and composed her own lengthy reply. For a woman whose intellectual capacities nobody, apart from Burnet, had appreciated until then, it was a remarkable performance: a clear, cogent and closely-reasoned attack on her father's faith which surprised and impressed James.

He replied complimenting her on her understanding: in the hope of appealing to her more directly, he sent her papers about their conversion written by her own mother, his first wife, and her uncle Charles II. In addition, he begged her to see a Jesuit priest at The Hague, a Father Morgan. Mary wrote back promising to read the papers and a book he had sent her, but she declined the talks with the Jesuit, rightly surmising that D'Albeville would at once give any such meeting the most sensational publicity. The envoy was already making himself a perfect pest, turning up unannounced in Mary's drawing-room, and boasting everywhere of the freedom with which they talked about religion together. Mary accordingly took the precaution of writing long explanatory letters about the whole incident to her sister Anne, the Bishop of London, and her chaplain Dr. Stanley, in London at this time.

She had shown these letters to William, together with a copy of her letter to the King. "The Prince", she wrote in her journal, "seemed so pleased with it and was so surprised by it, not thinking me capable of such a thing, that I confess it flattered not a little my vanity . . ."

In the New Year she sat down to read seriously through the book James had sent her – *Reflections on Differences in Religion*. She was not impressed by it, put off at the outset by its author's pious, ingratiating tone, but she read it dutifully, then on 17 February she sent her father a long eloquent rebuttal of its arguments: nothing in the book, she concluded, had given her the slightest inclination to change her views. She had by this time also read the papers of Charles II – "nothing in it to shake me" – and of her mother – "I found her reasons as strange as they were surprising for a woman of whom I had always heard it said that she possessed great intelligence." A final attempt – some extracts from St. Cyprian's writings – was demolished by her with equal spirit, and James acknowledged defeat. Deeply vexed, according to Mary, "he said he desired to send me no more books or papers. That was what I hoped . . ."*

THE YEAR 1688 OPENED QUIETLY ENOUGH. Apart from a palace revolution in Turkey, and another in faraway Siam, where the French were thrown out, very little was stirring in the world, as James was fond of saying. But the calm was only short-lived, and in the middle of January the King, frustrated in his efforts to win the support of the Prince and Princess of Orange, demanded from the States-General the return of the six English and Scottish regiments. He sent Colonel Wauchope, Elizabeth Villiers's former lover, over to Holland to bring them back.

James had been preparing this coup since the summer of 1687,* when he had asked Louis XIV to receive the regiments into the French army. Since they were mainly Protestant, and much better paid than the French soldiers, the French King refused the offer, but he undertook to pay for the upkeep of 2000 troops on their return to England.

The States-General thereupon disbanded the troops and made it known that those who wanted to were free to go. Many of the men, including almost all the Catholics who had little chance of promotion in William's army, returned to England. William was left with a strong body of English and Scots soldiers whom he knew to be loyal to the Protestant cause.

The rift between William and James was now complete. When Danby's son asked the King's leave to go to the Continent in March, James granted it, "but said with some heat, provided it be not into Holland, for I will suffer nobody to go thither."*

On the other side of the North Sea, mistrust was also deepening. The recall of the troops had destroyed the last vestiges of Dutch goodwill for James, and the follies of his ambassador did nothing to mend matters. One day, when William in conversation with D'Albeville referred to James's oath to maintain the laws and the established church, the ambassador answered recklessly, "Upon some occasions princes must forget their promises." When the Prince said that the King ought to take greater care of the Church of England which was the main body of the nation, D'Albeville answered, "That the body which he called the church of England would not have a being two years to an end."* Emanating from a man with James's record such a threat could not be disregarded, and William mentally added it to the growing list of James's follies and misdeeds.

Winter changed into spring, a wet and wretched season this year, which brought an epidemic of severe influenza to an England already feverish with discontent. The atmosphere at Whitehall was heavy with suspicion. In the previous December the English had learned that James's prayers at St. Winifrede's well had been heard – Mary Beatrice was pregnant. Most of her previous pregnancies had, however, ended in miscarriages and if James was elated, the English were not as yet too much alarmed. Months had now gone by, there was still no word of the expected miscarriage, and James and his Roman Catholic Cabal triumphed openly. But they were soon almost alone in their belief that the pregnancy was genuine, most people preferring the comforting theory that it was all a wicked plot. As Danby wrote to William in March: "Many of our ladies say that the Queen's great belly seems to grow faster than they have observed their own to do."*

Mary Beatrice was well aware of these sniggering rumours, but as a matter of personal pride refused to offer the Protestant ladies of the Court any visual proof. Her toilette was performed without the customary ceremonial, only the Roman Catholic ladies being admitted, and once, when the Countess of Clarendon arrived unannounced while the Queen was dressing, she was hustled away.

Princess Anne was one of the first, and the most willing, to believe the rumours, "there being so much reason to believe it is a false belly", she wrote to Mary on 20 March. "For, methinks if it were not, there having been so many stories and jests made about it, she should, to convince the world, make either me, or some of my friends feel her belly. But quite the contrary, whenever I happen to be in the room as she has been undressing, she has always gone into the next room to put on her smock."*

The Princess of Orange, who had been kept posted about the

rumours, was perturbed by her sister's letter. As she wrote in her journal, "I received such an account of the Queen's condition as to give me just cause to suspect there had been some trickery."* She had first learned of the Queen's pregnancy from Mary Beatrice herself, "still in rather doubtful terms" since she was not sure. A couple of weeks later, the King wrote about it to Mary in another style as she noticed "speaking of it in such an assured manner, and that at a time when no woman could have been certain, as to give rise to some slight suspicion".*

Her first reaction had been one of pleasure. She had always been the best of friends with her young stepmother, who had shown her kindness and sympathy during her own miscarriages, and Mary knew from experience how bitter the disappointment of a miscarriage or a mistaken pregnancy could be. In March 1688, indeed, there were fresh rumours that she herself was with child – followed by yet another painful denial.*

That Mary Beatrice's child might turn out to be a boy, who would take precedence of the Princess of Orange in the succession, did not at first disturb Mary either. "This news does not trouble me" she confessed to her journal, "God having given me such a contented mind and no ambition other than that of serving my Creator." But she soon understood that a new Prince of Wales would be born and brought up a Roman Catholic, and that she could not afford to remain indifferent in a question which involved the safety of the Protestant religion in England. "This drew me out of the gentle and satisfying tranquillity which I had been enjoying, and made me realize how much I was obliged to wish that I myself might come at the Crown." There was another consideration as potent: "The love I have for the Prince brings me to wish for him all that he deserves, and although I regret having no more than three crowns to offer him, its not my love that makes me blind; no, I can see his failings, but I say this because I also know his merits."*

In the circumstances, the rumours that Mary Beatrice's pregnancy was a wicked Catholic invention came almost as a relief to Mary who grasped at them eagerly.

While all this was going on William and Mary left The Hague for the house at Het Loo, but as in England the weather in the Republic this spring was appalling, and Mary wrote sadly to Lady Mary Forester: "I have bin once in the litle wood, where we playd at hide and seek since I came hithere, the ill wethere will not suffer much walking."* The worst possible weather, however, never deterred the Prince from going hunting, and it was not surprising that by the beginning of May he was in very poor health, suffering from a racking cough. Mary had the greatest difficulty in getting him to take anything for it, but she prevailed and gave him some remedies, which "by the blessing of God, did him a great deal of good".*

His illness, as the Emperor's ambassador Kramprich remarked, was possibly not only due to a cold. In April the Prince had had to interrupt his stay at Het Loo for an important visitor, Georg III, Elector of Saxony, who had come to The Hague for talks with William and his reception by the States had been magnificent. One witness told how only the host was less drunk than the guest, and Kramprich reported that the Prince's health "had been in danger through . . . the great number of banquets and the exaggerated drinking, while the Prince normally lives with great and praiseworthy sobriety."* The Elector followed William to Het Loo, a visit that put Mary in a dilemma. She and the Prince had the habit of keeping Easter according to the English calendar and the Elector arrived on 22 April, for the English the Thursday before Easter. The Prince, in consideration for his guest, had switched at once to the continental habit and already celebrated Easter a week earlier. His wife, who thought that she would hardly be disturbed by the Prince's guest, stuck to her own Anglican calendar, but while the Elector was at Het Loo she was completely distracted by the "novelty of meeting such a person" and by the Prince's insistence that she should dress up and put on all her jewellery. She enjoyed it very much, but afterwards noted sadly that her mind had been too far "from my duty and my devotion, which made me realize that I was not as determined and strong against the vanities of this world as I ought to be."*

The guest for whom all this fuss was made had a special importance for the Prince of Orange; he hoped to draw him, with many other princes, into a new alliance against France. Louis XIV had lost nothing of his aggressiveness in the last years and he had succeeded in alienating almost the whole of Europe by his imperious demands. He had antagonized the Pope by insisting on the right of the French ambassador in Rome to extend the embassy's diplomatic immunity; he had outraged the Emperor by siding with the Turks; the Spaniards had not forgiven the occupation of the fortresses in the southern Netherlands, and even the merchants of Amsterdam had turned their backs on him, following a tariff war imposed by the French.

Now, in the spring of 1688, Louis XIV put forward further territorial demands which made it clear to Europe that sooner or later a war was inevitable. He laid claims in the name of his sister-in-law Liselotte, the daughter of the Elector Palatine, to the whole Palatinate stretching up the Rhine from Strasbourg to Mainz, and at the same time he tried to get control over the Electorate of Cologne by foisting his candidate Wilhelm von Furstenberg, Bishop of Strasbourg, on the cathedral chapter as successor to the dying Archbishop.

This threat of a strong French presence on the Upper Rhine was almost enough to pull the German princes together in self-defence. The Prince of Orange, for once with the wholehearted support of the Dutch, made the most of this opportunity to cement a Protestant alliance, at which he worked tirelessly for the next few months. He badly needed the solidity and reassurance of neighbours united against France, because it was becoming clear that before very long he would have to give his full attention to the affairs of England.

CHAPTER XXII

Rock-a-Bye Baby

O N 7 MAY 1688 James published his Second Declaration of Indulgence. It was largely a repetition of the first with one sinister addition; speaking of freedom of conscience, the King announced that he had had to dismiss from his civil and military service those who refused to co-operate with his policy. There was only one interpretation of these words possible: for James, freedom of conscience meant absolute obedience to his wishes.

The Opposition at last decided on action. Admiral William Russell came over to The Hague, on pretext of visiting his sister. "He was desired by many of great power and interest in England to speak very freely to the Prince, and to know positively of him what might be expected from him. . . ."* The Prince explained that he was prepared "to come and rescue the nation and the religion" and that he believed he could be ready by the end of September. But he made it clear that he was not prepared to move unless he was formally invited "by some men of the best interest, and the most valued in the nation".*

Russell took this answer back to England, and William returned with a new sense of urgency to work for his alliance against France. He sent Van Amerongen to Saxony to renew the pressure on Georg III, only a month earlier a guest at Het Loo. The Elector was sympathetic but declined to commit himself. William received the same answer from the Elector of Hanover, who, however, gave an assurance that he would undertake nothing against the Prince of Orange. But from the most powerful state in Germany, Brandenburg, he obtained a promise of full co-operation.

William's uncle, the old Elector Friedrich Wilhelm, had died on 9 May and his son Friedrich had succeeded him. One of his first actions had been to ask the Prince to send someone trustworthy to him for talks, and for a mission on which so much depended William could rely on nobody but Bentinck. He sent him away reluctantly, since his friend's wife Anne and son Willem were both seriously ill. It was his intention, as D'Avaux guessed, to take Friedrich completely into his confidence about his plans for England and to ask him to cover the eastern frontier of the Republic with a force of 1000 men. The negotiations were protracted and Waldeck sighed cynically: "With the Elector of Brandenburg there is nothing to be done without money."*

The death of the old Archbishop-Elector of Cologne, on 3 June, shortly before Bentinck reached Berlin, brought the European crisis closer and gave fresh urgency to the talks in Berlin. The Prince wrote pressingly to Bentinck on 7 June: "The elector of Cologne is dead. France will try to cause the election of Cardinal Fürstenberg by force of arms. If the Emperor and the Princes of the Empire suffer the Chapter to be forced . . . they must no more think of German liberty." With the Empire still at war with Turkey, the German princes must save themselves, and William hoped that the Elector of Brandenburg could be talked into taking the lead.*

The Dutchman's mission achieved almost all that the Prince of Orange had hoped, but Friedrich asked for a secret meeting with his cousin before he committed himself. For Bentinck himself these had been heartbreaking weeks. While his wife was still desperately ill his son, who had never been very strong, died. The Prince broke the news to his friend: "Although I believe that you hardly expected poor Willemtie to live, that won't save you from great grief at learning that he died yesterday evening. I can assure you that I am deeply touched."* Two weeks later Bentinck, deep in tricky negotiations with the prince and ministers of Hesse-Cassel, Zell and Hanover, received another distressing letter from the Prince. "I found that Madam your wife had had a high fever all the previous night and that she was very weak . . . She is in danger." But three days later William hastened to reassure him: "I have real joy in being able to tell you at once, that Madam your wife is very much better, and that for two days and nights she has had no fever."*

While the Prince of Orange spared no effort in the construction of a strong anti-French coalition, his uncle the King of England was no less busy working out his own destruction. He no longer seemed a man open to reason. Even Sunderland, now a Catholic himself and James's most trusted adviser, remarked that there was no leading the King but "by a woman, a priest or both", while the foreign diplomats noticed that his stubbornness looked more and more like insanity. He continually told d'Adda, the Papal Nuncio, that all Charles I's troubles had come on him by his failure to act harshly enough – "*per la troppa indulgenza*" – and this thought became an obsession with him. "I will make no concession," he often repeated, "my father made concessions and he was beheaded."*

His insistence that his Second Declaration of Indulgence should be read out from the pulpit of every Protestant church in the country on successive Sundays in June, was typical of his determination to remain firm. He refused to listen to protests and when seven of the ten English bishops, headed by Archbishop Sancroft, petitioned him to withdraw the order, he responded by throwing them into the Tower on a charge of sedition. The bishops protested that the Declaration was "founded upon such a dispensing power, as hath often been declared illegal in Parliament" and they had added that: "Your petitioners cannot in prudence, honour and conscience so far make themselves party to it."*

The arrest of the bishops created a sensation in England. Crowds gathered to protest as they were taken down the river to the Tower on 8 June. "Some persons ran into the water to implore a blessing . . . both banks of the Thames were lined with multitudes, who, when too distant to be heard, manifested their feelings by falling down on their knees", wrote Van Citters to the States-General.* The indignation was general and even nonconformist ministers – once regarded by James as his wholehearted allies – came to visit the distinguished prisoners, which act earned them a sharp reprimand from the King.*

The English had hardly recovered from the shock when a long-dreaded event took place: Mary Beatrice gave birth to a son on 10 June. The birth had been premature and took everybody by surprise. Lord Clarendon wrote in his diary:

> In the morning I was at St. James Church, where I observed great whispering, but could not learn what the matter was. As I was going home, my page told me the Queen was brought to bed of a son: I sent presently to St. James (whither the Court removed but last night) and word was brought to me that it was true that her Majesty was delivered about ten this morning. As soon as I had dined, I went to the Court and found the King shaving. He said the Queen was so quick in her labour, and he had so much company, that he had not time to dress himself until now. He bid me go and see the Prince. I went into the room which had formerly been the Duchess' private bedchamber and there my Lady Powis (who was made governess) showed me the Prince; he was asleep in his cradle and was a very fine child to look upon.*

Almost immediately it was said that the child was not Mary Beatrice's at all but a changeling smuggled into the lying-in chamber in a warming-pan on instructions from the Jesuits. Suspicious circumstances were made much of: the last-minute move from Windsor to St. James's was because the Queen's bedchamber there had a convenient secret entrance, and almost all of those present had been Papists. It would have been normal to invite Clarendon and his brother Rochester to the lying-in as uncles of Mary and Anne. Other missing witnesses were Archbishop Sancroft, still in the Tower, and the Dutch ambassador. But the most important absentee was Princess Anne, who was said to have been sent to Bath by her father.

She hurried back to London all agog on hearing the news, and wrote to Mary: "My dear sister can't imagine the concern and vexation I have been in, that I should be so unfortunate to be out of town when the Queen was brought to bed, for I shall never now be satisfied whether the child be true or false. It may be it is our brother, but God only knows, for she never took care to satisfy the world, or give people any demonstration of it." She ended her letter: " 'tis possible it may be her child; but where one believes it, a thousand do not."* The letter threw Mary into a state of confusion in which one sentiment stood out – anger with Anne who "has committed an irreparable fault by her absence". She read and re-read the details Anne had supplied and tried to make up her mind. The birth of the child, coming only two days after the arrest of the bishops, struck her as very suspicious, as did the fact that it arrived "much too soon, since it still wanted a month to the Queen's time".*

In spite of her doubts, Mary gave immediate orders that the child should be publicly prayed for in her chapel, against the advice of her chaplain Dr. Stanley, but with the approval of the Prince, who sent Zuylestein to London to compliment James and Mary Beatrice on the birth. These prayers in the Orange Household were the only public acknowledgment made by the Dutch.

The English ambassador D'Albeville did his best to make up for this lack of enthusiasm. He lit huge bonfires and erected a triumphal arch in the street outside his house. The arch showed a royal crown under which a baby sat on a great globe, with a sceptre in one hand and in the other an olive branch. The Dutch people found it very significant that when the arch was lit up in the evening, both crown and sceptre crashed to the ground. The English consul Petit in Amsterdam had no better luck. His bonfires attracted the attention of the pro-Orange rabble, and his guests had to flee to safety through a neighbouring house to escape their fury.*

No representatives of the Court or the States had attended D'Albeville's party, of which he complained bitterly. His vexation grew when the Princess decided to have the prayers for her little step-brother stopped. She took this drastic step after consulting the Prince about the rumours which made it "impossible not to have strong suspicions, which upset me very much". D'Albeville's subsequent protest under instructions from James made the cautious Prince think again, and very much against Mary's judgment, the prayers were resumed, at least for the time being.*

The end of the month of June saw the trial of the seven bishops in London. Judge Jeffreys, notorious since the Bloody Assizes, was now Lord Chancellor but he could do nothing to prevent the defenders of the bishops making a brilliant attack on the legality of the King's dispensing power, and the jury declared them innocent. The streets of London and every town in England were filled with cheering crowds when the news arrived, and the bonfires that no one had troubled to light for the new Prince of Wales blazed everywhere, in defiance of strict orders.*

The general impression was that the acquittal of the bishops was by the same token the condemnation of the King's dispensing power, and "it was wished at Court that the thing had never been begun." Sir John Reresby was present the day afterwards when the King inspected his army in camp on Hounslow Heath. "Everybody observed he was disturbed."*

James had more reason to be disturbed than he knew. On that same day his former Rear-Admiral and ex-Master of the Robes, Arthur Herbert, disguised as a common sailor, crossed the North Sea carrying an invitation to William to come over and save England. The invitation had been drawn up in haste and it was signed by seven leading members of the aristocracy and the Church of England. Three men signed it on behalf of the outlawed but powerful Whig families – William Cavendish, Earl of Devonshire, Edward Russell, cousin of the famous Whig martyr under Charles II, and Charles Talbot, Earl of Shrewsbury, whose conversion to the Church of England from Catholicism in 1679 later cost him his public career under James. Three men signed it for the Tories: Thomas Osborne, Earl of Danby, Charles's brilliant minister, who had been living in semi-retirement for some time and was much opposed to James's pro-French policy; Richard Lumley, a Catholic until 1679 and once a loyal supporter of James, who had become one of his most outspoken critics; and Henry Sidney, always a great "Williamite". The church was represented by the suspended Dr. Henry Compton. Two other politicians had known of the invitation, but hesitated to commit themselves by signing it: Halifax and the Tory Daniel Finch, Earl of Nottingham. Since the paper was on the face of it a treasonable document, the seven signed by code-numbers only.

In their invitation, the seven asserted that they spoke for England: "Your highness may be assured, there are nineteen parts of twenty of the people throughout the Kingdom who are desirous of a change." And they gave him a solemn promise: "we who subscribe this will not fail to attend your highness upon your landing." More detailed suggestions about this landing were left for Herbert, the bearer of the invitation, to communicate to the Prince by word of mouth.

That the seven Revolutionaries had picked Herbert as their messenger was not so much for his Protestant fervour as for his reckless adventuring spirit. He was a one-eyed, loose-living, foul-mouthed hero of James's navy, who claimed to have fallen out with his King because he refused to support the repeal of the Test Act.

In fact a most unwelcome enquiry into his financial misconduct during a Mediterranean command hung over Herbert's head: he owed the Treasury more than £4000 and was unable to account for numbers of slaves he had starved and sold.* In the circumstances, he had been happy to resign, and even happier now to retire to Holland, where the Prince of Orange made him his Rear-Admiral of the States fleet, "which made the King very angry, a great many seamen going after him."*

A week after his arrival, Mary heard the latest news of James's son: "The Prince of Wales has been ill these three or four days" wrote Anne, adding hopefully "and if he has been as bad as some people say, I believe it will not be long before he is an angel in heaven."* But the little boy was stronger than Anne expected, and survived after his diet had been changed from an ill-advised "water-gruell", made with barley, water, sugar and currants, to a normal milk diet.* Zuylestein had by this time returned from his polite visit to London and brought Mary – as she wrote in her memoirs – "still more confirmation of the suspicion we had here". The Princess was determined now to put an end to her agonized uncertainty about the child's legitimacy, and after Anne's unsatisfactory accounts, she drew up a long list of eighteen detailed and technical questions. She numbered them carefully in order to extract methodical replies from her lazy sister. "Did any woman, besides the confidants, see the Queen's face when she was in labour?" was one of them. "Was there a woman called in to hold the Queen?" "Was there a screen around the bed?" "How long did the labour last?" and "Is the Queen fond of it?" were others.*

Anne obliged under protest as soon as she could and gave the answers on 24 July. Describing Mary Beatrice's labour she wrote:

> When she was in great pain . . . the Queen desired the King to hide her face with his head and periwig, which he did, for she said she could not be brought to bed and have so many men look on her.

There had been no screen in the room and according to Anne's account

> as soon as the child was born, the midwife cut the navel-string . . . and then she gave it to mrs Labaudie, who as she was going . . . to carry it

into the little bedchamber, the King stopped her, and said to the Privy Councillors, that they were witnesses there was a child born, and bid them follow it into the next room and see what it was, which they all did.

The only negative evidence of a plot Anne had been able to gather was that she had never heard of anyone feeling the child stir before birth, and that Anne herself had seen no milk.* Anne was conscious that she had made out a very weak case for the prosecution: telling Mary that much of her information had come from the midwife Mrs. Dawson, she summed up lamely: "All that she says seems very clear but one does not know what to think."*

To an unprejudiced reader Anne's answers prove almost conclusively that unless there had been a conspiracy among all the people present, Mary Beatrice had indeed given birth to a son. But Mary was not an impartial and detached reader: on the contrary, she wanted desperately to be convinced that the Prince of Wales was a fraudulent changeling.

The Prince by now had informed her of the invitation of the Seven and of his plans to invade England to save the State and Church. In Mary's eyes the best justification for William's action was "the horrible crime of which her father was guilty by his fraud". If the child were genuinely James's, Mary, with her innate respect for the hereditary principle, would have found it difficult to support the idea of an invasion. But England must not remain in the power of the Catholics, nor her husband, deprived of his three crowns, be thwarted in his European plans. She closed her mind therefore when she received a charming and affectionate little note from Mary Beatrice announcing the birth: "The first time I have taken pen in hand since I was brought to bed is to write to my dear LEMON." Mary's reply was cold and evasive on the subject of the new baby: "All the king's children shall ever find as much affection and kindness from me as can be expected from the children of the same father."*

James, who had protested to his daughter about the omission of prayers in her chapel, received an equally shifty note from Mary, who was just on the point of leaving for her country home at Het Loo:

> I see you had heard that the Prince of Wales was no more prayed for in my chapel; but long before this, you will know that it had onely bin sometime forgot. M. d'Albeville can assure you I never told him it was forbid, so that they wear only conjectures made upon its being sometimes neglected; but he can tell, as you find your Majesty already knows, that he (the prince) was prayed for heer before it was done in England. This excessive hot weather continues . . .*

It was obvious that the Princess's mind was made up. From now on she would wholeheartedly support the Prince in his plans even if it meant watching her husband turn her father off the throne of England. But she was a warm-hearted woman and while she felt that her husband was completely justified in his action, the idea of it horrified her. William had been prepared for this reaction and gave her all the sympathy and tenderness she needed: "The Prince . . . has seen my tears and pities me."*

The Prince by this time was used to discussing his plans freely with his wife and she was the first to know of his real intentions, "which is that my husband should go to dethrone [my father] by force".* To outsiders the Prince denied that he had such far-reaching plans. He wrote, for example, to Castanaga, the Governor of the Spanish Netherlands, around that time: "Although my enemies would have the world believe it, be assured that my intention is not to dethrone the King of England. . . . But I find myself obliged in honor and in conscience to go there to maintain the subjects in their laws and religion and to procure a liberty of conscience according to the laws."*

The Prince of Orange knew, however, that matters in England had gone too far for a temporary solution which would leave James on the throne. He knew the King's blind attachment to his romanizing policies too well to hope that he might have a change of heart. Without this change a revolution in England was inevitable, and William had understood this for months now. He knew, too, that a revolution which he did not lead himself was more likely to end in a republic than in the crowning of William III of England. A republican England would not only mean a direct threat to the Dutch as in the days of Cromwell, but was unlikely to be drawn into his ambitious design against France.

There was no choice. To safeguard Europe, the Republic and a Protestant England, he was obliged to interfere, whatever his personal feelings. He was not concerned about the newborn Prince of Wales – he had once said in a discussion with Witsen, the Burgemeester of Amsterdam that even if Mary Beatrice had a son "his rights would be as good as before" – and he was too realistic to accept the theory of a fraud. He knew very well that the birth of a Prince of Wales was not the miracle that was going to save James, but the final *coup* that would make the King's destruction certain. As they were singing in England:

> *Rock-a-bye baby, in the tree top,*
> *When the wind blows the cradle will rock,*
> *When the bough breaks the cradle will fall,*
> *And down will come baby, cradle and all.*

JAMES II MADE IT NECESSARY for the Prince of Orange to intervene
in the affairs of England in 1688; it was Louis XIV who made it possible.
By his menacing posture on the Rhine he gave William a pretext for
raising an army and a powerful inducement to lure the Protestant
German princes into an alliance. And by his trade restrictions on the
Dutch, the French King had alienated even his staunchest supporters
in the Republic, who rallied now in unusual unity around the Stadholder.

The French attack on Dutch trade had begun in the autumn of 1687,
when France forbade the import of herrings other than those salted with
French salt, and followed it up with a ban on manufactured linen
and woollen cloths. The States had been obliged in retaliation to
prohibit French brandy and sugars, but nothing could make up for the
loss of the herring industry on which 60,000 Dutchmen depended for a
living.

Even so, when Raadspensionary Fagel told Burgemeester Nicolaas
Witsen of Amsterdam in the beginning of 1688 that the Stadholder might
have to interfere in the affairs of England, the reaction of the Amsterdammer was cautious. After the birth of James's son and the invitation
of the Seven, the Prince himself talked to Witsen and told him that
matters had reached a crisis – "*Aut nunc aut nunquam*". But the Burgemeester still did not dare to commit himself and William left it to Dijkvelt
and Bentinck to try to convince him of the necessity of the expedition to
England. Witsen stubbornly maintained that they should trust providence and wait a few months, and there was now only one course open
to the Stadholder: to give Providence a helping hand.

The French army was on the move again and the Prince, pleading
the poor state of the Rhine and IJssel defences, asked the States-General
for a loan of four million guilders for their repair. The money was
collected in eight days. He called Witsen again, told him that delay
would only give James time to strengthen his position, and pointed out
that the four million guilders was more than enough to cover the cost
of his intervention in England. The Burgemeester finally gave in so far
as to promise grudgingly that as long as Amsterdam was not directly
involved, he would do what he could to "obtain for him such support as
might be consistent with their duty".*

The Prince tried to make it clear to Witsen that he was not undertaking this enterprise to satisfy his personal ambitions: he expected
nothing but labour for his reward. The Burgemeester, with the typical
distrust of the Amsterdammer towards the Stadholder, afterwards
observed sceptically that "considering the proximity of the Princess to

the crown he thought some richer reward than labour might be in store for him".*

With the half-hearted support of Amsterdam, William now began energetically to make his preparations. First of all he needed a reliable second-in-command – and once more it was Louis' policy that provided the solution. Frederick Herman, Count Schomberg, had been one of France's most brilliant commanders. Although he was a German and a Protestant he had become a Marshal of France, but he resigned at the time of the Huguenot persecution and fled to Berlin. He was known and respected in England, and in spite of his advanced age – he was in his seventies – he seemed to William the best possible choice. With the approval of the Elector of Brandenburg, Schomberg and his two sons came to Holland and on 22 July received instructions from the Prince to prepare for the descent on England.

Through the following three months an army was prepared, equipped and trained on the Mookerheide. There were eighteen infantry battalions, including six of the Anglo-Dutch brigade, partly made up of the former English and Scottish troops that had refused to go back to England to serve James. Four battalions were Federal regulars, and five the personal troops of the House of Orange, including William's famous Blue Guards. There was one battalion from Brandenburg, two Scandinavian and two composed of French Huguenot refugees. The cavalry consisted of fourteen Dutch regiments and one entirely composed of Huguenot officers, mounted at William's expense. Together with the artillery and numbers of Englishmen the total strength was over 15,000 on paper and in fact perhaps 12,000.*

This army had to be equipped in a matter of weeks, and hundreds of Dutchmen worked overtime to get everything ready. "All the bakers of Rotterdam toiled day and night to make biscuits. All the gunmakers of Utrecht were found too few to execute the orders for pistols and muskets. All the saddlers of Amsterdam were hard at work on harness and holsters."*

The Dutch fleet had to be made ready at the same time. In addition to the ordinary force of 25 men-of-war and 10 fire-ships, 24 other men-of-war were fitted out. For the transport of the troops, the horses and their equipment the Prince had at first calculated he would need just under 200 vessels. But by the time they had provided space for a portable bridge, a mobile smithy, the highly important printing press, moulds for striking money, the baggage of senior officers, extra provisions such as 4 tons of tobacco, 1600 hogsheads of beer and 50 of brandy, 10,000 pairs of boots, and the Prince's personal coach and horses, the number of

transports had risen to 225.* This impressive fleet with 7000 sailors was
divided into three squadrons, one under Arthur Herbert, one under
Lt. Admiral Van Almonde and one under Admiral Evertsen.

All these preparations could not be kept secret and they were reported
everywhere before they were complete, with everybody making his
own guess about their purpose. The army, the States hinted, was needed
for the defence of the Republic's eastern frontiers against the French army
marching to the Upper Rhine. The fleet, it was explained, had been
strengthened to combat the Algerian pirates, who had intruded into
German seas. The French did not believe a word of this last explanation
and Louvois thought it wise to strengthen his garrison on northern
coasts of France.

Throughout August d'Avaux had been sending detailed reports of
all this activity to Versailles with the repeated warning that it was
designed against England. He had passed on all his information to
Barillon for James's information, "because it seems to me that they are
on the point of falling asleep in England". But he was disregarded at
Versailles: an autumn invasion by sea was a hazardous enterprise which
they could not believe the cautious Prince of Orange would undertake.
A springtime descent seemed far more probable. And in London Barillon
and Bonrepaus, who shared the mistaken confidence of the English
Court, did not take d'Avaux's warnings seriously either. They reminded
Versailles that James had a powerful navy and a strong standing army.

But widespread rumours of the preparations certainly frightened
some of the English revolutionaries. Danby in particular got cold feet,
and at the end of August he sent the Prince an agitated letter expressing
his doubts. William sent the letter on to Bentinck at Zell, admitting
that the fact "that the thing is beginning to be talked about everywhere
and the little advance we have made with our preparations . . . fills me
with frightful dismay and uncertainty." He added that "more than ever
now I need divine direction, not being sufficiently enlightened to know
which way to decide."*

At this crucial moment Henry Sidney, his old friend and admirer,
arrived at Het Loo, full of the latest news from England, energetic and
optimistic. He was soon followed by Shrewsbury and Russell, who had
hired a boat to cross the North Sea in secret, while Shrewsbury brought
£3000 in cash which he had raised on his estates. Their support came at
the right moment and it encouraged the Prince to go ahead. In the
beginning of September he left for Minden in Germany for the meeting
which his cousin Friedrich, the Elector of Brandenburg, had requested
that summer. The Duke of Zell and the Landgrave of Hesse-Cassel were

also present and William succeeded in convincing them that it was in German interests to support the expedition to England. After he returned on 13 September to Het Loo – "in perfect health", Mary noted, "although he had done enough to upset it"* – d'Avaux with his excellent spy-system was able to report to Paris that "the Elector will furnish 12,000 men, . . . the elector of Saxony 6000, the Dukes of Zell and Wolfenbüttel 4000, Hesse-Cassel 3000."*

At last D'Avaux's warnings were heeded. Louis instructed him to ask the States-General for an explanation of these military preparations, and on 9 September gave them formal warning that any act of hostility against England would be regarded as a declaration of war against France. No statement from Versailles could have been more helpful to the Prince of Orange. The rumour of a revival of the Pact of Dover between England and France, that had been circulating for some time, appeared to be confirmed. The States asked England for clarification, and an angry and embarrassed James denied all knowledge of a pact and repudiated France's right to intervene. There were no more offers of help from Louis. He still did not seriously believe the Prince could be contemplating an invasion, and if he did James – according to Barillon – was quite strong enough to defend his throne, or at the very least to tie down the Prince and his armies in a long-drawn-out civil war.

Thus reasoning, Louis XIV removed the last obstacle to the Prince's enterprise on 27 September: French armies invaded the Palatinate to press the rights of his sister-in-law Liselotte, and advanced to besiege Philipsburg in support of the claims of the French protégé, Cardinal Fürstenberg, on Cologne. "Never has news more rejoiced the Prince of Orange," wrote a mournful d'Avaux, "for he feared that they would come into Flanders, or from the side of Cologne."* Not only was the way to England wide open, but even the most hesitant of the German princes were rallying to William's side.

For the Emperor, who had just invaded Belgrade, Louis's latest act of aggression was the final push he needed to approve William's designs against James, who had made the Emperor his enemy by siding with France in the Cologne affair.

The same mistrust of James, whose religious fanaticism had already done the Catholic cause in England more harm than good, and the same faith in William's promises of tolerance, had already earned the moral support of the Pope, Innocent XI. His sympathy for the Prince was strengthened by his own continual clashes with Louis XIV, which at the beginning of the year had culminated in a denunciation of papal power by the French Parliament, "setting forth that the Pope is not infallible

[and] that he hath no power to excommunicate princes or to use his priestly authority in temporal matters."*

The Pope's pro-William attitude even gave rise to the astonishing story, told by the French Cardinal d'Estrées to Versailles, that funds from the Papal treasury were reaching the Prince for his expedition, on condition that he would later take command of an anti-French allied force on the Rhine. The deal had been arranged between Cassoni, the Pope's secretary, and a Dutch agent disguised as a salesman of artificial flowers.* No evidence of this transaction has ever been found, and the authenticity of d'Estrées's letter to Louvois is doubtful.

With France engaged elsewhere and with such overwhelming support from almost all Europe, the Stadholder risked calling a secret session of the States-General to ask for their permission to use their troops and their fleet. According to international custom of the time, William might employ Dutch soldiers and sailors for a personal enter-prise without formally involving his country in war, but the States' approval was still necessary. On Wednesday, 29 September, Fagel – a desperately ill man for some time now – got up from his sick-bed to address the States of Holland on behalf of the Prince, and to assure them that "his Highness does not intend to dethrone the King or to conquer England, but only to ensure that by the convocation of a free Parliament . . . the reformed religion will be secure, and out of danger ". The Prince's only desire, said Fagel, was to restore good relations between the King and the English nation, so that England can be of service again to her friends and allies, and especially to this State.*

After a brief discussion the States of Holland gave their permission, swearing not to divulge the Prince's plans to outsiders, and the States-General followed suit on 8 October. Nearly two weeks later, a completely distorted version of these proceedings reached England. "We had an account of the Prince of Orange's speech to the States – that he went to reigne or dye; if he reign he would be theyr friend; if he dy'd he would dye their humble servant. This was in the publick Newes letter", wrote a certain Captain Bellingham in his diary.*

CHAPTER XXIII

Mary's Ordeal

E<small>VER SINCE AUGUST THE MOOD OF ENGLAND</small> had swung between
hope and fear. Rumours of the Prince of Orange's preparations, and
especially the fitting out of the fleet, had aroused expectation in some of
the English and fear in others. It was reported that "the Dutch begin to
enroll their 9000 seamen, and are in great forwardness", while "our fleet
now at sea are not near mann'd as they should be, the Dutch having got
away most of our best seamen."*

The least-concerned person in England seemed to be the King himself – at any rate in his letters to Holland. To William he wrote on 31
August from Windsor: "This place of itself affords little news, for tis
none now to tell you when the parliament is to meet", and two weeks
later he commented casually on William's decisive trip to Zell: "I find
you were come back . . . from a voyage you had made into Germany,
to speak with some of the Princes there."*

Those around him saw a different mood. When Sir John Reresby
waited on him at Windsor at the end of August he found that "The
Court was in some trouble and the King out of humour (though he was
always of so even a temper that it was hard to discover it) at the news of
the Dutch having set out a fleet as designed against us . . ."* It was
known at Court that the King and his son-in-law still corresponded, and
as late as 25 August one newsletter reported that the Prince of Orange
had written "a very obliging letter to His Majesty to assure him that the
States-General hath not the least thought of being the aggressors of this
juncture and would only act defensively."* And when four days later
French intelligence suggested in a message to Bonrepaus that the Prince
would not undertake anything against England this year, the King and
many of his court were eager to believe it.

At the end of September, however, this optimism disappeared.
"Fresh expresses doe confirm the design of the Dutch to be upon
England; that they have 16,000 men on board, besides sea men; that they

have several thousand of saddles and furniture for horses, and a vast treasure of money besides; that their printing house at Amsterdam is very busie in private", noted Narcissus Luttrell, that assiduous chronicler of his times.* On the same day, 28 September, James published the proclamation that the Government had received notice of "a great and sudden invasion from Holland on the pretended pretext of defending freedom, property and Protestantism purposing an absolute conquest of these Kingdoms."*

An English pamphlet sneered at the threat. "And truly what's the present hottest news? But a universal current talk of a bold neighbour now crossing the herring pond to make us a bolder visit."* A Jacobite commented: "What ought to incite our courage against [the Dutch] the more, is, that they are said to have a thousand Saxon horses on board; as if old England were to be conquered a second time by that nation . . ."* But he was one of the minority. The Emperor learned with grim satisfaction from his ambassador Hoffman at Whitehall that James had against him "all the clergy, all the nobility and all the people and all the army and the navy with a few exceptions".*

At last the King himself realized how vulnerable he was and started belatedly to make some of those "concessions" of which he had spoken with such scorn only two months earlier. He began by publishing a proclamation in which he undertook to uphold the laws of Church and State and summon a free Parliament. Other concessions came thick and fast. He cancelled Compton's suspension and made overtures to the Archbishop of Canterbury; dissolved the hated Ecclesiastical Commission and restored the Charter of the City of London. One of his most resented acts had been to turn Magdalen College at Oxford into a Catholic preserve the previous year; now the Catholic fellows were bundled out again, accompanied by spiteful rumours that they had "much embezill'd the plate belonging to the college".*

At one stroke James destroyed the carefully constructed network of City and County supporters. His loyal Lords Lieutenant were dismissed, cities up and down the country had their charters restored to them, and Justices of the Peace and magistrates who had been sacked for refusing to co-operate in the putting of the infamous Three Questions were reappointed.

The fearful haste of the King made the worst possible impression. Hoffman reported to Vienna: "Even if the Prince of Orange's plans are not directed against England, the King has already done himself great harm. The impression of exceptional firmness he gave up till now, has disappeared. Instead it is now one of extraordinary weakness."*

There were two concessions, however, that James did not make: he refused to renounce his claim to the dispensing power, and in his growing apprehensions he would not hear of the dismissal of the Roman Catholic officers of his 25,000-strong army. In addition he tactlessly emphasized the fact of the Catholic succession by having James Francis Edward, the Prince of Wales, baptized in St. James's Chapel on 15 October with the Pope and the Catholic Queen-Dowager as his godparents. And a week later he called a Council to hear evidence that his baby heir was not a changeling.

It was on the morning of 22 October that James assembled at Whitehall all the Lords Temporal and Spiritual that could be got together; they were fifty-four in all, including Clarendon, Nottingham, Bishop Compton and the Lord Mayor. James had tried to bring in Father Petre, the despised Catholic adviser from whom he still refused to be parted; at the insistence of his councillors, however, the priest was sent away again. Princess Anne, who pleaded pregnancy, was absent, but James led in the Queen-Dowager, Catherine of Braganza, and a discussion followed "which has no precedent in European history".

The King told the assembly: "I have summoned you for an extraordinary business, but unusual diseases demand unusual remedies. The intrigues of my enemies have so much poisoned the minds of my subjects that I am forced to believe that many of them think the son God has given me is not mine at all but a supposititious child." He told them that he had chosen this moment to put before them the evidence they would now hear, since the next east wind would bring over the Prince of Orange to descend on the Kingdom. He hoped that by acting thus he might leave the minds of his subjects at rest when he went to lead his armies against the invader.

The Queen-Dowager was the first of forty witnesses to whom the company listened with stunned attention. The King spared them no smallest gynaecological detail, and was so eager to convince them that he even offered to call Queen Mary Beatrice as witness. It was too much for the Council, who told him that they found the evidence adequate, and declared that the child was his legitimate son.*

A few years later James's court painter Kneller, who had seen the baby, was astonished that anyone could ever have believed otherwise. "His fader and moder have sate to me about 36 times a piece, and I know every line and bit in their faces," he wrote, "I sayh this child is like both, yt there is not a feature in his face, but wat belongs either to his fader or his moder; this I'm sure of, and be got, I cannot be mistaken. Nay ye nails of his fingers are his moders . . ."*

The proof of the child's legitimacy given at the council had indeed been overwhelming. "The unprejudiced were left no shadow of doubt", commented an Englishman, adding significantly: "But the number of the unprejudiced in England was small."*

Princess Anne was not of that small number. After the authentication had been registered with great festivities at Westminster, a deputation from the Privy Council waited on her with the documents, but the Princess refused to look at them, saying mockingly: "My lords, this was unnecessary. I have so much duty for the King that his word has more weight with me than all this evidence."*

As far as the people of England were concerned, the question of the Prince of Wales's legitimacy was now irrelevant anyway. A mood of apathy had descended on the country, and the idea of an invasion by the Prince seems to have been accepted by everyone. "It was very strange, . . . that neither the gentry nor common people seemed much afeared or concerned at it, saying, The Prince comes only to maintain the Protestant religion; he will do England no harm."* They waited almost with indifference for that east wind which was so much dreaded by James that he asked for regular weather reports and had "a weathercock of no ordinary dimensions" raised on the roof of the Banqueting Hall. It was placed there to be visible from his apartments, "that he may learn with his own eyes whether the wind is Protestant or Popish."*

At the same time he issued a further proclamation setting out instructions for the defence of the realm, and gave particular charge that the coasts should be carefully watched. The Sailor King, as he liked to consider himself, paid special attention to the fleet, bombarding its commander George Legge, Lord Dartmouth, with a stream of exhortations and suggestions such as the thought that the Dutch might try to repeat their success of 1667 when they sailed up the Medway and had landed at Chatham.

Dartmouth had, by the end of the month, a fleet of 37 men-of-war and 11 fire-ships, and reported complacently to the King: "Sirs, we are now at sea before the Dutch after all their boasting . . . I wonder to hear by so many letters of the frights that are ashore, though I thank God they have no effect upon us here . . . Your statesmen may take a nap, and recover, the women sleep in their beds, and the cattle, I think, need not to be drove from the shore."*

Once at sea, however, Dartmouth made no further move, an attitude certainly motivated by his doubts about the loyalty of the fleet. A skipper had reported to Burnet that, sailing to Holland through the English fleet, he had been told by the men from two ships that they would never fight the Dutch fleet and that they had drunk the Prince of Orange's health.*

England and the United Provinces both waited for the Protestant wind, James in Whitehall studying his weathercock, and William at The Hague settling the last details of his journey. He wrote his will, and signed it on 20 October, leaving Fagel a legacy of 100,000 guilders and his country house "De Kruidberg". Bentinck was to receive the town of Leerdam, which gave him the title of Count, and among others the lands of IJsselstein.* At the same time William composed a Declaration of his intentions, which was immediately printed and 50,000 copies sent over to England to be circulated throughout the country. The Declaration listed all the English grievances against James II's government, such as the appointment of Roman Catholics to civil and military posts and the introduction of arbitrary government. At the insistence of his English advisers, William reluctantly added a reflection on the legitimacy of the Prince of Wales stating that it was an imposture, but while his advisers considered this a very important point to make, William dealt with it in a few brief words and placed it at the bottom of the list. The Prince concluded his Declaration by saying that following an invitation from the Lords Temporal and Spiritual, he and the Princess had agreed that these grievances must be redressed by the calling of a free and legitimate Parliament.*

Mary was with William during these last weeks at The Hague. She forced herself to look as cheerful and happy as possible when she was in company, and although she found the prospect of the descent on England almost unbearable to contemplate, she had convinced herself that her husband's decision was right. But she still found it heartbreaking to read the last plea from her stepmother Mary Beatrice:

> I am much put to it what to say, at a time when nothing is talked of here but the Prince of Oranges coming over with an army . . . I never did believe it till now very lately that I have no possibility left for doubting it. The second part of this news I will never believe, that is, that you are to come over with him; for I know you to be too good, that I dont believe you could have such a thought against the worst of fathers, much less perform against the best, that has always been kind to you, and I believe has loved you better than all the rest of his children.*

Burnet was one of the few to whom the Princess could allow a glimpse of her feelings. When he called on her at The Hague a few days before the expedition's departure, he noted that "she seemed to have a great load on her spirits." He was afraid that her nerves might not stand up to the strain, and reminded her forcefully that her public approval of the venture was essential; he added that "if there should happen to be at any time any disjointing between the prince and her, that would ruin all." Mary reassured him that he need have no such fears. "She was very solemn and serious, and prayed God earnestly to bless and direct us."*

Only to the Prince could Mary open her heart without reserve. The couple who a year earlier had found it impossible to discuss the important question of the succession without embarrassment, had now grown so close together during these months of crisis that they dared to express their deepest feelings. And if Mary was grateful to William for his consideration and kindness, he discovered in turn how much he could rely on her.

William's health that autumn was undependable, and the tension had brought on a series of asthmatic attacks and headaches. Bentinck and other close friends were scattered on diplomatic or military business, and his most trusted confidant in Dutch political life, Casper Fagel, was a dying man. On the eve of this enterprise which would decide the whole course of his and Europe's future, he realized how terribly alone he was, and more and more it was to Mary that he turned for company and understanding – "*extrêmement obligeant*" as she said. He understood, too, how she must feel, seeing her husband about to confront her father and that perhaps on the battlefield.

On 25 October, the eve of his departure, the Prince called her into his study to give her some last words of advice. If she found herself in any difficulties during his absence, she was to consult Waldeck, the caretaker of William's army during his absence, or Raadspensionary Fagel, or his adviser Dijkvelt. But he had something far more important to tell her, and Mary, describing the conversation in her journal only a few days later, relived the moment: "He went on to say to me, that in case it pleased God, that I should never see him again (words which pierced my heart and caused me such a pang, that at the hour I write it has scarcely worn off), if that happened, he said, it will be necessary to marry again. If the first words struck me so cruelly, this last surprised and shocked me and reduced me to a state as if my heart had been broken."

William himself was no less moved.

There is no need, he continued, for me to tell you that it must not be a Papist. He himself could not utter these words without shedding tears and throughout this conversation he showed me all the tenderness I could wish. But I was so much astonished by this proposal that it was long before I was able to reply. He protested that it was solely the concern he had for religion which could make him speak as he did. I don't remember all that I said. The grief I felt made my answers confused, but I assured him that I had never loved any one but him, and would not know how to love any one else. And apart from that, having been married so many years without its having pleased God to bless me with a child, I believed that sufficient to prevent me ever thinking of what he proposed. I told him, that I begged God not to let me survive him; if however I should do so, since it had not pleased God to give me a child by him, I would not wish to have one by an angel.

Their conversation was long and loving. At its end Mary asked his pardon for all her shortcomings. "He responded with so much tenderness, that if it had been possible, that would have increased my love for him even more."*

The following day the Prince took leave of the States. In deep silence the deputies listened to his words of thanks for their loyalty and to his assurance. "I have always served you faithfully and kept the welfare of this state constantly before me", he told them, and deeply moved, he begged them: "What God intends for me I do not know, but if I should fall, have a care for my beloved wife who always has loved this country as her own."*

He left The Hague in the afternoon to dine with Mary at Honselaersdijck and afterwards she accompanied him down to the river, where he took a boat for Den Briel. Mary was overwhelmed to see him leave; she could not bear to order the coachman to go, and she stayed motionless inside her carriage "for as long as I could still see the Prince". She returned at last to The Hague and – like the Clorine of old – found some relief in pouring her heart out into her journal, with an account of the parting at Den Briel. "It was there that I saw him for the last time, and God alone knows, if we are to meet again. This thought is very dreadful and for some time robbed me of my senses."*

27 October was kept as a general fast throughout the Republic and Mary noted with pleasure that it was observed with great zeal, even by the Jews. The Spanish ambassador, Señor Colomba, had masses said for the success of this enterprise against the Roman Catholic King of England, and only d'Avaux and D'Albeville pointedly ignored these demonstrations.*

Three days later it seemed that the moment for sailing had come. The Protestant east wind was blowing, and the Prince's fleet left Den Briel on Saturday the thirtieth. It was hardly at sea when a tempest got up, and as Mary next day wrote: "Although it lasted only a few hours, the fleet was completely scattered and many horses perished, . . . On 31 at five in the morning the wind swung round and blew so strongly from the west, that in order to save the transports, they were obliged to return to the port . . . by the grace of God without further loss."*

The Prince at once sent his wife reassuring letters from Hellevoetsluys in which he expressed his resignation to God's will. He spared her the anxiety of knowing how close he had been to shipwreck. Burnet, who had been in the same ship, remarked gloomily to the Prince that it seemed predestined that they should not set foot on English ground, to which the Prince made no reply.* The Scotsman's was not the only downcast face. "There were few among us that did not conclude . . . that the whole design was lost" and Burnet wrote to Admiral Herbert, whose appointment he had strongly disapproved, suggesting that the storm was a judgment on his loose living.

At Hellevoetsluys the fleet was gradually reassembled and the losses counted. The biggest blow was the death of about 1300 horses, all suffocated when the hatches were battened down during the storm, but in the end the damage was less bad than was feared. Only one ship was lost.*

While waiting for a favourable wind, however, the morale of the troops and sailors began to suffer, and one of the accounts that reached London related that the Prince of Orange was sick and the men suffering from the "bloody flux".* It was news that rejoiced the Court and a Frenchman visiting London wrote:

> I was present when James received letters from Newport, informing him, with extravagant exaggerations of the dispersion of the Prince of Orange's fleet. At his dinner, he said to M. Barillon, the French ambassador, laughing, "at last the wind has declared itself Popish", and he added, resuming his serious air and lowering his voice, "you know that for these three days, I have caused the Holy Sacrament to be carried in procession."*

More practically, he had also given orders for lighthouses on the coast to extinguish their lamps and for the warning buoys to be removed.

It was at this time that James instructed his ambassador in The Hague, D'Albeville, to give Mary a copy of the evidence about his son's legitimacy that he had printed after the secret Council meeting. Obedient to the Prince's instructions she asked Dijkvelt for his advice and then sent back a message to D'Albeville by her secretary d'Allonne saying that she was not surprised that the King should take the trouble to try and satisfy the doubts of his subjects. She herself, however, was no competent judge of a question which only Parliament should decide.

Mary at The Hague lived for the Prince's letters, which brought her regular news. She had daily prayers said in her Household but they gave no relief to her spirits. "I found it very hard and disagreeable to love someone so much, when the loved person is absent." The Prince had assured her that he was just as impatient to see her as she was to see him, and he promised in every letter that he would not set sail again without having seen her. But as usual the uncertainty and strain were too much for her health. She was terrified that the wind would change before he had summoned her, and her sleeplessness and worry brought on a recurrence of her kidney ailment. Her doctor prescribed the popular remedy of bleeding, but a letter from the Prince on Tuesday, 9 November was a more effective remedy. He asked her to join him the next day.

> The tenth I went to Den Briel where the Prince had the goodness to come just for a couple of hours, his presence being very much needed at Hellevoetsluys [Mary wrote later]. The road was so bad that he had a great deal of difficulty in getting over it in a coach. The second separation was more painful to me even than the first and when he left me it was as if my heart had been torn out. I could not even shed as many tears as the first time. I stayed without moving in the room where he left me; all I could do was to recommend him to God. After having been about an hour and a half shut up alone like this, I at last opened the door of the room and having learned that there was a sermon in town, I went there as to the place that suited me best in my situation.

She stayed the night at Den Briel and attended next morning the public prayers that were said for the expedition. At twelve in the morning she climbed the 315 steps of the church tower, hoping that she might be able to see the fleet, but to her great disappointment only the masts of the ships were visible. At one o'clock the fleet sailed, with the most favourable wind possible.

Mary left her lookout to return to The Hague, where she arrived at nightfall and where next day she received the report that "the vessels were all out of sight, thank God, with a following wind, very good weather and ardent hopes for their lucky success."*

All Europe noted that the daughter of James II had publicly given her prayers and wishes to an expedition setting out to her father's ruin. "It is a Tullia", wrote Madame de Sévigné, "Ah, how boldly she would step over the body of her father. She has been the procuress of her husband in his bid to take possession of the Kingdom of England, of which she claims to be the heiress."*

CHAPTER XXIV

"William the Conqueror"

DAWN ON SUNDAY, 14 NOVEMBER revealed the cliffs of the Isle of Wight to the Dutch fleet. It was the thirty-eighth birthday of the Prince of Orange, and the eleventh anniversary of his marriage. The people, who crowded to the beaches and the cliffs to watch the Dutch Armada, nearly 300 strong, sailing slowly down the Channel, heard music coming faintly over the water. "They . . . are soe thick there is noe telling of them" said one eye-witness.* From the mast of the Prince's flagship, *Den Briel*, streamed a huge banner with the Orange family motto "*Je Maintiendrai*". Other ships carried great streamers with slogans in Latin such as "*Pro libertate et religione*" and "*Pro religione protestante*", or in English, announcing "The liberty of England and the Protestant religion".

The Protestant wind had brought them over safely and unopposed, keeping the whole English fleet under Dartmouth weatherbound in the Thames estuary. And now, on this Sunday morning, sails were slackened so that divine service could be held on every ship. For the rest of the day, and all through the night, the fleet kept steadily on its way for Torbay. But here, as all along the coast, the buoys had been removed at James's orders, and the first officer of the *Den Briel*, Sijmen Janszoon Hartevelt, overshot the bay. It was impossible to turn, and it looked as if they would have to sail on to the next port, Plymouth, which was heavily garrisoned under Lord Bath. But the Protestant wind came to the rescue and veered to the south, the ships were able to turn, and at noon the whole fleet dropped anchor in Torbay. It was 15 November; by the old-style English calendar it was the fifth, and Gunpowder Day, the date on which the English celebrated their deliverance from Popish conspiracy with bonfires.

One of William's commanders, Count von Solms-Braunfels, was rowed ashore with ten grenadiers, and when the villagers of Brixham put up no resistance, the Prince followed almost immediately. In his light armour, with the insignia of the Garter gleaming on his left shoulder, he was at once recognized, and some of the local women ran into the sea to kiss his hands, saying "God bless you!" Two horses were brought from the village and the Prince and Schomberg mounted to watch the disembarkation of the troops. Among the first to land was Dr. Burnet who rushed over to the Prince to congratulate him. He found him looking unusually cheerful and happy, and William – his thoughts going back to the storm and near-shipwreck of a few days earlier – grasped him by the hand and asked teasingly, "What do you think of Predestination now, Doctor?"*

It had been raining heavily and the ground was muddy and soggy, but by nightfall all the troops had been landed. The baggage, however, was still on board and the men had to sleep as best they could on the ground. The village of Brixham was tiny, just a handful of rough stone houses with slate roofs and one inn, the Crowned Rose Tavern, where Huygens with some difficulty managed to beg a corner to put down his mattress. The Prince found a bed in the neighbouring village of "Brixcumlay", and his personal standard floated incongruously over a small fisherman's hut.*

Next day the baggage and horses had to be landed, and it looked like a long and tricky task, until a local fisherman guided them to a deeply shelving bay nearby, where the transports could be brought in close enough for the horses to swim ashore. Twenty-four hours after they first dropped anchor, disembarkation was complete, and the advance on London could get under way.

The roads were appalling, winding through steep and hilly country, stony and muddy, but in spite of the pouring rain all the way people came out of their houses to welcome the Prince with shouts of "God bless you!" They gave apples to the soldiers, and one old woman went up to the Prince with a jug of cider and offered him a drink. The Dutch were astonished to see that many of the women were smoking pipes, even girls of thirteen or fourteen years old.

In spite of the hearty welcome, it was obvious that the people were frightened and one explained to Huygens: "If this thing do miscarry, we are all undone", telling him that after the Monmouth rebellion – only three years ago – a great many people had been hanged.*

The first stop was the small town of Newton Abbot where the advance was halted and the Prince's declaration was read. William, with Bentinck and his other friends, made his headquarters at nearby Ford for the next two days, where his hosts, the Courtenay family, entertained him lavishly* and where the officers used the delay for replacing the hundreds of horses that had been lost in the storm. At the same time the Prince sent Dr. Burnet and Mordaunt, with a small force, to the first important town on the route, Exeter, to find out what sort of welcome he could expect. Burnet discovered there that Bishop Lamplugh and the Dean had fled to London, but that the city was orderly and the annual fair – in spite of orders from James – was in full swing. It seemed good enough and the Prince decided to go there himself. He realized that a show was expected of him, and when on the Friday, 9 November he made his entry he gave Exeter a splendid one. First came 300 cavalry, mounted on impressive Flanders horses, followed by 200 of the first Negroes the country people had ever seen, brought over from the Dutch colony in Surinam, colourfully dressed in embroidered capes lined with fur and plumes of white feathers on their heads. Next came the same number of Laplanders from the Scandinavian contingent, in black armour with reindeer skins over their shoulders, and armed with broadswords. The Prince himself was preceded by his banner, supported by 100 gentlemen and pages, and by 50 war-horses, each led by two grooms. He was conspicuous in highly-polished armour and mounted on a white horse, with Schomberg riding at his side. After him came another contingent of 200 cavalry, 3000 Swiss mercenaries, the first 500 English volunteers, each leading two horses, and the Prince's 600 Blue Guards in full armour. The rest of the army, thousands of common soldiers, brought up the rear together with 21 enormous brass cannon, each one dragged along by 16 carthorses.*

The people of Exeter, who had never seen anything like it, were highly impressed by the parade. Crowds of them followed the Prince into the Cathedral, where Burnet had organized a solemn service of thanksgiving. The nervous canons stayed away, but the choristers and prebendaries were present until, after the Te Deum, William's Declaration was read and they left in a hurry. At the end of the service Burnet was carried away with enthusiasm and shouted "God Save the Prince of Orange!" Not everyone cried "Amen!"*

The parade and the solemn service had done nothing to improve the Prince's temper. The Seven in their invitation had assured him that they would not fail to attend him upon his landing. But while the common people had given him a warm if reserved welcome, people of any influence and standing had stayed aloof, and five days after his landing there was still no sign of this vital English co-operation. He admitted to Shrewsbury that he was embarrassed and concerned by the situation, and his friend tried to cheer him up by pointing out that nobody liked to be the first, but if one came, the rest would follow.

Gleeful reports of William's predicament reached London. One of James's supporters wrote to a friend in Ireland: "The country is not fond of him, nor forward to run in to him; they keep good order, but cannot prevail . . . to come at them, but they send their inviting letters unopened to the King." Three days later the same correspondent passed on the latest account: "Some of the scurf and meaner part run into them as they would see a show, but generally retreat the next day." He had another bit of news – the Prince had ordered 6000 pairs of boots in Exeter, famous for its tanning and leather craftsmen, but in London the order was explained as "a trick to drill on time, till they could see if any part of England would come in to them".*

The reluctance of William's supporters to come forward had already presented him with an unexpected problem: his funds were running low. He had issued strict instructions against pillaging and looting, everything his army needed was paid for in ready cash and by the time he reached Exeter the money he had borrowed from the States-General or raised from his own estates had almost all been spent. He had no more than about £45,000 left. As a short-term solution he appropriated the funds collected by the local tax-office, but even this was inadequate and not till the beginning of December, when Shrewsbury seized Bristol for him, could he solve his problems by confiscating the handsome sums yielded by the tobacco tax in this city, the principal port for the Atlantic trade.

By then the first important noblemen had at last appeared at William's headquarters in the Bishop's house at Exeter. They were only just in time: the humiliating wait had angered the Prince so much that he threatened to go home and leave the ungrateful English to their fate. The man who saved the day was, strangely enough, one of the Prince's former opponents, Sir Edward Seymour, the most influential man in the county. And as Shrewsbury had predicted, others were quick to follow. Lord Colchester, Thomas Wharton, Edward Russell and the Earl of Abingdon joined the Prince at the same time that the Earl of Bath, commanding the garrison at the important naval base of Plymouth, declared for him. Reports reached William of risings in other parts of England too. Danby had organized one in York, and Lord Delamere in Cheshire. The Earl of Devonshire raised an army in the North Midlands with his headquarters at Nottingham, where he was reinforced by the Earls of Manchester, Stamford, Rutland and Chesterfield. The first men in the kingdom were at last rising against James in strength.*

At Exeter they found the Prince of Orange in no mood to be flattered by their coming. When he addressed them he pointed out that he was there at their invitation, and he reproached them for not having appeared sooner. He went on to tell them that his duty to God obliged him to protect the Protestant religion, and that his love for mankind had brought him to the defence of their liberties and properties. He therefore intended to remain, even if he had "a bridge of gold to turn back".*

AT WHITEHALL James, after he had received the first news of the landing of his son-in-law, sent off hasty instructions to his armies at Hounslow and 25,000 men under the command of the French-born Louis Duras, Lord Feversham, were soon under orders to march for Salisbury. The King himself hesitated. At this crucial moment in his life, he seemed incapable of making any firm decisions. His long-held almost insane conviction that kings not only should be, but were obeyed, suddenly turned out to be baseless, and without this prop the whole structure of his authority and obstinacy crumbled. All that was left was a weak and frightened man, who realized that not only could he not trust many of his courtiers, but that even his beloved army and navy could not wholly be relied on.

His old haughtiness flared briefly when a number of peers and bishops asked at an audience that he call a free and legal parliament. James listened, but dismissed them with a few icy words of refusal. Then he sent his baby son secretly to Portsmouth – the idea of flight to France was already in his mind – and after appointing councillors to advise the Queen in his absence he left London to join his army, reaching Salisbury on Monday, 19 November.*

Even before he arrived, the first significant defection among his officers had already occurred – that of his nephew Lord Cornbury, Clarendon's son. When Clarendon learned the news he had exclaimed in distress "O God that a son of mine should be a rebel!"* But it was a situation in which one day's traitor seemed the next day's patriot, and when James reached his army headquarters he found that Cornbury was not the only man uncertain where his duty lay – the whole camp was buzzing with rumours about the disloyalty of the officers. Unnerved and dismayed, James succumbed to a violent nose-bleed, which kept him inactive for several days. When he finally recovered a little and – still undecided – asked his officers' advice, he found they could not agree. Churchill, seconded by Grafton, was all for action: the King must rouse himself and advance, after first inspecting in person his armies at Warminster, fifteen miles away.

James, who at once suspected a fresh plot, preferred Feversham's counsel of despair, retreat, and to the disgust of Grafton and Churchill announced that he would do so the next day. By morning, both officers had disappeared, taking 400 men over to the Prince of Orange with them. Churchill left a letter justifying his desertion to the Protestant cause as due to "the inviolable dictates of my conscience . . . which no good man can oppose".*

"Oh if my enemies only had cursed me, I could have borne it", exclaimed James pathetically on reading it.* He was prostrated by this betrayal, and George Clarke, Judge-Advocate of the army, visiting headquarters that day, found a scene of demoralized confusion in which most people were obviously now only thinking of how to save their own skins. James, appealing to Dr. Radcliffe to stop his nose-bleed somehow, seemed already a forgotten man.* News that Kirke, in command at Salisbury, was now refusing to accept the King's commands, came as a final blow to him, and James made up his mind to return to London.

He stopped for the night at Andover, where he dined with Prince George of Denmark and the Duke of Ormonde, son of William's old friend Ossory: he was no sooner retired to bed than the two took horse and rode off to join William. In the general horror, George's defection seemed almost light relief, and James took it calmly, only remarking, "A good trooper would have been a greater loss", before he obligingly sent the Prince's carriage and luggage after him.*

The arrival of the stout, lethargic Prince of Denmark was no surprise for William. He had just received a long letter from Princess Anne, assuring him of her support and good wishes in "so just an undertaking". The letter had been written on Sunday, 18 November, only the day after her husband had left London with James, and – as Anne blandly revealed – it was already decided that he should join the Prince "as soon as his friends thought it proper".*

When James arrived in Whitehall, he found that his youngest daughter, too, had fled. On hearing of the King's imminent return she had taken fright and, with Sarah Jennings for company, had fled to the Bishop of London, who had escorted her to join the rising at Nottingham. Anne left behind a letter of pious self-defence for Mary Beatrice, with whom she had hardly been on speaking terms for months now. She was gone, she said, "to avoid the King's displeasure, which I am not able to bear, either against the Prince or myself . . . Never was any one in such an unhappy condition, so divided between duty and affection to a father and a husband." She bitterly attacked James's Catholic advisers, "who, to promote their own religion, did not care to what dangers they exposed the King". And she expressed her confidence in the good intentions of the Prince of Orange: "I'm fully persuaded that he designs the King's safety and preservation. . . . God grant a happy end to these troubles."*

James was shattered by her defection. "God help me," he cried, "my own children have forsaken me."* And when on 27 November he summoned a Council of fifty peers and bishops, every one of them Protestant, to ask their advice, he had the air of a broken man ready to agree to anything. Rochester at once urged him to call a parliament, and Jeffreys and Godolphin seconded him. The King feigned enthusiasm: "What you ask is what I passionately desire. I promise on the word of a King to call a free and legal parliament the moment the Prince of Orange shall depart. But how can you have a free parliament now that a foreign Prince, at the head of a foreign force, has it in his power to return a hundred members?"* On this cue Rochester and Halifax at once pointed out the necessity of opening negotiations with William, and the King broke up the meeting, promising to think it over.

After a night of reflection he asked for Halifax whom he made a member of a three-man commission, with Nottingham and Godolphin, and sent them away to negotiate with the Prince of Orange. He issued writs for convoking a parliament for the New Year, and reluctantly proclaimed a free pardon for all in rebellion against him.* Nothing remained of the confident and assured King who had crushed the Monmouth rising with such speed and severity in 1685.

The Prince of Orange had in the meantime left Exeter at last on 27 November to march into Dorset. He was in no hurry and took the first day off to hunt in Lord Poulett's Park at Crewkerne.* By the thirtieth he had reached Wincanton, where he gave the astonished townspeople an example of his famous army discipline: he publicly hanged two soldiers for stealing a chicken, telling the others that they were paid well enough not to need to steal. "His soldiers are mighty civil", commented an officer in the English army.*

Hindon was reached on 1 December and he spent three nights there to allow his slow-moving army to catch up with him. When he left on the fourth he made a detour to visit Wilton, the house of the Earl of Pembroke, famous for its decoration and paintings. It was a freezing day, and by the time the Prince reached Salisbury in the evening – nine days after James had left – he had caught a violent cold, but it could not damp his enthusiasm for the Van Dycks he had seen, and he urged Huygens not to miss them.*

It began to look as if his march to London would be peaceful and unopposed. There was only one short sharp encounter near Reading between his advance guard of 250 Englishmen and 600 of James's detested Irish soldiers in which the Irish were beaten, but otherwise the Prince's march over the Berkshire Downs was simply an enormous parade, and on 7 December William reached Hungerford, where he took a room at The Bear, an old inn which had formed part of Henry VIII's dowry to Anne of Cleves. It was at this inn that James's three commissioners arrived next day. Their leader Halifax handed him a letter from James, written – for the first time – by an adviser and in formal French. The Prince, discovering this, said in surprise: "I have had many letters from the King, but they were all in English and in his own hand."

The letter was non-committal and said little apart from a reference to the Parliament James had called and a recommendation of his commissioners to William. "They will tell you in greater detail what I have instructed them, to which you will give entire credence in so far as it comes from me, and more especially when they assure you of my sincere disposition towards the establishment of a firm and solid peace." The King signed himself "Your affectionate father and uncle, James".* After reading the letter, William listened to the proposals of the commissioners: points in dispute were to be referred to a new Parliament, and William should not come within thirty or forty miles of London.

The Prince left the crowded rooms of the inn for a quiet weekend at Littlecote Manor two miles away, to consider James's proposals in peace. Twenty-four hours later, when the commissioners came to dine with him there and learn his answer, he brushed aside the King's suggestions as an irrelevancy and simply stated his own terms. All Papists were to be dismissed from office. All proclamations against the Prince were to be withdrawn, and his supporters who had been imprisoned set free. The Tower and Tilbury Fort were to be garrisoned by the City of London. Portsmouth was to be placed in the hands of a commander William could trust to prevent French intervention. The upkeep of William's army was to be at the public charge. Most important of all, troops of both King and Prince should stay at thirty miles' distance from town, and both King and Prince should be present at the opening of the new Parliament, accompanied by an equal number of guards or else completely unguarded.*

They were terms which James could not have accepted without forfeiting completely the respect of his people, all prestige, and all authority. In fact he had not the slightest intention of listening to any proposals that the Prince might make. As he admitted to Barillon, the

commission to his son-in-law was a mere feint to gain time to send
Mary Beatrice and their baby son to France, after which he himself
would take refuge in Ireland, Scotland or "with your Master".*

A week earlier, he had already instructed Dartmouth to have a yacht
ready to take the little Prince to France. But Dartmouth refused, writing
to the King on 3 December that he had no desire to be 'the unhappy
instrument of so apparent ruin to your Majestie and my country as an
act of this kind would be", and begging him: "Pray Sir, consider farther
on this weighty point, for can the Prince's being sent to France have
other prospect than the entailing of a perpetual warre upon your nation
and posterity, and giving France a temptation to molest, invade, nay
hazard the conquest of England . . ?"*

James was unmoved. Before his commissioners to the Prince of
Orange had had time to report back to Whitehall, the Queen and the
Prince of Wales were already on their way to France. In the small hours
of Monday morning, 10 December, Mary Beatrice, heavily disguised and
carrying her tiny son, slipped out of the Palace and, escorted by the
Comte de Lauzun, reached Gravesend where a boat waited to take them
across the Channel. By nine that night she was on French soil at Calais,
where she had been taken on her arrival to the house of the magistrate
Ponton. Almost immediately she sent a despairing appeal to Louis XIV:
"Monsieur, a poor fugitive Queen bathed in tears has not been afraid
to expose herself to the greatest perils of the sea to seek consolation
and refuge from the greatest and most generous Monarch in the world
. . . it is out of her singular regard that she desires to entrust to you all
that is most precious to her in the person of the Prince of Wales, her
son . . ."*

On the same day James learned the Prince's harsh terms, and with
the last hope of saving his crown destroyed, made up his mind to follow
his Queen. He burned the writs for the new Parliament and deposited
his most important papers, including his memoirs, with the Tuscan
minister. The Mayor and Sheriffs were told that he had no intention of
quitting Whitehall, and the Peers were invited to wait on him the next
day. Then he went to bed, giving orders that he was not to be disturbed.

London awoke on Tuesday the eleventh to find that their King had
fled. He had left Whitehall at 3 in the morning, gone by hackney coach
to Millbank, and crossed by boat to Vauxhall. From there he took
a carriage to Sheerness. On his way over the Thames, he threw his
Great Seal into the river to prevent the calling of a Parliament in his
name. Five months later it was found by a fisherman.*

Before he fled, James wrote to the two commanders of his forces,

Feversham and Dartmouth, blaming the disloyalty of army and navy for his plight. To Feversham he wrote: "Things being come to the extremity that I have been forced to send away the Queen and my son the Prince of Wales that they might not fall into my enemy's hands, which they must have done, had they stayed, I am obliged to do the same thing . . . If I could have relied upon all my troops I might not have been put to this extremity I am in." He thanked Feversham for his loyalty and freed him from any obligations of further resistance.* To Dartmouth he wrote in the same despairing strain: "Finding . . . that the poison is got amongst the fleet I could no longer resolve to expose myself to no purpose to what I might expect from the ambitious Prince of Orange . . ." He gave instructions that the fleet should go to Ireland and put themselves under the command of Lord Tyrconnel.*

Dartmouth refused to send his ships to Ireland, having gone over to William, but Feversham disbanded his troops at the height of the confusion the King had left behind him.

The news of James's flight spread fast throughout London, and anticipating trouble, a group of twenty-two peers and five bishops assembled hastily at Guildhall and constituted themselves an emergency government. With Sancroft in the chair they declared for the Prince of Orange and sent an urgent message asking him to come and take charge. The City of London followed immediately, and the guards were called out in an attempt to restore calm. These improvisations were not enough to stop the London mobs getting out of hand when they realized that authority in the person of the King had abandoned the capital. By nightfall disordered crowds were out in the streets eager to show their resentment of papists and foreigners. "The rabble . . . rose in prodigious numbers and . . . pulled down the chapels of that worship and many houses of such as did profess it, taking and spoiling their goods, imprisoning such as they suspected to be priests."* They gutted the Franciscan chapel at Lincoln's Inn Fields and two other chapels of St. John Clerkenwell and in Lime Street. "Having levelled them, they carried all the trumpery in mock procession and triumph, with oranges on the tops of swords and staves, with great lighted candles in gilt candlesticks . . ."* The house of the King's printer, Henry Hills, was burned to the ground, catholic chapels at foreign embassies were looted, and the French embassy in St. James was only spared because Barillon had had the forethought to ask for a strong guard, as did the Venetian envoy.

The worst sufferer was the Spanish ambassador, Ronquillo, whose house was plundered "of all its rich furniture plate, money and three coaches, to the value as is computed of £20,000", and afterwards burnt to the ground.*

There was astonishingly little bloodshed, but one man came near to being lynched: the Chancellor Jeffreys, loathed since the Bloody Assizes and the bishops' trial. He had cut off his prominent eyebrows and disguised himself as a sailor, but was nevertheless spotted as he waited for a boat at Wapping. He was rescued by soldiers and thrown in the Tower, where he was soon afterwards joined by Father Petre, the King's adviser and the Quaker Penn.*

After this night of anarchy the provisional council of the previous day assembled again at Whitehall and issued emergency orders to meet the crisis. These were sufficient to prevent new serious disturbances on Wednesday. But before daybreak on Thursday morning a new alarm ran like wildfire through the City: James's hated Irish soldiers, disbanded by Feversham, were marching on London, burning and killing as they came. People, shouting "Rise, arm, arm, the Irish are cutting throats", ran through the streets, and in "half an hour's time there was an appearance of above a hundred thousand men to have made . . . against any enterprise of that nature".* The streets were lit up by candles burning at every window. The panic subsided gradually only after scouts sent out by the provisional council returned to report that it was a false alarm, and after a fresh and calming rumour spread that an advance guard of the Prince of Orange was on its way.

News of James's flight had reached William on Tuesday at Abingdon, where he was dining at Marshal Schomberg's headquarters. The King had done what the Prince had hoped and half anticipated, and an eyewitness noted: "He was very cheerful and could not conceal his satisfaction at the King's being gone."* When William heard, however, that Feversham with James's implicit approval had disbanded the English army, and that numbers of James's undisciplined soldiers were at large, he burst out in anger. "I am not thus to be dealt with; and that my Lord Feversham shall find."* He prepared to leave for London at once.

The fleeing King had got no further than Faversham, a small village in Kent, where his companion Sir Edward Hales, the former governor of the Tower, was recognized. They were both dragged off the boat and only then did the crowd realize that the second man was King James. Word was at once sent to London. Under this final strain the King cracked completely. Obsessed by the thought that his son-in-law was coming after him to kill him, he begged his guards for a boat. He rambled confusedly, making the Bible text "He that is not with me is against me" the theme of a long wandering sermon about his subjects' disloyalty. Sometimes he recovered a little of his old pride, and told his astonished listeners that he might fall as Abel had done by the hand of Cain, but that he was confident he and his cause would be accepted by God.* His captors showed little respect: they stole his ring, watch and money and some of them cursed him, but in an apathetic daze he submitted to it all. At last he was rescued when Feversham, at the orders of Lords in London, arrived with a detachment of Life Guards to bring him to Rochester.

Encouraged by the fact that the Lords had sent some of his guards to rescue him, the confused and broken King made a last attempt to save his face. He wrote to William that he was on his way back to Whitehall and sent Feversham with the letter to Windsor, where the Prince was now staying. But William refused to receive him. He had not forgiven the commander for disbanding James's armies so irresponsibly, and the news that Feversham brought was not calculated to sweeten the Prince's temper. On the pretext that he had no safe-conduct, Feversham was placed under arrest.

William immediately sent Zuylestein to Rochester with orders that the King was to be detained there, but he arrived too late. James was already on his way to London, where he arrived on Sunday the sixteenth. His entry was hardly triumphant, but thousands of curious Londoners flocked to see him driving to Whitehall, and for James the reception was encouraging enough. His self-confidence returned, and over a festive dinner, before which a Jesuit priest said grace, he told his embarrassed courtiers gaily about his adventures since he had fled the palace.

Some of the Peers had not waited for his return. Halifax, whose sense and moderation made him a natural leader in this crisis, and who had taken Sancroft's place as president of the provisional Council, had already left for Windsor, and there, on Monday, William summoned a meeting of twelve peers to discuss what should be done with the King. Ever since his landing, the Prince had constantly insisted that any initiative should come from the English and not himself, and now once more he withdrew to let the King's fate be decided by his own subjects.

Some of the peers wished James to be imprisoned in the Tower, another suggestion was that he should be sent to Breda; both solutions which would have been unacceptable to Mary. And in the end it was agreed that the best course was simply to let him go away again. They advised William to send him to Ham House, near Richmond. The Prince approved and Halifax, Shrewsbury and Delamere were given the painful task of taking this message to James.

At Whitehall the Court was crowded that evening, but the festive mood of the former night had gone and the people who flocked to watch James dine whispered to each other: "Have you come to see the King for the last time?"* When James retired to bed, the Dutch guard in their blue uniforms had already taken over sentry-duty from his familiar Coldstreamers, who had been ordered to leave London with the rest of the Royal army.

He was hardly asleep when the three Peers arrived from Windsor with the news that he must go to Ham. James protested that in the depth of winter Ham House would be cold and uncomfortable, and asked if he could go back to Rochester instead. William, who realized that flight was once more in the mind of his father-in-law, readily sent his permission.

The following morning at noon, in drenching rain, James descended Whitehall steps to the Royal barge to be taken to Gravesend for Rochester. He looked composed and dignified, and Clarendon noted: "It is not to be imagined what a damp there was upon all sorts of men throughout the town. The treatment the King had met from the Prince of Orange, and the manner of his being driven, as it were from Whitehall . . . moved compassion even in those who were not very fond of him."*

Not everyone shared Clarendon's sentiments. To the west of the town huge crowds were gathering to welcome the Prince of Orange. William, who had spent the night at Syon House at Brentford as the guest of the Countess of Northumberland, set out for London at the time of James's departure. Huygens preceded him along muddy roads made almost impassable by the rain, and was thrilled by the great number of people waiting to welcome the Prince along the seven-mile route.

At the boundaries of the town the Prince was officially welcomed by the Aldermen and Sheriffs of London. From there the light carriage, in which he rode with Schomberg, was escorted into the town by crowds of coaches and gentlemen on horseback. Huygens described their arrival:

"We drove through the gates of St. James's Park, which his Highness reached at three o'clock to the loud cheers of the people. Among them were great number with orange ribbons on their hat and carrying oranges on a stick. The women, hanging out of the windows, wore orange headdresses."* Most of the Londoners, however, were deeply disappointed. They had stood for hours in the rain, expecting the Prince to follow the usual route down Piccadilly. But William, "who neither loved shows nor shoutings", had preferred the quiet, quick way through the Park.*

On the evening of that same day, 18 December 1688, while bonfires burnt all over London and bells pealed, the nobility hastened to St. James's to pay their respect as soon as possible – and to see the Prince for themselves. Evelyn was one of the many whose curiosity was too much for them: "All the world go to see the Prince at St. James's, where there is a greate Court. There I saw him and several of my acquaintance who came over with him." The Court's first impression at least was favourable. The Prince, it was noted by one of them, looked "very stately, serious, and reserv'd".*

CHAPTER XXV

Farewell to Holland

REPORTS FROM LONDON reached the Princess of Orange on 19 November, nine days after she had said goodbye to the Prince at Hellevoetsluys: they told her of her husband's safe landing at Torbay.

His departure had prostrated her, and while this news relieved her agony a little, nothing would ease her spirits completely until she had a reassuring letter from the Prince himself. After the tenderness and love he had shown her during their last weeks together, she had expected him to write at the first opportunity, "but I received no letter at all from him".

She waited weeks and weeks in vain, unable to bear company. In her misery she was haunted by her last conversation with him: "I confess", she wrote in her journal, "that the last words the Prince had said to me, about my marriage and his death, had sunk so deeply into my mind that I could not root them out; I imagined to myself that they had been uttered in a sort of prophetic manner, which made me suffer more than I can ever express."

The only comfort she had was from her religion. "My God was very gracious to me, who sustained me to bear, as I did, the not hearing in so long time from England." She threw herself into her devotions with ardour. Every morning she was present at the French prayers; at midday she heard Common Prayers in her chapel; at five o'clock she went out to a church to listen to a sermon in Dutch, and at half past seven, she heard Common Prayer again in her chapel. Wednesday was a special day in her week: an English sermon was preached for her.

Finally, a month after the Prince's departure, and even though she had still not heard from him personally, the constant stream of reassuring reports from England had calmed her spirits. She felt it her duty now, after all the good news, to appear in company again, looking as cheerful as possible as a sign of her loyalty to William's enterprise against her father. Four days a week were appointed to receive the ladies, Monday, Tuesday, Thursday and Friday, but there were no card games yet.

Once out of her isolation she was heartened by the warmth and extraordinary kindness of her Dutch friends: "There was never so much praying in these countries as is now daily for the success of the prince's enterprises", she noted with satisfaction.*

The silence of William was the worst of her trials, but it was not the only one. When the expedition sailed for England, Bentinck had left behind a wife who was desperately ill, Mary's friend Anne Villiers. Ten days after their departure, Anne died. Bentinck's secretary Thomer wrote to him in England:

> . . . it has pleased Providence – and on me falls the task of telling your Lordship – to call hence out of this world into eternal happiness on the 20th of this month, between 11 and 12 o'clock at night, your Lordship's highly-born wife, my highly-honoured mistress, to the great affliction not only of her Royal Highness who stayed with her till her last sigh and with bitter tears left the body, but also of all the bystanders and servants . . .

The secretary had asked Mary as she was leaving if she would take and look after Bentinck's children while he was away, "which the Princess, still bitterly weeping, said amidst her tears that she would do".

The death of Anne Villiers was marked by an unexpected incident. She and her sister Betty had not been on speaking terms since the scandal of Betty's liaison with the Prince had disrupted the Orange household three years earlier. But when Betty heard that her sister was dying, she could not stay away, and she was one of the company in the death-chamber, almost concealing herself. It was Mary, of all people, who called her from the window where she was standing, but the people around had to push her forward, to Anne's bedside, to hear the dying woman's forgiveness whispered in her ear.*

A week before Christmas, the Princess suffered a second loss. Caspar Fagel the Raadspensionary, who had been seriously ill for months, died on 18 December. William was much distressed by the news and wrote at once to Fagel's brother: "I lose the greatest friend that I can have in this world, and the States certainly their most faithful servant."* To Waldeck he wrote that he was so stunned by the loss "that I do not know what to say".* For Mary, Fagel's death was a heavy blow too: the Raadspensionary had been one of the three men William had told her to turn to for advice if she needed it.

The New Year, however, brought not only letters from the Prince but also company and distraction. On 1 January the Elector of Branden-burg and his wife Sophia Charlotte arrived at The Hague. The visit of the young Friedrich, a great admirer of William, was a public demon-stration of his support for the enterprise of the Prince, and at the same

time an effort to improve his chances of the succession to the Stadholdership.

Mary, who felt she must make a special effort to entertain this
cousin and valued ally of her husband, found to her surprise that the
visit cheered her up enormously. "I gave myself no time for any thing
else. The circumstances of the time were such we could have no publick
entertainments, but onely treating them at my severall houses, which I
did and played at cards . . . so late at night, that it was ever neer two
before I got to bed."* She even forgot to go to church in the afternoon
and towards the end of their visit gave a small private dance. She told
them that she herself "could not dance since her father was in such
distress" – a remark which later when Liselotte repeated it to him in
Versailles, brought the tears to James's eyes.* But she wrote afterwards
in her journal that "tho I had seen the electress dance, I was not tempted,
so that I believed I had overcome that which used to be one of my
prettiest pleasures in the world."

Mary and Sophia Charlotte took a great liking to each other. Mary
wrote: "The electrice I found not only to have a good face but also very
agreable, and I believe she does not want wit, but she had been educated
with so much neglect of religion, that I fear she has very little."* And
the Electress, for her part, reported to her mother, Sophia of Hanover,
that it was impossible to speak too highly of the Princess . . . "her beauty
equals her mental gifts".*

The Brandenburgs left on 10 January, and Mary returned with a
certain relief to her "old solitary way of living" – the quiet life which
always suited her so well. But she felt very much alone: of her three
advisers, Fagel was now dead, Waldeck had been called back to the
Dutch army by news of French military activities and Dijkvelt had been
sent to London by the States-General. "I had nobody I could rely on for
advice, and being so little used to business was in no small pain", she
complained in her journal.*

Only a few weeks later, she was faced with a completely unexpected
decision. Kept regularly informed by the Prince's letters that now
arrived regularly, and the news-sheets, she had been following events in
England as little more than an interested onlooker. Now a letter arrived
that plunged her into the heart of English affairs. Danby wrote to say
that if it was her wish, he was certain he could persuade Parliament
to set her alone on the throne. Her answer was eagerly awaited in
England.

*

Yes, mighty Prince, our fear and danger's fled,
Error and ignorance by thee struck dead,
No more th' old chaos o're our world shall spread.
Thy words bids there be light, and strait a ray,
All heavenly bright, calls forth a new-born day.*

Thus runs an exaggerated account of the relief felt in England after the Prince of Orange took command. Every day after his arrival in London on 18 December new delegations came to congratulate him, among them the aldermen of the City of London, all the bishops with the exception of Sancroft, a deputation of nonconformist ministers, and the lawyers.

The Prince himself paid two courtesy calls on 20 December. The first was to his aunt, the Queen-Dowager Catherine of Braganza, now established at Somerset House. He greeted her politely, begged her to let him know if he could do anything for her, and enquired if she still played her favourite game of basset? Catherine replied meaningly that she had not been able to play for some time now, because her chamberlain was absent and he always kept the bank for her. Her chamberlain was Lord Feversham, who had managed her affairs for so long and so devotedly that the Court joked about him, nicknaming him the King Dowager. William took the hint and Feversham, still a prisoner after his arrest at Windsor, was set free the following day to return to Queen Catherine's basset-table.*

The Prince's other visit was to his sister-in-law, Princess Anne, who had returned from Nottingham and was settled in her old apartments in the Cockpit once more. He came to thank her for her support before and after his arrival in England. She was the second to the throne after Mary, and the Prince, who was aware that good relations with her were of the first importance, was still determined to do what he could to preserve them.

He had also planned to pay a visit to the widow of his old friend Ossory, but Emilia van Beverwaert had died just a week earlier of a heart attack.*

The needs of government could not wait. A few days after his arrival the surviving members of all the parliaments Charles had had were assembled. The first action of this skeleton "Parliament" was to ask the Prince to take over the provisional government immediately and to send out writs for elections. On 27 December the Prince agreed: he would call a Convention in January.

A day earlier James II had at last escaped from Rochester. He had been there a week, very lightly guarded on William's orders by a contingent of Dutch troops. He was surprised to find so many Catholics among them and commented on the fact to their commander Dorp, who answered pointedly: "Yes Sire, but they have Protestant swords."*

His presence in the country had been an embarrassment to everyone, particularly for William, who could not wait for him to go. When a letter was intercepted from Mary Beatrice to James, urging him to come to France, the Prince had read it and passed it on as quickly as possible to his prisoner in Rochester. To his relief James at once had given secret orders to have a ship prepared, and on the night of 26 December he sailed to exile in France. He left lying on the table in his room a last appeal to his people, in which he declared that although he was going to seek foreign aid to help him recover his throne, he would not make use of it to overthrow either the Protestant religion or the laws of the land. And once more, he reproached the English for having deserted him.*

The Prince of Orange now settled down to give his attention to a number of problems, of which the most urgent was a shortage of money. Only £40,000 was in the Exchequer and the collection of the revenue being suspended, the army, navy and civil service had not been paid for weeks. The City of London came to his rescue. The Prince had always been a favourite of bankers and merchants, and they showed their confidence in him by lending him £200,000 on no security but his word.

Another question demanding his attention was the plight of England's Roman Catholics. Remembering his promise of tolerance William was anxious to soothe their fears, and although he dared not do much at this stage, with public opinion still strongly against them, he could at least save them from any further violence. He reissued the order he had given immediately after his landing: the persons and properties of Papists were to be unharmed.* By the time the Prince had been a month in London, peace and order had been restored all over the country.

The greatest problem of all remained unsolved: who was to wear the crown? Every Englishman, and politicians in particular, debated the question during these first weeks of January 1689, and by the time the Convention assembled on 22 January it looked as if there were three main schools of thought, with the debate in Parliament likely to follow the same lines. Most of the Tories and the High Churchmen – too strongly committed to the hereditary principle to abandon it – considered James II still to be King, but wanted a Regency. Another small group of Tories were of the opinion that James could be held to have abdicated by his irresponsible flight, and that the crown automatically passed to the next in line, Mary. The Whigs, who were the majority in the Convention, were more ruthless. True to their neo-republican ideas, they intended to seize this chance to establish an entirely new concept of monarchy, that of a contract between King and People. James's conduct, they reasoned, had broken this contract, and Parliament was free to choose a king to its liking. It might be Mary, William or both.* These three propositions were debated over and over while the weeks passed by.

The one man whose views no one yet knew was the Prince of Orange. He had made his headquarters in Mary's childhood home, St. James's Palace, from which he overlooked the Park and could see a sight that must have reminded him of Holland – in this cold winter the Londoners were skating on the frozen ponds.* He had moved into the large bed-chamber where only six months earlier the Prince of Wales was born. Huygens was fascinated and went snooping around to see whether the warming-pan plot had been geographically feasible. He discovered to his delight that next door to the bed-head was a door opening onto a narrow passage-way, which led into a small dressing room. This room, in turn, had a second door which gave on to the backstairs.*

The Prince was not interested in the escapades of his secretary. His temper had chilled with the weather and people were commenting unfavourably on the fact that he "shew'd little countenance to the noblemen and others, who expected a more gracious and chereful reception when they made their court".* If he was following the debate in the Convention, he gave no impression of interest, and Reresby wrote: "The Prince all this while seemed not much to concern himself, only desired that they would dispatch and come to an early resolution."*

But his letters to Waldeck revealed that he found it hard to sustain this air of detachment. "If I were not so scrupulous by nature I should have no hesitation to wind up the affair at once", he had written wistfully at the end of December and there must have been many times in these long weeks when the temptation to declare himself King *de facto* had been hard to resist; but resist it he did in spite of the fact that the whole pointless discussion irritated and affronted him. "If you knew the life that I lead", he wrote to Waldeck, "you would certainly pity me; the only consolation I have is that, God knows, it is not ambition that rules me."*

Bentinck was less discreet than his master. After an argument that kept them up till dawn Burnet had a very good idea of what the Prince of Orange really wished. Halifax had proposed that the crown should be given to the Prince, and only to Mary and then Anne after his death. Bentinck considered this the obvious solution – "A man's wife ought only to be his wife" – and felt that considering all William had done for the English, it was the least they could do for him. Burnet strongly

objected: "It was a very ill return for the steps the Princess had made
to the Prince three years ago."* Admiral Herbert was equally horrified
by the Bentinck proposal to make Mary a mere Queen Consort. "I
would never have drawn my sword in the Prince's favour", he exclaimed
from the sickbed where Bentinck had come to canvass his opinion, "if
I could have suspected him of acting in such a way towards his wife."
Bentinck realized that he had gone too far and came back next day to
assure Herbert that it was his impression that the Prince would be
content with a joint sovereignty as long as the administration was in his
hands.*

The deadlock was abruptly ended by the eagerly awaited reply from
The Hague of the Princess of Orange to the letter of Danby. His offer
to talk Parliament into setting her alone on the throne was indignantly
rejected. "She made him a very sharp answer; she said she was the
Prince's wife, and would never be other than what she should be in
conjunction with him and under him; and that she would take it extreme
unkindly, if any, under a pretence of their care of her, would set up a
divided interest between her and the Prince."* Mary was careful to send
Danby's letter together with a copy of her reply to her husband, and
the Prince now acted.

He sent for Danby, Halifax and Shrewsbury. "He had not", he said,
"come over to establish a Commonwealth or be a Duke of Venice."*
He rejected both the idea of a Regency and of being no more than a
Prince Consort to Mary. "No man could think more of a woman than
he did of the Princess, but he was so made, that he could not think of
holding anything by apron strings, nor could he think it reasonable to
have any share in the government unless it was put in his person, and
that for the term of life." In other words, he was not prepared to stay
except as King. If they preferred any other solution "he would go back
to Holland and meddle no more in their affairs".*

There was no other solution, and Parliament knew it as well as he
did. The throne was declared vacant and on 6 February 1689 the crown
was offered to William and Mary jointly, with the administration vested
in William for life. But he was not to enjoy the sweeping powers of his
Stuart predecessors. A Declaration of Rights, subsequently embodied
in a Bill, cropped the monarchy of its power to suspend the law of the
land or maintain a standing army in peace; parliaments must be called
frequently and the dispensing power was condemned. This Declaration
was a final demonstration of the Whig triumph: the choice of William
had been in accordance with the Whig doctrine that kings might be
appointed by Parliament and must reign with Parliament.

The Revolution was accomplished. The reign of William and Mary had begun.

ON 17 JANUARY Pepys had already issued orders to send Arthur Herbert to Holland with two yachts to bring back the Princess of Orange, and a naval squadron under Sir John Berry to escort her. The two yachts were the *Fubbs*, Charles's pleasure yacht to which he had given his nickname for his mistress, Portsmouth; and the *Isabella*, named by James after the daughter who had died in infancy. William had appointed Edward Villiers to accompany the Princess.*

It was reported to London that contrary winds kept Mary in Holland while Parliament was debating who should have the crown, but William's opponents accused him of keeping her out of the country deliberately. It was more than likely that the Prince preferred to deal with the issue single-handed: only after Parliament had voted finally to give the crown to William and Mary together, did he dispatch an express messenger to summon his wife to London.

Mary received the summons with mixed feelings. She loved Holland and its people, and told the Imperial ambassador Kramprich at a last audience: "It is very hard for me to leave this country, where for eleven years I have lived in peace and quiet."* She had wept when she left England as a fifteen-year-old bride; now she cried more bitterly at the idea of going back. Being reunited with her husband was her only consolation.

In her journal she wrote a poignant account of her feelings.

> . . . self love made me shed a flood of tears at the thought of leaving a country where I had the esteem of the inhabitants, where I had led a life so suitable to my honour, and as I think not unacceptable to my God, where in a word I had all earthly content, and sufficient means to bring me to Heaven, abundant cause to make me love it, and no small reason to doubt if ever I should be so happy in my own country, yet, even then, . . . I checked my self and was angry at so much distrust of Gods mercy . . .*

The news that she was leaving spread fast at The Hague and everyone flocked to the Binnenhof to say farewell. "They have difficulty in keeping the people away from Court. Everyone wants to see the Princess for the last time. The Princess has not been able to go through it all without being upset and shedding tears", reported Kramprich to Vienna.*

She left The Hague on 18 February, driving in a simple carriage drawn by two horses to Maassluis, and thence crossed the Maas in a small yacht to land at Den Briel, where the two English ships had been waiting for some time now. The wind delayed her at Den Briel for twenty-four hours, and some of the company suggested that she might like to go back to The Hague until it changed. Mary shuddered at the thought of living through the same partings again, and from on board the yacht *Isabella* she wrote her friend the Baroness van Wassenaer van Obdam:

> I'm afraid they accuse me of obstinacy in staying here with a contrary wind, but if only they knew what I suffered yesterday, nobody would be astonished that I prefer to wait for the wind here than to go back, because truly it is so great a grief for me to leave a country where I have been so happy, and also I was so moved by all the tears that I saw shed yesterday that I do not know how to express it . . .*

The two yachts were able to sail on Sunday, 20 February, and the Dutch were genuinely grieved to see the wife of their Stadholder leave. Panegyrics were composed and sermons preached to mourn her departure. "Everybody's love and affection followed the ships, that took her away. Everybody's gaze followed her as long as possible; and if she disappeared out of our sight, she has not disappeared from our hearts, in which she has left the marks of an ineradicable love", declaimed a Hague preacher, Johannes Brant, later.* And Professor Bidloo at Leiden rhymed:

> *All England now is full of cheer;*
> *As Prince's Faith comes to her aid*
> *To rescue her from grief and fear;*
> *But all the Dutch are sore dismayed*
> *Since Our Princess without a peer*
> *Has vanished into England's shade.*
> *Our love will never disappear,*
> *Or Mary's image ever fade.**

The crossing was rapid and uneventful and they reached Margate on Monday, the eleventh, o.s. A day later Mary was welcomed at Greenwich by William and her sister Anne.* All the way over, she had been torn by conflicting sentiments. "I wisht of all things to see the Prince, yet I had rather seen him [in Holland] than in England." The thought of seeing him hailed as her country's deliverer filled her with pride and satisfaction – until she remembered from whom he had delivered England, and was filled again with grief and guilt at the memory of her father.

At Greenwich she was alone with the Prince for a little while.

I had a joy greater than can be expressed to come to the Prince, but I found him in a very ill condition as to his health, he had a violent cough upon him and was grown extreamly lean. He could not restrain. As soon as we were alone we both shed tears of joy to meet, and of sorrow for meeting in England, both wishing it might have been in Holland, both bewailing the loss of the liberty we left behind and were sensible we should never enjoy here.

Before they emerged they dried their tears "lest it should be perceived when we went out".*

By nightfall Mary was once more after so many years in Whitehall palace, where "as may be imagined . . . she had great crowds of all sorts coming to wait on her." There had been rumours that she was unhappy about her father, and upset by the final settlement of the crown, and the crowds expected to find her looking at least subdued, if not visibly saddened. But the Prince, anticipating this, had written to her "that it was necessary she should appear at first so cheerful, that nobody might be discouraged by her looks, or be led to apprehend that she was uneasy by reason of what had been done." No doubt he had reminded her again when he met her at Greenwich. And the crowds who flocked to this first Court evening of their new King and Queen were startled, and some of them even shocked, to see how delighted with her new position Mary appeared to be. Burnet voiced the feelings of many when he wrote: "I thought a little more seriousness had done as well, when she came into her father's Palace, and was to be sat on his throne the next day."* Evelyn noted disapprovingly: "She came into White-hall laughing and jolly, as to a wedding, so as to seem quite transported."* And Dartmouth later testified "that she put on more airs of gaiety upon that occasion than became her, or seemed natural . . ."*

The next day, Ash Wednesday, before William and Mary were proclaimed King and Queen, Mary's behaviour continued to give offence. Evelyn heard that "She rose early the next morning, and in her undresse, as it was reported, before her women were up, went about from roome to roome to see the convenience of White-hall, lay in the same bed and apartment where the late Queene lay . . ."* Soon exaggerated and spiteful accounts of Mary's housewifely curiosity to examine her new home were circulating at Court, and Sarah Jennings in particular improved on the tale, comparing her behaviour to that of a traveller just arrived at a common inn.

The English were just as surprised by Mary's equanimity when she and William were proclaimed in the Banqueting House in the morning. They had expected nothing better of William, but Evelyn was not the only one who had thought that Mary, at least "would have shew'd some (seeming) reluctance . . . of assuming her father's Crown, and made some apology, testifying by her regret that he should by his mismanagement necessitate the Nation to so extraordinary a proceeding . . . but nothing of all this appear'd . . ." In the few days that followed, nothing altered his impression:

> . . . within a night or two [she] sate down to play at basset, as the Queene her predecessor used to do. She smil'd upon and talk'd to every body, so that no change seem'd to have taken place at Court since her last going away, save that infinite crouds of people throng'd to see her, and that she went to our prayers. This carriage was censur'd by many. She seems to be of a good nature, and that she takes nothing to heart . . .*

Burnet was surprised and "took the liberty to ask her, how it came that what she saw in so sad a revolution as to her father's person, made not a greater impression on her." Mary told him that "she felt the sense of it very lively upon her thoughts. But the letters which had been writ to her had obliged her to put on a cheerfulness, in which she might perhaps go too far, . . . acting a part which was not very natural to her . . ."*

Mary's air of gaiety was not in fact altogether assumed. She was delighted to be with her husband again, and she was gratified that through her, and by her self-abnegation, he had come to the three crowns. She admitted herself in her journal that she was extremely pleased that the government had been placed entirely in the Prince's hands. "Many would not believe it, so that I was fain to force my self to more mirth than became me at that time, and was by many interpreted as ill nature, pride and the great delight I had to be Queen." This last assumption she found particularly ludicrous: "My heart is not made for a kingdom and my inclination leads me to a retired quiet life . . . Indeed the prince's being made king has lessened the pain, but not the trouble of what I am like to endure."*

The Proclamation took place at half past ten in the morning. In a cavalcade of coaches came the Lords and the Commons from nearby Westminster to the Banqueting House on which James's weathercock still turned, but which was now guarded by Dutch soldiers. They were hardly seated when the southern door opened and the Prince and Princess of Orange came in and took their seats under the canopy of state. The Peers and the Commons rose and bowed deeply, and Halifax speaking for both, asked the Prince and Princess permission to have the Declaration of Right read aloud. After this had been done, Halifax asked them to accept the crown. The Prince answered for them both. "We thankfully accept what you have offered us" he said, promising to be entirely governed by the laws of England, to do his best for the welfare of the kingdom, and to be guided by the advice of both Houses. After these reassuring words, which were loudly cheered, William and Mary were declared King and Queen of England, Scotland, France and Ireland.*

At the Court gates outside the Banqueting House trumpeters sounded a call three times, "the last of which was answered by a great shout of the vast multitude of people there assembled." When the shouts had died down, the Garter King of Arms in a loud voice read the Proclamation and after this ceremony was repeated in the City, at Temple Gate, Cheapside, Wood Street and Royal Exchange, London celebrated in its usual manner – "the rest of the day being spent in the ringing of bells, bonfires at night and other expressions of joy, though a great many looked very sadly upon it."*

Huygens watched the Proclamation from his window in Whitehall. Describing the scene in his journal, he was very conscious of writing the word "King" for the first time before his master's name, and when he next came to see him, kissed his hand in the English manner, which William allowed reluctantly.*

TWO MONTHS LATER, on 11 April, William and Mary were crowned in Westminster Abbey. Those who remembered James's coronation thought that "this was much finer and in better order; and if the number of ladies were fewer, yet their attendance was with more application near the Queen all the time, and with more cheerful faces by a great deal."*

The King and Queen had left the Palace of Whitehall at seven o'clock in the morning by a private staircase, to travel by barge the few hundred yards to Westminster, where the nobility waited in the House of Lords, wearing their ermine-edged robes of state. Three hours later, the whole impressive procession emerged from the Palace of Westminster to tread over the long blue carpet leading to the West Door of Westminster Abbey and lined by the Dutch Blue Guards. The King wore a crown topped with a pleated velvet bonnet to match his robes, and the Queen a golden diadem. The King's Coronation Crown was carried by the Earl of Grafton, the Queen's by the Duke of Somerset. The pointed sword, emblem of temporal justice, was carried before them by the Earl of Pembroke. The Archbishop of Canterbury, Sancroft, had refused to be present, pleading illness, and his place was taken by Dr. Compton.

The Bishop of Winchester and the Bishop of Bristol walked at the side of William and Mary.*

The ceremony that followed was unique. Mary, as Queen Regnant, was inaugurated exactly like her husband in almost every respect: the Sword of State was girded round her as round him, she was raised into the throne as William was, and she too was presented with the Bible, the spurs and the heavy jewelled orb.* Instead of the light, elegant diadem of a Queen Consort, her Coronation Crown was massive and heavily jewelled. It was specially made by Robert Vyner, who had also made her diadem and her Crown of State. The cost of making these together with the two crowns for the King, an orb and two sceptres for the King and the same for the Queen, came to £7260, but the stones alone, part of the Crown treasures, were valued at £126,000, consisting of 2725 diamonds, 71 rubies, 59 sapphires, 40 emeralds, and 1591 large pearls. The most striking jewel in the Queen's crown was itself valued at £30,000.* The weight of so much gold and jewellery was oppressive during the long ceremony, and William looked tired and strained. His wife, who had begun by looking almost exalted, was soon also wilting visibly. Her sister Anne felt sorry for her and whispered her sympathy, but Mary, according to unkind rumours, snapped back irritably: "Sister, a crown is not so heavy as it seems."*

The ceremony was unprecedented in another respect as well. Previous kings of England had sworn to uphold the law made by their ancestors. William and Mary swore that they would govern according to "the statutes in parliament agreed upon and the laws and customs of the same", and as an extra security, they promised to uphold the Protestant reformed religion.

The deepest impression of the whole service was made by Burnet who preached the Coronation Sermon, a moving exercise in optimism.

> It is in your persons, and under your Reign, that we hope to see an opening to a Glorious Scene, . . . May you reign long in your persons and much longer in a glorious posterity . . . May you be long the support of the Church of God, and the terror of all its enemies. May you ever be happy in obedient subjects, in wise Counsellors, and faithful Allies. May your fleets be prosperous and your Armies victorious. But may you soon have cause to use neither . . .*

The day's ceremonies ended with a banquet in Westminster Hall that lasted till ten o'clock at night. But though most of London celebrated on this evening, there were scattered murmurs of discontent. James's sympathisers, already christened Jacobites, were loud in their objections to the use of Dutch soldiers to guard William and Mary when they were crowned King and Queen of England. And they muttered again when their Calvinist king refused to perform the traditional Coronation ceremonies of the washing of the feet of the poor, and touching for scrofula, the King's Evil, dismissing these time-hallowed rituals as mere superstition.

William felt nothing but relief that the whole business was over, and he asked Burgemeester Witsen of Amsterdam, who had been present in London, if he had seen "the comedy of the Coronation", and what he thought "of those foolish old Popish ceremonies".*

But the air of preoccupation and gloom he had shown in the Abbey was not only due to dislike of ceremonial. That same day, news had reached London that James had landed in Ireland with an army. According to a Jacobite source, the news gave rise to a quarrel between Mary and William, in which she told him that he had made a mistake in letting her father go as he had done. When James heard this, he believed it, and exclaimed, "My own children have lost all their feeling, not only of filial love, but of ordinary compassion."*

This uncharacteristic story was a Jacobite invention. If Mary had accepted the crown, she was certainly not indifferent to James's fate. Her loyalty to her husband overruled her loyalty to her father, but it was not a painless struggle.

Now, newly crowned Queen of England, Mary wrote to Sophia of Hanover: "Many people have the fortune to be able to talk of things about which I have to be silent. You must not doubt the sincerity of my feelings when I say that I cannot forget my father, and I grieve for his misfortune."*

CHAPTER XXVI

Settling Down

"Hee hath such a mind to France, that it would incline one to think hee tooke England onely in his way."* That was Halifax's impression after one of his many long political conversations with England's new King in the spring of 1689. William liked talking to this shrewd and moderate Englishman, asked his advice frequently in the first few months of his reign, and was more frank about his designs than with anybody else. To Halifax, William made no secret of the fact that as early as January, he had proposed to Holland that they should declare war on France, confidentially promising them English military and naval assistance. Upon this promise, the States of Holland had immediately begun negotiations with the Emperor Leopold I, who was being simultaneously courted by Louis XIV and the exiled James II.

To embroil the English in a costly European war would have been an impossible task for William, if James and Louis had not given him a helping hand by invading Ireland. For the English, it was an unpardonable French intrusion into their domestic affairs, and immediately after the Coronation the Commons debated the French aggression in Ireland. All the hatred and resentment which the English had been nursing for years against France now burst out in a diatribe against "the most Christian barbarian". And in an address to their new King, they assured him that when he "should think it fit to enter into war against the French King, they would give him such assistance in a parliamentary way as to enable him to support and go through with the same."* William thanked them warmly. Ambition, he said modestly, should never induce him to draw the sword, but he had no choice: France had already attacked England.* To his closest confidants he said jubilantly afterwards, "This is the first day of my reign."* And he was so carried away by the idea of this war that he admitted to Halifax: ". . . hee had a great mind to land in France and that it was the best way to save Ireland."*

In May the expected news travelled rapidly through England. Captain Bellingham in Preston noted calmly in his diary for the fourteenth: "A hot day. The kings declaration of warr against the French king. I sup't att cousen Pattens and eat chard."* Louis riposted by a declaration of war "upon the English and Scottish adherents of William of Orange, usurper of the crowns of England and Scotland."* But his courtship of Leopold I came abruptly to an end. The Emperor, appalled by the French ambitions so bloodily displayed in the Palatinate, chose to side with the English and declared war on France. After some hesitation, he followed the Spanish lead by recognizing William as King, giving him the title of "Majesty", a style he had never accorded to James.* By mid-summer 1689 all Europe was committed to war; France stood alone against England, the United Provinces, Spain and the Empire. As Liselotte wrote:

> *Le Prince d'Orange gouverne tout;*
> *Le Roi de France demande tout;*
> *Le pape refuse tout;*
> *L'Allemagne s'oppose à tout;*
> *Les Jesuites se mêlent de tout;*
> *Si Dieu ne met ordre à tout;*
> *Le Diable emportera tout.**

The Dutch were naturally delighted at first by the new order in Europe – they would never again have to fight the English, and in a war with France they could rely on English assistance. Already in January 1689 the States-General had sent an embassy to London to cement the relationship between the two countries. The embassy was headed by Nicolaas Witsen, the Burgemeester of Amsterdam, and they arrived in London on 18 January much shaken after a frightful crossing. William gave them an audience four days later, when they were recovered, and asked them cheerfully: "Now is it a good thing that you advised me to undertake this work? Are people pleased about it?" But when Witsen commented on William's apparent popularity in England, he answered wryly: "The cry is all Hosanna today, but soon perhaps it will be Crucify him."*

A month later Witsen was again received by William when he came to congratulate him on being offered the Crown. Witsen wished him "the wisdom of Solomon, the good fortune of David, and the years of Methuselah".* He ought to have added, the patience of Job: in Holland as in England, a certain disenchantment soon set in. While the English accused William of too close an attachment to Dutch interests, the

Dutch complained that he did not do enough for them. Witsen reported
to The Hague that the King only laughed when the Dutch envoys asked
for trading concessions and the repeal of the Navigation Act of 1651.
During the Anglo-Dutch negotiations that spring, the King was careful
to remain neutral, "to avoid displeasing the English", as the Dutch
noted resentfully. And in the end, the Republic had to accept that
England was the more important partner. In the Naval Agreement of
April 1689 it was laid down, for instance, that in any joint Anglo-Dutch
action at sea, the English admiral should always take command.

The Alliance Treaty of September, which bound the two countries
to make war and peace with France jointly, contained another affront
to Dutch feelings: it declared an absolute embargo on trade with
France. Witsen was so shattered by this defiance of the sacred Dutch
trade principle – "Free ship, free goods" – that his hand shook when he
added his signature to the treaty.

On the surface at least, all was cordiality and friendship. After the
Coronation, the States had elevated their envoys Witsen, Dijkveldt and
Odijk to the status of ambassadors and added two more, Schimmel-
penninck and Van Citters. On 27 May they made their magnificent
formal entry, blocking Whitehall with their eighty coaches. The English
crowds were wildly enthusiastic, and shouted "Away with popery!
God save King William and Queen Mary! Here are the real friends of
England, – the day has come – God bless the Protestant religion."* The
Dutchmen were officially received by William and Mary together, and
Schimmelpenninck was so impressed by the occasion that he kept
forgetting his speech and had to be prompted by Witsen in a whisper.

It was observed that the King raised his hat every time "their High
Mightinesses", the States-General, were mentioned in the speech.* And
if William could not favour the Dutch during the negotiations, at least
in private they knew where his heart lay. To Witsen he admitted that he
would rather "give up English interests altogether than see Holland
perish".*

The Dutch were the least of William's problems that year; Scotland
and Ireland made heavier demands on his attention. Mary might have
regretted that she had only three crowns to give her husband. Now, as so
often, he must have wished there had been only one. And now as always,
the affairs of Scotland were a distraction which he bitterly resented.
"The Scotchmen by their severall stories distracted his mind more than
anything" he told Halifax crossly.* He had attempted an immediate
settlement of Scottish affairs by ordering elections to a Convention of
Estates in the spring, which formally offered him the Crown on 11 April

under its President the Duke of Hamilton. If the Presbyterian majority in Scotland had eagerly abandoned James, however, the Highland clans were still loyal to their exiled king, and in Dundee they had an able and inspiring leader. Not for long. When at the end of July the Highland army encountered the disciplined Williamite troops commanded by Mackay in the Pass of Killiecrankie, "bonnie Dundee" was killed. The clansmen fled, and for the moment Scottish Jacobite resistance was broken. The Irish problem would take longer to solve.

IN THE LATE SEVENTEENTH CENTURY London smog was notorious. "The vapours, fogs and rains with which the atmosphere . . . is loaded, drag with them in their fall the heaviest particles of the smoke; this forms black rain and produces the ill effects that may justly be expected from it upon the clothes of those who are exposed to it."* So wrote a Frenchman who visited London in 1690. The air was so polluted with the smoke from domestic coal fires that the Londoners sometimes feared they would never see the sun shining again. And for the asthmatic William III the need to escape into fresh smokeless air soon became urgent.

His health had deteriorated rapidly since his arrival in England. Mary had been horrified to find how ill he looked when she arrived in England in February, and the Dutch envoys thought he looked wretched – "he's not the same man in England as he was in Holland."* William himself was worried, writing to Waldeck in March 1689, "My health is not of the best because my cough is getting worse in this climate, which makes me very weak."* Even the occasional hunt he managed to escape to brought him no relief. Dijkvelt told Huygens that during one hunt, the King had felt such oppression of his chest that he could not gallop.* Huygens was used to his constant coughing, but noted in London that the King was always having long coughing attacks and bringing up great quantities of phlegm.

His asthma tortured him, and he called in London's most celebrated physician, Dr. John Radcliffe, a brilliant diagnostician whose treatment gave the King so much relief that he offered him the post of Court physician with a salary £200 higher than any of his other doctors. Radcliffe, a Tory and a staunch Jacobite, refused, although he continued to treat William occasionally, making as much as 600 guineas a year out of his royal patient.*

What Radcliffe could not cure was the King's homesickness for Holland that first year. It sapped at his wellbeing even more than the

London smog and exhausted him mentally and physically, giving him an abstracted air. Courtiers saw an unusual sight: William, normally so rigidly self-controlled, began talking to himself, moving his lips soundlessly.* He made no effort to hide his nostalgia from Huygens, asking him one day if he was not already homesick himself. When his secretary said no, the King smiled sadly and said he could understand it if he were. A few weeks later – it was May and springtime – the King, dictating to his secretary, looked out of the windows and remarked: "It is warm weather, and the kermess is on at The Hague. Oh, if only we could fly over like birds through the sky. I would give a hundred thousand guilders for that" . . . and a little later, still daydreaming, he corrected himself, "Yes, I would give two hundred thousand guilders for that."*

There was no solace to be had for his longing for Holland but if he could not fly to The Hague or Het Loo, at least he was not obliged to put up with the stink and overcrowding of Whitehall, and shortly after his arrival in England, his eye fell on Hampton Court, the vast rambling Tudor palace of Henry VIII. He took Mary down there as soon as she came to London, and on 20 February the chronicler Luttrell reported: "Their Majesties goe frequently to Hampton Court, taking delight in that place."* Soon they moved in; and the courtiers grumbled loudly about the hours they now had to spend commuting between Whitehall and Hampton Court.

Halifax complained to Reresby that spring that "the Kings inaccessibleness and liveing soe at Hampton Court altogether, and at soe active a time ruined all the business." He pleaded with William to spend at least an occasional night in town, but the King answered shortly that "it was not to be done except he desired to see him dead."*

This indifference to public opinion gave great offence, but William either could not or would not make an effort to please for the sake of pleasing. And there were times in the early months of his reign when it seemed that his ungraciousness might even cost **him** his crown. "This King used noe arts", commented Halifax who, as one of William's rare English confidants, was appalled by the speed with which the King's standing had deteriorated. He remarked to Danby that if James would turn Protestant "he could not be kept out four months". Danby went even further and said that if James "would give the satisfaction in point of religion which he might, it would be hard to resist him as he was."* Burnet voiced the same anxious criticisms: he noted that the King "was apt to be very peevish, and to conceal his fretfulness put him in a necessity of being very much in his closet . . . many persuaded him to be more accessible. He said that 'his ill health made it impossible'."*

The Dutch envoys in London saw with distress and disbelief that their Stadholder, so much beloved at home, was fast losing all the love and affection of his new subjects. Dijkvelt told Huygens in May that "the love of the English, and especially of the Lords, for the King had not increased; they complained about his taciturn and reserved ways. . . ."* And Witsen related to the States of Holland how "in the coffeehouses here people are saying 'We have beheaded one king and thrown out another and we know how to deal with the third.'"*

Perhaps more than anything else, it was his obvious preference for Dutch company that irritated the English. "The King was thought to love the Dutch more than the English", reported Burnet, "to trust more to them and to admit them to more freedom . . . and the English being of more lively temper than the Dutch, grew to express a contempt and an aversion for them, that went almost to a mutiny."*

By September at last even William realized that he must make some attempt to conciliate his subjects. Accompanied by Prince George, several of the nobility and the Dutch ambassadors, he went for ten days to Newmarket Races. He enjoyed it much better than he had expected, tried hard to mingle naturally with the crowds as Charles had done, lost a fortune at betting, got himself reeling drunk one evening, and dined wherever he was invited. It needed no more than this small effort to please people, and Lord Coote wrote cheerfully about the new sociable King: "I hope his Majestie, by degrees will become a true Englishman."*

Back in London, William made another effort. On 19 October, he and the Queen were the guests of the City of London on Lord Mayor's Day. The traditional show was followed by a magnificent dinner which cost the Lord Mayor £300, the two sheriffs £150 each and the aldermen £50. Both the sheriffs and two aldermen were rewarded with knighthoods, and William and Mary were reported "very well pleased with their reception."* Next day they dined for the first time in public, and a few days later William, at his own request, was made a member of a City livery company – "he who was proud and a soldier pretended to derive honour from being chosen master of the grocers' company."*

The King's first birthday in England on 4 November was designed as the highlight of this new popularity campaign: the shops were closed, the bells rang and bonfires were lit. In the morning there was a special service at court, at which the Bishop of St. Asaph paid a glowing tribute to the King as the Church's great deliverer. And the ball given by the King and Queen that evening ought to have been the most splendid in years; unfortunately so many Londoners crowded to get a rare glimpse of their stand-offish King that it soon degenerated into chaos.*

The awkwardness and unease with which the King made even these gestures of good-will, however, robbed them of half their charm, and realizing this, he soon fell back into his old ways. He went hunting, busied himself with his troops at Hounslow – "one of his favourite places of resort"* – and once again saw almost nobody but his Dutch coterie. To the fury of the English noblemen, they were left standing at the King's table while he dined with Bentinck, Ouwerkerk, Zuylestein and his Dutch officers.

None of the Dutch were particularly popular, but easily the most hated man at Court was Bentinck, created Earl of Portland at the Coronation. The English realized soon after William's arrival how much he relied on the advice of this unbending foreigner, who was soon nicknamed "the Wooden Man"; Huygens remarked in his diary as early as January 1689 that Portland "gave great jealousy to the English", and referred again in March to the hatred that the "Favourit" aroused.* Witsen told Amsterdam how much the English Peers resented Portland's high-handed manner, and how well-disposed Englishmen had implored him to use any influence he might have with the King not to closet himself with Portland all the time.* One of the many lampoons of the day attacked Portland's jealous guarding of the King:

> *Make room crys Sir Thomas Duppa†*
> *Then Benting up-locks*
> *His King in a box*
> *And you see him no more till supper.**

The political influence of the Favourite was rightly guessed to be enormous. One English courtier told Witsen that the King did nothing without the approval of Portland. When the Dutch envoy protested weakly that he perhaps only asked his advice, the Englishman assured him: "No, we've watched them carefully."*

Nothing was too bad to say about "cringing" Portland,

> *whose earth-born race*
> *The coronet and garter does disgrace;*
> *Of undescended parentage, made great*
> *By change, . . . his virtues undiscovered yet.*
> *From his ignoble neck the collar tear*
> *Let not his breast the rays of honour wear.*
> *Of black designs and lusts let him remain*

† Sir Thomas Duppa was the King's gentleman-usher.

A servile favourite, and grants obtain;
While ancient honours, sacred to the crown
*Are lavished to support the minion.**

In the coffeehouses the gossip said that the Dutch favourite was making a fortune by selling offices – at least £35,000 in one year. They did him an injustice: it was the King's lavishness that soon made him one of the wealthiest men in the country. His office of Groom of the Stole at £5000 a year was among the first and smallest of his perks. He was made Treasurer of the Privy Purse too, and there was plenty more to follow.

If he had lived in ostentatious splendour the English might have forgiven him much, but according to them he took all and spent nothing, not even on fine clothes. The Spanish envoy mistook him at first sight for a servant.*

There was only one Englishman at the Court who could successfully compete with Portland for William's friendship: it was Henry Sidney, created Earl of Romney in the Coronation Honours list. Romney had been one of the first and most important of the Williamites in the times of Charles II and he remained loyal throughout James's reign against his own interests. He was "the great wheel on which the revolution rolled" and William rewarded him with a succession of important posts, beginning by making him colonel of his Foot Guards. More flatteringly, the King gave Romney his full trust and confidence.* Englishmen who knew this tall handsome man were amazed by the choice. They admitted his honour and honesty, but found him a man only of "moderate capacity, who promised everybody, but did for no one; which makes him the less pitied; constantly for many years, drunk once a day."*

Romney's influence belied the accusation that only the Dutch had any say in Court matters. In fact the plum jobs at court were shared out equally between the two nations. In William's Household, two other Dutchmen held important positions besides Portland. Zuylestein was Master of the Robes, and Ouwerkerk Master of the Horse. Three Englishmen filled other important posts: the Earl of Devonshire was Lord Steward, the Earl of Dorset was Lord Chamberlain, and the Earl of Montagu Master of the Great Wardrobe. In the lower ranks, the English were in the majority and only in the King's secretariat was he entirely served by Dutch staff. Huygens remained his principal Secretary, assisted by Pieter de Wilde and Samuel van Hulst.

Mary's household was predominantly English. The Duchess of Dorset was her Lady of the Bedchamber, the Marquis of Winchester was

Chamberlain, Jack Howe, the aggressive M.P. for Cirencester, was Vice-Chamberlain and the Countess of Derby, daughter of Ossory and an old friend of Mary, was Groom of the Stole. There were only two Dutch ladies-in-waiting, "Joffers" Goldstein and Agnes Vijgh van Ubbergen, and neither of them was very happy in London. Joffer Goldstein complained to Huygens, almost in tears, that the English ladies treated her and Joffer Vijgh with disdain, and she once said sadly that the Queen was becoming "too English".*

Like William, Mary kept the secretary who had served her in Holland: d'Allonne, half French and half Dutch, was now "Principal Secretary and Master of Request to the Queen".

One name was missing from the list of courtiers: that of Betty Villiers. She had not remained behind in Holland, however, journeying back to England soon after William and settling in London, where she spent her first few weeks at the house of her sister, Madame Puissars. When the King and Queen later moved to Kensington, she followed them, and quietly established herself in lodgings nearby.* Soon it was known that she was seeing the King at Hampton Court too, meeting him in the house of Zuylestein. But as always, William kept the affair as discreet as possible, and Betty received none of the honours and rewards which the King lavished on his male friends, and which a Royal mistress might have felt entitled to expect. Madame Puissars had received a handsome pension for life from the King, through Betty's intervention, but she told a friend bitterly that if Betty was now a "queen", little was done for her brothers and sisters who ought at least to have been earls and countesses by this time.*

Mary probably knew of Betty's presence nearby, but she had long since resigned herself to the existence of this shadowy other woman in her husband's life. And at this time, in any case, she had no leisure to brood over her emotional problems. She was very worried about William's health; and she was even more concerned by his growing alienation from her countrymen. In an attempt to ease the situation a little for everyone, she talked him into buying a country house much nearer Whitehall than remote Hampton Court, and in June he bought Kensington House from the Earl of Nottingham for 18,000 guineas.* This pretty brick-built villa lay at the western edge of Hyde Park, which was still filled with deer. It had its own large gardens, and Kensington itself was a pleasant country village surrounded by farms and market gardens.

During the first few weeks after her arrival in February, Mary had lived in the new apartments built by James for Mary Beatrice at Whitehall, facing the Privy Gardens. They were sumptuous, designed as a new block by Wren, and lavishly decorated by artists such as Grinling Gibbons, Verrio and Gennari. Mary's bedroom had as its most splendid feature a white marble mantelpiece surmounted by a mirror with a delicately carved frame, and picture panels enriched with leaves and flowers, for which work Grinling Gibbons had been paid £48. All the rooms were panelled, with the mouldings picked out in gilt, and the ceilings were covered with the florid and colourful paintings of Verrio.* But she abandoned these apartments without regret for Hampton Court and Kensington. And at both places she threw herself with enthusiasm into the task of preparing Royal residences which should not only be splendid, but homely and comfortable as well – a peculiar Dutch combination of qualities which Het Loo perfectly exemplified. The new residences were needed in a hurry, and architect Christopher Wren found the Queen an exacting client who hustled him mercilessly. Within three months of his first inspection Wren had his plan for Hampton Court ready, by June the building materials were ordered, and by July the foundations were already under construction.

According to Wren's plans, all the ramshackle old Tudor buildings with the exception of the Great Hall were to be demolished, and replaced by a tremendous new Renaissance palace with formal gardens and avenues in the best continental manner. Intentionally or not, it was to be England's rival to Versailles.

Mary supervised every stage of the work, making suggestions, "examining and surveying the Drawings, Contrivances and whole Progress of the Works" and giving her "own judgment, which was exquisite".* She took a special interest in the former Water Gallery which Wren had begun in April to remodel into a suite of pretty little rooms for her; they were decorated with Gibbons's delicate wood carvings, and they included what was still a rarity in England – a bathroom with a bath of white marble, "made very fine, suited either to hot or cold bathing, as the season should invite".*

With her passion for gardening she also took the keenest pleasure in planning the alleys, the flowerbeds and the shaded walks of Hampton Court. Hothouses were built for the tropical flowers, and shrubs sent to her from the Canary Islands and Virginia.* From the West Indies a whole collection of exotic trees and shrubs were dispatched to the royal gardens, their names as novel as their appearance: Jack in a Box and Sugar Apple, Silk Cotton and Leather Coat, Prickly Yellowwood and Sea side Grape, Galley Pear and Calamola.*

Mary, who sometimes felt guilty about the enormous sums of

money that she and William were spending on their palaces and gardens, soothed her conscience with the thought that it was her one extravagance, and "since this employed many hands, she was pleased to say that she hoped it wd be forgiven her."*

But, as she wrote in her journal, the "hand of God" punished her. They had taken a short lease of Holland House, also at Kensington, but Mary felt unsettled there and was so eager to move into Kensington House that she went almost every day to urge on the work. Her impatience had disastrous consequences. Wren, who was working at Hampton Court and Kensington simultaneously, began in desperation to cut corners, and to resort to fast but unreliable methods of construction. In November, as a result, a newly-built roof at Kensington which had just been covered in lead collapsed, killing some of the workers and injuring others.* And at Hampton Court only a month later a similar accident occurred – "occasioned by the slightness of the wall" – in which more workmen lost their lives.* Mary was deeply distressed and wrote: "All this as much as it was the fault of the workmen, humanly speaking, yet shewed me the hand of God plainly in it, and I was truly humbled."*

William was highly displeased by the news, which caused a public outcry, and Christopher Wren had to face not only a court of inquiry, but the King's wrath. He was summoned to Whitehall and reproached with his responsibility for the death of four men. Wren could only defend himself lamely with the fact that it had actually been no more than three.*

The King and Queen finally moved into their new home at Kensington just before Christmas 1689, when the place was still swarming with builders and covered with scaffolding. What Wren had done to the old house of Lord Nottingham was to tack pavilions onto its four corners. The two eastern pavilions were for the King; the north-west pavilion, together with the great hall, were for the Queen, and the south-west pavilion housed the great stairs and the royal chapel. "Architecturally, there was nothing remarkable about Wren's work at Kensington. It was a neat enough conversion job, but there was no attempt at grandeur";* Evelyn, who came to inspect it at the beginning of 1690, found it. "a patched building, but with the garden . . . a very sweet villa". He was impressed by "the straight new way through the park" which had been specially laid out for the benefit of King and Court. The road was wide enough for three coaches to drive abreast, and at regular intervals along it were set posts on which were glass cases for lamps, lit every evening when the Court was at Kensington.* This was not the extravagance it sounded: the road out to Kensington was notorious for its highwaymen and footpads.

The gardens at Kensington were in the Dutch style. A tree-lined avenue ran down from a black-and-white flagstoned terrace in front of the King's Gallery. On either side were four large parterres planted with miniature trees, shrubs and box hedges in elaborate patterns, one of them in the shape of classic designs for fortifications. The work was done by the celebrated gardeners London and Wise, and over the next seven years cost William £11,000.*

Inside, Kensington House soon took on something of the look of a museum. The King had already begun skimming off the cream of the royal collections and transferring them to his new home, filling the galleries with Titians, Raphaels, Holbeins and Van Dycks. The Queen contributed her collections of Chinese porcelain which she had brought over from Holland, thus launching a new national craze. She had a taste for rare and exotic furniture too; Evelyn went to admire the Queen's rare cabinets and collections of china a few years later, and found them "wonderfully rich and plentifull, but especialy a large cabinet, looking-glasse frame and stands, all of amber, much of it white, with historical bas-reliefs and statues; with medals carved in them, esteem'd worth £4000, sent by the Duke of Brandenburgh . . . divers other china and Indian cabinets, screens, and hangings".*

Blue and white china was not the only fashion for which Mary was responsible in England. When she sailed over from Holland, she brought with her a whole troop of the little dogs known in Holland as Mops-honden and soon nicknamed in England, where they had never been seen before, Dutch Mastiffs or Dutch Pugs. It was said that a Dutch pug had once saved the life of William's famous ancestor, William the Silent, by barking to warn him of the enemy's approach, and ever since the little dogs had been almost mascots of the Orange family and their supporters. Now they became a craze in England as well, and many courtiers were soon seen accompanied by a little pug sporting an orange bow in token of their loyalty. A few years later Mary was responsible for the introduction of another domestic pet, the goldfish, which an admirer had presented to her and which she showed proudly to Huygens.*

Another trend set by the new Queen, which was followed by many English ladies, was that of knotting, a primitive form of crochet that spared her weak eyes. She was seldom seen without her knotting, "and that sometimes with so constant a diligence as if she had been to earn her Bread by it", says Burnet. At first people found the sight astonishing, but soon ladies of fashion were to be seen knotting enthusiastically away even in their coaches.*

When her eyes allowed it, and when she could spare the time, Mary was a keen reader. In her library there was a large collection of books·in English, French and Dutch on a great variety of subjects.* She read with equal ease in all three languages, and had a special interest in history, that of England in particular. "Her Age and her Rank had denied Her Opportunities for much study", but she tried to make up the deficiencies of her courtly education by studying philosophy and mathematics. She found them hard going, however, and soon abandoned them in favour of natural history and geography. She loved to read poetry, and enjoyed an occasional light novel: as Burnet, tactful for once, put it in his Funeral Essay, "Lively Books, where Wit and Reason gave the Mind a true Entertainment, had much of her time."*

But most of her time was necessarily devoted to the organization and running of the Royal Households. Careful instructions were set out in writing in the first weeks of the reign. "The Establishment: The yearly charge of their Majesties Dyet, with incidents for Housekeeping . . . to commence ye 1st day of Aprl. 1689" was signed by William himself, and gave the minutest details of household expenditure and supply, down to the last candle and bottle of claret. Although former Royal Household precedents were constantly quoted, they were those of Charles II; James II was never mentioned.

The Royal menus, with seasonal variations, were specified. For dinner, ten meat dishes were served up to the King and Queen, which might include a pottage of capons, boiled beef, roast mutton, pheasants, baked buck or hen pie; at supper, eight meat dishes including plovers, larks, ducklings, pigeons and lamb. At both meals, three other dishes of seasonal delicacies like artichokes, asparagus or peas were served, and puddings like pistachio cream or a plate of Morello cherries. A royal sirloin of beef appeared regularly at dinner on Thursdays; and on Fridays, Saturdays and throughout Lent, fish was served. Extras to the Royal tables included new-laid eggs, butter, bacon and milk. The drink supply was lavish: the daily allowance included eight bottles of ale – which William enjoyed occasionally – six bottles of claret, and two bottles of Rhenish wine. Safe drinking water was fetched daily "from the best fountains" at an annual cost of £132 and ten shillings.

Both William and Mary were light eaters and seldom ate from more than three or four dishes. The abundant leftovers were a recognized perk of the Royal Household, carefully allotted to specific members. If, however, the King and Queen happened to be dining out or picnicking in their coaches, and there were thus no leftovers to be disposed of, the staff were not allowed to claim cash compensation.

The King and Queen dined and supped in style: their joint annual bill for the laundering of table linen was £200, and orange flower water and rosewater was provided for finger-bowls at table.

Lighting the house was enormously expensive: it cost £6500 a year, nearly double that for their Majesties' food. The number of candles or the more luxurious wax lights was therefore carefully regulated – William had eight wax-lights on his dining-room sideboard, eight in his bedroom.

The abuses common to large households were to be guarded against as far as possible: "Vagrants and Masterless Men" were not to be given shelter, but at the same time £219 a year was allowed for daily alms at the gate.*

Many of the supplies for the Royal table were sent over regularly from Holland, including the chocolate that both William and Mary liked at breakfast-time, good Dutch butter and fine Rhenish wines. Occasionally delicacies like the first asparagus of March were supplied from the King's Dutch estates.

Especially in the first months of their reign, ships from Holland were constantly bringing crates of household goods for the King and Queen. Chinaware cups and saucers, and Indian tea-tables for the Queen's collection, trees for her gardens, an odd seventy-three chairs, and – in April 1689 – his Majesty's horses, coaches, harness and hounds were shipped in five different vessels. They ran into stormy weather on the way over, and thirty-two of the horses were lost.*

Mary found all these domestic affairs absorbing and congenial. But despite the brave show of cheerfulness she kept up – any animation in Court life was due to her efforts – she was not a happy woman. Ever since her arrival in London, she had been faced with a constant succession of problems that made heavy demands on her energy and courage. And in the circumstances, it was hardly surprising that she looked back on her life in Holland as Elysium. "The more I find myself harassed and overwhelmed with people here" she wrote to Dutch friends, "the more I regret those happy days I passed in so much quiet in your country . . ."*

When her friends in Holland wrote to tell her how much she was still missed there, she replied nostalgically: "I find it a very great comfort to be regretted among people I think so much of, and in a country that I consider as much my own as if I were born there, since long habit and eleven years of happiness make me feel that I came into the world at the Hague. . . ."* She never stopped reassuring her Dutch friends: "I am as good a Dutchwoman as ever",* and in April she wrote to Waldeck, "I have not changed. I still love Holland and I shall always remember the tranquillity I enjoyed there and that I shall never find here."*

At least one aspect of her new life in England pleased her: she had nothing to do with politics, being more than happy to leave such matters to her husband in accordance with her principle: "Women should not meddle in government." Witsen was one of the first to discover this when after the Coronation he began to talk business with her. She stopped him politely, telling him that she knew nothing of State affairs.* When, during the first parliamentary session of their reign, the administration in case of the King's absence was put in her hands, Burnet observed that "the queen seemed to take no notice of the matter".*

Politicians and noblemen realized very quickly that she was not the slightest bit interested in politics and that the King was not a man to pay much attention to his wife's views in any case. They had been eager to court her at first, but when this became clear they soon stopped bothering, and "though she gave great content to all that came to her, yet very few came".*

It was exactly what Mary wished.

CHAPTER XXVII

Second Thoughts

MARY'S TRANQUIL DETACHMENT from political business lasted less than a year. Irish affairs were going from bad to worse and by Christmas 1689 it was apparent to the King that he must go over and take charge of the situation himself, leaving the administration in the hands of the Queen. But long before this, and without her knowledge, an impulsive decision by William had threatened to shatter her quiet for ever: he announced to some of his ministers that English political life disgusted him so much that he proposed to return to Holland for good, leaving affairs in the Queen's hands. As he told Shrewbury and Caermarthen, "he did not see how he could extricate himself out of the difficulties into which the animosities of parties had brought him." His ministers protested at this faint-heartedness. "They pressed him vehemently to lay aside all such desperate resolutions," reported Burnet, ". . . much passion appeared among them: the debate was so warm that many tears were shed."*

The King was not easily to be convinced. With himself back in his beloved Holland and Mary handling English affairs, he felt that both countries would be better off and a perfect union possible between them. Mary's charm and popularity, together with her Englishness, might succeed where he had failed and make the parties more flexible and co-operative. "Though he could not hit on the right way of pleasing the nation", William told Shrewsbury, "he was sure she could, and that we should all be very happy under her."*

His ministers did not share his belief in Mary's ability to cope with the situation and in the end their tears and pleas prevailed: the King abandoned his plan. He had not thought it necessary to tell Mary about it – possibly his threat to return to Holland was no more than a gesture intended to bring the hostile parties to terms – and she heard about it much later from the garrulous Burnet.

William's disillusionment was understandable. He had been invited over by leading Whigs and Tories to save England from a romanizing despot, but the gratitude he felt entitled to had been non-existent. The discussions about who should wear the Crown had given him a first irritating experience of English party politics, and ever since then the House of Commons seemed set on frustrating his wishes and limiting his kingly authority. In bitter contrast to their generosity towards the Catholic James II in 1685, Parliament to begin with refused to grant him a revenue for life. An enraged William told Burnet "with more than ordinary vehemence" that "he was not a King, till that was done; without that, the title of a King was only a pageant. . . . The worst of all Governments was that of a King without treasure and without power."* It was more than an attack on his authority: he saw it as a personal slight. "The Commons have treated me like a dog", he burst out after the debate to Halifax, who noticed how "their course usage boyled so upon his Stomach, that hee could not hinder himselfe from breaking out sometimes against them."*

Adding insult to injury at the end of 1689, Parliament put the Declaration of Rights on the statute book. The English have ever since considered the Bill of Rights as the charter of their liberties, but for William it was an exasperating curb on his Royal powers. His resentment on this occasion was evident to everyone and confirmed the unfortunate impression that his autocratic manner had already created. As Halifax once said: "the King had a great jealousy of being thought to be governed."*

But it was more than William's autocratic manner and ungracious behaviour which had created such bitter tensions between him and the two political parties. The Whigs in particular had reasons for resentment. For years they had been William's secret allies, and they felt that they, far more than the Tories, were responsible for placing him on the Throne. They were in the majority in Parliament, and for the first time in years they had hoped to taste the sweets of exclusive power. They were bitterly disappointed to find that their new King mistrusted the party of Republicans and Exclusionists quite as much as his predecessors, and counted on the Tories for their traditional support. His first Ministry was an uneasy coalition heavily weighted on the Tory side, with Danby, now Earl of Caermarthen, as President of the Council, and Nottingham as one of the two Secretaries of State. Shrewsbury, the other Secretary of State, was the only important Whig in high office, and their irritation was increased by the appointment of the Trimmer Halifax as Lord Privy Seal and Speaker of the House of Lords.

Whig feelings were summed up in an anonymous letter to William published at the end of 1689. "You have lost the hearts of a great part of your people . . . and what is yet worse, your court and your councils are filled and guided by such men as most of all seek your ruin . . ." The writer declared boldly: "We have made you King" and reproached William with his short-sighted and ungrateful dependence on Tory support.*

The Tories had no reason to be disappointed in William's generosity, but their support for him was half-hearted at best. They may have disagreed with James's policies, but their loyalty to the principle of hereditary monarchy made it difficult for them to see William as anything else but an usurper, and many of them were secretly in touch with James and his court, a fact that William had to learn to live with. Nottingham was a typical Tory: he served William loyally once he was king, but he had refused to vote for him.

If William could not bring himself to trust the Whigs, bitter experience soon taught him that it was equally unwise to trust the Tories. As a result it became more and more difficult for him to communicate with his Parliament, and when their animosity forced Halifax out of office William, feeling that he had lost one of his most trustworthy ministers, lost his last illusions about party politics.

Thanks to his decision to govern by coalition, the same divisions confronted him in his own Council. There were constant disagreements between Whigs and Tories, and William complained to Halifax "hee did not know of men who would speak freely before one another".* To Portland he remarked once with a sigh: "There are wise and honest men among the English as were in any part of the world, but they are not my friends."*

It was in this frame of mind that William threatened to go back to Holland. His bad health, his homesickness and the constant opposition in England had brought him to the verge of a breakdown. And although his ministers talked him out of giving up the government of England, he was determined to escape at least for a while. Parliament had voted £2,000,000 for the costs of settling the Irish problems, created by James's presence there, but things were still going so badly and criticism of the King's inaction was becoming so offensive, that William could now claim with every reason that his presence there was necessary. For once, the ministers agreed.

Sheer relief at the prospect of action, together with his move into a more congenial home at Kensington just before Christmas, raised William's spirit for a while. New Year's Day was celebrated with all the customary splendour of old. At Whitehall crowds of the nobility and gentry together with the Lord Mayor and the aldermen of the City turned up to wish the King and Queen a happy New Year "and there was a great consort of musick, vocal and instrumental, and a song composed by the poet laureate".*

William and Mary came again to town on the sixth to celebrate Twelfth Night at Whitehall. Both went after service in the chapel for dinner at Lord Shrewsbury's where Marlborough, Godolphin and other nobles were among the guests. The Queen retired to Kensington to play at cards and gamble with her sister Anne, and the formal dinner turned into a stag-party. "In the end they all became so drunk that there was not a single one who did not lose consciousness",* reported a Frenchman. Huygens saw Marlborough and Lord Selkirk staggering back to Whitehall dead drunk afterwards. Marlborough immediately fell asleep in the antechamber of the King's bedroom and when the King, who himself had been recovering in an armchair in front of the fire, swayed past him to return to Kensington, Marlborough never stirred. The party was a great success for William. Selkirk was full of drunken praise and told Huygens over and over again that the King had spoken *"en vray Roy"* that evening. The poor secretary, who had pursued his master unsuccessfully all day with urgent papers, was less enthusiastic. When he caught up with him he found that the King had "no inclination to do business".*

Business would not wait long. William's anxiety to return to Holland was not mere nostalgia after the Irish campaign; the Republic needed his presence. His absence had encouraged the anti-Orange party and the death of his strong supporter Fagel in December 1688 had – as William had foreseen – further weakened his position.

Michiel Ten Hove, who had succeeded Fagel as Raadspensionary, was a mortally sick man, totally unable to cope with a strained situation, and the appointment of the intelligent Antonius Heinsius after Ten Hove's death in March 1689 had been warmly welcomed by William. The new Raadspensionary, however, still lacked enough experience to deal with the mutinous and arrogant Regents and especially those of Amsterdam, who saw a new opportunity of cutting their Stadholder down to size.

Already in 1689 the city had protested against the fact that the Stadholder, although now in England, still appointed the seven sheriffs of Amsterdam. They claimed that the elections ought to be made by the Hof of Holland, the province's High Court, when the Stadholder was absent. They had unearthed a law dating from 3 January 1581 to support their point but did not push the matter too far that first year.

William and Mary's Coronation in Westminster Abbey,
April 1689. It was the only true
double coronation in English history.

*Project for a monument (never undertaken)
to William and Mary, by Grinling Gibbons.*

A Court Ball at The Hague in 1686, by D. Marot.

The departure of William's fleet from Hellevoetsluys
in November 1688 'for the restoration
of the Constitution and the true religion in England,
Scotland and Ireland'.

The Battle of the Boyne, July 1690, which ended
in the defeat of James II.

William at the Boyne: a heroic portrait, of which there are many copies still to be seen in Ulster.

*Hampton Court, started by Cardinal Wolsey
and much altered by William and Mary.*

Kensington Palace, selected as a home by the Royal couple
because its position, removed from the Thames,
benefited William's lungs.

Henry Sidney, Earl of Romney (1641–1704),
rake and charmer, reputed lover
of Anne, Duchess of York.

William Bentinck, Earl of Portland,
at the time of his Embassy to Paris in 1698.

William's mistress, Elizabeth Villiers
(1657–1733), 'the squinting dragon'.

Arnold Joost van Keppel,
first Earl of Albemarle, King William's
'constant companion' in later life.

Louis XIV.

John Churchill, Duke of Marlborough
(1650–1722), after Sir Godfrey Kneller.

Czar Peter the Great of Russia.

*Charles Talbot, twelfth Earl
and only Duke of Shrewsbury
(1660–1718).*

*William shortly after
the Coronation in 1689.*

*Daniel Finch, second Earl of Nottingham,
leader of the Council through which Mary
ruled England during William's absence.*

Daniel,
Earl of Winchilsea
& Nottingham.
1727.

Charlotte Elisabeth (Liselotte),
Duchess of Orléans, William's childhood
playmate and later one of his
rare admirers at the French Court.

Sir Thomas Osborne, first Earl of Danby
(1631–1712), who promoted the marriage
between William and Mary, by Sir Peter Lely.

The 'Paleis Het Loo', designed and built by William and Mary
near Apeldoorn as a Dutch rival to Versailles.
The English resented it and called it 'England's folly'.

William's entry into London after the Peace of Rijswijk.

The so-called Zoological Garden of William III,
by M. d'Hondecoeter. A favourite painting of the King, which used
to hang over the chimney in his private cabinet at Het Loo.

William's deathbed in 1702.

In 1690 William tried to prevent new incidents by sending Portland in January to The Hague with a signed letter of election with blanks for the names to be filled in by Heinsius. His main fear was that Amsterdam would use a conflict with their Stadholder as an excuse to support their old friend, Louis XIV, and in his first letter to Portland William emphasized the importance of his mission, "which is not only for me, but for the whole welfare of Europe".*

Amsterdam was not impressed by Portland's visit nor by the threat from their Stadholder that as King of England he had authority enough to arrest the city's ships "which are here now in great number and richly laden".* When Portland appeared on 20 January in the States of Holland, Amsterdam denied him the right to take a seat, pointing out that he was now in the service of a foreign nation. The other delegates rejected the point in vain: the Amsterdammers left the hall.

William was deeply worried "to see the tricks those Amsterdam people want to play you, which only proceed from enmity to me", he wrote Portland. "I hope that you will be able to surmount it and that the other towns will support you . . ."* They did so indeed, but Amsterdam still refused to give in, even when the States of Holland decreed on the twenty-eighth of that month that Amsterdam was obliged to send the nominations for the sheriffs to the Stadholder.

In February the City tried once again to persuade the High Court to appoint the sheriffs but the judges refused, and Portland wrote to William that the only solution was for him to come over in person and force Amsterdam to obey. The King, certain that the City fathers had "some intrigues with France", was all for it, but leaving England was impossible for the time being. He wrote to Portland on 10 March: "If it were possible without abandoning everything here, I would embark tomorrow to come and find you in Holland . . . but it is impracticable and so we must think of other means of bringing these Amsterdam people to reason . . ."*

Unexpectedly Amsterdam decided in March to stop her obstructive tactics, and her representatives returned to the States of Holland while Portland was still present. The letters of nominations for the sheriffs, they conceded, would in future be sent to the States to send on to William in England.

The authority of the Stadholder was thus maintained, thanks to the hard struggle Portland and Heinsius had put up for three months, and Portland was at last free to return to England. Before he left the Republic he paused to inspect two of William's palaces in the United Provinces. He reported to the King that at Het Loo everything is in "very good order and very neat", but at Dieren chaos reigned. "I discovered that I was much needed in view of the damage to the new dyke and to the little maze." He found the gardens in a sad state "thanks to the drunkenness of the gardener, who had never done a hand's turn". Portland sacked him on the spot and reassured the King: "Tomorrow I shall send another man to take his place."*

WILLIAM HAD MISSED his loved and trusted friend that winter more than ever. He was a very sick man. A combination of asthma, bronchitis and fever – "the illness which overcame me when we were on the point of landing"* – constantly plagued him and lowered his spirits terribly. He only dared to reveal his depression in his letters to Portland, writing in despair: "I shall not lose courage as long as I am able to sustain it, I hope that the good God will aid me and not abandon me."* Portland tried to console him and begged him to pull himself together: "I implore you, Sire, not to give in to the mood of which you complain . . . The man who possesses the treasure of interior peace, once he has done his duty, must with a quiet mind submit matters to Him who alone disposes of them."*

It was not only his sickness that depressed the King. He was also deeply alarmed by the acrimony in English party politics that led to a succession of crises that winter. The Whigs had touched off the latest furore when shortly after the New Year they tossed a bombshell into the House of Commons. A bill for restoring the rights of those corporations which had surrendered their charters in the reigns of James and Charles was before Parliament. The measure had been approved by both parties and many M.P.s, including most of the Tories, were still out of town keeping Christmas when, unexpectedly, the old Whig campaigner Sacheverell proposed an amendment by which anyone who had voted to surrender the charters should be excluded from any public office for seven years. Most of the Tories in local government up and down the country had loyally voted to surrender the charters to their King. The effect of the clause was thus "to make some thousands of the most opulent and highly considered men in the kingdom incapable, during seven years, of bearing any part in the government of the places in which they resided."*

By the same token it was almost a guarantee of a Whig House of Commons for the next seven years, a prospect that horrified William. He followed the debates with an anxiety which affected his health and wrote to Portland on 10 January, "I am so overcome by sleep, and my cough worries me so much that I don't know how to tell you any more about it", ending his letter with unusual emotion, "Yours till death".*

Fortunately for him – and for the peace of England – the Tories had been hastily warned of their danger, and as Macaulay vividly describes it: "A hundred knights and squires left their halls hung with mistletoe and holly, and their boards groaning with brawn and plum porridge and rode up post to town."* After a stormy session lasting fourteen hours, the clause was finally thrown out at midnight by a narrow majority.

William could breathe again – but not for long. The Tories thought the moment had come to reintroduce the Indemnity Bill, originally proposed by William and offering amnesty and oblivion for all political crimes. The Whigs had consistently opposed this Bill which would benefit the Tories as much as the Sacheverell Clause would have injured them, and they were now less inclined than ever to mercy for their opponents. William had to look on exasperated while the two political parties tore each other to pieces – "Men's minds are becoming more and more embittered against one another", he wrote sadly to Portland on 21 January.*

All this time he had been quietly working on his preparations for Ireland, down to the last detail: he had asked Wren, for instance, to design a little portable house for his use on campaign, "to be taken into pieces and carried on two wagons, and . . . quickly fixt up".* But apart from a few trusted ministers, nobody knew for sure whether he meant to go or not, and the question was hotly debated. On 25 January William wrote cynically to Portland that he would certainly have a unanimous address praying him not to go, as soon as he announced his intention. "And if I go without letting them know, they will not only find it ill-done, but it could have disastrous consequences. I am thus the most embarrassed man in the world, not knowing what to do."*

His conviction that his presence was needed in Ireland was nonetheless so strong that he finally decided to make it public. And since the party struggle had reached new heights of fury following the Indemnity Bill, he adroitly killed two birds with one stone: on 27 January he came down to Westminster unexpectedly, prorogued Parliament, and in the course of his speech revealed his decision to go to Ireland. William studied the stunned faces of the M.P.s with some amusement as he spoke, and reported a day later to Portland: "The Tories are fairly happy about it, but not the Whigs. They were all very surprised when I spoke . . . I saw faces as long as an ell changing colour twenty times while I addressed them . . ."* The dismay expressed by the Whigs did not impress

William, who wryly remarked that they feared "to lose me too soon, before they have done with me what they wish".*

THE QUEEN HAD KNOWN for some time of her husband's plans to go to Ireland, but had hoped that his ministers and his Parliament might dissuade him. The announcement on 27 January, which had taken M.P.s by surprise, came to her as shocking confirmation of her worst fears. "I grieve for the poor Queen, who is in a terrible state", the King told Portland on the same day.* Mary herself wrote in her memoirs: "This resolution being taken, I fell into great melancholy. I told the King all my trouble, he said there was no help, that it was but the same thing he had begun before and must now be finished; he said much to satisfy me." It was cold comfort for the Queen who longed for reassurance, but William, who always shrank from emotional scenes, cut the conversation short: he "desired to talk no more upon so sad a subject", he told her.*

This wet and rainy winter did nothing to improve Mary's spirits. Forbidden to discuss her misery with William and brooding about it for weeks, she made herself really ill. "All the crosses I met with in this world made me melancholly and even wish to dye or at last grow very indifferent to life, and this I found by a sore throat I had, so that the 7th of April . . . I did really thinck my self in danger." She had begun to feel ill the previous Saturday, and hurriedly put her affairs in order, to be ready for death, at the prospect of which, she admitted, "I was really rather glad than sorry."

In this morbid frame of mind, she struggled on with her ordinary life, hugging the thought of this imminent death while playing at cards. Finally somebody noticed her condition, doctors were called, and a simple blood-letting followed by a good dosing did the trick.* Luttrell dismissed the drama in a sentence: "The queen being lately indisposed was lett blood, and is since pretty well again."*

Mary's moment of weakness was hardly surprising; after her first difficult year in England, the future looked blacker than ever. Quite apart from her fears for William's health and safety and her dread of his absence, she was obsessed by "the sadness such to see my husband and my father personally ingaged against each other."* She was so haunted by the dread of this face-to-face encounter that she poured her heart out in a letter to the Electress Sophia: "I have every reason to be in distress for a husband, and I dare say – such a husband, but I am daughter as well, and I do not know what wishes I ought to make for a father . . ."*

The King was very well aware of these feelings, even though he was reluctant to discuss them with her, and he tried to shield her from upset. He told Caermarthen that "he must be very cautious of saying any thing before the queen that looked like a disrespect to her father, which she never forgave anybody." Halifax, said the King, had spoken slightingly of James to the Queen, and she had never forgiven him.* For the same reason he told Burnet how much he disliked going on campaign against Mary's father, "since it would be a vast trouble both to himself and to the queen, if he should be either killed or taken prisoner."*

The Jacobites always claimed that William had no intention of sparing his father-in-law if it came to the point, but although he would not in the least have minded James being taken prisoner and brought safely to Holland,* he was terrified of his suffering any physical hurt. And he rejected at least one plot proposed to him for kidnapping the ex-King, because he thought it likely to involve a struggle in which "some accident might happen to King James' person; in which he would have no hand".

As so often, the Queen only learned of her husband's thoughtful kindness from Burnet, and "she was much touched with the answer the king had made."* To those around her, her feelings of concern and guilt about her father – all the stronger for being unspoken – were apparent. Nottingham, a nostalgic Tory, confided his wishful thinking later to Dartmouth. If William was killed in battle, he was sure, "she would have done her utmost to have restored her father, but under such restrictions as should have prevented his ever making any attempts upon the religion or liberties of his country."*

In these weeks of apprehension Mary used to retire to her little closet at Kensington whenever she could, and put some of her feelings into writing. The only one of these intensely personal meditations preserved from this year of 1690 was dated 3 March: it was written after letters had been confiscated showing that there was a Jacobite party formed in which her uncle Clarendon was involved. "When I see how things are going at present, my husband going hence to risk his life, and that perhaps in person against my father, [and] when I know that there is a party formed here in favour of the latter, and that I am assured that there is another [party] which wishes for a republic, . . . is that not all enough to afright a personne much tougher than me."*

Quite as much as by her preoccupation with her father, Mary's peace of mind was destroyed by the public responsibilities she saw looming. After William had decided to go to Ireland he told her that it would be her choice whether in his absence the administration should be carried on in her name or if it should be left entirely to the Privy Council.

Some of Mary's supporters expressed to her their indignation that the King should not leave her in charge as a matter of course, but William knew Mary better, and she did indeed beg that "he should take care I should not make a foolish figure in the world".* She protested that it would make little difference whether she was nominally in charge or not, since she was "wholy a stranger in business" and although he gave her a kind and reassuring answer he obviously shared her doubts about her ability. He had told Halifax privately "there must bee a Councell to governe in his absence, and that the Queen is not to meddle", adding some time later that she was not to sit in the Commission he had appointed or have any control over what they did, but merely have a report made to her.* He stipulated that "all matters which may bear the delay, shall stay for his approbation. The Queen shall give no Bishopricks or Commissions. She shall have power to call the Parliament in case of a sudden emergency."*

His apparent mistrust of the Queen was construed by his enemies as a selfish desire to concentrate all power in his own hands, and William as usual disdained to explain his reasons. In fact he was chiefly moved by a wish to protect his wife from the savagery of the British political arena. He told Burnet: "For his own part, he trusted in God, and would either go through with his business, or perish in it; he only pitied the poor Queen, repeating that twice with great tenderness."*

As carefully as possible, he formed the Cabinet Council that was to advise the Queen. Five of them were Tories: Caermarthen, Pembroke, Nottingham, Marlborough and Lowther. Four of them were Whigs: Devonshire, Dorset, Monmouth and Edward Russell. The fifth Whig who would have balanced the parties had bowed out. It was Shrewsbury, on whom the King had relied more than anyone else to help the Queen, but who was so worn out by his year in office that he resigned at the beginning of May.

Shrewsbury, one of the first to join William in Holland in 1688, had served him loyally in the first months of his reign, but he was a sensitive man and found it hard to endure the conflicts with Tory colleagues such as Caermarthen. The fact that the King had objected that spring to the Whig proposal for an Abjuration Bill, obliging all office-holders to abjure James II, and had instead introduced an Act of Grace for all but a handful of political offenders, had been the last straw for Shrewsbury. William had taken the measure on the advice of Caermarthen, and Shrewsbury saw it as a personal slight.

A letter, later found among his papers, explained his feelings: "The toil and torture of so much business is a good bargain to no one but

those who are fond either of ambition, experience or money."* Shrewsbury was fond of neither, and retired on 5 May to his country house
near Newmarket, in bad health and "somewhat disgusted".*

If anybody sympathized with the reluctant minister it was probably
the Queen, but for her there could be no such escape. A few days before
he left for Ireland, William assembled the nine and leading the Queen in,
addressed them solemnly. "She wants experience, but I hope that, by
choosing you to be her counsellors, I have supplied that defect. I put
my Kingdom into your hands."*

On 4 June the King left on what Mary described as "the terriblest
journey to me that he ever took".* He drove away from Kensington in
his coach early in the morning, accompanied by Portland and Lumley.
Mary had decided that it was more practical for her to be at Whitehall,
at hand while she was in charge, and she moved back into the old
palace together with her sister Anne and the eleven-month-old Duke of
Gloucester, Anne's only surviving child.*

"The Queen was now in the administration", wrote Burnet years
later with evident satisfaction. "It was a new scene to her."*

CHAPTER XXVIII

The Irish Trouble

IN DECEMBER 1688 James II arrived a broken man in St. Germain-en-Laye, where Louis had generously given up his beautiful palace to Mary Beatrice. If the French King felt a secret triumph at holding these important English hostages, his manners were too good to betray the fact, and he greeted James with the utmost kindness.

In the following weeks the two kings saw each other frequently, most of the time at Versailles. But sometimes Louis and his court came to ride and hunt at St. Germain. The palace – as Saint-Simon describes it – was "unique in the world, unique in that it combined marvellous views and the immense background of its neighbouring forest, . . . the beauty of its trees, its grounds, its situation, the delights of its gardens."* The French courtiers treated James with all possible deference in obedience to Louis's wish, but they were not much impressed by this martyr to the cause of monarchy and catholicism. "Everyone agreed that he was a saint, but they looked in vain for his halo", was the comment. Mary Beatrice made a much better impression. "In looks and in spirit that is what a Queen should be", remarked Louis.*

News of the warm welcome James had received from the French King reached London soon after. William commented nastily: "When he has dragged that corpse around for three or four years, he will be as much embarrassed by him as I have been."* A keen hunting man himself, however, he did not have the heart to turn down one request made in a letter to Lord Dartmouth. "Howsoever the Prince of Orange uses me in other thing, sure he will not refuse me the common civility of letting all my coaches and horses come to me." His son-in-law sent them over immediately, together with the guns and pistols James had asked for as well.*

He might have hesitated had he known that ever since his arrival in France James had been planning a descent on Ireland as a first step towards the recovery of his kingdom. In February 1689 James began his practical preparations. He had hoped for the help not only of Louis but also of the Emperor – Catholic monarchs, he naïvely reckoned, should stick together – and he sent a moving appeal to Leopold. He had to wait two months for an answer, and when it came it was scathing. The Emperor's reply was addressed to "your most Serene Highness" and not to "Your Majesty". It was a bad start and worse followed. Although Leopold wrote that he was "sensibly touched and truly afflicted" by James's fate, he pointed out that "had your Serenity given more attention to the kind representations we made you . . . instead of hearkening to the fraudulent suggestion of France" these misfortunes might have been averted.*

James had to be content with French aid. It was lavish – "ships, frigates, troops, officers . . . toilet sets, camp beds, golden and silver dinner service and his own personal arms for the King", wrote Madame de Sévigné in astonishment. Even the cynical French court was touched when they saw the parting between King and Queen. "There was weeping, cries, tears, faintings", noted Madame de Sévigné in satisfaction and she added, "this is easy to understand . . . he has to win or die, because he has courage."*

With a fleet of fourteen men of war, seven frigates, three fire-ships and some transports James sailed from Brest on 16 March. As soon as he heard of James's departure William ordered out the Channel fleet under Arthur Herbert to try and intercept him. If they succeeded, Herbert had further instructions:

> In case you shall take any ship or vessel in which the late King James shall happen to be, you are to treat him with respect, . . . without expecting any further orders you are hereby required to transport him to some Port belonging to the States General of the United Provinces . . . and you are to dispose of the said King James into such hands as the said States shall appoint to receive him.*

James successfully evaded Herbert, and after a calm crossing landed at Kinsale in the south of Ireland near Cork on 22 March. D'Avaux, the former ambassador to the States and now chosen by Louis XIV as James's councillor, travelled with him on the *Saint Michael*, and immediately reported their safe arrival to the French King. In this same letter he expressed his misgiving about James's character as leader. "The only thing, Sire, which could land us in trouble, is the irresolution of the King of England, who often changes his opinion and does not always end up with the best one." In an earlier letter he had already complained about James's indiscretion – His Majesty could not keep any secret from anybody.* Travelling to Dublin the French could not believe their eyes – the countryside was poor, the villages empty and the fields untilled. But they were impressed by the warm welcome given James by his ragged Irish supporters all along the way to Dublin, where he arrived on 24 March.

The King entered the city riding on a nag, dressed in a plain cloth suit and a black slouch hat. Tyrconnel rode in front of him, bearing the Sword of State. At the castle gate James was greeted by four bishops carrying the Host: he dismounted and fell on his knees. Later a Te Deum was sung at the Cathedral. At a Privy Council next morning James convoked a Parliament to meet in Dublin on 7 May.* But before it met James, encouraged by his reception in Dublin, left on 14 April to take command of the Irish troops quartered a few miles from Londonderry, a stronghold of the Protestant English settlers in northern Ireland. He hoped that the mere sight of their Stuart King would win over the inhabitants of the town, but as he approached at the head of 20,000 men thirteen young apprentices gave the alarm and slammed the gate. They refused to surrender and James returned much disappointed to Dublin on the twenty-ninth. He complained bitterly about the Irish troops he had left to besiege the town, grumbling with his usual lack of tact that if they had been English soldiers Londonderry's decrepit fortifications would already have been dismantled stone by stone.*

He was back in time to open the Irish Parliament. His House of Lords hardly deserved the name. Of the hundred odd Irish Peers only fourteen turned up, of whom ten were Catholics; and seventeen more had to be hurriedly created. His House of Commons, he was confident, would be acquiescent; of its 250 members only six were Protestant. But he was to be disappointed: one of the first acts of James's Parliament was to abolish the supremacy of the English Parliament over Ireland.

It was a significant gesture. James's Irish supporters were not the slightest bit interested in helping him to recover his English throne. On the contrary they saw him as the Catholic deliverer from the hated English Protestants, and intended to use him only for their own aims. He tried in vain to calm his violently anti-English parliament and was so upset by the Irish attitude that his nose-bleeds started again. Unmoved, they repealed the Act of Settlement which had secured the grants of land to Protestant emigrants; English absentee landlords over the age of seventeen, and those who had already fled, were dispossessed of their lands; Protestant ecclesiastical property was handed over to the Catholic clergy; and in a final delirium of revenge, the Irish Parliament passed the sweeping Act of Attainder, which listed 3000 people including half the peerage and most of the Protestant ruling classes. Any of them who failed to give themselves up to Irish justice were sentenced to be hanged, drawn and quartered without trial.

News of these measures produced a storm of indignation that summer in England, and much of it was directed against William. The relief of Londonderry on 30 July by English ships rescued him for the moment from constant attacks by Parliament, and the city's heroic defenders certainly deserved the affectionate letter in which he acknowledged his debt to them.

By now William had reluctantly bowed to necessity and sent over his most trusted commander, Schomberg, who arrived at Carrickfergus at the end of August with a force of about 10,000 men. D'Avaux suggested to James that he retaliate by massacring all the Protestants in Ireland, in the hope of separating the two countries for ever by this bloodbath, but James rejected the idea with horror.

Schomberg's arrival changed little. In a lifetime of military service, the old marshal had never had troops under his command as ignorant, as untrained and as completely undisciplined as the Irish army. In addition, he had to cope with the consequences of massive frauds on the part of the Chief Commissary Henry Shales: food was uneatable, pikes were so rotten they broke in the hand, there were no carts for transport, the horses were all hired out to farmers, and when William wrote to urge action, Schomberg replied bluntly that the thing could not be done – "all the army is without shoes".

His letters to William, throughout the autumn and the long disastrous winter that followed, were a mounting crescendo of complaint. "I must tell your Majesty", he wrote early in October, "that if our Irish colonels were as able in war as they are to send to pillage the country, and not to pay the soldiers, your Majesty would be better served by them." And at the end of December came another cry of exasperation, "Never were so many people seen so desirous of stealing..."*

By that time he faced disaster. At Dundalk 2000 soldiers had died of "flux and fever", or dysentery. Many more were shipped to hospital at Belfast, 900 of them dying during the voyage; and between November 1689 and the following May, in the great hospital of Belfast alone 2762 died. The total of English deaths from disease was horrifying, more than half the number sent.* Schomberg exclaimed in despair: "The English nation is so delicately bred, that as soon as they are out of their own country, they die the first campaign."*

IT WAS FOR THIS unhealthy country that William left London on 4 June 1690. Not all the opposition in Parliament to the expedition had been based as the King had said on party interest. "Some did really apprehend the air of Ireland would be fatal to so weak a constitution."*

But William was not concerned. Those who travelled with him from Kensington were surprised by his unusual good humour – as he told Burnet before leaving London, going on campaign was a perfect pleasure to him, "he was sure he understood that better than how to govern England."* William left behind with relief the squabblings of politicians and the carping of courtiers, and rediscovered on the way the popularity he had enjoyed in Holland. His journey across an England green with early summer became a Royal progress: at every halt women surrounded his coach, mobbing him when he got out of it and fighting to kiss his hand.*

On Sunday 8 June after attending service at Chester Cathedral he arrived at Hoylake, where he inspected the fleet. Unfavourable winds detained him for three days without abating his high spirits – "the King seems very cheerful and vigorous", it was reported to Nottingham. But as the days went by he became impatient at the delay, being "soe intent on his voyage" that he even thought about going by Scotland "if the wind should long oppose him".*

On the evening of the tenth the wind changed at last, and William decided to board his yacht, the *Mary*, early next morning. The fleet of forty ships under Sir Cloudesley Shovell had hardly sailed from the little port of Hoylake when a new delay occurred: a thick fog, which compelled them to cast anchor until it lifted.* Not until the fourteenth, after a stormy crossing, did they reach Carrickfergus, north of Belfast. The fleet anchored in the bay before Whitehouse, and next day, in the evening, King William rode off to Belfast, where the whole city turned out to cheer him.

He had studied the countryside and liked it – "highly worth fighting for"* – but the people were less appealing to the eye. "We saw a great many poor and wretched men, women and children", noted Huygens, who accompanied his master, "they are half-naked, very ugly and look unhealthy, worse than I've seen in any other country. Their houses too are unusually dirty and miserable." What struck Huygens particularly was the fact that the people they met refused to describe themselves as Irish: they all claimed they were Scots who had come over and settled in Ireland.*

In Belfast the King stayed at the house of Sir John Franklin, a ramshackle old building only noteworthy for its bad paintings. Immediately after his arrival, he sat down to confer with Marshal Schomberg, who had been his Commander in Ireland since the previous year. The eighty-year-old soldier was still popular in England, but his constant grumbling and his reluctance to venture his troops in action against James had so irritated the King that he once remarked to Halifax: "hee was mistaken in him, else hee would hardly have brought him over, and bought him so dear."* Schomberg had plenty of excuses: the appallingly high casualty rate among his troops, the severe winter, and the elusiveness of the enemy. "Not having enough men and supplies," he told Huygens later, "he had not thought it advisable to risk matters which if they failed would harm the King's affairs."* But William had little time for these excuses: what he wanted now was action, and he told Schomberg briskly that he had not come to let the grass grow under his feet.*

He had brought over about 35,000 infantry and more than 9000 cavalry. Half his troops were English, including the Life Guards under the command of the Duke of Ormonde, the Scots Guards, and two of the English regiments that had served in Holland. Among the Dutch troops were Portland's and Van Ginckel's cavalry, and the famous Dutch Blue Guards commanded by Solms. There were troops from Germany, Denmark, Finland, there was a regiment of French Huguenots, and there were finally the Enniskilleners, the Irish troops dreaded by the natives for their cruelty and ruthlessness.*

With this impressive army to put against James's estimated 25,000, William determined to force a battle at the earliest opportunity. On Monday the sixteenth, the day after his arrival in Belfast, he wrote to the States-General: "I found affairs in a better condition than I expected, and hope to be able to march on Thursday next. I shall then be able to judge, in three or four days, whether the enemy wants a battle."*

Meanwhile he was kept busy at his headquarters in the castle dealing with an urgent administrative problem: the financial chaos into which James's rule from Dublin had plunged the whole of Ireland. The business class of the country was largely Protestant English, and many of them had fled the country. Ordinary commerce was virtually at a standstill, and inflation inevitably followed. James's solution to the scarcity of money was simplistic: he had increased the nominal value of the coins in circulation by decree, and as more and more of the original silver disappeared, most of it hoarded, he replaced it with brass money made out of melted-down guns. A total of £1,600,000 circulated in these detested coins, and even that was not enough; soon the half-crowns were being called in and after being stamped again were made to pass for crowns. Two hundred years later, the Protestant population of

Ireland still remembered with a shudder the brass money, together with the "popery, slavery, arbitrary power" of James, and the wooden shoes of his French soldiers.* Among the supplies that reached Belfast a few days after William's arrival were boxes containing tons of real money – tin halfpence and farthings to a total of £250,000* and William earned himself instant popularity when this money, issued to his army as pay, began to circulate.

When Thursday the nineteenth came, marching orders were given. It was a hot and beautiful day, and the huge army moved slowly south through Lisburn and the wild, lovely country round it, to make camp the first night at Hillsborough. By Monday the troops had reached Loughbrickland and paused there, while the King galloped ahead to reconnoitre as far south as Dundalk, where he had been told that James's army was lying. But James had already fallen back south, and after a deserter reported to William that his father-in-law had stopped at Ardee, he decided to move after him. On Thursday, 26 June, the whole camp at Loughbrickland was astir long before dawn, and by four a.m. the troops were on the march to Newry. The road was stony and narrow, and orders were given that transport wagons that broke down were to be pushed off into the swamps, together with their horses, so as not to hold up the columns. It was another scorching hot day, and the soldiers plotted sweating across hills and valleys where no tree was to be seen, only a few wretched little bushes that gave them no protection from the sun. Newry offered them little compensation: the little town near the picturesque bay of Carlingford had been burnt down by James a year earlier.

Next day they advanced to Dundalk, along a road even worse if possible – not only very narrow but for long stretches a mere causeway built up over the marshes. To make matters worse, they met hordes of refugees with horses and carts cluttering up the road, and progress was often slowed almost to a standstill while the two streams struggled to cross each other. At one point Huygens was almost pushed off the road into the swamp by a cart. Late in the afternoon they reached Dundalk, and again a miserable spectacle greeted them: the town had been mercilessly plundered by James's undisciplined Irish and French troops, and most of the adult population had been carried off as prisoners. The few people that were left behind were starving, and Huygens saw a little boy of seven or eight who looked more like a skeleton than a human being.* The cavalry and dragoons were not allowed to unpack and received orders to stand by for a surprise attack that same evening on James's camp at Ardee. But after a handful of dragoons had made a sortie and returned with the news that the enemy had retreated even further, William's men made camp.

It was obvious that a confrontation between the two armies was imminent, and the faintheartedness of James and his elusive army put William into an excellent humour. His English courtiers would not have recognized their surly monarch in the man described by one of his officers, who that evening waited on him at supper: "he discours'd me most of ye time, and was extremely pleasant and cheerfull."* He was even gracious to James's trumpeter, who came to request an exchange of a few prisoners. William enquired courteously after James's French commander – *"Comment se port M. de Lauzun?"* and he asked him *"de lui faire ses baise-mains"*.*

On Sunday, 29 June, the army reached Ardee, "miserably plundered by the enemy, leaving nothing but the houses with the bare walls, except some sick old bedridden people".* They were dying of hunger and misery, and William's army could spare little to help them. He had brought provisions for five days only, expecting to buy supplies en route, and the army had already run out of flour for its bread.* The troops were beginning to be restless, but news that James had halted his army a few miles away at Drogheda on the Boyne river, and clearly meant to give battle there, reached camp that night and raised everybody's spirits: it looked as if the long march was nearly at an end. By mid-morning the next day, 30 June, William was gazing down from high ground into the valley of the Boyne, flowing quietly towards the small walled town of Drogheda. Its green south banks were lined with the tents of James's army. "I am glad to see you, gentlemen", William is reported to have said as he surveyed them. "If you escape me now, the fault will be mine."*

While his troops made camp, William and his chiefs of staff rode down to the north bank of the Boyne to take a close look at the enemy. They dismounted and sat down for a picnic lunch. At that moment three of James's officers, Berwick, Lauzun and Tyrconnel, spotted the conspicuous figure of the King with his star of the Garter, had two cannon brought up immediately, and aimed at the party from behind a clump of bushes. The first shot was fired as William and his officers remounted, and it killed the horse of Prince George of Hesse. As the King cried out, "Oh the poor prince is killed", a second cannon-shot whistled over and ploughed through the sleeve of the King's uniform, grazing his shoulder.* William slumped forward on to the neck of his horse, and a shout of joy went up from James's army, who believed they had killed the arch-enemy. They did not know that the ball had only ripped his jacket and shirt and scorched his shoulder. A dressing was put on it after the party had retired to a dip in the road, and William dismissed it lightly: "Just as well it was not closer." As his shocked officers crowded around him he added with an impatient gesture "Why don't you move on?"*

Not only the enemy believed the King was dead. In his own ranks the news had spread consternation,* and when Lord Selkirk galloped back to reassure the soldiers he found Count Solms, one of William's friends, lying on the ground sobbing with grief. Selkirk told him that the King was alive, but Solms refused to believe it until William himself appeared, riding his big black horse.*

At the enemy camp they continued for some hours longer to believe him to be dead, and messengers were sent at top speed to Paris with the joyful news. The effect was electrifying, as Liselotte wrote her aunt Sophia weeks later. "The pleasure that the news of his death gave the canaille is quite impossible to describe . . . For 48 hours the people celebrated furiously and did nothing but feast and get drunk . . . some of them staged a mock-funeral. Others made a dummy out of straw and wax, named it the Prince of Orange and shot it all night long . . ."* Even the Pope pretended joy at the death of the Protestant King of England and the Earl of Melfort, sent to Rome by James as his ambassador, was witness of "all the expressions of a sincere joy in his Holiness for so important, so unexpected a success".*

Sadly for the Pope and the French, the confirmation of the news was not forthcoming. Only hours after this much-fêted shot, William was riding along the ranks of his army, waving his right arm to show that all was well. The same evening at nine o'clock he summoned a council of war to inform his officers that he had decided to attack next morning. Schomberg with his usual caution raised objections but was irritably overruled by the King. The old marshal walked out in a pique and when he received his orders later he commented bitterly that it was the first order of battle that had been sent to him.* It was also to be his last.

CHAPTER XXIX

The Battle of the Boyne

Tuesday 1 July dawned bright and clear, another hot, glorious summer day. By six o'clock the King was already on horseback, giving last minute instructions and encouragement. He had started his day at four a.m. by writing a letter to the Queen, and was now ready for battle.* His soldiers were ordered to wear a little green bough or sprig in their hats to distinguish them from James's men with their white feather.* The atmosphere was one of tense apprehension, and even Huygens did not know what exactly was going to happen. He was drinking raspberry lemonade with his friends when the order for marching was given, and rode immediately to a little ruin on a hill near the Boyne to watch coming events.

William had split his army into three sections, and it was the right wing that went into action first. Under the command of Schomberg's son, Meinhard, the cavalry had moved rapidly at dusk to Slane, about four miles to the right. The Irish battery guarding the bridge there for James had been withdrawn, and the 800 dragoons left to defend this strategic point fled when their commander was killed by one of the first bullets. The English crossed the river unopposed, thus creating a useful diversion which forced Lauzun to send reinforcements up to his left.

The main action started at nine o'clock, when William's Blue Guards were ordered to cross the Boyne. James's men fired from two empty houses and from behind bushes on the other side of the river, but the Guards pushed steadily through – Huygens from his safe post had for a moment the impression that the river was crawling with soldiers – and as soon as they had reached the south bank the Irish fled without a further shot. Only the French cavalry under Tyrconnel and Hamilton fought on, driving the Danes and Huguenots, who were attempting to cross, back into the river and killing their commander Caillemot. It was Schomberg who saved them. He had been watching from the rear and now rushed forward, crying to the Huguenots: "*Allons Messieurs, voilà vos persécuteurs"*, pointing with his sword to the French Catholics in the other army.* They were his last words. A group of thirty supporters of James, determined to kidnap or kill William, had succeeded in breaking through the lines and crossing the river. Most of them had been killed during their suicidal mission, but five survivors surrounded Schomberg, hacking at his head with their swords and killing him with a bullet in the neck.*

At that moment William reached the battle at the other side of the river. He had made a difficult and dangerous crossing near Oldbridge, lower down the Boyne, and it had taken longer than he had expected – his horse had got stuck in the morass and he had to dismount so that his soldiers could save the animal.* But his arrival was decisive. Unable to use his painful right arm, he drew his sword with his left and rode into the mêlée, inspiring his troops with the cry: "Men of Enniskillen, what will you do for me?"* They followed him without hesitation and together with the Blue Guards and the Huguenots routed James's army. By nine o'clock in the evening the Battle of the Boyne was over, and won by William. James's fleeing army was pursued for a few miles, but as Huygens reports, "the Irish ran so fast that our cavalry could not overtake them." They left their baggage and eight cannons behind.*

William had constantly been in the midst of his men and had only just escaped death when one of his own dragoons, not recognizing him, had pointed a pistol direct at the King's head. He had pushed it away with the words: "What, do you not know your own friends?"* One bullet had grazed his leg, taking away a piece of his boot.*

James, on the other hand, had stayed at a safe distance from the battle, watching it from the old church on the little hill of Donore. He did not wait till the end, and he was already on his way to Dublin when Hamilton, as one of the last defenders, was wounded and made prisoner.

The battle had been less bloody than might have been expected. Between 1500 and 2000 of James's men were killed, while William had lost no more than 400 men – "many of which were kill'd by our own men through mistake."* Their bodies were lying on the field and in spite of strict orders given by William not to molest the wounded, or touch the dead, Huygens discovered to his horror, when at last he descended from his lookout, that most of the dead had already been completely stripped by the women and the rabble that as usual followed the army. They had even started a market in their stolen goods on the battlefield.* One of the Dutch soldiers wrote later to his wife in Holland that the English hated the Irish and French so much that they killed all the prisoners, except the officers, while those who were wounded "were shot or beaten to death with their muskets". He could not believe his eyes when he saw the English drive their carriages over the bodies of the Irish, "who they consider less than dogs".*

William was appalled by this carnage, and did his best to stop it. As a deterrent he gave orders that one soldier, who had butchered three defenceless Irish soldiers, should be hanged on the spot.*

It was very late that night when the King at last retired, having pursued the enemy as far as Naul. He got to his quarters at Ballybog-hil, near Duleek, at about eleven o'clock, where his friends crowded round to congratulate him. William, who had been seventeen hours in the saddle, "with all the stiffness that his wound gave him", brushed aside these compliments. "He expressed neither joy nor any sort of vanity; only he looked cheerful," reported his physician, Dr. Hutton, later.* He went to bed in the tent of Count Solms at midnight, and slept late the next morning, not appearing before eleven, when he called all the officers together to thank them in person for "that service which they had rendered him the day before, and which he never would forget". He asked that his words should be repeated to the soldiers.* For the rest of the day he took it easy, walking about in slippers – as usual his ankles were swollen after so many hours booted and on horseback.

His Dutch friends were elated at his decisive victory, and dashed off jubilant letters with the news. Van Ginckel wrote to his father: "This is a great victory which will do good throughout Europe and give great satisfaction to the allies."* And Portland wrote to the King's Lord High Commissioner in Edinburgh: "You will have learned . . . the mercy that the good God has vouchsafed us, firstly in preserving the person and life of the King from so dangerous a shot . . . and then by giving him a so signal victory over his enemies by the gain of a battle."*

The King himself sent one of his officers, Captain Butler, to London to give the Queen and Nottingham a first-hand account of the battle and to reassure them about his health and safety.

By the time Butler reached London, James was already halfway back to Paris. On the day of the battle, he had arrived at ten in the evening at Dublin Castle, where he was met by Lady Tyrconnel who begged for details. He told her bluntly: "Madam, your countrymen have run away." Lady Tyrconnel was not Sarah Churchill's sister for nothing. "If they have, Sire," she hit back, "your Majesty seems to have won the race."*

Next morning James summoned the Mayor and Council of Dublin. "Gentlemen," he told them, "Tho' the army did not desert me here as they did in England; yet when it came to a tryal, they hastily fled the field, and left the spoil to my enemies . . . so that henceforward I never more determine to head an Irish army, and so now resolve to shift for myself."* His listeners were shocked by this plain speaking, but his reproaches were not unjustified. James's French officers had been appalled by the cowardice of the Irishmen in their command, and more than one wrote back bitter accounts to France of their mass desertions. "The enemy drove the Irish troops before them like sheep . . ." was one report.*

James had given up hope for the time being, and his decision was taken: he would return to France. Before he left, he asked the Irish not to burn and destroy Dublin, as they had done to other towns in the path of William's advance. Then he took his leave of them and rode through Bray to Waterford, where he took a boat to Kinsale. With his bastard son, the Duke of Berwick, he embarked there on a French frigate bound for Brest, looking, according to eyewitnesses, an old and haggard man.*

After his departure from Dublin the Protestants in the city, who had been imprisoned in their houses, realized they were unguarded, poured out into the streets and seized the key positions. Their leaders wrote an urgent appeal to William to come and take possession of the capital. When it reached him, he was still at Ballyboghil, waiting for his armies to assemble there. The good temper of the last few days had evaporated that morning when he received disastrous news from the Allied front in Europe. His allied troops under Waldeck had fought a great battle with the French at Fleurus, between Namur and Charleroi, and suffered a terrible defeat. During the long fight, which lasted nearly seven hours, it was said the Dutch losses had been as high as 13,000. Southwell wrote to Nottingham that the King was "much troubled at the misfortune of Prince Waldeck",* and William himself told Heinsius in his next letter to Holland that the news had destroyed all the satisfaction he had felt about his own victory.*

The King's dark mood did not last long. When next day his aide-de-camp, Captain Bellingham, presented him with the first basket of cherries, William accepted them with a smile.* The following day the march to Dublin could get under way and they made camp that Saturday afternoon at Finglas, a small town three miles west of Dublin. It was the last hot sunny day of the astonishing spell of good weather the English troops had enjoyed since their arrival in Ireland. On Sunday morning, when the King made his entry into Dublin, it was still stiflingly hot but the skies were overcast and gloomy, and later in the day strong winds sprang up, threatening to blow down the tents in the camp.*

But nothing could spoil the rejoicings of the Protestant citizens, who crowded into St. Patrick's Cathedral where the King, wearing his Crown of State, heard a sermon eloquently preached by Dr. King on the power of God, of which the mightiest earthly armies were but a faint shadow.* After the service William received the congratulations of the city's magistrates, who begged him to take up residence in Dublin Castle. He refused and returned to Finglas, where during the next days he concentrated on making his army ready for the final stages of Ireland's liberation and the formation of a provisional government. The constant flow of people to his little wooden house in the centre of the camp began, however, to irritate him greatly and news of another defeat, this time of the English and Dutch fleet by the French at Beachy Head, that only reached him now, did nothing to improve his temper. The guards around his tent received a violent scolding for failing to keep the curious at a distance, while a man who stopped to thank him for his deliverance, was impatiently pushed aside with the words: "What ails you, go away."*

With relief he gave the army orders on 9 July to march southward in the direction of Waterford. Progress was slow and the rain that started to fall turned the bad roads into muddy tracks. William had other worries too. The defeats at Fleurus and Beachy Head were followed by rumours that the French were preparing to invade Holland and England, while in London the supporters of James were ready to rise against Mary. He was particularly angry about reports that during the battle at Beachy Head the English fleet had left the fighting to the Dutch, and he immediately wrote a letter to the States assuring them that the English would be heavily punished for their misbehaviour. He informed them that he intended to return to England as soon as affairs here in Ireland permitted, followed by a visit to Holland.*

Meanwhile his army marched steadily on. Resistance was non-existent, and the only casualties were some soldiers caught while plundering the Irish population. One of them escaped with a caning by the King himself; four others, less lucky, were hanged.*

On 6 July Captain Butler returned from his mission to Mary. The news he brought from London was better than had been expected. Herbert, recently created Earl of Torrington, had been thrown into the Tower after his evasive behaviour at Beachy Head and the menace of a French invasion had rallied the English round the Queen.* William dared to relax again and on the nineteenth took a day off to visit Kilkenny, the ancestral castle of his friend Ossory, who had died exactly ten years before. Ormonde, Ossory's son, had gone a day earlier and had found his house undamaged, thanks to a gracious gesture of Lauzun, who had ordered his soldiers to spare it. William was much moved by his visit and Nottingham was told: "His Majesty seems extremely well pleased with the beauty and situation of the place."*

A few days later the King's armies reached Waterford, still occupied by some of James's troops. William, who had expected to have to fight for the town, worried about the women and children, but to his surprise Waterford surrendered almost immediately on the twenty-fifth. The whole eastern coast of Ireland was now in his hands – less than two months after his arrival from London.

It was time to return to England, where the threat of a French invasion still hung over the country and where he felt he was much more urgently needed than in Ireland. He wrote to the Queen that he was on his way back and set out for Dublin, riding comfortably in a coach for the first time during his campaign. But on the way he learned two pieces of news that made him change his mind. Public reaction had made it clear that a French invasion in England would almost certainly be unsuccessful, while the scattered troops of James had fallen back on the heavily fortified town of Limerick. He wrote to Heinsius: "I had come here with the intention of returning to England, as they were concerned there about a considerable descent of the French but now this fear has abated – although the enemy's fleet still lies at Torbay – I have decided to go back to the army, that marches to Limerick, where my presence is very necessary." In Holland too the threat of another French invasion had receded and William suggested to the Raadspensionary that the militia should be disbanded and sent back to their homes.* Reluctantly his plan to go to Holland was abandoned for the moment and he turned once more to concentrate on the problems of Ireland. Southwell reported to Nottingham that William was "resolved to turn back to the army, and having secured a passage over the Shannon, he then will hasten for England."*

Before he left Dublin for Limerick, he made an effort to settle Irish affairs by peaceful means. He had already issued a declaration in which he promised mercy in exchange for obedience. Now, in a second Declaration of 1 August 1690, he demanded the surrender of the last rebels and promised an amnesty to those who submitted to him, "as we abhor all manner of violence done to our loving subjects of what religion soever . . ." Leading citizens were ordered to go to certain towns and remain there while their future was considered, and foreigners were to be allowed a passport to return to their own countries.*

He reached Limerick a few days later. This port at the mouth of the Shannon was the second largest in Ireland and the key to the whole of the south-west. It could be easily supplied from the sea and as long as it remained in Jacobite hands it would be a rallying point for rebellion. Hopes that the town would fall easily into English hands rose when it was known that the French troops had pulled out, leaving it to the Irish to defend it – since the Battle of the Boyne, respect for the Irishman as a fighter was non-existent. As the town's fortifications were not more impressive than the defenders, the English troops were surprised by the determined resistance that met them. When William joined his armies in rainsoaked swamps before the city he sent a trumpeter to the governor of the town, Boiseleau, demanding his surrender. Back came the messenger with a guinea "to drink the health" of William, and a defiant message from Boiseleau: "Since King James had entrusted him with that garrison, he would recommend himself to the Prince of Orange by a vigorous defence."*

The English army found the siege of Limerick a miserable and depressing business. The rain poured steadily down day after day and the Irish gave them not a moment of rest, constantly harassing them with skirmishing parties. They sometimes came so near "that we could hear them talk with their damn'd Irish brogue on their tongues", complained an Englishman bitterly.* The Irish efforts were not confined to skirmishes; knowing that the King's troops were short of ammunition, the one commander of brilliancy on the Irish side, General Sarsfield, took out on 12 August a raiding party to intercept the reinforcements that he had learned were on their way from Kilkenny. The English now paid for their contempt of their Irish opponents: this train of wagons loaded with the urgently needed powder and several large guns was so lightly guarded that when Sarsfield swooped on it at dead of night he met almost no resistance. Both guns and powder were blown up and sixty of its English escort were killed.*

The siege dragged on for weeks, and ammunition ran low. On 27 August William, whose health was amazingly good, made a last desperate attempt to take Limerick, but after terrible fighting on the walls and in the streets, where the people of Limerick – even women and children – defended their town with murderous courage, the attackers were driven back. Three days later William decided to raise the siege. It was his first defeat in this campaign.

On 5 September William embarked at Waterford and after an uneventful crossing of only one day landed at Kingsroad near Bristol. He stayed the night at Kingsweston and travelled without haste towards London, interrupting his journey to be the guest of the Duke of Beaufort at Badminton and the Duke of Somerset at Marlborough. He made a last stop at Windsor and finally on Wednesday the nineteenth he arrived at Hampton Court, where he found Mary waiting for him.

Together they journeyed back to Kensington, arriving there at half past five in the afternoon.* They were enchanted by the warmth and enthusiasm of the welcome in London, where church bells were ringing and the crowds lined the streets to cheer them. "They made such fireworks and such prodigious number of bonfires to welcome King William as was never seen, all the town as if it were on fire", reported a Jacobite to Paris: adding: "They burnt King James and the Prince of Wales, which was a glorious sight for the daughter and the nephew son-in-law."* At Covent Garden an effigy of Louis XIV with a placard over his head with the words "Lewis the greatest tyrant of fourteen" was dragged in a procession before being solemnly burned.

Next day the Lord Mayor and the aldermen of the City of London came to congratulate the King at Whitehall on his safe return, followed in the afternoon by the Bishop of London and the clergy. Mary's name was constantly coupled with the King's in the praise and applause. But as she wrote simply in her memoirs: "The only thing that pleased me was that my husband was satisfied and told me that he was very much pleased with my behaviour."*

CHAPTER XXX

Mary Regnant

THE PRAISES OF THE KING and the country for Mary were more than deserved. That summer of 1690 this retiring and domesticated young woman, only twenty-eight years old, had surprised all England and its enemies by her cool command of public affairs. With no experience of politics or administration, she took charge in one of the most critical situations of her country's history. England was daily faced with a French invasion and a Jacobite uprising at home, but Mary displayed a courage and decisiveness which nobody had expected, and which proved that she was a born Stuart.

Outwardly cheerful through all these months of crisis, she never betrayed her continual and torturing anxiety about her husband on the battlefields of Ireland, and her misery at his absence. Her doubts and fears were kept for William's ears alone, poured out in a constant stream of letters to him; and at the end of the year, looking back on it in her memoirs, she summed up the full horror of her situation.

> I found my self now at White Hall as in a new world, deprived of all that was dear to me in the person of my husband, left among those that were perfect strangers to me; my sister of a humour so reserved, I could have little comfort from her; the great Council of a strange composition, the Cabinett Council not much better . . . The treasury was in a bad condition, there was no money, the fleet under the command of Lord Torrington, who lay drincking and treating his friends, til the French came on the coast and had like to have surprised him. In this condition I was left with this powerful fleet upon the coast, many enemies and discontented persons in the kingdom, and not above 5 or 6000 men to defend it, not secure of these at home; great reasons to apprehend danger from abroad; so I believe never any persons was left in greater streights of all kinds.*

From the outset she was, however, determined to keep up general morale by her own behaviour. After William's departure on 4 June, she dined every day in public at Whitehall, and often had company for supper too. She sometimes had herself rowed up the river to Chelsea, where she was "diverted there with a consort of musick".* And one evening she went to the theatre, having particularly asked for a performance of Dryden's play, *The Spanish Fryar*, which James had prohibited because of its anti-Catholic allusions, although it had often been performed in the reign of Charles II. It was an unlucky choice, which gave Londoners material for happy gossip for days afterwards. She had obviously not read the play, which contained an embarrassing parallel to her own situation. Lines such as "Very good, she usurps the throne, keeps the old king in prison and at the same time is praying for a blessing on the army", were not written to make her feel at ease in the circumstances, and the whole audience was soon much more fascinated by the spectacle of the Queen's discomfiture than by the play itself. In desperation, but determined not to admit the error of her choice by leaving, Mary was forced to "hold up her fan, and often look behind her and call for her palatine and hood, and anything she could next think of".* The play was taken off, and another play substituted. This time Mary stayed away.

She waited until she heard on the thirteenth that William had sailed for Ireland before she began to attend the meetings of the Cabinet Council, although at first she took hardly any active part in their consultations, "as I do not know when I ought to speak and when not" she confessed to William.* She found these Council meetings an ordeal, and as so often in times of crisis, she had a physical reaction. "I have got a swell'd face" she reported on 19 June, "though not quite as bad yet as it was in Holland five years ago." Two days later it was no better, and her doctors advised a painful remedy. "Yesterday I had leeches set behind my ears for it, which has done but little good, so that it mends but slowly."*

Her eyes, too, began to trouble her again, as they would do for the rest of the summer: sometimes, when she was writing to William late in the evening by candlelight, she had to keep breaking off to rest them, and the tears she shed when she was alone made them worse. Once, after a snatched visit to Kensington, she wrote sadly: "That place made me think how happy I was there when I had your dear company; but now . . . I will say no more, for I shall hurt my own eyes, which I want now more than ever." And when she wrote to him after he told her that battle was imminent, she ended her letter, "my eyes are at present in somewhat a worse condition than before I received your letter . . ."*

Writing to William and hearing from him was, as Mary often said, "the only comfort I have in this world". She wrote almost daily and if the King did not hear from her by every messenger from Whitehall, he worried and asked Southall to inquire if a letter had gone astray, "she being so punctuall a writer".* He himself wrote as often as possible in the beginning and even when he was too tired to answer Nottingham, he would still scribble "a little letter to the Queen" before he went to bed.* A great deal of their correspondence was necessarily devoted to affairs of State. But William knew how badly his wife needed encouragement and reassurance, and Mary's own letters make it plain that he was kind, understanding and often tender in his letters to her, although none of them has survived. "Judge then what a joy it was to me to have your approbation of my behaviour, and the kind way you express it in . . . when you tell me I have done well I could be almost vain upon it", Mary wrote happily upon one occasion.*

From her own family in London, there was no comfort to be had. Anne was distant and unfriendly, and William had been so uncertain of her loyalty that he felt obliged, much against his liking, to take her husband George of Denmark to Ireland with him, partly as a hostage and partly as a gesture to please her. There was no doubt where the Dowager-Queen Catherine of Braganza's loyalties lay, and she made no pretence of friendship towards her niece. The first storm which blew up after William's departure was caused by the action of her Chamberlain, Lord Feversham, who forbade prayers for the King's success to be said in the Protestant chapel at her residence, Somerset House. The Queen heard about it, and told Nottingham to send for him and, so wrote her counsellor to William, "tell him her Majesty's displeasure in the harshest terms I could express it".* Feversham was alarmed and appeared in Mary's bedchamber pale with fright just before dinner, flinging himself on his knees to beg her pardon. "I could not bring myself to forgive him" wrote Mary to her husband. "If it had been to myself, I could have pardoned him, but when it immediately concerned your person, I would not, nor could not." She pitied the poor man because he felt obliged to cover up for the Queen-Dowager, and following this incident all pretence of friendship between the two women ceased.*

Without William, with no support from her family, and – amazingly enough for the Courts of those days – without a personal favourite in whom to confide – Mary could only rely on the nine men whom William had left as his Cabinet Council. He had briefed her before he left about the personalities and loyalty of these politicians, but she soon formed her own estimate of her Council, which was quite often sharper than William's.

In her memoirs, she left a fascinating thumbnail sketch of the nine "Lord President (Caermarthen) was the person the King had particularly recommended to me, and he was one to whom I must ever own great obligations" noted Mary, who never stopped being grateful to him for having promoted her marriage to William, "yet of a temper I can never like." Lord Nottingham, the Secretary of State, was, as she well knew, "suspected by most as not true to the government".* But in spite of the fact that he had voted against the crown being offered to William and Mary, the King believed him an honest man and in the end Mary came to trust him more than most politicians: "I incline to have a good opinion of him; it may be his formal, grave look deceives me."* Caermarthen and Nottingham, both Tories, were the most powerful and ambitious men in the Council, and Mary soon realized that they wanted to exclude her from affairs as far as possible. "I find they meet often at the secretary's office, and do not take much pain to give me an account" she reported on 20 June.*

Marlborough she did not trust an inch, knowing all too well the mischievous role his wife Sarah played in Anne's household and his own personal ambition. Lord Monmouth was another she thought unreliable and when a series of anonymous letters, full of details of Council meetings and criticisms, began to arrive, she suspected that these "lemon" letters were his work.

Admiral Russell was a loyal supporter of William, but she found it difficult to know what to make of him at first and thought him edgy and unco-operative.

The remaining four she dismissed as lightweights. Dorset, the Lord Steward, "weak and obstinate, made a mere tool by a party"; Pembroke, "a man of honour, but not very steady . . ."; Devonshire, the Lord Chamberlain, "too lazy to give himself the trouble of business, so of little use"; and Sir John Lowther, the head of the Treasury, "a very honest but weack man". She summed up drily: "This was the Council I was to follow in all things."*

Mary had scarcely had time to form her own opinion of her ill-assorted Cabinet Council before crisis confronted her. On 22 June an express letter brought news that the French fleet was upon them, and had been seen off the coast of Devon, between Falmouth and Plymouth. The English fleet was at this time commanded by Lord Torrington, a touchy pessimistic man, more famous for his caution than for his courage. The fleet itself was in wretched shape, with many of the ships almost rotten and chronically undermanned, and the navy riddled by disease caused by dishonest victuallers. Torrington had no friends in the Cabinet: Mary's view of him – an idle and unreliable drinker – was certainly influenced by Nottingham, who fancied himself as an expert on naval matters, and by Russell, who was a professional rival.

When news of the French fleet's sighting reached Mary, she at once dashed off two notes to William, the first written at 10.30 p.m., the other an hour later, both despatched to the King by different routes. She told him that while she was worried by Torrington's lack of enthusiasm, she herself was "so little afraid, that I begin to fear I have not sense enough to apprehend the danger". She ended her letter: "What I fear most at present is not hearing from you. Love me whatever happens and be assured I am ever entirely yours till death."*

Two days later she wrote again. Torrington had reported that the English and French fleets were probably now only five leagues apart. He had added grimly that his force, which had now been joined by the Dutch under Admiral Evertsen, consisted only of 50 men-of-war and 25 fire-ships, while the French had 77 men-of-war and 30 fire-ships. "To-morrow probably will be the desiding day; lett them tremble at the consequence whose fault it was the fleet is noe stronger."*

"I cannot but be in pain" wrote Mary to William, commenting on Torrington's pessimism. "The loss of a battle would be such an encouragement to disaffected ones, that might put things here in disorder . . ."*

The prospect of this sea battle was overshadowed in her mind by the thought of the coming battle in Ireland. She knew that William had left Belfast with his army five days earlier on Thursday the nineteenth and she had had no word of him since. "I hope the easterly wind is the only cause I do not hear from you . . . I am in a million of fears, not knowing when you may be in danger . . ." Halfway through writing this she was called out to see Lord Nottingham who handed to her the long-awaited letter from Ireland, "which is so welcome that I cannot express it, especially because you pity me, which I like and desire from you, and you only . . ." In his letter he had asked about progress at Hampton Court, but Mary had no good news to tell: "I fear there will be many obstacles . . . especially since the French are in the Channel, and at present between Portland and us, from whence the stone must come."*

The public saw none of these fears and preoccupations. A newsletter of 26 June reports that "The Queen is extremely vigorous and cheerful under these great weights of government. Continual councils are held at Whitehall, and often expresses come from the fleet."* One of those expresses on that very day brought news that Torrington, who

had sailed at last with a favourable wind, had spent an entire day successfully evading an engagement with the French. Their superior strength,
he explained, "puts me beside the hope of success if wee should fight,
and really may not only endanger the ruine of the fleet, but at least the
quiet of our country too . . ."*

Mary's counsellors were beside themselves with indignation at what
they felt to be his cowardly behaviour. And at their insistence Mary
translated their wishes for an attack into a positive order to engage the
French, drafted by Russell in sharp terms, but softened at her suggestion:
"Her Majesty does not doubt his skill and conduct in this important
conjuncture, but thinks the consequence of his withdrawing to the
Gunfleet would be so fatal, that she rather chooses he should, upon any
advantage of the wind, give battle to the enemy."*

Next day Mary was just about to leave the Council Chamber when
she was handed a letter with shattering news from Loughbrickland: the
King might well at this moment be in the middle of a battle. "My heart
is ready to burst. I can say nothing but pray for you", she wrote back.
The same afternoon there was another blow to sustain: a letter from
Waldeck told her of the disastrous Allied defeat at Fleurus. Mary could
not sleep that night, and wrote to William imploring him not to leave
her without news about the battle against her father. "My impatience
for another [letter] from you is as great as my love, which will not end but
with my life."*

By Sunday, 29 June there was still no news of the expected sea-battle.
At an emergency meeting the Council came to a drastic decision: if
Torrington refused to fight, he must be replaced at once and the obvious
man was Admiral Russell. Instructions from the Queen to Russell were
drafted, ordering him to Dover "to take upon you the command of our
fleet and to oppose our enemies". Russell was to board Torrington's
flagship, and have him sent up to London under close arrest.*

Torrington, unaware that Whitehall had already ended his command,
sat down this same day to reply to the Queen's orders of the twenty-
sixth. "I this minute receive her Majesty's orders, which I will, soe soone
as I can gett the flag officers on board, communicate to them. I am very
certayne that they all will with my self with great cherefulnesse give due
obedience to her comands." But the rest of this letter betrayed no such
cheerfulness; he made it plain that he was going into battle reluctantly,
warning that "if wee are beaten all is exposed to their mercy".*

By dusk the next day it was all over. In obedience to the Queen's
orders Torrington had sailed out in the morning to meet the French,
with his own thirty-four ships and the twenty-two Dutch ships under

Evertsen. The Dutch squadron was in the van, and at once attacked the French under the command of Châteaurenault. Torrington in the *Royal Sovereign* found his squadron opposed to the French under the command of Tourville in the French flagship the *Soleil Royal*. But he was in no hurry to engage, and when Evertsen plunged on ahead, the French succeeded in cutting off the Dutch from the main body of the fleet, and in the violent battle that followed the Dutch bore the brunt of the action, while Torrington hovered just out of range. When the evening fell the French were victors and the scattered Dutch and English ships fled eastwards to take refuge in the mouth of the Thames. Ten of the Dutch ships and seven of the English were a total loss, and two Dutch admirals had been killed.

Torrington got in early with his own account of "this unfortunate battle". The fearsome damage suffered by the Dutch was due, as he wrote, to a sudden calm produced by a change of wind – "it gave the French an opportunity of destroying all their lame ships." And he generously conceded that the Dutch had behaved "in point of courage, to admiration".*

News of Torrington's defeat caused near-panic in London where everybody believed that a French invasion was now imminent. Orders were hurriedly sent off to Kent to muster and arm the entire militia, horse and foot of the county, and the Lords Lieutenant all over England were instructed to have half their mounted militia ready for action, and to round up Papists and suspected Jacobites.*

The full fury of the nation now fell upon Torrington. As Nottingham wrote to the King: "In plain terms, by all that yet appears, my Lord Torrington deserted the Dutch so shamefully that the whole squadron had been lost if some of our ships had not rescued them. . . . I find it is beleeved by all men that we should have ruined that fleet which is now pursuing us if my Lord Torrington had done his duty."*

The same evening the Queen wrote to Ireland: "What Lord Torrington can say for himself I know not, but I believe he will never be forgiven here." She reported in the same letter that Russell had got no further than Canterbury before hearing the news and returning, "so the nine are together again".* They decided next day that national amends must be made to the Dutch immediately, a view shared by Mary and a shamed England. The Queen personally issued orders that all possible care must be taken of the Dutch wounded, and resolved to send an envoy to the States "not to excuse the Lord Torrington, but to acquaint them with her resentment of his actions".* For this humiliating mission, she chose William Harbord, who sailed for Holland a couple of days later. Passing the English and Dutch ships sheltering in the Thames estuary, he wrote: "I am much out of countenance to see on one side of me a great 3rd rate and no damage and on the other the *Armes of Alkmaer* with 39 holes in one side visible and her mast shot down."*

Before he arrived in The Hague, Nottingham wrote to Lord Dursley, the English Envoy Extraordinary to the States of Holland, about the national resentment in England in unrestrained language, putting the blame for the Dutch sufferings on Torrington who, he said, is "wholly and only guilty . . . The Queen so highly resents it and all mankind express here so great indignation against him for it that the States will quickly see it revenged upon him . . ."*

Dursley hurried off to show this letter to the States "in which they took great satisfaction", he reported back to London, and which they wanted to have printed immediately "for the better quieting of the minds of the people".* Nottingham was embarrassed to have his hasty scribble, as he put it, "the subject of every alehouse talk",* but he was probably not sorry to have his opinion of the despised Torrington made known to the public. At least printing the letter saved Dursley from the fury of the Dutch mob, who wanted to destroy his house "when they heard how their fleet had been served". The Hague magistrates hurriedly produced Nottingham's soothing words, and the English envoy could breathe freely again.*

Meanwhile in London the Cabinet Council had agreed that a commission should be sent down to the fleet to order Torrington up to London, but they could not agree who was to go. Mary finally appointed Pembroke and Devonshire – the first time that she ventured to give her own judgment, as she rather diffidently told William.* She gave the two men special instructions to go and see Admiral Evertsen "to assure him of her esteem of his courage and conduct".*

Pembroke and Devonshire were also instructed to find out whether Torrington's officers would be willing to witness against him in a trial, but, as Nottingham wrote to William, "the very same persons who in their letters to their friends writ very freely and much blamed my Lord Torrington, would not speak of him."* And on 6 July Pembroke and Devonshire returned empty-handed: the navy had closed ranks against the two civilians.

But something had to be decided about Lord Torrington, and Mary wrote urgently to the King for instructions. "Whether you will think fit to confine him after his behaviour, I don't know, but all the Lords believe you will not."* At the same time she sent him a list of candidates for Torrington's post. Russell was the obvious choice, but would probably refuse to pick up the pieces. Others were Sir Richard Haddock, Sir John Ashby and Sir Cloudesley Shovell. There was even some talk of putting the command in the hands of a commission of three, with the third person a civilian.

While Mary dutifully listed the possible candidates, her thoughts were miles away. That morning, on her way to chapel, Nottingham had told her that the King had been slightly wounded at the Boyne, and she had burst into tears. "The thought that you expose yourself thus to danger, frights me out of my wits", she wrote to William. She knew that the decisive battle must by now have taken place; "I am not able to think of anything else."*

This agonizing suspense lasted till next morning, when Captain Butler arrived from Ireland with the glorious news of William's victory. Light-headed with relief, she sat down to scribble a long, almost incoherent letter to him. "I was yesterday out of my senses with trouble, I am now almost so with joy, so that I cant really as yet tel what I have to say to you, by this bearer who is impatient to return".*

Nottingham's news that her father was safe and unhurt completed her happiness, though Mary evidently believed him a prisoner, and pleaded with her husband: "I know I need not beg you to let him be taken care of, for I am confident you will for your own sake. Yet add that to all your kindness, and, for my sake, let people know you would have no hurt come to his person."*

The Council immediately sent a message to the King to congratulate him; they also strongly advised that "since his Majesty's affairs are so prosperous in Ireland, so far from being here", he should return at once, "since the French had it in their power to land when they please in England, and probably mean to do so."* Nottingham added a warning that discontent and disaffection were daily growing in the country. The Council's advice to the King to return was warmly seconded by Mary. "Methinks there is nothing more for you to do", she wrote to William, reflecting the general optimism about Ireland.

Already she was happily making plans for his homecoming: "I will hasten Kensington as much as it's possible." Two days later she repeated her plea and her hopes – "that you will have no more to do but come back here, where you are wish'd for by all that love you or themselves; I need not say most by me "* Heartened by the King's victory, by his praise for what she had done and her hope of seeing him soon, she tackled her heavy responsibilities once more with new vigour.

"In all this time of fear and disorder, the queen shewed an extraordinary firmness", wrote Burnet later admiringly; "her behaviour was in all respects heroicall: she apprehended the greatness of our danger; but she committed herself to God; and was resolved to expose herself . . . if she was forced to make a campaign in England while the King was in Ireland."*

The English felt her determination, and her example inspired the nation. Promises of support flooded in, and one of the first came from the City of London whose Lord Mayor and aldermen waited on the Queen to tell her "that it was the unanimous resolution of the City to defend and preserve their Majesties in case of invasion." Two days later the Mayor came back with a more concrete offer of support: "Their Militia, 9000 men, and their auxiliaries, 6000 more, should be in readiness to march upon her Majesty's command." They would immediately raise a regiment of 400 horse and another of 1000 dragoons, and pay for both.*

ON 10 JULY Torrington at last came to town to make what explanations he could: he was at once thrown into the Tower and a commission of enquiry appointed by the Queen to decide what should be done with him.* Then, with the French still masters of the Channel, Mary and Nottingham turned their attention to the urgent and tricky question of naming his successor.

William's wishes were known. He had twice written to name Russell as Admiral, with the competent and reliable Sir Richard Haddock under him. But Russell was understandably reluctant to take over command of the demoralized navy at such a unpromising juncture: "Not only the eye and expectation of all England, but all Europe, especially Holland, is upon this choice" he told Mary portentously. He urged on her a course which had already been suggested – the command should be put into a commission of three, two of them to be seamen, Sir Richard Haddock and Sir John Ashby, and one a person of quality, possibly Shrewsbury. Mary approved and put the suggestion before her Council – only to find herself immediately embarrassed by Caermarthen's eager offer of his services. She temporized, suggesting that Haddock and Ashby should be appointed but the third man left for the King's decision, since he was expected in London shortly.

This decision made, Mary fled to Kensington to inspect progress with the new buildings, delighted to have the thorny question settled. Her relief was short-lived. On her return to Whitehall that evening, she found the Admiralty commissioners waiting to insist once more that Russell be appointed to the sole command, and they stayed pestering

her till late that night. Even after Russell had reiterated his unwilling-
ness to serve the next morning, they still obstinately rejected the Council's decision, and a violent argument broke out between one of them
and the Queen. Sir Thomas Lee, a touchy and difficult man, refused
point-blank to sign the commissions, and went on to suggest insolently
that the King had no powers to name Torrington's successor, only the
Admiralty. Mary could not believe her ears, and – as always when her
husband's rights were questioned – was beside herself with anger. She
perceived, she told him sharply, that "the King had given away his own
power and could not make an admiral which the admiralty did not like".
Sir Thomas, equally angry, retorted "No, no more he can't."

Mary was on the point of snapping that in that case the King would
do better to appoint new commissioners, when Caermarthen hurriedly
intervened and asked the commissioners to retire. That night Mary wrote
urgently to William asking for a firm decision. "If I may say so", she
added bitterly, "I do not think people should be humoured to this
degree."* It took all Russell's persuasion to stop her sacking Sir Thomas.
Awed by her fury, the Admiralty eventually gave way; and the commission of three was appointed, with Killigrew as third man – the idea
of a civilian had been dropped.

It was the beginning of August, and after one French attack on the
little port of Teignmouth on 25 July the threat of a French invasion
seemed to have disappeared. With the question of command now
settled and the fleet – reorganized under Russell's stern eye – ready for
action, there was almost a feeling of regret in Whitehall at the departure
of the French. "We should have been glad to have had our revenge,
and repaired our honour and late misfortune", wrote Nottingham to the
King, who in spite of urgent demands for his return was still in Ireland.*

But if the French fleet had withdrawn for the moment, the Jacobites
in England were still active. Mary had taken stern measures against
them, ordering the arrest of several of them after a hostile demonstration
against herself in Hyde Park. She had even given orders for her uncle
Clarendon to be imprisoned in the Tower after incriminating letters had
been found, and she personally conducted the examination of a number
of important Jacobites. She was informed of all the plots against her,
most of them originating in Scotland, where, as one informer told her,
"there are not six men of note . . . that are not against the government",*
and she heard with horror about a plot much nearer home.

It was a vagrant, sleeping in St. James's Park, who discovered it
when he overheard the conversation of a group of nine people, including
a lady in a cloak and a Scotsman. In the darkness of the park they

discussed how to assassinate the King and Queen. According to the Scotsman, the Queen would be an easy victim. He had seen her going to chapel escorted only by one gentleman, and the swarm of "sixpenny beggars with their petitions" that always surrounded her would be excellent cover. The lady was enthusiastic and offered to account for William in Ireland. "As for that monkey", she promised, "I doe ingage . . . you gentlemen that he shall never returne."*

Not surprisingly, Mary's letters to William began to show an increasing edginess and a growing impatience for his return. On 20 July she had received his letter announcing his homecoming "with so much joy, that it was seen in my face by those who knew the secret",* and on 28 July the news had been confirmed by Captain Butler, "whose face I shall love to see ever hereafter, since he has come twice with such good news."* She was devastated four days later to learn that he had turned back to undertake the siege of Limerick – "unless I could express the joy I had at the thought of your coming, it will be in vain to undertake telling you of the disappointment 'tis to me that you do not come so soon . . .", she wrote to him in tears.*

Huygens' reappearance from Ireland on 12 August raised her hopes of the King's imminent return. She sent Sylvius at once to ask her husband's secretary to come and see her, but Huygens was so busy that Sylvius had to carry him off to the Queen two days later. Smilingly she reproached him for his delay, but he excused himself – he had hardly any news for her.

She was not the only person eager for news of William. When Huygens reappeared in London in mid-August his cousin Mrs. Becker, a friend of Betty Villiers, told him that she would bring Betty to hear his own account of events in Ireland. Huygens reacted coolly, and when next morning the King's mistress sent a messenger asking for the latest news, she received a curt reply that there was none. Undeterred she came in person two days later, and stayed for hours cross-questioning the disapproving secretary.*

The two women had to be patient for weeks longer. William was now at Limerick, and Mary's letters became almost cries of despair. "I must own the thought of your staying longer is very uneasy to me"; and three days later: " 'tis a terrible thought to me that your coming is put off again for so long time." She begged him: "for God's sake take care of yourself; you owe it to your own and this country." On 26 August, two days before the final assault on Limerick, she wrote: "My poor heart is ready to break every time I think in what perpetual danger you are,"

Letters from Ireland came sparsely now, and in her distress she forgot her last reserve, and poured out her heart to her husband:

> I never do any thing without thinking now, it may be, you are in the greatest dangers, and yet I must see company upon my sett days: I must play twice a week: nay, I must laugh and talk, tho' never so much against my will . . . all my motions are so watch'd, and all I do so observed, that if I eat less or speak less, or look more grave, all is lost in the opinion of the world; so that I have this misery added to that of your absence and my fears for your dear person, that I must grin when my heart is ready to break, and talk when my heart is so oppress'd I can scarce breathe . . . I can neither sleep nor eat. I go to Kensington as often as I can for air, but then I can never be quite alone: neither can I complain, that would be some ease . . . besides I must hear of business, which being a thing I am so new in, and so unfit for, does but break my brains the more, and not ease my heart.

As if all this were not enough to bear, casually glancing through a Dutch newspaper, she had come across the letter from William to the States in which he promised to come to the Republic soon: "I cant tell you how many ill hours I have had about that", she complained.*

The only other person to whom she dared give a sign of her distress was the Electress Sophia, to whom she confided: "things here aren't going too well . . . The personal animosities people have for each other are very unpleasant, and the different parties are too difficult for me to manage . . . I'm tired of it. The return of the King . . . will free me from all these burdens. . ."*

But at last she received news that the King was indeed on his way home: on 8 September, two days after he had landed, she heard that he was in England and dashed off a last note: "Nothing can express the impatience I have so see you, nor my joy to think it is so near; I have not slept all this night for it. . ."*

On 10 September they were together at last. Mary had left Whitehall the day before to move back into Kensington, but was too impatient to wait there and had gone by coach to their favourite palace outside London, Hampton Court, "where I found him, blessed be God, in perfect health". She was delighted to see how well he looked, tanned and untroubled by his asthma, and wrote afterwards of their reunion: "This was so great a joy to me that I want words to express it."

Mary had never been so happy: "My husband returned . . . I rid of all the troublesome business I was so little fit for."* With great relief she left London nine days later for a short holiday with William at Windsor.*

CHAPTER XXXI

Back to the Continent

IT WAS HIGH TIME FOR William to reappear on the international stage. During his absence in Ireland, the Allied campaign against France in Flanders under Waldeck had been disastrous, and it was obvious that without the King-Stadholder as its animating spirit the alliance faltered and lost heart. A congress of all Allied powers to restore morale and plan the next year's campaign was urgently necessary, and at the King's suggestion it was to assemble at The Hague.

William was anxious to get there as soon as possible, and it was homesickness as much as reasons of state that drew him. "We won't know Holland any more when we go there, and they won't know us any more", he remarked one evening in October to Huygens, who answered drily that the King might change his mind when there were crowds pressing around him, as they always did in Holland.*

Before he could get away there was urgent business to be attended to in England. On 2 October he opened the new session of a Parliament unusually good-tempered after his victories in Ireland. In his speech from the throne he asked them for generous supplies, reminding them of the French threat not only to the peace of Europe, but to the security of their own country. He told them almost buoyantly how, wherever he went in England, he had found "such Demonstrations of Affection, that I have not the least doubt but I shall find the same from the Representatives in Parliament".* He was not disappointed: within two days the M.P.s had voted the enormous and unprecedented sum of £1,800,000 for the navy and £2,300,000 for the army.

The heavy financial demands of the European war underlined the urgency of another task: that of putting the Treasury into capable hands instead of the party hacks who had mismanaged it for the last eighteen months. Godolphin, a born civil servant with a genius for administration, was the obvious choice, but since he had run the Treasury for James, he was unacceptable to many politicians and he himself was reluctant to serve. William, who liked and respected him, saw only one way to overcome the objections of Godolphin and the others: by getting them drunk. Early in November, following an uproariously convivial evening, Sidney Godolphin duly became First Lord of the Treasury.*

Another problem to be dealt with was the fate of Torrington, who had been in the Tower since 10 July. It was finally decided that he should face a court-martial, which was fixed for 9 December. By that time national resentment had cooled, and there had been a revulsion of feeling in his favour and against the Dutch. The navy particularly felt his trial as an injustice, and one of the key witnesses against him, Captain Carter, excused himself from attendance on the flimsiest of pretexts, leaving the main case for the prosecution in the hands of three Dutch officers. They gave their evidence against him with more passion than tact, and Torrington was acquitted by general consensus. As his yacht sailed up to London afterwards every ship in the Thames saluted him.* William, infuriated by the result of the court-martial, had the last word. Torrington was stripped of his commission as Admiral, relieved of the command of a regiment of marines, and never asked to serve again.

This autumn of 1690 at least, anti-Dutch feeling was not vented on the King himself, whose personal popularity indeed was at its height. His birthday on 4 November was celebrated with something like White-hall's old splendour. The King and Queen dined in public "where there was a great resort of nobility and gentry, and at night was a consort of musick, and a play afterwards."* It was a national holiday: the shops were closed all day and the great guns at the Tower were fired. And when he announced his forthcoming visit to Holland, many of the leading nobles and politicians decided that he should be escorted in style: "Some of his majesties coaches and baggage is gone to be shipt off for Holland; the Earl of Devonshire and other noblemen are preparing splendid equipages to attend his majestie thither", noted Luttrell on the seventh.* Accounts from Holland made it clear that his reception there would be magnificent too. "Great preparations . . . at The Hague for the reception of the King of England . . . the states have caused to be made an extraordinary rich chair of state for his majestie to sitt in, and which they intend to present him with. . ."*

By New Year 1691 William's preparations to leave for Holland were complete, and he could hardly wait to go. When Huygens came to "Kinsinghton" on 2 January with a bundle of letters, he could not get them signed: the King could talk only of his journey. It seemed like a dream to him, he said, that perhaps in eight days' time he would be at The Hague.*

His glee was not shared by Mary, who dreaded the loneliness and responsibility his absence would entail. After his return from Ireland, she had gladly given up all involvement in government to spend, as she admitted, "much time idle in going about to see several things". She was unaware of the panic her unexpected visits to friends occasionally created. One of the victims was Lady Wharton, whose husband, visiting Windsor to make his court, had found the Queen's coaches ready to take her and a party to his country seat at Woburn. He had guessed that the cupboards were bare after a week's heavy entertaining, and immediately sent a messenger "that found poor Lady Wharton just sat down to her own dinner", wrote a sympathetic member of her family afterwards, " 'Tis easy to imagine what her condition was . . . nothing in the house, nor nothing that on such a sudden could be got in the country. She sed if she would have given a pound for a partridge, 'twas not to be had . . ." As well as the Queen a huge company had to be fed. "Indeed, to heare my Lady Wharton tell the tragical story would almost have made one cry."

Other ladies were luckier. When the Queen dined a few days later at the Duchess of Monmouth's, "her entertainment . . . was very splendid, they having prepared for her above a week before she came."*

For Mary it was delightful to behave like a private person again, and she wrote of these weeks: "I minded so little bussiness, that I cant but wonder at what I have often heard said, that when any body was once used to it, they could not give it over." But she was not allowed to forget it altogether. Her husband, who had once never mentioned politics to her, had got into the habit of talking matters over with her, and with his own long absence in prospect, he was anxious that she should be kept in touch with what was going on.*

According to current gossip, however, it was something far worse than "bussiness" which spoiled Mary's pleasure in her husband's company. This winter, the scandalmongers of Whitehall were busy diagnosing a rift in the Royal marriage. William, it was said, was visibly out of love with his wife, and spent hours of his time with Elizabeth Villiers, with whom he was sleeping. She was pregnant by him, was showered with gifts of money through Portland, and held her own small court. Mary herself, so the gossip went on, had cooled from her once blind attachment to her husband; she had been heard to remark that girls who married at fifteen had no idea what they were about, and that they might be tired of their partners before they were thirty. (Mary was twenty-eight at this time.)

The gossip went further. Mary in her distress had raised false hopes in the heart of one of the courtiers: no less a person than Shrewsbury. She herself was unaware of his feelings, but the King of Hearts suddenly had no eyes for any other woman, and walked around Whitehall in a dream. Mary's Vice-Chamberlain, the spiteful John Howe, even described to a friend how Shrewsbury had great difficulty in disguising his agitation when he was in the company of the Queen. In his view, the Queen was not as naïve as everyone thought, and he had felt how she trembled at the sight of Shrewsbury when he led her into chapel.*

This gossip was reported to Dijkvelt in Holland by the Sieur Blancard, a Frenchman and diplomat who was a personal friend of his, and very highly thought of by both William and Mary. He emphasized in his letter that the Queen was certainly "virtue itself" and as much in love with the King as ever; but he was worried by the way she was always summoning Shrewsbury to keep her company or play cards, thus innocently encouraging the gossip. And what really disturbed him most, and prompted his letter to Dijkvelt, was one sinister detail of the gossip: Shrewsbury had been told by a fortune-teller that his love would be lucky after the King had died.

Was this another Jacobite plot?

Blancard's fears were unfounded this time. But although he had stoutly denied to his gossiping informant that there was any truth in her scandals, it seems clear that the Royal marriage was going through a particularly bad patch.

Elizabeth Villiers was certainly in town at this time, and confident enough of her position to have pestered Huygens for news of the King's return from Ireland. That she was pregnant seems unlikely, and that Portland was playing go-between equally improbable – he disliked her and disapproved of the liaison. But that the King spent hours with her and slept with her is by no means impossible. Mary was not very cheerful at the time, still suffering a reaction from the months of Irish crisis, and miserable at the idea that William was leaving her again. Besides, she was not looking her best: William teased her publicly about her "embonpoint".*

Blancard had done his best to kill the gossip, assuring everyone of the fidelity of both partners, but the fact that he found it worth while to report the matter to Dijkvelt, who had Portland with him at the time, is significant. If a serious rift in the marriage of William and Mary could be engineered, it might endanger the entire Revolution settlement, based as it was on Mary's willing submission to William's authority.

How much was true and how much mere Whitehall chatter, we shall never know. But certainly Mary's memoirs and letters for the early months of that year betray an exceptional unhappiness and in-security.

Mary had hoped that she might be going to Holland with William, but the international situation, as well as domestic politics, did not allow it and she wrote sadly to her Dutch friend Mlle. d'Obdam: "I don't like to talk about the departure of the King because I shan't be going along myself, but I hope that the time will come when things will be in such a state that I can go with him. What a satisfaction for me, what a joy, to see once more a country so dear to me . . ."*

When the King set out on 6 January 1691 she was very much fretted "considering the danger of the seas at that time of year", but to her surprise the King was back in Kensington only three days later, contrary winds having made it impossible for him to sail. He had to wait until the sixteenth before he left London again, embarking on his yacht *Mary* at Gravesend. On the seventeenth he sailed, escorted by a convoy of twelve men of war and accompanied by Nottingham, Devonshire, Dorset, Bishop Compton, Portland and Ouwerkerk.*

It was an appalling crossing. The ships had hardly left Margate when a violent storm blew up. For a whole day and night they struggled with the winds but the King refused to order their return. Gales blew them towards Dunkirk, which was in the hands of French privateers, and Sijmen Janszoon Harevelt, the same captain who had brought William to England in 1688, succeeded only at the last moment in altering course. On the 30 January n.s. the fleet arrived at the estuary. Dense fog and mountains of ice, however, made it impossible to sail into the river. Everybody advised the King to give up his reckless journey but he shrugged it off with the words: "For shame, are you afraid to die in my company?" and ordered his barge to be launched. Boarding it with Port-land, Ouwerkerk, Hartevelt, Devonshire and seven rowers, he set out for the coast. Although they reckoned to land within two hours they took seven bottles of beer and wine, two chickens and five loaves of bread – a sensible precaution, as the journey was to last fourteen hours.

Several times they neared the coast but the ice floes were so thick that they had to return to the open sea. At last they reached the island of Goeree near Zeeland, when fresh disaster struck: their boat went aground and could not be refloated until high tide. They had to wait till morning before they could begin to row again. When they were as close to the port of Goeree as the ice-floes allowed, Hartevelt jumped over-board in the darkness and scrambled over the ice to the beach to fetch help. William, who had argued against this dangerous act, sighed with relief when he fired a musket shot from the shore to signal his safe arrival. A few hours later, Hartevelt was back with carriages and the half-frozen group were able to land.

It was five o'clock in the morning when William entered the small farmhouse of Cortsiaen, where a blazing fire waited for him. He changed warmed himself and had something to eat. The dangers of the trip seemed to have made little impression on him, Hartevelt noticed – "it was remarkable that he had not once been dismayed during the whole journey."

At nine o'clock the King left again. The weather was clear and the four-hour crossing over the Maas to Oranjepolder was uneventful. At, the other side were two men waiting with horses and when one of them rode into the water to meet the barge, the King in high spirits greeted him warmly. "How are you, Jilles, do you still know me?" Jilles, a gamekeeper who had once worked for the Stadholder, was taken aback and stuttered: "Welcome, seigneur Prince, I did not see that it was you." It was not surprising: the King's face was covered by three days' growth of beard.

On shore the King and his party celebrated their safe arrival by finishing off the last bottles of wine and beer, after which William and Portland took the two horses and rode to Jilles' house, where his daughter welcomed them. The King, who had a heavy cold and by now could hardly speak, asked for something to drink, but the only thing that the girl could offer was buttermilk, which he accepted grinning. The others arrived shortly after him and while they warmed themselves around the fire, William retired to the stables, warm from the cows. He walked around and it was visible that he was deeply moved. After two years, he was back in his own country.*

He did not stay very long in the little house. A few hours later a coach arrived and at four in the afternoon the King arrived at Honselaersdijck. His cousin Hendrick Casimir, waiting to welcome him, fell on his knees, but William raised him quickly and kissed him on both cheeks. After having changed, he left immediately for The Hague, where thousands of people crowded out along the road to meet him with torches.

It was only a rehearsal for the formal entrance that took place on 5 February, much against William's wish but well calculated to dazzle the Englishmen in his entourage. Huygens, up early to look at the preparations with his wife, was astonished by the numbers of people already gathering despite the freezing cold, and the huge triumphal arches along the route. These showed all the Princes of Orange since William the Silent, and the history of the House of Orange from 1572 down to the Battle of the Boyne.

It was already dusk when the Stadholder-King reached the outskirts of the town, where the magistrates welcomed him on the beautifully-decorated Loosduynse bridge. Followed by thirty young men on horse-back – Huygens saw with pride that his son Tien was one of them – the King drove slowly down the Westeinde, past the Town Hall and under the arches along the Plaats and the Buitenhof to his residence. The entry was made even more impressive by the King's own entourage of English noblemen, who according to an eyewitness, "made a splendid appear-ance".* One of these noblemen, Nottingham, was struck by the warmth of the Dutch welcome, but when he said so to William, the King replied candidly: "Ah my Lord! If my queen were but here, you would see a difference. Where they now give one shout for me, they would given ten for her."*

The firework display from a platform floating in the Vijver that evening, however, was a fiasco: there was so much fog that the rockets were swallowed up in it before they exploded.*

Next day William was formally received by the States-General, and if any of the Englishmen in his party understood Dutch, his speech would not have made very pleasant hearing for them. Speaking with a warmth and emotion the English were not used to, the King assured the Dutch that "He would . . . sacrifice all that he had in the world for the good of this State; without sparing either his own Body or his own Life." If he had accepted the English crown, he told them, it was not out of personal ambition or greed, but to support and maintain their religion and peace, "and that he might be the better enabled more powerfully to assist his Allies, and more particularly this State, against the enterprise of France . . ."* Halifax had remarked shrewdly in 1689 that William "took England on the way to France": William now admitted as much.

Afterwards, William heard a sermon in the church nearby, and then strolled like an ordinary citizen in the Voorhout. His English friends were astonished again by his relaxed and genial manner: he seemed to know almost everyone they met, and greeted them all warmly.*

The Hague had never seen times like this. The small peaceful seat of the Republic's government was filled up with the rulers of half Europe, their entourages, and their servants; the streets were jammed with their coaches. Fourteen English lords came with William, there were the two Electors of Brandenburg and Bavaria, there was the Prince Regent of Württemberg, the Landgrave of Hesse-Cassel, the Prince of Brunswick and the flamboyant Governor of the Spanish Netherlands, the Marquis de Castanaga. In Paris, the royal heads were counted with some alarm – it was said that there had been twenty-eight princes at the *levée* of the

Majestas Potentissime – the title given William by the Emperor. As well as the princely guests, there were thirty ambassadors and numbers of princesses and ladies.

But for all its impressive guest list, the Congress itself failed to achieve much. The King had opened its proceedings with a stern warning that "not the decisions of a sterile congress, nor the unfounded hopes of statesmen, but soldiers, mighty armies and a speedy and close concert of all the allied powers must do our business here."* After days of talking, the Allies had agreed to put an army of 220,000 men in the field against France that season, but done little to ensure co-operation on diplomatic levels, and jealousies and divisions were dishearteningly evident in the Allied ranks.

During the negotiations, William was ably assisted by the Dutch Raadspensionary Antonius Heinsius. It was the first time the two men had been able to discuss matters face-to-face since Heinsius became Raadspensionary in 1689, although they had corresponded at length over the last two years. William had rapidly developed a warm liking and respect for this elegant and taciturn man, with his clear judgment and his diplomatic sangfroid. On foreign statesmen, too, Heinsius made an excellent impression: "simplicity of appearance, no luxury in his house. One secretary, one coachman, one maid, one lackey. Cool in his manners but never discourteous; even during an altercation, never losing control," so wrote the French minister de Torcy.*

For years to come, if William was the brains and heart of the alliance, Heinsius was its right hand, and his office at The Hague gradually became the nerve-centre of a Europe fighting against France.

The Congress lingered on until 4 March, when William was able at last to escape to his beautiful country palace, Het Loo. He took with him the Elector of Bavaria and other princes for a hunting holiday. Nottingham, who was one of the party, found it hard to keep up with him. "This morning I received yours of the 2nd, but am so tired with hunting that you will I hope pardon a short letter . . ." he reported to Russell.*

One incident spoiled the King's pleasure. Out hunting with William one day, a young Dutch Gentleman of the Bedchamber called van Keppel was thrown from his horse and broke his leg. Talking about it afterwards to Huygens, the King was most upset about it. "He's such a good boy", he said, "and he's in terrible pain."*

Arnold Joost van Keppel was the son of a distinguished Dutch family which could trace its patents of nobility back to 1179. His father was Osewolt van Keppel van der Voorst, his mother Reinira Anna

Geertruyd van Lintello tot de Mars. Joost was born in 1670 and succeeded his father in the Lordship when he was thirteen and already a
Page of Honour to William. His home, like Portland's, was an old castle
in Gelderland, not far from Het Loo, at Zutphen. He had come to
England with William in 1688, and he was now a lively, charming
twenty-one-year-old.* The portrait of him by Kneller shows soft, rather
effeminate good looks, with sharp intelligent eyes. His rise in the King's
favour had been rapid. From page he had become amanuensis, copying
William's letters, and now he was Gentleman of the Bedchamber and
indispensable companion of the King's leisure hours. His importance
was gradually dawning on the King's entourage, exciting jealousy and
suspicion: "something must be going on", concluded William's two
inquisitive secretaries, Huygens and De Wilde, when there was a letter
from William to be delivered to Keppel.* William was oblivious of these
jealousies, and impervious to the malicious gossip that his evident
affection for the young man excited. He was beginning to find Keppel
much more entertaining than Portland, always so serious and increasingly these days preoccupied by affairs of state. And he missed the young
man now very much, paying several calls to the sickroom to see how his
leg was mending.

The hours at leisure at Het Loo were, however, already numbered.
Everyone in England was daily expecting news of the King's return
when in mid-March Louis XIV with an army of 100,000 commanded by
Marshal Boufflers appeared at the gates of Mons, the most important
fortress in the south of the Spanish Netherlands. As usual, he caught the
Allies off guard. When William rushed to the army rendezvous at Halle,
south of Brussels, he found 50,000 soldiers assembled, but not a sign of
the 1000 transport promised by the Spanish, and he had to look on
helplessly while Mons capitulated. Louis XIV returned in glory to
Versailles while William, furious with his Spanish allies, took himself
off to England at last. A squadron of Dutch men-of-war escorted him
across the North Sea, and he reached London to the sound of "the firing
of cannon from the ships and round the Tower".*

Mary was delighted to see how well he looked. His absence this time
had been shorter, and her·responsibilities less overwhelming than the
previous summer. She had been cheered at first by the news from The
Hague, and proud of the figure her husband made there. "To let the
world see the difference I made between that journey and those wherein
his person was exposed", she wrote in her memoirs, "I went once or
twice to the play, I played every night at Comet or Basset . . ."* On her
sister Anne's birthday on 6 February, she played cards publicly with

Anne and Prince George at their apartments in the Cockpit, and afterwards gave a dance for them in her own drawing-room at Whitehall.* She paid visits: on 14 March she went to Chelsea College, "that stately fabrick which will . . . contain above 400 old and decrepit soldiers", and even when there were alarming new rumours of a French landing on the coast, she went bravely out to dine with the country's political leaders.* She did not enjoy it, irritated by "a generall peevishness and sylliness in them all".

The brief flush of William's popularity had already waned, Mary realized sadly. "I heard dayly . . . [that] the King and I were less loved, that we had many enemies and no friends . . ."*

She had longed to see him in England again at the end of the Congress, believing that "when he came back all would be well", and when the news came that he had gone to the army, "I looked on my case as the most deplorable in the world."* News of the fall of Mons swiftly followed and the spirit of the English Jacobites was revived by this humiliating blow. They came into the open again, boasting and intriging, and venturing out to their old meeting-place in Hyde Park. One of them Sir John Fenwick, even dared to insult the Queen publicly. While she was driving in the Park one afternoon, he ostentatiously stepped up to her carriage and instead of uncovering and bowing like any other gentleman, he stared directly and rudely at her and swept off his hat in her face. All the Queen could do was order the park-keepers not to admit him again.*

The only real support and sympathy the Queen felt at this time came from Romney. Before William left for Holland he had called him back from Ireland and given him the Secretaryship of State which Shrewsbury's resignation had left vacant. His nomination surprised everybody, and William admitted to Caermarthen that it was a makeshift: "he will do till I find a fit man." But he knew that if Romney was the least able of the ministers he was leaving behind, he was the most trustworthy, and a man on whom Mary could rely while her friend and ally "lord Nott" was with him in Holland.

NEWS THAT THE KING was at last on his way back home reached Mary just before Easter, but the pleasures of anticipation were spoiled for her by "a very sad accident". On 9 April, at eight o'clock in the evening, fire broke out at Whitehall, "occasioned, (as said) by the carelessness of a maid in burning of a candel from a bunch of candels, and leaving the other lighted". The fire blazed till four in the morning, destroying the greatest part of the Stone Gallery down to the waterside, and the apartments of the Duchess of Portsmouth and "other lodgings of such lewd creatures". In a desperate attempt to stop the fire spreading, several buildings were blown up in its path, including the lodgings of Portland who lost jewels in it valued at £6000.* Mary herself was "hartily frightened" – everybody thought at once of the Jacobite threats to her life.*

The King took the news of the Whitehall fire calmly on his return: he had never cared for living there, and had much too much on his mind to worry about it now. His stay in England was brief, hardly more than a flying visit, and its principal purpose was to form a stable new government before he took himself off to the Continent again for the summer campaign. His days were crowded with business, and with Romney at his side he dined with all the country's political leaders – Dorset, Shrewsbury, Marlborough and Godolphin. On the twenty-fifth he went out of his way to dine with his wife's uncle, the Earl of Rochester, one of the leaders of the still-hostile High Church party, in the hope of drawing him into his Ministry. He failed, as he also failed with the influential Whig Lord Sutherland.

Before he left again for Holland, he had to deal with a fresh conspiracy that had come to light in his absence. The chief of the plotters was Lord Preston, whom he personally examined in the presence of Lord Caermarthen. Preston's confession was alarming in its scope: he named among his Jacobite associates not merely those whose loyalty was already suspect, such as Clarendon, James's Admiral Dartmouth, Penn the Quaker and five of those bishops who had always refused to recognize William. He implicated also the prominent Whig Leaders Dorset and Devonshire, the Duke of Ormonde, and about a hundred M.P.s, most of them Whigs. The Tory Caermarthen was delighted, but William, sickened, stopped the hearing: "My Lord, there is too much of this", he said. He was realist enough to know that he could never count on the wholehearted loyalty of his English subjects, and he not only forgave Preston, but released most of the other conspirators, including Clarendon.

On 15 May, at about five in the morning, he left Kensington together with the Queen, who accompanied him as far as Ingatestone in Essex, and at nine the next morning he sailed from Harwich with a fair wind for Holland.*

"The return and the departure of the King followed so quickly upon the other, that it only seems a dream that he was here", Mary wrote afterwards to the Electress Sophia. She had seen little of him in London, and even during her last few hours with him, in the coach going to

Ingatestone, necessary "business" left little time for personal talk. She saw him go "with all the trouble and concern which can be felt in my circumstances".* And back in Kensington she wrote in her journal, *"Oh mon âme! je ne dois point souffrir que cette melancolie gagne tant sur moi . . ."**

For the first time for more than a century a King of England left his country to command an army in a war, and the English nobles, who unlike the French and German aristocracy were not used to battles, followed William eagerly to Flanders. Narcissus Luttrell noted that on 24 May "the Duke of Ormond, Earl of Essex, Marquesse of Winchester, Lord Villiers, Lord Hide, Lord Grey of Rolston, Earl of Drumlanrig, Earl of Scarborough, with other persons of quality, embarqu'd."* And going on campaign with the King's army suddenly became a fashion among "the gentlemen who combed their flowing wigs and exchanged their richly perfumed snuffs at the St. James's coffeehouses".*

Perhaps fortunately for them, no important battle took place that summer of 1691. The two armies circled each other warily, but Luxembourg declined to attack. In July the great Louvois died in Paris and was replaced by the twenty-three-year-old Barbesieux. The heart went out of the French war effort for that year and at the end of August William decided to leave the battlefield.

Everybody in England waited impatiently for him, assuming that he would now return. Instead, the King took two months off to go hunting at Loo with Portland and Romney, thus establishing the pattern of many years to come. Nottingham, who had stayed behind in London, tried as tactfully as possible to remind the King of his duty, writing to Romney: "I do not know whether I should wish you as much pleasure there [at Loo] as I had, least you should be tempted to stay too long",* but William did not take the hint. He stayed hunting happily at Loo, apart from occasional visits to The Hague for state business, while Romney repeatedly promised Nottingham that the King's "next remove will be into England".*

It was at Loo that the King received the news of the surrender of Limerick, the last Jacobite stronghold in Ireland.* For more than fifteen months the Irish had been defending this town against superior English forces under Van Ginckel, and it was only after Tyrconnel had died of a stroke and Sarsfield had taken over the command, that negotiations had started. On 13 October a treaty was signed, giving those Irish troops who wished leave to go to France, while the Roman Catholics were promised freedom to exercise their religion as under Charles II.

The surrender of Limerick, following Louis's loss of interest in

Ireland, was considered by the Jacobites the greatest error the French could have made. The Irish war, they thought, was the "best medium in the world for destroying the confederacy abroad, by reason that the confederal armies could not prolong the foraign warr without the arms and money of England, which were imployed in the warr of Ireland."* William, delighted by the victory, possibly shared their view: Van Ginckel was rewarded with the title of Duke of Limerick and Baron of Aughrim.

At last the King returned to England, where he landed at Margate on 19 October o.s. His coaches were, however, in Harwich where they had been waiting since the fifth, and he was obliged to hire one, in which he drove off with Portland and Marlborough. Near Gravesend, at Shooter's Hill, an accident happened. The coach suddenly overturned and Portland and Marlborough were thrown on top of the King. All three were slightly hurt – William wrenched his shoulder and Marlborough was concussed. He thought at first that his neck was broken, but the King reassured him that this could not be true "as he still could speak".* Without any further incidents the party arrived at eleven in the evening.

Rumours that the King was on his way had travelled faster, and the streets were filled with cheering people in their nightwear. Mary waited for him at Whitehall and William, jumping out of the coach, ran upstairs to her room, crying: "Where is the Queen?" Under the astonished eyes of the courtiers he kissed her twice, and they left immediately to sup together privately at Kensington.*

For Mary it had been a weary summer. Ever since the King's departure, she had been harassed by continual rumours of plots against herself and him, and some of the evidence suggested that her own sister Anne was a party to them. Under the strain her nerves gave way for the first time, plunging her into a state of morbid gloom. "I confess my weackeness was so great, that I was heartily troubled and frighted, but I kept it to my self", she noted in her journal. "I loockt over all my meditations, and burnt many of them fearing they might fall into hands I did not like. The journals I had kept, I put in a bag and tyed by my side resolving if any thing happened to have them ready to burn."

She had fled back to Whitehall to feel safer in its crowds, and as the hot summer wore on, worry and unhappiness made her ill again. In addition to these emotional strains, there were, as always, practical problems to deal with. The treasury was almost empty, the High Church party who had been antagonized by William's Calvinistic ways were showing signs of growing disloyalty, the English fleet under Russell achieved nothing against the elusive French and was almost destroyed by heavy storms, and the Tower of London, filled with prisoners, just escaped being blown to smithereens when a floor collapsed under the weight of hundreds of barrels of gunpowder.*

Worse disaster threatened at another moment. The four-year-old Duke of Gloucester, Anne's only child, fell seriously ill. It was Radcliffe who saved the boy, and the Queen was so grateful that she presented him with 1000 guineas.*

One other meditation, written that summer, reveals how completely she had lost her zest for life: "I do not know what will happen to me, but, life being so uncertain, I prepare myself for death. I bless God that the only thing which makes death uneasy to me is that some might suffer for it." She put this meditation among the journals she kept always with her, and added a note for the King: "I beg him to burn this and my other papers, and to preserve a tenderness for my memory, as for someone who has always been entirely his."*

William's return revived her almost miraculously, and her spirits were recovered enough to allow her to play hostess on William's forty-first birthday and their fourteenth wedding anniversary. It was one of the most brilliant and extravagant celebrations Whitehall had seen for years. "The court was all in their splendour, the Queen very rich in jewells . . . dined publicly", reported Luttrell.*

William himself was particularly nice to her, trying to make amends for the fact that in this year 1691 he had so far spent only three weeks with her in England, and Mary noted gratefully in her memoirs: "I must not forget to observe how kind the King is, how much more of his company I have had since he came home this time, than I used to have."*

The rumoured rift in the marriage had obviously been healed.

CHAPTER XXXII

The Sisters

"I FOUND MYSELF IN great order at Kensington, so that I thought I had done with the worckmen there", wrote Mary in the autumn of 1691. The weather was beautiful too, unusually mild and springlike for November; and looking at "the convenience of my house and the neatness of my furniture I thought myself as happy as one in my circumstances could be."* But the year was unlucky to the end, and after all the accidents and misfortunes of the summer, fire now destroyed part of another Royal palace. Whitehall was still in ashes when on 1 November Kensington Palace blazed.

At three in the morning the Earl of Essex burst into the King's bedroom to warn him that the Stone Gallery to the south of the courtyard was on fire. William and Mary hastily flung on nightrobes, and went to see what was happening. The fire, which had begun in an empty room next to the porter's lodge, had not gained much ground, but lack of water or powder hindered the fire-fighters, and Portland sent off to Whitehall for help. It only arrived three hours later, and by that time the whole of the newly-built south wing, with its offices and apartments for Court officials, had been severely damaged. "I was in the garden, where I saw their Majesties in deshabille, with about a dozen people", wrote one eye-witness. Nobody seemed to be taking the fire very seriously, except some "ladies in their chemises, who fled from fear where there was no danger", which made William and Mary laugh heartily.

The King had gone first to his Cabinet to reassure himself that his paintings were in safety, and found that they had already been carried out into the garden, together with Mary's porcelain. Everybody in the Household had rescued something and William walked around "to see the bundles which each one had packed up. He found among them provisions of Dutch cheese, bottles and bread, as if they had been going to stand a siege. That amused him very much."*

The fire was extinguished by eight o'clock, and when Huygens came to Kensington in the afternoon, he found that the King's apartments, from which all the hangings and furniture had been taken away to safety, were already looking perfectly normal again. The doors of his own office had been broken open, and a bundle of the King's papers had disappeared after being thrown out of the window in the panic. They turned up that same day in the house of a local Madam.*

Mary bore it all stoically: "This has truly, I hope," she wrote piously, "weaned me from the vanities I was most fond of, that is ease and good lodgings."* But, in fact, neither the King's nor her own apartments had been touched, and Wren was soon at work on plans for a new gallery.

While Mary devoted herself once more to her private meditations and the running of the Royal Household, William took over from her the burden of domestic politics which he found so little to his taste. He had opened Parliament on 22 October, asking them to vote supplies for an army of 65,000 men. The mood of this Parliament at its first meeting was fairly subdued after Ginckel's victory at Limerick, but in his speech from the Throne the King omitted the customary thanks for past generosity, and many M.P.s did not forgive him easily. They staged a concerted attack on the army estimates, arguing that England had no need for such an enormous army, and William sighed in a letter to Heinsius: "They are strange people one has to work with here."*

Like all Coalition governments, the King's ministry was under increasing attack from both sides of the House. But thanks to Caermarthen's brilliant management – he distributed pensions and offices freely to malcontents – the session at least gave the King almost all he asked for.

New Year 1692 was ushered in with the usual compliments of the nobility, and a great ball on Twelfth Night at Kensington, where the dancing went on till after one in the morning.* The King left his own party for a while for his traditional visit to the Groom Porter's gambling session, where he lost 200 guineas before his luck changed and he won back £100. Next evening the Queen went with the Queen-Dowager to hear Dryden's opera, while the King found more down-to-earth entertainment for himself. He went incognito to the House of Lords where the most sensational lawsuit of the century had just opened. The Duke of Norfolk was suing a man called Germain for £50,000 damages for enticing the Duchess away. He had already had twenty-eight witnesses sworn, and the whole of London was following the scandalous revelations with fascination. The day the King attended, he heard two witnesses swearing "that they saw Germain between a pair of sheets with the dutchesse . . ." (The case dragged on till the following November, when the jury awarded the Duke only token damages of 100 marks.)*

It was in this month of February that the King signed an order which was to blacken his reputation in England more than any other action of his reign. Since 1689 the Highland Clans of Scotland, almost all of them Jacobites, had been openly rebellious, but although William's two Scottish secretaries – the Earl of Melville in Edinburgh and Sir John Dalrymple in London – constantly recommended a policy of severity towards those lawless "cattle-thieves", William and Mary were anxious to reduce the Highlanders "by gentle methods to a submission". They had sent John Campbell, the Earl of Breadalbane, on a pacification mission to the chieftains in the summer, and in August 1691 the King had signed a general indemnity for those Highlanders who swore allegiance by 1 January 1692.*

Almost all the Highland chieftains took the oath by 31 December, and only MacIan, the Chief of the MacDonalds of Glencoe, came too late: arriving at Fort William to swear, he was sent on forty miles through the wintry mountains to Inveraray where – on 6 January – he finally took the oath. The certificate of his oath was forwarded to Edinburgh, where it mysteriously disappeared, and Dalrymple, who hated the Highlanders, learned with delight that the most notorious of the Highland robbers had technically failed to sign before the appointed date. On 16 January Dalrymple obtained William's signature to orders that those chieftains who had not taken the oath should be proceeded against, adding that "if MacIan of Glencoe, and that tribe, can be well separated from the rest, it will be a proper vindication of the public justice to extirpate that set of thieves." Dalrymple sent it to Edinburgh with a note that the MacDonalds were to be "rooted out in Earnest", and early in February the Campbells of Glenlyon – MacDonalds' most bitter enemies – arrived with a hundred men in Glencoe. For a week they enjoyed the traditional Highland hospitality of the MacDonalds, and then, at dead of night, rose and massacred their hosts in cold blood, men, women and children. Hardly any of the MacDonalds escaped.*

If William had known that his order was to be carried out in such an outrageous manner, he might well have refused to sign. But in all probability he did not enquire too closely into the fate of those remote Scotsmen. "The truth is", remarked Macaulay, "that the King understood Continental politics thoroughly and gave his whole mind to them. To English business he attended less, and to Scotch business least of all."* He found Scottish problems both incomprehensible and boring: months went by before he could be got to look at papers about Scottish affairs, and plans to go and visit Edinburgh were constantly put off. On this occasion, however, he certainly read the order: he signed it both above and below, unaware that MacIan had already submitted.

It was weeks before the full details of the massacre were known in Edinburgh, and months before news of it reached London. Mary was appalled by the news, but William seems to have learned it with a shrug of indifference, leaving it for the moment at that.

William's health that cold snowy winter was worse than usual. Mary was concerned about "the ill condition of health he was in" and desperately worried when he spat blood for a night and a day.* The ambassador of the Duke of Savoy, Monsieur de la Tour, who saw him at this time, described him to his master as "of medium height, very much stooped, always oppressed with a looseness of the chest, and of such a weak constitution that his life only seems to hang by a thread . . ."* For the King, and he was the one who best knew it, there was only one cure – to get away from London and English politics as soon as possible. A week after the Parliamentary session ended on 24 February, he was off.

The King set out at his usual early hour, four o'clock in the morning. Mary went part of the way with him, then travelled sadly back to Kensington alone in the afternoon. She had hoped that this year, for once, he might take her with him and she had even spoken to the King about accompanying him.* But in the circumstances it was impossible, and she resigned herself unhappily to another lonely spring and summer. To the Electress Sophia she wrote: "I am sure that my letters are always melancholy. The King is no sooner returned than there is only talk of his going away again, so that there is scarcely time to get over a horrid summer before one is dreading a sad spring . . ."*

This year she was to be lonelier than ever: in January, the breach between her and Princess Anne had become final.

Since Mary's first arrival in England relations between the two sisters, who had greeted each other with such "great appearance of kindness", had soon cooled. Temperamentally the two women had never had much in common, and they had grown further apart over the years. As the Duchess of Marlborough wrote with bitchy accuracy: "It was indeed impossible they should be very agreeable companions to each other, because Queen Mary grew weary of anybody who would not talk a great deal, and the Princess was so silent that she rarely spoke more than was necessary to answer a question . . ."*

The ambitious Sarah Marlborough capitalized on this difference, and egged on the passive Anne to assert her rights. The first collision came

in 1689 when Anne decided that her lodgings at the Cockpit were not
large and splendid enough. She asked for the sumptuous apartments of
the Duchess of Portsmouth in Whitehall, which the King gave her, but
when she also asked for the adjoining apartments for her servants, there
was a difficulty. They had been promised to Devonshire, the head of the
Royal Household. Sarah prompted Anne's furious answer, "that she
would then stay where she was, for she would not have my lord Devonshire's leavings". She stayed in the Cockpit, but used the Portsmouth
apartments as well, for the little Duke of Gloucester.

The next quarrel – in the same year – was over the question of
Anne's allowance. Sarah persuaded Anne that this ought to be settled
by Parliament, rather than left to William's generosity, and the matter
was raised in the House of Commons by Marlborough's friends without
either William or Mary being informed of it.* They were both deeply
insulted. "When I heard this," wrote Mary, "I thought it no longer time
to be silent, but upon her coming to me next night I spoke to her. She
could tell me no one thing in which the King had not been kind to her,
and would not own herself in the wrong for not speacking to either of
us, so that I found as I told her she had shewed as much want of kindness
to me as respect to the King and I both."*

"Pray what friends have you but the King and me?" Mary had asked
when Anne muttered that it was her friends' doing. They parted coolly,
and coming home, Anne found Sarah ready to convince her how deeply
she had been injured. "It was unjust in her sister not to allow her a
decent provision without an entire dependence on the King", said
Sarah warmly, and Anne, completely under her influence, agreed.
William was irritated by what he regarded as a women's quarrel. He sent
Shrewsbury to sort it out with Marlborough, who begged to be left out
of it – "his wife would by no means hear of it, but was like a mad
woman" – and the Secretary of State reluctantly called on Sarah herself.
He was instructed by the King to promise Anne £50,000 a year if her
friends would keep this family quarrel out of Parliament, but Sarah
refused insolently and in the end had her way. Out of a Civil List of
£600,000, Anne got her £50,000.*

Perhaps Anne's most burning grievance against William, however,
was the way he treated her husband, Prince George. If Anne and Mary
had little in common, their husbands had nothing at all, and William
never bothered to conceal his contempt for the man of whom it was
later said: "He is very fat, loves news, his bottle and the Queen [Anne],
. . . he hath neither friends nor enemies."* When William, much against
his will, took George in 1690 to Ireland with him, the Prince was never

asked to ride in his coach or join him at table, an affront that Anne, who was deeply devoted to her husband, never forgave.

There was worse to come in 1691. When the King left for Flanders with all his English nobles, George asked to go with him and was refused. He offered then to go to sea as a simple volunteer, but although William gave a non-committal answer, he told Mary to prevent him at all costs. Mary tried persuasion first, and had to ask Nottingham to intervene when this failed. George, who had already sent on his luggage had to have it brought back.*

There were many such incidents to feed Anne's resentment, and Sarah, hoping to strengthen her own and her husband's position, exploited them cleverly. When the Dutch guards at Whitehall once failed to salute Prince George it was no doubt Sarah who suggested that the omission was deliberate. "I cant believe it was their Dutch breeding alone . . ." wrote Anne furiously.*

By 1692 Anne found it impossible to think of submitting to William any longer. "Can you believe we will truckle to [him] who from the first moment of his coming has used us at that Rate as we are sensible he had done?" she wrote to Sarah,* and in this mood of revulsion, she made the gesture of a penitent letter to her father James. She was, she told him, "very desirous of some safe opportunity to make . . . a sincere and humble offer of my duty and submission . . .' and she ended: "If wishes could recall what is past, I had long since redeemed my fault."*

This letter was almost certainly written at the instigation of Sarah and her husband. The Earl of Marlborough was a bitterly disappointed man. Since the Revolution, one chance after another of high command had slipped past him, and William had only employed him once, in Ireland. He had brilliantly distinguished himself, and William had remarked "I know no man who has served so few campaigns, equally fit for command." But it had been Van Ginckel who was appointed to wind up the Irish wars, and when William named his commanders for Flanders, Marlborough was not among them. Frustrated, he decided at least to make his peace with St. Germain, and according to Jacobite sources, he got a message to James in which he wrote of "his sincere repentance . . . his crime appearing so horrid to him that he could neither eat nor sleep". He gave an account of the English military preparations, and told James that he was ready to abandon wife, children and country for his sake.* If it occurred to James that Marlborough might be merely hedging his bet, the letter from Anne to her father was, "considering the great power my Lord and Lady Churchill had with her", seen as "a more than ordinary mark of that Lord's sincerity in what he professed".*

Marlborough's disloyalty to William became public in England, when at the end of 1691 he moved an address in the House of Lords that the King should dismiss all foreigners from his and the Queen's service. James was ready to believe that this was the first step to bring him back and wrote later: "If the Prince of Orange had accepted this proposition, they would have had them in their power. If he refused it, the whole of Parliament would have declared against him; at the same time, milord Churchill would declare himself with the army for the Parliament, and the Fleet would have done the same; and I should have been called back."*

James certainly over-estimated the powers of Marlborough who only succeeded in stirring up a fresh wave of anti-Dutch feeling. William, who disliked Marlborough, had a shrewd idea what he was up to, telling Burnet that he had "very good reason to believe that he had made his peace with King James".* He called the Earl a "vile man", adding that "though he had himself profited by his treason, he abhorred the traitor".*

That the King was so well informed was mainly thanks to the Villiers family. One of them, Lady Fitzharding, was in Anne's service and she kept her sister Betty well informed. Betty who, like all the Villiers, hated the Churchills, in her turn "carefully related to William all the gossip to Marlborough's detriment".* Portland was another informer and when on 10 January the crisis came and Marlborough was dismissed, Sarah was convinced that, as she wrote in her memoirs, "this event might perhaps be well enough accounted for by saying that Lord Portland had ever a great prejudice to my Lord Marlborough, and that . . . Mrs. Villiers, though I had never done her any injury, except not making court to her, was my implacable enemy."*

For the English public, Marlborough's dismissal was a sensation, and William, who seldom chose to offer an explanation for his actions, gave no reasons for it. He merely told one M.P. that "the Earl had treated him in such a manner that he would have asked him for satisfaction with the sword if he had not been King."*

On the evening before Marlborough's dismissal, Mary had another painful confrontation with her sister Anne, who was then again pregnant, taxing her with complicity in the correspondence with St. Germain. Anne hotly denied it, and Mary was at first inclined to believe her, especially when Anne dismissed Sarah from her post as Groom of the Stole on 24 January.* But when a few days later Princess Anne attended the Queen's drawing-room, she caused a sensation at Court by bringing

Sarah with her. Mary, though very much upset by Anne's public discourtesy in bringing the wife of a disgraced officer to Court, said nothing at the time, but it soon leaked out that she had written almost immediately afterwards to insist that Anne should part with Lady Marlborough, * "since that gives her husband so just a pretence of being where he ought not". The tone of her letter was sharp: "I have all the reason imaginable to look upon your bringing her as the strangest thing that ever was done." She concluded pleasingly: "I have all the real kindness imaginable for you . . . I do love you as a sister . . . it shall never be my fault if we do not live kindly together."*

Next day was Anne's birthday, and she wrote a defiant refusal to part with her favourite: "A command from you to part with her must be the greatest mortification in the world to me." She asked her uncle Rochester to plead her case to the Queen, but Mary refused to listen. And Anne wrote again on the eighth to declare her resolve: if it was a question of choosing between a breach with her sister, or parting with Sarah, she would choose the first. She announced her intention of retiring to Sion House, taking Sarah with her.

For Anne, life without her fiery, domineering friend was no longer imaginable. Sarah had entered her life when Anne was seven years old, just a year after the death of her mother Anne Hyde. This playmate, five years older than herself, supplied all that was missing in the life of the plain, dull little Princess – affection, drama and attention – and Anne, for whom "friendships were flames of extravagant passion" fell completely under her spell. The girls grew up together and the spell grew stronger. Even Anne's marriage to Prince George did not diminish the influence of her favourite "Mrs. Freeman", so much more domineering than Anne's placid husband. The Princess treated Sarah, who was her Lady of the Bedchamber, as a complete equal, and begged her to be treated likewise, "which she thought belonged to friendship".

Anne's immediate removal to Sion House, taking Sarah with her, made the breach between the two sisters public. William himself made a last bid to make Anne see reason, and sent the Dukes of Ormonde and Somerset with a peremptory message to dismiss Sarah. "But the answer we hear not" wrote Luttrell. It had been no. The same day the Princess had her son, the young Duke of Gloucester, who was still staying with the Queen at Kensington, brought back to her at Sion House.*

Prince George did his best to keep up a show of normal relations between the two royal Households. He attended the House of Lords as usual, and came to kiss the King's hand on 3 March, the day before William left for Flanders. His personal guards had already been removed

at the King's order, and when he arrived at Kensington "'twas observed
the guards took no notice of him when he went into the court". When
he left, however, they sprang to their arms, "and beat their drums as
formerly". Two weeks later he attended a Privy Council meeting at
Whitehall, and afterwards led Mary back to her apartments where he
dined with her.*

But nothing he did could bridge the widening gulf between the two
women, or heal the sense of grievance they both felt. When in April
Anne was in labour she sent word to Mary with a message that she was
having a particularly bad time. The child died almost immediately, and
only then did Mary, who had been very ill and confined to bed herself,
appear at her sister's bedside. She asked her if she was still determined to
keep Sarah with her, but Anne refused to answer and she left soon after –
Mary could be as obstinate as her sister. A few days later Anne sent the
Bishop of Worcester with a request that she be allowed to visit the Queen
– without having parted with Sarah. Mary's reply was icy: "Don't give
yourself any unnecessary trouble . . . you know what I required of you.
And I now tell you, if you doubted it before, that I cannot change my
mind but expect to be complied with."*

Anne at once sent this letter off to Sarah, urging her spitefully to
spread the news – "sure never anybody was used so by a sister!"*

The Queen's displeasure went further than mere words. Anne's
guards were taken from her, and at Mary's orders no public honours were
paid to her. The minister of St. James's church, where Anne worshipped,
was ordered not to lay the day's text on her cushion and Mary forbade
her own Household to call on the Princess, making it known that anyone
who did so risked her displeasure. During a visit of the Prince and Princess to Bath that summer, the Secretary of State forbade the Mayor to
pay her any of the respect or honours normally shown to members of the
Royal family.* Efforts made to heal the breach were in vain. "Both had
engaged themselves", wrote Burnet "before they had well reflected on
the consequences of such a breach."*

Amazingly enough Mary's popularity in England did not suffer, and
when Marlborough was arrested on 1 May, it became clear where public
sympathies lay. "The Princess had very little following", noted the
Imperial ambassador soon afterwards, "and what little credit she had,
she has lost . . ."*

Not surprisingly, rumours circulated that Anne wanted to leave the
country. "We hear", reported Luttrell on 3 May, "the Prince of Denmark has asked leave of the queen in councill to goe for Denmark with
his princesse for 2 or 3 years; and that the lord President told his high-

nesse he believed the queen would return no answer till the King was acquainted therewith."*

It is unlikely that Anne should have wanted to leave Sarah while Marlborough was in the Tower, and her letters of this time say just the opposite. "If she should ever be so cruel to leave her faithfull Mrs. Morley, she will rob her of the joy of her life."*

Marlborough's stay in the Tower was brief. He had been accused of high treason, but his accuser was soon exposed as an impostor, and on 15 June Marlborough was released on bail of £6000. Halifax and Shrewsbury went bail for him, which displeased Mary so much that she struck their names off the list of Privy Councillors.

Three years of life as Queen had turned Mary from a gentle and diffident young girl into a woman capable of formidable firmness. "When I saw that no kindness would worck upon her", she wrote about her sister, "it made me change quite and grow (at least endeavour to grow) as indifferent as she is."*

In the autumn of that year the Prince and Princess of Denmark came back to London, and driving through Kensington, "the queen in her coach followed the same way and past by them and no notice taken on either side."* The two sisters never spoke to each other again.

CHAPTER XXXIII

Father and Daughter

"THE MORE I SEE OF THIS KING, the more excuses I find for the Prince of Orange, and the more admirable I think he is."* So observed Liselotte, the indefatigable letter-writing Madame of Versailles, to her aunt Sophia in 1691. "This King" was of course James, who since his precipitate flight from Ireland had become an object of general pity and derision at Versailles. Louis XIV had refused even to see him at first, and James's growing saintliness in adversity soon became a bore and a mark against him. "He lives always surrounded by friars and talks of his misfortunes with indifference", wrote a contemporary, "in this way he entirely lost the respect of the French."* But the cynics even had their doubts about his moral reform – it was well known, gossiped Liselotte, that there had been "two frightful old hags with whom he was always having it off" to entertain him in Dublin.*

Chances of any further French help in the reconquest of his kingdom seemed remote, especially since Louvois was violently opposed to the idea; and only after the death of this minister in 1691 did the future for James begin to look a little brighter. When he dutifully sent his condolences to Louis XIV on Louvois's death, the French King assured him that "his affairs and theirs would not fare any the worse for it", and Louvois's successor, his son the Marquis de Barbesieux, believed that a descent on England was feasible. He accepted at face value the Jacobite accounts of a discontented England ready to rise and cast off William and Mary; and through the winter that followed, James and the French worked hard at preparations for an invasion. By the New Year of 1692, 20,000 men were gathered together in a camp at La Hogue, on the Cherbourg peninsula, and in April James himself arrived at the camp with a contingent of Irish soldiers commanded by Sarsfield.

Details of these preparations were soon known in England, starting another invasion scare and putting fresh heart into the Jacobites – especially since William had left the country taking most of the army with him. But James now made another of his tactical blunders. He published a Declaration which made it clear that once restored, he would continue to behave precisely as before, and listing hundreds of people on whom his revenge would fall. Mary, with great presence of mind, promptly published the Declaration, with the Government's comments on it. The effect was so disastrous to the Jacobite cause that some of them hastily drafted another, much milder and more gracious, Declaration, which they said was the genuine one; but as Luttrell reported, "few give any credit to it but that party and some look on it as designed to amuse the people."*

Despite this propaganda victory, the possibility that the invasion might be successful could certainly not be ruled out. Mary had little confidence in Russell, now in sole command of the fleet, and she and her Cabinet Council were greatly alarmed by rumours of disaffection among the naval officers. Mary rose to the occasion: through Nottingham she sent a message to be read to all the officers, in which she dismissed the rumours of their disloyalty as foul slanders, and expressed her complete confidence in her navy.

It had the effect she hoped: the officers enthusiastically signed an address assuring her of their resolve to fight the French, and Russell himself, whose loyalties sometimes wavered back to James, swore to a Jacobite agent that if he met the French fleet he would fight, even though the King himself was on board.*

Preparations on shore were not neglected. Some regiments that had been about to sail for Flanders to follow William were stopped at the ports, and along the south coast the militia was assembled and armed, Papists were ordered to leave London and Jacobite suspects were rounded up. Among those arrested were a group of officers accused of a plot for "seizing the Queen's person immediately on King James's landing, who was . . . to be placed immediately on the throne".* Mary had lived in great fear when she heard about the plot and confessed in her journal: "I was told of dreadfull designs against me, and had reason to believe if their success answered their expectations, my life was certainly at an end."*

But she put her usual brave face on it, and even ventured out. On 10 May "the 6 regiments of the train'd band of the City marched of Hide Park," reported Luttrell, "where the Queen was pleased to take a view of them and complimented the Lord Mayor at the head of his regiment . . ."* In the whole of England there were now eight regiments of horse, two of dragoons and twelve of foot.*

The sight of them gave Mary fresh heart; better still, Portland arrived

from Flanders bringing William's promise to return himself if the worst
came to the worst.*

His presence was not needed. The French had had endless difficulties
in assembling and equipping their fleet, thanks to badly organized preparations on shore, and these delays lost them the sea battle before it
even took place. By 13 May the Dutch fleet under Lt-Admiral Van
Almonde – until then unable to sail because of contrary winds* – had
successfully rendezvoused with the English fleet at Spithead, and four
days later the combined Anglo-Dutch fleet, eighty-eight ships strong,
sailed for the French coast. On the morning of 19 May they encountered
the French fleet commanded by Tourville, who was still waiting for the
Mediterranean squadron to come up and had only forty-four ships
under him.

Despite these appalling odds, Tourville gave the signal to attack at
nine in the morning, hoping to divide the two fleets as in 1690, and his
own flagship, the *Soleil Royal*, opened the battle by engaging Russell's
flagship the *Britannia*.

The battle raged till four in the afternoon, when a dense sea-mist
halted the fighting. Everything had been against the French, including
the wind, and they were ready for flight as soon as the mist lifted.
Most of their ships were seriously damaged, and Tourville could only
give the order *Sauve qui peut*. Some of the French ships escaped to the
west; three of them including the *Soleil Royal* took refuge in Cherbourg, where they were destroyed by English fire-ships, and thirteen
of them reached the bay of La Hogue. The French defeat was complete
when three days later, the English fleet entered the bay and destroyed
the thirteen ships under the eyes of James, Tourville and other French
officers watching from the cliff. James did nothing to endear himself to
his allies by exclaiming in a passion of patriotic pride *"Ah mes bons
Anglais!"*

Even James realized now that the defeat of La Hogue must be a
final blow to his hopes, and he wrote to Louis XIV: "My unlucky star
has made its influence felt over the arms of Your Majesty, always
victorious until they battled for me. I beg you not to take any more
interest in a prince so unhappy . . ."*

The French King was ready to take him at his word. The defeat at
La Hogue was a blow to French dreams of naval supremacy, and the
destruction of the *Soleil Royal* especially he felt as a personal affront. This
ship with its 110 guns had been the pride of the French navy. It had
cost the French King £200,000 to build, it was magnificently decorated,
and – as they gleefully related in London – the commander's cabin was

dominated by a painting representing the French King with "several European Kings and princes in chains under his feet".*

The news of the defeat had reached Louis at Namur, which his armies were besieging, and William learned it on his way to relieve this stronghold. "The good God be thanked and praised" he wrote to Heinsius, "and may he grant that the enemy's fleet has been destroyed for ever."* The Dutch shared their Stadholder's joy and minted a medal to commemorate the victory, showing on one side the withered French lilies and a motto, *Non semper lilia florent.**

In London the bells rang all day long and the Queen ordered £30,000 to be distributed to all the seamen in the fleet and gold medals for those officers who had particularly distinguished themselves.* She now expected, like everyone in England, that the Anglo-Dutch fleet would make the long-planned descent on the defenceless coast of France. Immediately after the victory the ships had been refitted, and there were 14,000 troops at Portsmouth under the command of the Duke of Leinster ready to be embarked and landed in France. The attacks were to be aimed at the key French naval bases of St. Malo, Brest, or Rochefort, with the intention of deflecting the Franch war effort from Flanders.

Unluckily there was no general agreement in London about how exactly this plan should be carried out, and the instructions issued by the Queen and the Cabinet Council were in any case ignored by Russell, in charge of operations. In a stream of elaborate explanations about contrary winds and tides he justified his inaction, and when he heard of the strong resentment at his hesitation, he threatened to resign: "If they knew how litell I desired the honour they woud not fear I woud troubel them much longer in this station." He went on: "What can I doe . . . burne some foolish towne on the coast? I can see nothing else . . ."* Nottingham was horrified – "barely to burn a French Tingmouth is too mean a project for such a fleet"* – and on 6 June the Queen ordered Russell to hunt down and destroy the thirty French warships sheltering in St. Malo.

Russell did nothing of the kind: he found the enterprise too risky, and in the end the French ships succeeded in slipping out and escaping to Brest. After hanging about at Portsmouth all summer, the landing forces were finally embarked on 26 July and joined the fleet, but even now the landing at St. Malo was not attempted. Mary was desperate for action and did everything she could to encourage her vexatious commander. She tried tact – "[She] will only tell you that she thinks nothing so desirable and so much for the publick interest as a battle at sea" – and she tried irony – "If you can so contrive it as that it may be had without too great a hazard to the fleet . . . in respect of wind and weather"* – but it was all to no avail and she was continually exasperated by "Mr. Russell's strange letters", in which as she said "he seemed dissatisfied and did nothing but talck of retiring".*

The Cabinet Council eventually resolved that they should all go down to Portsmouth in a body to sort out the situation on the spot. "Their journey signified nothing" commented Mary: the Whig commander paid no attention to this group of Tory land-men, and in the end he won his point, and the whole idea of a landing was shelved. The Queen, who had displayed an astonishing energy and decisiveness all summer, was beside herself with angry frustration: "all the expence was thrown away, the troops came back as they went, having made us ridiculous to all the world by our great preparations to no purpose."*

In the midst of these trials, Mary was alarmed by news of yet another plot against William's life – but this time there was a sinister difference: her father was almost certainly directly involved. " 'Tis impossible for me to express what I then felt. I was ashamed to loock any body in the face", she wrote. "I fancied I should be pointed at as the daughter of one who was capable of such things, and the people would believe I might by nature have as ill inclinations."*

The plot was originally the brainchild of Louvois, and after his death Barbesieux, who suspected that his father's sudden death was the work of Orange agents, saw in it a possibility to combine personal revenge with a blow to the Allied cause. He engaged a young French officer called Grandval, who was to make his way to Allied headquarters in Flanders and shoot the King while he was making the rounds of his troops. He had two accomplices, a Catholic Dutch ex-officer, Leefdael, and a Walloon adventurer, Dumont. They were all to meet in Brabant, and Grandval, before he left Paris, paid a visit to St. Germain where he was presented to James. "I have been informed", said James, "of the business. If you and your companions do me this service, you shall never want."*

Dumont and Leefdael, however, had both betrayed Grandval, who was arrested as soon as he reached Flanders and court-martialled. William gave two orders: that he should not be racked when they questioned him, and that he should be silenced if he mentioned Louis XIV – a proof, as the Venetian ambassador remarked, of his greatness of soul.* Grandval made a free and full confession at his court-martial, revealing that James had given his approval to the scheme, and was executed soon afterwards.

The Cabinet – especially the Whigs – urged Mary to publish the details of his sensational trial in order to discredit the Jacobite cause, but

Mary shrank from doing so – "it was a hard thing . . . for me to publish my own shame." Her greatest fear during this whole affair was that it might alter William's feelings towards her, but his letters – frequent this summer – continued to be as kind as ever. "The pleasure of having a letter from the King this morning . . . had perfectly taken away all cloud from the Queen's face . . ." wrote the Countess of Rutland to her husband at this time,* and Mary herself wrote with relief: "he was so kind as not to take it ill of me or not to love me less for that my great and endless misfortune".*

Alienated from her father and her sister, separated from many of her dearest friends, Mary had now only her husband on whom she could depend emotionally, and the fact that she had never been able to give him the children they both longed for was a perpetual grief to her, although she never completely abandoned hope. Sitting in her little cabinet at Kensington once, while William was away in Flanders, she was reading the New Testament when she came to the passage in St. Luke's Gospel where Zachariah learns that his wife Elizabeth is to bear a child after years of barrenness. It was too painful a reminder of her own condition, and she poured her misery out on paper while she struggled to persuade herself that it was God's will. "Why are you so perturbed, o my soul, do you not know that the Lord does what He wishes in heaven and on earth . . . since it is not his will to bless you with a child, you must submit . . . I know that the Lord can still give me one, or even several, if he thinks fit; while I wait for it, I must have patience."*

William's presence could keep at bay these melancholy moods – "all my fears and troubles vanish by the King's return"* – but each time he went abroad the parting seemed harder to bear, and her melancholy harder to resist. Increasingly she was haunted by the feeling that everything that went wrong, like the quarrel with Anne, was God's punishment for the "irregularity" of the Revolution and she could only pray: "I trust the Church and nation shall not suffer, but that we in our private concerns and persons may bear the punishment . . ."* Even the failure of the attempted landing in France seemed to her "a just punishment upon . . . that too great desire I had, that some great thing should be done".*

But if Mary's religion sometimes made her a prey to guilt, it was still her greatest comfort and her only support. A deeply devout woman, she was never happier than when she could escape to the privacy of her study to read, write or meditate. She observed Sundays punctiliously, going to church three times a day and taking Communion once a month. "I know what loose people think of those who pretend to religion", she remarked once, "they think it all hypocrisie." But she was unaffected by the ridicule that her devotion excited in fashionable circles. "Let them think what they will . . . I thank God I can say it, I have not affected to appear what I was not."*

Religion was for Mary more than a private matter. She thought it her duty as Queen not merely to set an example but to do as much as possible for the church and for public standards of behaviour. William, preoccupied with more mundane problems, was happy to leave those questions more and more in her hands, which, as Burnet stated, "she managed with strict and religious prudence . . ."*

She always made careful enquiries into the private lives of candidates for ecclesiastical preferment and she was not easily fooled. During Romney's brief Lord Lieutenancy of Ireland, he once wrote to Mary recommending the son of some old family friend to a vacant see, and singing the man's praises. Mary at first agreed, but she had no great faith in Romney's moral standards and when she heard that his nominee had a bad reputation, she wrote sharply back to Romney refusing to confirm the appointment until he had forwarded references for the man in question from the six Irish bishops she named.*

Not all her appointments were approved by the King: her choice of his old enemy, her former chaplain Dr. Hooper, for the vacant Deanery of Canterbury in 1691, vexed William greatly. It was said that she was "chid by the King . . . and that it cost her some tears . . ."* But William confirmed the appointment all the same, and when the Archbishopric of Canterbury also fell vacant, it was another great friend of Mary's who was appointed by William, the excellent and pious Dr. Tillotson. The Cathedral of Canterbury afterwards enjoyed her special interest. Staying in the city once with William, she noticed that the altar furnishings looked threadbare, and quietly sent down workmen and materials to make new ones on the spot: a bill among her personal accounts for this kind gift, including the travelling expenses of the workmen, came to £106 12s 10d.*

No Queen of England, it might have been thought, could have done more to earn the respect of that Church whose titular head she now was, and to whose interests she was so devoted. But it was Mary's tragedy to be rejected to the end by some of the holiest and most esteemed Anglican leaders. Of the seven bishops who had been imprisoned in the Tower for their protest against her father's romanizing policy, only one, Bishop Lloyd of St. Asaph, took the oath to William and Mary after the Revolution. And Bishop Ken, Mary's former chaplain, considered a saint by many of the English, wrote sternly in 1692 to a woman he considered a great sinner: "I doe not give you the title of Majesty, not daring to doe it, because I thinke it justly belongs to none but to your royal father . . ."*

Mary's care for the souls of her subjects was not confined to England. After the Battle of the Boyne, she wrote to William to beg him not to forget the desperate need for schools and proper religious education in Ireland; and the William and Mary College in Virginia, founded to provide education for the settlers in the American plantations, was entirely her idea and her work.*

Mary had been horrified by the low moral tone of London society when she returned in 1689, and had determined that something must be done about it. In William's absence she issued Royal Proclamations for the more reverent observation of the Sabbath, and against swearing and profanity. She sent directives to magistrates throughout the country to use particular severity when dealing with drunks, and she had circular letters urging the general reform of manners read from pulpits everywhere. For a time the new Puritanism became almost fashionable: "Divers persons of quality entered into the Society for Reformation of Manners . . ." noted Evelyn.* And William himself did his best to give his wife's campaign a helping hand, issuing joint proclamations with her against "vitious, debauched and prophane persons", and personally ticking off a young man who swore in his hearing – the Court, he said piously to those around him, must set a good example.*

The Queen's campaign reached a crescendo in the summer of 1692, reflecting her own morbid preoccupation with the sins of the nation. "There came forth at this time several puritanical regulations for observing the sabbath in London . . . One was, that hackney coaches should not drive upon that day; by another, constables were ordered to take away pies and puddings from anybody they met carrying them in the streets; with a multitude of other impertinences . . ."*

Eventually the whole campaign for the reform of manners collapsed in ridicule, and even Mary began to feel that the hopeless task had better be abandoned for the time being: "seeing a violent Opposition, she thought that the putting her whole strength to it, might be reserved with great advantage to another time".*

CHAPTER XXXIV

Years of Struggle

THE YEAR OF 1691 HAD ESTABLISHED a pattern for the Royal Household in England. Every spring the King would leave London to confront Louis XIV and his generals in Flanders, while the Queen took over the responsibilities of government at home. In the autumn the King returned to face the other great struggle of his life – with the English politicians in Westminster. There were times when victory seemed hopeless on either front, and the only solace he enjoyed was his short hunting holidays with his friends at Het Loo.

It was a solace he badly needed after the campaigns of both 1692 and 1693. In the first of these years Louis XIV conquered the important fortress of Namur on the Meuse in May, celebrating it with a solemn Te Deum in Paris and his own maddeningly accurate boast: "My enemies had persuaded themselves . . . they should stop the current of my conquests; nevertheless I fail'd not to undertake, in Person, the Siege of the City and Castle of Namur; the taking of which they thought impossible . . ."* A month later the French army cut to pieces the English and Scottish battalions in William's army, a bloody battle which left 6000 dead on the fields of Steenkerk. While England angrily mourned her dead, France commemorated victory by a new fashion – the Steenkerk cravat, as carefully disarranged as possible.*

The one Allied initiative of 1692 – an attempt to root out the French privateers' raiding-base at Dunkirk – was a costly fiasco. It was altogether a dismal summer, made more so by the rains that teemed down day after day, and its end was suitably marked by an earthquake, at the beginning of September.* It happened while William was sitting at dinner in his camp in Flanders. His table shook, spilling wine out of the glasses, and several bricks came crashing down around him. An attack on the King's life was at once suspected, and people rushed to his house shouting "*Sauve le Roi!*" In the tumult the King was thrown to the ground, but it was all over in minutes.*

This freak earthquake was felt all over England and Europe, and it was excitedly reported that hounds in Enfield Chase lost the scent in full cry, and that in Middelburg in Zeeland "the streets quavered like the waves of the sea".* Most people simply thought they had had a sudden giddy spell.

The autumn that followed was exceptionally cold and dreary, with a bitter north-east wind blowing for days, and William, who had been suffering from bad headaches the whole summer, found even hunting a doubtful pleasure at Het Loo.* Disappointed, he was about to cut his holiday short and return to England when the French played him a last trick. They suddenly swooped on Charleroi, another of the great Meuse fortresses, and he had to hurry back to rejoin his army in Flanders.* The French attack was beaten off, but when they tried again a year later they succeeded.

The conquest of Charleroi in October 1693, which left the French solidly established along the Meuse, was the climax of another campaign disastrous to the Allies. At its outset William had written dismally to Heinsius from Flanders that "The enemy's superiority in numbers is incredible".* He had nevertheless foiled a French attempt to conquer Liège, the gateway to the Republic – Louis who had come in person departed furiously for Versailles, never to return to the battlefield – but had been beaten at the one major confrontation of the summer at Neerwinden. While the French suffered heavy casualties, the Allied armies were completely broken and fled. William himself had fought with more than his usual courage, taking off his heavy cuirass and narrowly escaping death three times when bullets whizzed through his peruke "which deafened him for a time", his sleeve and the knot of his scarf.* But the French under Luxembourg were too numerous for him, and bitterly William exclaimed: "Will it ever be possible to beat that nasty hunchback?" a remark that gave Luxembourg occasion for his famous retort: "Hunchback? How does he know that? He has never seen me from behind."*

It seemed there was no stopping France. In Catalonia the French armies inflicted a crushing defeat on the Duke of Savoy at Massaglia, while on the Rhine they overran and devastated the Palatinate, razing the beautiful city of Heidelberg to the ground.

In the United Provinces this succession of Allied disasters and defeats provoked bitter criticism. A leading Regent, Simon van Halewijn, the son-in-law of De Witt, had even started peace talks with the French on his own initiative. He was arrested for high treason and thrown into Loevestein prison, but his passionate words at his trial summed up the feelings of many Dutchmen: "He would rather be dead than look on any longer at our people being made to sacrifice their money and their blood in order to play the assiduous servants to the King of England . . ."*

The English themselves, up to their necks in European affairs for the first time in decades, reacted by occasional outbursts of frenzied chauvinism of which the Dutch were the principal targets. In the autumn of 1692, following the slaughter of Steenkerk, there were bitter attacks on William's Dutch commanders in both Houses, with the Whigs under the resentful Marlborough taking the lead. William was accused of giving the English troops in Flanders all the dirty work to do, and a pamphlet published that year described in vivid detail how the English soldiers were victimised – "hated in Flanders, abused at all rates by the Dutch, exposed upon all accounts as Forlorns".* In the following autumn of 1693 a Private Member's Bill for the naturalization of foreign Protestants, brought in by a Whig M.P., was the signal for another storm. It had been intended for the benefit of refugees from religious persecution, principally the Huguenots, but every opponent in the House of Dutch influence at Court at once pounced on it, declaring that it was obviously designed for the benefit of the Dutch who would come over in swarms to grab all the best jobs. "Already one of the most noisome of the plagues of Egypt was among us. Frogs had made their appearance even in the royal chambers. Nobody could go to St. James's without being disgusted by hearing the reptiles of the Batavian marshes croaking all round him . . ." So runs Macaulay's account of one of the more violent of the speeches, delivered by Sir John Knight, M.P. for Bristol. He ended his tirade with the appeal: "Let us first kick the Bill out of the House; and then let us kick the foreigners out of the kingdom." Even for the House of Commons, this was going too far, and Sir John was forced to apologize and the bill was quietly dropped.*

William, galling though he found these attacks, could afford to take them in his stride. At least politically, the situation was now much easier. The previous Parliamentary session of the winter of 1692–3 had seen ill-feeling between Whigs and Tories come to such a height, that, as Mary wrote in her journal, "it gives a very dismal prospect, and will make one almost despair of ever seeing matters accommodated."* The conflict between Russell and Nottingham had reached a climax that autumn, and was fought out as a party issue so violently in Parliament that it left hardly any time for other business. Finally, in despair, William overcame his personal prejudice and at the suggestion of Sunderland, James's old minister now making a discreet comeback as William's political adviser, began wooing the leaders of the strong Whig party.

Before he left for Flanders in the spring of 1693, he appointed the Whig Sir John Somers as Lord Keeper, and gave the vacant Secretaryship of State to another Whig, Sir John Trenchard. The staunch Tory Nottingham was shattered by these appointments, rightly guessing that they portended his own downfall, and in the autumn he resigned in disgust when the King, as a further gesture to the Whigs, reinstated the popular Whig Admiral Russell.

Thanks to this new understanding between William and the Whigs, the parliamentary session that opened in 1693 passed off almost tranquilly, and in December the increased army estimates were not only passed without a murmur, but with a huge majority.*

Early in 1694, William celebrated his conversion to the Whigs by making it known that he would withdraw his opposition to the Triennial Bill. This Whig measure enacted that Parliament must be called by the King at least once every three years, and that it should not have a life longer than three years. The Bill had been introduced in Parliament the previous year and passed both Houses, but William, who saw it then as an attack on a Royal prerogative, had for once exercised his royal veto. The Triennial Bill was, however, almost a matter of principle to the Whig party, and it was William's refusal to consider it that had alienated Shrewsbury, the one Whig he really trusted. William now desperately wanted him back in office, and he hoped that by climbing down on the Triennial issue, the reluctant Shrewsbury might be induced to accept the vacant Secretaryship of State.

At the same time he began to make approaches to Shrewsbury through more personal channels, using Betty Villiers – as far as is known for the first time – as his political go-between. Betty first wrote to Shrewsbury herself. "I am not vain enough, my Lord, to hope any reason I can give could change you . . . but . . . why should you show so much weakness where the nation is concerned?" she coaxed, hoping to persuade him to come to Kensington and see the King. Shrewsbury hesitated and Betty tried another tack.

A friend of hers, a Mrs. Lundee, was a close friend and perhaps the mistress of the politician. Betty worked on her till she agreed to go and deliver a carefully rehearsed exhortation at Shrewsbury's home, and Mrs. Lundee agreed, but made the mistake of announcing her mission in advance. Shrewsbury, who had a nervous dread of scenes, at once fled to the safety of his country home in the Cotswolds, pursued by Betty's reproofs: "Flying from hearing is a proof to me that you are in the wrong." After William had threatened his grave displeasure if she failed, she returned to the attack with another coaxing letter in which she painted a pathetic picture of William's need for his services. "I cannot think you can refuse him . . ." But even this letter and the personal appeal of its bearer, Mrs. Lundee, had no immediate effect. Neither did the persuasive appeal of a colleague, Thomas Wharton: "His Majesty . . . is more convinced every day that it is for his interest and that of the public to pursue such measures in the management of his affairs as he knows will be agreeable to you . . ."

Shrewsbury remained evasive, and Betty acknowledged defeat and withdrew, pursued by his consoling words: "When you, Madam, have failed, you may conclude the thing is impossible."* It was not so impossible as she believed. Possibly Shrewsbury was simply reluctant to be talked back into office by the King's mistress. At any rate he reappeared in London almost as soon as she stopped bullying him, and on 3 March Luttrell recorded: "His Majesty has been pleased to make the Earl of Shrewsbury Secretary of State . . . and yesterday morning had the seals of office delivered him."*

Five days later the King celebrated Shrewsbury's return to office by dining with him, the Earl of Bedford and the Earl of Devonshire. All three received Dukedoms a few weeks later. The next day he set out for Winchester with Shrewsbury and a triumphant Sunderland for company.*

Betty's intervention in the Shrewsbury affair was a rare departure from the obscurity to which this intelligent and forceful woman appears to have resigned herself. Many people were still unaware of her existence, and of those who knew, most of them doubted whether the liaison was still a physical one. If she was his mistress, it was certainly the most detached and coolly discreet relationship imaginable.

About another of his close attachments William never made the smallest effort to be discreet; and when the long and loving friendship of years with Portland showed signs of strain in the autumn of 1693, the fact was at once apparent to everybody in the King's entourage. The Wooden Man, they said triumphantly, was on his way out. One incident they related with relish had occurred when the King was at dinner with the Queen. Portland was standing behind him, leaning against the door, and someone tried to open it from the other side. The Queen noticed and remarked, "Look, someone is pushing my lord Portland." The King gave an irritable shrug: "Well, what is he doing, standing there like that? He never has any idea of the respect that is due to me."*

The fact was that this old friend's bluntness, which the King had once found so refreshing, was beginning to get on his nerves, like his ponderous manner, and more and more Portland found himself the butt of William's bad temper. Courtiers who had always been jealous of his monopoly of William listened delighted when the King, out hunting one day, failed to find and began to abuse Portland, who was responsible for the Royal parks, in the most violent terms.*

Keppel's rapid rise in the King's favour was not lost on Portland, who was bitterly resentful: "Portland and Keppel agreed as well together as fire and water" remarked Huygens in February 1693.* William, who was genuinely anxious not to upset his loved but irritating friend, did his best to soothe his ruffled feelings, sending him touching little notes after angry scenes between them: "I never was more shattered in all my life than I was yesterday. I hope that you are now completely convinced that it would be impossible to love you more than I do . . ."* And when Portland, convalescing from an illness, was left behind in England at the beginning of the 1693 campaign, William made a special visit to his friend's estates at Sorghvliet so that he could report reassuringly to their owner, "I have found everything in good order."*

But when Portland finally arrived in Flanders in May, he was very much upset to discover how indispensable to the King Keppel had clearly become, travelling in the King's carriage and constantly at headquarters with him. Nor was Portland much better pleased when the King's "third favourite", Romney, was summoned over from England to become Lieutenant-General of the English armies in place of Solms, killed at the Battle of Neerwinden. Portland, like everybody else, could never understand William's attachment to this agreeable but incompetent drunk, who had had to be hurriedly recalled from Ireland only a few months after being appointed Lord Lieutenant and Governor because there were such loud complaints of his administration.* Keppel and Romney, together with other agreeable courtiers like Ossory's son, the young Duke of Ormonde, and the Earl of Essex, made up a particularly merry party at Het Loo that autumn, while Portland, hurt and jealous, felt there was no longer a place for him. It was clear to him that his long reign was over.

Mary was always impatient for the end of these traditional hunting holidays at Het Loo. Every time when she received news of his landing at Margate or Harwich, she set out to meet him on the road. Usually they spent the night at Ingatestone, then travelled back together through London to Kensington House. The welcome they received from the London crowds who turned out to cheer them was always a comforting reminder of their solid popularity with the common people – however much politicians and nobles might hold themselves aloof – and this enthusiasm was not even diminished by military defeat. In 1692 – the disastrous year of Steenkerk – every window had been lit up in the City as they drove through, and the cheering crowds who escorted them to Kensington smashed those windows whose owners had been so foolish as not to illuminate them.*

William's return meant a delightful release for Mary from the strains of administration. "Being freed from care and business . . . I immediately gave my self to my own ease and carelessness . . . believing it very unnecessary for me to medle or trouble my head, when the King was here . . ."* There was time for agreeable outings: a few days after their return in October 1692 she wrote: "I've made some little trips to show him [William] the building at Hampton Court, he went down to Windsor to hunt, and I to keep him company, we have been to My lord Mayors show . . . where there was a huge crowd." There was even time for entertaining: apologizing to a friend at the beginning of November for not writing sooner, she explained, "the ball for the King's birthday ought not to be my excuse because I dont dance any more, but all the same its a day when there isnt a minute free for writing . . ."*

Their reunion on 30 October 1693 at Ingatestone brought her no such content. Both of them were tired, edgy and strained after a difficult summer, and Mary afterwards described it with a shudder as "the year I have met with more troubles as to publick matters than any other".* William's usual kindness and praise for her handling of state affairs in his absence was not forthcoming this time: on the contrary. "This year he disapproved allmost everything", she wrote in distress.*

Her months of administration had got off to a bad start. Mary shared to the full her husband's – and her father's – conviction that the Tories were the natural allies of the Crown, just as the Whigs were its natural opponents, and she was horrified when William, just before his departure for Flanders, had taken two of the hated Whigs, Sir John Somers and Sir John Trenchard, into his Ministry. She understood very well that the Tory Nottingham – "the only one who really toock the most gratest pains" to serve the King, in Mary's view – was on his way out, and Mary, who trusted him more than any other politician she had worked with, was indignant. "When I saw one who had served him longest and most faithfully so discouraged that he was ready to leave him . . . it was impossible not to be extremely melancholy and discouraged."*

The two new Whig members of her Cabinet Council, outnumbered by the Tories, were well aware of her sympathies; and the atmosphere at Council meetings was strained and tense as a result. "I found the Council more than ever divided" recalled Mary, "the old ones not mightely satisfied with the new comers, and they believing me to much inclined to t'other party, in a great coldness and strangeness to me . . ."*

She had encountered friction and opposition in her Council before, and was resigned to it, but this year she found herself, as well, at the centre of a public storm. In June 1693 the great Smyrna Convoy of Dutch and English merchant ships, loaded with valuable cargoes from the Levant, was successfully attacked by the French, suffering losses reckoned at over £1 million. The news touched off endless painful recriminations within the Cabinet itself, and in the country at large it "so inraged all kinds of People, that it is not to be expressed".*

The disaster was inexcusable, obviously the result of thoroughly bad management, "caused by the ill intelligence among those who were in bussiness, no orders being obeyed, no faults punished, every one glad to lay the blame on another", recorded Mary whose own anger was made plain at Council meetings.* When a deputation of City merchants came to represent their huge losses in the disaster, and their sense of grievance, Mary commanded Somers to promise them, in her name, that a Committee of the Privy Council would be immediately appointed to enquire into the whole business. And it was some balm to her shattered nerves when the Lord Mayor hurried to the Palace to assure her of the City's continuing loyalty.*

But more than ever this year, she had found the burden of government almost intolerable. The Electress Sophia had written urging her not to neglect her health, and Mary took her advice, escaping more often than usual from Whitehall, sometimes to Hampton Court to see how the new buildings and the gardens were coming on. Sometimes she walked all the way from Whitehall to Kensington – it was about the same distance as the House in the Woods was from The Hague. "I have walked more this summer than I had in three before", she reported to the Electress in the autumn, "tho at my first endevoring to do as formerly, I so heated my blood that I had an iresipilis upon an arm . . ."*

This had happened during a weekend visit to Hampton Court during that wet summer, in mid-June: "having got cold, [she] was indisposed on Sunday; and the symptoms of St. Antony's fire appearing, she was let blood, and is since perfectly recovered", recorded Luttrell.* But Mary's recovery was not as complete as the public believed, and early in July she retired to Kensington for a long spa-water cure, glad to forget for a while the general despondency and the acrimonies of party warfare.*

She longed very much for an end to the interminable war which took William away for months at a time every year, and in the winter of

1693–4 they both followed with intense interest the informal peace talks secretly taking place at Maastricht between the King's personal envoy Dijkvelt, and various French agents. The French seemed genuinely eager for an end to hostilities. The Allied blockade of the French Baltic trade with Sweden, Hamburg and Denmark was beginning to bite, and disastrous harvests for three years in a row had brought famine to many parts of France. People were starving to death in Paris, it was reported to London and The Hague,* and everybody read with interest Fénelon's burning accusations of Louis XIV: "Your people are dying of hunger, all France is no more than a great ravaged hospital, devastated and without supplies."*

Hopes of peace rose. William himself who knew his old enemies well enough to warn the Imperial envoy against optimism – "even going on as they do now, the French can hold out longer than we can"* – had allowed himself to indulge in a little post-war planning. Early in March 1693 when he travelled down to Winchester with his new Whig friends, he had inspected the palace at Winchester that Charles II had started to build in 1683.* It had been planned on a monumental scale by Christopher Wren as the finest palace in England, built in rosy Hampshire brick with stone dressings and three cupolas, looking towards the sea. The carcase of the building was already completed and roofed in when Charles died, and William was very much taken with its "incomparable prospect", and the broad avenue sweeping up to it from the Cathedral.* Quite as fond as Louis XIV of planning architectural splendours, he was intrigued by the idea of completing the first great modern palace to be built in England in decades, and during the winter months of 1693–4 he discussed the plans carefully with Sir Christopher Wren, whom he had taken to Winchester with him. The plans could only remain dreams as long as the wars continued: Hampton Court and Kensington were still undergoing costly alterations, and Whitehall was being restored at further expense – the Queen's "tarras walk" there, completed in the summer, alone cost £10,000.*

Meanwhile the French at the talks at Maastricht proved as stubborn as ever. They refused point-blank to give up the strongholds of Luxembourg and Strasbourg, and they insisted that William and Mary should declare the Prince of Wales as their successor if they died without children, in which case he would be sent to England to be brought up as Protestant. In exchange, Louis would quietly pension off James. Dijkvelt argued that the question of succession could not possibly be a matter for negotiation with a foreign power – events in Spain were soon to prove him wrong – and demanded French recognition of William. The French immediately countered that this could not be dealt with in a treaty any more than succession matters, and on these rocks of disagreement the talks foundered.*

In April 1694 it was already clear that the argument would have to be continued on the ravaged plains of Flanders. William had delayed his departure as long as possible this year, setting out only on 25 April after winding up the Parliamentary session. Among Acts which received his assent was the historic Act which established the Bank of England, proposed by another Whig addition to his Ministry, Charles Montagu. It freed William from then on from the problem of finding credit for his wars, since one of its statutes laid down that it should at any time lend the State £1,200,000 on a credit of eight per cent.* But for once, this year, William had no financial worries: Parliament had voted him supplies of £5,000,000 for the war, the largest sum ever.

Bad winds delayed his departure, keeping him commuting for days between London and Gravesend or Harwich in the hope of a favourable wind. Mary was delighted – for the first time in years, William was with her for her birthday on 30 April – her thirty-second – which they celebrated in great simplicity. And when he finally decided to go to Margate on 4 May and wait for the wind there, she went with him, taking lodgings in a small house. She very much enjoyed this unexpected little holiday with her husband, and was in the best of moods: when Huygens walked past their house, she leaned out of the window laughing, and teased him that all these delays to the King's journey were entirely his fault.*

At last on Sunday they said goodbye to each other; "he embarked for Holland, and the wind being fair was quickly out of sight." By Monday night she was back in London, and settled into Whitehall once more.*

The summer that followed was marked in June by yet another abortive English naval raid, this time on the French base of Brest. The English landed 400 troops under General Talmash, expecting no opposition whatever – and found 10,000 foot and 4000 horse waiting to greet them in fortifications specially laid out by Vauban. They were thrown back into the sea with heavy losses, the promising Talmash afterwards dying of wounds received. But the Allies pulled off a major coup at sea later: when an Anglo-Dutch fleet commanded by Russell appeared in the Mediterranean, the French abandoned Barcelona, only just occupied by them, in a hurry. It was the first fruit of a decision taken by William – Russell and the English fleet were to remain in the Mediterranean all winter – that was to revolutionize England's naval role for the future.

In Flanders too, the Allies were at least successful in holding the

French at bay, and they retook Huy. In the circumstances the States-General were in an acquiescent mood, although they grumbled about being "a province subservient to the English King" when news of William's secret peace initiative at Maastricht leaked out.* When he appeared before them in early November they thanked him warmly for his care of the State, and a few weeks later cheerfully voted the army estimates for 1695 that he had laid before them. Heinsius, as usual, had managed them brilliantly, and William wrote gratefully to acknowledge his debt: "it is a great blessing to God for your Honour that everything is going so well and speedily under your administration."*

In London too his House of Commons, where he now enjoyed the support of the Whigs, seemed almost too co-operative to be true. "I have opened Parliament yesterday," he wrote to Heinsius on 13 November, "and as far as I can see, affairs here are much better than I expected." William was particularly struck by a total change in their attitude to peace, "which they no longer wish but fear, thinking that our affairs have improved so much that we should not conclude a peace except on certain and advantageous conditions".*

For the first time in years, he looked forward to a quiet and relaxed winter.

CHAPTER XXXV

The Death of Mary

THAT AUTUMN OF 1694 the Queen was badly in need of a long rest. The responsibilities of state and the unpleasant bickerings of politicians had worn her out, and emotionally, too, she was an exhausted woman. The long separations from her husband and her fears for his life and health while he was away were a constant torture for her. "You will certainly pity me when the King goes away", she had written to a Dutch friend in April, two days before William left her, "and believe me, it's the only thing in the world one never gets used to . . ."*

She had been ill that spring with a feverish chill and this young woman of thirty-two wrote sadly: "I believe that I am becoming old and infirmities come with age, or with the chagrin or the inquietude which one has so regularly all the summer."* After William left, she took up her responsibilities with less enthusiasm than ever, perhaps disheartened by William's criticisms of her efforts the last year, and she attended only a few meetings of the Cabinet Council, relieved to know that Shrewsbury was back. For the first time, the diarists of that time record almost no public appearances, none of the play-going or musical evenings on the Thames of other years, or dinners in public at Whitehall. Most of the time she spent in semi-retirement, and for two weeks she shut herself up completely. "For a fortnighte together I was not able to do anything," she wrote to the Electress Sophia on 13 July, "I knew that too armys very neer . . . which kept me in perpetual expectation of a thousand fears of wat might have hapened."*

She was run down and she knew it. In May, on the advice of her doctors, she went on a long course of asses' milk which, according to her personal accounts, cost her £21 12s.* It was the fashionable tonic of the day. Her personal accounts reveal a more normal feminine cure for low spirits: plenty of new clothes. Her enormous dress bills are revealing. She might have been gloomy and melancholy at times, but she was at heart a cheerful woman, with a feminine love for the glitter of a silver ribbon, the gleam of a pretty little satin slipper, the flash of a golden girdle. She bought hundreds of yards of ribbon, was extravagant with gloves – she had a standing order for two dozen white pairs a month – and bought patches and painted fans as was expected of a lady of fashion. From one shoemaker alone she ordered seven pairs regularly every month, spending £68 10*s* on them in the first half of 1694, and her lingerie was luxurious: black embroidered stays stitched with silver, nightgowns or negligées made of quilted scarlet or red and white striped silk. She liked to mix her colours, but she had a preference for blue, olive green and "hair-coloured", or beige, trimming it with gold or silver lace. Her bill for accessories alone for the last nine months of 1694 came to £1321.*

She had a woman's love of jewellery too. On 7 September this year she went through her personal jewel-caskets, then wrote out a complete inventory of them in her own hand, starting with the necklace of fat pearls she was so often painted wearing, and that William had inherited from his grandmother Amalia. Her description of each item was short, and only once did she add a detail: "the ruby ring with which I have been crowned". This had been William's engagement present to her – "the first thing he ever did give me" she wrote on a piece of paper in which the ring was later found wrapped up. At her Coronation, she had had a bigger stone put in it, and by accident it was confused with William's coronation ring. That summer 1694 she considered it a very bad omen when the stone fell out during dinner and was lost, only to be replaced in October.

Another treasured possession was also a present from William: it was a huge beautifully cut rose-diamond pendant, hanging from a lovers' knot of small diamonds and half-circled with an enamel ribbon on which were the words, *"L'Amour en fait le lien"*. On the enamelled back were the interlaced initials W and M.

The most spectacular item in her inventory was the Little Sancy, one of the most famous diamonds in Europe: a faceted stone of thirty-seven carats, framed in gold. It had been for centuries a proud possession of the French Royal family, but in 1642 the ruined and exiled Marie de Medici sold it to William's grandfather Frederik Hendrik. William's mother Mary Stuart had pawned it to raise funds for her brother Charles II while he was banished from England. After his Restoration and her death in England in 1660, William, who was very much attached to this family jewel, begged his uncle Charles to help him retrieve it. His grandmother's secretary wrote on her behalf: "She begs you to let her know if there is no means of buying it back, because our little one never stops talking about it." He still had to wait a few years before he could buy it back himself.†

Among Mary's other jewels were rings of pearls, diamonds and emeralds, clips set with brilliants by her French Huguenot jeweller Richard Beauvoir – "Mr. Bevoir" – a black agate cross set with small diamonds, necklaces, bracelets, and numbers of jewelled buttons, a fashion of the times. Her favourite stone seems to have been the pearl, of which she possessed £13,000 worth. Her diamonds in 1694 had an estimated value of about £9000.*

In the rich silks and jewels in which William loved to see her dressed, Mary was an impressive figure, although she had lost some of her earlier good looks. "The Queen was perhaps a little on the heavy side," wrote a contemporary, "however, as she was very tall, this only gave a certain majesty to her figure."* Years of chocolate-drinking and lack of exercise had taken their toll, and though this kind observer called her features "regular", her face had become plump and double-chinned, she had a constant high colour, and her eyes were often red-rimmed and inflamed.

She had a great sense of humour – very evident in the excellent gossipy letters she wrote to her women friends when she had time – and she loved a good joke or an amusing piece of scandal. The Jacobites were far from thinking her a pious, devout young woman, and wrote accusingly of

> . . . *King James's Disobedient Daughter*
> *Who was addicted very much to Laughter*
> *And lived as if there was no world hereafter* . . .*

Clearly she was excellent company, and Burnet assures us that "whereas in most Courts, the Hours of strict Attendance are the heaviest parts of the Day, they were in Hers, the most Delightful of all others . . ."*

Mary loved going to the theatre and giving balls, though she no longer danced herself, and now and then she ventured on little shopping excursions and sightseeing trips as she had often done in Holland. Scandalized London once heard that she had visited a certain Mrs. Wise,

---

† The Little Sancy played an important role in the problems arising from William's will in 1702, and in the end it was given to his cousin King Friedrich I of Prussia, who had it set in the Royal Crown. Later it was removed, and set in a necklace worn by the Queens of Prussia. In an inventory in 1913, the Sancy was listed as the centrepiece of a necklace with thirty-two brilliants, in the possession of Emperor Wilhem II. After his abdication in 1918, he was allowed to keep it, but in 1945 it fell into the hands of Russians and disappeared from view.

"a famous woman for telling fortunes", who had refused to tell her anything "though to others she has . . . foretold that King James shall
come in again." Afterwards Mary had dined at Mrs. Granden's, a
lady of ill-repute. The King had rebuked her in public: "he heard she
had dined in a bawdy house." Mary replied with spirit that she had
done nothing that Mary Beatrice had not done, at which William asked
drily "if she meant to make her her example".

The little scene was followed by the whole Court: "more was said
on this occasion than ever was known before, but it was borne with all
the submission of a good wife . . ."* Mary was perfectly used to her
husband's cutting public manner, and saw no point in getting upset by
it, although members of her Household were often highly indignant at
"the insolent treatment she frequently received from him".*

The Jacobite satirists summed up their relationship: "A churle to his
wife, which she makes but a jest."* And Swift later, who had the
greatest admiration and friendship for Betty Villiers, while detesting
William, added a savage footnote to Burnet's remark about a perfect
union between Mary and William: "he proved a d—d husband for all
that."*

Swift never saw William and Mary together, however, as Burnet
did who spent a great deal of time with them, and who wrote that "There
was a Union of Their Thoughts, as well as of their Persons: and a con-
curring in the same Designs, as well as in the same Interests . . . He was
to Conquer Enemies, and She was to gain Friends . . . While he had
more business, and She more leisure, She prepared and suggested, what
He executed . . ."* And whatever anyone else thought of William as a
husband, Mary was deeply in love with him to the end of her life, writing
with feeling that year of 1694 to the Duchess of Hamilton whose husband
had just died: "I am really sorry . . . beleaveing the loss of a good husband
the dreadfullest thing that can happen in ye world . . ."*

William's health that summer, normally so good when he was on
campaign, had alarmed her. He had suffered from colds and from splitting
headaches, and he was hardly back in England when he caught a chill
which confined him to bed on 20 November. He took "the bitter
draught" – quinine – for it, and dieted on apples and milk.*

Mary was unable to nurse him, as she herself fell ill at the beginning
of December. Smallpox was raging through London that winter, and
for a moment everyone feared that the Queen might be suffering from
it – she had never had the disease.* It was a false alarm, and she was soon
up and about again. Then on 21 December she woke up feeling unwell.
She dosed herself and said nothing to anybody about it, even when she

noticed that a rash had broken out on her arms. That night, however, she locked herself up in her little study, and went through all her papers, burning some of them and putting others in order. She had done so twice before – when she left Holland, and again three years earlier, in 1691, when she expected the French invasion. Now her reasons for doing so were more serious: she seemed to be expecting death, and to be perfectly resigned to it.

Already in September, worn out by all the strains and emotions of the summer, she had spoken of her own feelings about death in a letter to a friend whose mother had just died. Mary called it a great loss for her children, then added with feeling: "It seems to me that she is happy to have been delivered by God from so much misery." She ended her letter – the last she is known to have written – with the significant words "I pray God to make us all ready [for death] as we ought to be."*

It was at this time that she made the inventory of her jewels, indicating in some cases how they were to be disposed of after her death,* and that autumn she listed her debts in detail, down to the smallest of them. In another paper, she calmly wrote directions for her own funeral.*

In other years, the autumn reunion with her husband and the prospect of several months of his company had helped her to recover her spirits. This time he had not only been in bad health ever since his return, but in the middle of December he had told her that he would soon be gone again. By 22 December it was public knowledge "His majestie has given directions for his equipage to be gott ready with all expedition, designing for Flanders sooner than any of the foregoing campaigns . . ."* For Mary, it was the final straw: she had lost her will to live.

When William went in state to Parliament on 22 December to give his assent to the Triennial Bill, he himself was slightly feverish. It was not for that reason, however, that he hurried back to Kensington instead of dining in Whitehall as was expected. It was already generally known that the Queen was ill again, and that smallpox was suspected.* The Londoners were deeply concerned, and those who were superstitious prepared for the worst when they heard that the eldest of the lions in the Tower, who had been there for twenty years, had suddenly sickened and died: exactly the same thing had happened at the death of Charles II.*

The doctors were sent for, and confirmed William's worst fears when he returned from Westminster. Smallpox, the disease that had killed both his parents, had now stricken his wife. Her calm astonished everybody – she had immediately given orders for all those in the Household who had never had the disease to be sent away for fear of infection. But William, who had himself survived smallpox, was so concerned that he had a bed put in her room, and, as it was related around town, "will not stir from her, but sees all things administered to her himself".* He could not disguise his terror, and when Burnet came anxiously to enquire after the Queen, William dragged him into the privacy of his closet and at once burst into tears. "He cried out", remembered Burnet later, "that there was no hope of the Queen, and that from being the happiest, he was now going to be the miserablest creature upon earth. He said, during the whole course of their marriage, he had never known one single fault in her."* The Scotsman was astonished to see how distressed this cold and undemonstrative man now was. To his friend the Prince de Vaudemont in Brussels, William expressed his feelings in even stronger terms. "You know what it is to have a good wife. If I were so unhappy as to lose mine, I should have to retire from this world."*

On Christmas Day, while in all the churches special prayers for her were said, her physicians were hopeful again. Mary felt better, the dreaded spots had disappeared and they thought it was measles after all. The King wrote in relief to Heinsius: "Thank God, she is much better and there is reason to hope that it will all turn out well."* That evening, however, when the doctors examined Mary again, their hopes faded completely. They diagnosed that the spots had not disappeared, on the contrary, they had sunk in too deeply, and after she had spent a bad night, the doctors attending her – there were now no fewer than nine of them – were in no doubt that it was smallpox "attended with St. Anthonie's fire, which caused some blew spots".

The distracted doctors prescribed every remedy they could think of for their important patient: she was bled, "scarifyed" with hot irons in her forehead, and "to prevent the effects of St. Anthony's fire . . . had diverse blisters made to keep it from her head".* In spite of all this and the draughts and potions prescribed for her, the doctors appeared to have had little confidence in their treatment and decided that she should be told to prepare for death. Tenison, the successor of Tillotson who had died in November, was entrusted with the task, but coming to the Queen's bedside, he found it unnecessary. She told him weakly: "I believe I shall now soon die, and I thank God I have from my youth learned a true doctrine that repentance is not to be put off to a deathbed."* She asked for the Collect of the Communion for the Sick –

"That when the soul shall leave the body it may be presented without stain before Thee" – to be repeated twice a day at her bed. "Everyone", she said, "needed to be reminded of death, and Princes as much as anyone."*

William, who did not leave her side for a moment and whose agony astonished everyone, broke down again and burst into tears. Mary in distress begged him to control himself and not to make her suffer the pangs of death twice, reminding him that he owed it to his country to take care of himself. He replied in tears that if God caused this blow to fall, everything would be over for him. "Breaking out into the most violent lamentations" and often fainting, he was finally persuaded to leave the room, and a camp-bed was put up for him in the anteroom, where he occasionally rested for a few minutes.

On the morning of the twenty-seventh, London's most famous physician, Dr. Radcliffe, was at last called to the dying woman. Surrounded by his nine colleagues, he examined her and told them bluntly that there was nothing he could do for her now: the torments to which they had submitted the Queen had been useless.*

Mary herself had had a fairly restful night but her husband's condition now alarmed everybody. He could not sleep, refused to eat, and "there is hardly any instance of so passionate a sorrow as the King has been overtaken with, which seemed excessive while life lasted . . ."*

That life was fading rapidly. About five in the morning, as it was soon known in London, her condition had suddenly changed for the worse, "in so much that her recovery is very much doubted".* She called for the Archbishop and received Communion again. She tried to pray but was too ill and whispered that others should do it for her, "seeing I am so little able to pray for myself".* She refused her medicine – "I have but a little time to live and I would spend it a better way"* – and had a last request to make of the Archbishop. The papers she had sorted out and preserved were in the small escritoire in her study, and she asked him to give it to the King after her death.*

Night came and growing weaker, she listened while the Archbishop read some of her favourite psalms. The clergyman had been standing at her bedside for most of two days now, and with a faint gesture she told him to sit down. Once or twice she tried to say something to William but had to give it up. "Even He who was more to her than all the World besides . . . could not now inspire Her with any desires of returning back to life",* and when he approached her in tears for a last time, she motioned him away.

An hour later, at quarter to one on the morning of Friday, 28

December, Mary died "after two or three small strugglings of Nature
without such agonies as are usual".* And to the waiting Londoners,
shivering in a snowbound city where all the coffee-houses and theatres
had been shut up, the news was carried by the tolling bells.* The reign
of William and Mary was over.

CHAPTER XXXVI

William's Grief

"IT IS IMPOSSIBLE" wrote Auersberg, the Imperial Envoy in London, to Vienna, "to describe the desolation which this death has caused to the whole nation . . . The love which everyone had for the Queen is indescribable." He added that "this sad occurrence has effaced the bad impression they had of the King, for they thought he only loved the Queen because she had helped him to the succession, but now people are quite undeceived about that . . ."*

The English were indeed beginning to wonder if they would not lose their King as well as their Queen. Immediately after Mary's death William had fainted, and Portland had had to carry him in his arms away from the deathbed. The cough so necessary to clear his lungs had stopped, and his condition alarmed everyone. "*On ne reconnoit plus le grand Guillaume à ses soupirs, à ses larmes, à son abattement*" wrote a Frenchman.*

For days afterwards he could only bear to see a few faithful friends, like Portland, Keppel and Shrewsbury, and kept breaking down while he talked to them. He found some relief in long talks with Archbishop Tenison about Mary and religion, telling him that "If I could believe any mortal man could be born without the contamination of sin, I would believe it of the Queen."* When the clergyman told him gently, "Sire, we must repent and mend our life", William replied with a touch of his usual asperity, "Ay sir, we must mend our life, I must mend my life and you must mend yours."*

It was noticed that he now went to prayers twice daily, and Burnet heard with satisfaction that he had "entered upon very solemn and serious resolutions of becoming in all things a true christian, and of breaking off all bad practices whatever . . ."*

Tenison had gone further than pious admonitions. One of the clergy in attendance on the sick Queen, Bishop Moor, revealed later that the Archbishop had taken his courage in both hands and brought up the subject of Betty Villiers, "with whom it was well known that William had been too familiar, and had given her great endowments". The Archbishop took the freedom "to represent to him the great wrong he had done to that excellent wife by his adultery with the Lady Villiers". According to Moor, William had taken it well and did not deny his crime, but faithfully promised the Archbishop he "would have no more to do with her".*

The Archbishop may have spoken on his own initiative, but it is possible that he had acted at Mary's suggestion. According to Burnet, Mary herself had left a letter for her husband among her other papers, in which "she had formerly wrote her mind in many particulars".* And a certain Lord Hardwick claimed to have seen a letter of hers "containing a strong but decent admonition to the King for some irregularity in his conduct". According to Hardwick, however, it was written in such general terms "that one can neither make out the fact nor the person alluded to".*

Whatever the letter contained, or however William interpreted it, one thing was certain: he kept his promise to Tenison and broke with his mistress, who was heard to remark one day that she "wondered she could never see that King after the Queen's death".*

The King's recovery was slow. He kept himself locked up in his room and when he was persuaded to go into the garden to get a little fresh air, he was so weak that Keppel had to carry him out.

He was spared the practical arrangements following the death of a Queen. A few hours after her death, her body was embalmed. Her heart was put in a small violet velvet-covered box and placed in an urn next to that of Charles II in the Henry the Seventh Chapel.* The Withdrawing Room had been hung in mourning, and on Saturday, 29 December the Queen's body was taken there while preparations were made for her lying-in-state. The same evening an order was published by the Earl Marshal of England requiring all persons to put themselves into deep mourning, and from 13 January, the Lords, the Councillors and all members of the Royal Household were ordered to have their coaches, carriages and chaises completely draped in black, any shiny ornaments on them painted black, and their servants put into black liveries.*

On the day of Mary's death both Houses of Parliament sat. Normally Parliament is dissolved by the death of a monarch, but England for the last six years had had a King and Queen who reigned jointly, and now all that was necessary to signify the change in power was to break the Great Seal of William and Mary and issue a new one, for William alone. Both sessions were brief and many of the men present were seen to have their handkerchiefs at their eyes.* The House of Lords and Commons alike sat for some time in silence, and then moved to present the King with an address of condolence, which was delivered next day. After expressing their grief at "the loss Your Majesty and the whole Kingdom do sustain, by the death of that Excellent princess . . ." they begged him "most humbly . . . that you would not indulge Your Grief, upon this sad Occasion, to the Prejudice of the Health of Your Royal Person; in whose Preservation, not only the Welfare of Your own Subjects, but of all Christendom is so nearly concerned."* The King broke down as he replied: "Gentlemen, I am very much obliged to you for the care you have of me and of the public good, and principally at this time but I can think of nothing else apart from the great loss we have just suffered."*

In the United Provinces, the death of the beloved wife of their Stadholder shattered everybody. " 'Tis impossible for me to tell you the sorrow that reigns universally in Holland", wrote the poet Matthew Prior from the English Embassy at The Hague. "These people, who had never any passion before, are now touched, and marble weeps . . .* The cruel news", he told Shrewsbury, "touches Holland to that degree that she may contend with England whose sorrow is greater . . . we are all abundantly convinced that we have lost the best of Princesses . . ."*

The States-General went into mourning and "we hear nothing but the dismal sound of bells". He himself went to look for solace on the shores of Scheveningen, near The Hague, where he wrote his own epitaph for the dead Queen, tracing it with the point of his sword in the sand:

> *Number the sands extended here;*
> *So many Mary's virtues were;*
> *Number the drops that yonder roll;*
> *So many griefs press William's soul.**

The cool composed Heinsius wrote a letter of unusual tenderness to William: "I know this is a great blow, and that your Majesty must grieve to the depths of your soul." He too was alarmed by reports of the failing health of their Stadholder and begged him "for the love that your Majesty has for his subjects, for this state, and for the reformed religion," to take care of himself. Heinsius like many statesmen on the Continent had speculated whether William's reign could survive the death of Mary Stuart, given his unpopularity with the English ruling classes and the continued strength of Jacobite feeling. In his letter he made it clear that if the worst had happened, the States-General would have given William all the support he needed, and now that Parliament's sole reaction had been a gesture of sympathy, Heinsius expressed the general relief of the Allies: "I hope that your Majesty will draw some consolation from the resolute declaration of the Parliament for your Majesty."*

By the New Year, the King's basic physical toughness had reasserted itself. He was sleeping normally again, and was seen walking in the snow-covered gardens of Kensington without leaning on Keppel's arm. He was still unable to face anyone but his closest friends, to the fury of many politicians who accused Portland of keeping the King under lock and key.* Huygens went over several times to Kensington with papers urgently needing the King's attention – with as little success as the politicians. Keppel, who found him waiting once, burst out impatiently: "The King doesn't want to see anybody and isn't doing anything. If he wants to see people, he will send for them."*

The turning-point came at last on 22 January, when the King dictated his first letter. It was to Heinsius, whom he thanked for his condolences. For the first time since Mary's death, he spoke of the war with France and his wish for peace. "I fear, however, that France in this my great unhappiness will be the more difficult than before, which must be dealt with. But I tell you in confidence that I am no longer capable of going to war."* In a letter to Vaudemont, written on the same day, the same doubts about his own strength were apparent. He hoped to be able to discuss various matters with him in person – "if God lets me live till my return to Holland".*

Kensington Palace was being put into mourning. To spare the King the sight of the black velvet being hung in every State room, he was taken by Portland down to Richmond Park on Wednesday the twenty-third, for a brief stay. He went hunting while he was there, "shooting flying on horseback, making 7 shotts all successful".* But it was so cold, he complained to Heinsius, "that I have had little benefit from it", adding: "Tomorrow I go back to Kensington, but I fear the walls will crush me."*

The change of scene had done him more good than he believed. On Sunday Huygens saw that the King was receiving people again, seeing four or five people at a time.* And in the evening, for the first time, "the King dined publickly and was very cheerful."* Huygens himself had to wait another two days before he could slip into the Presence Chamber where the King was giving an audience. "He didn't talk about his loss and signed a few things . . . Was reasonably kind . . ."*

Earlier that day, William had called an extraordinary session of the Privy Council. He had asked the lords of the Admiralty to be present and he gave instructions "to equip with all expedition all the men of warr in the ports of England that are fitt for the line of battle".* If France had hoped to take advantage of his weakness and England's grief, they had waited too long. The King had pulled himself together again.

He had done more. Mary's death had healed the breach with Princess Anne, and he had made their reconciliation public. During Mary's illness Anne had sent daily for news of her and had asked if she might come to her sister's bedside. Mary had been reluctant to see her and Anne's lady-in-waiting was given the reply that "it being thought so necessary to keep the Queen as quiet as possible", it was better to wait.*

The death of her sister had genuinely grieved Anne. She wrote immediately a letter to William: "Sir, I beg your Majesty's favourable acceptance of my sincere and hearty sorrow for your great affliction in the loss of the Queen. And I do assure your Majesty I am as sensibly touched with this sad misfortune as if I had never been so unhappy as to have fallen into displeasure . . ."*

William had been touched by her simple words and sent the Archbishop of Canterbury to see her on New Year's Day. As a first gesture of reconciliation he restored that same day her guards and soon afterwards she was received by him at Kensington. There was no stiffness or constraint left between them, reported an eyewitness later. "She told his Majesty in faltering accents, that she was truly sorry for his loss, who replied, he was much concerned for hers: both were equally affected, and could scarcely refrain from tears or speak distinctly."* Anne stayed for three quarters of an hour with the King behind closed doors and it was related afterwards that "on good authority . . . words had played much less part at this encounter than sobs and tears".*

This first visit was soon followed by others and the announcement that Anne would hold court again at Berkeley House "as if she were a crowned head" and that "as soon as the King appears in publick he intends to entertain their royal highnesses at dinner."* Even if relations between the King and his sister-in-law never became very cordial, William was realist enough to understand the importance of at least an appearance of understanding with the woman who was next in line to the throne.

Inevitably the return of Anne's favourites followed soon after, and on 29 March Marlborough kissed hands at an audience with William, a gesture that made it clear to everybody that in Marlborough's eyes Anne was the rising star and a much better bet than the ill-fated James.

At the exiled court in St. Germain the news of Mary's death had been welcomed as good news; their spies reported gleefully from London that the Prince of Orange "no longer having the right of his wife, becomes a stranger to the nation". William would certainly need the support of Dutch armies to maintain himself in power, the spies said, and an English uprising would then be inevitable "to preserve England from being overrun by foreigners". The King himself, of course, would no longer be able to take the field against France in person, "since there was no longer anyone to whom he could entrust the government in his absence".*

The Jacobites were over-optimistic: "One consolation remains to us in our misfortune", wrote Portland reassuringly from London to the English envoy in Vienna in mid-January, "our enemies will gain nothing by it either here or abroad. It seems indeed to have roused the spirit of all."*

Even at St Germain and Versailles, however, there were those who mourned Mary. Some of the gentlemen appeared at Court in black, claiming that they were mourning a relative.* James was not among them. To the indignation of Liselotte, he had not only forbidden his Court to go into mourning for his daughter, but he himself appeared "not the slightest bit moved by this death".* She made no secret where her own sympathies lay, writing in March relieved to her aunt Sophia that King William was in good health again. "His grief will certainly lessen with time."*

In London Mary's body was now lying in state in Whitehall Palace, where thousands of yards of black cloth and purple velvet had been used to cover the walls. Despite the bitter cold – the Thames had been frozen solid since the New Year – there were dense crowds queuing by six every morning, although they were admitted only between noon and 5 p.m. to see their Queen lying "in a bed of Purple all open". Over the bed was a canopy, "with rich gold fring, the middle being the armes of England curiously painted and gilt, the head piece embroyder'd richly with a crown and cyphers of her name, a cusheon of purple velvet at the head on which was the Imperiall Crown and Scepter and Globe, and at the feete another such a cusheon with the Sword and Gauntlets, on the corps . . ."* Round the bed was a balustrade covered in black velvet and thousands of candles burning. At the four corners of her bed her Ladies of Honour kept vigil, heavily veiled: they were relieved every half-hour.*

The streets outside, meanwhile, echoed to the sound of hammering. Sir Christopher Wren was supervising preparations for the funeral, having had order to prepare "rails from Whitehall to Westminster Abbey and the walks betwixt them to be gravelled, and the rails to be covered with black cloth".* Enormous sums were being spent – a total of over £100,000 – of which the smallest bills were £100 to Dr. Nobbs, "for opening the body of her late Majesty", and £250 to Dr. Harel, "for embalming the body".*

In the Palace itself a squabble was going on meanwhile about the distribution of perks. The King had already made generous provision for the Queen's personal staff, and ordered all her debts to be paid as soon as possible. But the furniture of the room she died in and all the rich velvet hangings in Whitehall were a bone of contention between her ladies-in-waiting. The Countess of Derby, "her most Darling Favourite", not only wanted to be Chief Mourner, but claimed this furniture as her due in her office of Groom of the Stole to the Queen. The distracted King had given in to her, but protests arose from all sides, and in the end the Privy Council had to intervene, giving the Duchess of Somerset the honour of being the Chief Mourner.*

Lady Derby was reluctant to give up her claims to the furniture and hangings, and on 28 February a Royal Warrant had to be issued "to take especial care that none of the goods of the late Queen Consort . . . be removed or any ways disposed of without the King's particular direction".* The row was only finally settled at the beginning of May, when the injured Countess was pacified by parcels of plate, 2457 ounces in all, and by "one pair of diamond earrings which were worn and used by the said late Queen; the present grant being in consideration of the great affection which the said Queen did bear to the said Countess", as the King's Warrant Book put it.*

The Queen herself would have been horrified by it all. Much too late, a paper was found among the documents she had left "wherein she desired that her body might not be opened, or any extraordinary expense at her funeral, whenever she should die."* By that time, she had been buried with all the pomp and splendour England could devise.

On 5 March, the long funeral procession set out from Whitehall to pace the short distance to Westminster Abbey in a driving snowstorm "so that the Ladies had but draggled trains by the time they got thither".* As custom dictated, the King was absent, but for the first time the funeral of a monarch was attended by both houses of Parliament, 500 members clad in black. Next came the Lord Mayor, the aldermen of the City, the judges, the officers of the Household and the guards, with the banners of England, Scotland, Ireland and France. Then came Sir Edward Villiers, the Queen's Master of the Horse, who led her favourite mount covered with purple velvet, and at last the hearse itself, an open chariot "made as ye bed was, the Canopy ye same all purple velvet, a high arch'd teister Ruffled, with ye Rich fringe and pall". It was drawn by six of the Queen's horses, and the six first Dukes of the Realm escorted it. At the head of the hearse lay the Crown and Sceptre on a cushion, and behind it walked the Duchess of Somerset as Chief Mourner, supported by the aged Lord Caermarthen and Lord Pembroke. Lady Somerset's train, six yards long, was borne by another Duchess and four young ladies, and after them the Lords, the Ladies and the Clergy in their long mourning cloaks streamed over the black-covered boards of Wren's footpath.

Inside the Abbey, the Queen's body was laid under a silver-fringed black velvet canopy, from which hung "a bason supported by cupids or cherubims shoulders, in which was one entire great lamp burning the whole tyme".* The crowds in the streets heard the great guns at the Tower firing every minute, while in the church, blazing with wax candles, sounded the sad music of Henry Purcell's specially composed Funeral Anthem, with its repeated muffled strokes of the timpani. "Thou knowest, Lord, the secrets of our hearts; shut not thy merciful ears unto our prayers, but spare us Lord most Holy . . ." sang the choir carefully rehearsed by Nicholas Staggins, the Master of the Music.*

After Tenison had preached the long funeral sermon, the coffin was lowered into the crypt and the Household officers broke their white staves and flung them together with their keys of office into the tomb. Then the tomb was sealed, and the long procession wound slowly out of the Abbey.*

The City of London had asked if they might commemorate the unique joint reign by raising a statue to Mary, with William, in front of the Stock Exchange.* The King had been against it. He had a better idea of how to honour his wife's memory: in 1691 Mary had given Christopher Wren an order to convert the palace at Greenwich, begun by Charles II in 1662, into a hospital for seamen.* Over the years she had followed the developments with the greatest interest, often to the despair of Wren himself. "The indefatigible Queen Mary was constantly at his elbow, . . . with most determined ideas", related Nicholas Hawksmoor, Wren's clerk-of-works, and no detail escaped her. She had forbidden him to pull down the original elegant Queen's House, designed by Inigo Jones, or to demolish the buildings which were erected for Charles by Webb and which fitted so well, she argued, into the garden-designs of "that most admirable Person Monsieur Le Nôtre".*

All these disagreements and discussions had certainly not speeded up the work, and when Mary died her favourite design was still far from being finished. William now decided that its completion would be the greatest tribute to her memory. Wren brought out his old designs, and work on Greenwich Naval Hospital was begun in earnest.

CHAPTER XXXVII

The Royal Progress

"MY HEALTH IS NEITHER VERY GOOD nor very bad", wrote the King to his friend Vaudemont in the middle of March 1695. "If it gets no worse, I shall be well content."* He had got over the worst shock of Mary's death, and although people noticed how sad and frail he looked, he had established a new pattern for his solitary life which evidently suited him. Kensington House with all its memories was still his home but he escaped every weekend now to Richmond or Windsor for hunting and shooting, and he kept up his new habit of having prayers said twice daily instead of once. He had resumed a close control of state affairs, and he now prepared himself for what he thought of as his last campaign.*

If the Jacobites had thought that he would not dare to leave England without Mary to rule the country, they were to be disappointed. The problem of a Regency was settled without any fuss and after William had prorogued Parliament on 3 May, he appointed a Council of seven men: Shrewsbury, Devonshire, Dorset, Pembroke, Godolphin, Somers and the Archbishop of Canterbury. On 12 May he set out for Flanders. He found there a French army of 100,000 men under a new commander, François de Neufville, Marshal Villeroi, the son of Louis's tutor and the King's personal friend. The great Luxembourg had died in January – "how glad the Prince of Orange will be" Louis had remarked – and Villeroi was a lightweight by comparison, "a man made for presiding over a ball" in Saint-Simon's opinion.* It was not difficult for William to fool him, and having kept the Frenchman baffled by the movements of the Allied army, he suddenly swooped on Namur.

For weeks on end Namur with its garrison under Marshal Boufflers was bombarded by the heaviest artillery fire ever known in a siege: at least 160 cannons battered relentlessly away, while charge after charge was undertaken. During one of the charges, William was furious to discover Michael Godfrey, the Deputy Governor of the Bank of England, in the front line under heavy fire. Angrily he ordered him to leave, but the civilian protested: "Sir, I run no more hazard than your Majesty." "I'm here where it is my duty to be", the King pointed out, "and I may without presumption commit my life to God's keeping, but you –" Before he could finish the sentence, a cannon-ball came whizzing past him and decapitated Godfrey on the spot.*

Namur finally surrendered early in September, after prolonged and savage assaults in which the English Grenadiers under Captain Cutts – nicknamed "the Salamander" because he was always where the fire was hottest – particularly distinguished themselves. William exclaimed delightedly as he watched them in action, "Look at my brave English!"

Four days later the 5000 survivors of the French garrison marched out of the town with flying colours, Boufflers at the rear. The Allied troops lined their path to where the King waited with the Elector of Bavaria and the Landgrave of Hesse. In accordance with his instructions Boufflers avoided saluting "the Usurper", and addressed himself to the Elector. Max Emmanuel at once turned to William and repeated the Marshal's words. The King, sitting in his coach, touched his hat and ordered that the soldiers should march on.

Boufflers was about to follow them when he was stopped by Dijkvelt who told him that he was now the King's prisoner. When the Frenchman protested volubly, Dijkvelt explained that since the French commander Villeroi had taken the Allied garrison of Dixmude prisoner a few weeks earlier, contrary to established military custom, the King of England was following French example. "How can he pay you a higher compliment", added Dijkvelt ironically, "than showing that he considers you as fully equivalent to the five or six thousand men whom your sovereign wrongfully holds in captivity?"*

Boufflers was taken to Huy, with Portland for escort. The two men got on extremely well, Boufflers – the first French Marshal ever to surrender – was treated with all respect, and after the garrison of Dixmude had been released on instructions from Louis – "the Prince of Orange is right", he observed* – the Frenchman was allowed to return to Versailles. Louis XIV made the best of a bad job, receiving his crestfallen commander with an embrace and a Dukedom, but for all that, it was William's credit which soared in France. "King William is spoken of in quite different tones now", wrote Liselotte. "Everywhere you hear remarks like 'a great man, a great King' and so on."*

The recapture of Namur was not only one of the rare victories in William's military career: it marked a turning-point in the Allied fortunes. "Our affairs have been at a great crisis", William wrote happily to Heinsius, "God be thanked for the outcome, and I don't doubt that this great success will give the affairs of Europe a new aspect."* He sent a messenger speeding to England with the good news, and his jubilant announcement in the *London Gazette* was a defiant riposte to Louis XIV and his Te Deums. "'Tis probable the French will now be willing it should be forgot with what Vanity and Boasting they fill'd all their public Relations, when they became Masters of this Town some Years ago . . ."*

The King himself hurried to Holland where after a short break at Het Loo, he went to The Hague to ask for funds for next year's campaign. He found that the capture of Namur had silenced the pacifists and given fresh heart to the Dutch war effort. Even Amsterdam readily voted the necessary supplies.

William hoped that his victory might yield the same encouraging results in England, and sent for his yachts at the beginning of October, anxious to get back early before the first glow of enthusiasm had faded. He landed on Thursday, 10 October o.s. and after a night in Canterbury at the Dean's house, where he and Mary had stayed a year and a half earlier, he reached Kensington to find "as great a confluence of the nobility and gentry as was ever known, who appeared generally in mourning".* He held a council meeting the same evening, and it was decided that a general election should be held at once, while the English were still in a good temper.

For once William was persuaded to do some electioneering himself. He explained to Heinsius a few days later: ". . . as most people are away and I have little to do, I have resolved to leave Thursday for a progress through the country to . . . divert myself . . . and to see a part of the country that I've never visited . . . which probably would have no bad effect."*

After a wet, chilly summer the autumn was mild and pleasant.* The King himself was in good health, the English were full of enthusiasm for the hero of Namur, and on Thursday, 17 October he left Kensington after taking leave of Anne, to arrive that same night at Newmarket. For four days he hunted and attended the horse-races and was convivial, before he continued his journey. His next stop was Althorp in Northamptonshire, the home of his political adviser Sunderland, where he stayed a week; then he went on to Stamford, then Lincoln, and on 30 October, Welbeck. From Welbeck the progress reached Warwick on his forty-fifth birthday, then Burford and Woodstock, to end at Oxford.

William was constantly in the best of moods. He hunted wherever he went, but never forgot that he was campaigning. To the fox-hunting nobles of Northamptonshire he said that their country was the finest in England and perhaps the whole world, adding like a good politician that "nothing made a gentleman look like a gentleman but living like one".* At Sherwood Forest where he hunted with 400 horsemen, he was appalled to see the many open "saw-pits" and, to the delight of the huntsmen, ordered them to be filled up.* Sometimes he found a door closed to him, like that of Burghley House: its owner, the Earl of Exeter, was a well-known Jacobite and had gone to London to avoid the King.* But others more than made up for him, and William was wined and dined by old friends like the Earl of Northampton at Castle Abbey, the Duke of Newcastle, and Lord Montagu at Boughton, who proudly showed him his collection of paintings. William was full of praise but with a touch of his usual melancholy remarked, "'Twas not good for one to set one's heart on any of them, for neither he nor his Lordship should be there forty years from hence to see them."*

It was the English people that made the Royal Progress the greatest success. Wherever the King went, huge crowds were waiting to give him a "great reception". They cheered him at Stamford, at Lincoln and at Welbeck; but they cheered him loudest of all at Warwick where Lord Brooke, his host, had organized a tremendous firework display in honour of the King's birthday, providing "a bowl of punch for the townspeople of one hundred and twenty gallons, made in a vessel call'd Guy Earl of Warwick's Pot".*

In Burford, where William's host was Shrewsbury, the King was presented with two masterpieces of the famous local saddlery, and it was with a certain regret that he left on the last lap of his tour. The only one to be pleased was his Under-Secretary of State, Vernon, who had found it difficult to maintain efficient communications between London and this roving Court. Wherever he went, the local Postmaster was enthusiastically celebrating the King's visit, and he once wrote in despair to London: "I have scarce seen any of them yet but they were drunk, and one has some trouble with them to get our packets dispatched."*

The last stop was at Jacobite Oxford, and William has specially asked that it should be brief and simple: no entertainment and certainly no dinner. Despite this request, the City did their best to turn the courtesy call into a State visit. After the King had been received in the Theatre where he was presented with a Bible, a Common Prayer Book and a pair of golden-fringed gloves, his hosts conducted him to a sumptuously laid dinner table, but William refused to sit down so emphatically that it was immediately rumoured he feared poisoning. Instead he drove straight off to Windsor.*

William himself was deeply touched by the unexpectedly warm welcome he had received everywhere in his adopted country and reported to Heinsius: "I got back yesterday night in good health, being very much satisfied with my journey, beautiful weather and everywhere I received much affection . . ."* Sometimes their reception had been a little more uninhibited that he was used to. On his way back to London from Windsor, a woman in the cheering crowds had pushed forward to peer at him in his coach. Astonished at the small, almost insignificant figure inside, she exclaimed in disbelief: "Is that the King? Why, my husband is a handsomer man than he is." William could not suppress a smile. He leaned forward and remarked gravely, "Good woman, don't speak so loud; consider I'm a widower."*

He had been out of London for his birthday, and at his return his friend the Earl of Romney, as Master of the Ordnance, had organized the most spectacular display of fireworks London had seen for many years, to celebrate his birthday and the victory of Namur together. The King supped at Romney's house in St. James's Square, where the display was held, and Princess Anne and Prince George watched it too, from a neighbouring house.*

Politically the Progress had been an unqualified success, and the new House of Commons that assembled on 22 November was at first ready to give him all the support he needed that year. After listening in satisfaction to the King's tactful opening speech, in which he attributed the summer's military successes largely to the extraordinary courage and spirit of the English troops, they voted him more than £3,000,000 to carry on the war.

After this initial show of complaisance, however, the House was unable to resist the opportunity which soon after offered itself of falling on the detested foreigners at Court. The King had made enormous grants of land in Wales – the domains of Denbigh, Bromfield, Yale and others – to Portland, and in December Parliament, led by the Welsh M.P.s, took up the question with relish. The gift of nearly five-sixths of the "ancient demesnes of the Prince of Wales", with all its coppermines and a yearly income of £6000, was too much, they protested, to be given away to a foreigner who was no more than a "mighty Favourite and a great Courtier".

Queen Elizabeth I had provoked an uprising when she gave Denbigh to her favourite Leicester – and he was at least an Englishman. She had not got away with it, and Parliament was determined that neither should

William. One of the most savage attacks was made by the Welsh M.P. Robert Price, whose speech against a "Dutch Prince of Wales" was later published in pamphlet form. It was, he said, his greatest fear that Wales would become "a colony of the Dutch".* Parliament shared his fears, and on 22 January 1696 the Commons passed a Bill laying down that the lands could only be given away by Act of Parliament. Reluctantly the King withdrew his gift. "I have a kindness for my Lord Portland", he told the M.P.s, "which he has deserved of me by long and faithful service, but I should not have given him these other lands if I had imagined the House of Commons could have been concerned . . . I will . . . find some way of showing my favour to him."* Three months later, his wealthy favourite received a grant of lands scattered over eight different counties in England.

That same winter a spectre from the past was rising to haunt the King. Three and a half years had passed since on orders personally signed by William, the MacDonald tribe of Glencoe had been cruelly massacred. Mary had learned the story in its full horror, and ordered an enquiry into the massacre, in the hope of saving the King's reputation.* A Commission had been appointed but its proceedings had been leisurely, and when she died, little had been done. In April 1695, however under pressure from public opinion in Scotland, the King had appointed a new Commission, which came to the conclusion that one man above all was responsible for the slaughter: Viscount Dalrymple, the Master of Stair. The Scottish Parliament had sent an Address to the King asking him to punish those responsible, but William was in no hurry to grasp this nettle, and it was not until December 1695 that it became clear what action he proposed to take: none. Dalrymple who had been suspended during the Enquiry was not reinstated, but he was virtually exonerated by the King's own words: "The Viscount of Stair . . . being at London, many hundred miles distant . . . could have no knowledge nor accession to the method of that execution . . ." and the King declared himself willing to "pardon, forgive and remit any excess of zeal . . ."*

In thus whitewashing Dalrymple, the King tacitly admitted his own responsibility, and it was probably a sense of guilt for his offhand treatment of Scotland that in June induced him to give his Royal Assent to an Act recognizing the Company of Scotland, newly founded by a group of Scottish visionaries in the hope of making their country's fortune by trade with the New World, which established a Scottish Colony on the Darien Peninsula. As might have been foreseen, the House of Commons violently objected to this Scottish threat to their overseas trade, and William, who could not afford to antagonize the strong City interests behind this protest, had to give way, sacking the men responsible for the Act. The English subscribers to the Company all withdrew their money in alarm, but the proud Scots refused to admit defeat, and in the space of six months this tiny and impoverished kingdom got together £400,000 – two-thirds of the capital needed. With the King's signed charter for the Company's existence, the ill-fated Darien venture was launched soon after.*

One way and another the amicable understanding between King and Parliament that had existed in the autumn had cooled considerably, when in mid-February the country was stunned by news of a dramatic Jacobite plot. The assassination of William was to be the signal for a general Jacobite rising, backed by invading forces from France. The rising was to have been masterminded from London by James's bastard son the Duke of Berwick, who had slipped quietly into the country; and the assassination, to be carried out by a Scotsman called Sir George Barclay, was planned for 15 February. At the eleventh hour one of the conspirators, a certain Fisher, lost his nerve and revealed the whole scheme to Portland. The King, on his way back from hunting at Richmond, with an escort of twenty-four men, was to be ambushed and slain at Turnham Green by a body of forty-six men led by Barclay. Portland, who had heard of a great many plots in his time, was sceptical but told the King, who dismissed the revelations as nonsense and refused to give up his precious weekend hunting. The day before his departure, however, another of the conspirators, Pendergrass, came to Portland late at night with exactly the same story, and further details. "The moment the fatal blow was given", he revealed, "there would be a general insurrection . . . and the King James was ready to embark at Calais with a French army to invade England."*

Portland, sceptical no longer, hurried to warn the King, and a few hours later it was announced that due to bad weather the King would not go hunting that weekend. At the news the conspirators panicked, and two more of them turned informer, coming to tell Portland that the attempt was delayed until the following weekend. Thanks to their revelations, fourteen of the ringleaders were rounded up in London, Barclay and Berwick fled the country, and the plot collapsed. "All the conspirators . . . allege that they had an order from King James, in his own handwriting, authorising them to strike the blow", reported a horrified Portland.*

At the first alarm, the trained bands in England had been raised and armed, and the fleet under Russell sent to cruise the Channel to intercept the French. These precautions were unnecessary. James waited in vain at Calais for the prearranged signal – a bonfire blazing on the Kentish coast – that would have launched the French armies across the Channel. It never came, the troops were disbanded, and James returned sadly to resume his devotions at St. Germain. In England the panic subsided, the emergency was declared at an end, and finally on 7 March William – who had not been allowed to put his nose out of doors for days without a strong guard – went hunting again. But the plot had far-reaching consequences.

James later told a Frenchman that he considered the murder of the Prince of Orange "at Richmond or Kensington the same as if Villeroy had laid an embuscade for him in Flanders".* Louis XIV, however, expressed the utmost horror when he learned that he was generally supposed a party to the plot. "The Prince of Orange will do me the justice to believe that I never wished to have him assassinated", he is reported to have said.* And he now washed his hands for good of all further interest in attempts to restore James to his throne by force.

William himself seems to have born no resentment against James or the French court for the threat to his life, and when in April that year Titus Oates rushed out a book denouncing James and offered to present it to him, he refused in horror as it spoke "so infamously and untruly of his late beloved Queen's own father".* He could afford to be generous: news of the plot had touched off an explosion of loyalty and patriotic fury throughout the country. "Though many did formerly pity King James's condition," wrote Evelyn, "this design of assassination and bringing over a French army alienated many of his friends."* And in Parliament, Sir Roland Gwyn, M.P. spontaneously proposed an Association for the defence of their Sovereign and their country. His suggestion was taken up with enthusiasm, and the Association snowballed: after it had been signed by 420 of the 530 M.P.s, their example was followed by tens of thousands of Englishmen all over the country and in the Colonies. Parliament itself, in a burst of anti-Jacobite feeling, passed an Act by which all M.P.s and all holders of office "solemnly recognised William as their rightful and lawful King, and bound themselves to stand by him and by each other against James and James's adherents".*

The upsurge of loyalty to William was due not so much to any particular love for his person as to the new national spirit which had been growing up quietly since the Revolution. Under this Dutch King, Parliament had been allowed to assert its independent self as never before, and the francophobe House of Commons of this time represented the interests of a business community with a vested interest in the maintenance of William. Millions of pounds had been lent to the State in his name, and the return of James would have meant that these loans could be written off as a total loss.

Politically, it was now clear to everyone that the restoration of the Stuart King would entail subordination to France and the enmity of the rest of Europe; and in the seven years that had passed since the Revolution, England had developed a proud awareness of its importance in the affairs of Europe.*

The loyalty of at least one of William's subjects, however, was not dictated by commercial or financial interests. It was that of the six-year-old Duke of Gloucester, the only surviving child of Princess Anne. As soon as he heard about the Association, he decided to make his own Address to the King his uncle. He asked one of the older boys in his small Household to write it out for him: "I, your Majesty's most dutiful subject, had rather lose my life in your Majesty's cause than in any man's else: and I hope it will not be long ere you conquer France. Gloster." He dictated another, to be signed by his young friends: "We, your Majesty's dutiful subjects, will stand by you as long as we have a drop of blood."*

The little Duke, born on 24 July 1689 and godson of the King in whose honour he was christened William Henry, had always had a great admiration for his uncle. He followed his military exploits in Flanders with keen interest. "Nothing pleased him but drums and arms, and stories of war", it was said, and when, for instance, he heard of the conquest of Namur, "the Duke was joyous, and ordered his guns should be fired six times round."*

The Duke was a frail little boy whose head was too big for his body – "insomuch that his hat was big enough for most men".* Now aged seven, he suffered from "a blood-shot eye which water'd very much, and occasion'd the lid to swell, nor could he see clearly with it".* For all his weakness, he was lively and active, and William and Mary adored him, spoiling him as though he were their own child. When he was only three, the Queen had given him a little sword, set with £200's worth of jewels, and publicly "girt it her selfe about his waste".*

Even the quarrel between Anne and Mary was never allowed to upset him, and he came regularly to stay with his aunt and uncle at Kensington House, where he had his own rooms. When one day he remarked to the Queen that his "mamma once had guards, but now had none", she pretended great surprise. The little boy was paying her a visit at the time; it was the spring of 1694 and William Henry had brought his two companies of soldiers to parade before her in honour of her birthday, just before the King went off to Flanders on campaign.

The soldiers, ninety little boys with red grenadier caps and armed with wooden swords and muskets, were formed into ranks in the garden by the beating of drums, and the King and Queen solemnly walked up and down inspecting them. William was especially impressed by one six-year-old boy, William Gardner, "remarkable for beating the drum, almost equal to the ablest drummer". He gave him two pieces of gold, distributing twenty guineas among the others.

Next day the King returned the visit. It was a Sunday, and the little boy excitedly gave orders for his toy fort and guns to be got ready. The fort was made of pasteboard, with tiny guns mounted on it, and there were also what he called his "great ones", four little brass cannons. "At this time he was wholly engrossed with a design of showing the King that he was a soldier, and would first salute him in a soldier-like manner, and afterwards compliment him." He had a manly talk with the King about horses and arms, and explained that one of his small brass cannons was broken. William promised to send him some others and the boy was thrilled. "My dear King, you shall have both my companies with you to Flanders", he said graciously.*

At the beginning of 1696, William had paid a New Year visit to Anne during which he promised to give the Garter to the Duke for his seventh birthday. The installation took place on Saturday, 25 July "in very great splendour at Windsor".* The little boy, proud as he was of his Garter and of the onyx and diamond George which the King had specially ordered for him, told Burnet, who congratulated him: "I am gladder of the King's favour."*

William had not been present. He left England on 14 May for the Republic, preoccupied by an urgent English problem: the shortage of ready money.

The state of the coin had been a grievance for years now, thanks to the practice of "clipping" surplus silver from their irregular edges. As a result of wartime inflation, the intrinsic value of the silver that English coins were made of had overtaken their face value, and they were simply disappearing from circulation to be melted down. Before William left London, he had given orders that the coin should be reminted in a form immune to this abuse, and from 4 May the old coins were withdrawn from circulation. While mints all over the country worked night and day churning out new coins, commercial life in England came to a standstill: Pepys wrote of "the gentlewomen, sitting with their arms across without a yard of muslin in their shops to sell while the ladies walk pensively by without a shilling (I mean a good one) in their pockets to buy."*

William himself had only been able to get together £44,000 in gold by paying the black market rate of 25s instead of 22s; and he simply could not afford to go to war. "If you cannot devise expedients to send contributions or procure credit, all is lost and I must go to the Indies", he wrote to Shrewsbury desperately.* No funds arrived and on 26 July he sent Portland back to London to see what could be done. After various ideas had been studied and dropped, Portland at last, with Shrewsbury's help, managed to talk the directors of the Bank of England into a loan of £2 millions, of which £50,000 would be immediately available. By the time these funds reached William in Flanders, however, it was too late in the season for anything to be done on the battlefield.

The financial situation was not much better in the United Provinces. Long years of war had drained the treasury of the States-General, and they had been forced to raise taxes. In Amsterdam this had led to rioting and disorder early in 1696, when the State of Holland decided to tax burials and marriages and the Regents of Amsterdam in protest at once made magnificent funerals illegal. Furious undertakers spread a rumour that all citizens in future would have to bury their dead in plain deal coffins, with the city's arms sewed on the shrouds. The mob of Amsterdam, always ready for a good riot, assembled on Dam Square to protest and went rampaging through the town, wrecking the house of Jacob Boreel, the Dutch envoy to France, whose son had signed "the Undertakers' Law", and the house of the English consul Kirby. The rioting went on for days, the militia had to be called out and five of the ringleaders were hanged.*

By the time William arrived the hated law had been annulled and calm restored. But the rioters had made a point which was not lost on William. All over Europe people were now heartily sick of war and high taxes, especially in Holland and England, the two countries on which the main burden of the war effort fell. And although the Emperor and the Queen of Spain made endless difficulties about possible terms, William himself was now determined to try and achieve a peaceful settlement. The French appeared equally eager to end this disastrous war, and had quietly made it clear that there would be no more difficulties about recognizing William as King of England. James made it easier for Louis XIV by publishing a document in which he stated that he could never come to terms with William or recognize the slightest diminution of his rights. As a sop to his pride, he had been offered the throne of Poland, made vacant by the death of John Sobieski, but he had refused, and Louis felt that he had now done all that decency demanded for his Royal and tiresome cousin.*

But the peace hopes of Europe were short-lived. On 29 August, Victor Amadeus, the Duke of Savoy, signed a peace treaty with France. French arrogance was restored by his treachery, and the peace talks ground to an abrupt halt. William retired to Het Loo a bitterly disappointed man. Another long winter of preparations, diplomacy, and endless arguments with Parliament now awaited him.

CHAPTER XXXVIII

Constant Companions

EUROPE'S SHATTERED HOPES FOR PEACE destroyed an illusion that Liselotte, the sister-in-law of Louis XIV, had been fondly cherishing that summer of 1696. The plump lady, known as "Madame" at Versailles, who once herself had been considered as a possible bride for William of Orange, had dared to propose her only daughter the twenty-year-old Elizabeth Charlotte, as the second wife of Europe's most eligible widower. Her Danish lady-in-waiting Christina de Meyercrone had written in veiled and discreet terms to Portland on the subject, suggesting that this Princess might be "a bird of peace accompanied with happiness". Portland grasped at once what she was driving at, and wrote back a polite but discouraging reply. "I can't think there is much hope of it, but you may assure the person of whom you speak that everything which comes from her will be very heartily received . . ."*

One obstacle was the religious difference – as Liselotte complained: "I find that religion spoils a great many things in this world, as my daughter at this moment cannot marry King William." But there was a much greater obstacle: William had no desire to marry again, and Liselotte, although very much disappointed, could well understand it after her own unhappy experience with Monsieur: "it's a big bore being married, and one can never be certain at the time that it will work out."*

The King had now been a widower for two years. He had faithfully kept his promise to Archbishop Tenison to break with Betty Villiers, infuriated according to malicious gossip by the fact that Betty, after the death of the Queen, had pulled a lock of hair out of Mary's head – presumably at her lying-in-state. "Sylvius told me", reported Huygens two weeks after the Queen's death, "that Betty is now completely in disgrace and that she will have to go and live in Ireland."* In 1691 the King had settled on his mistress the Irish properties that had belonged to his father-in-law, whose daughter – ironically – had signed the patents in October 1693 when William was on the Continent.

But Betty stayed on in London, and in November 1695 a match had been arranged for her with George Hamilton, fifth son of the Duke of Hamilton. He was a handsome dark-haired young man who stuttered and had nothing much to say for himself. But he had made the army his career and distinguished himself in almost every great battle of William's reign, from the Boyne down to the conquest of Namur where he was severely injured.

William thought highly of him, promoted him to Brigadier-General in 1695 and created him Earl of Orkney in January 1696. He was extremely rich for a younger son. As Swift learned years later: "The young fellow has £60,000 ready money, three great houses furnished, £7000 a year at present, and about five more after his father and mother die."* Betty herself brought him only £8000, and the Irish estates William had given her and which gave her an income of £5000 a year – hardly a fortune for a King's ex-mistress – but she went into the match with her head held high, telling her future husband "that she had been on very good terms with a certain person, but that she did not wish to hear any reproaches or insinuations on that score".*

Their marriage seems to have been a happy one, although some members of the Hamilton family were outraged by the connection, and her sister-in-law the Duchess of Hamilton would never speak to her. It was Swift, years later, who brought them together. He was a great admirer of Betty, writing about her: "Lady Orkney, the late King's mistress . . . is the wisest woman I ever saw."* He loved talking politics with her till far into the night, and thought her not merely shrewd, but kind as well – "like a mother". Only once did she touch on the subject of love with him, telling him of a saying of her sister's "that in men, desire begets love, and in women love begets desire . . ."*

Even after Betty's liaison with the King was broken off, she remained a force in politics, and kept up her friendship with Shrewsbury and other Whig leaders. Vernon, the Under-Secretary of State, mentions her intervention several times in letters to Shrewsbury, and twenty years later, her opinions were still valued by ministers like the Lord Treasurer.†

William, who had enjoyed talking to her, must have missed her amusing and entertaining company as he missed the love and tenderness of Mary. But he showed no eagerness to replace either mistress or wife

† Betty was never a beauty with her squinting eyes, and her looks certainly did not improve with age. At the Coronation of George II in 1727 Lady Mary Wortley Montagu describes her appearance: "She exposed behind a mixture of fat and wrinkles; and before, a very considerable protuberance which preceded her. Add to this the inimitable roll of her eyes, and her gray hair and 'tis impossible to imagine a more delightful spectacle." She died in 1733.

and seemed content for the moment with this state of affairs. The English and Dutch, however, were beginning to make it clear that they would appreciate it very much if their King and Stadholder would begin to think of marrying again, and Portland was instructed to draw up a short list of "Princesses of marriageable age and of the Protestant or Lutheran religion". He found six. There was the Princess Royal of Sweden, Hedwig Sophia, fifteen years old and very small; the Princess Royal of Denmark, Sophia Hedwig, eighteen years old, with a good figure, a nice character, beautifully brought up, and a sound Lutheran. In Hesse-Cassel there was the sixteen-year-old Sophia Charlotte, "*fort bien faite de corps et d'ésprit*"; the Saxe-Eysenac family had a much older Princess – twenty-five no less – Marie-Elisabeth, a good-looking pleasant girl, and the Holstein-Gotorp's another Marie-Elisabeth, twenty years old, and nothing known against her. The sixth was the daughter of William's old ally and cousin Friedrich of Brandenburg, a fourteen-year-old with the full name of Louise Dorothea Sophia.*

From a political point of view, the Brandenburg Princess was easily the most eligible – there was much to be said for a marriage alliance between Germany's most important state on one side, and England and the Republic on the other. And William himself, however little he liked the idea of a second wife, would have been happy to give England a Prince to secure the succession after Anne and the Duke of Gloucester, and the United Provinces a future Orange Stadholder.

For these reasons, he reluctantly came to the conclusion that he ought at least to have a look at the young girl. The first reports he heard of her were not very encouraging to a man who had been married to a recognized beauty and charmer: the Princess was said to be a lean bony girl with a gauche and unappealing manner. She had a cast in one eye and needed padding to give her a figure; she was well-read but not very amusing. Another later report by Portland himself, giving "no very favourable account of the lady as to her beauty" almost decided the King on calling off the idea. He "has no reason to be contented with a wife without" remarked Matthew Prior.*

But it was too late to get out of the visit gracefully – the Elector, his wife and children were already waiting at their house Moylandt at Cleves* – and William travelled in September 1696 to Tolhuis on the Rhine, where Friedrich was waiting to greet him. Together they drove to Moylandt, where they were received by the Electress in her own apartments. For about an hour they stood around talking – according to their own interpretation of protocol, both men had an equal claim to the only great armchair in the room but they were polite enough not to insist on it. Then Friedrich left the room and everyone sat down to a solid five hours' card-playing, the King in the great armchair, the Duke of Zell who had travelled with him in an ordinary one, the Electress on her bed, and Portland and Keppel on stools. The rest of the company stood around watching, among them Princess Louise – until Keppel broke protocol by gallantly pulling forward another stool for her and inviting her to sit down.

The Elector's Court, as the King's English suite now remarked, was dull and dowdy. The Electress herself, a pleasant dumpy woman, had a faint resemblance to Queen Mary in her looks and was full of chat and civility. But as Matthew Prior reported to Shrewsbury; "few of the women were handsome and all ill-dressed, in old-fashioned stiff-bodie gowns, too big for them, with their breasts and shoulders naked." He was just as merciless about the prospective bride: "The princess is not ugly, but disagreeable; a tall miss at a boarding school, with a straggy lean neck, very pale, and a great lover, I fancy, of chalk and tobacco-pipes."*

It was impossible to tell from William's manner what impression she made on him, but he was certainly kind and polite to the gawky young girl. That evening he dined with her and her mother and Keppel for male company, while Portland made polite conversation with their host the Elector in the next room. "There was a great deal of good meat and ill wine for every body else!" wrote Prior, "but they filled it in such mighty glasses, and it came about so fast, that people grew drunk before they had half dined."*

The next day, Sunday, however, the King's reaction to this German schoolgirl became apparent to everybody. It had been said that he would stay for at least twelve days, but he made his escape as soon as he decently could, after a long sermon in the morning and a stroll and talk with the Elector.* He returned alone to Het Loo not very far away, where, four days later, the seven-year-old Electoral Prince came to return his visit. His mother and his sister had already left for Berlin, their hopes dashed.†

The English and the Dutch were disappointed. In London they had considered the match a *fait accompli*, after it became known that the King had ordered "rich liveries for his domesticks", and "extraordinary rich furniture" for Kensington, including a great bed of state.* In Holland, the old Binnenhof Palace at The Hague had been refurbished

---

† Louise later married the Crown Prince of Hesse-Cassel, who became King of Sweden, but she died only five years after their wedding.

to lodge the parents of the bride, and at Het Loo they had received instructions from the King to get all the best furniture out of store.*

This disappointment was certainly not shared by the King himself; "Have the people then forgot the Queen so soon?" he exclaimed, "Well, if they have, I have not." Het Loo especially, the first home he had planned with Mary, was full of memories of her. She had laid the first brick of this palace in the middle of the Veluwe Forests, and it always had been his favourite. Since he had bought the property in 1684 he had lavished fortunes on having the house built according to the plans of the Dutch architect Jacob Roman and the French Huguenot Daniel Marot, and magnificent gardens laid out by Le Nôtre, and all his life he continued to pour money into furniture, decorations and paintings to make it even more ravishing. It was his personal fortune, raised from his Dutch estates, that he spent there, but the English, who resented the fact that he stayed there as long and as often as he could, chose to ignore the fact. Not only was he filling Het Loo with works of art plundered from English Royal palaces, they claimed, but he was squandering their hard-earned taxes on it; and Het Loo was dubbed by them "England's Folly". The Dutch, on the contrary, thought it Holland's pride, and the Province of Gelderland in 1695 gave him complete jurisdiction over the surrounding lands in gratitude for building such a noble palace.*

His passion for Het Loo was understandable. By Dutch standards it was a real Royal palace, built in the style that Versailles had made famous – at once formal in its lines and playful in its ornamentation. Its great gates, painted sky-blue and richly gilded, opened into a courtyard with a magnificent marble fountain adorned with dolphins splashing away in the middle. Nine broad brick steps led up to the dark green front door, which opened into a hall paved with black and white marble, and a large dining-room gloriously gilded and decorated with military devices carved in marble. The King's own apartments also reflected his military interests: the ante-chamber was hung with fine tapestries showing "the function or duties of cavalry, to wit, the incampment of horse, their foraging, their making of fascines, and the firing . . . of two parties of horse in an engagement". His bedchamber was hung with red silk, and one of its features was a curiosity – a clock that never had to be wound.

One of the most pleasant rooms was William's library with its simple polished oak bookcases filled by his books in fine French bindings. There were two great globes, and the ceiling was one large looking-glass.

On the other side of the building were the Queen's apartments, as Mary's rooms were still called although she had never set foot in them since she had sailed for England in 1688. Her bedroom was hung in light yellow silk, and the bedcover, in the same colour, had a border embroidered by Mary herself. Most of the rooms were furnished by the Frenchman Gole, according to her own taste. Below the windows of her apartment lay the Queen's garden, with another fountain playing in the middle, and in one corner was a little folly done up as a grotto, full of shells and exotic marine objects. Matching it on the other side of the palace was the King's garden, with a cascade of nine steps, while next to the stables a green for bowling was made. The Lower Garden was separated by a wall and a canal from the Upper Garden, where the centre-piece was a fountain with thirty-three spouts, that threw their water up to a height of 45 feet. The garden itself had the symmetry so typical of the French style, with drives rising to a little pavilion on a hill, shining with a blue cupola. When Dr Harris visited Het Loo that year he was deeply impressed: "The gardens are most sumptuous and magnificent, adorned with great variety of most noble fountains, cascades, parterres, gravel walks and green walks, groves, statues, urns, paintings, seats and pleasant prospects into the country."*

William knew no place where he loved to be more and if he always left this palace – and Holland in general – reluctantly, in this year 1696 he found it even more difficult. There was little to look forward to in England.

THE KING ARRIVED back in London early in October – to find Shrewsbury, his Secretary of State, gone. The revelations of Fenwick, the well-known Jacobite plotter, had driven the susceptible minister back to his house in the Cotswolds.

Fenwick, arrested in June, had been accused of high treason for his complicity in the assassination plot of the previous March. He had obligingly offered to reveal full details of the conspiracy, but when his account was read, it proved not so much a confession as a string of highly damaging assertions of Jacobite sympathies made against leading Whig members of the government, such as Godolphin, Marlborough, Russell and Shrewsbury. William, who had been sent a copy at Het Loo, read it without much surprise. He had always accepted the fact that many of his subjects were secretly flirting with St. Germain, and he was determined to frustrate this attempt to discredit his government.

"You know me too well to think that such stories as his can make any impression on me", he wrote soothingly to Shrewsbury on 10 September.* But all his kindness and assurances of complete trust could not induce Shrewsbury, nursing his shattered nerves in the country, to return to London, although his friends and colleagues pointed out that his flight was bound to be taken for an admission of guilt. Shrewsbury sent an unconvincing excuse – a fall from his horse had laid him up for a few days, he said – and his resignation. William refused to accept it but Shrewsbury could no longer face the strains of office, and remained Secretary of State in name alone, while the Under-Secretary James Vernon gradually took on all the responsibilities of the job.

The wrath of King and Parliament now fell on Fenwick's head. William had never forgiven him for once behaving insultingly to Mary in public, while Whigs and Tories alike felt that the sooner the embarrassing Fenwick was out of the way, the better. Since one of the two witnesses necessary for a conviction of high treason by the ordinary process of law had fled the country, Parliament voted a Bill of Attainder against him, to which arbitrary and later much-criticized measure, William gave his assent on 11 January 1697. Seventeen days later, Sir John was beheaded on Tower Hill.

It was the start of an unhappy winter for the King. His bad temper had been much commented on ever since his return from Holland, and it was particularly noticeable at the ball that Anne gave in honour of his birthday on 4 November. Vernon made excuses for his ungraciousness: "the King had no great satisfaction in the ball last night; he was in so many crowds, both in St. James's and Whitehall, and came back a little disordered to Kensington . . ."* The general impression was less kind: "His Majesty was extremely out of humour."*

His low spirits were not only caused by the political troubles of the session, which Fenwick's revelations and the loss of Shrewsbury had aggravated. He was a tired, unhappy man, who still missed Mary badly. On the anniversary of her death he shut himself up all day and saw no one, and he began drinking more heavily now to drive away his melancholy. Only late at night, sitting for hours over the table with his friends, did his gloom sometimes lift. An English friend once asked Keppel if he ever heard the King utter a word to anybody? Keppel answered, "Oh yes, he talks fast enough at night over his bottle, when he has no one about him but his Dutch friends."*

For a long time now, Keppel had been the indispensable companion of these drinking bouts. Huygens, who knew perfectly well that Keppel disliked him and wanted him replaced by d'Allonne, reported them disapprovingly from time to time in his journal: "The King hardly worked at all today, and it was said that he had been eating at Keppel's the night before, drinking more than normally."* On another occasion he noted with evident jealousy: "The King left at nine o'clock in a caleche for Het Loo . . . Saw Keppel sitting opposite him wearing a big powdered wig."* Two months later the secretary, now sixty-eight years old, left the King's service, saddened and aggrieved by the indifference William had shown him over the last two years. A year later he was dead.

Huygens was by no means alone in his jealousy of Keppel's growing importance. It was well-known in Court circles that the relationship between Keppel and Portland deteriorated by the day, and that the King had once had to separate the two favourites when they started to fight. There had been another spectacular dispute between them following the King's visit to the Elector of Brandenburg in September. Keppel had been constantly with the King but Portland, an older and wiser statesman, was appointed to keep the Elector company. He fretted about the situation so much that Keppel provoked him into a disgraceful scene on the return journey. "Our two favourites have had a quarrel", wrote Matthew Prior gleefully to Shrewsbury. "In coming home, Keppel being heated with wine, and heedless, made his coachman drive before Lord Portland, who was in one of the Duke of Zell's coaches; upon which Lord Portland said he would beat the coachman, who excusing himself upon his orders, my Lord Portland said, 'whoever gave those orders was an impertinent puppy, or some such words'."*

Matters went from bad to worse that winter, and the courtiers followed the situation with interest. Few of them had ever liked Portland very much – "he could never bring himself to be acceptable" – finding him too serious for their taste. They also accused him of being greedy for wealth, and much too possessive about the King, and they were not sorry to see his fall from favour now. Keppel, on the other hand, was a pleasant and amusing dandy, who managed to achieve a certain popularity despite the fact that he was one of the hated Dutch. The whole difference between the two favourites was once drily summed up by Sunderland, when Keppel brought him a message from the King: "This young man brings and carries a message well, but Portland is so dull an animal, that he can neither fetch nor carry."*

By the New Year of 1697 Keppel's influence on the King was enormous – "allmighty powerfull in the councils of his master", reported a contemporary. Less kind than Sunderland, he added, "and lacking the modesty of his predecessor he disposed of everything, with an independent haughtiness."* Another contemporary described the young man as "King William's constant companion in all his diversions and pleasures, intrusted at last with affairs of the greatest consequence, had a great influence on the King; is beautiful in his person, open and free in his conversation, very expensive in his manner of living."*

The Venetian ambassador, arrived in London in 1696, thought it advisable to include a note on Keppel in his report to Venice: "His Majesty regards him with pleasure as if he is a tender plant that he himself wanted to cultivate in the hope that it will bear fruit . . . Until now, the love of the King alone offers him a marvellous prospect for success."*

Burnet, not usually censorious, was much less impressed by this tender plant. He admitted that Keppel was a "cheerful young man, that had the art to please", but added that he was "so much given up to his own pleasures, that he could scarce submit to the attendance and drudgery that was necessary to maintain his post".*

Some of Keppel's pleasures were well-known at Court. He had a mistress – an attractive brunette – in Chelsea, to whom he paid £300 a year, and it was thought that she was not the only one.* He had once actually been discovered in bed with a married lady by her outraged husband, a cousin of Zuylestin, and had had to flee.* And William's great enemy at Anne's Court, Sarah Marlborough, said that Keppel was chiefly notable for his impudence and his vices.

If William knew about Keppel's escapades, he obviously did not mind. Keppel had been his greatest comfort after Mary's death, and was now a passable secretary and even better company. The King enjoyed talking to him, and sometimes spent as long as five hours chatting at his table, while letters piled up for the royal signature unheeded.

Not surprisingly, William decided in January 1697 to make his young favourite an English Earl. It was officially announced on the twenty-first; Keppel became Baron of Ashford, Viscount of St. Edmondsbury and Earl of Albemarle, the last title originally selected by the Plantagenets to grace their own line. The English were infuriated to see yet another Dutchman join the ranks of their aristocracy, and one of the lampoons of the times commented:

> *Proceed my muse, the story next relate,*
> *Of Keppech, the imperious chit of state;*
> *Of foreign birth, and undescended too,*
> *Yet he, like Bentir, mighty feats can do.*
> *Our ravished honours on his shoulder wears,*
> *And titles from our ancient rolls he tears.**

The Earl of Bath took action and protested, entering a caveat against the patent for the title. He was heard on 9 February, but to no avail.

The new Lord Albemarle took his seat in the House of Lords on 18 February.*

At the same time, William did not forget his old favourite. "I am told the King intends to give my Lord Staffords Garter to my Lord Portland", reported Vernon to Shrewsbury. "It is supposed this is conferred upon my Lord Portland at this time of the Earl of Albemarle's promotion to shew that he is still preferred a step above him."* On 20 February Portland was duly elected and installed at Kensington in the company of ten of the Knights.* It was the climax in the long series of honours and presents William had heaped on his friend over the years. Starting in 1664 as an ordinary page, he had first become Forester of the Stadholder in 1681, then Major-General in 1683, Groom of the Stole, Gentleman of the Bedchamber and Treasurer of the Privy Purse in 1689. That same year he was made Earl of Portland, Viscount Woodstock, Baron of Cirencester, and Ranger of the Royal Parks. In 1691 he was appointed General of the Dutch cavalry and made a member of the Privy Council. Now he was Knight of the Garter. On the more material side there were presents like Sorghvliet in Holland and certain buildings in Whitehall. After the failure to give him the greatest part of Wales at the end of 1695, he had received the manors of Grantham, Cracklow and Rudneth in Cheshire, of Torrington in Norfolk, of Partington, Hornsey, Thwing, Burnishley and of East Greenwich. It was no secret that Portland was the richest man in the land.

But all the honours and presents could not make up to Portland for the fact that he was no longer first among the friends and confidants of the King, and in March 1697 the man of whom Burnet had written "he bears his favour with great modesty and has nothing of that haughtiness that seems to belong to all favourites" determined to resign all his posts at Court.*

He did not have the heart and courage to tell the King himself, and left it to a third person. William was shattered. "I don't know how I restrained myself from coming to see you in your appartments", he wrote to him immediately. "Nothing is left me but to beg you, by all the ties that should be dearest to you, to change this pernicious decision and I feel sure that if you retain the least affection for me you will not refuse this prayer, however hard it may seem to you." He begged him for another year's trial – "I feel sure that you will not regret it" – and if Portland still persisted in his decision to resign after that, he would no longer oppose it. "If you will grant me this prayer, which I make with all imaginable earnestness, I shall, if that is possible, feel more obligation to you than I do for all the good and faithful service which you have

given me in the 33 years that you have been with me." He ended his
plea with a moving PS: "If you heart is hard enough not to give in to
my prayer, reply to me only tomorrow morning through Mr. Sunderland,
who is coming to see me. It would be too much for me to have so cruel
a refusal in your own hand."*

Portland gave in this time, but reluctantly; perhaps influenced by the
general anxiety about the King's health. It had been shaky all that winter,
and in April Vernon mentioned to Shrewsbury: "We have been appre-
hensive lest His Majesty might have a spice of a quartan ague: the first
appearance of it was on Wednesday last, and he had a kind of a fit on
Saturday again."* When he left for Holland he was still suffering from
dizzy spells, sleeplessness and lack of appetite, all most unusual in him,
and although he did not mention it to his doctors yet, he was concerned
by the way his feet and legs sometimes swelled. But as always, a few
days' hunting at Het Loo restored him in mind and body, and on 13 May
Vernon heard that the King was as good as recovered. "He sleeps well,
only his appetite is a little abated. He had been twice a-hare-hunting and
found himself the better for it."*

Portland had been with him at Het Loo, and seen his rapid recovery;
he had also noted that the King and Keppel, the new Earl of Albemarle,
were as intimate as ever. Almost sick with grief and jealousy, he announced to the King that he was still determined to leave his service,
and when William left for the army headquarters at Iseringen, Portland
took himself off to Brussels where he was the guest of William's friend,
the Prince de Vaudemont.

From Iseringen, he received a long pleading letter: "You have seen
the state I was in yesterday before your departure; I am not less grieved
by the uncertainty I am in at present about what you may resolve to do."*

Five days later, in a long and impassioned letter, Portland at last
revealed the true reasons for his decision to go. "I have always told
your Majesty that it was what was happening to me which made my
life unbearable; it's true, but it's not the only reason, Sire; it is your
honour which I have at heart." The point was, wrote Portland, that "the
kindness which your Majesty has for a young man, and the way in which
you seem to authorize his liberties and impertinences make the world say
things that I am ashamed to hear." He assured William that he believed
him "as far removed as any man in the world" from "these things", but
he had been thunderstruck when he had found that the same "malicious
gossip" that was going round in England, was also heard at The Hague
and in the army, "tarnishing a reputation which has never before been
subject to such accusations". He urged the King to act now "in order to

protect this reputation which has always been so dear to you", begging him finally "not to resent the freedom which you demanded from me and which, if it is fitting from anyone, is fitting for a man who loves you as I do".*

This letter reached the King on the road on 1 June, and it came like a thunderbolt. "It has so much astonished me that I hardly know where I am", William answered. "If I did not love you as much as I do, and I were not so strongly convinced of your good intentions I could not take it other than ill, and perhaps any man other than myself could only put a very bad interpretation on it." He wondered, however, why Portland if he really believed him "as far removed as any man in the world from these infamous suspicions" was staying away, leaving it to "my wisdom and prudence to protect my reputation". Portland's absence could only damage the reputation of the King further, "while everyone will censure your conduct". William finally promised to do anything to stop "such horrible calumnies" but made it clear that he was not willing to dismiss Keppel. "It seems to me very extraordinary that it should be impossible to have esteem and regard for a young man without it being criminal."*

Portland's letter the next day was long and almost incoherent, the letter of a man desperately upset and not used to putting his emotions down on paper.

> I fully expect Your Majesty to be extremely surprised and shocked by the things I warned you were being said, but not that you should find reason to take it ill that a man attached since all time to yourself should warn you of something of the nature, on the contrary I believed that I had been silent too long . . . I still have the unhappiness of seeing that you find there are contradictions in my letter which I do not perceive myself, because when I have the honour to tell you that I believe you so far removed from the thing, that does not prevent me wishing that Your Majesty should remedy by your own prudence those appearances which have given the world occasion for this infamous talk.

Sadly Portland reminded the King what he had promised after his first attempt to resign in March, when he had complained to William of Keppel's impertinence towards himself. Far from having improved, the situation had deteriorated since then, and he saw no reason to stay merely because of the sensation his departure might create. "It is not just recently, but for a very long time indeed now that these wicked rumours have been going round", and his own return would certainly not put a stop to them.*

William, however, had not waited for Portland's answer before involving others in the argument. Charles Henri, the Prince de Vaudemont, with whom Portland was now staying, had long been a close friend, as was his wife Anne Elisabeth; and like Portland, he was deeply in the King's debt. The bastard son of Duke Charles IV of Lorraine whom Richelieu had ruined, he had taken service with the Spanish forces in the Netherlands and had made his career with the help of William, who had even presented him with a richly furnished palace in Brussels.* The King now enlisted his help in persuading the indispensable Portland to return to his service, writing to Portland:

". . . I see to my great regret that you are so preoccupied by your own opinions that nothing I could say will have the slightest effect on you. This has made me resolve to hand over your letters to the Prince de Vaudemont so that at least a man of intelligence and sense can reason with you and make you see how wrong you are . . ."*

For all Portland's assurances that he alone could judge of the rights and wrongs of the case, Vaudemont successfully wore him down in the end. While Portland lay ill in the Vaudemont home – "I can't sleep and I can't eat and I'm getting weaker every day", he complained in one of his letters * – the Prince hurried up and down between Brussels and William trying to find a solution. It had taken him some time to extract the full story of his grievances from Portland, but finally he learned of the promises that the King had made his friend to improve matters, which, as he said bitterly, "had only served to increase the self-importance of this young man".*

If William agreed to remedy these grievances, he assured Vaudemont, he was ready to return. After another hurried conference with William, Vaudemont reported back to Portland: "I told his Majesty at great length of your powerful reasoning, your innermost feelings for him when you made these resolutions." William had appeared to accept them. "I told him very positively that if on your return to his personal service you should find things so unchanged that you could no longer endure them, you begged him in advance not to find it strange that you should carry out your intention of retiring."*

The King himself had already dashed off a few lines to express his delight: "I cannot adequately express the joy that I felt when the Prince de Vaudemont told me that you had resolved to come back to me; I hope that your health will soon permit it, and that you will never regret it, to which I will try to contribute as much as I can."*

Portland could not resist pointing out in a final letter what an effort this resolution had cost him, and that it was only "the strong assurances that your Majesty has given of your kindness for me, and of the remedy that you apply to the business in question" which had induced him to consider returning.*

William read between the lines: only one thing would satisfy Portland and it was nothing less than the dismissal of Keppel. He was deeply hurt and asked Vaudemont to answer Portland. "His Majesty tells me that he does not understand what sudden change you expect him to make before your return . . .", he wrote to Brussels, where Portland was now recuperating. The King would certainly do anything to please his friend, but Keppel was to stay and Vaudemont hinted as much: "I believe the King could hardly bring himself to take sudden and drastic action to which he would appear to have been compelled by your absenting yourself . . ."*

With this answer Portland had to be satisfied. He fretted for the rest of the summer but when at the end of June William made an appeal to him to play an important and secret role in the peace talks with France, he consented. At the end of August, having succeeded in his task, he joined the King at Dieren. For the moment, it seemed that the relationship between the two men had weathered the crisis. But Portland at least knew that it could never be the same again: he had to face the fact that Keppel was now as indispensable to the King as he himself had once been.

For the older man it was hard to accept. He had grown up with William since boyhood and in the household in Holland where there was hardly a woman to be seen, a great friendship and affection had developed between the lonely Prince and the Gelderland page, with his happily balanced family background. The early death of William's father and mother had left him with no one he could emotionally depend on until Hans Willem Bentinck came into his life, and even after their marriages William had found it difficult to let his friend go. While Portland adapted himself effortlessly to life with a wife and a family of his own, William's letters to him showed clearly the resentment he felt when family business took Portland away from his side. He found it impossible to imagine that any woman could have a greater claim on him or Portland, and however much he came to love Mary he never asked from her, or found it possible to give her, the same understanding as existed between him and Portland.

If William's feelings for Portland had homosexual overtones, this was almost certainly not the case with Portland. From the letters he wrote the King during the last crisis and his reluctance even to mention homosexuality by name – "*ces sanglantes choses*" – it is clear that his attitude was one of horror and disgust. He had grown up into a straitlaced man, who hated the decadent habits of many English noblemen and once expressed his desire to remove his son, Lord Woodstock, from England – "so that he would not learn the debauche of that country".* Even the scandalmongering Liselotte, who said "nothing is more ordinary in England than this unnatural vice", excluded Portland from her accusations when he came to Paris in 1698 with an English embassy, although she named several others.* And if Portland did not escape Jacobite insinuations about his friendship with William, more reliable observers in England never hinted that the relationship of the two men was anything but normal.

For William it was different. He was never very strongly attracted to women – his mother had more or less neglected him and his grandmother had been a distant and domineering figure. Throughout his life the rare women he found attractive were intelligent, witty and not always particularly feminine, like Charlotte van Beverwaert, whom he passed on to his friend Bentinck, boisterous Liselotte, and Betty Villiers. The ultra-feminine Mary seems almost to have frightened him in the beginning with the strength of her emotional demands. On the other hand, he gave himself without reserve in his friendship with men like Romney, Shrewsbury, Vaudemont, Portland and Keppel; men who combined great personal attraction with intelligence and ability were irresistible to him: apart from Portland, no friendship had been more important to him than that of Ossory, whom he met when he himself was only twenty, and whose memory he cherished for years afterwards, making a special pilgrimage to visit Ossory's boyhood home Kilkenny in Ireland in 1690. To what extent these relationships were homosexual is difficult to discover. In Holland William was surrounded by servants of outstanding loyalty, and Huygens was only once able to note the frequent private and lengthy visits to William's rooms of a handsome young captain of the cavalry, Dorp. It was in September 1683, but when he mentioned his suspicions to one of the Prince's staff, the man at once denied that anything was going on, adding, however, that he was not to mention it to anybody else.*

Huygens in any case was discreet in his journals less from choice than from lack of opportunity for observation – William was well aware of his secretary's inquisitiveness and kept him at a distance: Huygens was there when the King sent for him, and then only. It is also certain that William's marriage to Mary after the Villiers crisis was slowly gaining in intimacy and relaxation, while at the same time he had his intelligent mistress. From the evidence of Mary's private papers it is clear that his sexual relationship with her allowed her to go on hoping for a child.

And this relationship may have satisfied his physical needs for the time being and allowed him to suppress his homosexual inclinations. His affair with Betty may also have helped, although it is difficult to be sure how far, and for how long, sex entered into it. She certainly never had any children by him, yet when she married at the age of around thirty-eight in 1695 she presented her husband with three children in succession.*

After Mary's death and Betty's "dismissal" William found comfort and compensation in the company of Keppel, old enough to be talked to as an equal and still young enough to be stimulating to the tired and lonely King. Everybody noted Keppel's rapid climb in favour but hardly anyone thought any more about it at first – the King's agonizing grief at Mary's death was too evident. Liselotte, who had heard some earlier gossip, wrote around this time in reply to a reference from her aunt Sophia to the *"chateau de derrière"*; "it is true that people think of King William as belonging to that brotherhood, but they say he is less taken up with it now."*

But it was not long before all London was gossiping. When in 1696 Sir John Vanbrugh's comedy *The Relapse, or Virture in Danger* was first presented at the Theatre Royal in Drury Lane, its homosexual allusions were thought daringly topical. And the talk soon reached the Continent, where Portland heard it at The Hague, while the Jacobites at St. Germain made the most of it. "The King is said to have been in love with Albemarle as with a woman, and they say he used to kiss his hands before all the court", reported Liselotte later.*

Such displays of emotion were highly uncharacteristic of William, and talk of them can be dismissed as gossip. But Portland at least heard enough to be alarmed about the damage the King was doing to his own reputation. Keppel's familiar behaviour with the much older man, the King's obvious pleasure in this familiarity, and the hours they spent alone together, seemed to a jealous man final proof that the rumours were only too well founded. Portland's long letter of explanation is that of a man begging to be convinced that he is wrong. William, however, in his replies says nothing to reassure him, preferring to dwell on the damage that Portland's resignation will inflict on the reputation not only of Portland himself, but also of the King. He may not have been able to deny the accusation of a homosexual affair with Keppel – or he may not have wished to: throughout his life William never troubled to justify even his most criticized actions in public. But the fact that he refused to give even his best friend the satisfaction of a whole-hearted denial may be suggestive in itself. It is impossible to be certain. Burnet, speaking of a King he admired but never liked, says: "He had no vice but one sort, in which he was very cautious and secret" – and Swift, a friend of Betty Villiers and an enemy of William, added a footnote: "It was of two sorts – male and female – in the former he was neither cautious nor secret."*

For William's enemies there was no doubt that the King was a homosexual, and if his eulogists denied it strenuously – "To my certain knowledge he was as free from it as Lot when he left Sodom", according to one* – Portland's letter suggests that even his closest friends were not sure of the truth. The answer perhaps may be found in the triumph of Keppel, who remained closely attached to the King for the rest of his life, constantly rising in importance.

In August 1697 it was noted: "The Duke of Zell has presented the Earl of Albemarle with a rich chariot, and a sett of plate to fix in the same for a campagne; and the Elector of Brandenburgh presented him with a sett of fine horses."* They knew of no better way to please the King.

CHAPTER XXXIX

A Doubtful Peace

O N THE ROAD FROM THE HAGUE to Delft, William's grandfather Frederik Hendrik had built himself an elegant country mansion, designed by the famous Jacob van Campen and set in the wooded parklands of Rijswijk. It was built of deep rosy brick, decorated with bands and pilasters of creamy sandstone, and its interior had all the refined charm of noble Dutch mansions of the time, with decorations by Honthorst, Cornelius Delff and Kouwenburg.

Since the death of Frederik Hendrik, it had been little used by the Orange family, but on 9 May 1697 this pretty place became the focus of Europe's hopes for peace, when William III arrived there to open formal negotiations between the representatives of France and the Allies. Talks had already been going on for almost a year now, and the concessions that France had shown herself ready to make seemed to William to offer a sound basis for official discussion: in December 1696 Louis XIV had finally given way on the vital point of recognizing him as King of England. Only the Emperor still retained any enthusiasm for continuing the war, but in France, in England and in the United Provinces the clamour for peace was now too loud to be ignored.

When the negotiations opened at Rijswijk with Sweden as mediator, however, they soon developed into an elaborate diplomatic quadrille, with demand and counter-demand, concession and refusal coming from France and a pro-French Sweden on one side, England, the Republic, Spain and the Emperor on the other. William watched the futile proceedings with growing irritation, and learned almost with relief that the French armies were on the march again in Flanders. He hurried his armies there too late to save Ath from surrender on 5 June, but by a dramatic forced march overnight he succeeded in forestalling a French swoop on Brussels. It was a military master-stroke that put an end to war on the battlefield, and he felt that the time had come to be equally decisive at the conference table. Although the breach between himself and Portland at that moment was not yet completely healed, he called on his friend to put his diplomatic talents once more at his master's service.

There were two major obstacles to agreement between William and Louis, which the delegates at Rijswijk had not even touched upon. The lesser of them was Orange: William insisted that his principality should be restored to him with its civil and religious liberties intact, while Louis strongly objected to this Protestant haven and possible centre for rebellion in the heart of French territory. The second question was more crucial. The presence of James and his Court at St. Germain, so near to England and so accessible for discontented English Jacobites, was unacceptable to William, but Louis XIV, who believed strongly in the divine rights of kings and to whom recognition of William III had been a most painful concession, could not bring himself to dismiss this exiled King from his court.

These two questions could only be resolved by a more direct contact between the two Kings, and it was William who took the initiative. Portland had got on excellently with Marshal Boufflers when the Frenchman had been his prisoner after the fall of Namur in 1695, and Boufflers himself was now high in the favour of Louis XIV.

"They were saying yesterday", reported Liselotte on 11 July, "that my Lord Portland has begged the Marshal Boufflers to come and confer about some matter with him . . ."* On 8 July the two men met near Halle, not far from Brussels, and for two hours walked up and down an orchard together. It was the first of a series of private and informal conversations which by the end of a fortnight seemed to have broken the deadlock.

Louis promised to return Orange to the King, and even on the question of James's presence at St. Germain William had the impression that the French King was prepared to climb down. Boufflers had at first been reluctant to discuss it, but at a certain moment he murmured something vague about Avignon as a possible future residence for the exiled King. Portland took this for a commitment and wrote Shrewsbury: "Hence I doubt not he [James] will be removed from Paris, if France is sincere for peace."* In that case, he told Boufflers, the King would make no difficulty about a French claim – that Mary Beatrice's allowance of £50,000 a year should be regularly paid to her in future.

The King followed these negotiations from Brussels, where he relaxed with Keppel and with Portland when he was there. The three men were the guests of the Prince and Princess de Vaudemont and the King, looking fit and happy, was more at ease than anybody could remember in months. While Portland danced attention on a pretty

young widow, the Countess d'Aremberg, and Keppel flirted openly
with the Elector of Bavaria's mistress, the King escorted his hostess to
the Opera, and danced with her at a *fête champêtre* at their house.* "The
King grows gallant and popular. He was yesterday round the town at
Bruxelles to see all our ladies", it was reported to Shrewsbury,* who
wrote back tartly that the King and his friends would do well to pay
rather more attention to the ladies in England.*

When Portland returned from his last meeting with Boufflers with
news of Louis's concessions, William decided to spend the rest of the
summer at Het Loo, waiting for the results of the talks at Rijswijk.
There too matters were going more smoothly now. At the end of July
the French had offered favourable terms on the condition that a treaty
should be signed before 31 August. William agreed, and talked the
Spaniards into signing with him. The Emperor, however, refused and
when the final date came the paper remained unsigned. Louis announced
that the deadline would be extended till 20 September, adding that he
would now keep Strasbourg as a price for the delay occasioned by the
Emperor, but even this could not deter William from ending the war,
and on the appointed date France, England, the United Provinces and
Spain signed the peace treaty of Rijswijk. The Emperor was given one
more month to decide and followed on 30 October.

William learned the news at Het Loo, and Vernon wrote in great
relief to Shrewsbury: "There never came a peace so seasonable to any
people . . ."*

Vernon was wrong. At least one person was bitterly disappointed
that peace was made: the twenty-four-year-old Czar Peter of Russia,
who at that time arrived in Holland. This seven-foot-high monarch
came to pay homage and to offer him help against France. He was too
late, but his journey gave him at least a chance to gratify his curiosity
about life in Europe. This curiosity had been stimulated by François
Jacobiwitz le Fort, the Swiss Commander of his personal guard, who
had begun his military career in Holland and had introduced Dutch
shipbuilders in Leningrad. The young Czar, fascinated by everything
that had to do with ships, had spent many hours with these Dutch
craftsmen – even learning a smattering of their working-class Dutch.
He travelled incognito as a simple non-commissioned officer in a
company of 270 people, but his journey through Poland and Germany
had not passed unnoticed. "Blowing one's nose with one's hand must
be the height of fashion in Moscow if the Czar himself goes in for it",
wrote Liselotte after she had heard reports about Peter's visit to Berlin.*

As soon as he arrived in the United Provinces the Czar sent a message

to William expressing his desire to meet him, and the King invited him
to come to Utrecht on 11 September. The King, who had travelled
specially from Het Loo to Soestdijk, drove to the town where he
received the Russian delegation, headed by three ambassadors, in a
"publick house". After they had paid him their compliments, William
was led into a room where the Czar was waiting for him and the two
men "having embrac'd each other, conferred together by an interpreter
for two hours".*

The young Czar was deeply moved. "I have accomplished my wish
and I am sufficiently rewarded for my journey by having enjoyed your
presence", he told William. "It is your military genius that has inspired
my sword, and the noble emulation of your exploits has aroused in my
heart the first thoughts I ever had of enlarging my Empire." He promised
that if the war against France should be resumed he and his armies would
be at the service of William, and he offered free entry to Russia for all
Dutchmen.*

William listened straight-faced to the lyrical compliments, and invited the excited young man to dine with him at Soestdijk the next day,
which the Czar eagerly accepted. But when the meeting was over, the
sight of the curious crowds that had gathered outside provoked his
natural Romanov dread of a mob and he took the barge back to Amsterdam, excusing himself.* He had settled there after a short stay at Zaan-
dam, the little shipbuilders' town in North Holland, from where he had
also fled for the mobs that came to see him. As an English newspaper,
the *Post Boy*, reported: "He was ill-treated by the boys, who threw stones
at him; since which it has been forbid, upon pain of death to do any
harm to the Muscovites."* In Amsterdam "Pieterbaas" – as he was soon
called – stayed in a small boarding-house, the Oude Zijds Herenloge-
ment, and moved later to a little house on the Oostenburg wharfs of the
V.O.C., where he could be seen working like any common dockhand.*

When William sent him another invitation to dinner, this time at
The Hague, he accepted. "We hear the Czar was mightily pleased with
the magnificent dinner the King entertained him with", wrote Luttrell
afterwards, and the *Post Boy* added that he liked so much "our manner of
eating, that he merrily invited himself again".* During that second dinner
a huge crowd assembled to watch the two monarchs dining and Peter's
old fears returned. He offered to decapitate a few of them for William –
it was what he would have done in his own country, he explained – but
the King restrained him politely.

The Czar was still in The Hague when the Dutch celebrated the
peace of Rijswijk with a huge firework display. He had never seen

anything like it and to the great concern of William and his entourage, he borrowed a little boat and rowed fearlessly up and down the Vijver, while the fireworks crashed and sizzled around him.*

The peace treaty had been ratified on 5 October, but there were already grave reasons for misgiving. Nothing more had been said by the French about sending James away to Provence, and Vernon in concern noted on 8 October: "They talk of repairing the castles at Blois and Chambord, as if he were to retire no further."* William himself prayed in a letter to Heinsius that God might bless this peace, "but I confess that the way it has been made worries me not a little for the future".*

For all these doubts the King received the French ambassadors with great courtesy on 9 November, and assured them that he had never intended "any personal disrespect to so great a Prince, though circumstances had involved him in opposition to him; that he had always desired his esteem and asked for his friendship."* William was hatless during this interview – "I am not King in this country", he explained – and the conversation was relaxed and almost familiar. Callières, one of the French ambassadors, ventured to say that William appeared to him to be "so fond of war" that he could hardly believe that he would not wish to continue it. "He was no longer young", the King replied, "and had need of repose after so many labours as he had sustained during his life; that he knew the misery the people had suffered during the last war." "We told him that he had seen by the last war what France could do under a King like ours", reported Callières to his friend the Marchioness d'Uxelles. William had smiled – "He had been too sensible of it."

During the conversation the French ambassador had studied this dedicated opponent of their master with keen curiosity, and he was much impressed. "He speaks very well and to the point, and seems careful to choose the terms which he employs, so as to express neither too much nor too little. He speaks French very well and has no foreign accent. He speaks thick and very slowly." They had heard of his illness during the early part of that summer and the man in front of them now still showed traces of it. "He is thin, and appears to be of weak constitution, notwithstanding the great fatigue, which he daily undergoes in hunting, as he did yesterday in this cold weather, from morning till evening."*

The audience concluded with the King's assurance that "during the war he did what he could to gain their masters esteem; since a peace was concluded, he would doe the like to obtain his friendship." Instructions were sent off to Whitehall and Versailles for an exchange of Royal portraits.*

The formalities were now over, but the festivities continued. Anne, Princess de Vaudemont, had arrived in The Hague to act as hostess for William, and immediately after his audience with the French he took her off to the comedy. As always in her company he was relaxed and agreeable and he even enjoyed the great ball she organized for his birthday on 14 November at the palace at Noordeinde, rewarding her with a splendid present of diamonds.* "Everything was marvellous", he wrote to Portland, now back in England, "except for some of those squabbles among women, which are inevitable on these occasions."*

While the Dutch and English celebrated the Peace of Rijswijk, the French had little heart for festivities. Louis XIV tried to make the best of a bad job: "peace was the only point I had in view in every thing I undertook", he claimed; he had decided accordingly, "to sacrifice the fruits of my victory to the Repose of Europe". The Allies, so he boasted, "seeing the Vanity of their false Hopes and smarting with the real Sufferings, have accepted the Conditions I so frequently offer'd them . . ."*

But these fine phrases could not disguise the unpalatable reality: France had had to give up all the territories gained in the Low Countries since the Peace of Nijmegen in 1678; all her conquests in Spain beyond the Pyrenees; and many of the towns conquered in the Empire, with the exception of Strasbourg. The Rhine fortresses were razed, the Duke of Lorraine was given his estates back and Orange was restored to William.

Louis XIV minded even more, perhaps, the embarrassment of having to face his Royal guest James II after recognizing William, and as ill luck would have it, James and Mary Beatrice arrived at Fontaine-bleau for their annual autumn stay with the French King at the same time as the courier bringing news of the peace from Rijswijk. Louis, much mortified, was particularly kind and attentive, and promised that they would be allowed to stay at St. Germain. Mary Beatrice was sceptical: "For truly, after all we have seen happen, how can one believe oneself sure of anything in this world?" she wrote to her friend, Mère Priolo of the convent at Chaillot.* She could not fail to notice that the French court had already got into the habit of referring to her son-in-law as King William.

One of his staunchest fans there, as always, was Liselotte, whose hopes of marrying her daughter to the King of England had by no means been extinguished by Portland's courteous discouragement a year earlier, and had even revived a little that summer when it was rumoured round Paris and Versailles that William was considering her daughter. "I can't believe it" she wrote wistfully to Sophia of Hanover, "even if it were true, Madame Whore† would never permit it."* Nevertheless she thought it worth a try, and a month later her lady-in-waiting Christina de Meyercrone wrote another long letter full of elaborate compliments to Portland, stressing the great admiration Liselotte had always felt for this prince "with whom she had once hoped to be herself allied", and which had inclined her daughter in his favour. Madame de Meyercrone only finally came to the point in a postscript, and then in roundabout terms: "I would like to know if there are any laws against two people of different religions being married, as long as one does not give them a Jesuit for a director . . . and specially when one can confirm the peace of Europe with a princess who is well made and has a good character. . . .'*

Portland obligingly passed the letter on to William who answered him at leisure: "I'm sending back to you the letter of Madame Meyercrone, to which there is no other reply to be made but a compliment; you know well enough my feelings that such a marriage would not suit me . . ."* Portland translated this refusal into kinder terms, but it was all the same an unmistakable no.*

For William, it was no more than an incident in an autumn crowded with political and social obligations from beginning to end. In the brief intervals he hurried back to Het Loo not just to hunt, but to nurse his health, never fully restored since the springtime attacks of ague. It was now his legs that worried him particularly, and he called the distinguished Leedín Professor of medicine, Dr. Govaert Bidloo, to Het Loo to examine them. The doctor was appalled by what he saw: the left foot was swollen up above the ankle, the right one up to the heel, and the King told him that they had been inclined to swell in this way for the past two years. "But of late 'tis grown somewhat worse", he added. Dr. Bidloo questioned him about his general state of health, exercise and diet. William told him almost apologetically, "Everyone tells me that I do myself an injury by hunting hard; but if I do not follow violent exercises, the freedom of my respiration is much impair'd, and thereupon my feet swell more than at other times. Faint exercises do not avail me; but you'll see, that as soon as I have hunted hard, this swelling will abate." The doctor asked him how he looked after himself after a hard day's hunt. "From my infancy I have all along loved shooting, and have often been wet up to the knees", replied the King, "after which I always fed heartily, without shifting myself, and then sleep in a chair,

---

† Liselotte, Duchess of Orleans, was at daggers drawn with Madame de Maintenon, her sister-in-law, and invariably referred to her thus or in similar terms.

being very tired. Now my legs being always cold, I believe that has occasioned the swelling of my feet."*

Many of William's friends were in fact more and more worried by William's over-indulgence at table – he was eating huge meals these days, washed down by quantities of wine and strong ale. And the man who had once been noted and admired for his moderate drinking habits now liked to boast to his friends of his evenings over the bottle. "In the evening, we went on a debauch – at least for those who hadn't already celebrated the day's hunting too enthusiastically" he wrote to Portland that November.* Occasionally he lost all control in these drinking bouts and once, waving his glass, hit one of his companions in the face with it, spilling the wine all over the man's clothes – "he walked away sobbing with regret".*

As a young Prince, he had had nothing but disapproval for the debauched revels of his friends. Now he showed more understanding, and when Lord Pembroke came with a splitting head one morning to apologize for a display of drunken temper the evening before, William laughed it off. "No apologies," he said. "Make not yourself uneasy; these accidents over a bottle are nothing among friends."*

His growing intimacy with Keppel did nothing to discourage these habits. He was supping or dining with the young man two or three times a week, sitting on for hours afterwards drinking and talking.* And his doctors, who were always urging him to cut down on his eating and drinking, had no success. As he told Bidloo during his consultation at Het Loo: "Every one that is above 30 or 40 years of age ought to be his own Physician", adding defensively: "So long as I eat well, I am of the opinion 'twill do me no great harm."*

Bidloo realized that it was hopeless to try and restrain this difficult patient, and allowed him to drink freely of cider, ale and strong beer. At the same time, he prescribed that the King's swollen legs should be rubbed night and morning with flannel covered with a powder of crabs' eyes, flour and cummin seed, together with occasional hot poultices. William made free use of the first part of Bidloo's advice, and continued to drink as before, but he refused absolutely to follow the second part – the hot poultices kept him awake, he complained.*

When Dr. Radcliffe examined the King some weeks later in London, it was not surprising that the legs were no better, and he had also suffered "some small fits of gout in his knee". "I would not have your Majesty's two legs for your three Kingdoms" the English doctor exclaimed with his usual bluntness. The King was not pleased, and he was even less pleased when he was firmly lectured about his drinking and eating habits. Dr. Radcliffe was dismissed and William's legs continued to bother him.*

Their swollen and uncomfortable state had forced him to give up the idea of making his triumphal entry into London on horseback, as Portland had announced – hard hunting was one thing, but hours spent gently jogging along the cobbled streets of the capital was another matter. Instead he went by coach.

For weeks London had been preparing itself for one of the most glorious receptions of a monarch since Charles II's entry at the Restoration. News of the Peace of Rijswijk reached the city on 14 September o.s., when Matthew Prior presented the peace treaty to the Lords Justices at Whitehall. The great guns of the Tower boomed out the good news, flags were hoisted all over town and the bells were rung. The price of Bank of England stock shot up from 84 to 97, and euphoria seized the English, tired to death by nine years of war.

"The people are now in much better humour", commented Vernon, who did not share the popular illusions, "and relish the peace more than they will a year hence, when they shall find taxes in a good measure continued, troops lying heavie upon them as being in great numbers dispersed about the country, and that there will not be so quick a consumption for their goods, nor can cattle bear so high a price as in time of war . . ."*

But in their festive mood, most of the English had no time for these gloomy thoughts, and the celebrations went on for two months. One of the highlights was a king-sized bonfire organized by the Dutch ambassador at the end of October, in front of his house in St. James's Square. It was made with 140 barrels of pitch, built up into a pyramid on seven scaffolds; while it blazed merrily away trumpets were sounded, and "two hogs heads of wine were kept running continually amongst the common people".*

The climax of the celebrations was planned for the King's return from the Continent: "the lord mayor and aldermen of London", it was announced, "have resolved to receive his majestie on horseback in their scarlet gowns and gold chaines, with the citty companies in all their formalities, as they did King Charles."* Plans for huge triumphal arches were made, but later discarded at the request of the King, partly because they would block the view from the upper storeys of houses along the route, but also because his innate dislike of such shows had been increased "by what he had heard of the gross excesses of flattery to which the French have run . . . in honour of their King".*

Despite William's "modesty", his entry was as regal as the City could make it. On Sunday, 14 November o.s. he landed at Margate and on Tuesday, the sixteenth, he began his entry from Greenwich "in great splendour". With him in his coach went the Prince of Denmark; at his side sat Keppel, while Portland waited at Whitehall and Anne watched from a window at the house of a city merchant near the Exchange at Cornhill. On St. Margaret's hill in Southwark, the King and his retinue were greeted by the Lord Mayor in full regalia, and from there the procession moved slowly through the city – "horse grenadeers, the two citty marshalls with their men, 3 trumpets . . . citty sword bearer, the aldermen, recorder and sherifs all on horseback in their scarlet gowns . . . gentleman usher of the black rodd, lord mayor bearing the citty sword, garter king at arms". At last the King himself in his coach, attended by the Gentlemen Pensioners, footmen and equerries, and followed by "nobility and gentry in coaches with 6 horses each to the number of 80".*

The public loved it. London had never seen such crowds, and the crowds had never seen such a show. They cheered themselves hoarse for their hero and Portland wrote to his friend Vaudemont: "He entered London today amid extraordinary acclamations of joy, and the greatest concourse of people that I think can ever have been seen."* The King himself reported more modestly that evening to Heinsius: "It is impossible to conceive what joy the peace causes here . . ." He was particularly gratified by the fact that there had been so many "people of quality" among the cheering crowds.*

Two days later he announced that Thursday, 2 December, would be kept as a day of public thanksgiving, a holiday. He had intended to celebrate it himself by attending service in the newly-consecrated St. Paul's Cathedral, which – after Wren on special orders sent from Holland had doubled the number of workmen – was almost completed. Its sheer size staggered visitors. One foreigner quipped, it should be "capable of putting a stop to all the corruption of London, provided the efficacy of the sermons is answerable to the largeness of the building".* But it was this "largeness" that obliged the King to abandon the idea of attending the inaugural service of Thanksgiving there – it was pointed out to him that the whole of London would flock to St. Paul's to see him – so in the end he attended service in his own chapel at Whitehall where Burnet preached a sermon "somewhat too eulogistic for the place", as Evelyn put it.*

In the evening, there was another great firework display in St. James's Square, in front of Romney's house, where the King dined. It had cost £10,000, some estimated – but it ended in tragedy. Several people were injured crushing into the small square, and at least three died.*

Next day it was back to business for the King when Parliament met again, and if he had imagined that the uncritical adulation of the ordinary people would be wholeheartedly echoed by the House of Commons, he was soon disillusioned. As far as they were concerned, peace raised one major question: what to do with the huge armies built up during the war years? To leave such a weapon in the hands of their King was contrary to every English political instinct, and to keep so many Dutch soldiers in the country was contrary to every English prejudice. Discussion of this question was to rage on for months to come, to the grief and disgust of the tired King, and in the circumstances the arrival of Czar Peter from Holland, still in pursuit of his hero, was almost light relief.

The English were every bit as curious as the Dutch to see this scruffy giant, but he did everything in his power to disappoint them. When he disembarked on 10 January 1698, he ordered all the crew of the ship to go below deck before he would appear, and when he dined two days later with William at Kensington in public he got up and left the table at once, complaining later: "'twas strange he could not eat without being stared at".* In deference to his paranoia, William himself only went to see him in private and arranged for him to watch from a small room when he came to Anne's birthday ball at Kensington on 6 February. When Peter wanted to see the King in Parliament, but refused to go inside the building, he was put in "a gutter upon the house top, to peep in at the window, where he made so ridiculous a figure that neither King nor people could forbear laughing".*

Dread of crowds was not his only whim. When William called on him once in York buildings, he was confronted with Peter's pet monkey who jumped angrily on the King as soon as he sat down. Nobody could talk of anything else for the rest of the visit, and the Czar exhausted himself with apologies.*

It was a relief to everyone when he moved to Deptford, in order to be near the shipyards which fascinated him so much, and settled into Evelyn's charming house, Sayes Court. He turned it almost immediately into a pigsty, and Evelyn's servant wrote in despair to his master: "The Czar lies next your library, and dines in the parlour next your study." When the King came to visit him there, hurried efforts were made to put at least one room into some sort of order, and in the end the disgusted Evelyn had to call in Wren and the King's gardener, Mr. London, to estimate the cost of repairing the appalling havoc, then sent in a bill for £150.*

As in Amsterdam, a sham naval battle was laid on for the Czar during a visit to Portsmouth; but when he asked for a demonstration of keel-hauling, it was politely refused. He visited the Mint; and he turned out to have a keen eye for technical details – calling on the King at Kensington he fiddled incessantly with the sash-windows, a revolutionary novelty for him, and Burnet said scornfully, "The Czar . . . seems designed by nature rather to be a ship-carpenter than a great prince."*

He had, however, one taste that Whitehall might consider civilized – he loved going to the theatre, and he had an eye for a pretty actress; after he had seen Mrs. Cross playing, he insisted on meeting her, and an affair was the result. And even by Whitehall standards he was a formidable drinker – the company watched in awe one evening as he sank a pint of brandy, a bottle of sherry and eight bottles of sack before going to the theatre.*

He took his leave at last on 23 April, giving William a ruby valued at £10,000, wrapped up in a "piece of brown paper".* Then he sailed on board the *Royal Transport* that William had given him, returning to Holland where he lingered till June before turning his back on Western civilization again.

It is doubtful if this civilization had made a great impression on him. A year later, news reached the West of a magnificent entertainment, lasting three days, that Peter had put on for the Imperial envoy at Moscow. He "caused the 1st day, while they were at dinner, 1500 men to be beheaded: the 2nd day, 700 to be strangled; and on the 3rd, 400 had their ears and noses cutt off, in sight of the company." It was his punishment to those who had rebelled against him while he was absent paying homage to the King-Stadholder.*

CHAPTER XL

The Spanish Succession

O N TUESDAY, 4 JANUARY 1698, nearly two centuries of English history went up in smoke. A Dutch maid, at four in the afternoon, lit a charcoal fire to dry off some linen in one wing of Whitehall Palace, partly restored after the fire of 1691. Within minutes the panelled room was ablaze and the fire spread with horrifying speed through the whole ramshackle complex of buildings. A hard dry frost had set in two days earlier, and the firefighters found the Thames almost frozen over. The King came down from Kensington and watched from the Park while frantic efforts were made to save at least parts of the Palace by blowing up buildings. But by midnight his apartments, the new wing the Queen had occupied and most of the offices had already been destroyed, and when dawn broke Whitehall was a smouldering pile of ashes, in the middle of which the one building that had been saved, Inigo Jones's beautiful Banqueting House, rose blackened by the flames.*

However rambling and inelegant the Palace, its destruction was felt as a major catastrophe by the Londoners. Even if their present King no longer cared to live there, it was still the centre of government, and it was familiar territory to almost everybody. Now nothing was left of so much splendour – priceless art treasures had perished while only dull archives had been saved. The King himself had no personal regret but he was sensitive enough to appreciate the feelings of the English. "This loss would be greater to any other person than to me, because I could not reside there", he wrote to Heinsius, "However the loss is considerable."* And visiting the smoking ruins next day, he promised "if God would give him leave he would rebuild it, and much finer than before".*

Almost immediately gangs of labourers were set to work clearing away the rubble, and Sir Christopher Wren was called in to survey the ruins with a view to rebuilding it. Working at his usual speed, he soon came up with a scheme for a new Whitehall on a scale of Louvre-like grandeur, with the Banqueting House as its centre-piece and a long colonnade to connect it with the Houses of Parliament.* Whether William seriously contemplated spending hundreds of thousands of pounds on rebuilding a palace he had always disliked seems doubtful. In any case it reawakened his interest in other Royal palaces, like Windsor Castle, for which the indefatigable Wren shortly afterwards produced another stupendous scheme: a new Italianate addition to this neo-medieval castle. Huge tracts of land round about were bought up to be laid out by the master-gardener of Versailles, Le Nôtre, who came over later on to take a look.*

Windsor Castle had become the King's favourite country palace – he seldom went back to Hampton Court after Mary's death – and he was in the habit of going down from Kensington for three or four days at a time when he could get away. Just before the fire at Whitehall, he had taken Portland down with him to Windsor to discuss the important mission his friend was about to undertake. He had appointed Portland to be his first official ambassador to Paris and no one could have been better qualified than Portland for this job. His French was faultless and his manners polished, but even more important, he was Dutch: for the delicate negotiations ahead, an English politician would have been unacceptable to Louis XIV as a man who had broken his oath to James.

It was believed by the unkind at Court that there was yet another reason for the choice of Portland. He was once more finding it impossible to conceal his jealousy and resentment of Albemarle, and the King found the situation too painful to tolerate. Portland himself evidently believed that the King wanted him out of the way and when he left on 10 January – his departure had been delayed by the fire at Whitehall – the King sent a note after him to try and cheer him up: "Rest assured that I am more touched by your going than you could possibly believe, and if you suffered as much at leaving me as I do when I see you go, I should be very happy . . ."* Portland was not convinced and said so in his reply before he sailed, hinting once more at his wish to leave the King's service. "I have found an expression in one of your letters from Dover, which has upset me terribly", William wrote back anxiously. "I beg you to decide nothing, not even in your thoughts, until I have a chance to see you again. I always love you the same."*

William who knew how to impress the Sun King, had spared no expense for Portland's mission. "The embassy to France will cost . . . £40,000", it was reported, "he has four coaches made here; the best cost £600; and two more made in Holland, beside the coach of state made at Paris, which costs £6000 . . ."* Portland also took an enormous personal retinue: a gentleman of the Horse, twelve pages and fifty-six footmen.* A great number of English noblemen followed him.

In Paris Portland was lent the magnificent Hôtel d'Auvergne in the Rue de la Planche, but it was not impressive enough, and in three weeks a state dining-room was built on in the garden, where he began immediately to entertain.* Knowing better than to compete with French cuisine and wines, "his Excellency had frequently sirloins of English beef sent from Dover, which being landed at Calais, were despatched from thence by messenger on purpose to come fresh to Paris", reported a contemporary historian. "He also had large quantities of the finest Herefordshire cider and Burton ale, which were so fine that the custom-house officers on the Seine said it was vin d'Espagne, and would have seized it if it had not belonged to his Excellency."*

The French were duly impressed, and Saint-Simon gave him full marks: "His suite was numerous and superb, his expenditure on the most magnificent scale at table . . . and he displayed besides exquisite taste and refinement . . ."* His Dutch secretary Van Leven wrote complacently back to London that the French "do all the honour to his Excellency that can be desired".*

Portland's dazzling success would have amazed Whitehall, where he had been written off long since as a dull and grasping boor. In Paris, on the contrary, he was soon all the rage, and everyone admired "a personal distinction, a polish, an air of a man of the world and of a courtier, gallant and graceful manners . . ."* One of his most enthusiastic admirers was Liselotte who, as Portland wrote to William, received him "with demonstrations of joy and satisfaction of which she made no secret", saying loudly in front of her friends how much she had admired his master, even during the war.*

When Portland made his public entry in March, driving in full splendour through Paris on his way to Versailles, public interest was enormous and the irony of the moment was not lost on the Parisians when they saw the arms of England glittering on his coach. "What do we see today", exclaimed someone on the Pont Neuf, who remembered the joyful celebrations of William's "death" at the Boyne in 1690, "the solemn entry of a King that we burned at this same bridge eight years ago."* Arrived at Versailles Portland sailed gracefully through the maze of Court etiquette and Louis made the unprecedented gesture of speaking first, saying how glad he was to see so many English and French together.

It was not the first meeting between Louis and Portland: they had met in private at the beginning of February. The ambassador had as his mission to try and find a solution for the Spanish succession question; to talk Louis into sending James II away; and to get him to agree to stop countenancing Jacobite conspirators in France. At his first audience Portland made the error of starting with the last two questions. Louis denied then that he had ever promised to send James away, and Portland had replied that in that case there could be no question of the £50,000 allowance being paid to Mary Beatrice. Louis had been displeased and answered that whatever happened, he would never agree to dismiss the Royal exiles. Portland met the same negative response when he mentioned Jacobite plotters at Versailles: the King replied coldly that he knew of none.*

William was annoyed by Louis's reaction, as he made clear in a letter to Heinsius, but he felt at the same time that it had been tactless of Portland to raise these questions so early in his embassy. He told him so in his next letter, softening his reproof with an expression of affection "I begin to be extremely impatient to have you with me again, loving you always the same."* The King had been unwell all week, having lost his appetite, and his swollen legs had been bothering him so much that for three weeks he was unable to leave his room – "in all my life I have never been more grieved and melancholy than I am at the moment", he confessed in one of his letters.*

What worried the King most was that Portland's tactlessness in the question of James would make it more difficult to reach agreement over the most important part of his mission: the question of the Spanish succession. And indeed it took Louis and Portland a long time before they reached this subject which was beginning to preoccupy every statesman in Europe.

Charles II, the King of Spain – a sick man since he had come to the throne in 1665 – had no heir despite two marriages, and in March 1698 he was once more reported to be at death's door. The future of the enormous Spanish Empire – it comprised all Spain, the Spanish Netherlands, chunks of Italy and North Africa and huge territories in the New World – thus hung in the balance.

Before his death in 1558 the Emperor Charles V had split up his Habsburg Empire into a Spanish and an Austrian branch, and through a series of dynastic marriages, both Louis XIV and the Emperor could now put forward strong claimants to the Spanish throne. For Louis XIV the fact that his wife Maria Theresa, sister of Charles II, had renounced her rights on marriage was irrelevant, since her dowry had never been paid by Spain, and he now claimed on behalf of the Dauphin.

The Emperor had no intention of conceding the French pretensions and he had two candidates of his own: his grandson by the daughter of his first marriage, the six-year-old son of the Elector of Bavaria, and his son Charles by his third marriage (the older son Joseph was destined for the Imperial Crown). As his daughter Maria Antonia had renounced her rights and those of her little son, the Emperor's son Charles was the rightful candidate in his father's eyes, but Madrid recognized neither the claims of the Dauphin nor Charles, and had already named the Electoral Prince of Bavaria as heir to Charles II.

Both England and the United Provinces supported the Madrid view, since the presence of either a Habsburg or a Bourbon on the Spanish throne would destroy the balance of power in Europe. William, however, understood that the French King would certainly not allow the entire prize to escape him, and that if war was to be prevented on the death of Charles, at least some part of the Spanish inheritance had better be conceded in advance to the Dauphin. And he was prepared to agree to this on the condition that in no case should the Spanish Netherlands – the vital "*barrière*" – fall into French hands. He was also anxious to gain England a foothold in the Mediterranean – Ceuta, Port Mahon or Oran – to counterbalance the dangerous new French presence there. But his main objective was to keep the peace in Europe: "I own that I have so great an inclination to see no more war for the little time that remains to me to live," he told Portland, "that I would do anything in honour and conscience to that end . . ."*

Louis himself was realist enough to know that however exhausted Europe – and King William – might be by war, it was unlikely that he would be allowed to swallow up the whole Spanish Empire without resistance from the Allies. And on 14 March he sent his two ministers, Pomponne and de Torcy, to Portland to find out William's views on the Spanish succession. It was the start of discussions that lasted for months.

THE FRENCH KING AND William's ambassador got on remarkably well. Whenever Portland came to Versailles Louis paid him every possible mark of respect. "Every time he saw me", wrote Portland to William, "sometimes three times in one day, he greeted me and had long conversations with me, laughing and talking about all kinds of things."* To the great surprise and jealousy of the French Court, Portland was even handed the royal candlestick at the King's *couchée* one evening – "a favour only shown to the most considerable persons, and those whom the King wishes to distinguish".*

Even more gratifying to the English embassy was the admiration the French obviously felt for King William. As Portland wrote: "I may say without flattery that your Majesty is generally more esteemed, honoured and respected by this Court than in our own countries."* And Matthew Prior wrote in astonishment to the Earl of Pembroke: "it is incredible what true respect and veneration they bear to King William: '*Le plus beau prince du monde*' are the least things they say of him . . ."*

Nothing like the same respect was shown to James, he reported. "Poor King James is hardly thought on or mentioned . . . he is so directly the same man he ever was."* He gave a cynical description of the exiled King: "You never saw such a strange figure as the old bully is, lean, worn and rivel'd . . . the Queen looks very melancholy, but otherwise well enough; their equipage are all very ragged and contemptible . . ."*

But the irreverent young Englishman was not much more impressed by the splendours of Versailles and the Sun King himself: "The monarch as to his health is lusty enough, his upper teeth are out, . . . and he picks and shows his under teeth [with] a good deal of affectation, being the vainest creature alive even as to the least things." The famous palace of Versailles was, wrote Prior, "the foolishest in the world: [Louis] is strutting in every panel and galloping over one's head in every ceiling, and if he turns to spit he must see himself in person or his Vicegerent the Sun with *sufficit orbi*, or *nec pluribus impar*."*

The Dauphin he dismissed – "much like our Prince George, except that the one only makes love to the Princess, and the other every girl at the Opera without distinction."* But he was amazed by the importance of Madame de Maintenon, "our good friend" as he always called her in his letters to Keppel. "It is prodigious what power this old governess has over the mind of her royal pupil of sixty. He dares not do anything without her, refuses her nothing that she wants . . ."*

Madame de Maintenon was a close friend of Mary Beatrice, and resolutely refused to acknowledge the presence of Portland, but to his surprise not all James's followers appeared to share her feelings – "the Duc de Lauzun, the principal counsellor to King James, affects to be civil to me to a degree that surprises everyone", wrote Portland. And he was surprised to learn that James, "by the favourable manner in which everyone says he speaks of me", would not have been at all embarrassed to find himself in Portland's company.* He himself was anxious to avoid such encounters and his efforts to do so made his embassy to Paris something of a strain. He was thoroughly relieved when it came to an end in June. Like every visitor to Paris he had a shopping list to get through before he left, mostly commissions from William who had asked him to order some furniture for Dieren, damask and fine brocades and a horse. But he found it all too expensive and bought only the horse, an Arab from the King's own stables – big, beautiful and as strong as he'd ever seen – a good stud, Portland thought.*

On his own account – one of his jobs was Superintendent of William's gardens – he ordered fruit trees, sending all the way to Orléans for them, and with the grand new gardens at Windsor to be planned, he had taken a keen look at the gardens of the Sun King soon after his arrival in February, sending a long description of them to William. "The orange trees at Versailles are extremely beautiful and large and numerous, the trunks fine and high, but the heads not like those at Honselaersdijck . . . Of all the thousands of flowers of which your Majesty has heard so much, that the flower gardens were full of them all seasons, I have not seen a single one, not even a snowdrop." He was amazed by the way the gardens were left untouched all winter, and by the colossal sums spent on them.*

On 17 June he paid at last a farewell visit to Louis and they had a final long talk. The French King had already given him his portrait set in diamonds – of a value of at least 32,000 crowns – and he now took a friendly interest in Portland's journey home, urging him to see some of the great beauties of France on the way. He begged him not to miss some particularly fine towns in Flanders – Cambrai, Valenciennes, Condé, Tournai, and Ypres – names all too familiar to Portland from former battles. It only meant a small detour, he pointed out.* Ten days later Portland was back in London. His embassy, it was agreed by everyone, had been a great personal triumph.

"THE KING OF ENGLAND is very far from being master here; he is generally hated by all the great men and the whole of the nobility . . . It is not the same with the people, who are very favourably inclined towards him, yet less so than in the beginning." So wrote Camile d'Hostun, Comte and Duc de Tallard, from London that spring of 1698.* This shrewd and polished diplomat had been sent by Louis XIV as his own envoy to William. It had not taken Tallard very long to measure up the court, with the help of a careful briefing by the French Foreign Office from which it becomes clear how well informed Versailles was about the political situation in England.

"The Secretaries of State, with the exception of the Duke of Shrewsbury, had been, properly speaking only clerks, employed in writing the dispatches without having anything to do with the secrets," so ran

Tallard's brief, "the councils only meet for the form's sake, and important affairs are not discussed in them, thus all centres in the King of England alone." Tallard was warned about the importance of the Dutch at Court, and especially of Portland and Albemarle – "The credit of the latter has considerably increased of late; he takes cognizance of all affairs . . . it seems that he is at present in very high favour, while that of the Earl of Portland is on the decline."*

Only a few weeks after Tallard had arrived in April, he was able to confirm his brief from Versailles. It was, so he said, "the friendship this Prince shows to the Dutch, the intimacy in which he lives with them and with foreigners, the immense benefits which he confers on them, and the declared favour of the Earl of Albemarle, who is a very young man", that had produced the hatred the English nobility felt for their King.* Commenting some time later on the dispute between Portland and Albemarle, he told Versailles, "I am persuaded that when the Earl of Portland returns, he will find a place, though in this country he is looked upon as ruined."*

Tallard had rented the splendid house of the Duke of Ormonde in the fashionable St. James's Square and was soon as much the social rage in London as Portland was in Paris, when William went in April to the Newmarket races. The King put a show on for his guest – it was the most glittering visit Newmarket could remember – taking the whole court with him. The Prince of Denmark was there, the Dukes of Somerset, Grafton, Richmond and St. Albans, the Earls of Marlborough, Albemarle, Jersey, Orkney and seven other earls. The Dutch ambassador came with all the other foreign ministers; even Shrewsbury had dragged himself from his sick bed to be there.* Special orders were given for the furnishing of the King's house. "A crimson damask bed, chairs, stooles, screenes, window-curtaines, Looking Glasses . . ." were ordered to the value of about £600.*

The Royal gardeners had been busy: £235 8s 6d was spent "for work done at Newmarket, carriage and digging of earths, gravel and for looking after the said gardens and furnishing several trees and flowers for the use of the same".* This year too, Dutch bulbs made their first show in the Royal gardens here.

William had sent his hounds to the meeting and ordered falcons to be sent over from Holland. But the principal interest at Newmarket, then as now, was horses, and the King was proud of his. Ouwerkerk, his Master of the Horse, had a lavish budget, spending thousands of pounds in buying up champions all over Europe for the Royal Mews, and this season, as usual, they did not let him down. *Stiff Dick* and *Turk* were absolute masters of the course; *Turk*, in particular, was raced against Lord Carlisle's *Spot* for £500 and beat him unexpectedly – the odds had been 3 to 1 against him.* As always, betting was heavy, and fortunes changed hands at Newmarket, not just on horse-racing but as much on cockfights. The King himself saw six of these one afternoon before going to the races.

In the mornings everyone hunted, not always with great success – such numbers of people crowded to see all these swells, it was reported on the first day of the Royal visit by the *Post Man*, that the hare coursing was a fiasco – "it was impossible to run one hundred yards without starting others and changing."*

In all these amusements Tallard was the guest of honour: his place at table was next to the Royal armchair, and the King graciously drank his health.* No business, of course, was talked at Newmarket, but once back in London, negotiations began in earnest. At the outset, Tallard had been reserved and wary in his dealings with William, but now he knew him better and he was very much impressed by his direct and straightforward manner. "He is very quick on the uptake, his judgment is sound, and he will soon perceive that we are trifling with him if we protract matters too much", he reported to Louis XIV, adding a little later: "The King of England had hitherto acted with great sincerity, and I venture to say, that if he once enters into a treaty with your Majesty he will steadily adhere to it."* This treaty, of course, dealt with the business of the Spanish Succession: like Portland in Paris, Tallard had been instructed to sound out the King's opinions and see what solutions might be agreed on between London and Versailles.

Talks about this complicated matter continued intermittently throughout the summer, and when William left for the Continent in July, he gave Tallard an invitation to join him later on at Het Loo, since there was still much to discuss.

William's departure that summer of 1698 was resented even more than normally by the English who could see no reason for their King to leave the country now that the war was over. Tallard reported in the spring already that "people murmur here at the journey to Holland",* but the King was completely indifferent to such sentiments and was determined to escape from the irritation of English politics for as long as possible. On 29 July Tallard watched him go from Margate – "His countenance was expressive of the joy which he felt at going to Holland; he took no pains whatever to conceal it from the English, and to say the truth, they speak very openly about it . . ."*

To the fury of the English William spent two months at Het Loo with his friends followed by a visit to Zell. This visit had as first aim a possible match between the Duke of Gloucester and the small grand-daughter of the Electress Sophia of Hanover, to strengthen the Prot-estant succession and bind Hanover and England closer together. Sophia came to Zell in the company of her son George, a lazy, not very intelligent, and obstinate man of thirty-eight with fair hair and bulging blue eyes, and William studied him with interest: if Anne's ailing son did not survive, George – after Sophia – would succeed Anne on the throne of England.

Before the King had left Het Loo for Zell the question of the other succession, that to the throne of Spain, had at last been settled and the First Partition Treaty between England, France and the United Prov-inces had been signed in secret at Het Loo. The electoral Prince of Bavaria was the triumphant candidate. To him was allotted Spain, the Spanish Netherlands and the colonies; Naples and Sicily went to the Dauphin, and Milan and the Milanese to the Emperor's son Charles. The possibility that neither the Emperor nor Spain would quietly sit back and accept this division of the spoils was dismissed by both Louis and William as irrelevant. The most important thing was that war appeared to have been avoided – as long as Louis was prepared to keep his word.

William, as was his habit in foreign affairs, had consulted no English minister before making up his mind: only when the treaty was already drafted was the Chancellor Somers informed of it, and although he and other Whig ministers hastily composed and sent off to William a letter expressing their doubts whether the proposed division of the Spanish inheritance would do much to safeguard the peace of Europe, the King went ahead. William had his own misgivings, for that matter: "We are making very arbitrary decisions in matters of which we are not the masters", he told Tallard. But for the moment, it seemed the best that could be done.

Like Portland in Paris, the King raised the question of James's position at Versailles, but unlike his ambassador he waited until the Spanish succession question was safely out of the way before turning to this matter on which he knew that Louis XIV had strong personal feelings. "The King of England said to me", reported Tallard in November, "that he could not conceal his astonishment that at the time he was entering into the closest and most important engagements with us, more honours than ever were paid to King James." William was careful to make it clear that he spoke from no personal animus: "he pitied King James . . . but . . . in truth there could not be two Kings of England."* Louis did not budge. "Ill fortune cannot take the title or quality of King from a person who has once received it", he wrote back firmly.*

It was Edward Villiers, now Lord Jersey, Portland's successor in Paris, who that autumn had emphasized in a letter how Louis surrounded James and Mary Beatrice with his special care. "King James and his Queen are highly caressed at Fontainebleau, . . . the main court was made to Queen Mary, everybody being at her toilet in the morning . . . and '*à boire pour le roi d'Angleterre ou pour la Reine*' is spoke out as loud and with as much ceremony as for the King of France."*

The appointment of Jersey to this important embassy had been a blow to Portland's influence at Court. The Englishman, brother of Betty, had never been a friend of Portland, cultivating a great friendship with Albemarle. William liked this pleasant, amusing man – "a good figure in his person, being tall, well-shaped, handsome" – and despite what was generally considered as a "weak capacity", Jersey's rise to eminence was spectacular. He was no more than the Queen's Master of Horse in 1689 but became one of the Lords Justices of England by 1700.* William used to dine often at his lodge in the Park, and it was said of him that he could do "wonders on the slightest occasion".*

He had to perform one of these wonders in November of that year. To the astonishment and delight of the court at Het Loo, William and Albemarle had a row, and the young man retired from Court to go and sulk in the country. The occasion of this row was Portland's triumph – the last he was to enjoy – over his rival in the matter of William's Dutch Secretariat. Since Huygens's retirement, more and more of these duties had been taken over by Albemarle until now, at Portland's strong suggestion, the King appointed a full-time professional, his wife's former secretary d'Allonne, to the post. Vernon echoed the general surprise: "I must needs say that this is not what I expected, that a place which my Lord Albemarle had executed so long, should be given to a creature of my lord Portland. I suppose it must cost the King something considerable to set the balance even."*

Tallard, like everyone else, assumed that Albemarle had lost and that it was now Portland "who gets the upper hand".* Even William's great indulgence was strained by Albemarle's childish behaviour, and although at the request of Albemarle's mother, he had promised that her son should be enrolled that year in the highly distinguished Equestrian Order of Holland, he now refused absolutely to be hurried. "I beg you assure him that I am inclined towards it", he wrote to Heinsius, who had been approached by Albemarle at The Hague, "but at the same time tell him that, on account of the formalities, you fear that the matter cannot take place before my departure for England."*

Jersey was called from Paris to mediate. A compromise was found: from now on, d'Allonne remained Dutch Secretary, but his instructions were given to him by Albemarle, and not by the King, a fact that, as Tallard noted, would be "a source of an infinity of disputes, because the said d'Allonne is entirely devoted to the Earl of Portland, and never would consent to see Lord Albemarle".*

For the moment, peace had again been restored in the Royal Household. And when the King arrived back in England at the beginning of December, Albemarle was once more in his usual place at William's side.

The crossing had been a slow one – "I took two days and two nights to make the passage because there was little wind", reported William to Heinsius. But he was in no great hurry to get back to London and the problems that had piled up during his long absence. He knew that he could look forward to another winter of trouble at home: "The parliament meets today for the first time", he added in sombre apprehension.*

CHAPTER XLI

Xenophobia

To pay our just taxes was once thought too much,
But now extraordinary charity is such
*We bankrupt ourselves for maintaining the Dutch.**

T HIS WAS ONE OF MANY anti-Dutch ballads, lampoons and cartoons circulating in London in the autumn of 1698. English jealousy of the Dutch, "restrained during the war by the associated interests of England and Holland, now broke forth with the utmost violence,"* wrote an English historian looking back one hundred years later on those times. And it was in this mood that William's fourth House of Commons waited for his return.

The General Election of the summer had returned a House with a strong Tory majority, anti-war, anti-army, and indeed anti-Dutch. They had been summoned for 29 November, and they came up to London thirsting for action, only to learn that the King was still lingering in Holland with his Dutch favourites. When he at last returned and assembled his parliament on 6 December, it was the worst-tempered Commons of his reign. Almost their first action was to propose cutting the army down to seven thousand men only, and to insist that every one of them should be a native-born Englishman. The King was shattered. By this vote the House of Commons stripped England of its necessary defences, scattered a carefully built-up and experienced army, and confirmed their xenophobic ingratitude to the foreigners who had fought for them, such as the many French Huguenots and the King's own Dutch troops.*

"I am so upset by what's happening in the House of Commons about the troops that I can't think about anything else", he wrote just before Christmas to Heinsius.* He found it difficult to sleep, his appetite went, headaches tormented him, and a worried Vernon reported to Shrewsbury: "The King is not very right in his health . . . he cannot overcome himself under what he thinks a hard usage."* William in fact was seriously considering going back to Holland for good, and leaving this ungrateful and hostile people to their fate.

At first his ministers could not believe he was serious, but when the King wrote out an Abdication speech in his own hand, they realized with alarm that he meant it. William himself had already given a strong hint in his letters to Heinsius: "Business in Parliament is so desperate that in a short time I shall have to do something that will make a great noise in the world", and he warned that the Raadspensionary would see him in Holland earlier than he had expected.*

The Abdication speech composed by William was a dignified reproach. ". . . seeing . . . that you have so little Regard to my Advice, and that you take no Manner of Care of your own Security, and that you expose yourself to evident Ruin, by divesting yourself of the only Means of your Defence, it would not be just nor reasonable that I should be Witness of your Ruin", were his words. He asked that a Regency Council should be appointed to govern the country in his absence, promising that "when I can judge that my Presence will be necessary for your Defence, I shall be ready to return and hazard Myself for your Security."*

The speech was never delivered. However irresistible William now found the prospect of spending the rest of his days in happy retirement at Het Loo, his strong sense of duty forced him to change his mind. It had been his life work to save Europe from the hegemony of France; he would not throw it over in a fit of pique. At the end of January, too, there came a reminder that the peace of Europe was poised on a knife-edge: the seven-year-old Electoral Prince of Bavaria, named as principal heir to the Spanish crown in the first partition Treaty, died suddenly at Brussels in suspicious circumstances. One afternoon perfectly well, he was suddenly racked by vomiting and convulsions in the evening, sank into a coma, and was dead by two the next morning.*

It was an event of European significance, but to the English parliament it meant absolutely nothing, and they refused to change their minds about the army. William wrote in despair to Heinsius: "It's impossible to credit the serene indifference with which they consider events outside their own country . . ."* but he had no choice. At the end of January 1699 Tallard reported triumphantly to Versailles that the English King no longer opposed the reduction of the troops. "The Earl of Portland", he added, "speaking the other day on this subject, said to me that the King might have put them on another footing at a time when he was younger, and his passions were ardent; but that now he was old, he preferred calmness and mildness to what appeared to be the best for his own interest."*

On 2 February the King appeared in the House of Lords sternfaced to sign the disbanding Bill. He asked them, however, at least to reconsider their decision to send away his own troops, the famous Dutch Blue Guards who had fought under him in every major battle of his career. For a moment the House of Lords wavered, but under pressure from the Commons they hardened their hearts: the Dutch Guards were to go.* William felt it as a bitter personal slight. He told Lord Galway, "It is not possible to be touched more sensibly than I am . . . assuredly on all sides my patience is put to the trial." And he burst out bitterly, "By God if I had a son they should stay."* He made one last attempt to keep his faithful Dutchmen, sending Lord Ranelagh, Paymaster of the Forces, to the House of Commons on 18 March with a final plea: "H.M. is pleased to let the House know that the necessary preparations are made for transporting the Guards who came with him into England; that he intends to send them away immediately, unless, out of consideration to him, the House is disposed to find a way for continuing them longer in his service, which H.M. would take very kindly."*

The House was not disposed: on the contrary – "this attempt has had the opposite effect", wrote the King to Holland, "and the House has resolved to send me a very impertinent address on the subject . . ."* The address, when it was made to him, was not so much impertinent as malicious: "It was an unspeakable grief to them", the Commons claimed respectfully, "that his Majesty should be advised to propose anything in his message to which they could not consent with due regard to that constitution which his Majesty came here to restore." They pointed out that as "the happiness and welfare of this kingdom" depended mainly on the confidence between King and people, this could "in no way be so firmly established as by entrusting his sacred person with his own subjects".*

It was small consolation to the angry and resentful King that not all his subjects shared the view of his M.P.s. A City preacher remarked in a sermon that the King seemed "born to have his person exposed to his enemies abroad, and his patience tryed by his subjects at home", while Vernon told Shrewsbury that "there are more that shew a tenderness towards the Dutch guards and think it a hardship to deprive the King of them."* And when in March the Dutch Guards, whose blue uniforms had only just been replaced by new scarlet ones in deference to national taste, marched through London on their way to embark, plenty of people turned out to cheer them. An eyewitness wrote touchingly of this march "thro' London streets, taking a long farewell of the friends they left in England, with kisses, and tears in their eyes," adding that "whoever has seen this as I did must be shocked to hear it said that the driving them away thus gives great satisfaction to the people."* Some of the comments were less kind, however. How marvellous it was, commented one journalist, to be able to stroll through the Parks after breakfast-time without the smell of herring-bones everywhere, and without the smoke of Dutch tobacco to insult "the nostrils of our squeamish ladies".*

Still grieving for his Dutch Guards, and weakened by a winter of intermittent ill-health, the King took himself off to Newmarket in April for a short break. Many of the English noblemen went with him, but one familiar face was missing. Portland had gone to Windsor claiming that he was "ill of a cold". This excuse convinced nobody, and there were soon fresh rumours of his resignation. "I suppose it is a spice of the old jealousy against my Lord Albemarle's increasing favour", wrote Vernon.*

Vernon had hit the nail on the head. After his return from Paris, Portland had discovered that Albemarle replaced him in every sense of the word, even moving into those apartments adjoining the King's at Kensington which had always been his. It had been the work of the anti-Portland clique which included Betty Villiers, still meddling in English political affairs and detesting her former brother-in-law as much as ever.* The King did little to save Portland's face and continued to shower favours on the young man with complete disregard of public opinion. He bought him a country estate, made his brother colonel of a regiment of foot, and in March 1699 promoted Albemarle, over the Duke of Ormonde's head, to be the first commander of the Guards. This last, however, produced such a storm that even William had to bow before it and restore Ormonde to his commission.*

As Albemarle rose in the King's favour, his popularity with the English sunk, and people who had found him charming two years earlier now said nastily that his only merit was to be young and handsome.* All the old gossip about Albemarle's amorous relations with the King was dug out again and circulated freely. Portland heard it all, and suffered. In March he decided that he could stand it no longer. "For my part I am so weary of the world", he wrote to his former secretary Prior in Paris, "that if there were cloisters in our religion, I believe I should withdraw to one."* The tension between the two Dutch favourites of the King was so great and so evident that Tallard, who knew of Louis's esteem for Portland, wondered on one occasion if he ought not to interfere on Portland's behalf. He put the dilemma to Louis who told him sternly to stay out of "private court intrigues" and concentrate his attention on the new negotiations about the Spanish succession that

Tallard had embarked on with Portland after the death of the Electoral Prince.* William found it increasingly difficult to keep the peace between them – he even had to ask Heinsius to write about Albemarle on a separate sheet of paper, "for I might possibly have to show your letter to the Earl of Portland".*

Plainly, such a situation could not last for long, and while William was at Newmarket for the races, Portland finally made up his mind to go. The King had expected to find him at Kensington as usual when he returned on 20 April, and when his friend failed to appear wrote anxiously off to him: "I am very impatient to see you again, and . . . I am yours for ever . . ."* Next day he received a letter from Portland's house at Windsor in which he announced his decision to retire without delay. The King's first reaction was cool, only reminding him of the grave political implications of such a step: "the welfare and peace of Europe may depend on the negotiations you are engaged in with the Count de Tallard . . ."* Portland rushed to Kensington to justify his decision, and to hand over the keys of his office; the King refused to accept them, and when Portland returned to Windsor, a sad letter from William followed him. "I cant forbear expressing my extreme grief which is much keener than you could possibly imagine, and I am sure that if you only felt half what I do, you would think again . . ."*

He even sent d'Allonne off to Windsor after him "to try to bring him back", as Tallard managed to discover. "Every offer is made for himself and his family: he is promised considerable rewards. Never shall he meet with the Earl of Albemarle in any thing that might cause him annoyance." Albemarle himself was anxious for his unsuccessful rival to stay – "in order that he himself may not be solely and chiefly exposed to the jealousy of the English."* But it was all in vain, and on 5 May d'Allonne returned from Windsor with Portland's keys, as Shrewsbury learned from Vernon, who added with a touch of malice, "I presume he will keep the lodge and the superintending of the gardens."*

The King wrote sadly off to Heinsius with the news:

> I have to tell you with great grief that the Earl of Portland has finally retired, and that I have not been able to keep him. I have with great difficulty persuaded him to carry on the negotiations with Tallard. I cannot express to you how much all this has distressed me, especially as I had done everything within reason to give the Earl of Portland satisfaction, but a blind jealousy has prevailed above all that ought to be precious to him.*

In France the news created a sensation. Portland, who had many friends there, himself wrote personally to some of them, and Madame de Meyercrone begged him to stay and stop taking Albemarle so seriously – "you ought to behave as big dogs do, despise the yapping of the small ones."* And Liselotte added her pleas: "you will make yourself unhappy and you will be reproached for leaving so great and deserving a King as your master."* The sharp-tongued Prior found Portland's decision ridiculous; it "will give him all the uneasiness of a cast favourite without the quiet of a country gentleman." But like all sensations, it was soon forgotten at Versailles, and by June Prior could report "this court begins to grow more reasonable upon his subject. Villeroy only thinks England cannot subsist without him, and expects a revolution by the middle of next week."*

Portland never disappeared completely from the King's life. The two men dined together occasionally, and kept in touch about progress with the Second Partition Treaty. But Portland spent the rest of his life for the most part in quiet retirement at his lodge at Windsor, the charming Byfield House, and kept on his job as Ranger of Windsor Great Park and Supervisor of the Royal gardens for a salary of £2600 and annual expenses of £10,000.*

With Albemarle at his side, but Portland no longer of the company, William left England on 3 June. Sunderland had done his best to convince him what a disastrous impression this departure would make – "it will create a great deale of dislike and men will conclude he cannot beare the being in England" – but the King sailed just the same.*

That summer his main concern was to get a second Partition Treaty firmly agreed. Its outlines had been hammered out in the negotiations between Tallard and Portland: Spain and the Indies were now to go to the Archduke Charles, and the Dauphin would take all the Spanish territories in Italy. If William had hoped that Austria might be persuaded to accept the Treaty this time, he was to be disappointed: the Emperor at once objected to increased French influence in Italy, and angrily refused. Amsterdam supported him to the great embarrassment of William, who was being hard-pressed for Dutch agreement by the French. Only in January 1700 did Amsterdam give in, and the Treaty was signed by England, the Republic and France in March of that year.* It did not improve the outlook for peace very much. The Emperor protested in the strongest possible terms, while in Madrid "the King came close to dying of chagrin, and the Queen his wife flew into such a towering rage that she smashed up the furniture in her apartment, paying special attention to the mirrors and other ornaments that were of French origin."*

While these negotiations dragged on through that unusually hot summer of 1699, the King spent most of his time hunting at Het Loo with Albemarle in constant attendance – "the young favourite flutters with 8 horses and a gilt coach."* As usual William's temper was markedly better, but not, this time, his health. His legs were bothering him again, and the slightest change in temperature was apt to bring on a feverish chill. On horseback he was no longer the man he had been: the mettlesome hunters in his stables were too much for him to handle now, and orders were rushed back to England to find horses that were "very temperate . . . with a very easy motion in their gallop".* Tallard had already noticed in England that after a day's hunting, the King had to be carried upstairs. And when London's most celebrated physician, Dr. Radcliffe, went over to Holland, it was immediately rumoured that he had been summoned to attend the King. The doctor, however, had been called to attend Albemarle's mother.* William still believed that he was his own best doctor and refused to be fussed over.

At the end of October he felt well enough to face England again, arriving at Margate on the twenty-seventh – "I never had a more pleasant or agreeable passage" he said afterwards.* Perhaps he hoped that this passage was a good omen: at any rate he went out of his way that autumn to keep the atmosphere of his Court agreeable and relaxed. He took a keen interest in his domestic building projects, no doubt reasoning that if the English refused to spend the national wealth on armies, it might as well produce a little splendour instead, and at Hampton Court especially, work on the new buildings was speeded up while in the park a hare and pheasant covert was planted, "that there may be always game at hand for his majestie's diversion".* His forty-ninth birthday was celebrated at Court with particular style. In the morning the King was complimented "by the nobility and gentry, who appeared very gay on this occasion"; in the afternoon he dined with Anne and George at Kensington, "diverted with a fine consort of musick", and in the evening here were bonfires, illuminations, and a ball at St. James in his honour.*

Five days later he had a special treat for the Duke of Gloucester – a military review. While the little boy watched, the King and Prince George inspected the three troops of Horse Guards in Hyde Park in the presence of their commanders, Ormonde, Rivers and Albemarle. Luttrell reported that "his Majestie was extremely well pleased with them, and a vast number of people there as spectators."* The Guards must have looked particularly splendid. William had sent orders from Het Loo that summer that the soldiers were to be "new clothed . . . their coats to be laced with gold lace finer than heretofore . . . the gentlemen of the 3 troops of guards are ordered to wear feathers in their hatts; the 1st troop red, the 2d green, and the 3d yellow . . ."*

Before Christmas he began to entertain regularly at Kensington Palace, for the first time since Mary's death, and M.P.s and their wives were among the guests at his drawing-rooms, where Princess Anne acted as his hostess. Card tables for basset and other gambling games were set up and William, who detested ceremony, succeeded in keeping the atmosphere relaxed and informal, walking about and chatting to his guests, who were asked to remain seated. "I desire to miss not a Kensington day if ther be more than next" wrote the Countess of Rutland after one of those evenings. She had been charmed by the King who, when she was standing in his way and was about to move back, had stepped over a stool with the words "No matter, milady Rutland, for I can come over the stool." He told her that she was looking "mighty well" and added that "I was so grat a stranger he hopeed I would not leve them."*

But no amount of social activities could hide the fact that William had now effectively lost contact with the English nation. Even among the common people his popularity was at a low ebb, "by his going so constantly beyond sea, as soon as the session of parliament was ended; though the war was now over". And everybody said he made it only too obvious "that he loved no Englishman's face, nor his company".*

Politically, he was almost isolated. The great Whig ministers who had run his affairs so efficiently for him in the last years of the war had deserted him – Montagu had left the Treasury, Orford the Admiralty, Wharton had not been reappointed, and Shrewsbury, after a brief comeback, had dropped out again, this time for good. In their place were a handful of mediocre Tories, such as Lord Jersey, Lord Lonsdale and the Earl of Bridgewater. This weak Ministry was unable to handle the aggressively Tory House of Commons, and when that autumn the question of the King's grants in Ireland to his favourites was raised, they bungled the business badly.

The House of Commons had already had one go in February 1699 at the King's Dutch favourites, when a Bill was introduced to annul all grants of Crown property made since the Revolution. William's more able ministers of that time killed the Bill in one stroke by the simple suggestion that it did not go far enough, and should be stretched to include all grants of Crown lands made since the Restoration. Since many of the Tory leaders in the House owed their fortunes to the lavishness of Charles II or James II, they dropped it like a hot brick. But William's ministers now were unable to save him from the humiliation of an inquest on his generosity to his friends.

After the pacification of Ireland in 1691, more than a million Irish acres had been forfeited. A proportion had been given back to their former owners, but the rest had been handed over by William as personal gifts to those who had served him in Ireland, like the Earl of Athlone, and to his favourites, Albemarle, Portland and Romney, in spite of a plea from Mary, who wished to "keep some for public schools, to instruct the poor Irish". A commission of seven M.P.s was now appointed by the House of Commons to inquire into the grants, and from the outset the majority was openly hostile to the King. The Crown territories in Ireland were outside their brief, but when they discovered that the King had given to Betty Villiers 90,000 acres of the Irish estates of James II, they could not resist including these in their attack. Three of the commissioners objected, considering the matter an insult to William – "for it will fly in the King's face". They were shouted down: "Fly in the King's face? If you won't fly in his face, you can't execute this commission."* And the parliamentary storm lasted all winter, only to be concluded when in February 1700 the House voted that the grants should all be taken back and put into the hands of trustees, so that the national debts could be paid out of the revenue, which was wildly overestimated by the Commission.

The King made a last effort to justify the grants, telling the Speaker, "that he was not only led by inclination but thought himself obliged in justice to reward those who had served him well, and particularly in the reduction of Ireland, out of the estates forfeited by the rebellion there."* But his pleas made no impression, and in April 1700 Parliament sent fourteen commissioners into Ireland "to dispose of the forfeited estates there, towards payment of the debts incurred by the late war".*

Adding insult to injury, the House then voted that an address should be presented to the King asking him to remove all foreigners except Prince George from his councils. It was too much for the long-suffering William. He hurried down from Kensington to the Treasury, put on his robes and crown, and prorogued Parliament before they knew what was happening. He was too angry to make even the briefest of speeches from the throne, writing to Heinsius: "Its the ugliest session I have ever had . . . it is impossible for anyone who has not been here to imagine the intrigues – they're quite indescribable."*

As a gesture of defiance he announced soon afterwards that one of the two vacant Garters would be given to Albemarle, and gave orders that the installation should be "performed with greater splendour than ever was known, and all the foreign ambassadors to be present", and on 5 June Albemarle was duly installed.*

It was noticed on this occasion how unwell the King looked, pale and feverish, and he himself was longing to get away as soon as possible to Holland. "I shall become ill if I have to remain here longer", he wrote to Heinsius.* And Vernon mentioned that the King seemed to be "under a load of thoughtfulness, which perhaps may have an ill influence upon his health".*

It was not surprising. Not only in England but in Scotland too, animosity against the King was stronger than ever, following the collapse of Scotland's colonial adventure at Darien. His northern kingdom was in fact on the verge of revolution, and the King's own evident impatience and lack of sympathy had done nothing to improve the situation. Despite an address the previous October from the desperate leaders of Scotland, he had refused to call his Scottish Parliament earlier than March, and then put it off again. The Scots sent a delegation to Kensington at the end of March, but William, on the point of leaving to hunt at Hampton Court, received them coldly, and dismissed them after a few minutes. One of the delegates was determined not to have his country's grievances brushed aside in this careless manner, and told the King that the Address they brought him from Scotland was more than just a petition for Parliament, but evidence too of the deep discontent of Scotland. The King showed no concern, merely replying that that would be seen when the Parliament met in May. But when the Scottish Parliament finally met on 24 May, it was for a week only, and the King, who had ordered Holyrood House in Edinburgh to be fitted up for his reception earlier that year, was conspicuous by his absence.*

As a result of this cavalier treatment by their sovereign, Scottish discontent and fury grew. "The Scotch look as they were ready for any mischief, and that nothing will please them, but setting up for themselves", observed Vernon in early June.* But the King's patience with Scotland, always meagre, was now completely exhausted. "People there are like fools on the subject of their colony of Darien", he wrote contemptuously to Heinsius, and his only concern was that the whole fuss was delaying his departure from England. "I cannot express to you how ardently I long to breathe the air of Holland", he added wistfully.*

It was the selfishness of a sick man. Plagued for months by colds and fevers, swollen legs and constipation, William at the age of forty-nine was a worn-out old man. Dr. Radcliffe, who saw him in June, told some of the court with his usual bluntness that "he thought the King could not live three months to an end". And Vernon, who went to see William every day, was one of the few English who told him to go as soon as possible to Het Loo, "that he might be a little eased of the cares and chagrins he met here". William laughed and said that he was growing to be like Shrewsbury – "never at quiet for thinking what will be troublesome and vexatious hereafter". He was, as usual, of the opinion that he would be much better if only the doctors would stop giving him remedies, and he may have been right.* His English doctors could not even agree on what treatment would be effective, and carried their arguments into the sickroom. Radcliffe thought William was suffering from dropsy, and prescribed purges and asses' milk; another doctor, Sir Thomas Millington, argued that such treatment was completely wrong for the King, and suggested garlic. "Radcliffe says, that it will destroy lungs so weak as the Kings," it was reported to a sympathetic Shrewsbury, "and Millington thinks the Kings lungs the soundest part about him. The first says the King will be worse for going to sea; and the other says he will be better for going to Loo." They were getting nowhere and Millington suggested calling in Dr. Hutton, the King's first physician, for consultation, but at the mere mention of his name, Radcliffe "flung out of the room in a passion, and so they broke up resolving nothing".*

In the end William made his own decision and on 4 July left Hampton Court at six in the morning on his way to Holland, after a final consultation of his doctors as inconclusive as the first. "I hope the King will be better when he is out of their hands and at Loo", wrote Vernon with feeling.* Next day he sailed from Margate, arriving on the seventeenth n.s. at The Hague. It had been a stormy crossing, and according to news from Holland, "the King was very sick in his passage over sea."* But as soon as he arrived in The Hague he began to feel a little better, and when Jersey saw him at Het Loo in August, he noted with satisfaction that "the King is very well in his health, except his legs, which are mightily swelled."*

CHAPTER XLII

End of a Reign

"LETTERS FROM HOLLAND agree that his majestie continues in perfect health, and daily takes the divertisement of hunting; but upon news of the death of Glocester, exprest great sorrow, and confin'd himself to his chamber from company two dayes."* So Luttrell recorded in his chronicle on 13 August 1700. William's little nephew, never very strong, had fallen ill after his birthday party on 25 July. It was believed that he had smallpox, but his doctors failed to agree in their diagnosis, and their little patient was "bled, blistered and cup't, tho to no purpose . . ." In the morning of 30 July he died, eleven years old.*

The King felt his loss deeply. He had always been very fond of the little Duke, named after him – only two months earlier he had given him Mary's apartments at Kensington, "that he may have him under his protection".* He had taken special care of his education, and when he nominated Marlborough as his governor in 1698, he told the man he now recognized as England's most brilliant commander and diplomat, "My Lord, teach him but to know what you are, and my nephew cannot want for accomplishments."* Now he wrote grief-stricken to this man: "It is so great a loss to me as well as to all England, that it pierces my heart with affliction."* London went into mourning, and the crush to see the Lying-in-State of Anne's only child and heir was so great the Lord Chamberlain ordered that only persons dressed in mourning should be admitted. He was interred at Westminster Abbey on 9 August at nine at night, with a guard of honour lining his route with lighted torches in their hand.*

All over Europe speculation began immediately about the future of the English throne. Liselotte summed it up, writing to the Electress of Hanover: "The princess of Denmark is said to drink so heavily that her body is quite burnt up. She will never have any living children, and King William's health is so delicate that he can't live long. So you will soon sit on your grandfather's throne."*

In England, however, they hoped that William might now think seriously of marrying again and providing England with an heir to the throne, after Anne, who could be brought up like a good Englishman. There were plenty of candidates. "Many wish he would take the Princess of Denmark . . . she is a lady of three or four-and-twenty, as fit an age as any for children", wrote Vernon to Shrewsbury. The daughter of the Landgrave of Hesse was mentioned as well, but "she has so many brothers and kindred that would not be very welcome here".* There was even talk of a match between William and a respectable Dutch Princess, the widow of Hendrik Casimir who had died in 1696 and mother of Friesland's Stadholder Jan Willem Friso; but she was already thirty-four.*

Vernon knew that a more dependable solution had to be found to the succession problem. The French were already pushing their own two candidates, the little Pretender Prince of Wales at St. Germain, and the Savoy family whose Duke had married the daughter of Charles II's sister Henrietta. "I hope people will at last resolve that it is better to have a prince of Germany than one from France" he wrote, hoping that the Hanovers, the immediate Protestant successors after Anne, might be recognized as soon as possible, even if many English were already objecting against "more foreigners".*

William felt the same way about the Hanovers. He had no intention of marrying again, and was soon secretly in touch with Sophia, now Dowager-Electress. She and her daughter Sophie Charlotte, married to the Elector of Brandenburg, came to see him at Het Loo in October. It was certainly not easy for William to convince Sophia that she ought to accept the succession to the English throne for the sake of Protestant Europe. She was old, she was reluctant to leave her country and family and she still had a loyal if slightly contemptuous attachment to James, with whom she kept up an intermittent correspondence. James felt the same attachment to her and once, as Liselotte wrote to her aunt: "with tears of love for you welling up in his eyes and raising both hands in the air", he told her, "*o-o-o pour-pour cela eh-eh-eh-elle m'a toujours aimé*", adding "his stutter is worse than ever".*

But William won his point with Sophia, making it more attractive by promising her daughter Sophie Charlotte to acknowledge her husband as the first King of Prussia.† And satisfied he left Het Loo to return to England. Hardly back there Europe's other succession made the problem of England's crown suddenly seem minor: on 1 November o.s. William received an express from Paris telling him that the King of

† The Coronation took place on 18 January 1701.

Spain had died eleven days earlier, aged forty, "having, as it's said, by his last will, given all his countreys to the duke de Anjou (2d son of the dauphin)".* The burning question now was whether Louis XIV would stick to the Second Partition Treaty that gave the Crown of Spain to Archduke Charles of Austria, and the Spanish possessions in Italy to the Dauphin.

Europe was not kept in suspense for long. After hours of discussion with Madame de Maintenon and his son the Dauphin, Louis XIV graciously accepted on behalf of his grandson, Philippe d'Anjou, and presented him to the Spanish ambassador and the whole court as the new King of Spain.* Liselotte had guessed beforehand and teased the solemn little prince about it during a hunt. "When I heard the Duc d'Anjou coming up behind me in a narrow path," she wrote, ". . . I pulled up and said 'Pass, great King. May your majesty pass.' You should have seen his surprise at my knowing about it. His little brother the Duc de Berry almost died, he laughed so hard."*

There was little else to laugh at in the situation. It was clear to everybody that the Emperor was unlikely to take this settlement lying down, and Louis was already preparing himself to defend his grandson's claim. "The French King is buying horses, raising men, laying up great magazines in all his garrisons, fitting out his fleet; which makes many apprehend a new war", it was related in London.* Louis still hoped that at least England and the United Provinces might be persuaded to accept his grandson as Philip V of Spain. In a personal letter to the States-General on 4 December he wrote that he had acted "in the spirit of the Partition Treaty, to preserve peace and he was confident that instead of protesting, they would be grateful to him for sacrificing to the common wealth such considerable states which he could have added to his Crown." He made it known at the same time that the crowns of France and Spain would never be united.*

The English and the Dutch were anxious to believe him, and the stock markets in both countries rose on a wave of optimism. But their King-Stadholder could not share it. "I have never had much dependence on treaties with France", he wrote deeply shocked to Heinsius, "but that this solemn undertaking should be torn up in the eyes of all the world I never would have believed possible."*

The New Year of 1701 proved to the British and the Dutch that William's pessimism was well-founded. The Spanish Regency Council made the unwise and tactless gesture of inviting Louis XIV to govern Spain for the time being on behalf of his inexperienced sixteen-year-old grandson, and the Sun King had been unable to resist this chance of levelling the Pyrenees. In February this step was followed by the French occupation of the fortresses in Flanders. By the terms of an agreement between the Dutch and the Governor of the Spanish Netherlands, Maximilian of Bavaria, these fortresses had been garrisoned by States troops; now they were compelled to march out at a day's notice. "You can well imagine how deeply this has affected me", wrote William to Heinsius. "For twenty-eight years I have toiled unceasingly to preserve this barrier for the State . . . and now I have to watch it swallowed up in one day without a single blow being struck."*

Unlike the dark and distant intrigues of the Escorial, this brazen peace-time occupation of Flanders woke up Europe with a shock. In Amsterdam the stock market index fell 30 per cent, and English shares followed suit. Only the English M.P.s seemed to be unable to grasp the drama. The General Election returned a Parliament with a small Tory majority, but instead of discussing measures to deal with the menace hanging over Europe, they were preoccupied with the past, and the House of Lords made an indirect attack on the King when they attempted to impeach Portland for his role in negotiating the Second Partition Treaty without Parliament being consulted. Portland, who had married for the second time the previous year, taking as his wife the niece of Sir William Temple, Martha Jane Temple, did not improve the situation by his defence in the House in which he named three ministers – Somers, Orford and Montagu (now Lord Halifax) – together with Vernon, as having been equally involved. It won him no sympathy – it was obvious to everyone that the Englishmen had been brought in too late to do more than rubber-stamp this treaty which they considered, in the light of subsequent events, to have been disastrous for European peace.

The House of Commons gave their warmest support to the Lords' attack on one of the detested Dutchmen, and only one voice was raised in his defence: "I am not a friend of the Earl of Portland", said the speaker, "but it provokes me almost to compassion that amongst so many persons, who once in the time of his favour and power, counted themselves happy to receive from him a smile or a slight nod, or to drink chocolate with his lackeys in his anteroom, here not a single one stands up for him."* He made no impression on the excited M.P.s and on 1 April the House of Commons moved that "William Earl of Portland by negotiating and concluding the Treaty of Partition is guilty and shall be impeached of high crimes and misdemeanours."

The impeachment of the three Whig ministers was still being discussed in Parliament when the English people at last lost their patience. Apart from following the Dutch example in recognizing the Duc d'Anjou

as king of Spain, Parliament had done nothing. The Kentish people –
worried by rumours about a French invasion – were the first to voice
their disquiet and anger. They composed a petition begging the House
to stop their quarrels, provide for the safety of the country and vote
supplies that would allow the King to come to the defence of England's
allies. When on 8 May the petition was handed in, the furious M.P.s had
the five gentlemen who presented it at once arrested. But their impulsive,
high-handed reaction could have had no better effect from William's
point of view. The English were seething with indignation, and the
Kentish petition was followed by a far more impressive memorial,
drafted by the satirist and journalist Daniel Defoe. It was "the voice of
the people", condemning the arrest of the Kentish petitioners, attacking
Parliament for its inertia and shortsightedness, and for allowing "saucy,
indecent reproaches" to be made to the King. Defoe demanded that if
the French King refused to listen to reason, King William should declare
war on him, and he signed his memorial "Legion – for we are many".*

Defoe presented this memorial in person, at the head of a delegation
of sixteen gentlemen, and the House, listening in astonishment, had just
enough sense left not to arrest him, and continued the quarrel.

In mid-May, the States-General sent a memorial to William to ask
for English assistance in the face of growing French aggression in
Flanders. The hated d'Avaux had arrived at The Hague in March to try
to negotiate a separate treaty between France and the Republic. "We
have refused to enter into separate negotiations", reported the States to
William, "because England and the Republic have a common interest in
keeping the general peace. But we desperately need support." The States
pointed out that France was daily strengthening its position in Flanders,
working hard to secure the allegiance of the former allies of England
and Holland, and doing its best to foment discord in Germany. "We are
therefore besieged from all sides save that of the sea. Our situation is worse
now than in the last war. We have already been obliged to flood parts
of our country, and to open our dykes for the safety of our frontiers."*

William sent a copy of this memorial to both Houses. The Commons
were still too preoccupied with the impeachment proceedings to take
much notice, and it was left to the Lords to show a little more responsibility. They sent an Address to the King asking him to implement the
treaties between England and Holland, and to open negotiations for a
triple alliance between the Dutch, the English and the Emperor. The
King reported the news to Heinsius: he had a partial mandate from
Parliament for a war that he had done his best to avert, and that he would
certainly not survive.

Before he could sail for Holland and begin the urgent consultations with the Allies, two outstanding problems remained to be settled by Parliament: the impeachment of the three ministers, and the question of the English succession. The first was finally dealt with in June by the Lords. Following weeks of bitter wrangling about procedure between the two Houses, the Lords suddenly took matters into their own hands, and acquitted first Somers, then Halifax and Orford. The succession question was settled amicably on 12 June, when the King gave his Royal assent to the Act of Settlement, which named the House of Hanover as heirs after Anne to the English Crown. The Act included eight articles providing for new limitations on the Royal power, several of them clearly dictated by Parliament's resentment of William's Dutch ways – a future sovereign should, for instance, not be allowed to leave the country without Parliament's permission, and his chief advisers were to be English. But William was too old and too tired to be bothered by these insults, and thanked the House gracefully.†

On 14 July, William arrived at The Hague after a bad crossing. For the first time in years he brought Marlborough with him, as Ambassador Extraordinary. Whatever William's suspicions of this man had once been, he knew only too well that as soon as he himself was dead, Marlborough, husband of Anne's most intimate friend and her chief confidant, would become the first man in England. William was anxious to involve him now as far as possible in European affairs, and train him as the future leader of the Allied coalition against France. He left it to him, therefore, after he had presented him at The Hague to the foreign ambassadors, to begin talks with Heinsius and others, while he went to inspect the Dutch armies that he would never lead in person again. His Dutch and English friends were reluctant to let him go – the alarming decline in his health was apparent to them all, and people at The Hague who had not seen him for months were horrified by what they saw. "He looked like a dead man" commented a French agent. His legs were now so swollen that he could only walk with the greatest difficulty, and the painful gout that had attacked his left hand since March made it equally difficult for him to ride, since he had trouble holding the reins. After the physical ordeal of the inspection tour, he was exhausted, retiring to Het Loo to rest and following the negotiations at The Hague from a distance.

The French followed them too. D'Avaux had made a last effort to

† On 14 August, the Earl of Macclesfield arrived in Hanover to notify the Electress-Dowager Sophia of the passing of the Act, presenting her with a beautiful illuminated copy. Her son the Elector was given the Garter.

reach agreement on the eventual partition of the Spanish Empire, but the French terms were too high to be acceptable to the Allies, and the Ambassador was recalled to Paris on 11 August.

His recall lent added urgency to the Allied discussions, and a few weeks later, on 7 September 1701, a new Grand Alliance was signed at The Hague. With the aim of securing the Spanish possessions in Italy and the Spanish Netherlands – the Dutch Barrier – for the Emperor, the Republic undertook to raise an army of 120,000 men, England of 40,000 men, and the Emperor of 90,000. The Allies also pledged themselves to ensure by concerted action that the crowns of France and Spain should never be united, and it was decided that other European princes should be invited to join them. But they left the door open for peace by negotiation.

It was firmly slammed by Louis XIV. Nine days after the Grand Alliance was signed, James II died at St. Germain, and on his deathbed Louis told him that the young Prince of Wales would now be, in his eyes, the rightful King of England.

James's death had been expected for some time at the French court. He had been unwell since March, but refused to spare himself the exhausting devotions which had now become the chief interest of his life. "Good King James will do himself a mischief one day with his boundless piety", observed Liselotte cynically two weeks before his death. "The day before yesterday he spent so long kneeling and praying that he fainted clear away, and he was unconscious for so long that everyone thought his last hour had come."* It had indeed, and after hearing Louis's promise to recognize his son, and declaring that he pardoned all who had injured him, especially the Prince of Orange and Princess Anne, the luckless James died.

Louis's recognition of the Prince of Wales, a credit more to his heart than to his head, was a slap in the face for William. The news was sent to him at Het Loo by Lord Manchester, English ambassador to Paris, and it arrived when William was dining with his friends. He grew red with anger, and pulled his hat down over his eyes to hide it. Instructions were at once sent off to Lord Manchester to quit France, and to London to expel the French ambassador Poussin.*

At Mary's death, James had forbidden the French Court to go into mourning. William, with commendable restraint, refused to be so provocative himself, and ordered partial mourning – "as for a relation: persons of quality not to put their liveries into mourning".* It was not good enough for Princess Anne who had received a moving letter from Mary Beatrice, in which her stepmother told her that her father had pardoned her and sent her his last blessing from his death-bed.* She now expected that the Court at least should go into full mourning, as she herself had already done. When William's instructions arrived she had to take down the signs of mourning from her apartments at St. James's and she protested violently at "the ill-natured, cruel proceeding of Mr. Caliban", telling Godolphin: "I am out of all patience when I think I must do so monstrous a thing as not to put my lodgings in mourning for my father."* The reconciliation between William and Anne had never been wholehearted.

Anne's indignation at William's decision only to put on violet mourning was not shared by most of the English. Their fury was directed at Louis's outrageous interference in the succession to their Crown. He had gone back on his solemn word given at Rijswijk in 1698, and it was a new proof that the French were simply not to be trusted. What William could never have achieved by the most eloquent speeches, Louis – as so often in the past – had now effected for him by a single gesture: he had united the English in a determination to make war on France. And impatiently they waited for their King to return to London so that they might demonstrate their loyalty to him in person.

William himself prepared to leave Holland in October but his health, shaky all that summer, held up his departure. A few days before he was due to leave Het Loo for The Hague, he went for a last long energetic day of hunting at Dieren. It was pouring with rain and when he arrived at the house of his host at Voorst, he was soaked to the skin and shivering with cold. After a hot drink, he went early to bed and was up the next morning for another long day in the saddle – "scarce any body that was with him could hold it till the Chace was over." It had rained hard all day again, but the King was not deterred, and boasted next day, after a sound night's sleep: "I find myself very well. I knew . . . that this hunting bout would do me good. I was wet in my knees and toes, and yet I am much better than I was yesterday." His triumph was short-lived; he caught a raging cold, lost his appetite even for his favourite fish and fruit, and eventually had to leave Het Loo to go back to The Hague and see his doctors.*

Like everybody, they were amazed that a man in his broken state of health could even contemplate undertaking such a hard bout of hunting. His legs had now almost completely failed him. Since November the previous year the doctors in England had tried everything possible to get down that ominous swelling: frictions with elder-flower water; "spaw-water", pills made of extract of gentian and lesser centaury, powder of crabs'-claws compound, huge pills made of salt of wormwood, crabs' eyes, tartar vitriolate, steel prepared with sulphur. They fed him Epsom salt in chicken broth, purged him with rosin of jalap and extract of rhubarb, and dosed him with tincture of steel. But it was all to no avail and his legs remained as swollen as ever, while his cough got worse. The French ambassador, who had seen him in May coming out of St. James's church, had commented, "I find him very decrepit, his eye dulled, and he had the greatest difficulty getting into his coach."*

Before William had left England, his English doctors had given him a thorough examination, writing down their findings and the treatments they had prescribed for him as a guidance for any doctor he might see in Holland. "Within these Ten or Twelve Years last past . . . the Asthmatick Paroxysms have in a manner quite left him", they reported, "Though his Expectoration is much more considerable than formerly." They had been impressed by the resilience of the King: no headaches or upset stomach, a good sleeper and – almost unknown in that age – "never troubled with a looseness and but seldom with a costiveness". He suffered occasionally, they noted, from feverish colds in winter, but his appetite was excellent even though more moderate than it used to be: "He still ate most of the first Service, viz Soop made of pulse, potherbs and stew'd Meat; of the Second Service he used to eat but little; but he ate a great deal of Fruit, though never or very seldom between Meals. Confections or Sweet-Meats . . . never or seldom." His breakfast consisted simply of a dish of chocolate.

His drinking habits however, bothered them – the King liked to drink both his wine and his bottled beer well iced except in the depths of winter.

But the swollen legs baffled them. They had once recommended tight bandaging, with disastrous results – it simply drove the swelling higher. It was, as his doctor described it, "a soft pale swelling that retains Pits, after there being pressed with one's finger", and they now suggested massage and resting for an hour or two with his feet up when he came in from hunting. It did not help and by July, when he was at Het Loo, the legs were worse than ever, "swell'd a great way above the Knee, lead-colour'd and cold", while the dosings and purgings and diuretic spa-water cures had exhausted him and ruined his appetite. "When I complain of the Spaw-water, they tell me I must drink more of it", William told his Dutch doctor, the sound and sensible Bidloo, "and drink it faster, that the Quantity may make its way. But the more I drink the worse I am; and for that reason I am against it." He was appalled by these symptoms of his own decline, and anxiously asked

Bidloo for his opinion: "Do you think that my disease is no Dropsie? What I have used of late has done me more harm than good . . ." And after Bidloo had consulted with other doctors, he asked them impatiently: "But now what have you concluded upon among yourselves? I shall try it for a week or two, and if I find no benefit, then I'll leave it off."

The Dutch doctors at once took him off the purgatives and "all other strong evacuation"; they prescribed a fortifying medicinal wine made with herbs and citron peel and infused with Rhenish wine; and they begged him to eat less fruit and moderate his iced drink, although one doctor admitted "that an unwholesome diet, recommended by long use, is preferable to uncustomary things". For his legs they suggested massage twice daily with warm flannel, or Hungary water, and bandaging with more flannel. His breeches in winter should be lined with "good English lamb-skins". Their treatment had some success; within a few weeks, to William's relief, his legs were much improved.*

There were cynics in Holland who wondered if his illness was not a diplomatic one. It was known that he was anxious for the States to appoint the young Prince Jan Willem Friso of Nassau-Dietz, Stadholder of Friesland since the death of his father Hendrik Casimir, as his sucessor for the Stadholdership of all the United Provinces. He had already made the boy sole heir to most of the huge Orange estates. But when William started to talk at The Hague about him, he met with little response, and "many began to suspect that he pretended to be ill to force the States of Holland."* William was obliged to give up the idea, remarking they must wait till after his death "to adopt a measure so salutary to the nation."*

When in October William returned to The Hague on his way back to England, it was obvious to everybody that his illness was no pretence. On his arrival "he was for some days in so bad a condition that they were in great fear for his life."* His amazing constitution pulled him through once more, but he looked like death. One eye-witness remarked to one of his doctors: "It seems to me that our master, who walks so slowly, is leaving us at a very great pace." The doctor answered, "Even quicker than you would think."* And when the poet Droste saw him in his coach riding down the Voorhout, he felt instinctively that he would never see him back in The Hague.*

The crossing to England prostrated him. He had to be carried off the boat at Margate and was put straight to bed at Greenwich. London had been preparing a rapturous welcome for their King for weeks now, but it would have exhausted him, and instead of riding through the City he went directly to Hampton Court, arriving on 5 November o.s. Exactly thirteen years after his landing at Torbay as a young and vigorous Prince, an ageing, ailing King was carried into his country palace.

The enthusiasm of the English was not to be damped. They celebrated his return with bonfires and pealing bells, while deputations from all parts of the kingdom travelled to Hampton Court to deliver their speeches and addresses. He could not decently refuse to see them and complained bitterly to Heinsius how tiresome it was listening to so many harangues.

Once more fresh air and exercise were his best doctors. Four days later he was remarking, proudly, "I did not think one could recover so soon. I rode out yesterday on horseback and eat lustily."* That same evening Princess Anne and Prince George were his guests at Hampton Court, as they were often to be that winter when he dined in public. Everyone was struck by a new gentleness in his manner to them; ill-health had softened this outwardly cold and surly man. He lived quietly now at Hampton Court, surrounded by friends like Albemarle who that summer had married the daughter of one of William's officers, Gertruida Quirina van de Duyn, and was now looking forward to the birth of his first child. Portland came down regularly from his Ranger's lodge in Windsor Great Park, where he lived with his second wife and their first child; the two men had resumed something of their old intimacy, and during a stroll in the gardens at Hampton Court one day that winter, William confided to his friend of so many years, "that he found himself so weak that he did not expect to live another summer", begging him at the same time not to repeat what he had said.*

He made the remark after his legs had suddenly swollen up again, to his great alarm. He sent for Bidloo, the only doctor he really trusted and whom he had brought to England with him, and asked again if it was dropsy and if there was really nothing to be done. "It if reaches above my knees," he complained, "I shall walk like a sprain'd Hair and if it goes further, I shant be able to walk at all." The ingenious Bidloo thought hard about the problem, and then had a little stove specially made. It was a box made of oak big enough so that the King could sit with his legs and thighs inside it. It was lined with flannel, and on either side burned little lamps filled with spirits of lavender – a smell William liked. It worked wonders; William was delighted with it at first, and when Romney, Ormonde and other friends came to see him, he proudly demonstrated it to them: "do but see, one may moderate the heat as he pleases". But soon the novelty wore off; always a bad patient, he could not be bothered to go on using it regularly, and his legs swelled again.*

Bad health could not prevent him following political developments in England with the closest attention. At his return he had been impressed by the degree to which public opinion was now with him in his opposition to French imperialism. It encouraged him to dissolve the quarrelsome, factious Parliament of the previous year and to issue writs for a general election at the end of the year. On 31 December 1701 a new House of Commons assembled in which there was a Whig majority of about thirty, and the King's new Ministry was once more largely Whig in composition, headed by Somers. He went down in person to open Parliament, and made what many MPs thought the most effective and moving speech they had ever heard from him. "He laid it upon them to consider the dangers they were in, and not to increase these by new divisions among themselves", wrote Burnet afterwards, and "he expressed a readiness to forgive all offences against himself, and wished they would as readily forgive one another, so that no other divisions might remain but that of English and French, Protestant and Papist."*

He reminded them of their responsibilities: "The eyes of all Europe are upon this Parliament; all matters are at a standstill till your resolutions are known"; and he ended his speech in words worthy of the first great European that he had always been: "If you do in good earnest wish to see England hold the balance of Europe, and to be indeed at the head of the Protestant interest, it will appear by your right improving the present opportunity."*

Parliament and people were moved alike by the appeal from this shadow of a man and the Commons appeared to have taken to heart the King's words about the dangers of party divisions at this time. They voted unanimously that all necessary supplies for the preservation of Europe should be forthcoming.

William's words rang through Europe: his speech was printed and illuminated, translated into French and Dutch "and hung up in frames in almost every house in England and Holland, as his Majesty's precious legacy to his own and all Protestant people."* Belatedly, in this moment of crisis, even the English forgot their national prejudices and realized for the first time that their once-detested Dutch King was the man to whom Protestant Europe looked for leadership. Daniel Defoe, always an admirer of William, was one of the instigators of this new wave of appreciation that swept the country with his "True-Born Englishman". In biting terms he castigated the xenophobia of his countrymen, pouring scorn on their resentment of William's foreign advisers and their fickleness:

> *We blame the King that he relies too much*
> *On strangers, Germans, Huguenots and Dutch;*
> *And seldom would his great affairs of state*
> *To English councillors communicate.*
> *The fact might very well be answer'd thus*
> *He has so often been betray'd by us*
> *He must have been a madman to rely*
> *On English gentlemen's fidelity.*

Defoe, never a man with any patience for sycophants, spoke of William in terms the King was painfully unused to hearing from his English subjects:

> *He needs no character but his own fame*
> *Not any flattering titles but his name*
> *William's the name that's spoke by every tongue*
> *William's the darling subject of my song.**

The pamphlet became an instant best-seller, and William who read it summoned Defoe to Kensington to thank him.

Now with the full backing of Parliament and people, he began to make preparations for the campaign that would be inevitable that summer. The French were fortifying themselves in Flanders, at the same time penetrating deep into the Rhineland around Cologne, while the Austrians were already fighting the Spanish in Italy. But although the Allies presented a formidable coalition against France – the original core of Austria, England and the Republic had been strengthened by Denmark, Brandenburg, Hesse and Münster; Sweden and Poland were on the verge of joining them, and Portugal wavered – yet no general strategy had been decided upon. Negotiations about military preparations were going slowly at The Hague, and in February the King sent Albemarle over to get them moving faster, and to co-ordinate the Allied plans.

He did not live to see them carried out. On 20 February Bidloo was suddenly sent for in the evening to Kensington, and found the King with his arm in a sling. The King told him: "I was riding this afternoon in the Park near Hampton Court, and I was urging the horse into a gallop when she fell on her knees. I tried to pull her up by the reins, but she fell first forward and then sideways, and I fell on to my right shoulder on the ground. It was odd, because it was level ground."

The horse Sorrel, which William had been riding for the first time, had in fact stumbled on a mole-hill, and the King had broken his collar-bone in his fall. His surgeon Dr. Ronjat set it at Hampton Court, but William insisted on returning to Kensington that evening as he had planned, and during the long coach-ride it had been jolted out of place again. Bidloo had to reset it, and afterwards William went to bed and slept perfectly soundly, apparently unaffected by his accident.

Next day he felt well enough to work as usual, and thought no more of his fall until on 27 February they took the bandages off and discovered that the fracture had not mended and was slightly swollen: his right hand and arm – the same side as the fracture – looked odd and puffy too. William refused to take much notice of this and of his growing weakness, dictated letters as usual, including one to the Duke of Mecklenburg to thank him for joining the Allies, and next day sent a message to the House of Commons apologizing for not being there in person but urging them to bring about a union between his kingdoms of England and Scotland to avert the war which he felt to be otherwise inevitable. With the help of Bidloo, he limped about, and sometimes he felt strong enough to leave his rooms and walk slowly through the galleries of Kensington to look at his favourite paintings.

On 2 March, after he had appointed a commission of five Lords to deal with some urgent outstanding parliamentary matters, among them the Abjuration Bill to exclude the Pretender Prince of Wales from the succession, he made one of his slow strolls and this time the effort was too much for him. He sat down on a chair to get his breath back, and fell asleep near an open window. When he woke up, he was coughing and feverish, and next day in the evening the doctors had to be called to his bed again. That night he slept badly, coughing a great deal, and it was obvious to everybody that he was a very ill man. His doctors prescribed every remedy they thought might be effective – medicines and powders and herbal decoctions and juleps. William refused them all, and on 6 March he was so weak that he could no longer keep his food down and vomited often. New medicines were tried, like powdered crabs' eyes, and pearl'd julep, and sal volatile to revive him. For all their exotic names they were equally useless, and when the doctors begged the King to eat a little and keep his strength up, he replied with a touch of impatience: "Believe me, gentlemen, I know particularly well that forced feeding does me no good." That night, reported one of the Court next day, he was "taken so ill with a purging and vomitting that there was small hope of his recovery, being brought to extream weak-ness". In the morning he was given "Sir Walter Rawley's cordial", and quinine for his fever; he was able to swallow some milky tea and a cup of chocolate, and it was noted that "he now spits as he used to do which was stopped, and he has no feaver." It was Saturday, and the Commons who had assembled to discuss the Union of England and Scotland were told of the King's desperate condition. They wondered anxiously if he would be able to sign his assent to the Abjuration Bill, but William summoned enough strength that evening to put a specially prepared stamp on the parchment giving a commission the power to act for him, and the Bill became law.

Albemarle had hurried back from Holland, arriving at the King's bedside in the morning of the seventh, but when he reported how well the Allied discussions were going at The Hague, the King showed little interest. Only a few days earlier he had told a friend: "You know I have never been afraid of death. There have been times that I wished to die, but now there is a future, I would prefer not to go." Weakened and exhausted, he had now resigned himself to death, telling Albemarle, who was painfully distressed, "*Je tire vers ma fin*". Members of the Privy Council were assembled in his bedroom, and they questioned the doctors anxiously about his condition. The doctors, eight in number, shook their heads: "All their hopes, under God", they declared, "depended on the taking of some food and the taking of their remedies." Some of the noblemen urged Bidloo to try and persuade the King to eat a little, and William this time gave in. "Lift me up", he said, "and I'll take as much as I can of what is thought proper."

Later he slept a little, only to wake again at three in the morning and sent for Bidloo again. "I have a bad night, I do not sleep" he whispered, struggling to breathe through lungs already infected by pleurisy. The doctor propped him up in bed and leaning against him the King remarked, "I could sleep in this posture, sit nearer me, and hold me so for a little time." For an hour and a half the devoted doctor sat without moving until William woke and realized how uncomfortable Bidloo must have been. "You can bear me up no longer" he protested. Two servants, one of them his page Sewel, supported him with pillows from then on. The doctors consulted together soon afterwards and agreed that it was time to summon Tenison, the Archbishop of Canterbury, who arrived at five in the morning, together with Burnet, to give him the Sacrament.

As word spread through London, the dying King's sickroom filled with friends and courtiers, but William never lost his ordinary calm. "Amidst the Tears of all the Bystanders, his Majesty did not betray the least concern, but was very devout and friendly . . ." wrote Bidloo later.

The King said a quiet farewell to his closest friends, to Ouwerkerk and to Albemarle, to whom he gave his personal keys with the words "You know what to do with them"; and some of his servants were summoned to be specially thanked. At seven in the morning, struggling for breath, he took Bidloo by the hand, "return'd him hearty thanks for all his faithful services", and asked him "if this could last long". The doctor reassured him – "an hour, an hour and a half, though you may be snatch'd away in the Twinkling of an Eye." When Bidloo felt his pulse, he held on to him and said "I do not die yet, hold me fast".

At the last moment Portland arrived at his bedside. It was afterwards said that Albemarle had refused to send for him earlier, but according to another account, the servant dispatched to warn him lost his way to Windsor in the dark. When William saw him, he was already almost beyond speech but with a look the King asked him to approach. Portland bent down, putting his ear to the King's mouth. It was too late: he could distinguish only a few incoherent words. With a last gesture, William took Portland's hand and pressed it weakly against his heart. Then his head fell back on his shoulder, and "shutting his eyes, he expir'd with two or three soft Gasps". It was eight o'clock on Sunday, 8 March o.s., and after weeks of grey and overcast weather, the sun was rising into a cloudless sky.*

CHAPTER XLIII

Epilogue

Mysterious fate how canst thou reconcile
Earth's sullen grief and heaven's cheerful smile
While Albion her loved Nassau has resigned,
Mourning to lose what Angels joy to find . . .

Printed on black paper, and sold for twopence, this was one of the many tributes all Europe paid to the dead king. The English Court went into deep mourning, and theatres were closed.

The body of King William III was opened, and after an autopsy had been performed, it was embalmed and taken to the Prince's Chamber at Westminster for the lying-in-state. The doctors who performed the autopsy were astonished by the emaciated condition of the body, although the legs and right arm were still swollen. The stomach, liver, gall-bladder, spleen and kidneys were all in splendid condition, but both his lungs adhered to the pleura, which were inflamed, and the upper half of one lung was infected – "the immediate cause of his death". Even more surprising to the doctors was the small amount of blood they found: "it is rare to find a body with so little blood as in this, there being in the lungs more blood than in all other parts together", ran their report. As for the heart that had kept life pumping through this wasted body for such a long time, it was found to be amazingly small, "but firm and strong". When the King was undressed after death, the attendants found that he was wearing Mary's small gold ring with a lock of brown hair in it on a black ribbon round his neck, that he had had made in 1684 by Loofs.*

Portland and Albemarle were among the small handful of people by whom William was mourned in earnest. Portland retired to Windsor to nurse his grief in private, a sad and embittered man, who according to rumours in Paris might be thrown out of England at any time, and who a few weeks later indeed lost his job as Superintendent of the Royal gardens on the orders of Queen Anne.

Albemarle was so much affected by the death of his master and patron that days afterwards, a courtier reported that he continued "still very ill of greife for the Kinge".* And Liselotte, who had always been intrigued by the close relationship between King and young man, wrote sympathetically: "Milord Albemarle was on the point of following his master, he was ill to death with grief."* Even at Versailles there was surprisingly little public jubilation at the death of this "*perturbateur universel du repos public de la Chrétienté*".* Louis XIV, in deference to the English Court of St. Germain, forbade mourning, though many of the French nobility were related to the House of Orange; but he was too magnanimous to rejoice openly at the death of the man who had consistently thwarted his Grand Design.

The Jacobites found it harder to hide their pleasure, and it was Mary Beatrice who, with commendable generosity, restrained them: "Many of the English, when the news came, wanted to make some demonstration of their joy [but] the Queen has forbidden all display of delight, and she speaks of this Prince without animosity."*

Among those at Versailles genuinely upset by the death of William was Liselotte. "King William's death has made me sad" she wrote about the man whom she had always admired, and had once expected to marry. But his death was not a surprise to her: "Last autumn Lenor sent me an almanach for this year and King William's death is clearly predicted as follows: 'NB ♂h ⊙ March 20th 1702; a potentate goes to his grave,/This pleases not a few,/That's how it goes when one departs To make room for the new'."* To her aunt Sophia she dashed off an excited letter: "Now you are one step nearer the throne, with only a single person before you and it looks as though she is almost ready for the next world too."*

Sophia was less excited. In a letter of condolence to Portland, she wrote: "I cannot think that I shall live to see yet another calamity for England of the same kind; for Queen Anne is much younger than I am, who have entered my seventy-second year . . ."*

Anne had learned the news of William's death from Burnet, who had been the first to hurry to St. James's and throw himself upon his knees before England's new Sovereign. Since the King's accident, she had visited him with Prince George three times, but she was not present at his death-bed.* Instead, she sat with Sarah Churchill at St. James's waiting for the half-hourly bulletins sent to her by Lord Romney which told her how William's breath "grew shorter and shorter".* Immediately after Burnet's visit, delegation after delegation crowded to St. James's, while Vernon formally notified both Houses of Parliament that the King was dead. After a short silence one of the members rose to say

"Sir, we have lost a great King, and we have got a most gracious Queen."*
The same afternoon Anne was proclaimed in the presence of both houses
and received with such deafening cheers that her reply to the Speaker
could not be heard. These cheers and rejoicings were echoed all over the
country, drowning the half-hearted laments for the dead Dutch King –
"after so great a thunderclap surely never was there so quick a calm",
wrote one of William's ministers, adding, "there will no doubts remain but that the true interest of England will have preference to any
other."*

Even the mourning for the Dutchman became the occasion for a last
display of English nationalism. "For the encouragement of our English
silk, called *à-la-modes* his Royal Highness the Prince of Denmark and the
nobility appear in mourning hat-bands made of that silk, to bring the
same in fashion in the place of crapes, which are made in the pope's
country, whither we send our money for them."* Anne herself made it
clear that the deep mourning she was wearing was for her father James:
only the violet trimmings were in memory of William. And when she
announced that the Coronation would take place in just over a month,
on 23 April – exactly seventeen years after her father James had been
crowned – she commanded that "the very deep mourning was to cease
after that ceremony".

Excessive displays of mourning would have been out of place, and
Anne knew it. The death of William's Queen, just over seven years
earlier, had plunged the whole country into woe: there was no such
reaction now. "Noe king can be less lamented than this has bin" wrote
a contemporary, "even by thos that was his greatest admirers in his life
time . . . the very day hee dieid, ther was several expressions of joy
publicley spok in the strets – of having one of ther own nation to rain
over them . . ."* And the English Jacobites began to drink a new toast –
to the "little gentleman in black velvet", the mole on whose hill Sorrel,
William's "Illustrious steed", had stumbled. They immediately spread
malicious stories that the King had left nothing but debts, that Mary's
funeral bills were still unpaid, the Crown jewels pawned or spirited
away, and that William had thought of having Anne his sister-in-law
arrested so that the Hanovers should succeed him immediately.

In Holland, the mourning was more widespread. Heinsius wrote to
Anne of "the consternation, so great here everywhere", and church
bells tolled three times a day for the dead Stadholder.* But even among
his own people, who had grieved so much for his English wife, William's
death was not felt as a personal loss: over the last few years especially,
he had become remote to them, absent on campaign or in England, or

retired in the privacy of Het Loo. The Dutch remembered him less as the Saviour of the Fatherland of 1672 than as the belligerent leader who had dragged them repeatedly into wars that exhausted their resources, ruined trade and sunk their national pride by forcing them to play second fiddle to England. They looked back with growing nostalgia to the fifties – their Golden Age – and concluded once more that a Prince of Orange as Stadholder was a liability with which their country must never again be saddled.

In so reasoning, the Dutch did less than justice to William's memory. Without the House of Orange, there would have been no United Provinces, and without William III, the Republic would have become little more than an outpost of the French Empire. It is true that within the Republic itself, although his powers were almost absolute, his rule had produced no constitutional or administrative improvements of any significance – after 1689, Heinsius more and more took over effective government at home – and "William's War", as it was known both in England and Holland, had raised taxation to an unprecedented level. But he had left the Dutch with an army respected on the battlefields of Europe, a navy more powerful and better equipped than it had ever been, and most important of all, a sense that it was their national duty to defend their frontiers and to maintain the barrier of the Spanish Netherlands. It was thus with great relief that they learned that even after William's death, England's new sovereign intended to carry on the struggle against their common enemy, France: one of Anne's first actions after her accession had been to dispatch Marlborough to The Hague to reassure her Dutch allies.

It has been said of William that he was "King of Holland and Stadholder of England".* During a conversation between an English and a Dutch courtier overheard at Versailles, the Englishman enlarged on this epigram: "There is a Parliament in England which knows all too well how to clip his wings if he shows signs of going too far."*

It was indeed during the reign of William and Mary together, and later of William alone, that Parliament began to assume the importance that it has never since lost. After the whims of Charles and the tyranny of James, England's M.P.s made sure that no English sovereign should enjoy such absolute powers again – by voting William supplies for only one year at a time they forced him to summon regular parliaments – and however much he resented his dependence he was wise enough to accept this diminution of the Royal prerogative. From 1688 onwards Parliament acquired new responsibilities, and began to learn how to carry them out. For the first time, they began to play an active part in framing the foreign policy of England – up to that time, the King's privilege alone.

William saw England mainly as a weapon to be used against France's imperialism in Europe; and he needed English naval and military strength. When he arrived in 1688 he found a nation entirely preoccupied by its own internal conflicts and political dissensions. When he died he left a nation that he had compelled to accept an active role in European affairs. England was now a leading member of the Grand Alliance, she had established herself in the Mediterranean, she had a disciplined army fast acquiring its own military traditions and earning its battle honours in international wars.

It can be said that William III took England into Europe, as it can certainly be said that he was the first European. He was often called the Protestant Champion, but this was the tribute of a Europe that still thought in medieval terms. He himself was no religious fanatic, and the wars against France into which time and again he plunged Europe were certainly no crusades. They had only one object: to check the imperial ambitions of a French King. "It almost seemed", wrote Winston Churchill of William, "that a being had been created for the sole purpose of resisting the domination of France and the Great King."*

Such an objective completely justified the invasion of 1688 and the Glorious Revolution, in William's eyes. Both were essential if England was to be retained in the Protestant camp, on the side of the Allies; and the fact that they necessitated the deposing of his own father-in-law was tiresome but irrelevant.

Mary could not share her husband's detachment, and she was haunted by guilt towards her father until the end of her life. But she was too loyal ever to display these doubts in public, and she threw herself whole-heartedly into the demanding role assigned to her. Her Stuart blood and her close legitimate claims on the throne helped soothe the conscience of many of those who might otherwise have felt compelled to oppose the Revolution settlement; her charm, her dignity and her sheer goodness helped reconcile the entire English nation to the change. And during the long absences of William, she overcame her natural diffidence to display a forcefulness, an assurance and an instinct for rule which, in the view of several historians, would have made her one of England's great Queens if she had survived her husband to reign alone.

But her considerable abilities were appreciated only by her immediate circle, and when she died she left little more than a gentle memory and a fashion for blue-and-white china, while William left his imprint on the whole map of Western Europe. By rousing the Dutch against France, by forming the opponents of Louis XIV's expansionism into a strong aggressive coalition, and by involving England decisively in the affairs of the Continent, he created a new balance of power in Europe. Frontiers blurred and indistinct before his time were drawn with clarity and precision in the course of those struggles to which he gave the impetus.

William is thought of as a soldier-king, and he was one of the last European monarchs to lead his armies in person, but on the battlefield he was constantly outmatched by the superior strategy of Louis's generals commanding greater armies than he could muster. His desperate personal courage could not make up for an initial lack of experience and a mediocre military skill. Where he excelled was in diplomatic warfare. To have built up from nothing a strong and determined coalition against France was the achievement of a man of whom Churchill said: "Perhaps he has never been surpassed in the sagacity, patience and discretion of his statecraft. The combinations he made, the difficulties he surmounted, the adroitness with which he used the time factor, or played upon the weakness of others, the unerring sense of proportion and power of assigning to objectives their true priorities, all mark him for the highest fame . . ."*

He was a man born to lead, and his whole personality seemed formed with this object. While he was still a child, he already understood the role that destiny had given him, and he acted out this role to the end of his life with passionate single-mindedness. His body was weak, but he mastered this disability with the strength of a will to carry out what he felt to be his life's purpose, and he allowed nothing to stand in his way. He had no pity for himself, little for his wife, his friends and allies, and none at all for those who opposed him. By the standards of his time he was a humane king, but he was certainly no saint. He had the courage of his ruthlessness, and where he felt his own moral responsibility, he refused to visit public punishment or condemnation on those who had been his tools. In any case, he never allowed public opinion to be the guide of his behaviour. Criticisms of his generosity or rumours of homosexuality arising from his evident partiality towards his Dutch favourites left him completely unmoved.

His loyalty towards his friends – warm, strong and unaffected – was among the more attractive of his qualities. When he loved, he loved without reserve, expecting the same unquestioning devotion in return.

It was perhaps his tragedy that he was destined to be a war-time leader. Neither he nor Mary were intellectuals, but he was a sensitive and intelligent man, and shared with her a genuine taste for painting, architecture and gardening. If he had had the time and leisure to cultivate these interests, and she had lived longer, they would certainly have left England and the Dutch with more than Kensington Palace, Het Loo and some unfinished schemes to remember them by. The interest William and Mary took in their palaces was not only inspired by the aesthetic pleasure of creation, or – for William – a desire to compete with the Sun King; it was the enthusiasm of a man and a woman whose home life was precious to them. Until their reign, the Kings and Queens of England had lived in the full glare of the public gaze, but William and Mary were determined to be as private as possible, and they set a new pattern of domestication which, on the whole, the English monarchy has followed ever since. By the same token, they succeeded in giving a higher moral tone to English public life by making decadence and immorality no longer acceptable at Court. William, good Calvinist Dutchman that he was, was offended by profanity or ostentatious loose living, and he and Mary both tried to check the immorality of English life by decree. They were laughed at for their pains, but their influence was felt all the same, and it was just as much true of their tolerance in religious matters. If Parliament had allowed him to do so, William would certainly have abolished the worst disabilities from which Catholics and Dissenters suffered, and although his actual achievement was limited, he took much of the sting out of English religious conflicts, and left behind a country in which minority groups like Jews and Quakers were allowed to practise their religion according to their own conscience.

In spite of these admirable achievements and qualities, William was never much loved by the English, either in his own time or later, and while Mary is remembered with a certain affection to this day, William is the least appreciated King England ever had. Kings in England are allowed to be despotic, eccentric, or even mad; they can be extravagant, debauched or stupid; they can be drunkards, perverts or murderers, and still cut a passable figure in their country's history. William's crimes, in English eyes, were less forgivable than any of these – he was cold, he was reserved, and worst of all, he made almost no effort to win their hearts. They felt that he rejected them by his long absences in Holland. His irritated indifference to their party difference ensured his unpopularity in political circles, and his offhand treatment of the English nobility alienated the upper classes. His contempt for ceremonial display was another deeply-felt grievance. And all Mary's efforts could not atone for these deficiencies.

His funeral on Sunday, 12 April was thus an appropriate end to his reign. While his wife had been buried with Royal pomp and glory, his own funeral, which took place in private at midnight, as was customary for the great, was ordered with such complete absence of ostentation that Burnet thought it "scarce decent". The funeral procession began at Kensington, and went its slow way to Westminster with a wax effigy of the dead King lying on the funeral chariot; the coffin containing the King's body was only introduced when they reached Westminster Palace. The pall was carried by six dukes, Prince George was chief mourner, and the procession, moving silently through the dark streets, reached the doors of Westminster Abbey almost unnoticed by the population of London. It was met by the Dean and conducted to the Henry VII chapel where the service was read by the Dean and the Bishop of Rochester. But if a funeral sermon was preached, it has not survived, and uncertain tradition suggests only the name of one anthem: "I beheld and lo!" set to music by John Blow. Then the vault was opened, the coffin was lowered into it, and the officers of the dead King's household broke their staves and threw them in afterwards, shouting "God Save Queen Anne".* Thus William III silently reached his last resting-place in England, a stranger to the end. He was born a "passionate Dutchman" and he had remained one.

Eleven days later, Queen Anne was crowned amid the tumultuous celebrations of her subjects. The English once more had an English monarch, and they rejoiced in the fact. Anne herself understood them perfectly. In her first words after her accession, she had told them: "As I know my own heart to be entirely English, I can very sincerely assure you there is not anything you can expect or desire from me which I shall not be ready to do for the happiness and prosperity of England."* It was noticed that she was careful to emphasize the word "English".

*Notes
and Bibliography*

Notes

REFERENCES

References begin with the relevant page-number and cue-words. They refer to the works listed in the Bibliography, and are cited as briefly as possible. Besides the abbreviations of manuscript sources listed at the beginning of the Bibliography and those in general use (*EHR* = *English Historical Review*; HMC = Historical Manuscripts Commission, etc.) the following has been used:

Arch. = *Archives de la Maison d'Orange-Nassau*, 2nd ser., 5 ed. G. Groen van Prinsterer, The Hague, 1861; 3rd ser., 3 vols, ed F. J. L. Krämer, Leiden, 1907-9.

CHAPTER 1: *Death and Birth*

1 *in the Hague* Davies 453.

1 *had seemed inappropriate* Japikse, *Prins Willem III* 1 21.

1 *Heer van Heenvliet* Kerckhoven 552.

1 *the baby's head* BM Birch MS. 4460.

1 *House of Orange* Ontknoopinghe van den valstrick, van S.H. den Prince van Orangie, voor hem geleydt van sijner jeugt af, tot dese huydigen tydt toe, 1672, cit. Bilderdijk 9 282.

2 *plenty of wind* Kerckhoven 556.

2 *at the Hague* Zuylen van Nyevelt 146.

2 *hatred and dissatisfaction* Geyl, *Orange and Stuart* 11.

3 *but royal child* ibid. 10.

3 *opinion that triumphed* Fruin, *Verspreide Geschriften* 4 103.

4 *good as dead* Kerckhoven 544.

4 *sad and inconsolable* ibid. 545.

4 *skin and bone* Elizabeth of Bohemia 179.

4 *than eighty past* Zuylen van Nyevelt 145.

5 *of the Provinces* Groen van Prinsterer, *Handboek* 1 327.

5 *would be sovereign* ibid.

5 *will be deliberated* ibid.

5 *about its division* Japikse, *Prins Willem III* 1 22.

6 *for every campaign* Groen van Prinsterer, *Handboek* 1 327-33.

6 *after their coaches* Geyl, *Netherlands* 2 25-6.

6 *and without disputes* Kerckhoven 600.

7 *William Henry* Elizabeth of Bohemia 181

7 *pretentious royal ermine* Montanus 1 27; Japikse, *Prins Willem III* 1 38.

7 *for 5000 guilders* Aitzema 3 551.

7 *for her person* ibid. 567.

7 *and at peace* ibid. 574.

8 *treat a demoiselle* ibid. 616, 617, 628.

8 *relieved and triumphant* ibid. 639.

8 *it so expensively* Witt, *Brieven* 1 19.

8 *for the Prince* Japikse, *Prins Willem III* 1 27.

8 *of her child* ibid. 45.

CHAPTER 2: *The Triumph of Amsterdam*

11 *any given situation* Churchill 1 72.

12 *to the poor* Mountague 148.

12 *burning my sails* Blok 4 273.

14 *in May 1652* Elizabeth of Bohemia 190.

14 *sent him away* Witt Huberts 22.

14 *stadholder after all* Blok 7 8.

15 *the Dutch Navy* Davies 453.
15 *in a pamphlet* Geyl, *Netherlands* **2** 31.
15 *but in pieces* Bowen, *William of Orange* 38.
15 *or finer man* Groen van Prinsterer, *Handboek* **1** 315–16.
16 *promise from Holland* Fruin *Verspreide Geschriften* **4** 225.
16 *for his protection* ibid. 248.
16 *of Prince William* Aitzema **3** 298.
16 *evidente necessiteit* Secrete Resolutien *Holland* **1**, 142, 159, 160; cit. Japikse, *Prins Willem III* **1** 50.
16 *in this country* Fabius 39.
16 *was fine enough* KHA f. 2583.
17 *brought him home* Elizabeth of Bohemia 213.
17 *favorit of mine* ibid. 215.
17 *than she did* ibid. 229.
17 *was a failure* Geyl, *Orange and Stuart* 28–9.
17 *guilders a month* R. A. Nass. Dom 601. f. 34, cit. Baxter 21.
18 *of a nurse* Witt Huberts 46
18 *Reservedness and Moderation* Boyer 10.
18 *taken with him* Elizabeth of Bohemia 227

18 *most chaste manners* Trigland 10.
19 *his everyday life* Huygens, "Discours".
19 *with great fear* Japikse, *Correspondentie*, **2** i 1.
19 *are in it* Thurloe **1** 664.
19 *worth 80,000 guilders* KHA f. 2583 Krämer, "Je Maintiendrai" **2** 270
19 *than he intended* Beresford, *Downing* 94.
20 *her in Breda* Witt Huberts 46.
20 *act verie well* Elizabeth of Bohemia 286.
20 *resenting the nomination* ibid. 281.
20 *sens et d'esprit* Arch. 2nd ser. **5** 187.
21 *replied William* Chevalier **1** 11.
21 *red-velvet bound album* Alphen, "Anthony Smets".
22 *the whole Court* Oman, 428, 430.
22 *Prince and her* Elizabeth of Bohemia 290.
22 *of these expectations* Japikse, *Prins Willem III* **1** 64.
23 *treatie of Munster* Elizabeth of Bohemia 290.
23 *summoned to Honselaersdijck* Arch. 2nd ser. **5** 196.
23 *Spoke for him* Wicquefort **2** 667.

CHAPTER 3 : *William Alone*

24 *of the state* Japikse, *Verwikkelingen* 11.
24 *more to him* Elizabeth of Bohemia 307–308.
25 *men of honour* Bowen, *William of Orange* 65.
25 *their own course* Witt, *Brieven* **4** 108.
25 *munitions of war* Blok **7** 176.
25 *attention from passers-by* Bowen, *William of Orange* 64.
26 *the poised axe* Goes **1** 87.
26 *by the prince* Witt Huberts 60.
26 *not be equal* Arch. 2nd ser. **5** 205.
27 *in the world* KHA MS. 15 14.
27 *behaviour beneath her* Arch. 2nd ser., **5** 169.
27 *of old friends* Silvius, cit. Geyl, *Orange and Stuart* 128–9.
28 *saying a word* Faugere, *Voyage à Paris* 12, cit. Jorissen 62.
28 *of the Prince* Fabius 57.
28 *his small household* Pepys **1** 139 (14 May 1660).
28 *air de grandeur* Japikse, *Prins Willem III* **4** 75.
28 *his intelligence keen* Monconys **2** 127, cit. Blok **7** 127.
28 *wrote Clarendon* Zuylen van Nyevelt 127.

28 *could well succeed* Bowen, *William of Orange* 62.
29 *his own barge* Elizabeth of Bohemia 327.
29 *endeavoured to please* Gramont 107, 173.
29 *as this marriage* Clarendon, *Life* **1** 384.
29 *it by another* Jesse **4** 474.
30 *of his son* Clarendon, *Life* **1** 384.
30 *back to France* Krämer, *Maria II Stuart* 21.
30 *respect and love* Pepys **2** 3 (1 Jan. 1661).
30 *in Westminster Abbey* Elizabeth of Bohemia 334.
30 *his country's good* KHA MS. 16 18.
31 *communication with England* Goes **1** 122.
31 *in his treasure-house* Japikse, *Correspondentie* **2** i 2.
31 *wrote Elizabeth* Elizabeth of Bohemia 334–5.
31 *than ever before* Fabius 60.
31 *his chief guardians* Japikse, *Prins Willem III* **1** 89–890.
32 *hands of it* Geyl, *Netherlands* **2** 55.
32 *be its ruin* Arch. 2nd ser. **5** 235.
32 *verie good natured* Elizabeth of Bohemia, 342.

32 *of his uncle*   Japikse, *Prins Willem III* 1 101.

33 *in the future*   Goes 1 149.

33 *love of dancing*   Jesse 3 14.

33 *find nobody pleased*   Pepys 3 75 (1 May 1662).

CHAPTER 4: *War and Peace*

34 *Gallus non Vicinus*   Arch. 2nd ser. 5 234; Fabius 65.

34 *still their slaves*   Arch. 2nd ser. 5 213.

35 *d'Estrades protested vigorously*   Huygens, *Briefwisseling* 6 61.

35 *Downing to Clarendon*   Clarendon Papers, cit. Zuylen van Nyevelt 224.

35 *without asking her*   Huygens, *Briefwisseling* 6 64; *Nederlandse Spectator* (1875) 334; Krämer, "*Je Maintiendrai*" 2 272

36 *have my friendship*   Japikse, *Correspondentie* 2 i 6.

36 *faithfully carried out*   Grimblot 1 516–517.

37 *art of riding*   Huygens, *Briefwisseling* 6 170.

37 *of his birth*   ibid. 159.

37 *stem the tide*   Geyl, *Netherlands* 2 87.

37 *Declaration of War*   Estrades 3 465–6, cit. Fruin, *Verspreide Geschriften* 5 9.

38 *were talking about*   Blok 7 150, 189.

38 *cares of power*   Beresford, *Downing* 190.

39 *friends and allies*   Estrades 3 186, 202.

39 *ni son lit*   ibid. 202.

40 *for Years together*   Ralph, *History* 1 129.

40 *pour son age*   Grimblot 1 (app. i).

40 *will have Merit*   Ralph, *History* 1 129.

40 *Child of William*   Aitzema 5 787, cit. Fabius 74.

40 *off her bonnet*   Charlotte-Amelia de la Trémouille, *Mémoires*, cit. Witt Huberts 86.

40 *Elector of Brandenburg*   Herzogin Sophie, *Briefwechsel*, cit. Fabius 80.

41 *punish their insolence*   Davies 3 45–9.

41 *fled to England*   Proces van Buat, cit. Fruin, *Verspreide Geschriften* 2 261–305.

42 *a horrified witness*   Pepys (2 September 1666).

42 *tread on them*   Evelyn, *Diary* 2 202 (4 September 1666).

42 *vaine, empty, carelesse*   Wood 127.

42 *ordinary private father*   Pepys 5 268 (12 September 1664).

44 *do to parchment*   Blok 7 239.

44 *been more evident*   Groen van Prinsterer, *Handboek* 1 357.

45 *very well regulated*   Hoogewerff 133–7.

45 *to the spectators*   Droste 1 41.

45 *he can rule*   Japikse, *Prins Willem III* 1 144.

45 *deportment and self-assurance*   Hoogewerff 135–7.

CHAPTER 5: *Visit to England*

46 *Huygens to Amalia*   Huygens, *Briefwisseling* 6 16.

46 *De Witt's authority*   Bowen, *William of Orange* 111.

47 *de ma santé*   Japikse, *Prins Willem III* 1 150.

48 *at that time*   Temple 1 285, cit. Sidney 1 42.

48 *sort of wine*   ibid.

48 *of many virtues*   ibid. 1 194, cit. Sidney 1 91.

48 *or of artifice*   ibid.

49 *the whole world*   Bodleian MS. 10493 f. 250, cit. Woodbridge 64.

49 *Orange sovereign there*   Goes 2 6.

50 *behind the other*   ibid. 2 20.

50 *with something indigestible*   ibid. 2 154.

50 *and our persons*   Bowen 117.

50 *and higher one*   ibid. 119

51 *respectfully round him*   Goes 2 134.

51 *emissary to Arlington*   Japikse, *Correspondentie* 2 i 26.

51 *the Minister's garden*   ibid. 27, 31.

51 *upon his Highness*   ibid. 26.

51 *England one day*   ibid. 32.

52 *only by royalty*   Goes 2 159.

52 *in his eyes*   Sommier en Waerachtigh *Verhael* (1670–1) pamphlet, which has been used as a principal source for this chapter.

52 *of the Court*   L.C.C., *Survey of London* 13 41.

52 *faded and stained*   Droste 43.

53 *nasty and stinking*   Evelyn, *Diary* 2 444–445 (4 February 1685).

53 *on the chairs*   Droste 154–5.

53 *sort of trap* Reresby 93.
53 *who you love* Jesse **3** 195–6.
53 *to them enough* Sommier en Waerachtigh Verhael.
53 *been timely rescued* Reresby 82.
53 *courageous, wise countenance* Evelyn, Diary **2** 253 (4 November 1670).
53 *like those popinjays* Sommier en Waerachtigh Verhael.
53 *of his own* Newton, *Diary* 58, cit. Bowen, *William of Orange* 124.
54 *paid by Charles* Hore **2** 300–1.

54 *and was acquitted* Sommier en Waerachtigh Verhael.
54 *civil servants involved* Japikse, *Prins Willem III* **1** 168.
55 *a wholehearted welcome* Fabius 88–92.
56 *generosity and politeness* RA St. Gen. 6922, cit. Japikse, *Prins Willem III* **1** 169.
56 *his Dutch blockheads* Burnet, *History* **1** 495.
56 *have hindered him* Dalrymple **1** 47.

CHAPTER 6: *Clouds Over Europe*

57 *and christened Catherine* Sommier en Waerachtigh Verhael (1670–1), pamphlet.
57 *only eleven months* Jesse **3** 468.
57 *him his job* Krämer *Maria II Stuart* 69–70.
57 *about her eyes* PRO, *CSP Dom.*, SP 277.
57 *the Lady Mary* Reresby 82.
57 *banished to France* Jesse **1** 195.
58 *the Back Stairs* Jesse **3** 476.
58 *were so good* Pepys (2 April 1669).
58 *find it out* Fea, *James II* 53.
58 *for love letters* HMC Rutland **2** 11.
59 *to see her* Gramont 274.
59 *in their despatches* Krämer, *Maria Stuart* 67–8. He also mentions Pufendorf the historian of Frederick III of Brandenburg, as well as Bonrepaus and Kramprich; and Count Gallas speaks about it in a letter in 1711
59 *retire from public* HMC Rutland **2** 10–11.
59 *sense of things* Burnet **1** 298.
59 *near the throne* Gramont 110.
59 *invest in jewels* Pepys (27 January 1668).
60 *praying at Dover* PRO, *CSP Dom.*, SP 277.
60 *the last word* Oldmixon, *Critical History* **2** 560.
60 *that I have* Stuart Papers **2** 286.

60 *a poor wretch* Evelyn, *Life of Mrs Godolphin* 13.
60 *the stately carcase* ibid.
61 *Castle of Loevestein* Coronelli 11 (9 April 1671).
61 *free of suspicion* Goes **2** 201.
62 *part in it* M. C. Trevelyan 73.
62 *love of change* Fruin, *Verspreide Geschriften* **5** 16.
62 *declared Arlington* Haley 32.
63 *see us destroyed* Japikse, *Correspondentie* **2** ii 37.
63 *more and more* ibid. 38.
63 *me Captain-General* ibid. 39.
63 *dependentie" on England* Fruin, *Verspreide Geschriften* **4** 347; Japikse, *Prins Willem III* **1** 175.
63 *them of Holland* Beresford 252.
64 *of the Republic* Japikse, *Correspondentie* **2** i 40–1.
64 *hard to describe* Japikse, *Prins Willem III* **1** 180.
64 *became prized souvenirs* Goes **2** 353.
64 *lasted eight hours* ibid.
64 *for good hope* ibid. 356.
64 *and open way* Japikse, *Correspondentie* **2** i 43.
65 *William to Ossory* ibid. 41.

CHAPTER 7: *The Disaster Year*

66 *a good bleeding* Ségur 58.
66 *warned De Witt* Lefèvre Pontalis **2** 194.
66 *were almost unmanned* Anon. "Dagelijkse Aantekeningen" 253.
67 *I am dead* Witt, *Brieven* **4** 345, cit. Japikse, *Prins Willem III* **1** 188.
67 *States and me* Japikse, *Correspondentie* **2** i 48.

67 *25,000 wretched troops* Voltaire **1** 327.
68 *a powerful force* Witt, *Brieven* **2** 628–9, cit. Japikse, *Prins Willem III* **1** 188.
68 *things but envy* Evelyn, *Diary* **2** 283 (2 June 1672).
68 *let Holland fall* Japikse, *Prinse Willem III* **1** 188.
69 *then they prayed* Blok **7** 277.

69 *flood the countryside* Ségur 61.
69 *artificial man-made country* Niox, *Géographie Militaire* **3**, cit. Ségur 61.
70 *on 29 June* Jonge 449; Lefèvre Pontalis **2** 395.
70 *sorry for you* Wagenaar **14** 75; Wicquefort **4** 490.
70 *of the Rampjaar* Gebhard, *Dagboek* 53.
71 *have been made* Fabius 116.
71 *De Groot's return* Rousset **1** 387, cit. Fruin **4** 349.
72 *was made Stadholder* PRO, SP 84/189 ff. 143–58; Japikse, *Correspondentie* **2** i 220.
72 *before his obligations* Bowen, *William of Orange* 219.
72 *of his own* ibid. 220.
72 *the last ditch* M. C. Trevelyan 258.
73 *aimez la vôtre* Jesse **3** 98;
73 *than accept them* Fruin, *Verspreide Geschriften* **5** 30.
73 *more glorious existence* Macaulay **1** 164.
73 *him as sovereign* Fruin, *Verspreide Geschriften* **4** 344–5.
73 *of the government* Japikse, *Correspondentie* **2** i 86.
74 *you my heart* Anon, "Aantekeningen Betreffende het Voorgevallene" 442.
74 *Duke of York* Fruin, *Verspreide Geschriften* **5** 43.
74 *establish the Prince* ibid. 44; Krämer, *Maria Stuart* 75.

75 *Prince of Orange* Bowen, *William of Orange* 31.
75 *a well-deserved death* Gebhard, *Dagboek* 89.
76 *are dead men* Fruin, *Verspreide Geschriften* **4** 375–6.
76 *that awaits them* Bilderdijk **9** 290.
76 *sold as souvenirs* Goes **2** 410; Gebhard, *Dagboek* 89–90.
76 *fifteen years later* Japikse, *Correspondentie* **2** ii 275.
77 *towards De Witt* Geyl, *Netherlands in the Seventeenth Century* 134.
77 *un peu soulagé* Grimblot **2** app. i, 524–5.
77 *ambassador as well* Japikse, *Correspondentie* **2** 96.
78 *for several reasons* ibid. 103.
78 *that poor people* ibid. 108–9.
78 *faint-hearted by nature* ibid. 115–16.
78 *Heer van La Leck* Bourdon 93–4.
79 *the local interest* Fruin, *Verspreide Geschriften* **4** 353, 376; Groen van Prinsterer, *Handboek* **1** 37; Fouw 99.
80 *into a duck* Ségur 126.
80 *replied William* Anon, "Aantekeningen Betreffende het Voorgevallene" 459–60.
80 *action si hardieuse* Japikse, *Prins Willem III* **1** 278–9; Ségur 168.
80 *on distant adventures* Ségur 167.
81 *the King's troops* Sylvius, cit. Grew, *William Bentinck and William III* 28.
81 *carefully looked after* Japikse, *Prins Willem III* **1** 286.

CHAPTER 8: *The European War*

83 *Frenchman to Louvois* Ségur 234.
84 *follow this Fleet* Fabius 146.
84 *the Seven Provinces* Japikse, *Prins Willem III* **1** 303.
84 *the general verdict* Rousset, cit. Ségur 239.
85 *during the siege* Huygens, *Journalen* **4** 17.
85 *of the state* Japikse, *Correspondentie* **2** i 310.
85 *my distant conquests* Louis XIV, *Œuvres* **3** 454, cit. Ségur 239.
86 *houses of Vreeswyk* Ségur 263.
86 *Prince of Orange* Ségur 215.
86 *except these two* Dalrymple **1** 154.
86 *against the French* Oerizonius, *Laudatio Funebris* 26, cit. Fruin, *Verspreide Geschriften* **5** 209.
87 *most faithful ministers* Fruin, *Verspreide Geschriften* **5** 135–6.
88 *any human creature* Robert Halstead, "Memoirs of Peterborough" in *Succinct Genealogies of the House of Alno* (1685), cit. Turner 112.
88 *of your piety* Haile 21.
88 *of the Pope* Fea, *James II* 71; Williamson **2** 63.
88 *husband and all* Oman, *Mary of Modena* 31.
88 *our religion unblemished* Krämer, *Maria Stuart* 74.
88 *the French King* Reresby 92–3.
89 *their customary bonfires* Williamson 82.
89 *emerging Protestant champion* Woodbridge 117.
89 *you so established* Fruin, *Verspreide Geschriften* **5** 49; Japikse, *Prins Willem III* **1** 336, 337.
89 *des quoquins d'Hollandais* Japikse, *Correspondentie* **2** i 338.
89 *so much disdain* ibid. 342.
90 *as I live* Jesse **1** 48.
90 *for the Allies* Bulstrode 119.

90 *than the enemy*　Japikse, *Prins Willem III* **2** 25–9.

91 *our baggage train*　Japikse, *Correspondentie* **2** i 119.

91 *did very little*　ibid. **2** i 472.

91 *of a Marius*　Japikse, *Prins Willem III* **2** 25–9.

91 *his own example*　Jesse **1** 49–50.

91 *was all fire*　Burnet, *History* **4** 562.

91 *have of me*　Japikse, *Correspondentie* **2** i 477.

92 *Things this Campaign*　Bulstrode 114.

92 *very badly seconded*　Japikse, *Correspondentie* **2** i 527.

CHAPTER 9: *The Princess of England*

93 *view in Europe*　Ralph, *History* **1** 258.

93 *the Loevestein Faction*　ibid.

93 *the best uneasy*　Japikse, *Prins Willem III* **2** 35.

94 *the Flanders fortresses*　Ralph, *History* **1** 257.

94 *the battlefield is*　Temple, *Memoirs* **2** 300.

94 *in his loyalties*　Bulstrode 142.

94 *throne before him*　Huygens, *Journalen* **2** 8.

95 *to the prince*　Temple, *Memoirs* **2** 272.

95 *Lotte never married*　Japikse, *Correspondentie* **2** ii 4–5, 16.

95 *William of Orange*　Huygens, *Journaal* **3** 8.

95 *mixed with sweetness*　Japikse, *Correspondentie* **2** i 335.

96 *were available*　Pontbriant 227.

96 *not their bastards*　ibid.

96 *proudly and often*　Dalrymple **1** 148.

96 *between the two*　PRO, *CSP Dom.* (1677–1678) 540.

96 *and shipped off*　Anon, *Secret History of Whitehall* **1** 178.

97 *is his W.*　Bathurst 32–3.

97 *mightily to harte*　ibid. 37–8.

97 *covered with jewels*　Evelyn, *Diary* **2** 305 (15 December 1677).

98 *have proceeded further*　Evelyn, *Life of Mrs Godolphin* 96.

98 *ready to cry*　Bathurst 54–5.

98 *your humble trout*　ibid. 60–1.

99 *"very ingenius" girl*　ibid. 64.

99 *but a daughter*　Oman, *Mary of Modena* 48.

99 *one admirer's opinion*　Japikse, *Prins Willem III* **1** 335.

99 *dutiful and hardworking*　Fabius 177.

100 *to be lavish*　Huygens, *Journaal* **3**

100 *a little paradise*　Montague 44.

100 *but Bentinck answered*　Temple, *Memoirs* **2** 309.

100 *fell ill himself*　Gaeto 203.

100 *constancy of mind*　Temple, *Memoirs* **2** 97

101 *of his health*　Coronelli 12.

101 *had for him*　Fabius 190.

101 *not allowed it*　Japikse, *Correspondentie* **2** ii 27–9.

101 *is piled up*　Müller **2** 247.

101 *neglected their duty*　Japikse, *Correspondentie* **2** ii 65.

102 *related Huygens*　Huygens, *Journaal* **4** 47.

102 *he rides on*　Correspondence of Sophia of Hanover, December 1674, cit. Ségur 319.

102 *made that winter*　Japikse, *Correspondentie* **2** ii 71.

102 *Prince of Condé*　Ségur 103–5.

103 *of the Midianites*　Davies **3** 147–8.

103 *in Holland waves*　Japikse, *Prins Willem III* **1** 347.

103 *rectify his ideas*　in Grimblot **1** 2 pp., 525.

103 *done for Israel*　Japikse, *Correspondentie* **2** ii 12–13.

CHAPTER 10: *Fading Hopes*

104 *this poor nation*　Evelyn, *Diary* **2** 107 (30 March 1676).

104 *his wife's chapel*　HMC, *Report* **7** 467, cit. Turner 126.

104 *his second marriage*　Temple **2** 345.

105 *tell him freely*　ibid. 343

106 *near each other*　Japikse, *Correspondentie* **2** ii 98.

107 *Most Christian Majesty*　Correspondence of Père Quesnel, cit. Ségur 262.

107 *plus haï qu'aimé*　Japikse, *Prins Willem III* **2** 54.

107 *a greater nightmare*　ibid. 48–54.

108 *aren't yet spoiled*　Japikse, *Correspondentie* **2** ii 132–3.

108 *were no falls*　ibid. **1** i 16.

108 *it years later* Japikse, *Prins Willem III* **2** 115–16.

108 *make the peace* Haley, "Rapprochement" 617.

109 *terms were his* Temple **4** 316.

109 *of this alliance* Japikse, *Correspondentie* **2** ii 144.

110 *hang you later* Anon, *Royal Diary* 60.

110 *this vigorous commander* ibid.

110 *else spotted them* Ségur 440.

110 *un peu embarrassé* Huygens, *Journalen* **4** 151.

110 *to buy M.P.s* Forneron 187–8.

110 *to the world* Reresby 120.

110 *by the war* Dalrymple **1** 138.

111 *likes it not* HMC Rutland **2** 33.

111 *the Lady Mary* PRO *CSP Dom.* 1676–7 592.

112 *to the King* Huygens, *Journalen* **2** 121.

112 *in the army* Japikse, *Correspondentie* **2** ii 180.

112 *from an attack* Japikse, *Correspondentie* **2** ii 199.

112 *dealing, is intolerable* Japikse, *Correspondentie* **2** ii 205.

113 *gardens of Enghien* Huygens, *Journaal* **3** 211.

113 *with H. H. convenience* Japikse, *Correspondentie* **1** ii 6.

113 *The Hague* ibid. **2** ii 207.

113 *nephew at Newmarket* *Arch.* 2nd ser. **5** 348.

CHAPTER 11: *The Marriage*

114 *a common one* Evelyn, *Diary,* **2** 248 (22 July 1670).

114 *he drove through* Oprecht verhaal (pamphlet) 6–8.

115 *that know least* BM Add. MSS. 25119 f. 116.

115 *entered into affairs* Temple **2** 293.

115 *badly brought up* Baschet, cit. Turner 131.

115 *of his father-in-law* Fruin, *Verspreide Geschriften* **5** 44.

115 *up for him* L.C.C., *Survey of London* **13** 80.

115 *upon former enquiries* Temple **2** 294.

115 *his fruitless visit* Klopp **2** 455–6.

116 *as Temple said* Temple **2** 294.

116 *and William himself* ibid. 295.

116 *the Catholic Spanish* Barillon, cit. Haley, "Rapprochement" 643.

117 *in Protestant arms* Anon, *Royal Diary* 33.

117 *he must consent* Clarke **1** 509–10.

117 *I obey him* Temple **2** 295.

117 *The following day* Lake 5.

117 *very well together* HMC Atholl, 34.

118 *thick brown hair* Verney **4** 237.

118 *wife Mary Clorine* Bathurst 78.

118 *of building Versailles* Temple **2** 297.

119 *would be made* Barillon, cit. Haley, "Rapprochement" 644.

119 *from the castle* PRO *CSP Dom.* 1677–8 422, 427.

119 *knighted by Charles* Dring.

119 *not believe it* Oprecht verhaal (pamphlet) 18–22.

120 *observed this condition* Montanus **1** 282; HMC Finch **2**.

120 *a foregone conclusion* Fruin, *Verspreide Geschriften* **5** 58.

120 *goodness of heart* ibid. 213.

120 *most part false* KHA Prins Willem III **13** 2.

120 *very well satisfied* PRO *CSP Dom.* 1677–1678 438, 449.

121 *of coarse pleasantries* Halifax **2** 257.

121 *all clear gain* Lake **1** 6.

121 *St George for England* ibid.

121 *had been gambling* Orléans, *Letters from Liselotte* 32.

122 *the present time* Ségur 466.

122 *William of Orange* Burnet **2** 124.

122 *were no children* PRO, SP 104/66.

123 *her conqu'ring eyes* Waller, *Works* (Glasgow, 1752) 145.

CHAPTER 12: *Mary in Holland*

124 *least before folkes* Hatton Correspondence 10 November 1677, cit. Airy (ed.) Burnet, *History* (1900) 131 n. 2.

124 *was another comment* Verney **4** 237.

124 *state of intoxication* Hare **2** 348.

124 *into her closet* Lake 8.

124 *likely to live* ibid. 7.

125 *of his children* ibid. 14–15.

125 *all her family* ibid. 9.

125 *sullennesse and clownishnesse* ibid.

125 *to read them* ibid. 10.
125 *must dy condemed* Bathurst 81.
126 *out of England* Lake 10.
126 *scene of grief* Lady Chaworth, cit. Fea, *James II* 88.
126 *where they dined* Lake 10; *Oprecht verbaal* (pamphlet).
126 *of the delay* Oprecht *verbaal*.
126 *favourable wind there* Arch. 2nd ser. 5 351.
126 *in this country* ibid. 352.
126 *from the coaching-inn* Danby 153.
126 *a good passage* Arch. 2nd ser. 5 352-3.
127 *Mary never forgot* Strickland 7 47.
127 *the same reason* Lake 9.
127 *the Orange Household* Evelyn, *Diary* 2 333 (19 November 1677).
127 *into the War* Arch. 2nd ser. 5 354.
128 *hot meal ready* Lake 12.
128 *might be peace* Oprecht *verbaal*.
128 *the young girl* Droste 124. Oprecht *verbaal*.
129 *descending from Heaven* Krämer, *Maria Stuart* 87.
129 *back to Holland* Nippold *Regierung der Königin Maria* 3 n. 2.
129 *for her hand* ibid.; Klopp 2 70.
129 *fluency of conversation* Zuylen van Nyevelt 304.
129 *ennobles its possessors* ibid.
129 *(by the French)* Japikse, *Correspondentie* 2 ii 214.
130 *doing my duty* Japikse, *Prins Willem III* 2 80.
130 *herbs it yields* Bathurst 66.

130 *a prince's house* Vernon to Williamson, cit. Beresford 254.
131 *of the forests* Krämer, *"Je Maintiendrai"* 2 224-5.
131 *of the Princess* RA Resolutien Staten-Generael 8 January 1678, cit. Japikse, *Prins Willem III* 2 124.
131 *applying the adder* Vernon to Williamson, cit. Beresford 252.
132 *of the province* Fabius 183-4.
132 *trees about it* Mountague 201-2.
132 *blanc et vuide* Huygens, *Briefwisseling* 6 403.
132 *care and expense* ibid.
132 *for its elegance* Anon. *Dagelijkse Aantekeningen* 255.
133 *in perfect order* Geyl, *Netherlands* 2 191.
133 *not for use* Fruin, *Verspreide Geschriften* 4 250.
133 *to much breeding* Mountague 7.
133 *very ill-natured fellow* Saint-Évremond 42-4.
133 *his own way* ibid.
133 Marvell, "Character of Holland"
134 *very beautiful withal* Lake 26.
134 *the strict Dutch* Lake 22.
134 *marry Madam Villars* Danby 185-7.
134 *on the bride* Japikse, *Prins Willem III* 2 127; BM Egerton MSS. 708 1 f. 1.
135 *and so cheerful* Japikse, *Prins Willem III* 2 80.
135 *Highness allows yourself* Arch. 2nd ser. 5 364.
135 *that I lead* Bathurst 88-9.
136 *herself another time* PRO *CSP Dom.* 1678 126.

CHAPTER 13: *Peace in Europe*

137 *was continually rejected* Cobbett, *Parliamentary History of England*. cit. Turner 135.
137 *in a Yatcht* Danby 38-40.
138 *frogs is ended* Correspondence of Sophia of Hanover, cit. Ségur 475.
138 *biased Electress Sophia* ibid. 472.
138 *you think fitt* Japikse, *Correspondentie* 2 ii 260.
138 *we do too* ibid. 254.
139 *did not expect* Dalrymple 1 243.
139 *well as invincible* Ralph, *History of England* 1 369.
140 *of his Highness* Bowen, *William of Orange* 75.
140 *peace was concluded* Japikse, *Correspondentie* 2 ii 270.

140 *what they contained* Ségur 497.
140 *a good lesson* (app. Grimblot 1 525-6.)
140 *war so unluckily,* Ségur 523-5.
141 *of his letters* PRO *CSP Dom.* 1678 277
141 *it to you* Bathurst 91-2.
142 *post be gone* PRO, *CSP Dom.* 1678 411-412.
142 *they last met* Oman, *Mary of Modena* 56.
142 *young breeding woman* PRO *CSP Dom.* 1678 411-12.
142 *not for them* Dalrymple 2 i 201.
143 *me to say* Japikse, *Correspondentie* 2 ii 285.
143 *and to acquaintances* Droste 178.

143 *to inspire respect* Zuylen van Nyevelt 313

143 *of good Humour* Burnet, *Essay*.

144 *start to finish* Zuylen van Nyevelt 313.

144 *to the Princess* Orléans (Brunet) 1 456.

144 *sweetness and majesty* Bourdon 82.

145 *me with kindness* Huygens, *Journalen* 4 51, 52, 145, 211, 231.

145 *at all times* Burnet, *History* 4, 562.

145 *constant dry cough* ibid.

145 *by your hump* *Kronijk van het Historisch Genootschap*, Utrecht, 1854, 39.

146 *Burnet put it* Burnet, *History* 4 563.

146 *trumpet or drum* Harris, *History* 500.

146 *be given up* Bourdon 83.

146 *I not sweet* Bentinck 148.

147 *and poky parlour* Hooper ed. Prowse, cit. Plumptre 1 141.

147 *in the nation* Evelyn, *Diary* 2 386 (5 November 1681).

CHAPTER 14: *The English Rival*

148 *Introduction of Popery* Evelyn, *Diary* 2 343 (1 October 1678)

148 *Court more brave* ibid. 2 345 (15 November 1678)

149 *to the chapel* ibid. 2 343 (1 October 1678).

149 *Prince of Orange* Reresby 178,

149 *the popish party* ibid. 156–7.

150 *fuss of them* Japikse, *Correspondentie* 2 ii 295.

151 *knaves by consequence* Ailesbury 1 76–84.

151 *family are gone* Grew, *Court of William III* 98.

151 *the Crown interrupted* Reresby 156–7.

151 *to our party* Sidney 1 43.

152 *and his daughter* ibid. 1 16–17.

152 *Duchess of York* ibid. 1 19–20.

152 *became very public* Burnet, *History* 3 277.

152 *truth or honour* Swift footnote in Burnet, *History* 3 277.

152 *to his satisfaction* Sidney 1 43.

152 *of his friends* ibid. 1 54.

153 *out of danger* Japikse, *Correspondentie* 1 i 9.

153 *wants any remedies* Sidney 1 45–6.

153 *strongly displeases us* Oman, *Mary of Modena* 61.

154 *to hide them* Bathurst, 92–101.

154 *Frenchmen lodged here* Japikse, *Correspondentie* 2 ii 298.

155 *at their reunion* Sidney 1 131.

155 *having it himself* ibid. 130–1.

155 *King of England* ibid.

155 *William told Sidney* ibid.

155 *else he would* ibid. 154–6.

156 *Parliament at all* ibid. 161–3.

156 *going into England* ibid. 73.

CHAPTER 15: *The Exclusion Crisis*

158 *weary next day* Sidney 1 199.

159 *my house tomorrow* ibid. 1 139–40.

159 *of the last* ibid. 2 16–17.

159 *she had been* ibid. 2 4–5.

159 *mends a pace* *Arch.* 2nd ser. 5 387–8

159 *it with interest* Dartmouth note in Burnet, *History* 4 11.

160 *out of doors* Sidney 2 19–20.

160 *give his consent* ibid. 2 26.

160 *play that game* ibid. 2 77.

161 *in this country* ibid 2 78–9.

161 *of his recovery* Japikse, *Correspondentie* 2 ii.

162 *the Holy Sacrament* Evelyn, *Diary* 2 366–7 (26–30 July 1680).

162 *wrote Evelyn sadly* ibid.

162 *his person was* Japikse, *Correspondentie* 2 ii 353

162 *of the country* Sidney 2 93–7.

163 *supper one evening* Huygens, *Journaal* 3 54; Japikse *Prins Willem III* 2 14.

163 *moment for business* Huygens, *Journaal* 3 53

163 *he himself disappeared* Huygens, *Journalen* 4 43.

164 *for his country* ibid. 44.

164 *Hanover to matchmaker* Sidney 2 78–9, 103–4.

164 *of appearing old* Huygens, *Journaal* 3 27.

164 *Frances herself again* Bathurst 125.

165 *afords no other* ibid. 130–1.

165 *Clergy, no University* *Arch.* 2nd ser. 5 421.

165 *be my heir* Jesse 116–21.

165 *the Parliament sitts* *Arch.* 2nd ser. 5 420.

165 *name with patience* ibid. 422.

165 *by following them* ibid. 428.
166 *Charles's bastard son* Sidney **2** 119–21.
166 *should for him* ibid. 123.
166 *a pretty figure* ibid. 124.
166 *ever return again* ibid. 126–7.
167 *to the other* Arch. 2nd ser. **5** 459.

167 *in good harmony* Fruin, *Verspreide Geschriften* **5** 73.
167 *of civil war* Reresby 205, 207.
167 *thing ever writ* Sidney **1** 162.
167 *and a compromise* Fruin, *Verspreide Geschriften* **5** 79–80.

CHAPTER 16: *A Wasted Journey*

168 *Come to England* Sidney **2** 148
169 *in it himself* ibid. 141 ff.
170 *chaplain with dismissal* Zoutelandt 77–78.
171 *all your temper* Plumptre **1** 143–5.
171 *his good opinion* Sidney **2** 209–19.
171 *by the meeting* Dalrymple **1** 68.
171 *is with child* PRO *CSP Dom.* 1682 34.
172 *on the spot* Clarke **2** i 690.
172 *game for him* Bulstrode 327–8.
172 *presently to Windsor* ibid.
172 *he would go* Clarke **2** i 690.

173 *to be convinced* ibid. PRO 31/3/149 ff. 213–16.
173 *very great Disappointment* Bulstrode 327–8.
173 *his nephew prophetically* Burnet, *History* **2** 415.
173 *in one letter* Arch. 2nd ser. **5** 512.
173 *after his restoration* ibid. 513.
173 *of his family* ibid.
174 *earlier that year* Kenyon, "Earl of Sunderland" 78.
174 *for you here* Sidney **2** 211.

CHAPTER 17: *Conflict with Amsterdam*

175 *to believe it* Hanover, 363
175 *claim the Stadholdership* from a minute inserted in North's *Examen* 120, cit. Ralph, *History* **1** 254.
175 *by other discourse* Doebner 23.
175 *with innocent Mirth* Anon, *Royal Diary* 10.
175 *than her own* Burnet, *Memorial* 155–6.
176 *thought the Dutch* Groen van Prinsterer, *Handboek* **1** 411–12.
177 *blockade of Luxembourg* Japikse, *Correspondentie* **2** ii 446.
177 *lose his interest* Barillon to Louis XIV, PRO 31/3/150 ff. 323–42.
177 *make of it.* Arch. 2nd ser. **5** 536.
177 *memory of man* Reresby 248; Luttrell **1** 161.
177 *of the lose* Arch. 2nd ser. **5** 540–1.
178 *at the Hague* ibid. 548; Fruin, *Verspreide Geschriften* **5** 121.
178 *ill-bred and unreliable* Avaux **2** 97
178 *an unkind interpretation* Arch. 2nd ser. **5** 548; Fruin, *Verspreide Geschriften* **5** 121.
178 *commented William drily* Müller **1** 143; Fruin, *Verspreide Geschriften* **5** 106.
178 *from his allies* Arch. 2nd ser. **5** 547; Fruin, *Verspreide Geschriften* **5** 106.

179 *the Royal table* Erlanger 175–98 passim,
179 *had once belonged* Pontbriant 235.
179 *of doing so* Huygens, *Journaal* **3** 62–3.
179 *Prince of Orange* Jesse **1** 59.
179 *him no more* Avaux **1** 260–1.
174 *Haye en Hollande* Ralph, *History* **1** 104–105.
180 *affairs of Europe* Dalrymple **1** 104–5.
180 *the dinner ended* Huygens, *Journaal* **3** 70.
180 *argue the matter* Dalrymple **1** 104–5.
180 *of his principality* Pontbriant 236.
180 *audience of congé* Dalrymple **1** 105.
181 *people in England* Avaux **1** 311.
181 *What he wanted* Arch. 2nd ser. **5** 567.
181 *peace and quiet* ibid. 569.
181 *heaven than Versailles* Baxter 187.
181 *to be valiant* Evelyn, *Diary* **2** 414 (25 July 1683).
182 *quiet life somewhere* HMC *Report* IX, App. 2, cit. Green, *Queen Anne* 35.
182 *than in Holland* Grew, *William Bentinck and William III* 70.
182 *about the ring* ibid. 69.
182 *mount for Mary* Japikse, *Correspondentie* **1** i 14.
182 *had been made* ibid. 12.
182 *been in peace* Dalrymple **1** 108–9.

182 *for subjecting them* Avaux **2** 191.
183 *no longer William* ibid. 209.
183 *of the country* ibid. 380.
184 *City of Amsterdam* ibid 14–16.

185 *duty or not* Heim **1** lviii.
185 *will be over* II, 431
185 *Fifth Universal Monarchy* Evelyn, *Diary* **2** 413 (15 July 1683).

CHAPTER 18: *The Fall of Monmouth*

186 *head", he protested* Jesse **3** 128.
186 *in no others* Dalrymple **1** 118–19.
186 *must obey him* Avaux **4** 57.
187 *as I did* Dalrymple **1** 123–4.
187 *the Prince altogether* Burnet, *History* **3** 13.
188 *you did not* Dalrymple **1** 125.
188 *the three kingdoms* Baschet, cit. Ashley, *Glorious Revolution* 56.
188 *to convert people* Japikse, *Correspondentie* **2** ii 681.
188 *never be brought* ibid. 694.
188 *it had been* Jesse **3** 131–4.
189 *M. de Monmouth* Avaux **4** 211–12.
189 *on the other* ibid.
189 *for our vices* Evelyn, *Diary* **2** 413 (15 July 1683).
190 *and other parts* Dalrymple **2** 411.
190 *the whole kingdom* Reresby 352.
191 *very unaccountable manner* Jesse **3** 428–9.
191 *an English king* Evelyn, *Diary* **2** 465 (22 May 1685).
191 *this autocratic streak* Fox xviii.
191 *displays of power* Turner 235.
191 *to the nation* Evelyn, *Diary* **2** 481–2 (17 September 1685).
191 *drinking and wenching* Letters illustrative of the Herbert Family **1** 125, cit. Jesse **3** 426.
192 *our family requires* Dalrymple **1** 117.

192 *manner so noble* ibid. **2** 6.
193 *of ugly trollops* Orléans, *Correspondance* (Brunet), **2** 94.
193 *spring of 1685* Jesse **3** 135–7.
193 *in my cause* ibid.
194 *regiments from Holland* Japikse, *Correspondentie* **1** i 28.
194 *King believed him* ibid. **1** i 23.
194 *may be deceived* Letters in possession of Duke of Portland, cit. Sandars 124–5.
194 *followed his scent* Boyer **2** 28.
194 *in a ditch* cit. Jesse **3** 144.
194 *showing his delight* Reresby 385.
195 *which God grant* Japikse, *Correspondentie* **1** i 28.
195 *mercy and compassion* Jesse **3** 144.
195 *afraid of death* HMC Rutland **2** 93–4.
195 *two more blows* Omstandig en seecker verbael (1685) pamphlet (BM 8122).
196 *critics, John Evelyn* Evelyn, *Diary* **2** 471–2 (15 July 1685).
196 *William the Conqueror* Boyer **6** 33.
196 *pieces of Whitehall* Macaulay **1** 495.
196 *sent me thither* Jesse **3** 431–5.
196 *right of Kings* Ashley, *England in the Seventeenth Century*, 170.
196 *see them exercise* Evelyn, *Diary* **2** 473 (18 July 1685).

CHAPTER 19: *Scandal at Court*

197 *she was better* PRO *CSP Dom.* Oct. *1683–Apr. 1684* 216–17.
197 *of improving them* PRO *CSP Dom.* May *1684–Feb. 1685* 120.
198 *Bentinck in London* Japikse, *Correspondentie*, **1** i 13.
198 *we did together* HMC Stopford-Sackville **1** 29–30.
199 *have write soner* Bathurst 188.
199 *my dear Aurelia* ibid. 186.
199 *smiling to Huygens* Huygens *Journaal* **3** 69.
199 *could not bear* Bathurst 190.
199 *louse no time* ibid. 186.

199 *a blacke gowne* ibid. 189.
200 *women as well* Avaux **4** 241, cit. Krämer, *Maria Stuart* 114.
200 *was d'Avaux's story* Correspondance de Madame (2 September 1718), cit. Grew, *William Bentinck and William III* 96.
201 *by James's standards* Fruin's notes to Droste **2** 461.
201 *for several days* Bourdon 84–6.
202 *Madame Zuylestein's chamber* Clarendon, *Correspondence* **1** 165.
203 *and Dr Covell* Bourdon 86–7.
203 *if the beter* Bathurst 189.
204 *still not over* Sidney **2** 253–5.

204 *back to Holland* Zoutelandt 71.
204 *me in speaking* Bowen, *Third Mary Stuart* 98.
204 *him from here* Clarendon, *Correspondence* 1 163–4.
204 *daughter and son-in-law* ibid.

205 *the King's eyes* Fruin's notes on Droste 2 461.
205 *long white neck* Bourdon 83–5.
205 *refused to interfere* Japikse, *Prins Willem III* 2 131.

CHAPTER 20: *A Crown at Stake*

208 *of his nose* Erlanger 219.
208 *fields and substance* Evelyn, *Diary* 3 8 (3 November 1685).
209 *wrote to Louvois* Pontbriant 243.
209 *had not fled* Burnet, *History* 3 86.
209 *was his incontestably* Dalrymple 2 49.
209 *longer in heresy* Turner 346.
209 *such small importance* Burnet, *History* 3 86.
209 *against my husband* Mazure 3 44.
209 *as his successor* HMC Ormonde 2 334.
210 *step by step* Turner 258.
210 *the Chapel Royal* Reresby 404.
210 *Parliament", stated* Fagel Heim 1 xcv.
211 *Prince of Orange* Baschet 10 January, 17 May 1686, cit. Ashley, *Glorious Revolution* 101.
211 *by each other* Macaulay 1 559–60.
211 *assistance to them* Luttrell 1 375.
211 *his Majesty's pleasure* ibid. 385.
211 *in such matters* Burnet, *History* 3 111–112.
212 *little stirring here* PRO *SP Dom. January 1686–April 1687* 8/3 no. 172, 27.

212 *thought very indecent* Burnet, *History* 3 133–4.
212 *plain, downright idolatry* Brown, *Letters of Anne* 16–17.
212 *open my eyes* ibid. 21.
213 *sum of £500* Luttrell 1 121.
213 *right of marriage* Burnet, *History* 3 131–9.
215 *a great deal* Foxcroft, *Burnet* 223.
215 *that she made* Burnet, *History* 3 133–4.
215 *all the world* Foxcroft, *Burnet* 223.
216 *to the church* Heimans 147.
216 *stayed at home* Japikse, *Correspondentie* 2 ii 738–9.
216 *love of repose* Japikse, *Prins Willem III* 2 207.
217 *what he could* Burnet, *History* 3 275.
217 *the royalist party* Dalrymple 2 147.
218 *repeal those laws* Burnet, cit. Carswell 83.
218 *he possibly can* Cavelli 2 113.
218 *strike bold strokes* Barillon, cit. Macaulay 1 584
218 *terrible than lovely* Chesterfield 2 237.

CHAPTER 21: *The Turning Tide*

219 *or of truth* Burnet, *History* 3 172.
219 *on the princess* ibid. 173–4.
219 *of the prince* ibid.
220 *was freely resumed* Trevelyan, *England under the Stuarts* 420.
220 *to his father-in-law* Japikse, *Correspondentie* 2 ii 750.
220 *wished of him* Fruin, *Verspreide Geschriften* 5 157.
220 *the King intended* ibid.
220 *London to Paris* Bonrepaus, cit. Macaulay 2 55.
220 *myself the trouble* Fruin, *Verspreide Geschriften* 5 157.
221 *in our misfortune* Somerville 42.
221 *change her religion* PRO *CSP Dom. no. 1774* 426.

221 *of a martyr* ibid.
221 *denunciation of war* Burnet, *History*, 3 166–7.
222 *1 September 1687* Japikse, *Correspondentie* 2 ii 166–7.
222 *matters of business* Macaulay 1 537–8.
222 *by Arabella Churchill* Japikse, *Correspondentie* 2 ii 742.
223 *to the Prince* Japikse, *Correspondentie* 2 ii 781.
224 *to translate it* Japikse, *Correspondentie* 1 i 34.
224 *Stewart to Fagel* *Hollandsche Mercurius 1688* 164–5.
225 *what I hoped* Bentinck 4–65 passim.
225 *summer of 1687* Luttrell 1 432.
225 *to go thither* Dalrymple 2 94.

226 *to an end* Burnet, *History* 3 218–19.
226 *own to do* Ashley, *Glorious Revolution* 161.
226 *own her smock* Brown, *Letters of Anne* 35.
227 *been some trickery* Bentinck 71.
227 *some slight suspicion* ibid. 62–3.
227 *another painful denial* Luttrell 1 433.

227 *know his merits* Bentinck 62–3.
227 *suffer much walking* HMC Stopford-Sackville 1 31–2.
228 *deal of good* Bentinck 72.
228 *and praiseworthy sobriety* Klopp 4 28.
228 *ought to be* Bentinck 70.

CHAPTER 22: *Rock-a-Bye Baby*

230 *expected from him* Burnet, *History* 3 240–1.
230 *in the nation* ibid.
231 *done without money* Grew, *William Bentinck and William III* 106.
231 *taking the lead* ibid. 108.
231 *am deeply touched* Japikse, *Correspondentie* 1 i 38.
231 *had no fever* ibid. 1 i 43.
231 *he was beheaded* Macaulay 1 547.
232 *party to it* Carswell 139.
232 *to the States-general* BM Add. MSS. 34512 f. 131, cit. Carswell 144.
232 *from the King* Reresby 500.
232 *to look upon* Clarendon, *Diary* (10 June 1688).
233 *thousand do not* Brown, *Letters of Anne* 37.
233 *the Queens time* Bentinck 72–3.
233 *escape their fury* Montanus 2 82.
234 *the time being* Bentinck 74–5.
234 *of strict orders* Reresby 501.
234 *he was disturbed* ibid 502.
235 *starved and sold* Bryant 199.
235 *going after him* Reresby 503.
235 *angel in heaven* Dalrymple 2 176.
235 *a normal milk-diet* Krämer, *Maria Stuart* 166.
235 *were others* Dalrymple 2 177–84.

236 *seen no milk* Brown, *Letters of Anne* 39–42.
236 *what to think* Dalrymple 2 177–84.
236 *the same father* Oman, *Mary of Modena* 111, 115.
236 *hot weather continues* BM Add. MSS. 4163 f. 1, cit. Strickland 7 139–40.
237 *and pities me* Bentinck 74–5.
237 *by force* ibid.
237 *to the laws* Miscellanies, Philobiblon Society 1, cit. Pinkham 57.
238 *with their duty* Davies 3 203.
239 *store for him* ibid.
239 *fact perhaps 12,000* Carswell 170.
239 *harness and holsters* Macaulay 2 209–10.
240 *risen to 225* Carswell 169.
241 *way to decide* Japikse, *Correspondentie* 1 i 49.
241 *to upset it* Bentinck 78.
241 *4000, Hesse-Cassel 3000* Grew, *William Bentinck and William III* 126.
241 *side of Cologne* Avaux, cit. Grew, *William Bentinck and William III* 127.
242 *in temporal matters* Reresby 483–4.
242 *of artificial flowers* Dalrymple v 122, cit. Carswell 126.
242 *to this state* Fouw 132–3.
242 *in his diary* Hewitson 21.

CHAPTER 23: *Mary's Ordeal*

243 *the best seamen* Luttrell 1 457.
243 *the Princess there* Dalrymple 2 104.
243 *designed against us* Reresby 506.
243 *only act defensively* Ashley, *Glorious Revolution* 179.
244 *of his times* Luttrell 1 463.
244 *of these Kingdoms* Klopp 4 162.
244 *a bolder visit* Alphen *Stemming* 12.
244 *by that nation* Ellis 4 128.
244 *a few exceptions* Cavelli 2 66.
244 *to the college* Luttrell 1 469.
244 *of extraordinary weakness* Klopp 4 164.

245 *his legitimate son* ibid. 169–20.
245 *are his moders* Killanin 18.
246 *England was small* Klopp 4 169–70.
246 *all this evidence* Clarendon, *Life* 2 196.
246 *England no harm* Reresby 522.
246 *Protestant or Popish* Jesse 3 436
246 *from the shore* HMC Dartmouth 2 5, 58; Powley; both cit. Ashley, *Glorious Revolution* 202.
247 *of Orange's health* Huygens, *Journalen* 1 9.

247 *lands of IJsselstein* BM Egerton MSS. 1708 f. 7, cit. Japikse, *Prins Willem III* **2** 257.
247 *and legitimate Parliament* Klopp **4** 157
247 *of his children* Jesse **1** 202.
248 *and direct us* Burnet, *History* **3** 311.
249 *him even more* Bentinck 80–2.
249 *as her own* RA Nass. Dom. 743 ff. 247, 260.
249 *of my senses* Bentinck 82.

249 *ignored these demonstrations* ibid. 82–3.
250 *without further loss* ibid. 83.
250 *made no reply* Burnet, *History* **3** 327–8.
250 *ship was lost* Huygens, *Journalen* **1** 6, 7, 8.
250 *the "bloody flux"* Ellis **4** 135.
250 *carried in procession* Jesse **3** 436.
251 *their lucky success* Bentinck 85–7.
251 *be the heiress* Pontbriant 247.

CHAPTER 24: *"William the Conqueror"*

252 *said one eye-witness* Carswell 183.
253 *Predestination now, Doctor* Burnet, *History* 327–8.
253 *small fisherman's hut* Montanus **2** 112; Huygens, *Journalen* **1** 14; Macaulay **2** 242–3.
253 *had been hanged* Huygens, *Journalen* **1** 15–16.
253 *entertained him lavishly* Macaulay **2** 243.
254 *by 16 carthorses* Jesse **1** 78; Macaulay **2** 244–8.
254 *everyone cried "Amen"* Macaulay **2** 248.
255 *in to them* Ellis **4** 143.
255 *James in strength* Macaulay **2** 262–3.
256 *to turn back* Pinkham 171–2.
256 *Monday, 19 November* Macaulay **2** 257–60.
256 *be a rebel* ibid. 253–6.
257 *man can oppose* Grew, *Court of William III* 181–2.
257 *on reading it* ibid.
257 *a forgotten man* HMC Leybourn-Popham 267.
257 *luggage after him* Macaulay **2** 265–70.
257 *thought it proper* Jesse **1** 272.
257 *to these troubles* ibid. 270–1.
258 *have forsaken me* Macaulay **2** 265–70.
258 *a hundred members* Mazure **3** 180–1, cit. Carswell 195.
258 *rebellion against him* Macaulay **2** 271–4.
258 *Park at Crewkerne* BM Le Fleming MSS. 1890 f. 224.

258 *the English army* ibid. 225.
258 *to miss them* Huygens, *Journalen* **1** 35–6.
259 *and uncle, James* Macaulay **2** 284–5.
259 *else completely unguarded* Huygens, *Journalen* **1** 40.
259 *with your Master* Macaulay **2** 274–6.
260 *conquest of England* HMC Dartmouth **5** 276.
260 *Wales, her son* Bosq de Beaumont 2–10.
260 *by a fisherman* Ashley, *Glorious Revolution* 232.
261 *of further resistance* Turner 442.
261 *of Lord Tyrconnel* HMC *Report* **2** App. Part 5, 226, cit. Baxter 241–2.
261 *to be priests* Reresby 537.
261 *as gilt candlesticks* Ellis **4** 172.
262 *to the ground* ibid.
262 *the Quaker Penn* Reresby 537.
262 *of that nature* Ellis **4** 174.
262 *King's being gone* Clarendon, *Life* **2** 113.
262 *Feversham shall find* Macaulay **2** 305–6.
263 *accepted by God* BM Add. MSS. 3209 f. 302.
264 *the last time* Montanus **2** 139.
264 *fond of him* Clarendon, *Diary*, cit. Jesse, *Court of England* **1** 90.
264 *wore orange headdresses* Huygens, *Journalen* **1** 50–1.
264 *through the Park* Burnet, *History* **2** 339.
265 *serious, and reserv'd* Evelyn, *Diary* **3** 62 (18 December 1688).

CHAPTER 25: *Farewell to Holland*

267 *noted with satisfaction* Bentinck 89–91.
267 *in her ear* BM Add. MSS. 34516 ff. 13 ff.
267 *most faithful servant* Japikse, *Prins Willem III* **2** 257.

267 *what to say* Müller **2** 119.
268 *got to bed* Doebner 4–5.
268 *to James's eyes* Klopp **4** 377.
268 *has very little* Doebner 5.
268 *her mental gifts* Klopp **4** 376.

268 *in her journal* Doebner 6.
269 *a new-born day* A Congratulatory Poem to His Highness the Prince of Orange on his Arrival at London, 1688.
269 *Queen Catherine's basset-table* Jesse **3** 29.
269 *a heart attack* Ellis **4** 168.
270 *have Protestant swords* Huygens, *Journalen* **1** 53.
270 *having deserted him* Burnet, *History* **3** 363.
270 *to be unharmed* Macaulay **2** 327.
271 *William or both* Burnet, *History* **3** 373–6.
271 *the frozen ponds* Huygens, *Journalen* **1** 53.
271 *to the backstairs* ibid. 55.
271 *made their court* Evelyn, *Diary* **3** 67 (29 January 1689).
271 *an early resolution* Reresby 546.
271 *that rules me* Japikse, *Prins Willem III* **2** 270.
272 *three years ago* Burnet, *History* **3** 390–1.
272 *in his hands* Mazure **3** 351.
272 *and the Prince* Burnet, *History* **3** 390–7.
272 *Duke of Venice* Foxcroft, *Halifax* **2** 203.
272 *in their affairs* Grew, *William Bentinck and William III* 150–2.
273 *accompanying the Princess* Huygens, *Journalen* **1** 58; Bryant 372.
273 *peace and quiet* Klopp **4** 377.
273 *of Gods mercy* Doebner 4.
273 *Kramprich to Vienna* Klopp **4** 377.
273 *to express it* Bentinck 115.

273 *Johannes Brant, later* Fruin, *Verspreide Geschriften* **5** 195.
274 *image ever fade* Bidloo, *Op het vertrek.*
274 *her sister Anne* Montanus **2** 170.
275 *we went out* Doebner 7–10.
275 *the next day* Burnet, *History* **3** 406–8.
275 *seem quite transported* Evelyn, *Diary* **3** 69 (21 February 1689).
275 *or seemed natural* Dartmouth footnote in Burnet, *History* **3** 407.
275 *late Queene lay* Evelyn, *Diary* **3** 69 (21 February 1689).
276 *nothing to heart* ibid.
276 *natural to her* Burnet, *History* **3** 408.
276 *like to endure* Doebner 11.
277 *France and Ireland* Macaulay **2** 373–4.
277 *sadly upon it* Reresby 554.
277 *William allowed reluctantly* Huygens, *Journalen* **1** 86.
277 *a great deal* Russell 452.
278 *William and Mary* Misson de Valbourg 83; Montanus **2** 192–200; Macaulay **2** 270.
278 *heavy jewelled Orb* Macaulay **2** 469.
278 *valued at £30,000* PRO *Treasury Papers 1689* **9** 83, 119.
278 *as it seems* Jesse **1** 203; Huygens, *Journalen* **1** 112–13; Japikse, *Prins Willem III* **2** 277.
278 *to use neither* London *Gazette* 14 April 1689.
279 *old Popish ceremonies* Gebhard, *Witsen* 358.
279 *of ordinary compassion* Clarke **2** 328.
279 *for his misfortune* Klopp **4** 379.

CHAPTER 26: *Settling Down*

280 *in his way* Foxcroft, *Halifax* **2** 210.
280 *with the same* Traill 66.
280 *already attacked England* Macaulay **2** 477–8.
280 *of my reign* Japikse, *Prins Willem III* **2** 228.
280 *to save Ireland* Foxcroft, *Halifax* **2** 220.
281 *and eat chard* Hewitson 63.
281 *England and Scotland* Thomson 25.
281 *accorded to James* Baxter 252.
281 *Diable emportera tout* Orléans, *Letters from Liselotte* 52.
281 *be crucify him* Macaulay **2** 233; Gebhard, *Witsen* 341.
281 *years of Methuselah* Gebhard, *Witsen* 352.
282 *the Protestant religion* ibid. 363–4.
282 *in the speech* Fabius 324.

282 *see Holland perish* Japikse, *Prins Willem III* **2** 293.
282 *told Halifax crossly* Carswell 221.
283 *exposed to it* Smith 75.
283 *was in Holland* Japikse, *Prins Willem III* **2** 278.
283 *me very weak* ibid.
283 *could not gallop* Huygens, *Journalen* **1** 111.
283 *his royal patient* Hone 55–6.
284 *his lips soundlessly* Huygens, *Journalen* **1** 118.
284 *guidlers for that* ibid. **1** 122, 95.
284 *in that place* Luttrell **1** 504.
284 *see him dead* Reresby 577.
284 *as he was* ibid. 565–6.
284 *made it impossible* Burnet, *History* **4** 152.

285 *and reserved ways* Huygens, *Journalen* 1 132.
285 *with the third* Gebhard, *Witsen* 3 ii 156.
285 *to a mutiny* Burnet, *History* 4 152–3.
285 *a true Englishman* Hore 3 200–1.
285 *with their reception* Luttrell 1 593–7.
285 *the grocers' company* Dalrymple 2 143.
286 *degenerated into chaos* Evelyn, *Diary* 3 80 (5 November 1689); Luttrell 1 600; Huygens, *Journalen* 1 203.
286 *places of resort* Ralph, *History* 2 165.
286 *the "Favourite" aroused* Huygens *Journalen* 1 57, 77, 98.
286 *all the time* Alphen, *Stemming* 230
286 *more till supper* ibid.
286 *watched them carefully* Alphen, *Stemming* 230.
287 *support the minion* Jesse 1 15.
287 *for a servant* Ranke 4 15.
287 *trust and confidence* Ralph, *History* 2 21; Burnet, *History* 4 7–8.
287 *once a day* Macky, *Memoirs* 34.
288 *becoming "too English"* Alphen, *Stemming* 81–3; Japikse, *Prins Willem III* 2 318.
288 *in lodgings nearby* Huygens, *Journalen* 1 138.
288 *by this time* ibid. 190–1.
288 *for 18,000 guineas* Luttrell 1 549.
289 *paintings of Verrio* Turner 246.
289 *which was exquisite* Parentalia, cit. Briggs 182–6.
289 *season should invite* ibid.

289 *Islands and Virginia* BM Sloane MSS. 2370–1 3343.
289 *Pear and Calamola* BM Sloane MSS. 2346.
290 *be forgiven her* Burnet, *Memorial*.
290 *and injuring others* Luttrell 1 602.
290 *lost their lives* ibid. 616.
290 *was truly humbled* Doebner 17.
290 *more than three* Huygens, *Journalen* 1 220.
290 *attempt at grandeur* Hayes 5.
290 *was at Kensington* Evelyn, *Diary* 3 83 (25 February 1690).
291 *cost William £11,000* Hayes 7.
291 *screens, and hangings* Evelyn, *Diary* 3 110 (13 July 1693).
291 *proudly to Huygens* W. H. Goodger, *The Pug Handbook* (London, 1959).
292 *in their coaches* Alphen, *Stemming* 58; Burnet, *Essay* 83.
292 *variety of subjects* Evelyn, *Diary* 3 110 (13 July 1693).
292 *of her time* Burnet, *Essay*.
293 *at the gate* BM Harleian MSS. 5010; Luttrell 1 519.
293 *horses were lost* PRO *Treasury Papers 1689* 9 24, 144, 574.
293 *in your country* Bentinck 119.
293 *at the Hague* ibid. 116.
294 *Dutchwoman as ever* ibid. 122.
294 *never find here* Müller 2 224.
294 *of State affairs* Gebhard, *Witsen* 361.
294 *of the matter* Burnet, *History* 4 78.
294 *very few came* ibid.

CHAPTER 27: *Second Thoughts*

295 *tears were shed* Burnet, *History* 4 70–71.
295 *happy under her* BM Harleian MSS. 6584, cit. Strickland 7 242.
296 *and without power* Burnet, *History* 4 60–61.
296 *sometimes against them* Foxcroft, *Halifax* 2 207.
296 *to be governed* ibid.
297 *on Tory support* Dalrymple 2 198.
297 *before one another* Foxcroft, *Halifax* 2 244.
297 *not my friends* Grew, *William Bentinck and William III* 158.
298 *the poet laureate* Luttrell 2 1.
298 *not lose consciousness* Churchill 1 370.
298 *to do business* Huygens, *Journalen* 1 225.

299 *welfare of Europe* *Arch.* 3 i 45.
299 *and richly laden* Japikse, *Correspondentie* 1 i 63.
299 *will support you* Grew, *William Bentinck and William III* 162–3.
299 *people to reason* ibid. 169.
300 *take his place* Japikse, *Correspondentie* 1 i 157.
300 *point of landing* Japikse, *Prins Willem III* 2 105.
300 *not abandon me* Grew, *William Bentinck and William III* 169.
300 *dispose of them* Japikse, *Correspondentie* 1 i 153.
300 *which they resided* Macaulay 3 106.
301 *Yours till death* Grew, *William Bentinck and William III* 162–3.
301 *post to town* Macaulay 3 108.

301 *on 21 January* Grew, *William Bentinck and William III* 165.
301 *quickly fixt up* Luttrell **2** 12.
301 *what to do* Japikse, *Correspondentie* **1** i 74.
301 *I addressed them* Japikse, *Correspondentie* **1** i 95.
302 *what they wish* Grew, *William Bentinck and William III* 162–3.
302 *the same day* Japikse, *Prins Willem III* **1** 95.
302 *he told her* Doebner 22.
302 *did the trick* ibid. 25–7.
302 *pretty well again* Luttrell **2** 28.
302 *against each other* Doebner 21.
302 *for a father* ibid. 78–9.
303 *never forgiven him* Dartmouth footnote to Burnet, *History* **4** 241.

303 *or taken prisoner* Burnet, *History* **4** 83–84.
303 *king had made* Burnet, *History* **4** 84–85.
303 *of his country* ibid. 241.
303 *tougher than me* Bentinck 95.
304 *in the world* Doebner, 22.
304 *made to her* Foxcroft, *Halifax* **2** 246–8.
304 *a sudden emergency* ibid. 252.
304 *with great tenderness* Burnet, *History* **4** 83–4.
305 *experience or money* Somerville 66.
305 *and "somewhat disgusted"* Luttrell **2** 38.
305 *into your hands* Macaulay **3** 167.
305 *he ever took* Doebner 29.
305 *only surviving child* Luttrell **2** 52.
305 *scene to her* Burnet, *History* **4** 87.

CHAPTER 28: *The Irish Trouble*

306 *of its gardens* Saint-Simon, cit. Bosq de Beaumont 44–5.
306 *remarked Louis* Bosq de Beaumont 46.
306 *I have been* Bib. Nat. Fonds Clairambault **290** f. 509, cit. Bosq de Beaumont xix.
306 *for as well* Grew, *English Court in Exile* 84; Montanus **2** 158.
307 *have been averted* ibid. 106–7.
307 *he has courage* Bosq de Beaumont 68–70.
307 *to receive him* Ellis **4** 186.
308 *secret from anybody* Bosq de Beaumont 71–2; Macaulay **2** 509.
308 *on 7 May* Askin 8; Macaulay **2** 513.
308 *stone by stone* Askin 9; Ralph, *History* **2** 86.
309 *desirous of stealing* Dalrymple **2** 167–87.
309 *the number sent* Harris, *History of William-Henry* 247.
309 *the first campaign* Dalrymple **2** 167–87.
310 *weak a constitution* Burnet, *History* **4** 71–2.
310 *to govern England* ibid. 46.
310 *kiss his hand* Klopp **5** 339.
310 *long oppose him* HMC Finch **2** 293.
310 *until it lifted* Huygens, *Journalen* **1** 284.
310 *worth fighting for* Anon., *Royal Diary* 75.

310 *settled in Ireland* Huygens, *Journalen* **1** 303.
311 *him so dear* Foxcroft, *Halifax* **2** 206.
311 *the King's affairs* Huygens, *Journalen* **1** 287.
311 *under his feet* Anon., *Royal Diary* 71–5.
311 *cruelty and ruthlessness* Macaulay **3** 187.
311 *wants a battle* *Arch.* 3rd ser. **1** 68–9.
312 *his French soldiers* Grew, *English Court in Exile*.
312 *total of £250,000* Mullenaux 7.
312 *a human being* Huygens, *Journalen* **1** 290–2.
313 *pleasant and cheerfull* Hewitson 129.
313 *M. de Lauzun* Huygens, *Journalen* **1** 293.
313 *old bedridden people* Mullenaux 8.
313 *for its bread* Huygens, *Journalen* **1** 294.
313 *will be mine* Macaulay **3** 186.
313 *grazing his shoulder* Bosq de Beaumont 85.
314 *you move on* Huygens, *Journalen* **1** 295.
314 *had spread consternation* Hewitson 130.
314 *big black horse* Jesse **1** 109.
314 *all night long* Orléans, *Letters from Liselotte* 56–7.
314 *unexpected a success* Ellis **4** 193.
314 *sent to him* Jesse **1** 110.

CHAPTER 29: *The Battle of the Boyne*

315 *ready for battle* Hewitson 130; Huygens, *Journalen* **1** 296.
315 *their white feather* Anon., *Royal Diary* 75.

316 *the other army* Traill 88–9.
316 *in the neck* Mullenaux 9; Anon., *Glorious Life* 126–7.
316 *save the animal* Askin 14.

316 *do for me* Traill 89.
316 *eight cannons behind* Huygens, *Journalen* 1 297; Mullenaux 10.
316 *your own friends* Jesse 1 111.
316 *of his boot* Harris, *History of William-Henry* 270.
316 *men through mistake* Hewitson 131.
316 *on the battlefield* Huygens, *Journalen* 1 297.
317 *less than dogs* Alphen, *Stemming* 96–7.
317 *on the spot* Macaulay 3 197.
317 *Dr Hutton, later* Burnet, *History* 4 106–7.
317 *to the soldiers* Huygens, *Journalen* 1 297
317 *to the allies* Huisarchief Amerongen, portefeuille x 219, cit. Baxter 266.
317 *of a battle* Grew, *Bentinck* 178–9.
317 *won the race* Askin 15; HMC Finch 2 344, 352.
318 *shift for myself* Mullenaux 13.
318 *was one report* Macaulay 3 193.

318 *and haggard man* Huygens, *Journalen* 1 302.
318 *of Prince Waldeck* HMC Finch 2 338.
318 *his own victory* *Arch.* 3rd ser. 1 69.
318 *with a smile* Hewitson 133.
318 *in the camp* Huygens, *Journalen* 1 299
319 *a faint shadow* Mullenaux 14–15.
319 *you, go away* Huygens, *Journalen* 1 301.
319 *visit to Holland* ibid. 308.
319 *lucky, were hanged* ibid.
319 *round the Queen* ibid.
319 *of the place* HMC Finch 2 371.
320 *to their homes* *Arch.* 3rd ser. 1 80–1.
320 *hasten for England* HMC Finch 2 388.
320 *their own countries* Mullenaux 18, 19.
321 *a vigorous defence* ibid. 23.
321 *an Englishman bitterly* ibid. 22.
321 *escort were killed* ibid. 24.
322 *in the afternoon* Luttrell 2 102.
322 *the nephew son-in-law* HMC Finch 2 465.
322 *with my behaviour* Doebner 33.

CHAPTER 30: *Mary Regnant*

323 *of all kinds* Doebner 29–30.
324 *consort of musick* Luttrell 2 57.
324 *next think of* BM Add. MSS. 14195 ff. 100–1.
324 *confessed to William* Dalrymple 3 75.
324 *mends but slowly* ibid. 68–72.
324 *received your letter* ibid. 88, 83.
325 *punctuall a writer* HMC Finch 2 301.
325 *went to bed* ibid. 321.
325 *upon one occasion* Dalrymple 3 115.
325 *could express it* HMC Finch 2 305–6.
325 *two women ceased* Dalrymple 3 70–1, 73.
326 *to the government* Doebner 29–30.
326 *look deceives me* Dalrymple 3 95.
326 *on 20 June* ibid. 79–80.
326 *in all things* Doebner 29–30.
327 *yours till death* Dalrymple 3 73.
327 *is noe stronger* HMC Finch 2 308.
327 *here in disorder* Dalrymple 3 75.
327 *stone must come* ibid. 75–6.
327 *from the fleet* BM Le Fleming MSS. 275.
328 *our country too* HMC Finch 2 314–16.
328 *to the enemy* ibid. 318.
328 *with my life* Dalrymple 3 80–2.
328 *under close arrest* HMC Finch 2 322–3.
328 *to their mercy* ibid.
329 *courage to admiration* Dalrymple 3 67.
329 *and suspected Jacobites* HMC Finch 2 335.
329 *done his duty* ibid. 334.

329 *are together again* Dalrymple 3 84.
329 *of his actions* HMC Finch 2 335–6.
330 *mast shot down* ibid. 351.
330 *revenged upon him* ibid. 340.
330 *of the people* ibid. 351.
330 *every alehouse talk* ibid. 355.
330 *breathe freely again* Luttrell 2 76.
330 *diffidently told William* Dalrymple 3 85–88.
330 *courage and conduct* HMC Finch 2 335–336.
330 *speak of him* ibid. 342–3; Luttrell 2 68.
330 *you will not* Dalrymple 3 90.
331 *of anything else* ibid. 90, 92.
331 *impatient to return* ibid. 92.
331 *to his person* ibid.
331 *to do so* HMC Finch 2 347.
331 *most by me* Dalrymple 3 93, 97.
332 *was in Ireland* Burnet, *History* 4 98–9.
332 *pay for both* HMC Finch 2 354–5.
332 *done with him* ibid. 353; Luttrell 2 73.
333 *to this degree* Dalrymple 3 103–10.
333 *still in Ireland* HMC Finch 2 405.
333 *against the government* ibid. 391–2.
334 *shall never returne* ibid. 349.
334 *knew the secret* Dalrymple 3 103.
334 *such good news* ibid. 111.
334 *him in tears* ibid. 113.
334 *The disapproving secretary* Huygens, *Journalen* 1 322–3.

335 *she complained* Dalrymple **3** 123–9 passim.
335 *all these burdens* Doebner 80.

335 *night for it* Dalrymple **3** 129.
335 *little fit for* Doebner 33.
335 *William at Windsor* Luttrell **2** 106, 108.

CHAPTER 31: *Back to the Continent*

336 *did in Holland* Huygens, *Journalen* **1** 340.
336 *Representatives in Parliament* Ralph, *History* **2** 245; Klopp **5** 109, 210.
337 *of the Treasury* Huygens, *Journalen* **1** 336.
337 *Thames saluted him* HMC Finch **2** 494–495.
337 *a play afterwards* Luttrell **2** 125.
337 *on the seventh* ibid. 130, 134.
337 *present him with* ibid. 135.
337 *at the Hague* Huygens, *Journalen* **1** 388.
338 *before she came* HMC Rutland **2** 131–2.
338 *was going on* Doebner 34.
339 *her into chapel* Dartmouth note to Burnet, *History* **5** 451–3.
339 *about her "embonpoint"* HMC Denbigh 83–5.
340 *dear to me* Bentinck 123–4.
340 *Portland and Ouwerkerk* Luttrell **2** 154–159.
341 *his own country* Japikse, *Prins Willem III* **2** 325–6.
342 *a splendid appearance* Huygens, *Journalen* **1** 395–6; Japikse, *Prins Willem III* 327–8; Jesse **1** 149–50.
342 *ten for her* Macaulay **4** 5.
342 *before they exploded* Huygens, *Journalen* **1** 395–6.
342 *enterprise of France* Ralph, *History* **2** 264.
342 *them all warmly* Droste **2** 530.
343 *our business here* Wagenaar **14** 141.
343 *minister de Torcy* Groen van Prinsterer, *Handboek* **1** 426.
343 *reported to Russell* HMC Finch **3** 29.
343 *in terrible pain* Huygens, *Journalen* **1** 401.

344 *twenty-one-year-old* Albemarle **1** 31.
344 *delivered to Keppel* Huygens, *Journalen* **1** 428.
344 *round the Tower* Luttrell **2** 208.
344 *Comet or Basset* Doebner 36.
345 *drawing-room at Whitehall* ibid.; Luttrell **2** 172.
345 *country's political leaders* Luttrell **2** 196.
345 *and no friends* Doebner 36.
345 *in the world* ibid. 37.
345 *admit him again* Macaulay **3** 290–1.
346 *valued at £6000* Luttrell **2** 206; Evelyn, *Diary* **3** 93 (10 April 1691).
346 *to her life* Doebner 37.
346 *wind for Holland* Luttrell **2** 219.
347 *in my circumstances* Doebner 84, 38.
347 *tant sur moi* Bentinck 98.
347 *of quality embarqu'd* Luttrell **2** 233.
347 *St. James's coffeehouses* Macaulay **3** 315.
347 *stay too long* HMC Finch **3** 260.
347 *be into England* ibid. 271–8 passim.
347 *stronghold in Ireland* Ralph, *History* **2** 309.
348 *warr of Ireland* Grew, *English Court in Exile* 235.
348 *still could speak* PRO *CSP Dom. 1690–1* 547; HMC Portland **3** 477.
348 *privately at Kensington* Grew, *William Bentinck and William III* 198; Luttrell **2** 296.
349 *barrels of gunpowder* Doebner 38–42.
349 *with 1,000 guineas* Hone 53.
349 *been entirely his* Bentinck 97.
349 *publicly", reported Luttrell* Luttrell **2** 302.
349 *used to have* Doebner, 43.

CHAPTER 32: *The Sisters*

350 *circumstances could be* Doebner 43.
350 *him very much* Grew, *William Bentinck and William III* 199; Huygens, *Journalen* **1** 516; Luttrell **2** 305.
351 *a local madam* Huygens, *Journalen* **1** 516.
351 *and good lodgings* ibid. 517
351 *work with here* Arch. 3rd ser. **1** 212.

351 *in the morning* Huygens, *Journalen* **2** 9; Luttrell **2** 331.
352 *of 100 marks* Luttrell **2** 331, 342, 344, 623.
352 *1 January 1692* HMC Finch **3** 125, 213.
352 *the Macdonalds escaped* Japikse, *Prins Willem III* **2** 313–14.

352 *least of all* Macaulay 3 421.
353 *and a day* Doebner 46.
353 *by a thread* Arch. 3rd ser. 1 xxxiii.
353 *about accompanying him* Huygens, *Journalen* 1 527.
353 *a sad spring* Doebner 88–9.
353 *answer a question* Marlborough 18.
354 *informed of it* ibid.
354 *and I both* Doebner 18.
354 *got her £50,000* Ralph, *Other Side* 36.
354 *friends nor enemies* Macky, *Memoirs* 3.
355 *it brought back* Marlborough 27.
355 *wrote Anne furiously* Green, *Queen Anne* 72.
355 *wrote to Sarah* Ralph, *Other side* 111–12.
355 *redeemed my fault* Grew, *Court of William III* 202.
355 *for his sake* ibid. 183–4.
356 *what he professed* ibid. 202.
356 *been called back* Macaulay 3 392.
356 *with King James* ibid.
356 *abhorred the traitor* Strickland 7 219.
356 *to Marlborough's detriment* Wolseley 2 120, 244, 260.

356 *my implacable enemy* Marlborough 29.
356 *not been king* Alphen, *Stemming* 109.
356 *on 24 January* Luttrell 2 343, 357; Doebner 45.
357 *with Lady Malborough* Huygens, *Journalen* 2 21.
357 *live kindly together* Grew, *Court of William III* 197.
357 *at Syon House* Brown, *Letters* 53–4; Luttrell 2 373.
358 *dined with her* Luttrell 2 376, 391.
358 *be complied with* Marlborough 32.
358 *by a sister* ibid.
358 *the Royal family* ibid. 65, 70; Luttrell 2 434.
358 *such a breach* Burnet, *History* 4 163.
358 *she has lost* Grew, *William Bentinck and William III* 202.
359 *was acquainted therewith* Luttrell 2 438.
359 *of her life* Grew, *Court of William III* 203–4.
359 *as she is* Doebner 45.
359 *on either side* Luttrell 2 595.

CHAPTER 33: *Father and Daughter*

360 *think he is* Orléans, *Letters from Liselotte* 57.
360 *of the French* Cavelli 2 504.
360 *him in Dublin* Ranke 1 94.
361 *amuse the people* Luttrell 2 431–5.
361 *was on board* Grew, *Court of William III* 190.
361 *on the throne* Luttrell 2 444–5.
361 *at an end* Doebner 48.
361 *of his regiment* Luttrell 2 447.
361 *twelve of foot* ibid. 428–31.
362 *to the worst* Doebner 48.
362 *of contrary winds* Arch. 3rd ser. 1 275–7.
362 *prince so unhappy* Bosq de Beaumont 102.
363 *under his feet* Luttrell 2 466.
363 *destroyed for ever* Arch. 3rd ser. 1 277.
363 *semper lilia florent* Luttrell 2 463.
363 *particularly distinguished themselves* ibid. 464.
363 *see nothing else* HMC Finch 3 93.
363 *such a fleet* ibid. 95.
364 *wind and weather* ibid. 221.
364 *talck of retiring* Doebner 52.
364 *to no purpose* ibid. 54.

364 *as ill inclinations* ibid.
364 *shall never want* Macaulay 3 482.
364 *greatness of soul* Japikse, *Prins Willem III* 2 342.
365 *at this time* HMC Rutland 2 137.
365 *and endless misfortune* Doebner 55.
365 *must have patience* Bentinck 92–3.
365 *the King's return* Doebner 43.
365 *bear the punishment* ibid. 45–6.
365 *should be done* ibid. 54.
366 *I was not* Anon, *Royal Diary* 10.
366 *and religious prudence* Burnet, *History* 4 211–12.
366 *bishops she named* ibid. 214–15.
366 *her some tears* Heimans, 30.
366 *£106 12s 10d* BM Add. MSS. 5751. A.
367 *your royal father* Plumptre 2 309.
367 *and her work* Burnet, *Essay* 140–1.
367 *Manners", noted Evelyn* Evelyn, *Diary* 3 150 (24 March 1700).
367 *a good example* Luttrell 2 345–6.
367 *of other impertinences* Dartmouth footnote to Burnet, *History* 4 181–2.
367 *to another time* Burnet, *Memorial*.

CHAPTER 34: *Years of Struggle*

368 *they thought impossible* Ralph, *History* **2** 363.
368 *disarranged as possible* Macaulay, **3** 480.
368 *beginning of September* Evelyn, *Diary* **3** 105 (15 September 1692).
368 *over in minutes* Huygens, *Journalen* **2** 124.
368 *of the sea* Luttrell **2** 560–71 passim.
368 *pleasure at Loo* Evelyn, *Diary* **3** 105 (1 October 1692).
369 *army in Flanders* Luttrell **2** 578–91 passim.
369 *numbers is incredible* *Arch.* 3rd ser. **1** 321.
369 *of his scarf* Jesse **1** 155.
369 *me from behind* Ségur 99.
370 *King of England* Geyl, *Netherlands in the Seventeenth Century* **2** 264.
370 *accounts as Forlorns* Ralph, *History* **2** 422.
370 *was quietly dropped* Macaulay **4** 81–2.
370 *seeing matters accommodated* Doebner 56.
371 *a huge majority* Kenyon, "Earl of Sunderland".
372 *thing is impossible* Shrewsbury 19–30; Somerville 85–8.
372 *office delivered him* Luttrell **2** 278.
372 *Sunderland for company* ibid. 281.
372 *due to me* Huygens, *Journalen* **1** 337; Grew, *William Bentinck and William III* 225.
373 *most violent terms* Huygens, *Journalen* **2** 37.
373 *in February 1693* ibid. 176.
373 *than I do* Grew, *William Bentinck and William III* 212.

373 *in good order* Japikse, *Correspondentie* **1** i 176.
373 *of his administration* Sidney **1**, introduction.
373 *to illuminate them* Luttrell **2** 593–9.
374 *King was here* Doebner 55–6.
374 *free for writing* ibid. 94–5.
374 *than any other* ibid. 58.
374 *wrote in distress* ibid. 59.
374 *melancholy and discouraged* ibid. 58–9.
375 *strangeness to me* ibid. 59.
375 *to be expressed* Kenyon, "Earl of Sunderland" 586.
375 *at Council meetings* Doebner 60.
375 *City's continuing loyalty* Sandars 347.
375 *upon an arm* Doebner 102–7.
375 *recovered", recorded Luttrell* Luttrell **3** 115; Evelyn, *Diary* **3** 110 (24 June 1693).
375 *of party warfare* Luttrell **3** 133.
376 *and The Hague* ibid. 276.
376 *and without supplies* Erlanger 99.
376 *than we can* Klopp **6** 348.
376 *build in 1683* Luttrell **3** 280–1.
376 *from the Cathedral* Fiennes 47; Briggs 161–4.
376 *above cost £10,000* Luttrell **3** 174.
377 *the talks foundered* Thomson 32.
377 *eight per cent* Japikse, *Prins Willem III* **2** 355.
377 *entirely his fault* Huygens, *Journalen* **2** 344; Luttrell **3** 299–306.
377 *Whitehall once more* Luttrell **3** 308.
378 *Maastricht leaked out* Klopp **6** 371.
378 *under your administration* *Arch.* 3rd ser. **1** 371.
378 *and advantageous conditions* ibid. 366.

CHAPTER 35: *The Death of Mary*

379 *gets used to* Bentinck 149.
379 *all the summer* ibid. 146.
379 *might have happened* Doebner 111.
379 *her £12 12s* BM Add. MSS. 5751 A.
380 *came to £1321* ibid.
381 *of about £9,000* Gans 116–18, 428–30; KHA A16.
381 *to her figure* M***, *Relation*.
381 *no world hereafter* BM Add. MSS. 5540 f. 26.
381 *of all others* Burnet, *Essay* 85–6.
382 *a good wife* BM Add. MSS. 14195.
382 *received from him* Hardwicke footnote to Burnet, *History* **4** 249.

382 *but a jest* Macaulay **2** 421.
382 *for all that* Swift **12** 206–7 "Remarks on Burnet".
382 *what he executed* Burnet, *Essay* 36–8.
382 *in ye world* BM Add. MSS. 35618.
382 *apples and milk* Luttrell **3** 402–3.
382 *had the disease* Heim 348; Evelyn, *Diary* **3** 119 (29 December 1694).
383 *ought to be* Bentinck 149–50.
383 *after her death* Gans 428–30.
383 *her own funeral* Evelyn, *Diary* **3** 120 (8 March 1695).
383 *the foregoing campaigns* Luttrell **3** 416.
383 *smallpox was suspected* ibid.

383 *of Charles II* Dring.
384 *to her himself* Luttrell 3 417.
384 *fault in her* Burnet, *History* 4 277.
384 *from this world* Japikse, *Prins Willem III* 2 360–1.
384 *turn out well* Arch. 3rd ser. 1 537.
384 *from her head* Luttrell 3 417.
384 *to a death-bed* Anon., *Royal Diary* 11
385 *much as anyone* Tenison.
385 *had been useless* Hone 57.

385 *while life lasted* Lexington 35.
385 *very much doubted* Luttrell 3 417.
385 *pray for myself* Anon., *Royal Diary* 11.
385 *a better way* ibid.
385 *after her death* Burnet, *History* 4 248.
385 *back to life* Burnet, *Essay* 177.
386 *as are usual* Tenison.
386 *the tolling bells* Luttrell 3 417; Evelyn, *Diary* 3 119 (29 December 1694–20 January 1695).

CHAPTER 36: *William's Grief*

387 *undeceived about that* Klopp 8, 9.
387 *wrote a Frenchman* Dring.
387 *of the Queen* Anon., *Royal Diary* 2.
387 *must mend yours* Huygens, *Journalen* 2 51.
387 *bad practices whatever* Burnet, *History* 4 249–50.
388 *do with her* Whiston 1 100.
388 *in many particulars* Burnet, *History* 4 248–9.
388 *person alluded to* ibid.
388 *the Queen's death* Whiston 1 100.
388 *the Seventh Chapel* M***, *Relation.*
388 *into black liveries* ibid. 13–14; Luttrell 3 419.
388 *at their eyes* Macaulay 4 117.
389 *so nearly concerned* *Journal of the House of Lords* 15.
389 *have just suffered* M***, *Relation.*
389 *and marble weeps* *Lexington Papers*, cit. Bickley 36.
389 *best of Princesses* HMC Bath (Prior Papers) 3 46.
389 *press William's soul* Bickley 36–7.
390 *for your Majesty* Fouw 146.
390 *lock and key* Huygens, *Journalen* 2 447.
390 *send for them* ibid. 448.
390 *going to war* Arch. 3rd ser. 1 578.
390 *return to Holland* Japikse, *Prins Willem III* 2 362.
390 *shotts all successful* Luttrell 3 430–3.
390 *will crush me* Arch. 3rd ser. 1 578.
390 *at a time* Huygens, *Journalen* 2 451–3.
390 *was very cheerful* Luttrell 3 430–3.
390 *was reasonably kind* Huygens, *Journalen* 2 451–3.

391 *line of battle* Luttrell 3 433.
391 *better to wait* Marlborough 75.
391 *fallen into displeasure* ibid. 76.
391 *or speak distinctly* Lewis 66.
391 *sobs and tears* M***, *Relation.*
391 *highnesses at dinner* Luttrell 3 419–29.
392 *in his absecne* Alphen, *Stemming* 222.
392 *spirit of all* *Lexington Papers*, cit. Grew, *William Bentinck and William III* 235.
392 *mourning a relative* Anon., *Secret History of Whitehall* 78.
392 *by this death* Orléans, *Correspondance* (Brunet) 1 14.
392 *lessen with time* Ranke 1 123.
392 *on the Corps* Fiennes 294–5.
392 *relieved every half-hour* Luttrell 3 442.
393 *with black cloth* Luttrell 3 420–2.
393 *embalming the body* PRO Treasury Papers 12 519–25.
393 *the Chief Mourner* Luttrell 3 432.
393 *King's particular direction* PRO Treasury Papers, King's Warrant Book 18 83.
393 *Book put it* ibid. 140–2.
393 *she should die* Evelyn, *Diary* 3 120 (8 March 1695).
393 *they got thither* Grew, *William Bentinck and William III* 236.
394 *the whole tyme* Fiennes 295.
394 *of the Music* PRO Treasury Papers, Disposition Book 12 191.
394 *of the Abbey* Fiennes 295.
394 *the Stock Exchange* Nippold, *Regierung* 99.
394 *hospital for seamen* PRO Treasury Books 9 part iii 1226.
394 *Monsieur Le Nôtre* Briggs 201–8.

CHAPTER 37: *Royal Progress*

396 *be well content* Japikse, *Prins Willem III* 2 363.
396 *his last campaign* Huygens, *Journalen* 2 491.

396 *in Saint-Simon's opinion* Erlanger 256.
397 *on the spot* Macaulay 4 158–9.
397 *holds in captivity* ibid. 165–6.
397 *right", he observed* Ranke 1 128.

397 *and so on* Orléans, *Letters from Liselotte* 70.

398 *a new aspect* Arch. 3rd ser. 1 329.

398 *some years ago* Ralph, *History* 2 607.

398 *generally in mourning* Luttrell 3 536.

398 *no bad effect* Arch. 3rd ser. 1 410.

398 *mild and pleasant* Evelyn, *Diary* 3 123–125 (28 July–25 October 1695).

399 *living like one* Anon., *Royal Progress* 4–5.

399 *be filled up* ibid. 9–11.

399 *avoid the King* ibid. 7–8.

399 *to see them* ibid. 6.

399 *of Warwick's Pot* ibid. 12.

399 *our packets dispatched* Somerville 104–106.

400 *off to Windsor* ibid.; Evelyn, *Diary* 3 124; Anon., *Royal Progress* 13–15.

400 *received much affection* Arch. 3rd ser. 1 412.

400 *I'm a widower* Jesse 1 87.

400 *a neighbouring house* Luttrell 3 550, 555; Evelyn, *Diary* 3 125 (13 November 1695).

401 *of the Dutch* Alphen, *Stemming*, 232–4.

401 *favour to him* ibid.; Huygens, *Journalen* 2 569.

401 *the King's reputation* Papers illustrative of the Highlands of Scotland, cit. Waterson 89.

401 *excess of zeal* Prebble 252–3.

402 *launched soon after* Mackenzie 68–70.

402 *to invade England* Lexington Papers, cit. Grew, *William Bentinck and William III* 251–4.

402 *a horrified Portland* ibid.

403 *him in Flanders* HMC Bath (Prior Papers) 3 239.

403 *to have said* Ranke 1 142.

403 *Queen's own father* Evelyn, *Diary* 3 129 (28 April 1696).

403 *of his friends* Evelyn, *Diary* 3 128 (26 February 1696).

403 *and James's adherents* Macaulay 4 217–31.

403 *affairs of Europe* Ogg 427–8.

404 *drop of blood* Lewis 105.

404 *six times round* ibid. 94.

404 *for most men* ibid. 41.

404 *clearly with it* ibid. 106.

404 *about his waste* Luttrell 3 589.

405 *he said graciously* Lewis 42–4.

405 *splendour at Windsor* Luttrell 4 89.

405 *the King's favour* Strickland 8 47.

405 *pockets to buy* Pepys, *Correspondence* 1 110.

406 *to Shrewsbury desperately* Somerville 115–18.

406 *ring-leaders were hanged* Davies 3 242.

406 *and tiresome cousin* Thomson 35–6; Arch 3rd ser. 2 12.

CHAPTER 38: *Constant Companions*

408 *very heartily received* Japikse, *Correspondentie* 1 ii 282–3.

408 *will work out* Ranke 1 156.

408 *live in Ireland* Huygens, *Journalen* 2 456.

409 *and mother die* Swift 3 74.

409 *on that score* Huygens, *Journalen* 2 563.

409 *I ever saw* Swift 3 47.

409 *love begets desire* ibid. 62–3.

409 *the Lord Treasurer* Vernon 1 33, 43.

410 *Louise Dorothea Sophia* Japikse, *Correspondentie* 1 i 80–1.

410 *wife without it* Wickham Legg 36.

410 *Moylandt at Cleves* Huygens, *Journalen* 2 622.

411 *chalk and tobacco-pipes* Wickham Legg 67.

411 *had half dined* ibid.

411 *with the Elector* Huygens, *Journalen* 2 624.

411 *bed of state* Luttrell 4 94–113 passim.

412 *out of store* Huygens, *Journalen* 2 624.

412 *a noble palace* RA Nass. Dom. 888f. xviii.

413 *into the country* Harris, *Description of Loo.*

413 *on 10 September* Macaulay 4 256–60.

414 *disordered to Kensington* Vernon 1 45.

414 *out of humour* HMC Report 12, app. ii 365, cit. Green, *Queen Anne* 74–5.

414 *his Dutch friends* Carte papers, cit. Strickland 7 218–19.

414 *more than normally* Huygens, *Journalen* 2 567.

415 *big powdered wig* ibid. 627.

415 *some such words* Grew, *William Bentinck and William III* 269.

415 *fetch nor carry* Dartmouth footnote to Burnet, *History* 4 412.

415 *an independent haughtiness* Bourdon 91–92.

416 *manner of living* Macky, *Memoirs* 68.

416 *prospect for success* Gaeto 204–5.

416 *maintain his post* Burnet, *History* 4 412.

416 *the only one* Huygens, *Journalen* 2 565, 581.

416 *had to flee* ibid. 4.

416 *rolls he tears* Jesse 1 251.
417 *on 18 February* Luttrell 4 176; Vernon 1 205.
417 *step above him* Vernon 1 209.
417 *of the knights* ibid. 212–16.
417 *posts at Court* BM Harleian MSS 6584, cit. Grew, *William Bentinck and William III* 101.
418 *your own hand* Japikse, *Correspondentie* 1 i 197–8.
418 *on Saturday again* HMC Bath (Prior Papers) 3 104.
418 *better for it* Vernon 1 247.
418 *resolve to do* Japikse, *Correspondentie* 1 i 198.
419 *as I do* ibid. 198–9.
419 *it being criminal* ibid. 199–200.
419 *stop to them* ibid. 201.
420 *palace in Brussels* Coronelli 23.
420 *wrong you are* Japikse, *Correspondentie* 1 i 202.

420 *of his letters* ibid. 212.
420 *this young man* ibid.
420 *intention of retiring* ibid. 213.
420 *as I can* ibid. 202–3.
421 *to consider returning* ibid.
421 *your absenting yourself* ibid. 213–14.
422 *of that country* Huygens, *Journalen* 2 43.
422 *named several others* Orléans, *Letters* (Stevenson) 1 217.
422 *to anybody else* Huygens, *Journaal* 3 78, 81.
423 *children in succession* Jesse 1 chap. xiii.
423 *with it now* Orléans, *Letters from Liselotte* 70.
423 *reported Liselotte later* Orléans, *Letters* (Stevenson) 156–7.
424 *cautious nor secret* Swift 12 206 "Remarks on Burnet".
424 *according to one* Anon., *Royal Diary* 50.
424 *of fine horses* Luttrell 4 260.

CHAPTER 39: *A Doubtful Peace*

426 *matter with him* Ranke 1 170.
426 *sincere for peace* Grimblot 1 93.
427 *at their house* HMC Buccleuch 2 ii 487, 497.
427 *reported to Shrewsbury* ibid. 486.
427 *ladies in England* ibid. 497.
427 *to any people* Vernon 1 410.
427 *visit to Berlin* Orléans, *Letters from Liselotte* 79–80.
428 *for two hours* Luttrell 4 273 ff.
428 *for all Dutchmen* Leo Loewensen "The First Interview between Peter I and William III, 1697: some neglected English material: "William III and Peter in 1697" *Slavonic and Eastern European Review* 36 308; Luttrell 4 291.
428 *Amsterdam, excusing himself* Luttrell 4 273–80.
428 *to the Muscovites* Post Boy 13 October 1697.
428 *any common dockhand* Gebhard, *Witsen* 430.
428 *invited himself again* Leo Loewensen "People Peter the Great met in England" *Slavonic and Eastern European Review* 37 459.
429 *sizzled around him* Droste 234.
429 *retire no further* Vernon 1 410.
429 *for the future* Arch. 3rd ser. 1 623.
429 *for his friendship* Grimblot 1 134–6.
429 *morning till evening* Luttrell 4 307.
429 *of Royal portraits* ibid. 309.

430 *present of diamonds* Droste 238.
430 *on these occasions* Japikse, *Correspondentie* 1 i 214.
430 *frequently offer'd them* Ralph, *History* 2 761.
430 *convent at Chaillot* Stuart 1 27–9.
431 *never permit it* Orléans, *Letters from Liselotte* 80.
431 *a good character* Japikse, *Correspondentie* 1 ii 283–4.
431 *not suit me* ibid. 1 i 209.
431 *an unmistakable no* ibid. 1 ii 285.
432 *of my feet* Bidloo, *Verhaal* 5; BM Add. MSS. 5724.
432 *Portland that November* Heimans 168–170.
432 *sobbing with regret* Huygens, *Journaal* 3 80.
432 *nothing among friends* Dalrymple 3 vii 183.
432 *drinking and talking* Heimans 168–70.
432 *no great harm* BM Add. MSS. 5724.
432 *awake, he complained* ibid.; Hone 58.
433 *to bother him* ibid.; Luttrell 4 310.
433 *time of war* Vernon 1 414.
433 *the common people* Luttrell 4 298.
433 *did King Charles* ibid. 286 ff.
433 *of their King* Burnet, *History* 4 373–4.
434 *number of 80* Luttrell 4 286–307.
434 *have been seen* BM Egerton MSS. 24205.
434 *the cheering crowds* Arch. 3 ser. 2 3.

434 *of the building* Smith 77.
434 *Evelyn put it* Macaulay **4** 322.
434 *least three died* Luttrell **4** 315.
435 *being stared at* Luttrell **4** 330–5 passim.
435 *could forbear laughing* Jesse **1** 161–8.
435 *himself with apologies* ibid.

435 *bill for £150* Evelyn, *Diary* **3** 138–9 (30 January–9 June 1698).
436 *a great prince* Jesse **1** 161–8.
436 *to the theatre* ibid.
436 *of brown paper* ibid.
436 *to the king-Stadholder* Luttrell **4** 469.

CHAPTER 40: *The Spanish Succession*

437 *by the flames* Fiennes 276, 292; Luttrell **4** 335; Montanus **2** ii 259; L.C.C., *Survey of London* 13 38–9.
437 *loss is considerable* Grimblot **1** 144.
437 *finer than before* Luttrell **4** 335.
437 *Houses of Parliament* Luttrell **4** 334, 351; Briggs 174–6.
438 *take a look* Luttrell **4** 380, 387, 407; Briggs 165–7.
438 *be very happy* Grimblot **1** 145.
438 *you the same* Grimblot **1** 150.
438 *which costs £6,000* Luttrell **4** 326–9.
439 *and fifty-six footmen* Grimblot **1** 162.
439 *immediately to entertain* Grimblot **1** 216.
439 *to his excellency* Jesse **1** 241.
439 *taste and refinement* Saint-Simon, cit. Grew, *William Bentinck and William III* 320.
439 *can be desired* Grimblot **1** 227.
439 *and graceful manners* Saint-Simon, cit Grew, *William Bentinck and William III* 320.
439 *during the war* Japikse, *Correspondentie* **1** i 223.
439 *eight years ago* Grew, *William Bentinck and William III* 322–3.
440 *knew of none* Grimblot **1** 169.
440 *always the same* ibid. 181.
440 *of his letters* Japikse, *Correspondentie* **1** i 250.
441 *to that end* ibid. 400; Grew, *William Bentinck and William III* 327.
441 *kinds of things* Japikse, *Correspondentie* **1** i 299.
441 *wishes to distinguish* Grew, *William Bentinck and William III* 320–1.
442 *our own countries* Japikse, *Correspondentie* **1** i 300.

442 *say of him* HMC Bath (Prior Papers) **3** 279.
442 *he ever was* ibid. 306.
442 *ragged and contemptible* ibid. 259.
442 *nec pluvibus impar* ibid.
442 *Opera without distinction* ibid. 195.
442 *that she wants* ibid. 201, 205.
442 *in Portland's company* Grimblot **1** 204.
443 *stud, Portland thought* Japikse, *Correspondentie* **1** i 288, 290, 298.
443 *spent on them* Grimblot **1** 192.
443 *he pointed out* Japikse, *Correspondentie* **1** i 335.
443 *spring of 1698* Grimblot **1** 466.
444 *on the decline* ibid. 249–50.
444 *for their King* ibid. 466.
444 *upon as ruined* ibid.
444 *to be there* Luttrell **4** 364; Hore **3** 213.
444 *of about £600* Hore **3** 221.
444 *of the same* ibid. 231.
445 *I against him* ibid. 282–3, 361 ff.
445 *others and changing* ibid. 213.
445 *drank his health* ibid. 211.
445 *adhere to it* Grimblot **2** 56.
445 *journey to Holland* ibid. 470, 355.
445 *openly about it* ibid. 91.
447 *Kings of England* Grimblot **2** 183.
447 *wrote back firmly* ibid. 187.
447 *King of France* Vernon **2** 197.
447 *England by 1700* Macky, *Memoirs* 28.
447 *the slightest occasion* Grimblot **2** 57.
447 *the balance even* Vernon **2** 209.
447 *the upper hand* Grimblot **2** 184.
448 *departure for England* ibid. 188.
448 *see Lord Albemarle* ibid. 189.
448 *in sombre apprehension* ibid. 207.

CHAPTER 41: *Xenophobia*

449 *maintaining the Dutch* Alphen, *Stemming* 203.
449 *the utmost violence* ibid. 247.
449 *own Dutch troops* Macaulay **4** 426–51 passim; Burnet, *History* **4** 3, 98–9;

Kenyon, *Robert Spencer* 307–8; Japikse, *Prins Willem III* **2** 405.
449 *Christmas to Heinsius* Arch. 3rd ser. **2** 258–9.
449 *a hard usage* Vernon **2** 250.

450 *he had expected* Arch. 3rd ser. **2** 275;
Burnet, *History* **4** 377; Ellis **2** 216.
450 *for your Security* Ralph, *History* **2** 807.
450 *the next morning* Arch. 3rd ser. **2** 302–3.
450 *their own country* ibid. 22–3.
450 *his own interest* Grimblot **2** 236.
451 *were to go* Luttrell **4** 481; *Vernon* **2** 263.
451 *they should stay* Jesse **1** 173.
451 *take very kindly* Ralph, *History* **2** 809–
810.
451 *on the subject* ibid.; Vernon **2** 269.
451 *his own subjects* Grimblot **2** 310–11.
451 *King of them* Luttrell **4** 502; Vernon **2**
241–4.
452 *to the people* Alphen, *Stemming* 263.
452 *our squeamish ladies* Edward Ward in
The London Spy, cit. Alphen *Stemming*
263.
452 *favour", wrote Vernon* Luttrell **4** 505;
Vernon **2** 274.
452 *much as ever* Grew, *Court of William III*
228.
452 *to his commission* Luttrell **4** 288;
Evelyn, *Diary* **3** 142 (30 March 1699);
Grimblot **2** 62.
452 *young and handsome* Ranke **1** 192.
452 *withdraw to one* Grew, *William Bentinck and William III* 359.
453 *the Electoral Prince* Grimblot **2** 245–6.
453 *Earl of Portland* ibid. 279.
453 *yours as ever* ibid. 313–14.
453 *Count de Tallard* Japikse, *Correspondentie* **1** i 338.
453 *could think again* ibid. 339; Vernon **2**
276.
453 *of the English* Grimblot **2** 320.
453 *of the gardens* Vernon **2** 278.
453 *precious to him* Arch. 3 ser. **2** 406.
454 *the small ones* Japikse, *Correspondentie*
1 ii 316.
454 *as your master* ibid.
454 *of next week* Wickham Legg 289–90.

454 *expenses of £10,000* Hore **3** 232.
454 *just the same* Japikse, *Correspondentie*
1 ii 111–12; *Prins Willem III* **2** 406.
454 *of that year* Japikse *Prins Willem III* **2**
407–11; Arch. 3rd ser. **2** 509.
454 *of French origin* Voltaire, cit. Erlanger
282–3.
455 *a gilt coach* Wickham Legg 295.
455 *in their gallop* HMC *Report* **8** 83
Vernon **2** 357.
453 *attend Albemarle's mother* Luttrell **4**
554–67 passim.
455 *he said afterwards* Grimblot **2** 360.
455 *his majestie's diversion* Luttrell **4** 574–5,
581.
455 *in his honour* ibid. 578–9.
455 *there as spectators* ibid. 583.
455 *the 3d yellow* ibid. 547–8.
456 *not leve them* RA Heinsius 623, cit.
Baxter 373–4.
456 *nor his company* HMC Rutland **2** 166.
457 *execute this commission* Vernon **2** 386;
Alphen, *Stemming* 272.
457 *the rebellion there* Vernon **2** 440.
457 *the late war* Bense 192.
457 *they're quite indescribable* Japikse, *Prins
Willem III* **2** 410.
457 *was duly installed* Luttrell **4** 647–53
passim.
458 *wrote to Heinsius* Grimblot **2** 416.
458 *upon his health* Vernon **3** 73.
458 *by his absence* Luttrell **4** 603; Prebble,
Darien 294–5.
458 *in early June* Vernon **3** 77.
458 *he added wistfully* Grimblot **2** 415, 417.
459 *have been right* Vernon **3** 105.
459 *up resolving nothing* ibid. 97.
459 *Vernon with feeling* ibid. 107.
459 *passage over sea* Luttrell **4** 666.
459 *are mightly swelled* HMC Bath (Prior
Papers) **3** 43.

CHAPTER 42: *End of a Reign*

460 *company two dayes* Luttrell **4** 676.
460 *eleven years old* ibid. 671–2; Vernon **3**
118–19.
460 *under his protection* Luttrell **4** 664.
460 *want for accomplishments* Coxe **1** 68, cit.
Rowse 238.
460 *heart with affliction* ibid.
460 *in their hand* Luttrell **4** 674–6.
460 *your grandfather's throne* Orléans, *Letters
from Liselotte* 95.
461 *very welcome here* Luttrell **4** 673; HMC

Bath (Prior Papers) **3** 414; Vernon **3** 128.
461 *already thirty-four* Luttrell **4** 679.
461 *against "more foreigners"* Vernon **3** 129,
141.
461 *worse than ever* Orléans, *Letters from
Liselotte* 93.
462 *of the dauphin* Luttrell **4** 703.
462 *King of Spain* Orléans, *Letters from
Liselotte* 94; Erlanger 286.
462 *laughed so hard* Orléans, *Letters from
Liselotte* 93.

462 *related in London* Luttrell **4** 703–6.
462 *never be united* Groen van Prinsterer, *Handboek* **1** 445.
462 *have believed possible* Japikse, *Prins Willem III* **2** 415–16.
463 *blow being struck* Groen van Prinsterer, *Handboek* **1** 445.
463 *up for him* Grew, *William Bentinck and William III* 380–2.
464 *we are many* Defoe, *Legion's Memorial*, cit. Ogg 463.
464 *of our frontiers* Groen van Prinsterer, *Handboek* **1** 445–8.
466 *hour had come* Orléans, *Letters from Liselotte* 101.
466 *French ambassador Poussin* Macaulay **4** 533.
466 *liveries into mourning* Brown, *Letters of Queen Anne* 68.
467 *from his death-bed* Bosq de Beaumont 235.
467 *for my father* Green, *Queen Anne* 86–7.
467 *see his doctors* BM Add. MSS. 5724.

468 *into his coach* Macaulay **4** 529.
469 *were much improved* BM Add. MSS. 5724.
469 *States of Holland* Wagenaar **17** 104.
469 *to the nation* Davies **3** 256.
469 *for his life* Burnet, *History* **4** 544.
469 *you would think* Bourdon 78.
469 *in The Hague* Droste 227.
470 *and eat lustily* BM Add. MSS. 5724.
470 *he had said* Anon., *Royal Diary* 87.
471 *legs swelled again* BM Add. MSS. 5724.
471 *Protestant and Papist* Burnet, *History* **4** 296.
471 *the present opportunity* Ralph, *History* **2** 1006.
471 *all Protestant people* Oldmixon 253, cit. Burnet, *History* **4** 296.
472 *of my song* Alphen, *Stemming* 288–94.
475 *a cloudless sky* Japikse, *Prins Willem III* **2** 523; HMC Rutland **2** 169; Vernon **3** 183–92 passim; Green, *Queen Anne* 90, 94; Fabius 392–3; BM Add. MSS. 5724;

CHAPTER 43 : *Epilogue*

476 *joy to find* The Mournful Poem (pamphlet).
476 *1684 by Loofs* Bidloo, *Verhaal* 110; BM Add. MSS. 5724; Anon, *Royal Diary* 36.
477 *for the Kinge* HMC Rutland **2** 170.
477 *death with grief* Orléans, *Letters from Liselotte* 107.
477 *de la Chrétienté* Thomson 107–9.
477 *Prince without animosity* Orléans, *Correspondance* (Brunet) **1** 65.
477 *for the new* Orléans, *Letters from Liselotte* 107.
477 *next world too* ibid. 106–7.
477 *my seventy-second year* Ward 365.
477 *at his deathbed* Post Boy; Macky, *Characters* 140, cit. Strickland **8** 120.
477 *shorter and shorter* Strickland **8** 126.

478 *most gracious Queen* Onslow notes on Burnet, cit. Strickland **8** 129.
478 *to any other* HMC *Report* **11** 242.
478 *money for them* Postman cit. Strickland **8** 132.
478 *rain over them* Verney, *Memoirs*, cit. Alphen, *Stemming* 308–9.
478 *the dead Stadholder* Japikse, *Correspondentie* **1** i 524–5.
479 *Stadholder of England* Gaeto 218.
479 *going too far* Ranke **1** 191–2.
480 *the Great King* Churchill **1** 341.
481 *the highest fame* ibid. 542.
483 *Save Queen Anne* Robb 504; Burnet, *History* **4** 570; Strickland **8** 133; Anon., *Royal Diary* 88–9.
483 *prosperity of England* Post Boy, cit. Strickland **8** 131.

Bibliography

MANUSCRIPT SOURCES IN ENGLAND

British Museum: Birch, Bodleian, Egerton, Le Fleming, Forster, Harleian, Sloane and Additional MSS.

Public Record Office: *Calendar of State Papers Domestic (CSP Dom.)* and Treasury Papers.

MANUSCRIPT SOURCES IN HOLLAND

Koninklijk Huisarchief (KHA); Koninklijk Bibliotheek (KB); Algemeen Rijksarchief (RA); Algemeen Rijksarchief, Nassau Domeinen Ordonnanties (RA Nass. Dom.).

PAMPHLETS AND OTHER PRINTED DOCUMENTS

Aanmerkelijk Verhael der Staats-omkeringen nu Laatst in 't jaar 1688 in Siam Voorgevallen (1689).

A True Relation of the Late King's Death (1702).

Brief van H. M. Maria aan S. M. Willem.

Copie de la lettre du Duc de Luxembourg écrite au Roy de France (1690).

Des véritables nouvelles du voyage de sa Majesté vers l'Irlande (1690).

Een Verhael van een Kroon van Licht, die Boven de Stad van Oranje is Gezien.

Exorbitant Grants of William III (1703).

Extraits des nouvelles d'Angleterre, d'Irlande et d'Écosse (1690).

Form of Proceeding at the Funeral of Queen Mary (1695).

His Majesties Most Gracious Speech to both Houses of Parliament (1685).

The Mournfull Poem on the Royal Funeral of King William the Third.

Omstandig en Seecker Verhael van 't Gepasseerde in en Omtrent de Executie van de Persoon van Jacob Schot (1685).

On the Death of the R. Hon. Thomas, Earl of Ossory (Dublin, 1680).

Oprecht Verhaal van 't Gepasseerde op de Reyse van de Prins van Oranje (1677).

Pertinent Verhaal van de Vuurwerken den 5e Februari 1691 's avonts naar de Heerlijke Intrede van Koningh Willem III in 's Gravenhage.

Seecker en Omstandigh Verhael van het Gepasseerde, Zedert het Overgaan van S. H. naar Engelandt in 1688.

Sommier en Waerachtigh Verhael van de Reyse van S. H. de Heere Prince van Oranje in Engelandt (1670–1).

The Speech of the Prince of Orange to some principal gentlemen of Somersetshire and Dorsetshire (Exeter, 1688).

Waaragtig Relaes van de Overkomst van Zijne Majesteit William de Derde (1691).

BOOKS

AILESBURY, THOMAS BRUCE, 2ND EARL OF: *Memoirs* (Roxburghe Club, 1890).

AITZEMA, LIEUWE VAN: *Saken van Staet en Oorlog* (The Hague, 1669).

ALBEMARLE, GEORGE THOMAS KEPPEL, 6TH EARL OF: *Fifty Years of my Life*, vol. 1 (London, 1876).

ALPHEN, GREGORIUS VAN: *De Stemming van de Engelschen tegen de Hollanders in Engeland* (Assen, 1938).

— 'Anthony Smets, Bibliothecaris van de drie prinsen van Oranje (1636–1689)', *Gedenkboek van de Koninklijke Bibliotheek*, 119–60 (The Hague, 1948).

ANON: 'Dagelijkse aantekeningen van een reisje ter bezichtiging van de verdedigingswerken van den IJssel, 1672', *Kronijk van het Historisch Genootschap*, 233–63 (Utrecht, 1861).

— 'Aantekeningen betreffende het voorgevallene in de maanden juli tot december 1672', *Kronijk van het Historisch Genootschap*, 5 ser., deel 4, 439–72 (Utrecht, 1868).

— *Engelands Godsdienst en Vrijheid Hersteldt* (Amsterdam, 1689).

— *Willem III te 's-Gravenhage in 1691* (2 vols, Amsterdam, 1905).

— *The Royal Progress; or, a Diary of the King's Journey* (London, 1695).

— *The Glorious Life of William III* (London, 1702).

— *The History of the Republic of Holland from its First Foundation to the Death of King William* (2 vols, London, 1705).

— *The Royal Diary; or King William's Interior Portraicture* (London, 1705).

— *The Secret History of Whitehall* (2nd ed., London, 1717).

— *The Lives of the Princes of the Illustrious House of Orange* (London, 1734).

— *The History of England during the Reigns of King William, Queen Anne and King George I* (London, 1784).

ANTHEUNISSEN, W.: *Historische Opstellen* (Zutphen, 1927).

ASHLEY, MAURICE: *The Glorious Revolution of 1688* (London, 1966).

— *England in the Seventeenth Century* (London, 1968).

— *The Golden Century, Europe 1598–1715* (London, 1969).

— *Charles II, the Man and the Statesman* (London, 1971).

ASKIN, PAUL: *King William and His Times* (Dublin, 1890).

AULNOY, M. C., BARONNE D': *Memoirs of the Court in England in 1675* (2nd ed., London, 1927).

AVAUX, JEAN-ANTOINE DE MESMES, COMTE D': *Négociations depuis 1679 jusqu'en 1684* (6 vols, Paris, 1752).

BATHURST, B.: *Letters of Two Queens* (London, 1924).

BAXTER, STEPHEN: *William III* (London, 1966).

BELLOC, HILAIRE: *James II* (London, 1928).

BENSE, J. F.: *Anglo-Dutch Relations from the Earliest Times to the Death of William the Third* (The Hague, 1925).

BENTINCK, MECHTILD, COMTESSE (ed.): *Marie, Reine d'Angleterre, Lettres et Mémoires* (The Hague, 1880).

BERESFORD, JOHN: *Gossip of the Seventeenth and Eighteenth Centuries* (London, 1923).

— *Sir George Downing, the Godfather of Downing Street* (London, 1925).

BEVAN, B.: 'Queen Mary of Orange', *Contemporary Review*, May 1962.

BICKLEY, FRANCIS: *Life of Matthew Prior* (London, 1914).

BIDLOO, GOVAERT: *Op het vertrek van haar Kon. Hoogheid de Princesse van Oranje naar Engeland* (1689).

— *'s-Graavenhaage legevierende, op de dag der Krooning van Haare Majesteyten Willem en Marie* (The Hague, 1689).

— *Verhaal van de Laatste Ziekte en het Overlijden van Willem III* (Leiden, 1702).

BILDERDIJK, WILLEM: *Geschiedenis des Vaderlands* (vols 9, 10), ed. H. W. Tijdeman (Amsterdam, 1836).

BLOK, P. J.: *Geschiedenis van het Nederlandsche Volk* (8 vols, Leiden, 1892–1908).

BODEMAN, E.: *Briefwechsel der Herzogin Sophie von Hannover mit Ihrem Bruder dem Kurfürsten Karl Ludwig von der Pfalz* (1885).

BOSQ DE BEAUMONT, G. DU et M. BERNOS: *La cour des Stuarts à St. Germain-en-Laye (1689–1718)* (Paris, 1912).

BOURDON, DANIEL DE: 'Mémoires de Monsieur de B.' ed. F. J. L. Krämer, *Bijdragen Historisch Genootschap* (vol. 19, The Hague, 1898).

BOXER, C. R.: *The Dutch Seaborne Empire (1600–1800)* (2nd ed., London, 1966).

BOWEN, MARJORIE: *William of Orange* (London, 1928).

— *The Third Mary Stuart* (London, 1929).

BOYER, ABEL: *The History of King William III* (3 vols, London, 1702).

BRIGGS, MARTIN: *Wren the Incomparable* (London, 1953).

BROWN, BEATRICE CURTIS: *The Letters of Queen Anne* (London, 1935).

BROWN, THOMAS: *The Lives of All the Princes of Orange* (London, 1693).

BROWNING, ANDREW: *Life and Letters of Thomas Osborne, Earl of Danby* (Glasgow, 1951).

BRYANT, SIR ARTHUR: *Pepys, the Saviour of the Navy* (London, 1949).

BULSTRODE, SIR RICHARD: *Memoirs and Reflections* (London, 1721).

BURNET, GILBERT: *An Essay on the Memory of the Late Queen* (London, 1695).

— *A Memorial Offered to her Royal Highness the Princess Sophia* (London, 1815).

— *History of his own Time, with notes by the Earls of Dartmouth and Hardwicke, Speaker Onslow and Dean Swift to which added other Annotations* (2nd ed. enlarged, 6 vols, Oxford, 1833).

BURTON, ELIZABETH: *The Jacobeans at Home* (London, 1962).

CAMPBELL, KATHLEEN: *Sarah, Duchess of Marlborough* (London, 1932).

CAMPBELL, R.: *The Life of Dr. John Radcliffe* (London, 1950).

CARREL, ARMAND: *History of the Counter-Revolution in England (History of the Reign of James II)* (London, 1846).

CARSWELL, JOHN: *The Descent on England* (London, 1969).

CARTE, THOMAS: *The Life of James, Duke of Ormonde* (6 vols, Oxford, 1851).

CAVELLI, MARCHESE CAMPANA DE: *Les derniers Stuarts* (2 vols, Paris, 1871).

CHAPMAN, HESTER: *Great Villiers* (London, 1949).

— *Mary II: Queen of England* (London, 1953).

— *The Tragedy of Charles II in the Years 1630–1660* (3rd ed., London, 1965).

CHESTERFIELD, PHILIP STANHOPE, 2ND EARL OF: *Letters* (2 vols, London, 1837).

CHEVALIER, N.: *Histoire de Guillaume III par médailles* (Amsterdam, 1693).

CHEVENIX TRENCH, CHARLES: *The Western Rising* (London, 1969).

CHURCHILL, SIR WINSTON S.: *Marlborough, His Life and Times* (2 vols, London, 1933).

CLARENDON, EDWARD HYDE, 1ST EARL OF: *Life* (3 vols, London, 1827).

CLARENDON, HENRY HYDE, 2ND EARL OF: *Correspondence of Clarendon and his Brother, Laurence Hyde, Earl of Rochester* (2 vols, London, 1828).

CLARK, SIR GEORGE NORMAN: *The Dutch Alliance and the War against French Trade (1688–1697)* (Manchester, 1923).

— *The Later Stuarts, 1660–1714* (2nd ed., Oxford, 1965).

CLARKE, JAMES STANIER (ed.): *Memoirs of James II* (2 vols, London, 1816).

CORONELLI, VINCENT: *The Royal Almanack* (London, 1696).

COURTENAY, THOMAS PEREGRINE: *Life of Sir William Temple* (2 vols, London, 1836).

CRAGG, GERALD R.: *The Church and the Age of Reason, 1648–1789* (revised ed., London, 1970).

CUNNINGTON, C. WILLETT and PHILLIS: *Handbook of English Costume in the Seventeenth Century* (London, 1955).

DALRYMPLE, SIR JOHN: *Memoirs of Great Britain and Ireland* (3 vols, Edinburgh, 1771–88).

DANBY, THOMAS, EARL OF: *Copies and Extracts of Some Letters Written to and from the Earl of Danby (now Duke of Leeds) in the Years 1676, 1677 and 1678* (London, 1710).

DAVIES, C. M.: *History of Holland* (3 vols, London, 1841–4).

DEFOE, DANIEL: *A Tour through England and Wales* (London, 1927).

— *Journal of the Plague Year* (London, 1969).

DOEBNER, DR. (ed.): *Mary of Orange, Memoirs* (London, 1886).

DOHNA, FRÉDERICK DE: *Mémoires*, ed. Borkowski (Königsberg, 1898).

DOORN, JACQUELINE: *Mary Stuart, 1631–1660* (Zaltbommel, 1966).

DOUMIC, RENÉ: *Saint-Simon: La France de Louis XIV* (Paris, 1920).

DRING, DANIEL: *The Life of that Incomparable Princess Mary* (London, 1695).

DROSTE, COENRAET: *Overblijfsels van Geheugchenis, der bisonderste voorvallen, In het leeven van den heere C. Droste*, ed. Fruin (Leiden, 1879).

DUTTON, RALPH: *English Court Life, from Henry VII to George II* (London, 1963).

EIJSTEN, J.: *Het Leven van Willem II* (Amsterdam, 1916).
ELIZABETH, QUEEN OF BOHEMIA: *Letters*, compiled by L. M. Baker (London, 1953).
ELLIOT, J. H.: *Imperial Spain, 1469–1716* (London, 1970).
ELLIS, HENRY: *Original Letters Illustrative of English History*, 2nd ser. (vol. 4, London, 1827).
EMERSON, WILLIAM RICHARD: *Monmouth's Rebellion* (London, 1951).
ERLANGER, PHILIPPE: *Louis XIV* (London, 1970).
ESTRADES, COMTE D': *Memoirs and Letters* (3 vols, London, 1711).
EVELYN, JOHN: *Life of Mrs. Godolphin*, ed. S. Wilberforce (London, 1874).
— *Diary*, ed. W. Bray (4 vols, London, 1906).

FABIUS, A. M. J.: *Het Leven van Willem III (1650–1702)* (Alkmaar).
FARMER, D. L.: *Britain and the Stuarts* (London, 1965).
FEA, ALLAN: *King Monmouth* (London, 1902).
— *James II and his Wives* (London, 1908).
FEILING, KEITH: *History of the Tory Party (1640–1714)* (Oxford, 1924).
FIENNES, CELIA: *Diary*, ed. Christopher Morris (London, 1947).
FINCH, ALLAN G.: *Report on the Manuscripts of the late Allan G. Finch* (2 vols, London, 1922).
FLEMING, ROBERT: *Discourse on the Death of King William* (London, 1703).
FORNERON, HENRI: *Louise de Kéroualle, 1649–1734* (Paris, 1886).
FOUW, A. DE, jr.: *Onbekende Raadpensionarissen* (The Hague, 1946).
FOX, CHARLES JAMES: *A History of the Early Part of the Reign of James the Second* (London, 1808).
FOXCROFT, HELEN C.: *The Life and Letters of Sir George Savile, Bart, First Marquis of Halifax* (2 vols, London, 1898).
— *A Life of Gilbert Burnet* (2 vols, London, 1907).
FRANSEN, J.: *Les Comédiens Français en Hollande* (Paris, 1925).
FRUIN, ROBERT JACOB: *Prins Willem II in zijn verhouding tot Engeland* (1889).
— *Verspreide Geschriften* (vols, 4, 5, The Hague, 1901–2).
FUNCK-BRENTANO, FRANTZ: *Liselotte* (Paris, 1936).

GAETO, FRANCO: *Relations des ambassadeurs Vénitiens* (Paris, 1969).
GANS, MOZES HEIMAN: *Juwelen en Mensen* (Amsterdam, 1961).
GEBHARD, J. F.: *Het Leven van Nicolaas C. Witsen* (Utrecht, 1881).
— 'Een dagboek uit het rampjaar 1672', ed. J. F. Gebhard, *Bijdragen van het Historisch Genootschap*, **8** 45–116 (Utrecht, 1885).
— 'Het aansprekersoproer in 1696', *Amsterdams Jaarboekje* (1898).
GEYL, PIETER: *The Netherlands in the Seventeenth Century* (vol. 2, London, 1967).

— *History of the Low Countries* (London, 1964).

— *Orange and Stuart (1641–72)* (London, 1969).

GOES, WILLEM VAN DER: 'Briefwisseling tussen de gebroeder van der Goes (1659–1673)', ed. C. J. Gonnet, 2 vols, *Historisch Genootschap*, 3rd ser., no. 11 (Amsterdam, 1909).

GRAMONT, COUNT ANTOINE CHARLES: *Memoirs of the Court of Charles the Second*, ed. Sir Walter Scott (London, 1846).

GREEN, DAVID: *Queen Anne* (London, 1970).

GREEN, EMANUEL: *The March of William of Orange through Somerset* (London, 1892).

GREW, EDWIN and MARION: *The Court of William III* (London, 1910.)

— *The English Court in Exile* (London, 1911).

GREW, MARION: *William Bentinck and William III* (London, 1924).

GRIMBLOT, PAUL: *Letters of William II and Louis XIV* (2 vols, London, 1848).

GROEN VAN PRINSTERER, G.: *Handboek der Geschiedenis van het Vaderland* (2 vols, Amsterdam, 1852).

— *Archives de la Maison d'Orange-Nassau*, 2nd ser., 5 vols (The Hague, 1861); 3rd ser., 3 vols, ed. F. J. L. Krämer (Leiden, 1907–9); cited as *Arch.*

GROOT, PIETER DE: 'Lettres de Pieter de Groot à Abraham de Wicquefort (1668–1674)', ed. F. J. L. Krämer, *Historisch Genootschap*, 3rd ser., no. 5 (The Hague, 1894).

GUICHE, COMTE DE: *Mémoires* (London, 1714).

GUTTRIDGE, GEORGE HERBERT: *The Colonial Policy of William III* (2nd ed., London, 1966).

HAILE, MARTIN: *Queen Mary of Modena, her Life and Letters* (London, 1905).

HALEY, K. H. D.: *William of Orange and the English Opposition (1672–1674)* (Oxford, 1953).

— 'The Anglo-Dutch Rapprochement of 1617', *EHR*, 614–48, October 1958.

HALIFAX, GEORGE SAVILE, 1ST MARQUIS OF: *Complete Works*, ed. J. P. Kenyon (London, 1969).

HALLEMA, A.: *Amalia van Solms* (Amsterdam).

HAMILTON, COUNT ANTHONY: *Memoirs of the Comte de Gramont* (London, 1930).

HAMILTON, ELISABETH: *William's Mary* (London, 1972).

HANOVER, ELECTRESS SOPHIA OF: *Briefwechsel*, ed. E. Budeman (1885).

HARRIS, WALTER: *A Description of the King's Royal Palace and Gardens at Loo* (London, 1699).

— *The History of the Life and Reign of William-Henry* (Dublin, 1749).

HAUCK, CARL: *Elisabeth, Königin von Bohemen* (1905).

HAYES, JOHN: *Kensington Palace* (H.M.S.O., London, 1969).

HAZARD, PAUL: *The European Mind, 1680–1715* (London, 1964).

HEIM, H. J. VAN DER: *Het Archief van de Raadpensionaris A. Heinsius* (The Hague, 1867).

HEIMANS, H. E.: *Het Karakter van Willem III, Koning-Stadhouder* (Amsterdam, 1925).

HEWITSON, ANTHONY (ed.): *Diary of Thomas Bellingham, an Officer under William III* (Preston, 1908).

HIBBERT, CHRISTOPHER: *The Court at Windsor* (London, 1966).

HILL, CHRISTOPHER: *The Century of Revolution (1603–1714)* (7th ed., London, 1967).

HONE, CAMPBELL RICHARD: *The Life of Dr. John Radcliffe 1652–1714* (London, 1950).

HOOGEWERFF, G. J.: 'De Twee Reizen van Cosimo de Medici, Prins van Tuscanie, door de Nederlanden', *Historisch Genootschap*, 3rd ser., no. 41 (Amsterdam, 1919).

HORE, JOHN PHILIP: *The History of Newmarket* (3 vols, London, 1886).

HUIZINGA, JOHAN: *Dutch Civilisation in the Seventeenth Century* (London, 1968).

HUYGENS, SIR CONSTANTYN: *Briefwisseling* (vols 5, 6) uitgegeven door J. A. Worp (The Hague, 1916–17).

— *Correspondance* (vols 6, 7, The Hague, 1899, 1901).

— 'Discours sur la Nourriture de son Altesse Monseigneur le Prince d'Orange', 1674, KB, MS. 73 J 11.

HUYGENS, CONSTANTYN: *Journalen (1, 2) van 1688 tot 1696* (2 vols, *Historisch Genootschap*, n.s. 23, 25, Utrecht, 1876–7).

— *Journaal (3), gedurende de veldtochten der jaren 1673, 1675, 1676, 1677, 1678* (*Historisch Genootschap*, n.s. 32, Utrecht, 1881).

— *Journalen (4), 1649, 1650, 1680, 1682* (*Historisch Genootschap*, n.s. 46, Utrecht, 1888).

ISING, ARNOLD L. H.: *Het Hof te 's-Gravenhage* (The Hague, 1898).

JAPIKSE, NICOLAAS: *De Verwikkelingen tussen de Republiek en Engeland van 1660–1665* (Leiden, 1900).

— *Correspondentie van Willem III en Hans Willem Bentinck* (5 vols, The Hague, 1927–37).

— *Prins Willem III, de Stadhouder-Koning* (2 vols, Amsterdam, 1933).

— *De Geschiedenis van het Huis van Oranje-Nassau* (2 vols, The Hague, 1937–8).

JESSE, JOHN HENEAGE: *Memoirs of the Court of England During the Reign of the Stuarts* (4 vols, London, 1855).

— *The Court of England from the Revolution in 1688 to the Death of George II* (4 vols, London, 1901).

JONES, DAVID: *A Continuation of the Secret History of Whitehall* (London, 1697).

— *Tragical History of the Stuarts* (London, 1697).

JONGE, J. C. DE: *Verhandelingen en onuitgegeven stukken betreffende de geschiedenis der Nederlanden* (2 vols, Delft, 1825).

JORISSEN, T.: *Historische Werken* (4 vols, Haarlem, 1912).

KANNEGIETER, J. Z.: 'Amsterdam en de vrede van Rijswijk', *Bijdragen Historisch Genootschap*, no. 48, 99–136 (Utrecht, 1927).

KENNET, WHITE: *History of England, Charles I–William III* (London, 1706).

KENYON, JOHN P.: 'The Earl of Sunderland and the King's Administration 1693–1695', *EHR*, 576–602, October 1956.

— *Robert Spencer, Earl of Sunderland, 1641–1702* (London, 1958).

— *The Stuarts* (4th ed., London, 1969).

KERCKHOVEN, JOHAN VAN, HEER VAN HEENVLIET: 'Journaal', *Kroniek van het Historisch Genootschap*, 5th ser., no. 5, 541–647 (Utrecht, 1869).

KILLANIN, MICHAEL MORRIS, 3RD BARON: *Sir Godfrey Kneller and his Times* (London, 1948).

KINGSTON, RICHARD: *A True History of the Several Designs and Conspiracies against His Majesties Sacred Person and Government* (London, 1698).

KLOPP, ONNO: *Der Fall des Hauses Stuart* (vols, 4, 5, 6, Vienna, 1877).

KNOOP, W. J.: *Krijgs– en Geschiedkundige besch. van Willem III* (1895).

KNUTTEL, W. P. C.: *Catalogus van de pamflettenverzameling berustende in de Koninklijke Bibliotheek* (9 vols, The Hague, 1889–1920).

KRÄMER, F. J. L.: *Maria Stuart, gemalin van Willem III* (Utrecht, 1890).

— *'Je Maintiendrai', Geschiedkundige bijdragen* bijeengebracht onder leiding van prof., F. J. L. Krämer, E. W. Moes en Dr. P. Wagner (2 vols, Leiden, 1905–1906).

KURTZ, G. H.: *Willem III en Amsterdam, 1683–1685* (Utrecht, 1928).

LAKE, DR. EDWARD: *Diary*, ed. G. P. Elliot (London, 1846).

LANE, JANE: *King James the Last* (London, 1943).

LAW, ERNEST: *Hampton Court* (London, 1849).

— *Kensington Palace* (London, 1899).

LEFEVRE PONTALIS, EUGÈNE: *Jean de Witt* (2 vols, London, 1884).

LEVER, SIR TRESHAM: *Godolphin, his Life and Times* (London, 1952).

LEWIS, JENKIN: *Queen Anne's Son, Memoirs of the Duke of Gloucester*, ed. W. J. Loftie (London, 1881).

LODGE, RICHARD: *The Political History of England* (vol. 8, London, 1905).

LONDON COUNTY COUNCIL: *Survey of London* (vol. 13, London, 1930).

LUNSINGH SCHEURLEER, T. H.: 'De Stadhouder-koning en zijn tijd', *Catalogus van de Herdenkingstentoonstelling* (Rijksmuseum, Amsterdam, 1950).

LUTTRELL, NARCISSUS: *A Brief Historical Relation of State Affairs, 1678–1714* (6 vols, Oxford, 1857).

M***, MONSIEUR: *Relation de la Maladie, de la mort et les funérailles de Marie Stuart, Reine d'Angleterre* (1695).

MACAULAY, THOMAS BABINGTON, LORD: *The History of England, from the Accession of James II* (Everyman ed., 4 vols, London, 1966).

MACKENZIE, WILLIAM COOK: *Andrew Fletcher of Saltoun, His Life and Times* (Edinburgh, 1935).

MACKY, JOHN: *Memoirs of the Secret Services* (London, 1733).

— *A View of the Court of St. Germain* (London, 1696).

MARLBOROUGH, SARAH CHURCHILL, DUCHESS OF: *Memoirs*, ed. William King (London, 1903).

MAZURE, F. A. J.: *Histoire de la Révolution de 1688 en Angleterre* (3 vols, Paris, 1825).

MISSON DE VALBOURG, H.: *Mémoires et observations faites par un voyageur en Angleterre* (The Hague, 1698).

MITFORD, NANCY: *The Sun King* (3rd ed., London, 1966).

MONTANUS, ARNOLDUS: *Het Leven, Bedrijf en Oorlogsdaden van Willem den Derden* (2 vols, Amsterdam, 1703).

MOUNTAGUE, WILLIAM: *The Delights of Holland* (London, 1696).

MULLENAUX, SAMUEL: *A Journal of the Three Month Campaign of His Majesty in Ireland* (London, 1690).

MÜLLER, PIETER LODEWIJK: *Wilhelm II von Oranien und G. F. von Waldeck* (The Hague, 1873).

NABER, J. W. A.: *Onze vorstinnen uit het Huis van Oranje-Nassau* (vols 1, 2, Haarlem, 1911).

NIPPOLD, W. K. A.: *Die Regierung der Königin Maria Stuart* (Hamburg, 1895).
— *Wilhelm III* (Berlin, 1900).
— *Oliver Cromwell, Wilhelm III und Ihre Feinde von Heute* (Berlin, 1901).

OGG, DAVID: *England in the Reigns of James II and William III* (London, 1969).

OLDMIXON, JOHN: *The Critical History of England* (2 vols, London, 1724–6).
— *History of the Stuarts* (London, 1730).

OMAN, CAROLA: *Mary of Modena* (London, 1962).
— *Elizabeth of Bohemia* (London, 1964).

ORLÉANS, CHARLOTTE ELISABETH, DUCHESSE D': *Correspondance de Madame*, ed. de Ranke and Holland (Paris, 1880).
— *Correspondance complète de Madame*, trans. M. G. Bruner (2 vols, Paris, 1886).
— *The Letters of Madame*, ed. Gertrude Scott Stevenson (2 vols, London, 1925).
— *Letters from Liselotte*, trans. and ed. M. Kroll (London, 1970).

OUDENDIJK, J. K.: *Willem III* (Amsterdam, 1954).

PELET-NARBONNE, G. VON: *Friedrich Wilhelm, der Grosse Kurfürst von Brandenburg* (Berlin, 1905).

PEPYS, SAMUEL: *The Diary: A new and complete transcription*, ed. Robert Latham and William Matthews (11 vols, London, 1970–).
— *Private Correspondence and Miscellaneous Papers*, ed. J. R. Tanner (2 vols, London, 1926).

PINKHAM, LUCILLE: *William III and the Respectable Revolution* (Cambridge, Massachusetts, 1954).

PITTIS, WILLIAM: *Some Memoirs of the Life of John Radcliffe* (London, 1715).

PLUMB, J. H.: *The First Four Georges* (London, 1966).

— *The Growth of Political Stability in England, 1675–1725* (London, 1967).

PLUMPTRE, EDWARD HAYES: *The Life of Thomas Ken* (2 vols, London, 1890).

PONTBRIANT, COMTE A. DE: *Histoire de la Principauté d'Orange* (Avignon, 1891).

POSTMUS, J.: *Een Eenzaam Strijder, Prins Willem III* (Amsterdam, 1909).

POWLEY, EDWARD B.: *The English Navy in the Revolution of 1688* (Cambridge, 1928).

PREBBLE, JOHN: *Glencoe* (London, 1968).

— *The Darien Disaster* (London, 1970).

PREUSS, G. F.: *Wilhelm III von England und das Haus Wittelsbach* (Breslau, 1904).

RALPH, JAMES: *The Other Side of the Question* (London, 1742).

— *The History of England During the Reign of King William* (London, 1744–6).

RANKE, LEOPOLD VON: *Englische Geschichte* (7 vols, 1859–68).

REID, STUART J.: *John and Sarah, Duke and Duchess of Marlborough* (London, 1915).

RENIER, G. J.: *William of Orange* (London, 1932).

— *The Dutch Nation* (The Hague, 1944).

RERESBY, SIR JOHN: *Memoirs*, ed. A. Browning (Glasgow, 1936).

RIJPERMAN, H. H. P.: *Uit de correspondentie van Willem III* (Amsterdam, 1938).

ROBB, NESCA: *William of Orange* (2 vols, London, 1966).

ROUSSET, CAMILLE F. M.: *Histoire de Louvois* (4 vols, Paris, 1862).

ROWSE, A. L.: *The Early Churchills* (London, 1969).

RUBINI, DENNIS: *Court and Country 1688–1702* (London, 1967).

RUSSELL, LADY RACHEL: *Letters*, ed. T. Selwood (London, 1792).

RYAN, JOHN: *The Life of William the Third* (Dublin, 1836).

SAINT-ÉVREMOND, CHARLES DE SAINT-DENIS, SIEUR DE: *Letters*, ed. John Hayward (London, 1930).

SAINT-SIMON, LOUIS DE ROUVROIS, DUC DE: *Mémoires* (4 vols, Paris, 1953–4).

SAMSON, P. A.: *Histoire de Guillaume III, Roi d'Angleterre* (3 vols, The Hague, 1703–4).

SANDARS, MARY: *Mary II, Princess and Queen of England* (London, 1913).

SANDERSON, ROBERT: *Original Letters from William to Charles II, Lord Arlington, etc.* (London, 1704).

SAUCK, KARL: *Elisabeth, Königin von Bohemen, in ihre letzten Lebensjahren* (Heidelberg, 1905).

SCHELTEMA, JACOBUS: *Geschied- en letterkundig Mengelwerk* (6 vols, Amsterdam, 1817–36).

SCHOTEL, GILLES DENIS JACOB (ed.): *Journal de l'ambassade extraordinaire de son Excellence Mylord Comte de Portland en France* (The Hague, 1851).

SÉGUR, PIERRE DE: *Le Maréchal de Luxembourg et le Prince d'Orange (1668–1678)* (Paris, 1902).

SHREWSBURY, CHARLES TALBOT, DUKE OF: *Private and Original Correspondence of Shrewsbury with William III*, ed. W. Coxe (London, 1821).

SIDNEY, HENRY: *Diary and Correspondence* (2 vols, London, 1843).

SIJPESTEIJN, J. W. VAN: *Enige Gebeurtenissen gedurende het Leven van Prins H. Casimir II van Nassau* (The Hague, 1865).

SITWELL, SACHEVERELL: *British Architects and Craftsmen* (London, 1960).

SMITH, EDWARD: *Foreign Visitors in England* (London, 1889).

SOMERS, BARON JOHN: *Collection of Tracts* (vol. 10, London, 1813).

SOMERVILLE, D. H.: *The King of Hearts* (London, 1962).

STORY, GEORGE: *An Impartial History of the War of Ireland* (London, 1693)

STOYE, JOHN: *Europe Unfolding, 1648–1688* (London, 1969).

STRICKLAND, AGNES: *Lives of the Queens of England* (vols. 7, 8, London, 1885)

STUART: *Calendar of the Stuart Papers at Windsor Castle* (7 vols, London, 1902–1923).

SWIFT, JONATHAN: *Works* (2nd ed., 19 vols, London, 1883).

TEMPLE, SIR WILLIAM: *Observations upon the United Provinces of the Netherlands* (London, 1673).

— *Memoirs* (London, 1700).

TENISON, THOMAS: *A Sermon Preached at the Funeral of Her Late Majesty Queen Mary* (London, 1695).

THOMSON, MARK A.: *William III and Louis XIV, Essays 1680–1720* (Liverpool, 1673).

THURLOE, JOHN: *State Papers*, ed. T. Birch (7 vols, London, 1742).

TORRIANO, WILLIAM HARCOURT: *William the Third* (2nd ed., London, 1887).

TRAILL, HENRY DUFF: *William the Third* (London, 1915).

TREVELYAN, GEORGE MACAULAY: *England under the Stuarts* (revised ed., London, 1946).

— *The English Revolution, 1688–1689* (London, 1965).

TREVELYAN, MARY CAROLINE: *William III and the Defence of Holland 1672–4* (London, 1930).

TREVOR, ARTHUR: *Life and Times of William III* (2 vols, London, 1835–6).

TRIGLAND, DR. CORNELIUS: *Laudatio Funebris* (Leiden, 1702).

TURNER, FRANCIS CHARLES: *James II* (London, 1948).

TUTCHIN, JOHN: *The Foreigners* (London, 1700).

VERNEY: *Memoirs of the Verney Family* (vol. 4, London, 1899).

VERNON, JAMES: *Letters Illustrative of the Reign of William III, from 1696 to 1708 addressed to the Duke of Shrewsbury*, ed. G. P. R. James (3 vols., London, 1841).

VOLTAIRE: *Siècle de Louis XIV* (*Œuvres Complètes*, vols. 17, 18, Paris, 1819).

WAGENAAR, JAN: *Vaderlandsche Historie* (24 vols, Amsterdam, 1790–6).

WARD, ADOLPHUS WILLIAM: *The Electress Sophia and the Hanoverian Succession* (2nd ed., London, 1909).

WATERSON, NELLIE M.: *Mary II, Queen of England, 1689–1694* (Durham, North Carolina, 1928).

WEDGWOOD, C. V.: *William the Silent* (London, 1967).

WENEWITINOFF, M. A.: *Russen in Holland* (1897).

WESSEM, CONSTANT VAN: *Koning-Stadhouder Willem III* (The Hague, 1939).

WHISTON, WILLIAM: *Memoirs . . . and Writings by himself* (London, 1749).

WICKHAM LEGG, LEOPOLD G.: *Matthew Prior* (Cambridge, 1921).

WICQUEFORT, ABRAHAM DE: *Histoire des Provinces-Unies des Pays-Bas*, ed. L. E. Lenting (4 vols, Amsterdam, 1861).

WILLIAMSON, SIR JOSEPH: *Letters*, ed. W. D. Christie (2 vols, London, 1874).

WITT HUBERTS, F. DE: *Uit de Jeugdjaren van Stadhouder Willem III* (The Hague, 1925).

WITT, JOHAN DE: *Mémoires* (Regensburg, 1709).

— *Brieven,* bewerkt door R. Fruin (3 vols, *Historische Genootschap*, 3rd ser. nos., 18, 25, 31, Utrecht, 1906–12).

WOLF, JOHN B.: *Louis XIV* (London, 1968).

WOLSELEY, GENERAL VISCOUNT: *Life of John Churchill, Duke of Marlborough* (London, 1894).

WOOD, ANTHONY À: *Life and Times* (London, 1932).

WOODBRIDGE, HOMER EDWARDS: *Sir William Temple* (London, 1940).

ZOUTELANDT, MADAME DE: *Mémoires* (Paris, 1709).

ZUYLEN VAN NYEVELT, BARONESSE SUZETTE VAN: *Court Life in the Dutch Republic (1638–1669)* (London, 1906).

Index

Index

A Note on the Type

The text of this book was set on the Monotype in a type face called Garamond. Jean Jannon has been identified as designer for this face, which is based on Garamond's original models but is much lighter and more open. The italic is taken from a fount of Granjon, which appeared in the repertory of the Imprimerie Royale and was probably cut in the middle of the sixteenth century.

A Note about the Authors

Henri and Barbara van der Zee are both working journalists based
in London. A native of Holland, he is the London correspondent of
Amsterdam's *De Telegraaf*, and the current president of the Foreign
Press Association in England; she writes for the London *Daily Mail*
under her maiden name, Barbara Griggs. Their collaboration in
William and Mary was the result of a common interest in historical
biography: Dutch-born William of Orange and his English wife,
Mary Stuart, were a natural subject for Anglo-Dutch writing part-
ners. The Van der Zees, both in their thirties, live in Hampstead,
London, and have a baby daughter.